Handbook of Research on End–to–End Cloud Computing Architecture Design

Jianwen "Wendy" Chen
IBM, Australia

Yan Zhang
Western Sydney University, Australia

Ron Gottschalk
IBM, Australia

A volume in the Advances in Systems Analysis,
Software Engineering, and High Performance
Computing (ASASEHPC) Book Series

www.igi-global.com

Published in the United States of America by
 IGI Global
 Information Science Reference (an imprint of IGI Global)
 701 E. Chocolate Avenue
 Hershey PA, USA 17033
 Tel: 717-533-8845
 Fax: 717-533-8661
 E-mail: cust@igi-global.com
 Web site: http://www.igi-global.com

Library of Congress Cataloging-in-Publication Data

Names: Chen, Jianwen, 1969- editor. | Zhang, Yan, 1962 November 25- editor. |
 Gottschalk, Ron, 1959- editor.
Title: Handbook of research on end-to-end cloud computing architecture design
 / [edited by] Jianwen (Wendy) Chen, Yan Zhang, and Ron Gottschalk, editors.
Description: Hershey, PA : Information Science Reference, [2017] | Series:
 Advances in systems analysis, software engineering, and high performance
 computing | Includes bibliographical references and index.
Identifiers: LCCN 2016024311| ISBN 9781522507598 (hardcover) | ISBN
 9781522507604 (ebook)
Subjects: LCSH: Cloud computing--Handbooks, manuals, etc. | Computer
 architecture--Handbooks, manuals, etc.
Classification: LCC QA76.585 .H3635 2017 | DDC 004.67/82--dc23 LC record available at https://lccn.loc.gov/2016024311

This book is published in the IGI Global book series Advances in Systems Analysis, Software Engineering, and High Performance Computing (ASASEHPC) (ISSN: 2327-3453; eISSN: 2327-3461)

British Cataloguing in Publication Data
A Cataloguing in Publication record for this book is available from the British Library.

For electronic access to this publication, please contact: eresources@igi-global.com.

Advances in Systems Analysis, Software Engineering, and High Performance Computing (ASASEHPC) Book Series

Vijayan Sugumaran
Oakland University, USA

ISSN: 2327-3453
EISSN: 2327-3461

MISSION

The theory and practice of computing applications and distributed systems has emerged as one of the key areas of research driving innovations in business, engineering, and science. The fields of software engineering, systems analysis, and high performance computing offer a wide range of applications and solutions in solving computational problems for any modern organization.

The **Advances in Systems Analysis, Software Engineering, and High Performance Computing (ASASEHPC) Book Series** brings together research in the areas of distributed computing, systems and software engineering, high performance computing, and service science. This collection of publications is useful for academics, researchers, and practitioners seeking the latest practices and knowledge in this field.

COVERAGE

- Virtual Data Systems
- Software Engineering
- Network Management
- Distributed Cloud Computing
- Engineering Environments
- Storage Systems
- Human-Computer Interaction
- Computer graphics
- Enterprise Information Systems
- Computer System Analysis

IGI Global is currently accepting manuscripts for publication within this series. To submit a proposal for a volume in this series, please contact our Acquisition Editors at Acquisitions@igi-global.com or visit: http://www.igi-global.com/publish/.

Titles in this Series

For a list of additional titles in this series, please visit: www.igi-global.com

Innovative Research and Applications in Next-Generation High Performance Computing
Qusay F. Hassan (Mansoura University, Egypt)
Information Science Reference • copyright 2016 • 488pp • H/C (ISBN: 9781522502876) • US $205.00 (our price)

Developing Interoperable and Federated Cloud Architecture
Gabor Kecskemeti (University of Miskolc, Hungary) Attila Kertesz (University of Szeged, Hungary) and Zsolt
Nemeth (MTA SZTAKI, Hungary)
Information Science Reference • copyright 2016 • 398pp • H/C (ISBN: 9781522501534) • US $210.00 (our price)

Managing Big Data in Cloud Computing Environments
Zongmin Ma (Nanjing University of Aeronautics and Astronautics, China)
Information Science Reference • copyright 2016 • 314pp • H/C (ISBN: 9781466698345) • US $195.00 (our price)

Emerging Innovations in Agile Software Development
Imran Ghani (Universiti Teknologi Malaysia, Malaysia) Dayang Norhayati Abang Jawawi (Universiti Teknologi
Malaysia, Malaysia) Siva Dorairaj (Software Education, New Zealand) and Ahmed Sidky (ICAgile, USA)
Information Science Reference • copyright 2016 • 323pp • H/C (ISBN: 9781466698581) • US $205.00 (our price)

Modern Software Engineering Methodologies for Mobile and Cloud Environments
António Miguel Rosado da Cruz (Instituto Politécnico de Viana do Castelo, Portugal) and Sara Paiva (Instituto
Politécnico de Viana do Castelo, Portugal)
Information Science Reference • copyright 2016 • 355pp • H/C (ISBN: 9781466699168) • US $210.00 (our price)

Emerging Research Surrounding Power Consumption and Performance Issues in Utility Computing
Ganesh Chandra Deka (Regional Vocational Training Institute (RVTI) for Women, India) G.M. Siddesh (M S
Ramaiah Institute of Technology, Bangalore, India) K. G. Srinivasa (M S Ramaiah Institute of Technology, Ban-
galore, India) and L.M. Patnaik (IISc, Bangalore, India)
Information Science Reference • copyright 2016 • 460pp • H/C (ISBN: 9781466688537) • US $215.00 (our price)

Advanced Research on Cloud Computing Design and Applications
Shadi Aljawarneh (Jordan University of Science and Technology, Jordan)
Information Science Reference • copyright 2015 • 388pp • H/C (ISBN: 9781466686762) • US $205.00 (our price)

www.igi-global.com

701 E. Chocolate Ave., Hershey, PA 17033
Order online at www.igi-global.com or call 717-533-8845 x100
To place a standing order for titles released in this series, contact: cust@igi-global.com
Mon-Fri 8:00 am - 5:00 pm (est) or fax 24 hours a day 717-533-8661

List of Contributors

Alam, M.Afshar / *Jamia Hamdard University, India* 222

Buyya, Rajkumar / *The University of Melbourne, Australia* 410

Calheiros, Rodrigo N. / *The University of Melbourne, Australia* 410

Chen, Shiping / *CSIRO Data61, Australia* 455

Cook, Jim / *IBM Corporation, USA* 279

Dastjerdi, Amir Vahid / *The University of Melbourne, Australia* 410

Easton, John / *IBM Corporation, UK* 15

Egwutuoha, Ifeanyi P. / *The University of Sydney, Australia* 455

Ehrhardt, Richard / *IBM, Australia* 105

Eigenbrode, Shelbee / *IBM, USA* 326

Graf, Florian / *IBM Corporation, Switzerland* 254

Hamidine, Hicham / *University of Bridgeport, USA* 189

Hinton, Heather / *IBM Corporation, USA* 159

Huber, Rebecca / *IBM Corporation, Germany* 254

Hunt, Anthony / *IBM Corporation, USA* 254

Jain, Prashant / *IBM, Singapore* 56

Jaluka, Rajesh / *IBM Corporation, USA* 348

Khandelwal, Prateek / *BITS – Pilani, India* 130

Mahmood, Ausif / *University of Bridgeport, USA* 189

Marzantowicz, Karolina / *IBM, Poland* 39

Mukherjea, Sougata / *IBM, India* 1

Nassar, Suheil / *IBM Cloud, USA* 326

Paciorkowski, Łukasz / *IBM, Poland* 39

Pang, Yan / *IBM, Singapore & National University of Singapore, Singapore* 56

Parmar, Rashik / *IBM Corporation, UK* 15

Pfitzmann, Birgit / *IBM Corporation, Switzerland* 254

Piraghaj, Sareh Fotuhi / *The University of Melbourne, Australia* 410

Richardson, Laura / *IBM, USA* 1

Schlatter, Marcel / *IBM Corporation, The Netherlands* 254

Schrøder-Hansen, Claus / *IBM Corporation, Denmark* 254

Shalan, Mohammad Ali / *Jordan Engineers Association, Jordan* 376

Shamsolmoali, Pourya / *Advanced Scientific Computing, CMCC, Italy* 222

Somani, Gaurav / *Central University of Rajasthan, India* 130

Thio, Choong / *IBM Corporation, USA* 279

Venkateswaran, Sreekrishnan / *IBM Corporation, India* 73

Wolfe, Martin / *IBM Corporation, USA* 300

Zareapoor, Masoumeh / *Shanghai Jiao Tong University, China* 222

Zolotow, Clea / *IBM Corporation, USA* 254

Table of Contents

Foreword *by George Africa*.. xvii

Foreword *by Rhonda Childress*... xviii

Preface... xix

Acknowledgment xxiii

Section 1

Chapter 1
Enterprise Mobility Reference Architecture: Mobility Services Overview... 1
Laura Richardson, IBM, USA
Sougata Mukherjea, IBM, India

Chapter 2
Navigating Your Way to the Hybrid Cloud... 15
John Easton, IBM Corporation, UK
Rashik Parmar, IBM Corporation, UK

Chapter 3
Community Cloud: Closing the Gap between Public and Private 39
Karolina Marzantowicz, IBM, Poland
Łukasz Paciorkowski, IBM, Poland

Chapter 4
Cloud Computing Architectural Patterns.. 56
Prashant Jain, IBM, Singapore
Yan Pang, IBM, Singapore & National University of Singapore, Singapore

Chapter 5
Industrial Patterns on Cloud 73
Sreekrishnan Venkateswaran, IBM Corporation, India

Section 2

Chapter 6
Cloud Build Methodology 105
  Richard Ehrhardt, IBM, Australia

Chapter 7
Virtual Machine Placement in IaaS Cloud 130
  Prateek Khandelwal, BITS – Pilani, India
  Gaurav Somani, Central University of Rajasthan, India

Chapter 8
Security and Compliance: IaaS, PaaS, and Hybrid Cloud 159
  Heather Hinton, IBM Corporation, USA

Chapter 9
Cloud Computing Data Storage Security Based on Different Encryption Schemes 189
  Hicham Hamidine, University of Bridgeport, USA
  Ausif Mahmood, University of Bridgeport, USA

Chapter 10
Multi-Aspect DDOS Detection System for Securing Cloud Network 222
  Pourya Shamsolmoali, Advanced Scientific Computing, CMCC, Italy
  Masoumeh Zareapoor, Shanghai Jiao Tong University, China
  M.Afshar Alam, Jamia Hamdard University, India

Section 3

Chapter 11
Transition and Transformation into a Cloud Environment 254
  Clea Zolotow, IBM Corporation, USA
  Florian Graf, IBM Corporation, Switzerland
  Birgit Pfitzmann, IBM Corporation, Switzerland
  Rebecca Huber, IBM Corporation, Germany
  Marcel Schlatter, IBM Corporation, The Netherlands
  Claus Schrøder-Hansen, IBM Corporation, Denmark
  Anthony Hunt, IBM Corporation, USA

Chapter 12
Workload Migration to Cloud 279
  Choong Thio, IBM Corporation, USA
  Jim Cook, IBM Corporation, USA

Section 4

Chapter 13
Establishing Governance for Hybrid Cloud and the Internet of Things 300
   Martin Wolfe, IBM Corporation, USA

Chapter 14
Design and Implementation of Service Management in DevOps Enabled Cloud Computing
Models.. 326
   Shelbee Eigenbrode, IBM, USA
   Suheil Nassar, IBM Cloud, USA

Chapter 15
Enterprise IT Transformation Using Cloud Service Broker 348
   Rajesh Jaluka, IBM Corporation, USA

Chapter 16
Risk and Governance Considerations in Cloud Era... 376
   Mohammad Ali Shalan, Jordan Engineers Association, Jordan

Chapter 17
A Survey and Taxonomy of Energy Efficient Resource Management Techniques in Platform as a
Service Cloud... 410
   Sareh Fotuhi Piraghaj, The University of Melbourne, Australia
   Amir Vahid Dastjerdi, The University of Melbourne, Australia
   Rodrigo N. Calheiros, The University of Melbourne, Australia
   Rajkumar Buyya, The University of Melbourne, Australia

Chapter 18
Cost of Using Cloud Computing: HaaS vs. IaaS 455
   Ifeanyi P. Egwutuoha, The University of Sydney, Australia
   Shiping Chen, CSIRO Data61, Australia

Compilation of References 473

Index.. 502

Detailed Table of Contents

Foreword *by George Africa*..xvii

Foreword *by Rhonda Childress*...xviii

Preface... xix

Acknowledgment xxiii

Section 1

Chapter 1

Enterprise Mobility Reference Architecture: Mobility Services Overview... 1
    Laura Richardson, IBM, USA
    Sougata Mukherjea, IBM, India

The smart phone has become one of the most important devices in our day to day lives. Mobility is also impacting business significantly and most enterprises are providing services to facilitate the mobile workforce. This chapter introduces an enterprise mobility reference architecture. The architecture highlights the key aspects of enterprise mobility such as platform and application development, end user support, collaboration, virtualization, mobile security, monitoring and mobile analytics. The architecture is presented from several viewpoints to cater to different needs of clients. The relationship of the mobile architecture to a cloud reference architecture is also explained. Finally, a use case to demonstrate how a real world scenario maps to the architecture is also discussed.

Chapter 2

Navigating Your Way to the Hybrid Cloud... 15
    John Easton, IBM Corporation, UK
    Rashik Parmar, IBM Corporation, UK

The authors believe that cloud computing systems should become hybrid in nature for organisations to realise the full business potential that the cloud offers: increased agility, velocity and innovation in business IT. Yet hybrid environments are complex to design, implement and run. To the organisations implementing them, these systems present many architectural challenges that must be solved if the resulting solution is to deliver desired business outcomes. This chapter defines the different types of hybrid cloud: those seen to date as well as those that will emerge in the near future. Using seven key business use cases as a framework, the authors propose a high-level architecture for hybrid cloud computing environments that is practically illustrated with real-world client examples.

Chapter 3

Community Cloud: Closing the Gap between Public and Private 39

Karolina Marzantowicz, IBM, Poland
Łukasz Paciorkowski, IBM, Poland

Should you turn to a public or private cloud solution? Discussions prizing the first or the second option are endless. Public cloud means flexibility, unlimited scalability, frictionless consumption and less worry for your CIO. On the other hand, private cloud gives you full control over the environment and keeps your data close to you, preferably under your nose—or at least within the borders of your country. Public cloud is relatively cheap, while a private cloud might get pricey. But what if neither of those two options fit your needs? You may not trust public cloud providers, but at the same time you are searching for the way to cut through complexity of the private cloud. The answer to your needs might be a community cloud.

Chapter 4

Cloud Computing Architectural Patterns 56

Prashant Jain, IBM, Singapore
Yan Pang, IBM, Singapore & National University of Singapore, Singapore

Cloud computing has been one of the most disruptive technologies, which has changed the way IT is consumed by enterprises, both small and large. The ability to subscribe to "as-a-service" consumption model, while converting capital expenditure to operational expenditure, has been a key driver for Cloud adoption. Rapid provisioning and deprovisioning of services, elastic scaling of infrastructure resources and self-service ability for users are some of the key characteristics and benefits offered by Cloud. Infrastructure as a Service (IaaS) provides the basic building block, with Platform as a Service (PaaS) providing a layer of abstraction on top of IaaS and similarly Software as a Service (SaaS) providing a layer of abstraction on top of PaaS. Moving up the layers reduces complexity and enables users to tap into a much larger spectrum of benefits that Cloud computing has to offer. While Cloud opens the door for "as-a-service" consumption model, there are many additional benefits that can be realized by enterprises beyond the typical IaaS, PaaS and SaaS. A number of these benefits can be realized by leveraging Cloud in different scenarios and use cases. For example, an enterprise may continue to pursue a traditional non-Cloud based infrastructure deployment strategy, however, it could use a public Cloud for storage elasticity. Such use cases exemplify many atypical benefits that Cloud can provide, which often got overlooked. This paper will present a number of such cloud deployment use cases that go beyond the typical IaaS usage of cloud. A hierarchical architectural model of cloud solution pattern is proposed to describe both the business requirements and technical considerations of these use cases. These cloud architectural patterns are further elaborated through real-life case studies and examples.

Chapter 5

Industrial Patterns on Cloud 73

Sreekrishnan Venkateswaran, IBM Corporation, India

Cloud Computing is rapidly gaining traction today as the preferred platform for deploying both development and production workloads. Every industry has started adopting hybrid hosting models to leverage benefits that accrue from a convergence of technologies; Cloud is being used as a flexible springboard to mount a defense against disruptive digital trends. The use cases and associated gains are industry specific, ranging from leveraging auto-scaling to assuage seasonal spikes in Retail, and creating software-defined network functions in Telecom, to aggregating and analyzing sensor data in Automotive, and deploying multi-site disaster recovery in Government. In this chapter, we will embark on an expedition spanning ten industries, searching for patterns where Cloud enables advantageous solutions to business-specific categories of use cases. The observations are based on actual case studies chosen from hundreds of real Cloud deals across industries.

Section 2

Chapter 6

Cloud Build Methodology 105
Richard Ehrhardt, IBM, Australia

The cloud build methodology chapter provides an introduction to the build methods for hybrid clouds. It does this by first introducing the concept of a hybrid cloud and the different types of services provides by clouds. It then overviews the components of hybrid clouds and how these components get incorporated into the design. It takes a brief look at the cost drivers with building a cloud to provide background with design decisions to be made. With the background on the design, it takes the reader through the build of a hybrid cloud and how automation can be used to reduce the cost. Lastly, it takes a brief look at a possible direction of cloud builds.

Chapter 7

Virtual Machine Placement in IaaS Cloud... 130
Prateek Khandelwal, BITS – Pilani, India
Gaurav Somani, Central University of Rajasthan, India

A crucial component of providing services over virtual machines to users is how the provider places those virtual machines on physical servers. While one strategy can offer an increased performance for the virtual machine, and hence customer satisfaction, another can offer increased savings for the cloud operator. Both have their trade-offs. Also, with increasing costs of electricity, and given the fact that the major component of the operational cost of a data center is that of powering it, green strategies also offer an attractive alternative. In this chapter, the authors will look into what kind of different placement strategies have been developed, and the kind of advantages they purport to offer.

Chapter 8

Security and Compliance: IaaS, PaaS, and Hybrid Cloud 159
Heather Hinton, IBM Corporation, USA

Despite a rocky start in terms of perceived security, cloud adoption continues to grow. Users are more comfortable with the notion that cloud can be secure but there is still a lack of understanding of what changes when moving to cloud, how to secure a cloud environment, and most importantly, how to demonstrate compliance of these cloud environment for regulatory purposes. This chapter reviews the basics of cloud security and compliance, including the split of security responsibility across Cloud provider and Client, considerations for the integration of cloud deployed workloads with on-premises systems and most importantly, how to demonstrate compliance with existing internal policies and workload required regulatory standards.

Chapter 9

Cloud Computing Data Storage Security Based on Different Encryption Schemes 189

Hicham Hamidine, University of Bridgeport, USA

Ausif Mahmood, University of Bridgeport, USA

Cloud Computing (CC) became one of the prominent solutions that organizations do consider to minimize and lean their information technology infrastructure cost by fully utilizing their resources. However, with all the benefits that CC promises, there are many security issues that discourage clients from making the necessary decision to easily embrace the cloud. To encourage the use of CC, clients need to be able to strategically plan their future investments without the uncertainties of security issues that come with hosting their data in the cloud. This chapter will discuss different mitigation techniques and the common proposed security algorithm schemes for data storage encryption based on classical "symmetric and asymmetric" and with an emphasis on fully homomorphic encryption schemes.

Chapter 10

Multi-Aspect DDOS Detection System for Securing Cloud Network 222

Pourya Shamsolmoali, Advanced Scientific Computing, CMCC, Italy

Masoumeh Zareapoor, Shanghai Jiao Tong University, China

M.Afshar Alam, Jamia Hamdard University, India

Distributed Denial of Service (DDoS) attacks have become a serious attack for internet security and Cloud Computing environment. This kind of attacks is the most complex form of DoS (Denial of Service) attacks. This type of attack can simply duplicate its source address, such as spoofing attack, which defending methods do not able to disguises the real location of the attack. Therefore, DDoS attack is the most significant challenge for network. In this chapter we present different aspect of security in Cloud Computing, mostly we concentrated on DDOS Attacks. The Authors illustrated all types of Dos Attacks and discussed the most effective detection methods.

Section 3

Chapter 11

Transition and Transformation into a Cloud Environment 254

Clea Zolotow, IBM Corporation, USA

Florian Graf, IBM Corporation, Switzerland

Birgit Pfitzmann, IBM Corporation, Switzerland

Rebecca Huber, IBM Corporation, Germany

Marcel Schlatter, IBM Corporation, The Netherlands

Claus Schrøder-Hansen, IBM Corporation, Denmark

Anthony Hunt, IBM Corporation, USA

It is a challenge to migrate and transform existing workloads into the cloud, especially those requiring the higher standardization of managed services. Covered here are the various types of transition and transformation into the cloud from lift and shift to automated migration; the tooling and automation for the cloud environment; and the migration services via wave planning and check-pointing to the cloud for customers. Transition and Transformation is an integral part of cloud services, and creating a repeatable, reusable, factory model for a customer ensures a successful cloud migration.

Chapter 12
Workload Migration to Cloud 279
Choong Thio, IBM Corporation, USA
Jim Cook, IBM Corporation, USA

Workload migration to cloud is a critical area in increasing the adoption of cloud. In order to fully leverage the power of cloud computing, clients need to determine what workloads and applications are good candidates in the cloud and migrate them quickly and in an efficient manner into the cloud. The main goal of this chapter is to explore and study how workloads can be migrated into cloud. In addition, this chapter will also describe the overall end-to-end process for cloud migration and its resulting benefits.

Section 4

Chapter 13
Establishing Governance for Hybrid Cloud and the Internet of Things 300
Martin Wolfe, IBM Corporation, USA

This chapter is focused on the current and future state of operating a Hybrid Cloud or Internet of Things (IoT) environment. This includes tools, data, and processes which allow an organization to use these assets to serve business goals. Examining governance in this context shows how it works today and how it should change, using some real-world examples to show the impacts and advantages of these changes. It is a high level overview of those important topics with prescriptive detail left for a future and follow-on analysis. Finally, all of the lessons learned, when combined together form a governance fabric, resulting in a set of techniques and actions which tie together into a supporting framework and set of processes. The important questions include: Why does governance matter in the deployment and operation of Hybrid Cloud and IoT? If governance already exists how must it change? What are the important and salient characteristics of governance which need special focus? Thus, this analysis gives a context of how today's governance approach should change when moving to a Hybrid Cloud or IoT model.

Chapter 14
Design and Implementation of Service Management in DevOps Enabled Cloud Computing
Models.. 326
Shelbee Eigenbrode, IBM, USA
Suheil Nassar, IBM Cloud, USA

This chapter examines the importance of including value-add service management practices early in the Continuous Integration/Continuous Delivery (CI/CD) pipeline. The authors will also address the importance of establishing a balance between the development and delivery of features with the development and delivery of practices that support overall infrastructure and service management capabilities. Without fully encompassing all of these practices, the DevOps benefits of reducing time-to-market for a set of features can be negated by a potential increase in security exposures as well as overall quality issues. Within this chapter, several key service management practices are identified as well as the importance of fully incorporating those practices into a DevOps adoption.

Chapter 15
Enterprise IT Transformation Using Cloud Service Broker 348
    Rajesh Jaluka, IBM Corporation, USA

Cloud is significantly changing the economics as well as delivery and support model for Information Technology. Every enterprise needs to come up with a plan to transform their current IT and embrace cloud. The road to transformation poses many challenges and there is no one right answer. The objective of this chapter is to describe some of the key challenges and provide a methodology based on IBM Design Thinking to address the challenges. The author will also enlighten the readers on how a Cloud Service Broker can help smoothen the journey.

Chapter 16
Risk and Governance Considerations in Cloud Era 376
    Mohammad Ali Shalan, Jordan Engineers Association, Jordan

Cloud Computing (CC) has recently emerged as a compelling paradigm for managing and delivering computing services over the internet. It is rapidly changing the landscape of technology and ultimately turning the long-held promise of utility computing into a reality. Nevertheless, jumping into the cloud is never a trivial task. A special approach is required to discover and mitigate risks, also to apply controls related to the cloud jump. The main objective of this chapter is to specify some of the phenomena associated with the CC paradigm and associated business transformation. It looks at the motivations, contracting, obstacles and the agile project rollout methodologies. It then provides an in-depth analysis for the allied risks and governance directions. CC governance is being more crucial as the CC paradigm is still evolving. In this context, this chapter build few bricks toward a full Cloud Computing Risk and Governance Framework (CCRGF).

Chapter 17
A Survey and Taxonomy of Energy Efficient Resource Management Techniques in Platform as a Service Cloud 410
    Sareh Fotuhi Piraghaj, The University of Melbourne, Australia
    Amir Vahid Dastjerdi, The University of Melbourne, Australia
    Rodrigo N. Calheiros, The University of Melbourne, Australia
    Rajkumar Buyya, The University of Melbourne, Australia

The numerous advantages of cloud computing environments, including scalability, high availability, and cost effectiveness have encouraged service providers to adopt the available cloud models to offer solutions. This rise in cloud adoption, in return encourages platform providers to increase the underlying capacity of their data centers so that they can accommodate the increasing demand of new customers. Increasing the capacity and building large-scale data centers has caused a drastic growth in energy consumption of cloud environments. The energy consumption not only affects the Total Cost of Ownership but also increases the environmental footprint of data centers as CO_2 emissions increases. Hence, energy and power efficiency of the data centers has become an important research area in distributed systems. In order to identify the challenges in this domain, this chapter surveys and classifies the energy efficient resource management techniques specifically focused on the PaaS cloud service models.

Chapter 18

Cost of Using Cloud Computing: HaaS vs. IaaS 455

Ifeanyi P. Egwutuoha, The University of Sydney, Australia

Shiping Chen, CSIRO Data61, Australia

With the recent advancement in computing technologies, business and research applications are not only executed in the traditional systems such as enterprise systems and supercomputers (HPC systems) but also in the cloud. The traditional HPC systems are expensive and sometimes require huge start-up investment, technical and administrative support and job queuing. With the benefits of cloud computing, cloud services such as Infrastructure as a Service (IaaS) and Hardware as a Service (HaaS), enables business, scientists and researchers to run their business and HPC applications in the cloud without upfront investment associated with the traditional infrastructures. Therefore, in this paper we analyze the computational performance and dollar cost of running HPC applications in the cloud when IaaS or HaaS is leased. We find that HaaS significantly reduces the cost of running HPC application in the cloud by 20% compare to IaaS without significant impact to application's performance. We also found that there is a substantial improvement in computational performance in HaaS compare to IaaS.

Compilation of References 473

Index 502

Foreword

Cloud computing is a rapidly growing business and technology area. It has been one of the most challenging technologies and has changed the way IT is consumed by enterprises. More and more enterprises are willing to step into the cloud business and realize the full business potential that the cloud offers: increased agility, velocity and innovation in business IT. Cloud computing has made possible the extensive automation of managing and administering IT systems, thereby providing many unique benefits when compared to traditional IT models. The ability to subscribe to "as-a-service" consumption model has been a key driver for cloud adoption.

The cloud systems and related services are complex to design, implement and run. Challenges include establishing cloud reference architectures, implementing cloud platforms and services, migrating application workloads into clouds, designing hybrid cloud service frameworks and providing cloud service brokerage. We are facing these challenges and we are working through and overcoming these challenges in order to deliver the desired cloud platforms and services in our real world business.

The challenges in cloud computing are both difficult and interesting. This book has great value in providing an end-to-end and systemic study on both architectural design and implementation of cloud computing. It offers a reference handbook of state of the art industrial and research knowledge to IT professionals and researchers, and helps the audience to find out the key challenges of cloud worlds and explore the ways to overcome these challenges using the best industrial practices validated in real enterprise use cases.

George Africa
IBM Corporation, Australia

George Africa *is a Solutioning Executive Leader and Executive IT Architect in IBM Australia. He is a recognised business leader and technology innovator especially in cloud business. George provides leadership to establish corporate cloud architecture and deploy new cloud business capabilities, and provides the vision, direction and strategy to ensure effective delivery of cloud platforms and services.*

Foreword

In this new era of Cloud Computing, we are currently facing a number of major challenges in the architectural design and implementation of Enterprise Cloud systems and services. These challenges include: the reference architecture of cloud computing, cloud models for enterprises, the methodologies to build cloud systems, the best practices of architectural and industrial patterns, risk and security management of cloud systems and services, service management and migration of applications to the cloud.

This handbook provides detailed studies of cloud computing and explores every aspect and component involved in the design and implementation of the cloud computing system - including system models, methodologies and patterns, workload placement, data storage, security and compliance. The handbook also provides perspectives into the designing and implementing service management functions, integration models and the use of brokerage services over clouds.

Security and risk control in cloud computing are always a major concern for enterprises. Despite a rocky start in terms of perceived security, cloud adoption continues to grow because users see the benefits of the cloud as greater than the risk. Although enterprise users are becoming more comfortable with the notion that cloud can be secure, there is still a lack of understanding of how to secure a cloud environment and how to demonstrate compliance of these cloud environment for regulatory purposes. This handbook covers a number of security, risk controls and governance topics. It also provides insight into the recent research and industrial practices as to how security control and risk mitigation can be designed and implemented for cloud environments and services.

Rhonda Childress
IBM Corporation, USA

Rhonda Childress *is an IBM Fellow and CTO of Security Services in IBM Security Business Unit. She is a Master Inventor and has over 80 granted patents in different technology areas. She provides direction, strategy and reference architecture for the IBM Global Technology Services group, especially in the security service area.*

Preface

Cloud computing is a continually evolving subject in both industry and academic research. This handbook is an original and comprehensive reference handbook and aims at covering major aspects of end-to-end architectural design and implementation of cloud computing. Topics range from cloud computing reference architectures, different cloud models, cloud system build methodologies, architectural and industrial patterns, workload and application cloud migration, service management and brokerage of cloud service, to security, risk and cost of cloud system and service. This handbook will be of broad interest to both industrial and research communities.

CLOUD COMPUTING ARCHITECTURE DESIGN

Cloud computing is a model for enabling ubiquitous, convenient, on-demand network access to a shared pool of configurable computing resources (e.g., networks, servers, storage, applications, and services) that can be rapidly provisioned and released with minimal management effort or service provider interaction. In terms of deployment models, Cloud can be typically defined as three different types, i.e. Public Cloud, Private Cloud and Hybrid Cloud.

Although the current cloud computing model has established some elements for cloud system build and cloud services, IT people are facing a number of real major challenges on the end-to-end architecture design and implementation to provide appropriated enterprise cloud systems and services. These challenging areas include: evolving reference architecture of cloud computing; selecting appropriate cloud models for enterprises; developing end to end cloud system build methodology; developing and choosing the best practice of architectural and industrial patterns; the risk and security management of cloud system; service management and brokerage of cloud services; and workload and application migration to clouds. This handbook aims to cover and address these challenging topics through the latest industrial and research practice.

OBJECTIVES

The main purpose of this handbook is to provide an end-to-end deep dive and systemic study on architecture design and implementation of cloud computing. It offers a reference handbook of state of the art industrial and research knowledge concerning the key issues surrounding current and future challenges associated with the cloud computing.

To achieve this goal, this handbook contains a collection of contributions from leading experts in the world aiming at:

1. Presenting current industrial and research results on cloud computing reference architecture, cloud computing model, cloud system build, service management in cloud and application cloud migration;
2. Providing a comprehensive description and deep dive of some leading-edge industrial and research practice that related to cloud computing models, builds, services, securities and cost;
3. Offering an overview of the current well-defined architectural design and the emergent trends in areas of cloud computing.

CONTRIBUTION

This handbook provides an excellent contribution to industry and research by making the best industrial practice and research results available in an area where there is a clear industrial and research gap for the architectural design and implementation of cloud computing. The theme of this handbook is strategic, and of central importance in establishing end to end architecture design, implementation and systemic study for the emerging cloud computing technology.

This book provides an end-to-end deep dive and a systemic study on architecture design and implementation of cloud computing systems and services. It provides and highlights the latest industrial practices and research studies of cloud computing from architecture design models to implementation technologies, from cloud system builds to cloud services managements, and from strategic reference architectures and models to detailed cloud build patterns and application migration methods.

This handbook provides unique values in the following areas:

As one key challenge of cloud computing research, there is no one book published to study the design and implementation of cloud computing from the end to end approach. This handbook studies and presents the end to end architecture design and implementation of the cloud computing, from designing and building of cloud systems, provisioning service management and orchestration, developing cloud pattern, to migrations methods and models for cloud applications and workloads, risk and security consideration, and financial analysis of using cloud system and service.

This handbook provides deep dive studies of cloud computing, especially in a number of areas that are facing challenges in the current cloud computing research such as the best practice of industrial patterns for cloud builds, service management and brokerage over hybrid clouds, orchestration and integration model across hybrid clouds and legacy environments, and migration methodologies and models for cloud workloads, applications and data.

This handbook also addresses the needs to have a publication for the systemic study on all important perspectives of cloud systems and services, from industrial standard open stack architecture and reference architectures in cloud computing to the best practice of architecture designs, solutions and implementations in using and evolving Infrastructure/platform/Software/Business Process as the Service models.

AUDIENCE

This handbook is intended for people interested in the architecture design, implementation, operation, and management of cloud computing systems and cloud applications at all levels, including: IT professionals, IT architects, researchers, scientists, practitioners, managers, educators and students who are looking for the state-of-the-art information in cloud computing trends and development for architecture design and implementation, and require access to current information in this emerging field. The audience can learn industrial standard and reference architecture of cloud computing, and find the best practices in designing and implementing cloud systems and service management, and applications. The audience can learn architecture design and implement of the major areas of cloud computing sysmetically and in depth, and form an end to end view of cloud computing. In particular, technology innovators can take advantage of the leading-edge research ideas, results and case studies described in this handbook. The combination of theoretical and practical content will enable a broader audience to take advantage of this handbook and apply received knowledge in their own cloud projects.

CONTENT

Firstly, This handbook studies the architectural design and implement of both cloud systems and cloud services in private, public and hybrid clouds; presents cloud computing reference architecture; studies open stack architecture as one of industrial open standards in cloud computing; explores the design and implementation how computer nodes, storage, network, security, software and business applications can be provisioned and consumed in Infrastructure/Platform/Software/Business Process As A Service models.

Secondly, this handbook presents the design and implementation of the management perspectives of cloud systems and services. It studies service management and service brokerage in cloud computing for a range of ITIL service management functions. Especially, the book explores how system and service orchestration, integration and aggregation can be designed and achieved in hybrid clouds.

In addition, the handbook studies the cloud computing from the data and application perspectives. It explores the method of analyzing the applications and workloads for the fits of different cloud models and introduces available migration methods and tools for the application migration to cloud environments.

Chapter 1, 2, 3, 4 & 5 focus on the studies of enterprise reference architecture, different cloud models for private, public, hybrid and community clouds, and the architectural and industrial patterns in cloud systems.

Chapter 6, 7, 8, 9 & 10 explore every aspect and component involved in the design and implementation of the end to end cloud system build such as IaaS/PaaS/SaaS models, end to end build methodology, VM placement, security compliance and data storage.

Chapter 11 & 12 provide the transition and transformation strategy, method and tool to migrate data, applications and workloads into cloud environments.

Chapter 13, 14, 15, 16, 17 & 18 present the design and implementation of the management, governance, brokerage and financial management of cloud service and systems.

Jianwen Chen
IBM Corporation, Australia

Yan Zhang
University of Western Sydney, Australia

Ron Gottschalk
IBM Corporation, Australia

Acknowledgment

The editors would like to acknowledge the help of all the people involved in the development of this book and, more specifically, to the authors and reviewers that took part in the review process. Without their support, this book would not have been completed.

We would like to thank each one of the authors for their contributions. Our sincere gratitude goes to the chapter authors who contributed their insights, expertise and time to this book. We have 12 chapters contributed by IBM Distinguish Engineers (DE), Senior Technical Staff Members (STSM) and senior cloud technical leaders from IBM U.S., Europe, India, Australia and Singapore. Sincere thanks to them for bringing the real world cloud experience and the best industrial practice to our audience. We have 6 chapters contributed by the global researchers from different universities and organizations, sincere thanks to them for bringing the leading edge research results to us.

We wish to acknowledge the valuable contributions of the reviewers regarding the improvement of quality, coherence, and content of chapters.

In particular, we are indebted to Rhonda Childress (IBM Fellow and CTO of Security Service) and George Africa (IBM Australia Solutioning Executive Leader and Executive IT Architect), for their contribution in writing Forewords for this book. They are well known global cloud business and technology leaders that design and deliver cloud platforms and services for the enterprises.

Last, we would like to thank our families for their love, patience and support throughout the realization of this book.

Jianwen Chen
IBM Corporation, Australia

Yan Zhang
University of Western Sydney, Australia

Ron Gottschalk
IBM Corporation, Australia
August 2016

Section 1

Chapter 1
Enterprise Mobility
Reference Architecture:
Mobility Services Overview

Laura Richardson
IBM, USA

Sougata Mukherjea
IBM, India

ABSTRACT

The smart phone has become one of the most important devices in our day to day lives. Mobility is also impacting business significantly and most enterprises are providing services to facilitate the mobile workforce. This chapter introduces an enterprise mobility reference architecture. The architecture highlights the key aspects of enterprise mobility such as platform and application development, end user support, collaboration, virtualization, mobile security, monitoring and mobile analytics. The architecture is presented from several viewpoints to cater to different needs of clients. The relationship of the mobile architecture to a cloud reference architecture is also explained. Finally, a use case to demonstrate how a real world scenario maps to the architecture is also discussed.

INTRODUCTION

The purpose of this chapter is to discuss the essential cornerstones of mobile enterprise architecture as they relate to End-to-End Cloud Computing Architecture Design. It is based on IBM's architectural best practices in mobility and covers aspects such as application development, end user support, collaboration, virtualization, device management, and mobile analytics.

Mobility can be defined in many ways. It is about business in motion; business with anyone, anywhere, anytime. Today's Mobile leaders are doing more to integrate mobile into the fabric of their business. Mobile is also about transacting business, driving revenue and leveraging insights from mobile usage to identify and capture new business opportunities.

DOI: 10.4018/978-1-5225-0759-8.ch001

This Reference Architecture Overview uses mobile infrastructure, mobile platforms, mobile software, and mobile services to implement mobile solutions for the enterprise. It is intended to be used by a wide range of clients and architects who are involved in building an end-to-end mobile solution. It shows how IBM builds a solution for the client one level above the technical speak.

The target mobile architecture is based on IBM project experiences in building and supporting mobile and workplace infrastructure, and while being a prescriptive blueprint, it can be implemented with multiple points of variability based on architectural decisions, use cases, requirements and budget. These points of variability do not change the nature of the reference architecture that is designed to maximize the value realized from the IBM experience in building mobile solutions.

Reference Architectures typically provide several views for clients. These can be tailored to client interest or need. Views included in this chapter are:

- Capabilities,
- Functional,
- Cloud-aligned, and
- End user experience

BACKGROUND

Mobile's Disruptive Influence on Business

It's no secret that mobile has fundamentally changed the ways that we live, work and play. Mobility is bringing to light important new features and functions required by the mobile workforce. From an enterprise perspective, if we look beyond the new world of our more mobile workforces, we can see mobile impacting business in even bigger and more profound ways.

First, Mobility is changing and disrupting traditional business models with new data and insight. Employees are interacting, making decisions and taking action in real time. As a result, IDC FutureScape estimates that 100% of the Line of Business apps in customer-facing roles will be built for mobile-first consumption by 2017 (IDC, 2014) .

Second, because of incredible adoption, particularly in growth markets, mobile is bringing consumerization to business. A few years ago simply having a mobile application was sufficient. Now consumers want a superior personalized experience. It is impacting not only their decision to do business with a company in the present, but in the future as well. In fact, according to *"IBM Mobile App Consumer Survey"*, a commissioned study conducted by Forrester Consulting on behalf of IBM in September 2014, 65% of app users said that a poor mobile experience will stop them from making other purchases from a company (IBM, 2014).

Third, mobile is having a huge impact on enterprise IT. Mobile has accelerated the speeds at which applications must be developed and while application demand booms, development is slowed by manual processes, cross platform requirements and complicated integrations with backend data. Also, now applications, data and devices are often not directly within company control. Moreover skills availability continues to plague most organizations. Mobile requires a new approach to IT and organizations that cannot quickly and adequately adapt will fail to fully realize the benefits of mobility (Buckellew, Custis, Esposito & Lesser, 2013).

Because of the increasing importance of mobile in the enterprise the focus of this chapter is the reference architecture for enterprise mobility and the mobile services that can be provided for the enterprise.

Mobility Impacts on Infrastructure

Now consider characteristics of mobile workloads. Mobility means increased web traffic and mobile applications drive an increase in overall transaction rates. For example, when users can check their bank balance anytime, they tend to do it more often. Add to this sensors and actuators; mobility is more than just smartphones. It is estimated devices relaying information to a server will push into the tens of billions in the next few years.

With the increase in mobile traffic, mobile applications can create new and huge increases in transactions. More than simply a concern in the growing average transaction volumes, now the magnitude of peak transaction volumes is a factor as well.

Mobile applications are often first deployed to cloud-based servers. This has led to many new servers being required for smartphone or tablet purchases. With the global adoption of Mobile, IT is now being exposed to a much larger group of new and untrusted users than traditionally seen with web apps and e-commerce.

End User Expectations Evolution

What are we looking for as the mobile workforce? Users want a superior personalized experience. We want systems to be persona driven – in other words to address the goals and behavior of groups and individuals. We want our experience to include real time status updates and seamless connectivity. We also want the systems to be self-maintained and contextually intelligent. For example, banks with automated teller machines (ATMs) can benefit from social data by understanding major sporting events because such events can drive up ATM usage locally. They can adjust maintenance schedules for these ATMs to ensure all machines are in good working order, as well as increasing cash held during these times.

There is a broad set of systems of engagement, including mobile and business applications, which need to be connected in a coherent way so that users can have the same experience from any device, so they can get to data and applications they need from these devices in order for business processes to transform and really leverage the capability of mobility. We once considered mobile components as discreet elements of how you might connect a user and a device to some an application. We now need to think about mobility in terms of systems of engagement. Both end user expectations and systems of engagement are key elements to consider as companies try to:

- Extend business to mobile customers and their workforce,
- Improve operational efficiencies and reduce costs,
- Differentiate the customer experience, and
- Enable new services and business models.

The needs of the mobile business are varied. In our work with 5,000+ enterprise mobility clients, we fine-tuned our approach to enterprise mobility to allow clients to build mobile applications and connect to and run backend systems, while also managing and securing their business, extending capabilities to mobile devices, and transforming their businesses.

Along with its tremendous impact on the enterprise, mobile is also opening up valuable new opportunities. With mobile we can reinvent how we work. More of us are using mobile technologies at work. In fact, use of mobile in the enterprise is growing at about 25% per year (Markets and Markets, 2014). Unfortunately, many companies that have developed strategies for mobile haven't yet moved beyond using mobile as a new way to transact with customers or communicate with employees. But by combining mobile and analytics to serve up rich data on location and in context, we can empower employees to quickly acquire new skills, work better with their organizations and improve decision making.

We can also enable relevant engagement in real time. The ubiquity of mobile and the proliferation of applications are creating an intense battle for mobile mind share. If everyone has an app – and research shows that out of the two dozen apps each of us has on our phones that we spend 80% of our time on just five of them (Husson, 2015). How do you stand out? Successful companies are using data to design engagement systems that seamlessly connect with customers across all channels and turn each new mobile touch point into an opportunity to attract new customers and deepen relationships with existing ones.

Additionally, we can prioritize speed and agility. In 2015 enterprise application development doubled compared to 2014. Organizations are already struggling to keep pace with app requests thanks to the complexity of multiple platforms, the need to continuously update and improve apps, and complex and time consuming backend integration requirements. As a result, 85% of companies have a mobile app backlog of up to 20 apps. With speed and agility as top requirements, now is the time to design a unified approach to mobile systems, platforms and operating models to deliver new levels of integration while managing all manner of complexity.

It is important to make security as important as convenience. For most of us, our mobile device is within arm's reach 90% of the time. In the race for mobile mind share, it is tempting to prioritize speed over security. In fact, about 65% of companies admit that the security of mobile applications is sometimes put at risk to meet customer demand. But at any given moment, malicious code is infecting 11.6 million of our mobile devices (Ponemon Institute, 2015). A mobile first approach is reliant on enterprise-grade security robust enough to ensure that the apps, devices, data and transactions involved in mobile interactions are trustworthy, secure and compliant

MOBILITY SERVICES

A Capabilities View

IBM worked with 5,000+ enterprise mobility clients, to develop our approach to enterprise mobility. The most successful mobile enterprises do four things exceptionally well:

1. They use mobile to fundamentally reinvent the way they do business.
2. They use insights to engage their customers wherever they are.
3. They build applications that unlock core business knowledge for mobile users.
4. They protect and securely manage the mobile enterprise and optimize performance.

We can provide the infrastructure and the services to help achieve these four goals – to reinvent, engage, to build, and secure. New capabilities are needed to introduce the new features and functions of this approach. Let's look at Mobility Services from a capabilities perspective. In Figure 1, we group both new and existing capabilities into multiple domains.

This capability view depicts a set of capabilities clients must consider as they embrace the mobile space – they include capabilities around management, security, analytics, and an application platform. It also shows that these capabilities can be offered as cloud and hosted services. While we're speaking about core mobility services for completeness, we have also highlighted some complimentary services.

Strategy and Design

When a client starts its mobility journey it is critical to explore, assess and plan the mobile solutions. To help clients reinvent and transform, we need to have services to assess the infrastructure to help build a strategy and roadmap. Moreover we need to have services for defining the appropriate Mobile policies. For example, enterprises may define the authentication requirements for accessing enterprise system of records based on the type of network access; a person logging in from the office LAN will need fewer authentication steps than a person using a public Wi-Fi system.

Application and Data Platform

The Mobile application development capabilities enable clients to develop rich mobile applications without lock-in. We should provide the ability to develop both native applications across all popular

Figure 1. Mobility services capabilities view

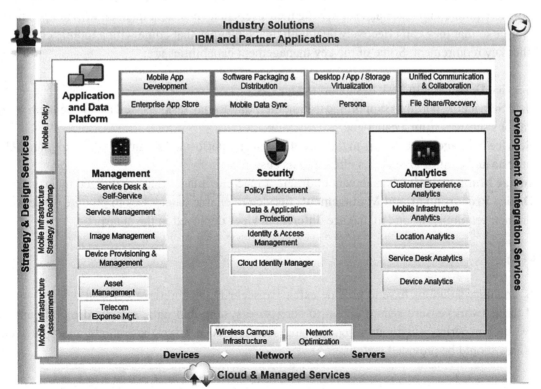

mobile device platforms as well as hybrid applications. The ability to provide an enterprise app store where enterprise clients can provide various applications to facilitate the day to day activities of their employees is also essential. Moreover, we need to allow the developers to seamlessly package the software and distribute it as required. Since users utilize multiple devices to perform their work, the ability to synchronize data across the multiple devices is another key requirement.

Many types of applications are useful for mobile users. Of these some are becoming critical for global enterprises with geographically distributed mobile workforce. Firstly, desktop and application virtualization enables separation of the desktop environment and applications from the client devices that are used to access them. These systems enable employees to perform their job roles from anywhere. Storage virtualization is another key requirement for the mobile workforce. Unified communication and collaboration platforms and applications are also becoming essential for global enterprises since they enable the employees to collaborate across multiple channels and share different files and other information seamlessly irrespective of their geographic locations.

The mobile ecosystem is used by different user personas. The different personas use different devices, require different levels of support and accesses different types of applications and data. The mobile environment should have the ability to adapt itself to serve all different types of user personas effectively.

Management

Management is primarily focused on helping the client to build Mobile Device Management (MDM) capabilities, on bringing "Bring Your Own Device" (BYOD) into the business, and dealing with all the challenges that come with an untrusted mobile environment. These are capabilities that enterprise customers need to ensure that their data is protected, devices are managed, and the enterprise feels confident that they are within compliance and supporting their users in a consistent manner. Providing support to the end user so that they can effectively deal with the challenges that come with a mobile environment is another key requirement. Some of the key management capabilities are:

- **Service Desk:** A help desk to support the end user
- **Self-Service:** A portal to support the user in their day-to-day tasks as well as enable them to order various services from a catalogue.
- **Service Management:** Refers to the activities that are performed by an enterprise to plan, deliver, operate and control IT services offered to its customers.
- **Image Management:** Management of different machine images that are utilized in an enterprise.
- **Device Procurement and Management:** Service to enable enterprises to procure devices based on their requirements and to manage different devices deployed in the enterprise.

Security

Clients' mobility solutions have to provide extensive security capabilities to protect devices and data, defend the network, ensure secure access to enterprise system and data, safeguard mobile apps and preserve user experience without compromising security. To achieve these goals, multiple security capabilities should be provided including:

- **Policy Enforcement:** Enforcing the enterprise security policies
- **Data & Application Protection:** Protection of the sensitive data and applications stored in the devices including facilities to wipe corporate data if the device is lost or stolen.
- **Identity and Access Management:** Identifies and authorizes the user providing risk and context based access to mobile and cloud services. It also blocks unauthorized access.

Analytics

Analytics is very important in order to improve the quality of the mobile application, infrastructure, and support services. In this functional area, we consider the multiple analytics capabilities including:

- **Customer Experience Analytics:** One of the key success criteria for the popularity of a mobile application is to quickly determine the experience of the customers while using a mobile application and correcting any problems that they may be facing.
- **Mobile Infrastructure Analytics:** Analysis of the mobile infrastructure is critical to correct any errors in the applications because of backend issues as well as optimizing the infrastructure to effectively serve the mobile users
- **Location Analytics:** In recent times we can easily monitor the user's location using technologies like Wi-Fi and GPS. Location analytics can enable our clients to determine the best way to serve the customers better by utilizing the location data. Obviously such analysis should ensure that privacy of the end users.
- **Service Desk Analytics:** Service desk analytics utilizes data from various sources like chats, problem tickets to determine root causes of user problem as well as trying to predict problems even before they occur. An effective solution can greatly enhance customer satisfaction, and can provide a personalized experience, as well as efficiency of end user support systems.
- **Device Analytics:** Captures metrics on the actions performed by users on devices that can help improve management of devices.

Development and Integration

There are three stages in the mobile app lifecycle that need to be considered:

1. Developing a mobile application,
2. Running / hosting a mobile solution, and
3. Supporting mobile application end users.

In this chapter we will not get into further details of the application development process. Our focus is on the running and hosting of these applications as well as the mobile end user support.

Other Services

In this document our focus is on Mobility services. Other services which are complimentary have also been highlighted in Figure 1. For example services like asset management and telecom expense management while not core Mobility services, may be useful. Also other security measures, like cloud identity manager may also be required by the clients.

Functional View

Now, let's look at a functional view of the mobile architecture. In this view IT functions that are split into four topology areas as shown in Figure 2.

Devices

The end user interacts with various types of devices. The devices have various types of applications including business, communication and service enablement applications. The devices also have frameworks that provide various types of Application services that are provided by device manufacturer or Mobile Network Service provider or other vendors. These services can be utilized by all types of applications. For example security services can be provided for managing the authentication sequence and for securing the application data and its link to the mobile server. The device itself has OS, containers for enterprise and personal usage, as well as agents to manage the device. Depending on the types of device, it has several capabilities – for example, most smartphones today have different types of sensors as well as storage to enable the user to work offline.

Figure 2. Mobility services high level functional view

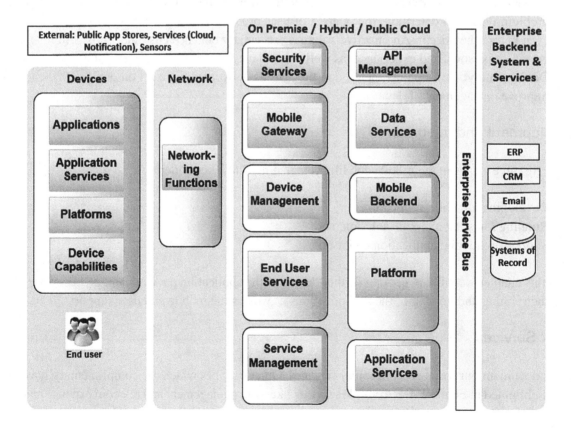

Network

The device interacts with the backend through the Network layer which controls security through the firewall and access management and enables performance using the Load Balancers.

On-Premise/Public/Hybrid Cloud

The mobility services can be hosted either on the client premise or in a public or hybrid cloud. The key components to enable the Mobile ecosystem are:

- The Mobile Gateway marks the entry point from a mobile application to the mobile specific services for the solution, typically offering a set of internet-accessible APIs.
- Device Management focuses on managing devices, mostly in Business to Employee (or B2E) scenarios.
- The Mobile Backend provides runtime services to mobile applications like notification and data sync.
- The Mobile Platform provides some core applications like Mobile application development and Virtualization services.
- Application Services represent the enterprise or industry specific capabilities that need to be available to devices that consume mobile services or drive communications with users of devices. These include various types of analytics services.
- End User Services are services to support the end user like print services and communication & collaboration services.
- Service Management services are performed by an enterprise to plan, deliver, operate and control IT services offered to its customers.
- API Management capabilities advertise the available services endpoints to which the mobile gateway has access.
- Data Services enable mobile application data to be stored and accessed efficiently.
- Security Services enable management of access so that only authorized users can securely access mobile cloud services.

Enterprise Backend

The mobility services interact with the enterprise backend using the enterprise services bus. The enterprise backend contains multiple enterprise applications as well as systems of record.

Those IT functions are shown here in greater detail, again in terms of topology in Figure 3.

Mobility Cloud View

Cloud services are a good match for supporting mobile devices. Mobile applications tend to have time variable usage patterns that are well handled by the scalability and elasticity of cloud computing - increasing and decreasing the backend resources to match the level of requests from the mobile devices. It is also characteristic of mobile applications to make use of server-side data.

Figure 3. Mobility services detailed functional view

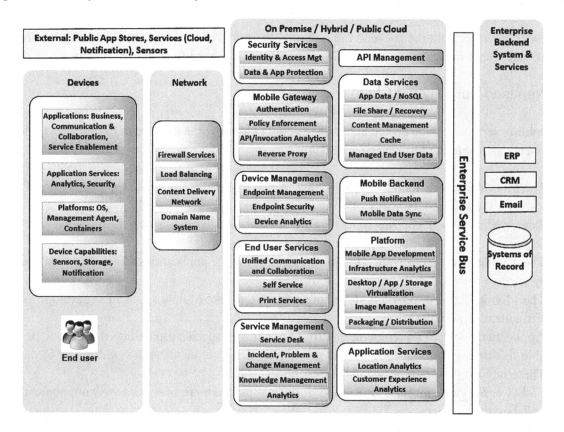

The Cloud Standards Customer Council (CSCC) provides guidance to multiple cloud standards-defining bodies. The CSCC establishes criteria for open standards based cloud computing. One of their 2015 projects was Mobile Cloud Architecture and a Customer Reference Architecture was developed as part of the project (Cloud Standard Customer Council, 2015).

Figure 4 shows a high level view of the Mobile Cloud Customer Reference Architecture that is derived from the CCSC project. The figure shows how a mobile device, containing the platform and applications, connects to the core cloud components including mobile gateway, mobile backend, application and end user services, data services and security services while transformation and connectivity gets relevant data from enterprise systems and puts it in a format that can be leveraged on mobile devices. Note that this view is consistent with the Functional view that was described before. This Cloud view is also consistent with ISO/IEC 17789 International Standard Cloud Computing Reference Architecture and IBM Customer Cloud Reference Architecture (CCRA).

End User View

While capabilities reflect the technology needed, often our clients approach us in the framework of their organization and their need to improve and transform the user experience. Users are increasingly becoming accustomed to instant gratification when using technology in their personal lives, whether for gaming, shopping or managing their daily activities. They want the same kind of immediate service

Figure 4. Mobile cloud customer reference architecture high level view

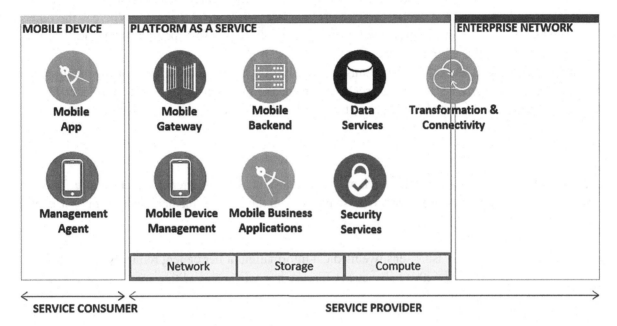

when they go to work. To address this expectation, IT support needs to adapt, evolve and even revolutionize itself or become outdated.

Figure 5 is the client needs view and it is also a good operational view. Customers can easily recognize their own organization within this structure. This could also be seen as a governance view.

Customers today are driving towards a superior, personalized end user experience. If we look at this from an end users' experience view, end users are served in a variety of ways. And today that's through desktop as a service, mobile devices, thin clients, and thick clients. The services that they receive on that platform are driven by personas and include analytics and policies.

Figure 5. End user experience view

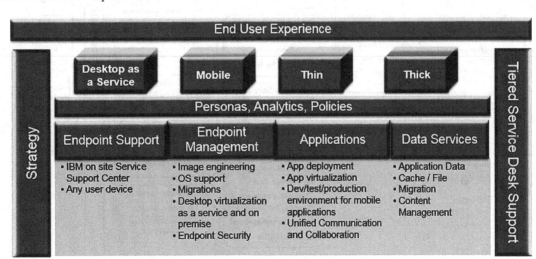

The services that we provide (underneath that area) include endpoint support, endpoint management, applications and data services. This is an end user services view of what we do. Whereas the others views are an overall Mobility architecture views, this is really from a standpoint of the legacy end user experience, and how this all translates.

In order to transform and exploit the promise of mobility, the enterprise systems of engagement should present a seamless experience to the end user based on enterprise policies and the role of the user. IT support must reinvent itself into a friendly, proactive service that is tied directly to a business' profitability.

Use Case

Let us now look at a use case and discuss how the scenario maps to the reference architecture. This use case presents a healthcare scenario and represents a day in the life of a medical doctor. It consists of 3 scenes:

- A doctor securely accessing sensitive medical information of her patient remotely.
- A doctor collaborating with a colleague to discuss her patient's condition
- A doctor working remotely

Figure 6 highlights the architecture components that are being utilized during the scenario.

Figure 6. Components of the reference architecture utilized in the healthcare scenario

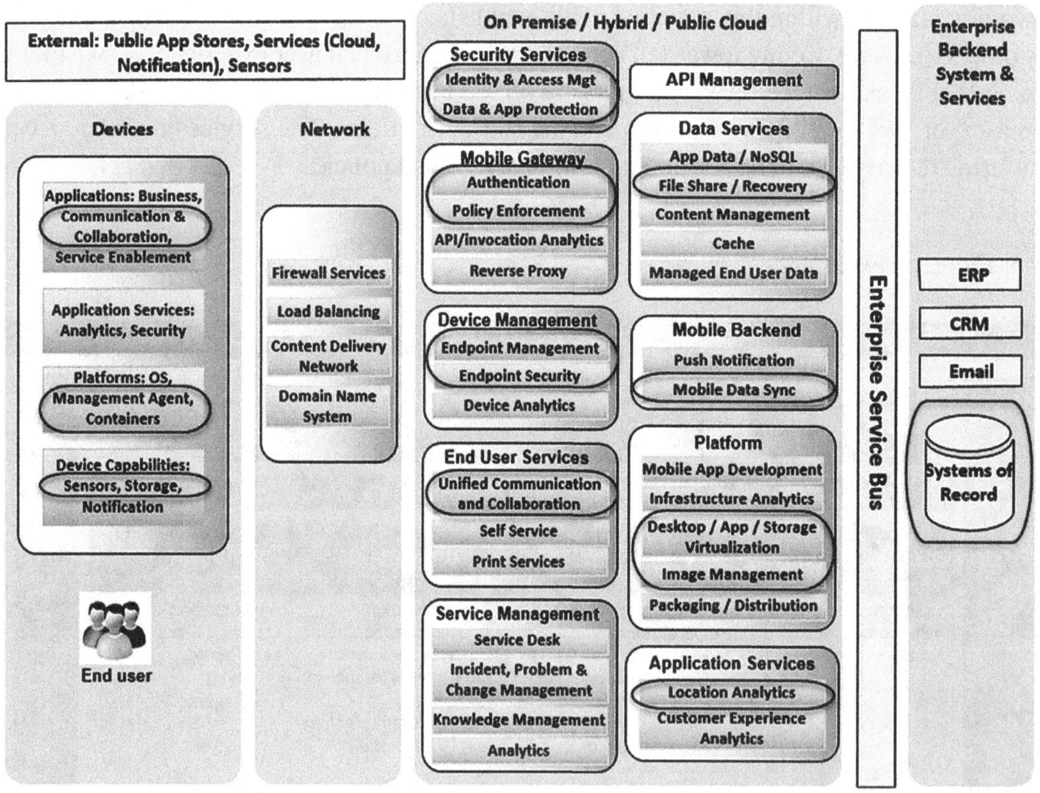

When the doctor is accessing the medical records of her patents she accesses the data using the secure enterprise container on her device. The mobile gateway marks the entry point from a mobile app to the mobile specific services for the solution and identifies, authenticates and authorizes the user, using a variety of methods and token types using the Identity and Access Management security services. The Mobile Gateway also enforces corporate policies during invocations from mobile devices.

After the user is authenticated she can access the Enterprise Systems of Record for the patent data. During this interaction between the device and the backend the management agent on the device interacts with the device management and security services at the backend to ensure the security of the data. The user has the option to download a version of a file to work offline. While the file can be downloaded to the device to ensure security it can only be accessed within the secure container in the device. When the user is again online this file is synced to the backend automatically so that any other user accessing the data with have the latest version.

To collaborate with colleagues the doctor needs to utilize the Communication & Collaboration application on the device to interact with the corresponding service at the backend. This service enables the users to share files if required over a secure channel. If the doctor requires the patient to refer to a specialist for consultation, the GPS on the device can be used to determine the user's location and the location analytics service can determine a doctor with the required expertise in the proximity.

The ability to work remotely is a key requirement for enterprises. The Virtualization framework provides a virtual desktop that allows an employee to access to confidential and compliance-related information that isn't stored on the device, reducing their exposure should it ever be lost or stolen. This enables the employee to work efficiently in remote locations.

CONCLUSION

It should be emphasized that there has been and continues to be rapid advancement in the field of mobile technology. For example cognitive computing will start to play a major role in mobile end user services. Moreover with the explosive growth of mobile data secure storage and management of the data will become essential. Therefore the reference architecture needs to be constantly refined so that it can represent the start-of-the-art.

As consumers and the workforce become more mobile and utilize multiple devices for their day to day activities, End-to-End Cloud Computing Architecture Design can benefit from a Mobility perspective on Reference Architecture. The goal of this reference architecture overview is to provide practical guidance on how common business applications can be achieved and to act as stabilizing force or foothold in a rapidly evolving mobile landscape We believe that the different mobile reference architecture views that have been presented in this chapter will enable architects and developers to effectively design end-to-end mobile solutions.

REFERENCES

Buckellew, P., Custis, K., Esposito, R., & Lesser, E. (2013). *The upwardly mobile enterprise: Setting the strategic agenda*. Retrieved from http://www-01.ibm.com/common/ssi/cgi-bin/ssialias?infotype=PM&subtype=XB&htmlfid=GBE03574USEN

Cloud Standard Customer Council. (2015). *Customer Cloud Architecture for Mobile*. Retrieved from http://www.cloud-council.org/CSCC-Webinar-Customer-Cloud-Architecture-for-Mobile-6-16-15.pdf

Husson, T. (2015). *Five Myths about Mobile Apps*. Retrieved from http://blogs.forrester.com/thomas_husson/15-01-30-five_myths_about_mobile_apps

IBM. (2014). *IBM Mobile App Consumer Survey*, a commissioned study conducted by Forrester Consulting on behalf of IBM. Retrieved from http://www.ibm.com/mobilefirst/us/en/good-apps-bad-apps.html

IDC. (2014). *IDC Reveals Worldwide Mobile Enterprise Applications and Solutions Predictions for 2015*. Retrieved from http://www.idc.com/getdoc.jsp?containerId=prUS25350514

Markets and Markets. (2014). *Bring Your Own Device (BYOD) & Enterprise Mobility Market Global Advancements, Market Forecast and Analysis (2014 – 2019)*. Retrieved from http://www.marketsandmarkets.com/PressReleases/byod.asp

Ponemon Institute. (2015). *The State of Mobile Application Insecurity*. Retrieved from http://www.workplaceprivacyreport.com/wp-content/uploads/sites/162/2015/03/WGL03074USEN.pdf

Chapter 2
Navigating Your Way to the Hybrid Cloud

John Easton
IBM Corporation, UK

Rashik Parmar
IBM Corporation, UK

ABSTRACT

The authors believe that cloud computing systems should become hybrid in nature for organisations to realise the full business potential that the cloud offers: increased agility, velocity and innovation in business IT. Yet hybrid environments are complex to design, implement and run. To the organisations implementing them, these systems present many architectural challenges that must be solved if the resulting solution is to deliver desired business outcomes. This chapter defines the different types of hybrid cloud: those seen to date as well as those that will emerge in the near future. Using seven key business use cases as a framework, the authors propose a high-level architecture for hybrid cloud computing environments that is practically illustrated with real-world client examples.

INTRODUCTION

Many organisations that have begun to adopt cloud computing have run into problems when faced with systems and workloads that don't easily move into the cloud paradigm. These organisations have tried to adopt a hybrid cloud approach according to the definition described by the National Institute of Standards and Technology (NIST) but fail because their environments don't correspond to this model. The main challenge with both of these approaches is that they assume one or both of the systems being integrated are cloud-like in nature. There is also a seeming unwritten bias that assumes that cloud is "new" and hence "good," whereas the more traditional systems are "old" and hence "bad." By understanding the ways that these types of systems are used by businesses, an architecture for these hybrid cloud systems that cuts through these problems can be defined. Readers of this chapter will gain a better understanding of the challenges of hybrid cloud and be shown a hybrid cloud architecture that illustrates a solution.

DOI: 10.4018/978-1-5225-0759-8.ch002

BACKGROUND

Whilst IT automation techniques for systems and software are well understood, cloud computing has made possible the extensive automation of the IT support processes for managing and administering information technology (IT) systems, thereby providing many unique benefits when compared to traditional IT models. Cloud services can automatically reconfigure infrastructure components to cope with rapidly changing workload demands. The time required to move a suite of computer programs to a state in which the users are able to use the systems can be dramatically reduced through automation. These are the primary advantages of cloud computing as a tool to support businesses. Additionally, cloud provides a new way of exposing business services to customers, partners and suppliers. These business services are presented as application programming interfaces (APIs). A new API economy is emerging in the cloud, where digital services are purchased and combined with additional data or programs to support business activities. The innovation potential of cloud computing allows new business patterns to emerge. These are explored in "The New Patterns of Innovation" (Parmar, McKenzie, Cohn & Gann, 2014).

Organisations want to build on their prior IT or cloud investments. To do this, they must eventually adopt an approach that is inherently hybrid in nature. In this section the authors explain the rationale for this belief.

To understand the different ways that organisations deliver cloud services to their customers and users requires the authors to first describe the differences in IT delivery for organisations whose IT is "born on the cloud" and those using "traditional IT" delivery models.

The born-on-the-cloud model is typically found within newer, "startup" type organisations that have developed their IT relatively recently and are using new or non-traditional approaches to create applications, deliver infrastructure and services, etc. Instead of owning any IT themselves, they may procure what they need, when they need it from a service provider. They likely develop applications in modern or emerging programming languages and are focused on the rapid delivery of minimum viable products using agile development approaches. They are also consumers of many different open source technologies, and they consume these services from wherever they deem most appropriate.

Organisations with born-on-the-cloud IT tend to operate in ways very different from those following a traditional IT approach, which is the approach that most readers would think of when business IT is mentioned. Though there are many ways that the traditional IT approach can be realised, these tend to be less agile and process-driven as well as use a much wider range of hardware, software and service components to deliver services. Organisations with traditional IT tend to use open source less often and most have relationships with a relatively small number of hardware and software vendors. Programming, if done at all, likely follows a waterfall delivery model and is supported by traditional project management methods.

These born-on-the-cloud and traditional IT approaches are not mutually exclusive; each delivers value to organisations. It is important to understand the differences in the architectural aspects of each approach, which are mainly related to how applications are designed, created and managed.

Traditional enterprise IT applications tend to be built on the assumption that they will be running on a resilient infrastructure platform. The way in which that resilience is delivered may vary—resilient server, high availability cluster, etc.—but the application itself isn't devoting resources to how it's going to recover from failures. If a disk fails, the underlying RAID array in a disk subsystem masks this from the application. If a network adapter fails, a second adapter is available to take over the network traffic, moving IP and/or MAC addresses such that the application only sees a delay in the arrival of network packets. Even failures of entire servers may be masked by the use of commonplace failover techniques.

In contrast, an application that was born on the cloud can make very few assumptions about the availability of the underlying platform. To deliver the lowest cost offered by some cloud providers, there is no inherent systems availability built into the servers or virtual machines delivered to the user. Failures are left to the application writer to deal with. The only assumption an application can make is that things will change; components will come and go. This type of application is designed to be aware of and cope with changes as they emerge so that it can continue to offer its service to users.

Data in these two environments also tends to be handled in different ways. Say an application uses a database to store information. The traditional IT approach is often based on the atomicity, consistency, isolation, and durability (ACID) of the database. The ACID properties of a transaction rely on the infrastructure being available to store data reliably. This leads to the database being consistent at all times. At the other end of the spectrum, the born-on-the-cloud approach is based on an "eventual consistency" model where the database will become consistent at some point in time, but it is not guaranteed when that will be. A born-on-the-cloud application should be able to manage potential inconsistencies in its underlying data.

Traditional IT systems tend to change relatively infrequently. There are many reasons for this, but it is most often because of the service level agreements (SLAs) that are in place for the services that such systems provide. An IT organisation managing to an SLA tends to avoid doing anything that might put that SLA at risk. Consequently, all changes, systems maintenance requests and updates are reviewed, managed through change control processes, and implemented with appropriate back out plans should anything go wrong. SLAs might also require the system to be available for use at all times, so there would be minimal opportunities to take a system offline to make changes. All of these factors combine such that change is infrequent.

Born-on-the-cloud IT is frequently synonymous with DevOps. DevOps is a new delivery paradigm characterised by frequent delivery of small changes in a highly automated and agile fashion. A developer might create a new application function or fix a bug in his or her code. This new code is tested using automated tools that ensure the function is safe before being deployed into production. The monolithic codebases of a traditional enterprise application are not well suited to such an approach. Any update could potentially require the entire program to be retested. This is one reason why DevOps approaches are hard to adopt for more traditional kinds of applications. Born-on-the-web applications tend to be much more modular with a high degree of independence between modules. Interfaces tend to be the only points of consistency. This modular approach and the emerging microservices trend allow for modules to be developed and changed at different speeds and on different timescales.

The colliding worlds of born-on-the-cloud and traditional IT paradigms have given rise to a range of terms: bimodal IT (Gartner), multimodal IT (Ovum), and "third platform" (IDC). Regardless of the name that it has been given, there are many challenges involved in bringing these worlds together. In order to understand the architectural challenges involved in designing, building and running a hybrid cloud, it is necessary to investigate what one means by "hybrid cloud." The National Institute of Standards and Technology (NIST) provides the following definition (Mell & Grance, 2014):

The cloud infrastructure is a composition of two or more distinct cloud infrastructures (private, community, or public) that remain unique entities, but are bound together by standardized or proprietary technology that enables data and application portability (e.g., cloud bursting for load balancing between clouds).

Experience with a wide range of clients has told the authors that a definition this simple is insufficient to describe the range of different environments that organisations wish to implement today. Almost all of the previous cloud literature (Grozev, & Buyya, 2014; Hamdaqa, & Tahvildari, 2014; Kertesz, 2014; Lunawat & Patankar, 2014; Rao, Naveena, & David, 2015; Serrano, Gallardo, & Hernantes, 2015; Tarannum & Ahmed, 2014; Toosi, Calheiros & Buyya, 2014) in this space uses the NIST definition, so many of the types of environments being created by businesses today have been ignored. These hybrid environments tend to fall into two main categories: cloud of clouds and cloud to non-cloud.

Types of Hybrid Cloud

- **Cloud of Clouds:** A hybrid IT environment containing components that originated in different cloud computing environments. For example, an organisation is consuming two separate software-as-a-service (SaaS) offerings from different providers, an ecommerce application and a web analytics platform, and combines them to generate new business insights.
- **Cloud to Non-Cloud:** A cloud computing environment linked to existing systems. For example, connecting onsite customer relationship management and transaction processing systems to a cloud-based platform that supports mobile devices. These types of existing systems are not likely to be cloud platforms, making it necessary to understand the ways in which cloud and non-cloud platforms can be integrated into a single system.

Though these two categories appear to be simple to comprehend at first, the following factors add complexity to this categorisation scheme:

- **Single Ownership and Multi-Ownership Hybrids:** Hybrid clouds in which a single organisation owns or controls all of the components should be treated differently from those where different components are under the ownership or control of different organisations. This may be as simple as an organisation consuming services from a cloud service provider. Different ownership leads to different policies around issues such as the security measures being applied to different components within the hybrid arrangement.
- **On-Site and Off-Site Hybrids:** A hybrid cloud with all of its components physically located in a single geographic location has different architectural implications as opposed to one in which the components are in different locations. A hybrid cloud located within an enterprise's perimeter security will likely have very different security characteristics to one where the enterprise security domain must be extended to encompass external services. Likewise, the latency implications of a connection to a remote service on the overall performance or throughput of a business service will be different from one where all components are in the same physical location.
- **Managed Versus Unmanaged Hybrids:** Cloud computing is often described as a significantly cheaper way to deliver IT services. Descriptions such as this tend to result from the low headline prices offered for many services; this makes them look cheaper than their more traditional counterparts. However, this perception usually isn't based on a like-for-like comparison. Most traditional IT platforms have a complex supporting management discipline involving people, processes and tools. Cloud options, particularly those that are the cheapest, offer no management. To be more correct, the cloud platform itself may be managed to a certain level—typically to the hypervisor—but there is no management from the cloud service provider above that. If there is, it costs

extra. Rather than describing this as "unmanaged," the term "user managed" is more accurate: the user of the cloud service takes the responsibility for its management. Different management disciplines for different components within the hybrid arrangement lead to more complexity.

- **API Hybrids:** Providers hold very different perspectives on cloud services as opposed to consumers. However, much of the hybrid cloud discussion to date has been very consumer-centric in nature. As organisations use cloud as a key to innovation in the areas of new business models and new revenue streams, consumers of cloud services may find themselves acting as cloud service providers in their own right. For example, they might consume infrastructure services from one cloud provider and use these, plus their industry expertise or specialised in-house developed software, to deliver software as a service (SaaS) or business process as a service (BPaaS) to their customers. Increasingly, these services will be delivered via an API rather than a traditional application. This allows consumers of the service to incorporate specific application services from the provider within their own application without needing to consume that application as a whole. One can then conceive of an application that is offered via a cloud service to a consumer that is using an application and data services from multiple other underlying cloud providers. The management and control of such an API hybrid application gives rise to many challenges that organisations must address in order to exploit this approach to business innovation.

INTRODUCING THE SEVEN HYBRID CLOUD USE CASES

Through the analysis of many hybrid cloud projects, the authors have identified seven common use cases for hybrid clouds. The authors discuss these use cases and in particular highlight the similarities and differences that affect a hybrid cloud's architecture. The seven use cases are:

1. Independent workloads,
2. SoE-SoR integration,
3. Portability and optimization,
4. Hybrid cloud brokerage,
5. Backup and archive,
6. Capacity access, and
7. Disaster recovery.

These use cases define how the cloud operates to support a particular client business need and are described in more detail in the next sections.

Independent Workloads

This use case, as its name suggests, arises in a hybrid cloud environment where different workloads run independently on different parts of the hybrid system and require little or no integration between them. As an example, consider the case in which an organisation is consuming an email service from one cloud provider and an accounting application service from another. While there may be some desire to link these two environments together to support specific user needs, each workload can run independent from the other. Should either service become unavailable, the other will continue to run as before.

SoE-SoR Integration

To better understand this use case, it is important to first explain the terminology. The terms "systems of record" (SoR) and "systems of engagement" (SoE) were first introduced in the paper "Systems of Engagement and the Future of Enterprise IT: A Sea Change in Enterprise IT" (Moore, 2011). "System of record" are defined as "conventional enterprise systems designed to contain the authoritative data source for a given piece of information." These systems are those that are typically required to run an enterprise. They would be the key transaction processing systems of a retail bank, for instance. These systems tend to have very high service levels associated with them, and the nature of the data stored within them requires them to be highly secure. To meet these requirements, they tend to be highly managed and change infrequently.

The same paper describes a "system of engagement" as very different from a SoR and as having a "focus on people, not processes, and by harnessing mobile, social and big data to deliver apps and smart products directly". The nature of these systems is that they must change frequently to meet the needs of their users or customers. Consider a web retailer that interacts with a wide range of users via web browsers and app interfaces on mobile devices. The user experience is paramount, so the services offered change regularly in response to the actions of competitors, new marketing activities and new services being delivered through the platform.

The SoE-SoR hybrid cloud use case is typically found where an existing, traditional enterprise system is integrated with a cloud platform that offers more agile customer engagement attributes; for example, where a "web shop" and ecommerce platform acts as a front end to legacy order processing and enterprise resource planning (ERP) systems. Combining these two environments delivers synergistic benefits beyond what a single system can offer. In its initial form, this is simply an integration between two applications running on different systems. More advanced use combines data from both system environments and applies analytical techniques to deliver greater insight than what one could gain from either system on its own. This form of integration is referred to as a "system of insight" (SOI).

A frequently cited example of such would be something called "next best action," which raises the question, what is the best thing I could do next to generate a desired customer outcome? That outcome could be leading a customer to purchase more in a single visit to an ecommerce website or to retain a valuable customer while encouraging a less-valued one to leave. This combines data from both systems of record (such as a customer transaction history) with activities in the system of engagement, and performs a real-time analytical calculation to determine what offer can achieve the desired business goal.

Portability and Optimisation

This use case is based on an organisation having the ability to run applications or consume equivalent cloud services from a number of different platforms or providers. The use case describes not only the capabilities required to gain that ability, such as the equivalence of the services being provided (for example, an x86 virtual machine delivered by an infrastructure-as-a-service provider), but also the decision-making process that an organisation should go through to determine where best to run a workload. This could be as simple as a least-cost determination, in which the cloud provider is chosen on the basis of whomever is offering the lowest price per virtual machine at the time the service is requested. It could likewise be a more complex decision driven by a requirement to store different data objects within different cloud storage services in a way that ensures that legislative compliance is maintained.

Hybrid Cloud Brokerage

If an organisation intends to consume services from different cloud providers, then a mechanism that hides the complexities of this sort of environment from general users and makes the management of the environment simpler is a necessity. The optimisation and portability use case can be regarded as a simple example of a brokerage in which the two services are functionally equivalent. Typically, this functional equivalence only occurs at the level of the underlying infrastructure services, where 10 TB of storage or an x86 virtual machine with 4 GB of memory can easily be compared. Such technical services are likely to be unsuitable for a general business user to consume directly, and are typically hidden within a higher-level cloud service to meet a specific business need. For example, wanting to create a website or run a marketing campaign are tasks described in simple terms, but they may require the complex orchestration of lower-level services from multiple cloud providers to complete. Cloud brokerage can hide this complexity from the user and can occur on multiple levels, each of which have different implications for a hybrid cloud architecture.

Backup and Archive

This describes the use case where a hybrid cloud exists to provide a backup for the data created by one or more other systems.

Capacity Access

The capacity access use case is a generic description of the model that many would understand or describe as "cloud bursting." It is typically identified as a solution in which an existing system environment has insufficient resource capability to meet current workload demands. A cloud provider adds capacity to the running system to augment the resource-constrained environment. The nature of the workloads being run and the speed at which the cloud provider can provision resources lead to capacity access models being operated in different ways. Consider the case of a life sciences company doing drug discovery. The process is computationally intensive and runs on a compute grid. Now assume that the company has such a cluster on its own premises, but needs to analyse more potential drug molecules than it has the capacity to do within the time allotted. The company might extend its grid by using additional systems from a cloud provider. Depending on the software environment, this could be a dynamic extension invoked by automation code run by the system or one that is manually invoked in advance. Another example would be a web retailer that adds more capacity for a few months to support the increased workload expected during Christmas and New Year's sales.

Disaster Recovery

The final use case is of a cloud platform that is used to provide a disaster recovery platform to another system, cloud or non-cloud. This could itself be regarded as a hybrid of both the "backup and archive" and "capacity access" use cases.

DEFINING A NEW HYBRID CLOUD ARCHITECTURE

The use cases clarify the definition of high-level architecture for a hybrid cloud by describing the different hybrid cloud environments. This high-level architecture will be elaborated through discussion of the following:

- Architectural components or "key building blocks" that comprise the hybrid cloud platform. Each building block will be described in detail, along with its relationships and interconnections to other architectural building blocks.
- Key considerations for selecting an architectural model and its components.

The building blocks "agile edge" and "industrialised core" represent the two types of IT systems that a business must have to be successful. The industrialised core is made up of traditional IT systems that have been engineered over many years, such as ERP or CRM systems. The agile edge provides rapidly changing systems that enable rapid experimentation and new capabilities, as can be found in born-on-the-cloud organisations. These two building blocks must share information and services, which is the role of the integration building block. The brokerage building block provides the overall orchestration and management of the hybrid cloud environment. The traditional security perimeters of IT systems are no longer sufficient in the hybrid cloud. A new security approach is required, which is provided by the security building block. To achieve the overall agility and velocity needed for the hybrid cloud, a DevOps approach that spans an organisation's entire IT environment is required. That approach is represented by the development and operations building block. Finally, organisations will want a level of confidence in the long-term viability of these technologies. The standards component defines the current dominant standards and highlights areas for growth (see Figure 1).

BUILDING BLOCKS IN THE HYBRID CLOUD ARCHITECTURE

The hybrid cloud architecture building blocks defined in the previous section are described in detail.

Figure 1. The high-level hybrid IT architecture

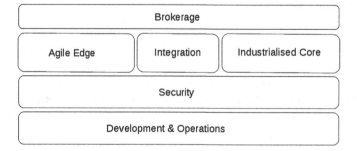

Standards

Once technologies have matured, standards drive commoditisation of the common technology components. In many cases, open ecosystems provide free access to the software that implements the standards. Commercial organisations add value to this open software by providing choice and confidence in the services to administer, maintain and manage these systems. The pace and scale of the innovation of these standard components make them a compelling choice for the hybrid cloud building blocks.

Standards are evident in all the building blocks within the hybrid cloud architecture. The NIST cloud computing reference architecture describes a range of standards within the three common layers of a cloud computing environment: infrastructure as a service (IaaS), platform as a service (PaaS) and software as a service (SaaS).

The lowest level of the standard to be considered is the technology to virtualise hardware components into a software-defined environment. OpenStack has emerged as the dominant open standard for the delivery of the IaaS component, but there are many alternatives available from commercial companies. Hybrid cloud interoperability is greatly facilitated by the use of open standards. Alongside OpenStack, it is worth mentioning other open technologies such as the KVM hypervisor and container support from Docker.

Specific to the hybrid cloud, organisations should consider which standards allow them to implement the building blocks in an efficient and affordable manner. Implementations should create a unified pool of hardware resources that can be housed in the organisation's data centres, be dedicated resources for the sole use of that organisation, or be shared, public resources. Using a standard allows systems to be dynamically provisioned to any of the resource pools based on defined enterprise rules.

In the hybrid cloud context, PaaS abstracts middleware components to simplify and automate the deployment and provisioning of a unique platform needed for any application. Cloud Foundry is a common and growing open standard for PaaS. Unique to the hybrid environment, PaaS must be customised to expose the middleware needed for integration with traditional IT systems and across various clouds.

Each SaaS component will build on a range of PaaS and IaaS standards, and will have its own domain-specific standard. It will also likely conform to a number of common approaches, such as the use of security assertion markup language (SAML) for authentication and authorisation or representational state transfer (REST) APIs for interoperability. The standards to be considered here are the interfaces of these SaaS components, which are typically specific to industry domains.

The final standard that should be considered in the hybrid cloud is the application container. These containers can be dynamically provisioned to one or more cloud environments, allowing new levels of resource optimisation and efficiency. Docker is the growing standard for application containers.

Selection of the applicable standards for a hybrid cloud allows businesses to meet expectations while giving them confidence in future viability, choice and competitiveness.

Development and Operations

The combined development and operations building block is often referred to as DevOps. This provides the capability to develop, deploy and manage all the resources in the hybrid cloud environment. DevOps should be extended across multiple cloud environments and traditional IT components. Common or standards-based technology components can simplify and, in some cases, make the hybrid cloud viable. The components for this building block are shown in Figure 2.

Figure 2. The development and operations building block

Developers use a range of integrated development environments (IDE) and source code management (SCM) tools. In an ideal world, only one IDE and SCM would be required for the overall hybrid scope. That scenario is unlikely in reality; organisations should develop approaches for combining all the code and resources for applications to flow through the automated stages. A unified repository such as GITHUB is often used as the entry point to the hybrid DevOps process.

Release management defines the approach for staging code from development into testing and production. The hybrid scope covers systems that change on a rapid (perhaps daily) cycle, such as in the agile edge building block, as well as those released on monthly or annual cycles, such as the industrialised core building block. The releases are designed to achieve new business outcomes by providing new or improved IT capabilities. If one considers the requirements of these two different deployment platforms, one can better understand how it works in practice. Consider the industrialised core. Here, much of the functionality is well proven and required to be reliable, secure and performant. Changes made here are infrequent and typically associated with improving efficiency. Given its non-functional characteristics, any changes are likely to be highly reviewed, tested and implemented with comprehensive contingency plans. This ensures the system can still deliver its business functions in case a release does not go according to plan. Contrast that approach with the agile edge, where changes are often about delivering new business functions on a codebase that is less proven and tested. Defects reported by users are likely addressed in the same code deployments that implement new functions. The agile nature of its development and delivery relies on a much higher percentage of automated testing, such that when tests pass, code can automatically be promoted into the production systems that make up the agile edge.

As each code drop is released, changes are integrated into the package and move along to automated testing. The Continuous Integration component ensures the integrity of the code and supporting middleware components. Developers write scripts to ensure the required middleware and supporting systems are available. Any additional resources needed for automated testing are included with the release.

Unit testing is typically unchanged in the hybrid environment. Additional testing stages, such as integration testing, system testing and regression testing, are often more complex. Those stages must include multiple clouds or traditional IT systems, provision all the test components, instantiate test databases, execute the tests, and review results against expectations. The goal should be that the whole process for the hybrid cloud environment, including any traditional IT environment, can be completed without manual intervention. This requires automated provisioning of all the components within the scope. This may not be possible in some traditional IT environments.

Integration, performance and security testing are the three areas that require special consideration in the hybrid cloud environment. Each must cater to cases that are relevant to the various cloud models and traditional IT.

Once an application has completed the testing, it can be provisioned to live environments.

Access to a comprehensive suite of the operational metrics for components within the hybrid cloud is made possible through instrumentation. Consider what metrics are needed for each component in each state. How can one capture those metrics? Creating a repository of all metrics over time allows one to use analytics tools to identify trends and predict future demands or constraints. The repository also aids in the identification of problems. The hybrid cloud requires a mature and effective problem management process because of the additional complexity of multiple cloud and traditional IT environments.

The traditional processes of service-level management, capacity management, service planning and service monitoring should be adapted to the hybrid cloud environment. Though the metrics repository provides a foundation to adapt these practices, interactions between the dynamic cloud environments and traditional IT systems often require the development of predictive models. The embedded instrumentation allows a comprehensive data store of all operational information. Automated dashboards that use analytics provide an instant view of the overall health of services and allow for the creation of automated actions, such as increasing or reducing resources for a service.

Determining the root causes of any issues requires a comprehensive view of the components and their interactions. The increased number of components and the types of components makes problem determination increasingly complex. Having standards for the logging of information and log record content is critical.

Just because this is a cloud platform does not remove the need for those traditional IT management components also found in a tradtional IT systems environment: Event Management, Incident Management, Change Management, Request Management and so on. Whilst many of these competencies operate very differently within a cloud environment does not remove the requirement for these capabilities to be supported within this building block. The cloud platform provider may provide tooling as part of the platform to achieve these goals or this may be an addition needing to be brought to the platform by the service consumer

Security

Traditional security systems focus on establishing boundaries by only allowing authorised users to access systems, protecting the privacy of data and application functions by limiting access through a control list. In addition, physical security limits physical access to the infrastructure. The evolution to a hybrid IT creates a much wider range of security threats and requires additional security capabilities. Security systems should have forensic algorithms to identify potential threats and learning algorithms to initiate automated responses. Figure 3 shows the components of a hybrid cloud security building block.

Identification determines the characteristics of an individual or service attempting to access a service. Important information about the source includes biometric information, user location and other unique identifiers. Depending on the service being protected, the range of identification factors can be increased.

Figure 3. The security building block

Security					
Identification	Analytics		Audit	Encryption
Authentication	Access Control	Risk Management	Logging	Compliance

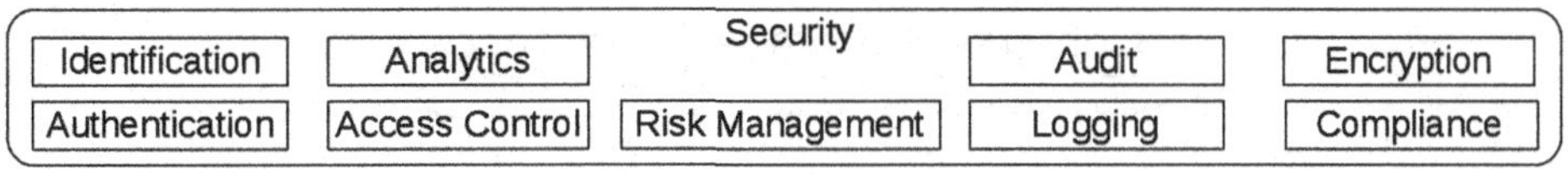

Authentication uses the details captured by the identification component along with a passcode to validate an identity. In the hybrid cloud, the user may need to use services that require a range of different mechanisms. The credential token is often used to authenticate those services. For higher levels of security, multi-factor mechanisms are used.

Access control defines the services and users that may access any service, data or resource. In the hybrid cloud, the access control list details should be kept consistent across different clouds and traditional IT systems to avoid creating unexpected vulnerabilities.

Encryption complements other services by providing a range of mechanisms to ensure data cannot be tampered with en route and can only be read by the intended recipient. In the hybrid cloud, encryption keys should be kept consistent.

Logging involves keeping detailed records of all security events. In the hybrid cloud, there will be multiple logs with multiple formats. This log information should be combined to identify significant security events. Establishing a consistent format is ideal, but rarely possible. The various formats should be mapped to a common format for analysis, either as a service or as an integrated data store. Logging and Audit go hand in hand when it comes to proving that the system is being operated in accordance with the required policies and legislative frameworks that the organisation may need to operate within.

Analytics includes a range of algorithms that analyse logging databases and additional data to identify the range of the security threats. Creating simple dashboards is the primary result of those analytics. The majority of the security data is unstructured text that requires textual analysis algorithms to identify events and create structured metadata. Trend analysis is used to identify the normal operating parameters, so alerts can be generated for unexpected changes which could indicate security threats.

Finally, Compliance ensures that security procedures adhere to legislative, commercial and organisational policies. This also uses the logging and audit information along with the analytics technologies. Security at its core is about Risk Management, hence the existence of this as the final component within the Security Building Block.

Agile Edge

The agile edge is a cloud computing environment that hosts rapidly changing services. The edge can be accessed via web, mobile devices, embedded devices for Internet-of-Things networks or APIs. The ability to cope with rapidly changing development tools and techniques distinguishes the agile edge from traditional IT environments. It provides an ideal place to experiment with or test prototypes of new services. Being able to provide new releases of these services on a daily or hourly basis is an essential capability of the agile edge (see Figure 4).

Figure 4. The agile edge building block

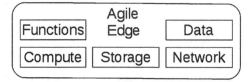

The functions often combine software-as-a-service components with proprietary components. The cloud capabilities of compute, network and storage provide the ideal platform for an agile edge. PaaS allows the middleware capabilities to be dynamically instantiated to satisfy the requirements of the functions.

Data within the agile edge represents a wide range of non-traditional information. Social media interactions, mouse movements, location information and sensor data are good examples of the data that is captured in the agile edge. As this data can rapidly grow, data storage and management requires careful consideration. For example, is all the data necessary? Can the data be compressed? What is the backup requirement?

Integration

The integration component facilitates the interconnection of services across the hybrid cloud. The primary interconnections are between the industrialised core and the agile edge building blocks. Integration also plays a critical role in security, DevOps and brokerage (see Figure 5).

Four primary types of integration are required. At the simplest level, data integration transforms data from one format into another or combines data from multiple sources to create a simple and consistent data interface. It can also translate data from one type to another, such as from JSON to XML. Master data management techniques allow the creation of a simple, consistent data store, hiding the underlying physical data.

For example, one could generate a unified, single view of the overall customer relationship using data integration services by combining information from multiple state stores in relational databases from traditional IT systems and data in object stores from cloud native systems. One can also use data integration to manage the challenge of data updates and ensure the consistency of data across all systems.

Data transfers can create technical challenges in the design of hybrid cloud systems and data integration services should cater to the transfer of data from one data store to another to provide an efficient service.

Process integration is the integration of rudimentary services to create higher-level services, aiming to simplify programming efforts or to translate from multiple service models to a single, consistent model. This occurs in a similar manner to the enterprise service bus often found in service-oriented architectures.

Data and process integrations are both commonly used in the hybrid cloud to combine functions from traditional IT systems and make them available to cloud-native systems.

Workflow integration builds on process integrations to manage multiple, complex interactions and map to a business process step. The workflow component identifies component or interaction failures and determines the next steps based on defined flows.

Figure 5. The integration building block

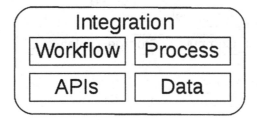

The final elements of integration are the APIs, which aim to provide comprehensive access to a function through a single request. The request would provide all the contextual information required, and the requestor would assume that the request will be completed once it has been sent using the API.

Representational state transfer is the most common protocol for APIs. In the hybrid cloud, APIs hide the underlying complexity of the established IT systems, providing simple, consistent interfaces. Agile edge systems or external partners use APIs to develop new client interactions or business applications to increase user productivity.

Industrialised Core

The Industrialised core houses the IT functions that are established and critical to the operation of the business. Systems such as financial ledgers, enterprise resource planning, and human resource management are good examples of industrialised core applications. Though these systems are constantly changing to meet regulatory and business demands, changes are grouped into releases that are implemented at regular intervals. These are traditional IT systems built with enterprise Java, relational databases, COBOL or transactional processing systems. In the hybrid cloud, these systems are refactored to cloud enabled or cloud native. The focus of this refactoring is:

- To increase the agility of these systems to cope with the unpredictable demand from agile edge systems. This can be achieved by migrating to an IaaS platform.
- To simplify access to the systems. This is achieved by creating new or simpler interfaces and providing consistent APIs.
- To optimize the operations of the systems to increase the productivity of the operational staff while increasing the resilience of the service (see Figure 6).

The components within the industrialised core building block are the same as those in the agile edge. However, the operational characteristics are often very different. The compute network and storage components can either be an IaaS, if the systems have been refactored to cloud native, or can remain as traditional, virtualised environments with cloud management instrumentation to allow integration with the overall hybrid cloud operations components.

Data management subsystems and middleware prerequisites for the functions can often be migrated to an IaaS. The technique for state management within the functions will determine if the functions can operate within the IaaS.

Figure 6. The industrialised core building block

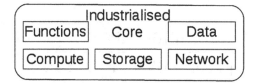

Brokerage

One of the aims of the hybrid cloud is to create a marketplace of cloud service providers that allows clients to choose the provider that can best deliver a certain service. The brokerage building block creates a unified cloud platform from multiple cloud providers or cloud-enabled, traditional IT systems (see Figure 7).

The service catalog component allows the user to find and use all the services provided. Virtual compute resources to business services are listed in the catalog, along with descriptions of the services provided and considerations that are unique to the organisation and pricing.

The billing component records all the costs incurred from the usage of all the components within the hybrid cloud. While complex with cloud native environments, cloud enabled or traditional IT environments typically do not provide metering or billing information at a granular level. Estimation techniques should be used to determine the metering information.

The service orchestration component manages the instantiation, transition and deactivation of any service. The detailed steps for each of the stages are coded in scripts that are followed. The ability to cope with failures or error conditions is an essential element of these scripts. For the hybrid cloud to be effective, there should be no manual activities that need to be performed.

The Service Management component handles the backup, recovery and any specific management activities for a service. This could include isolating resources to allow for hardware maintenance. The Systems Management component provides the primary interface for the hybrid cloud operations staff. It provides a dashboard that shows the overall health of the services, consolidates log information from all the building blocks and provides problem determination tools to investigate any failures.

ILLUSTRATIONS FROM GENERIC CLIENT EXAMPLES

In this final section, the authors will consolidate learnings from the previous sections and exercise this architectural model with several client use cases that illustrate each of the seven hybrid use cases described above. These practical client examples will demonstrate how this approach delivers business value and how the underlying architectural model facilitates this.

In Figure 1, the authors introduced the architectural model and subsequently described the components that exist within the high-level building blocks. If all this is brought together, the high-level hybrid cloud architecture can be represented in Figure 8.

The authors will now show how these components interact to support the client use cases. Note that only the key component interactions will be shown in the following figures. We intentionally use show a subset of the components in each building block within the following figures to aid readability. Regarding security specifically, only authenticated users who have the appropriate access rights should be able

Figure 7. The brokerage building block

Figure 8. The complete Hybrid IT architecture model

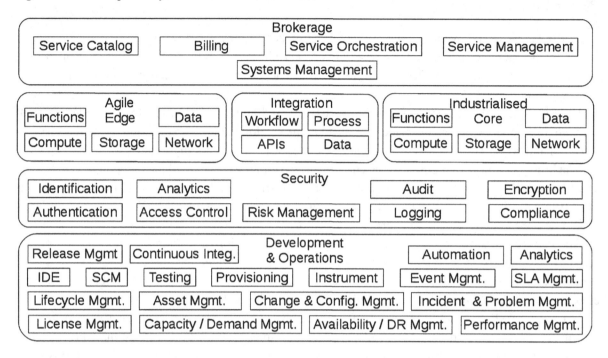

to access each component. Showing each of these interactions with the Security building block would have made the figures illegible, so they have been omitted.

Independent Workloads

The user selects the service that he or she requires from the service catalog (1). This invokes the service orchestration component (2), which drives the underlying platforms to instantiate the respective instances of the workload (3a) on those platforms. At the same time, the service is registered with the service management component (3b) and with the billing component (3c). Different users can instantiate different services (shown in red and green in Figure 9) from either the agile edge or the industrialised core, which are independent of one another.

This use case is typical of general office users invoking a number of cloud services to perform the different tasks that they need to perform each day. For example, a user in the accounting department might invoke an email service to check his inbox or to pick up new work items for the day. Then he might invoke an accounting application run on the cloud to perform his work tasks. A colleague in the marketing department might invoke the same email services or different services such as marketing analytics from cloud providers. A production engineer might interact with on-premises systems in the industrialised core that collect data from the core production systems that run the business.

Systems of Engagement (SoE) – Systems of Record (SoR)

"Next best action" is a well-known analytical use case that describes using intelligence based on previous interactions—say between a customer and a retailer—to tailor a current interaction. In Figure 10, the customer is interacting with functions in the agile edge (1). When required, the function requests data

Figure 9. *Component interactions for the independent workloads use case*

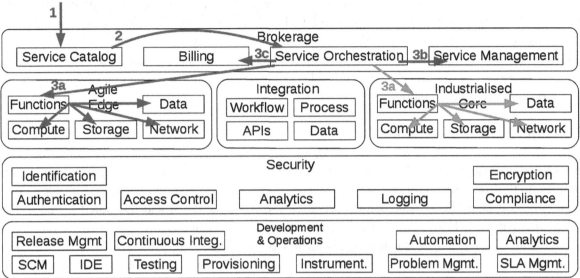

For a more accurate representation of this figure, please see the electronic version.

Figure 10. *Component interactions for the SoE-SoR use case*

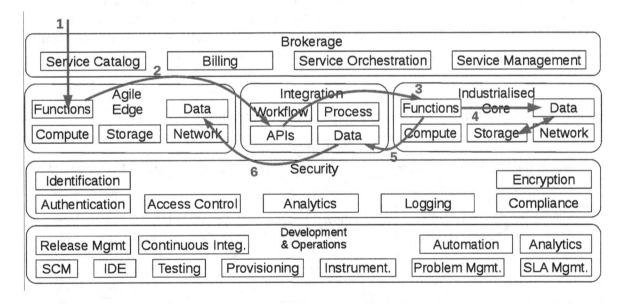

via an API call (2) from the backend system of record (3). This retrieves the relevant data (4) and returns it via the integration functions (5). Some reformatting or transformation may be required to ensure the agile edge function can consume the requested data (6).

To illustrate this use case with a practical example, consider the case of an aircraft manufacturer. Commercial airlines need to keep their aircrafts operational to fly passengers or freight and maximise their revenues. Time spent on the ground, while necessary, is costly. Being able to rapidly turn around an aircraft—to return it to a "ready to fly" state after cleaning, refueling, repairing, etc.—delivers immediate value. The engineer attends the plane with a mobile device running applications in the agile edge. From this device, he can access both the data downloaded from the engine as well as historic engine data from the industrialised core. The applications determine what the best action to take is to safely and quickly ensure all aircraft components are checked and that the plane is able to take its next load of passengers on to their destination.

Portability and Optimisation

One of the early use cases for cloud was as a test and development platform for on-premises production systems. In this use case, a user interacts via an IDE (1) to develop code that is stored in a source code management system (2). As development progresses, the code is tested and integrated (3) until it is complete and ready to be released to the environment. All of these functions are performed in the cloud.

To deploy the code into production (4) a workflow is run (5). The workflow invokes other functions in the cloud (6), which copy the program data (executables, code etc.) via the integration capability (8) into the on-premises systems (9). At this point, the new code becomes available as a new or updated function in the system (10) (see Figure 11).

Consider an organisation that runs a substantial part of its business on a large ERP system such as those provided by SAP or Oracle. For an organisation such as this, many systems are often allocated to developing and testing the functionality of new applications that will run within industrialised core systems. Key business benefits of running these development and test activities in cloud-based systems include being able to deploy resources for use only when development and testing activities are running, as well as being able to set up new environments in a predictable, automated fashion in a much shorter

Figure 11. Component interactions for the portability and optimisation use case

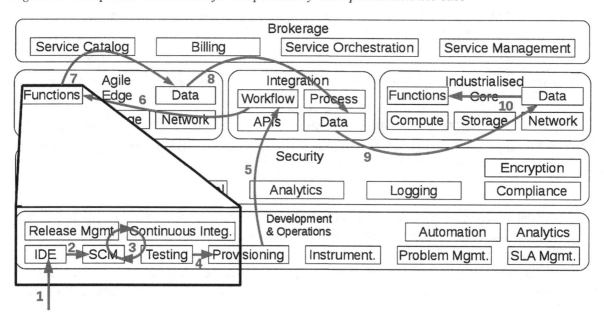

period of time. The increased efficiency and agility offered by the cloud drive down costs and make IT systems more responsive to rapidly changing business needs.

Hybrid Cloud Brokerage

In this use case, a user identifies the business service required from the service catalog (1). It won't be clear in which cloud this may be deployed. This then invokes the service orchestration component (2), which makes a policy-based decision to determine what cloud platform is the most appropriate to use. The service orchestration component in turn drives the underlying platforms to instantiate respective instances of the workloads (3a) on the different cloud platforms. At the same time, the service is registered with the service management component (3b) and with the billing component (3c) (see Figure 12).

Note: The service orchestration component may identify that deploying a service in the industrialised core is the most appropriate action to meet a given policy rule. This interaction is not shown to make Figure 12 clearer.

For many business users and IT organisations, the complexities of cloud computing are daunting. When services are being delivered to an organisation from multiple cloud platforms, this problem only gets larger. Hybrid cloud brokerage aims to solve many of these problems, perhaps by presenting all cloud (and on-premises) services in a single service catalog or displaying a single bill that brings together all of the charges from multiple cloud providers. For this reason, many industry watchers believe that cloud brokerage will be the primary means through which enterprise users consume cloud services in the future.

Consider a retailer who wishes to run a series of marketing and advertising campaigns concurrently in a number of different media: print, online, mobile, broadcast TV, etc. Different specialist service provid-

Figure 12. Component interactions for the hybrid cloud brokerage use case

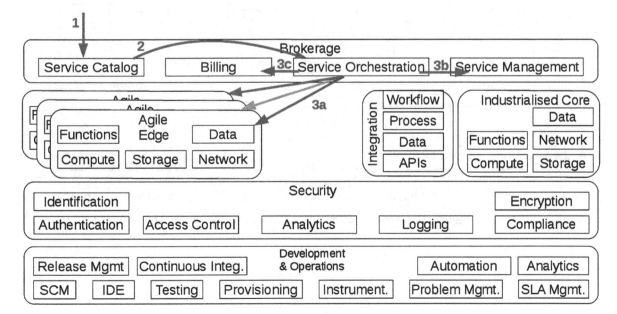

ers are likely to consume these services, given the different channels involved. A typical retail marketer is unlikely to understand how to consume the infrastructure-as-a-service components needed to build the systems to run such services. The marketer may not even know the software-as-a-service required to deliver an advertising campaign or marketing action. This complexity is hidden by the brokerage service, which might present services to users whose goal is "I want to run a web advertising campaign."

Backup and Archive

A backup action is initiated by a function running in the industrialised core (1). This drives a backup workflow (2) that starts a process to manage the backup action. This calls a different function (3), which interacts with the local storage (4). Data from the industrialised core (5) are transferred via the integration capability (6) to the agile edge systems (7) where the data are placed in storage in the cloud (8). The final stage of the workflow (9) drives functions in the agile edge to define things like retention policies. Note that this can also run in reverse; data in the cloud can be backed up to an industrialised core if that is the core business of a data retention company (see Figure 13).

This use case could be illustrated by the case of a car manufacturer that is creating CAD (computer-aided design) drawings for a new car. These must be backed up in case of a disaster or failure of the industrialised core systems. The data could also be backed up to the cloud to permit sharing with a multitude of component providers or other car manufacturers with whom designs are being shared. For example, there could be a case in which two manufacturers share components across different car models in separate ranges. In this case, cloud backup offers greater flexibility to facilitate such collaboration than would an on-premises backup and archive solution. Another use case might be one in which data must be retained offsite for an extended period of time, possibly to meet specific legislative requirements.

Figure 13. Component interactions for the backup and archive use case

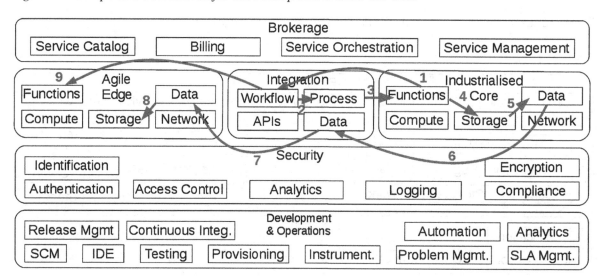

Capacity Access

Computation is performed on systems (1) which consume compute, storage and networking resources. When a given threshold – whether predetermined or ad hoc – is reached, a local function is invoked to request more resources (2). This drives a workflow (3) to the service catalog (4) to identify the source of these resources. Once these resources are identified, service orchestration capabilities (5) call local provisioning functions (6) in the agile edge. These functions provision the necessary compute, storage and networking resources to support the new business workload needs (7). In parallel and illustrated in red, there is likely a requirement to provision the data with which the computation will be performed into the agile edge. The same workflow that was used to identify and provision the compute resources drives the movement of data (8) from the industrialised core to the data integration capability (9) and into the agile edge (10), from which it is delivered to storage (11) so work can begin. At a future trigger point—again predetermined or ad hoc—a similar workflow is run to return the data to the Industrialised core and deprovision the resources in the agile edge (see Figure 14).

There are a great many examples of the capacity access use case across many industries, but for the purpose of this discussion, the authors will consider the needs of a pharmaceutical company performing drug discovery, in which there are a large number of computationally intensive jobs to be run against a list of target molecules. One can assume that the company's on-premises capability allows researchers to process 5,000 molecules per week. Imagine a case in which researchers are required to process 8,000 molecules over the same period. This might be an unusual occurrence, and thus doesn't justify an investment in the capacity to perform this work on the company's own systems. At the infrequent rate this extra need occurs, it is simpler to rent excess capacity from a cloud provider and link the on-premises and cloud systems together to provide sufficient capacity when required to meet business needs.

Figure 14. Component interactions for the capacity access use case

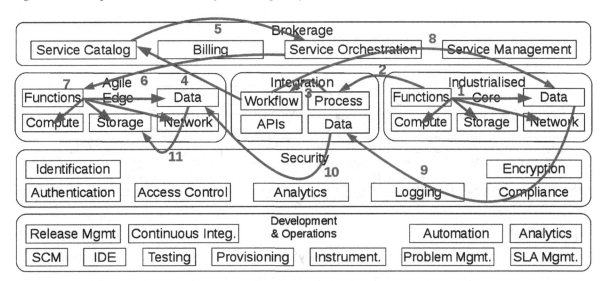

Disaster Recovery

Data updates and other changes are backed up periodically via a function running in the industrialised core (1). This drives a workflow (2) to start a process to manage backup activity. This calls a different function (3), which interacts with the local storage (4). Data from the industrialised core (5) is transferred via the Integration capability (6) to the agile edge systems (7), where is it placed in storage in the cloud (8). The final stage of the workflow (9) drives functions in the agile edge to define things such as retention policies. This process continues over time.

When a disaster is declared, the disaster recovery service is selected from the service catalog (10). This then invokes the service orchestration component (11), which drives the underlying platforms in the disaster recovery capability in the agile edge to instantiate the compute resources necessary to run the recovered workloads (12a) on those platforms. At the same time, the service is registered with the service management component (12b) and with the billing component (12c) (see Figure 15).

This final use case applies to all industries. As such, there are many possible industry examples. The advantages of using a cloud for disaster recovery are the ability to keep a minimal presence in the disaster recovery facility and opportunity to rapidly provision new systems and services when a disaster occurs. In more traditional approaches to this problem, organisations must invest in hardware, software and facilities that are idle for the majority of their operational lifetimes. The cloud approach is a significantly more cost-effective solution.

WHERE TO START

Hybrid cloud architecture is an ideal target for many enterprises. However, determining the stages of the journey, particularly the all-too-important starting point, requires careful consideration. Mapping the

Figure 15. Component interactions for the disaster recovery use case

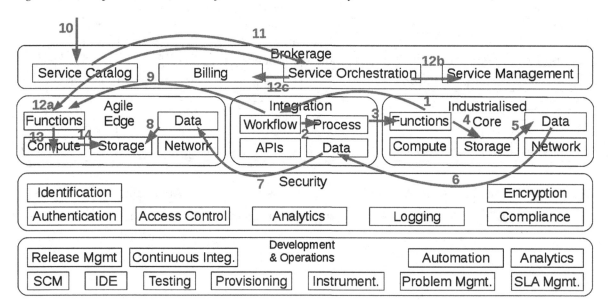

journey purely on the basis of business pressures may not be the only option, though many organizations tend to do so. In many cases, born-on-the-cloud solution providers offer solutions that address business uses. Often, traditional IT organisations are unaware of those options. The reality of the existing IT environment must be taken into consideration when developing the strategy.

Questions that one should be able to answer about an existing IT environment before considering hybrid cloud include:

1. What level of change can the IT staff absorb while ensuring the IT service continues to keep the business running?
2. What elements of hybrid cloud architecture could be implemented to achieve a step up in productivity and create capacity to establish other elements?
3. How can the current IT environment be adapted to more readily integrate with newer, born-on-the-cloud services?
4. Will a viable and timely change require a partner?

These four questions, plus the hybrid cloud architecture and seven use cases discussed in this chapter provide organisations with the ingredients required to plan their journey to the hybrid cloud.

REFERENCES

Grozev, N., & Buyya, R. (2014). Inter-Cloud architectures and application brokering: Taxonomy and survey. *Software, Practice & Experience, 44*(3), 369–390. doi:10.1002/spe.2168

Hamdaqa, M., & Tahvildari, L. (2014, November). The (5+ 1) architectural view model for cloud applications. In The IBM Centers for Advanced Studies Conference (pp. 46-60). IBM.

Kertesz, A. (2014). Characterizing Cloud Federation Approaches. In *Cloud Computing* (pp. 277–296). Springer International Publishing.

Lunawat, S., & Patankar, A. (2014, February). Efficient architecture for secure outsourcing of data and computation in hybrid cloud. In *Optimization, Reliability, and Information Technology (ICROIT), 2014 International Conference on* (pp. 380-383). IEEE. doi:10.1109/ICROIT.2014.6798358

Mell, P., & Grance, T. (2011). *The NIST definition of cloud computing*. Retrieved from: http://csrc.nist.gov/publications/nistpubs/800-145/SP800-145.pdf

Moore, G. (2011). *Systems of Engagement and the Future of Enterprise IT: A Sea Change in Enterprise IT*. Retrieved from http://www.aiim.org

Parmar, R., McKenzie, I., Cohn, D., & Gann, D. (2014, January-February). The New Patterns of Innovation. *Harvard Business Review*.

Rao, T. V. N., Naveena, K., & David, R. (2015). A New Computing Environment Using Hybrid Cloud. *Journal of Information Sciences and Computing Technologies, 3*(1), 180–185.

Serrano, N., Gallardo, G., & Hernantes, J. (2015). Infrastructure as a Service and Cloud Technologies. *IEEE Software, 32*(2), 30–36. doi:10.1109/MS.2015.43

Tarannum, N., & Ahmed, N. (2014). *Efficient and Reliable Hybrid Cloud Architecture for Big Data.* arXiv preprint arXiv:1405.5200

Toosi, A. N., Calheiros, R. N., & Buyya, R. (2014). Interconnected cloud computing environments: Challenges, taxonomy, and survey. *ACM Computing Surveys, 47*(1), 7. doi:10.1145/2593512

KEY TERMS AND DEFINITIONS

Agile Edge: The cloud computing environment that hosts rapidly changing services, typically supporting new workloads.

API: Application Programming Interface. The means by which functions from different systems are invoked and integrated.

Hybrid IT: The IT system that combines functions from the agile edge and industrialised core to deliver a greater functionality than can be achieved by either component on its own.

Industrialised Core: Those systems that run the established IT functions that are critical to the operation of a business.

Integration: A key component in any hybrid IT environment that allows services from the industrialised core and agile edge to be brought together.

System of Engagement: Those systems that are rapidly changing to meet the desires of the business to offer new services to their customers. May be synonymous with an Agile Edge system.

System of Record: Those systems which are highly reliable, secure and resilient that support key business functions. May be synonymous with the Industrialised Core.

Workload: The functions and processes that make up an application or business service running in an IT system. Migration to the cloud is always done on a workload-by-workload basis.

Chapter 3
Community Cloud:
Closing the Gap between Public and Private

Karolina Marzantowicz
IBM, Poland

Łukasz Paciorkowski
IBM, Poland

ABSTRACT

Should you turn to a public or private cloud solution? Discussions prizing the first or the second option are endless. Public cloud means flexibility, unlimited scalability, frictionless consumption and less worry for your CIO. On the other hand, private cloud gives you full control over the environment and keeps your data close to you, preferably under your nose—or at least within the borders of your country. Public cloud is relatively cheap, while a private cloud might get pricey. But what if neither of those two options fit your needs? You may not trust public cloud providers, but at the same time you are searching for the way to cut through complexity of the private cloud. The answer to your needs might be a community cloud.

BACKGROUND: WHY CLOUD DISCUSSION IS IMPORTANT

Cloud dominates IT related discussions. The promise of lower operational costs, flexibility and the access to the innovative capabilities attracts more and more organizations. There is a good reason for it. IT, once a competitive advantage for the firms, is gradually becoming a commodity. Challenging market situation forces organizations of all sizes to search for the cost reduction opportunities. At the same time rapid digitization requires more storage, computation power and new advanced software solutions. Virtually all major IT vendors are shifting their strategy towards cloud technologies. But they are not the only ones. Smaller but much more dynamic challengers are entering global IT market every day. Competition in the cloud market is taking part on multiple levels. Price wars are won be the biggest players – the

DOI: 10.4018/978-1-5225-0759-8.ch003

economy of scale works on their advantage. Smaller players can compete by using new, innovative solutions, platforms and tools. All of the cloud providers are trying to establish their position on the market.

This global trend of cloudification is not purely technology driven hype. Organizations around the world are searching for new business models based on the digitized offerings. Innovation cycles were drastically shortened during last decade. New versions of products and services are deployed every week. For the traditional IT addressing the business demand on time became increasingly difficult. Standard procedure-driven and mostly manual work of IT specialists is not enough for the new generation, internet-based businesses. Many of them turn towards cloud as enabler for growth and innovation.

More traditional organizations and institutions like banks and governments are lagging behind in the cloud adoption journey. The reason for this is that a lot of inhibitors exist for them. Companies from highly regulated industries require specific approach, which often cannot be accommodated by public cloud providers. As the cloud platforms work due to high level of standardization any major deviation from those standards does not make economic sense. As a result organizations like banks or governments are often left alone with the options of a standard outsourcing or private, on-premises cloud.

In this chapter we will look at the specific scenario for the cloud platform – a Community Cloud – which is closing the gap between public/private and on/off-premises scenarios. Before we will discuss the specifics, lets first have a quick look at the cloud ecosystem, its players and different models existing today on the market.

Figure 1. Public cloud

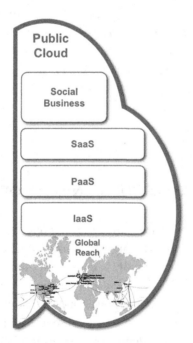

PUBLIC, PRIVATE, AND THE MISSING PART

Although cloud does not have one, precise definition, some common characteristics are used to describe it. Most common ones are division between Private and Public one and on-premises versus off-premises.

Private cloud model assumes that the resources used by this platform (compute, network, storage, virtual machines, middleware, application) are dedicated exclusively for one customer or organization. Public (or multitenant) cloud assumes that resources are shared among different customers and organizations. On-premises cloud is the model in which resources are placed within the customer organization (e.g. in the organization owned data center). In off-premises model resources are delivered by the external cloud service provider using provider's data centers. There many other characteristics which help do describe cloud models but in our discussion we will focus on those 4, described above.

Figure 2 summarizes the general cloud characteristics and the relationship between them.

Another disputable topic is the border between traditional IT and the cloud. Is virtualization of resources in your datacenter enough to call it a private cloud? Are simple hosting services enough to call it off-premises cloud? No straightforward answer to such questions exists. Nevertheless it is safe to assume that when talking about cloud 3 main characteristics are important:

Figure 2. General cloud characteristics

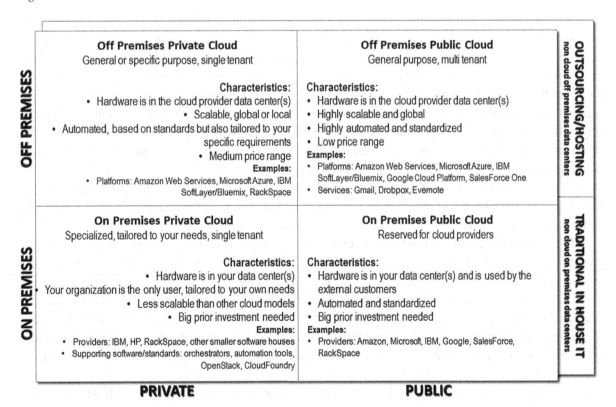

OFF PREMISES

Off Premises Private Cloud
General or specific purpose, single tenant

Characteristics:
- Hardware is in the cloud provider data center(s)
- Scalable, global or local
- Automated, based on standards but also tailored to your specific requirements
- Medium price range

Examples:
- Platforms: Amazon Web Services, Microsoft Azure, IBM SoftLayer/Bluemix, RackSpace

Off Premises Public Cloud
General purpose, multi tenant

Characteristics:
- Hardware is in the cloud provider data center(s)
- Highly scalable and global
- Highly automated and standardized
- Low price range

Examples:
- Platforms: Amazon Web Services, Microsoft Azure, IBM SoftLayer/Bluemix, Google Cloud Platform, SalesForce One
- Services: Gmail, Drobpox, Evernote

OUTSOURCING/HOSTING
non cloud off premises data centers

ON PREMISES

On Premises Private Cloud
Specialized, tailored to your needs, single tenant

Characteristics:
- Hardware is in your data center(s)
- Your organization is the only user, tailored to your own needs
- Less scalable than other cloud models
- Big prior investment needed

Examples:
- Providers: IBM, HP, RackSpace, other smaller software houses
- Supporting software/standards: orchestrators, automation tools, OpenStack, CloudFoundry

On Premises Public Cloud
Reserved for cloud providers

Characteristics:
- Hardware is in your data center(s) and is used by the external customers
- Automated and standardized
- Big prior investment needed

Examples:
- Providers: Amazon, Microsoft, IBM, Google, SalesForce, RackSpace

TRADITIONAL IN HOUSE IT
non cloud on premises data centers

PRIVATE   **PUBLIC**

- **Simplicity:** Cloud computing should simplify management of the underlying technology platform. It would be naive to think that the IT solutions itself will become less complex. In contrary, the advancement in technology and software will require even more technicians and highly specialized engineers than ever before. But this complexity should be covered by the easy, simple to use management layer allowing for quick and frictionless consumption of cloud resources.
- **Standardization:** Building highly scalable, robust and flexible cloud platform requires high level of standardization. Each deviation from the standard results in more possible errors, bigger cost associated with automation and management and requires more resources to operate and manage the change. Componentization is a very important as the excessive standardization can lower the flexibility. In order to build specific and distinct solutions standard components are used. Microservice architecture pattern is a great example how standardization and flexibility can coexist in the cloud environment.
- **Automation:** This is probably the most important of all cloud computing characteristics. Automation lies in the heart of the cloud. It allows for customer self service, rapid resources provisioning and simplification in the management area. It also helps to lower the costs making cloud platforms commercially attractive. Automation requires standards (like OpenStack or CloudFoundry), tools and procedures and requires focus, determination and time to be setup properly (OpenStack, 2016; CloudFoundry, 2016).

In recent years public cloud platforms gained immense market share mostly because of the very attractive commercial models and the ease of consumption. Suddenly managing technological platform became so easy, fast and non-problematic. This is a significant shift from the standard model where the most of the changes and adjustments to the technical landscape required involvement of procurement, multiple IT departments, business and, very often, external consultants and advisors. The gains were so great and obvious that the organizations accepted the general terms, conditions and limitations imposed by the public cloud providers. But not all customers can agree on the open and multi-tenant platforms. Some of those require very specific solutions, which cannot be accommodated by the public cloud providers, as they do not fit the standards imposed by their cloud platform. Others are bounded by the laws and regulations which requires specific data placement policies, security mechanisms etc. For those special cases the old traditional IT is still a default choice. Alternatively those organizations and companies can think about setting up their own private cloud platform.

Off-premises private cloud is a bit more expensive but still very attractive option for the customers who do not want to share their sensitive workloads with others. As with many other terms in cloud world this model is also not well defined and can mean different things for different customers and service providers. In the Software as a Service space private cloud would mean that the application instance is dedicated to the only one customer. On the Platform as a Service level it would mean that the instances of the services are running as an independent entities. On Infrastructure as a Service it gets even more complex. For example Amazon Virtual Private Cloud allows for deploying AWS workloads in the dedicated private virtual network, which would be separated from the rest of the customers. It does not mean that the underlying resources like storage and compute would be not shared with others. On the other hand IBM and few other cloud providers allow for renting dedicated server (so called bare metal server), which assures that your workload is separated from the other customers workloads. Unfortunately those options might be still not sufficient for the most demanding customers. On-premises private cloud could be the answer.

The most expensive version of the cloud is the one where the organization is building it for itself. Although it gives the most control over the technical features, data and the governance model it requires significant funds, time and resources to setup. Unless your company operates a substantial number of systems, environments and servers it might be very difficult to defend commercial viability of building your own private cloud platform. It is because cloud works well at scale. It is attractive commercially only if the critical mass is achieved. Automating and standardizing entire IT stacks for only few tens of systems is simply overkill. Also flexibility which cloud platform brings makes sense only if you have enough "clients" to keep the utilization of the underlying IT structure on the appropriately high level. Nevertheless there are organizations, which system landscapes are big enough that private on-premises cloud platform is a commercially viable option.

Probably the biggest disadvantage of the on-premises versus off-premises cloud is the access to the innovative services. Without a doubt the speed of delivery for the new tools, solutions and services increased drastically over the past few years. Also many of the big corporations and startups they expose their services only through the public off-premises platforms. As a result access to the innovative solutions is much more difficult for the organizations which do not want to open themselves to the public cloud.

One option, which should be also taken under consideration, is a hybrid cloud. Some service providers (like IBM) argue that hybrid is the only possible scenario as there will be always some on-premises systems to be integrated with off-premises platforms and services. That might be true unless you are organization born-on-internet and your business model does not require any local systems. Unfortunately private+public cloud does not help customers from highly regulated industries for which setting up private on-premises cloud is simply too expensive and using public cloud is too risky.

Trying to cut through the complexity of the cloud deployment and consumption models, while searching for the best option for your organization, it is worth to look at all available scenarios. For the highly regulated industries the best option would be a cloud where benefits of public platforms meet security

Figure 3. Public cloud pros and cons

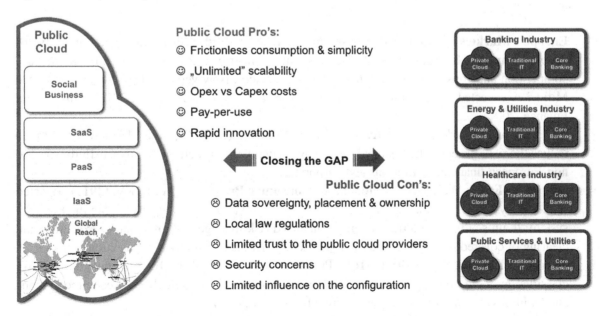

and requirements achieved by private and on-premises solutions. The answer to that question might be community cloud concept. But before we will get to the details of this concept let's look at some of the inhibitors of a cloud adoption from the perspective of a highly regulated industries like banking, government and utilities.

REGULATIONS, RESTRICTIONS, AND LIMITATIONS

For the organizations from highly regulated industries like banking, government or utilities it is very difficult to accept the openness and globalization proposed by the public cloud providers. Questions regarding required compliance certifications, data placement, interpretation of the local law inhibit wide adoption of the cloud computing. Although regulatory bodies can issue appropriate certifications confirming that the given cloud platform meets the specific industry requirements organizations (especially in European Union) are very careful with the interpretation of local laws. As a result many barriers regarding public cloud consumption are based on the fear of non-compliance rather then a concrete requirements regarding security, data placement or governance model. Nevertheless those fears need to be addressed by the cloud providers. Let's look in details at the specific industry.

Financial services sector is intensively regulated industry where many cloud adoption inhibitors exist. There are many regulations, which in specific apply to the cloud computing. Most of them are concerning personal data protection. Information security is a key concern, but the location & lack of control over the data as well as access and audit requirements are broadly discussed.

Banks in European Union are bound by the international laws, EU specific regulations, local in-country regulations and the bank internal regulations. Those can differ depending on the region and country. European Union is considered to have the strictest regulations in the world. Other countries following similar regulatory concerns are Israel, Australia & Canada. The United States and Asian markets have a fundamentally different philosophy towards data protection regulations and many inhibitors present in EU do not exist there.

The examples of the EU regulations for financial institutions are:

- **Europe's Markets in Financial Instruments Directive (Mifid) (2007):** EU regulators responded to crisis in 2008 by creating the Markets in Financial Instruments Directive (MiFID) to increase competition and consumer protection in financial services. New version of this regulation called Mifid 2 is expected to be implemented in all European banks by the end of 2016 (Banking and Finance, 2007).
- **The European Markets and Infrastructure Regulation (EMIR) (2012):** EU law that aims to reduce the risks posed to the financial system by derivatives transactions. It impacts European and non-European financial institutions and corporates.
- **The Dodd-Frank Wall Street Reform and Consumer Protection Act (DFA) (2011):** Enacted to reduce systemic risk, increase transparency, and promote market integrity within the financial system. It aims at increased transparency, enhanced risk management, mandatory execution and clearing of covered products, market integrity, customer and counterparty protection
- **European Banking Authority (2016) :** Provides an overview of the EBA's regulatory activity classified by topic, ranging from binding Technical Standards to Guidelines, Recommendations and Opinions. http://www.eba.europa.eu/regulation-and-policy

- **Germany's Federal Data Protection Act (1990) :** Known as Bundesdatenschutzgesetz or BDSG, the laws were reformed significantly in 2009 to cover a range of data protection-related issues. The key principles of the 2009 amendments state that organizations cannot collect any personally identifiable information without express permission from an individual. To help with the legal complexities, in 2011 the German Data Protection Authority (DPA) issued a set of guidelines to help would-be cloud users and service providers structure their business arrangements (Germany's Federal Data Protection Act, 1990).

In summary constrains and requirements around financial data processing are complex enough to successfully discourage banks from wide adoption of a public cloud computing. And it is a shame. Many of the next generation services, analytics capabilities and platforms are available only through the public cloud. As a result banks cannot fully utilize the potential of new technologies available on the market. It impacts the quality of service and the ability to innovate.

On the other hand European Commission encourages the European companies to use cloud computing to increase institutions mobility. To close the gap between data protection requirements and the will to capitalize on the cloud computing financial sector is likely to request an extra security guarantees from cloud providers. Industry specific Community Cloud concept might be the answer satisfying all cloud market participants.

SECURITY, FEARS, AND TRUST ISSUES

Discussion around cloud security is very vivid. For some cloud platforms are not to be trusted and using them poses the biggest threat to data security. Others are stressing from-the-ground-up design of cloud data centers, which are built with the security in mind. Data breaches, successful attacks on known corporate and governmental portals are adding unnecessary emotions to this discussion. But as with every technical topic there is no one, single definition about what is secured and what is not and if the cloud model is vulnerability in the data security.

Obviously the most secured system is such one, which does not have the connection to the external world with very limited access for the users. But with most of the systems such limitations are irrational and are missing the point. Systems are there to aid users and to allow people to perform their work. In the era of mobile and social business systems tend to be more open and accessible from outside of your organization's firewall. Of course security is a very important part of the cloud discussion. But it should not be the only factor driving the decision about cloud adoption.

It is also important to understand different types of security breaches, which are widely discussed in the news. It is crucial to differentiate between application security and the underlying technology platform. It does not matter where the external facing portal will be installed if the application-level security is poor. Also difference between hacking frontend portals and the backend critical business systems are two different things. Internet access to the backend systems can be always restricted (also using public cloud) but the frontend systems by definition will be available publically. Finally distinction between technical platform and the human-factor vulnerabilities is needed. Attacks based on social engineering, which are still the most common ways of getting unauthorized access to the systems, require yet another considerations.

One of the major misconceptions of the public cloud is that it can be accessible through the Internet by everybody. For the end customer Software as a Service like DropBox or Gmail it is true. But for the enterprise grade software delivered as a service often dedicated connections are used prohibiting access from the outside of your organization network. In such case "public" means that underlying infrastructure (and potentially software platform) is shared between many customers. Many hardware and software based techniques exist to filter, block and detect unwanted connections and attacks from public network.

Furthermore very often discussions labeled with "security concerns" are touching the point of trust towards the platform steward (or simply cloud service provider). At the end no matter how secured is the cloud platform your data will reside on the infrastructure managed by the external party. This means that your sensitive information can potentially be accessed by anybody (with appropriate authorizations) from the cloud provider's organization. Putting it in the context of industrial espionage, data trading practices or governmental surveillance it might discourage many organizations from using off-premises cloud.

COMMUNITY CLOUD: CONCEPT AND BENEFITS

Looking at both benefits and risks associated with cloud platforms it is worth to consider community cloud concept. It brings the best from the public and private worlds. The main idea is to build a community of organizations, firms or institutions that share similar characteristics and requirements towards IT platform. Examples of such communities might be the governmental institutions, banks, energy &

Figure 4. Community cloud concept

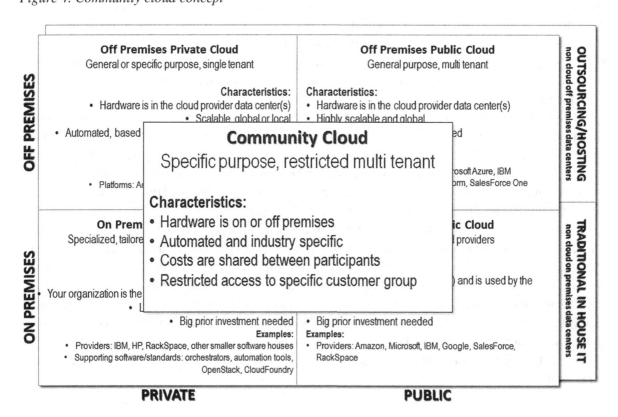

utilities companies and telecommunication operators. Each of this group has a very specific set of expectations, requirements and needs towards cloud platform.

To address the industry specific requirements each organization can build its own private, on-premises cloud. Unfortunately it might be very costly approach and might not bring the savings and flexibility one could expect from the cloud platform. Alternatively those organizations could start using cloud platform shared only among community members. Such approach should give more confidence to the cloud consumers as the other users are known and respected.

One important aspect needs to be address: will companies, which compete with each other on daily basis, cooperate to benefit from cloud computing. There are a few factors which convinced me that – yes – they will cooperate.

All highly regulated industries, even if they are commercial organizations, they provide services to citizens. Those services are partially basic services for all people. They need to be provided to allow people to collaboration with government (banking services) and to achieve minimal level of living (utilities). All those industries face disruption not only from startups (in many cases based on innovative technology, or innovative usage of common / known technology). In many cases, disruptors come from other industries, and they are not regulated in the same way. So in many cases industry has new competitors, and to fight with them cooperation with other industry players can be one of the options.

Peer 2 peer services become more popular. And they gain certain market share in each industry. Of course it is difficult to replace for example government services – it can be illegal in many cases. But with other services like crowdfunding in place of taking a loan from bank, there is more freedom and possibilities.

All those challenges put a pressure on organization to be more flexible, and agile. They need to adapt innovative technologies (like analytics, social, mobile, cloud) to provide more business value, optimize costs and improve business results. In the need digital economy ability to share and collaborate is important more than in the past.

As an example; let's take a Community Cloud for Banking. Such offering would provide services relevant to the financial sector. It would also assure appropriate level of security required by the banks and regulators in a given country/region. Additionally other market participants like clearing house or payment platforms could have full or limited access to this platform. As a result a closed ecosystem of financial institutions would gather around technological platform enabling new ways of collaboration and tighter integration.

In highly regulated industries; security, data placement, governance model, transparency concerns and the industry-specific requirements are the main inhibitors for the cloud adoption. Community cloud address them in the following ways:

- **Security:** In contrary to the public platforms, community cloud platform can be adjusted fairly easy to accommodate all participants security concerns. Common agreement between participating organizations should assure that the platform is considered safe.
- **Data Placement:** Due to its nature most community cloud will be bound to the specific geographic location. For example government community cloud will most likely be dedicated for the government institution from one country. For this reason community cloud is perfect for the organizations which need to assure that the digital data is stored and processed within the boundaries of a given region or country.

- **Governance Model:** There are many approaches towards governing the community cloud. No matter which model will be used it is possible to assure that interests of all participants will be represented. In comparison to the public cloud platforms it is also much easier to adopt model tailored to the specifics of the industry. Possible governance models are discussed in details in the following section.

- **Transparency and Auditability:** For highly regulated industries it is very important to have clear and transparent rules on how the cloud platform works. Depending on demands from the community participants and external regulatory bodies it is possible to address all of their concerns. Potential auditors and supervisory bodies (e.g. clearing house for the banking sector) can be invited to participate in definition of procedures and audit capabilities.

- **Industry Specific Requirements:** In case of other specific requirements industry community cloud can be designed to accommodate them from the very beginning. No matter if it is redundant data storage or specially secured access to the physical servers such demands can be reflected in the community cloud platform design.

Above points should convince potential customers that the community cloud is a safe environment even for their sensitive workloads. It is also important to understand what benefits community cloud can bring. Starting from the most obvious:

- **Lower Entry and Operational Costs:** While building the community cloud platform initial costs are covered either by the cloud provider or are shared between community participants. Either way entry costs are much lower than in case of private, on-premises cloud. Also due to multi-tenant nature of such platform, by using appropriate level of automation and standardization it is possible to achieve a higher operational efficiency. This in turn leads to the lower price per usage.

Figure 5. Community cloud strengths

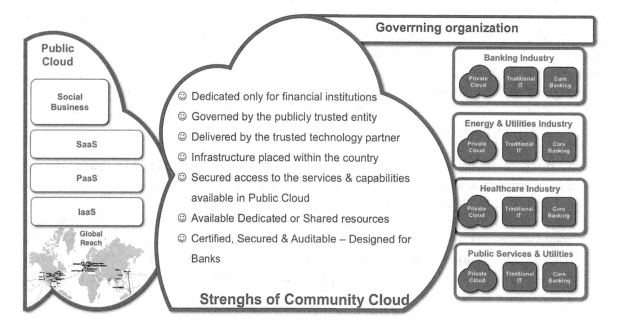

- **Higher Return on Investment in Infrastructure:** In comparison to the private, on-premises cloud, thanks to the greater number of users, higher utilization of the underlying infrastructure is possible.
- **Greater Flexibility and Scalability:** Community clouds are built with growth in mind. Technical platform should have enough capacity to accommodate unplanned picks in workloads and demands. Unexpected requests for additional environments, servers or storage.
- **Reuse and Best Practices:** Leveraging prior investment and lessons learnt it is important to reuse already existing solutions, modules, patterns, methods and processes proved during previous projects.
- **Enhanced Responsiveness to the Security Threats:** By exchanging information and data related to the attacks, misuse and cases of system abuse CC community is able to protect itself better.
- **Common Innovation Platform with Access to External APIs:** CC can bring services and capabilities which typically would be unavailable or very expensive to deploy them on premises. Sharing the costs between CC participants can give access to cutting edge technologies like cognitive computing platforms.
- **Cross Industry Integration Platform:** CC can help to bring capabilities from different industries in order to extend the standard portfolio of finance-focused organizations.
- **Proxy to the Public Cloud:** To meet needs of participants who would like to consume external services but are reluctant to expose their internal systems directly to the public internet.

Summarizing the community cloud is a specific purpose, restricted multi-tenant cloud environment. It can be based on IT infrastructure on or off premises. It is automated to support industry specific needs and requirements. It can have restricted or open access. Costs of community cloud are shared between participants.

GOVERNANCE MODELS FOR COMMUNITY CLOUD

Governance model is crucial for the success of the community cloud. There are few possibilities to choose from. Community cloud can be governed by a cloud service provider, or IT service provider. It can be managed by an independent organization which is trusted and respected by all participants. There is also the possibility to create a consortium, which will manage and govern entire platform.

No matter which option is be chosen the most important factor is that there should be clear responsibilities split between Community cloud members and the governing body. Also the involvement of the regulatory body is crucial for building the trust. Once all formal requirements and concerns are addressed community cloud can become fully usable platform, safe, auditable and lawful alternative to public or private cloud.

ENGAGEMENT MODELS FOR COMMUNITY CLOUD

For Community Cloud there are following engagement models proposed based on estimated market needs:

- Only services associated with the infrastructure are provided (customized version of IaaS). Minimal business value is provided in comparison to public or private cloud in this model. It can be more expensive then public cloud providers offering.
- On top of first option, there is development platform and services (including managed services) provided (customized version of PaaS). Participants get more value and synergy from sharing some of components in this scenario.
- On top of 2nd version, there are business applications and business services provided. It is the most advanced scenario. Participants can share business solutions, business data, APIs, etc and get much more from collaboration.

COMMUNITY CLOUD CAPABILITIES

Community cloud shares many common characteristics with other cloud services (IaaS, PaaS, SaaS). They are paid per use. Participants can have both: dedicates and shared resources.

Figure 7 shows IBM CC proposition for Banking industry.

There are following key element of CC:

- **Integration point with Public Cloud:** Controlled and secure,
- **Community Marketplace:** Similar concept to the App Store known from the mobile phone market, a place where CC specific applications, extensions and modules are published being available for other ecosystem participants,
- **Automation:** Process, testing and operations automation,

Figure 6. Proposed engagement models for community cloud

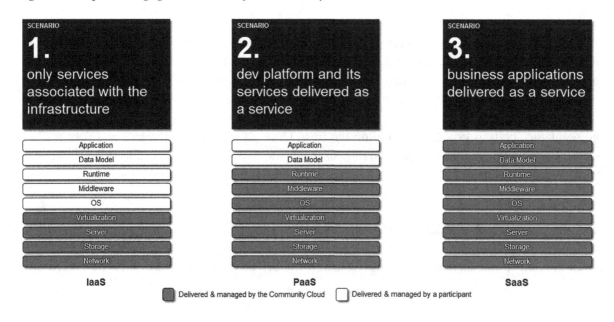

Figure 7. Community cloud capabilities: IBM banking community cloud

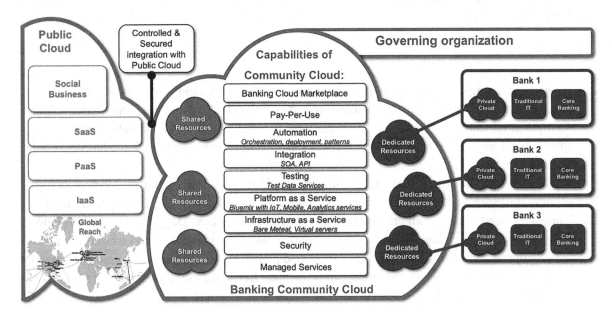

- **Integration:** Shared and dedicated APIs, API management tools, shared and dedicated integration services,
- **Test Services:** Test Data Services such as data anonymization, and others,
- **Security Services:** Security services covering community needs and legal requirements,
- **Managed Services:** Managed, remote services for community,
- **Analytics Services:** Additional analytics services provided by CC,
- **PaaS:** Faster development and prototyping platform providing common services for developers and administrators,
- **IaaS:** Virtualized network, compute and storage critical for rapid infrastructure provisioning.

SPECIFIC COMMUNITY CLOUD USE CASES

For the early adopters of cloud there are specific use cases, which make a lot of economic sense. They allow for a slow cloud adoption strategy: Starting with less essential workloads and non-mission critical systems, later on moving towards full hybrid model. The most basic use cases are:

- **Test and Dev Environments:** Without production data, development and test seem to be the first use case where CC can be applied.
- **Proof of Concepts and Innovation:** Innovation is extremely important in current times. All companies need a place for experimenting and fast prototyping. CC can be an answer for it. Common platform can result with new business models between participants, because they will discover easier new ways of business collaboration.

- **Systems of Engagement:** Leveraging organization core data, with users interactions to create new level of experiences.

The more advanced use cases are:

- **Internet of Things:** IoT will drive data growth in next few years. And it will impact all industries. Standardization is one of key challenges for sensors and devices manufactures which impacts their potential usage by others. Common platform to build solutions for all industry players in a standardized way can be breakthrough for new business models generation, and additional values for customers.
- **Advanced Analytics (incl. Cognitive Computing):** More and more cognitive, machine learning services are offered only via cloud. There is no option to buy them for on premise installation. All companies need to deal with amount of data generated every day. Deep algorithms will help to better understand data and discover hidden patterns and values. Secured and trusted integration with them can allow for faster and less expensive implementation. There are also industry specific areas where common analytics solution can be applied, like anti money laundering, fraud prevention or cybercrime in financial sector.

Figure 8 shows example of implementation community cloud as a tests environment shared between many parties. We see dedicated and shared resources there.

Figure 8. Community cloud: Test use case

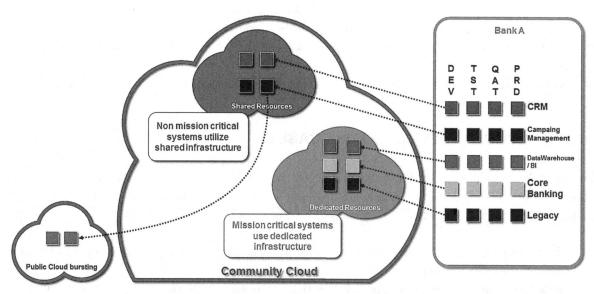

CONCLUSION

Community cloud is a viable alternative for many market sectors and many organizations. In the center of this concept lies sharing. Reusing resources, joint investment and learning from each other is a great benefit, which comes with the community cloud. It is true that not all organizations are willing to share their IT resources with others, especially not with the competition. But in the modern economy sharing, open source and tight integration is more often perceived as a competitive advantage rather than a threat to your market position. Appropriate governance model enhanced with the security measures should assure that your organization's data stays safe and confidential.

For the highly regulated industries community cloud helps to bring common & standardized way of governing, managing and securing IT resources. If set appropriately, regulatory bodies should accept the security and auditability of the entire system beyond any doubt. Open standards and transparency do help to gain general trust towards community cloud platform. Additionally sharing costs and building demand for the additional services gives possibility to create financially attractive offer for all participants.

Community cloud is viable opportunity for all organizations working in the highly regulated industries. No matter if you search for the operational cost efficiency or the possibility of frictionless growth this cloud model can fit your needs. In governmental and banking sectors it can also help achieving better transparency of operations and transactions. Together with the rise of the blockchain-based procedures community cloud can lead the new level of security and auditability.

In the future all transactions done between any publicly trusted entities will be logged and stored in the cloud. Certified community clouds will become platform of choice for all sensitive businesses for both, public and private entities.

REFERENCES

Amazon Web Services. (2016). *Platform overview*. Retrieved from: https://aws.amazon.com/

Banking and Finance. (2007). *Europe's Markets in Financial Instruments Directive (Mifid1 & 2). Investment Services and Regulatory Markets*. Retrieved from: http://ec.europa.eu/finance/securities/isd/index_en.htm.Europa.eu

Bundesinisterium der Justiz und fur Verbrauchenschutz. (2016). *What is Openstack*. Retrieved from: http://www.openstack.org/software/

BusinessDictionary.com. (2016). *Service Provider definition*. Retrieved from; http://www.businessdictionary.com/definition/service-provider.html

CloudFoundry. (2016). *What is CloudFoundry*. Retrieved from: https://www.cloudfoundry.org/

European Bank Authority. (2016). *Regulation and Policy*. Retrieved from: http://www.eba.europa.eu/regulation-and-policy

National Institute of Standards and Technology. (2011). *Definition of Cloud Computing*. Retrieved from: http://nvlpubs.nist.gov/nistpubs/Legacy/SP/nistspecialpublication800-145.pdf

Senate and House of Representatives of the United States of America. (1990). *Germany's Federal Data Protection Act - known as Bundesdatenschutzgesetz or BDSG*. Retrieved from: http://www.gesetze-im-internet.de/bdsg_1990/index.html#BJNR029550990BJNE001503310

The Dodd-Frank Wall Street Reform and Consumer Protection Act (DFA). (2011). *Financial Stability Act*. Retrieved from: https://www.sec.gov/about/laws/wallstreetreform-cpa.pdf

The European Markets and Infrastructure Regulation (EMIR). (2012). *Derivatives/EMIR*. Retrieved from: http://ec.europa.eu/finance/financial-markets/derivatives/index_en.htm.Europa.eu

Wikipedia. (2016). *Platform as a Service*. Retrieved from: http://en.wikipedia.org/wiki/Platform_as_a_service

KEY TERMS AND DEFINITIONS

Cloud Service Provider: A company that offers component of cloud computing –to other businesses or individuals. Amazon was the first major cloud provider, with the 2006 offering of Amazon Simple Storage Service (Amazon S3). Other cloud providers include Apple, Cisco, Citrix, IBM, Google, Microsoft, and Salesforce.com.

IaaS: The definition of Infrastructure as a Service is simple. You rent infrastructure—servers, storage and networking provided over cloud — on demand, in a pay-as-you-go model. National Institute of Standards and Technology (NIST, 2011) defines IaaS as "The capability provided to the consumer is to provision processing, storage, networks and other fundamental computing resources where the consumer is able to deploy and run arbitrary software, which can include operating systems and applications. The consumer does not manage or control the underlying cloud infrastructure but has control over operating systems, storage and deployed applications; and possibly limited control of select networking components (e.g., host firewalls)."

PaaS: Platform as a Service is a platform for delivering operating systems and associated services over the Internet without downloads or installation. Platform as a Service brings the benefits over to the software development world. PaaS can be defined as a computing platform that allows the creation of applications quickly and easily and without the complexity of buying and maintaining the software and infrastructure underneath it. There are a number of different characteristics on what constitutes PaaS but some basic points include (http://en.wikipedia.org/wiki/Platform_as_a_service): Services to develop, test, deploy, host and maintain applications in the same integrated development environment. All the varying services needed to fulfil the application development process: (1) Web based user interface creation tools help to create, modify, test and deploy different UI scenarios; (2) Multi-tenant architecture where multiple concurrent users utilize the same development application; (3) Built in scalability of deployed software including load balancing and failover; Integration with web services and databases via common standards; (4) Support for development team collaboration – some PaaS solutions include project planning and communication tools; (5) Tools to handle billing and subscription management.

SaaS: Software as a Service is a software distribution model in which applications are hosted by a vendor or service provider. They are made available to customers over a network (the Internet). SaaS lets companies use software tools without having to install, operate and maintain them on premises, freeing customers to concentrate on creating business functions and value. Organizations can potentially start using software more quickly than waiting for the installation of on premises software. The SaaS approach enables them to expand their systems as usage grows without having to make any capital-equipment purchases. SaaS can be a good choice when there's little or no budget money available for buying software and related hardware. Overall SaaS costs will depend on the amount of usage tools get. SaaS can stand for at least three different "as-a-service" offerings. The original use of the acronym was to refer to Software as a Service (described above). The term has since been used in reference to Storage as a Service and Security as a Service.

Service Provider: Definition based on the Business Dictionary (http://www.businessdictionary.com/definition/service-provider.html) is *1. General:* Organization, business or individual which offers service to others in exchange for payment; *2. Internet:* A company that provides customers with an internet connection.

Workload: In computing, the workload is the amount of processing that the computer has been given to do at a specific time. As cloud computing evolves, so does its capabilities, which means not all workloads are currently appropriate for a cloud-based model. To deploy a workload multiple components need to be wired together: application code, middleware, management agents, preexisting services, virtual machines, data, disks, and networks. Workload availability and performance depends on the correctness of the wiring and on how the components are provisioned and maintained by the cloud management system.

XaaS: The collection of things available "as-a-service" is referred to as XaaS which refer to "anything as a service" or "everything as a service".

Chapter 4
Cloud Computing Architectural Patterns

Prashant Jain
IBM, Singapore

Yan Pang
IBM, Singapore & National University of Singapore, Singapore

ABSTRACT

Cloud computing has been one of the most disruptive technologies, which has changed the way IT is consumed by enterprises, both small and large. The ability to subscribe to "as-a-service" consumption model, while converting capital expenditure to operational expenditure, has been a key driver for Cloud adoption. Rapid provisioning and deprovisioning of services, elastic scaling of infrastructure resources and self-service ability for users are some of the key characteristics and benefits offered by Cloud. Infrastructure as a Service (IaaS) provides the basic building block, with Platform as a Service (PaaS) providing a layer of abstraction on top of IaaS and similarly Software as a Service (SaaS) providing a layer of abstraction on top of PaaS. Moving up the layers reduces complexity and enables users to tap into a much larger spectrum of benefits that Cloud computing has to offer. While Cloud opens the door for "as-a-service" consumption model, there are many additional benefits that can be realized by enterprises beyond the typical IaaS, PaaS and SaaS. A number of these benefits can be realized by leveraging Cloud in different scenarios and use cases. For example, an enterprise may continue to pursue a traditional non-Cloud based infrastructure deployment strategy, however, it could use a public Cloud for storage elasticity. Such use cases exemplify many atypical benefits that Cloud can provide, which often got overlooked. This paper will present a number of such cloud deployment use cases that go beyond the typical IaaS usage of cloud. A hierarchical architectural model of cloud solution pattern is proposed to describe both the business requirements and technical considerations of these use cases. These cloud architectural patterns are further elaborated through real-life case studies and examples.

DOI: 10.4018/978-1-5225-0759-8.ch004

INTRODUCTION

Cloud computing has been one of the most disruptive technologies, which has changed the way IT is consumed by enterprises, both small and large. The ability to subscribe to "as-a-service" consumption model, while converting capital expenditure to operational expenditure, has been a key driver for Cloud adoption. Rapid provisioning and de-provisioning of services, elastic scaling of infrastructure resources and self-service ability for users are some of the key characteristics and benefits offered by Cloud. Infrastructure as a Service (IaaS) provides the basic building block, with Platform as a Service (PaaS) providing a layer of abstraction on top of IaaS and similarly Software as a Service (SaaS) providing a layer of abstraction on top of PaaS. Moving up the layers reduces complexity and enables users to tap into a much larger spectrum of benefits that Cloud computing has to offer. More importantly, while Cloud opens the door for "as-a-service" consumption model, there are many additional benefits that can be realized by enterprises beyond the typical IaaS, PaaS and SaaS. A number of these benefits can be realized by leveraging Cloud in different scenarios and use cases.

A pattern describes a solution for a recurring problem in a given context. Patterns help capture best practices in solving problems in almost every domain. Using patterns can help identify and document design principles that are repeatable given a well-defined problem statement. Using patterns provides a concise way of documenting solutions to repeatable problems. As a result, it becomes much easier to refer to a well-defined pattern as the solution to a problem, instead of repetitively detailing out the solution each time the problem is encountered. This reuse of successful patterns also facilitates avoidance of common mistakes and pitfalls in solution design.

While the use of patterns is most common in software design, however, their use is not restricted to software domain only. Patterns have been applied to areas ranging from the architecture of buildings (Alexander, 1979) to teaching (Bergin, 2012). In this chapter, we use patterns to describe a number of cloud deployment uses cases that go beyond the typical Infrastructure-as-a-Service (IaaS) usage of cloud. For example, an enterprise may continue to pursue a traditional non-Cloud based infrastructure deployment strategy, however, it could use a public Cloud for storage elasticity. Such use cases exemplify many atypical benefits that Cloud can provide, which often got overlooked.

USE CASE SCENARIOS

We use the pattern format of (Buschmann, Meunier, Rohnert, Sommerlad, & Stal, 1996) to capture the following key components for each cloud deployment use case scenario:

- **Problem:** Identifies the key issue(s) that must be resolved
- **Context:** Describes when it makes sense to apply the pattern
- **Solution:** Describes the key steps to address the problem
- **Benefits:** Highlights the impact and advantage of applying the pattern
- **Offerings:** Describes some of the offerings and products that are relevant or required in applying the pattern

The format provides a well-defined structure to capture the recurring problem, its solution and when it makes sense to apply the solution. Note that the list of offerings covered in this chapter should only be regarded as a representative set.

Use Case Scenario 1: Compute Capacity Optimization for Development and Test Workloads

Problem

Development and test workloads typically represent 10% to 20% or sometimes even more of an enterprise's environment. A common practice in an enterprise is for developers to have their own sandbox development environment to work in. A sandbox provides developers their own technical environment, which is separate from an integration or staging environment, thereby helping reduce the risk of inadvertent errors seeping in and adversely affecting a larger group of people. An integration environment is a build and test environment, where all developers commit code changes. The goal of this environment is to integrate and validate the work of the entire project team so it can be tested before being promoted to the staging environment.

Most of these development, integration and test environments are not required all the time. Furthermore, many times the infrastructure requirement changes during a development or test phase, which cannot always be anticipated. Enterprises can invest in providing dedicated development and test environments as well as over-provision infrastructure capacity in anticipation of additional requirements. However, not only does this add cost, it also leads to suboptimal use of resources.

Given that the workloads are variable in nature, how can development and test environments be built such that the cost as well as the utilization of the infrastructure is optimized?

Context: Highly variable environments that can be quickly set up and/or taken down

Solution

A Cloud based environment can help optimize the infrastructure requirement and utilization for development and test workloads. Rapid provisioning and de-provisioning of capacity along with elastic scaling of infrastructure resources is a key benefit offered by Cloud. These capabilities can be leveraged by development and test workloads to optimize the required infrastructure footprint.

A public or private Cloud should be leveraged to deploy development and test environments. However, a development or test environment and the underlying infrastructure should only be provisioned when actually required. When migrating to Cloud from a traditional IT environment, an enterprise should evaluate how many of the existing development test servers are really required. When not active, the development and test servers should be de-provisioned, thereby freeing up capacity as well as reducing the overall operational expenditure.

Depending upon the Cloud provider, a server can be provisioned in a few minutes to a couple of hours. Therefore, if a new development environment is required, it should be set up on demand. Once the development activities have been completed, the environment should be removed, after persisting any required data so that it can be restored at a future date, if required. A Cloud based environment also allows existing capacity to be increased or decreased. For example, if a developer has a requirement to increase the compute capacity of the provisioned servers, that can be done dynamically with minimal disruption and in very little time.

Benefits

Using Cloud for hosting development and test environments offers a number of benefits:

- Reduction in the absolute number of development and test servers/images by moving in-house dedicated images to Cloud, where they can be de-provisioned or hibernated when not required, while keeping storage around.
- Lower price of development and test servers in Cloud compared to in-house, given the servers are not required to be running all the time. Additionally, this leads to lower operational, asset and management costs.
- Standardized Cloud image catalog, which can help improve development quality.
- Faster provisioning time (from weeks/months to minutes/hours).
- No capital investment with pay-as-you-use charging model.
- Ability to scale up and down as needed.
- Integrated billing and metering as part of Cloud capability.
- No need for hardware refreshes.

Offerings

All Cloud providers support hosting of development and test workloads. Many of the Cloud providers offer additional offerings and capabilities that can support agile development and testing:

- **Physical Servers:** SoftLayer offers bare metal servers and Rackspace offers OnMetal servers, which are both physical servers hosted in Cloud. These can be useful when a test environment needs to be on a physical server to mirror a production environment that is non-virtualized and on-premise.
- **Bluemix:** IBM Bluemix is an open-standard, cloud-based platform for building, managing, and running applications of all types (web, mobile, big data, new smart devices, etc.).
- **AWS Developer Tools:** AWS offers a number of tools on its Cloud that can assist developers during software development lifecycle. This includes, CodeCommit for source code management, CodeDeploy for code deployment and CodePipeline for software release using continuous delivery.

Use Case Scenario 2: Compute Capacity Augmentation

Problem

Many enterprise customers experience variable demand for compute capacity. This may be triggered by some workloads exhibiting seasonal variability for required system resources such as processing power or memory. For example, an online retailer may experience burst in compute requirement during a promotion period or holiday season when there is a surge in online traffic. Similarly, the demand for additional compute capacity may also be required for running short-term tasks and processes such as batch jobs or business analytics.

Similar to the earlier pattern, in this scenario the requirement for additional compute capacity is short-lived. Furthermore, there may be variability in the amount of additional compute capacity, which cannot always be anticipated. Many enterprises that have invested in traditional IT infrastructure address these requirements by over-provisioning infrastructure capacity in anticipation of the additional compute capacity requirement. This typically results in underutilized infrastructure as for a large period of time the excess capacity lies idle.

How can such short-term compute capacity requirements for enterprises be fulfilled such that the cost as well as the utilization of the infrastructure is optimized?

Context: Workloads with variable system requirements, with variability as granular as hourly basis

Solution

A public Cloud can be leveraged to augment an enterprise's existing compute capacity seamlessly. There are three possible options that an enterprise can explore in this scenario:

- **Migrate Partial Workload to Cloud:** This option can be considered when the workload can be split, such that part of it that requires additional compute capacity can be moved to a public Cloud. For example, in a three-tier application, the web tier components of the user interface can be moved to a public Cloud, while the remaining parts of the workload (middleware and database) remain in the existing on-premise environment. The web tier would benefit from the elastic compute capacity provided by a public Cloud. As there is a requirement for compute capacity, additional resources can be provisioned and similarly, once the requirement goes away, these resources can be released. This is a typical example of the Systems of Engagement (SOE) and Systems of Record (SOR) integration scenario, where the end users would access the application as hosted in the Cloud environment (SOE), and the application would interface back to the on-premises environment for the core data and business functions (SOR).
- **Migrate Complete Workload to Cloud:** This option can be considered when the entire workload can be migrated to a public Cloud. This allows all the components of the workload to scale and benefit from elasticity offered by a public Cloud. Of course, an enterprise would need to evaluate whether the entire workload, including the database and/or file storage can be hosted on a public Cloud. This would involve assessing whether there are any regulatory or legal constraints, as well as whether the Cloud capability can fulfill any specific performance requirements.
- **Leverage Cloud-Based Capability:** An increasing number of software and business applications are now available in Cloud-based or software as a service (SaaS) editions. For example, business analytics is offered as a service hosted on Cloud by a number of providers. Instead of building large and complex data warehouses, enterprises can leverage these Cloud-hosted analytics offerings and capabilities to analyze data rapidly and in real time. The Cloud based software and applications not only help augment an enterprise's on-premise compute capacity, it allows customers to consume it on-demand, with several hosting options to choose from. An important point that needs to be evaluated is if there is any tight dependency between the Cloud-based capability and on-premise workloads. For example, an enterprise's data warehouse may need to be on-premise,

in which case a Cloud-based analytics solution would imply significant network traffic and hence bandwidth requirement.

For all of the above options, some degree of integration would be required between the on-premise environment and the Cloud environment. This is likely to be both at the time of implementing the solution as well as during steady state operations.

Benefits

Using Cloud for augmenting compute capacity offers a number of benefits:

- Ability to extend local compute capacity with on-demand Cloud infrastructure.
- Ability to scale capacity up and down as needed.
- Leverage advanced capabilities, such as analytics as a service with minimal infrastructure, implementation and reduced administrative cost.

Offerings

A large number of Cloud providers offer various software as a service, including business applications, middleware and databases.

- **IBM Cloud Marketplace:** IBM provides a rich portfolio of Software-as-a-Service, with over 400 offerings and software hosted on Cloud. This includes, Watson analytics, Bluemix, Cloudant, IBM Commerce, MaaS360 and Verse.
- **Oracle Analytics:** Oracle offers a number of analytics software on Cloud, which includes HCM Analytics, CRM Analytics, ERP Analytics and SCM Analytics
- **Salesforce:** Salesforce offers its CRM solutions through SaaS deployment. In addition, its offering Force.com is a PaaS that allows developers to create multitenant add-on applications that integrate into the main Salesforce.com application. Similarly, others systems such as Data.com, Desk.com and Do.com are all deployed in Cloud and hence can be consumed without the expense of purchasing hardware and IT support.

Use Case Scenario 3: Storage Capacity Augmentation

Problem

The increasing volumes of both structured and unstructured data getting generated in enterprises is fueling the need for secure, reliable, and cost-efficient storage infrastructure. While per unit cost of storage has been going down every year, the rapid growth of storage volume has been increasing the overall cost of procuring and maintaining the storage infrastructure. As enterprises purchase additional storage infrastructure, they also need to wrestle with data center space and cost. In fact, many enterprises face physical space constraint in their data centers as they try to add additional storage.

Moving workloads to Cloud can address the challenge as long as the existing data for these workloads can also be migrated to Cloud. Unfortunately, for many enterprises there may be a challenge in doing so, since the footprint of the existing storage infrastructure may be too large to merit migrating to Cloud.

Therefore, how can enterprises augment their existing storage capacity without adding additional storage infrastructure in their data center?

Context: Workloads that can leverage remote storage either for short-term or long-term basis

Solution

A public or private Cloud storage can be leveraged to augment an enterprise's existing on-premise storage capacity seamlessly. A Cloud storage gateway provides integration between the on-premise storage and the Cloud storage. The Cloud storage gateway can be devices, appliances or virtual machines, which reside on the local network of a customer and act as a local storage array, while interfacing with Cloud-based storage. The gateway can make the Cloud storage appear as locally mounted storage accessible using traditional SAN and NAS protocols.

The Cloud storage gateway interfaces with many different Cloud providers as well as different types of storage. For example, object storage is a very cost effective storage option that is offered by most major Cloud providers. However, even though object storage is great for scaling out storage infrastructure, it isn't interoperable with the block storage typically seen on an on-premise SAN. Cloud storage gateways can help integrate with object storage offered by a Cloud provider such that Cloud storage is presented on the network as block or file storage, while the gateway translates to objects and sends them back to the object storage hosted by the Cloud provider. A Cloud storage gateway can also help integrate with the API requirement of various Cloud providers, making storage access seamless.

A public or private Cloud storage can also be used for implementing a backup or archival solution. By using a Cloud storage gateway, an enterprise can take regular offsite backup, which would be kept in the storage of one or more Cloud providers. In fact, many of the Cloud storage gateway providers support keeping the data on-premise in-sync with the data in the Cloud. When required, data can be restored from Cloud to on-premise. To address the issue of bandwidth cost as well as time taken for large restores, some Cloud backup service providers offer an option to restore data to disks, which are then sent to the customer for local on-premise recovery.

Benefits

Using Cloud for augmenting storage capacity offers a number of benefits:

- Ability to scale storage capacity up and down as needed, without incurring capital expenditure.
- Provides an additional tier of storage, such that local storage can be used for performance sensitive workloads, while Cloud storage can be leveraged for capacity and data protection.
- Support for thin provisioning, which helps provide savings through better granularity and capacity management
- Support for many advanced storage features such as backup and recovery, caching, compression, encryption and storage de-duplication.

Offerings

A number of vendors have products and offerings that support on-premise storage augmentation by integrating into various public and private Cloud.

- **EMC CloudArray:** CloudArray is an offering from EMC that utilizes storage from over 20 different public and private Cloud providers to extend an enterprise's existing on-premises storage infrastructure. Using CloudArray, enterprises can add an additional tier of cloud storage to their arrays that is cost-effective, scalable, and seamless.
- **Panzura Global File System:** Panzura's Global File System (GFS) turns Cloud storage into a local file system. Panzura GFS behaves like local storage appearing as a large file share to users, however, it is backed by a central cloud data repository and can span hundreds of sites.
- **Nasuni Cloud NAS:** Nasuni Cloud NAS combines local storage controllers and Cloud storage to provide enterprises global access to data. The Nasuni architecture allows multiple local storage controllers at multiple locations to access the same live volume, while providing appropriate levels of access control.
- **CTERA Cloud Storage Gateway:** CTERA's Cloud Storage Gateway (CSG) is a hybrid appliance that combines an enterprise's local storage with Cloud storage. The appliance features a full set of NAS capabilities and comprehensive backup functionality, utilizing on-premises storage capabilities for speed and local sharing, while taking advantage of Cloud storage for off-site backup, universal access, file sharing, and folder synchronization.

Use Case Scenario 4: Cloud-Based Disaster Recovery

Problem

Implementing Disaster Recovery (DR) is a key part of Business Continuity for most enterprises. Most DR services work by replicating application and database states between two sites – primary and secondary data centers. In case the primary site becomes unavailable, the secondary site takes over with the applications getting activated using the latest version of the replicated data. Depending upon the required Recovery Time Objective (RTO) and Recovery Point Objective (RPO), the DR approach taken by enterprises can be costly with the need to provision additional servers at a secondary site and keeping them running or on standby. More importantly, for most enterprises, keeping these servers running or on standby in the secondary site results in sub-optimal resource utilization, since in most cases the servers are idling most of the time.

Therefore, how can enterprises implement disaster recovery by minimizing the infrastructure footprint required in the secondary data center?

Context: Workloads with loose or relaxed RTO requirement, typically of 2 hours or more, although a more aggressive RTO may also be possible

Solution

A public Cloud can be used as the secondary site to implement disaster recovery. Under normal operating conditions, minimal infrastructure footprint in the Cloud would be required, while ensuring that the data is replicated between the primary and secondary sites. If the RTO is loose and the Cloud provider is able to support fast provisioning of servers, then during normal operating conditions, very few servers need to be active in the Cloud. When a disaster actually happens, the full set of servers are provisioned in the Cloud, and the applications and data are restored from replicated storage. The use of Cloud allows the servers, applications and data to be rapidly brought online once disaster is declared. Even in case the applications need to be kept running on the secondary site, a cost effective approach can be to multiplex a single replication server for multiple applications. In case of disaster, additional servers and infrastructure capacity can be provisioned in the secondary site to augment the single server.

A variant to the above solution is to deploy both primary production and disaster recovery instances in different Cloud data centers. In this case, the data replication would take place over the network between the two Cloud data centers. Some Cloud providers such as SoftLayer provide unmetered bandwidth over their private network connecting their various Cloud data centers. Using this, enterprises can implement a cost effective disaster recovery solution by deploying production and disaster recovery instances in two different SoftLayer data centers. This would help eliminate the network cost associated with data replication between the primary and the secondary sites.

Benefits

A Cloud based disaster recovery approach can provide a number of advantages:

- Eliminates need for dedicated hardware at DR site, by paying only for the disaster recovery capacity/servers as needed.
- Having DR sites in the Cloud reduces the need for data center space, IT infrastructure and IT resources, which leads to significant cost reductions, enabling smaller companies to deploy disaster recovery options that were previously only found in larger enterprises.
- Deploying both primary production and disaster recovery instances across two Cloud data centers of the same provider, can potentially eliminate or reduce network data replication cost, which can be substantial depending upon the type of applications.
- Cloud resources can be quickly added with fine granularity and have costs that scale smoothly without requiring large upfront investments.

Offerings

Most of the public Cloud providers can be leveraged to implement a DR solution. However, a number of key considerations should be taken into account when selecting a Cloud as the secondary site. These include, the server provisioning time supported by the provider, network data replication cost and the ability to reconfigure the network in the Cloud deployment in case of disaster.

- **VMWare Site Recovery Manager (SRM):** SRM supports data synchronization between multiple sites and can be leveraged to implement disaster recovery across private cloud environments. VMware SRM automates the process of synchronizing data between the primary and secondary sites and in case of a disaster, helps start the servers in the correct order, while specifying network configurations.
- **Amazon Web Services (AWS):** AWS supports many popular DR architectures from "pilot light" environments that are ready to scale up at a moment's notice to "warm standby" and "hot standby" environments that enable rapid failover.
- **IBM SoftLayer:** IBM provides Virtualized Server Recovery (VSR) managed service on SoftLayer, using which enterprises can replicate entire systems in real-time including system files, databases, applications and user data in a way that is independent of the make and model of the underlying hardware.

Use Case Scenario 5: Load Balancing and Auto Scaling

Problem

Load balancing is the distribution of load across a pool of servers. It is used to share processing across multiple servers as traffic or workload increases. It is also used as a form of high availability, such that in the event that one of the servers in the pool experiences any kind of hardware or software failure the load can be redistributed among other servers. One of the most common use cases of load balancers is in distributing HTTP traffic, however, that is not the only type of scenario supported by load balancers.

Load balancing can be implemented through both hardware and software appliances. Hardware appliances perform well, however, they have several drawbacks. They are expensive and lack flexibility in adding custom load balancing algorithms. They also lack multi-tenancy support. To address these issues, most enterprises have adopted software load balancers that provide a lot more flexibility.

A load balancer is configured with a pool of servers among which it distributes the incoming requests using one or more algorithms such as round robin, least connections or IP hash. In case the workload grows beyond what can be handled by the pool of servers, an additional server would typically need to be added to the pool and then the load balancer configured to route traffic to the new server. Similarly, if the workload would fall below a certain threshold, it is likely that many of the servers would be left underutilized. For example, a social networking website may require a minimum of three servers available at any time. These three servers can be added to a pool, and a load balancer configured to distribute workload among these servers. Over the weekend as the website traffic spikes, let's say an additional two servers are required to handle the load. If a total of five servers is set up in the pool, then during the week the servers would remain underutilized. On the other hand, adding two servers every weekend and then removing them is also not a practical solution.

Therefore, how can a server pool associated with a load balancer be dynamically scalable to optimize the infrastructure footprint required?

Context: Environments requiring dynamic horizontal scalability of infrastructure

Solution

A public Cloud can be used to implement horizontal scaling tied to a load balancer. Many Cloud providers support a feature called auto scaling, which helps scaling a system either vertically or horizontally in case of a load spike. When load reduces or goes back to its normal state, some of the running instances of the application can be automatically stopped or deprovisioned to ensure that the Cloud tenant does not incur extra costs for running idle instances.

Figure 1. illustrates the concept of horizontal scaling, where additional identical servers are added to a load balancer.

Auto scaling in pubic Cloud is typically integrated with the load balancer service. As a result, any time new servers are added or removed from a load balancing pool, the load balancer is automatically notified so that it can add or remove them from its load balancing pool.

There can be a number of triggers for auto scaling to kick in. For example, triggers may be tied to a specific time of the day or day of the week. In the example above, auto scaling would kick in automatically at the start of the weekend, resulting in two servers to be provisioned. Similarly, auto scaling would automatically deprovision two servers at the end of the weekend. Triggers can also be based on rules or policies such as volume of network traffic per second or the total number of active network connections.

Compared to vertical scaling, which usually results in application downtime and non-linear improvements, horizontal scaling is typically achievable without downtime and near-linear scaling results. However, the applications have to be designed for scalability. This design is critical, because it will greatly affect the performance of the application, and sometimes the application might not even function correctly when horizontal scaling is on.

Benefits

Software load balancing and auto scaling are fundamental services in the Cloud and bring a lot of benefits to cloud users:

Figure 1. Horizontal scaling

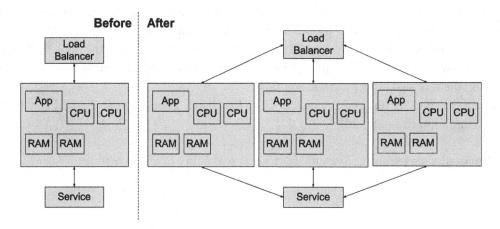

- Optimizes performance to meet the SLAs without overprovisioning resources. It helps ease management overhead by automatically monitoring the performance of the system, and by making decisions about adding or removing resources without operators' involvement.
- Enables pay per use by ensuring that resources are only provisioned and run when needed.
- Supports high availability by ensuring that resources change without downtime.
- Optimizes the workload among multiple instances to provide high performance on the cloud.

Offerings

Many of the public Cloud providers support some form of auto scaling coupled with load balancing service.

- **IBM SoftLayer:** Auto Scale is SoftLayer's complimentary service built into the Customer Portal and API that allows clients to create a series of parameters that, when triggered, automatically provision or cancel hourly Virtual Servers.
- **Amazon AWS:** AWS's implementation of Auto Scaling is integrated with Amazon CloudWatch. Groups are created with Launch Configurations that are set by the client. For example, a condition can be set to add new Amazon EC2 instances in increments to the Auto Scaling group when the average utilization of an Amazon EC2 fleet is high. Amazon CloudWatch can send alarms to trigger scaling activities.
- **Rackspace:** Rackpace's Auto Scale solution includes Scaling Groups that are configured using Scaling Rules. The Scaling Rules set thresholds based on Rackspace's monitoring tools and scaling policies that define how the client's environment should be scaled.

Use Case Scenario 6: Leveraging Cloud for Data Center Migration and Consolidation

Problem

Enterprises migrate or consolidate data centers in order to move out of an outdated, legacy data center, to overcome shortage of space as a result of infrastructure growth, as well as a means to reduce IT cost. Data center migration and consolidation provide a unique opportunity for enterprises for cost take-out as well as infrastructure refresh. However, at the same time data center migration can become a high risk project that must be executed without impacting business operations, availability of applications and infrastructure and ensuring minimal impact to data.

How can the complexity and timeline for data center migration and consolidation be managed, while optimizing or potentially eliminating the build-out costs for a new data center?

Context: Migration of some or all of the existing workloads as part of data center consolidation and migration strategy

Solution

A Cloud can be leveraged to reduce the required data center footprint and at the same time eliminating the need for procuring "bubble" hardware to support application migration. Migrating or consolidating data centers can be a good opportunity to migrate workloads to Cloud. Workloads should be assessed for migration to Cloud based on functional and non-functional requirements, including any regulatory constraints. For a target workload the following should be taken into consideration: type, complexity and criticality of the workload, migration duration and potential impact due to factors such as network latency.

The workload migration strategy can also be tied to infrastructure refresh strategy, such that applications that are deployed on servers that are due for refresh can be migrated directly to Cloud. This would help reduce the capital expenditure associated with infrastructure refresh. Applications deployed on servers that are not due for refresh can also be considered for migration to Cloud. The servers that are not due for refresh and that get freed up can be repurposed and used to support scalability requirement of any applications that cannot be migrated to Cloud. Alternatively, some of the freed up servers can be used as "bubble" hardware when migrating applications to the new data center.

The end result would typically be a hybrid cloud deployment, where some of the workloads would be deployed in Cloud, while the remaining would be deployed on-premise in the new data center.

Benefits

Leveraging Cloud can provide a number of benefits at the time of data center consolidation and migration.

- Reduces data center footprint and corresponding cost by migrating existing workloads to Cloud.
- Eliminates the need for procuring "bubble" hardware by migrating applications directly to Cloud. Similarly, some of the freed up servers can be used as "bubble" hardware when migrating applications to the new data center.
- Implements hybrid Cloud providing scalable capacity to support future expansion for new workloads. Provides additional capacity from freed up servers to support scalability requirement of applications that cannot be migrated to Cloud.
- Refreshes infrastructure for the migrated workloads.

Offerings

Most of the Infrastructure-as-a-Service (IaaS) Cloud providers can be leveraged to support data center migration and consolidation. Some of the popular providers include:

- **SoftLayer:** SoftLayer, an IBM Company, provides IaaS from a growing number of data centers and network points of presence around the world. Products and services include bare metal and virtual servers, networking, turnkey big data solutions and private cloud solutions.
- **Amazon Web Services (AWS):** AWS provides a reliable, scalable, low-cost IaaS Cloud with data center locations in the U.S., Europe, Brazil, Singapore, Japan, and Australia.
- **Microsoft Azure:** Azure is an IaaS and PaaS Cloud built on a global network of Microsoft-managed and Microsoft partner hosted datacenters. Azure provides integrated cloud services covering analytics, computing, database, mobile, networking and storage.

Use Case Scenario 7: Cloud Analytics

Problem

Using analytics discovers patterns, trends and associations in data that help an organization understand the behavior of the people and systems so as to optimize its business operations. Cloud deployments offer a choice of private, public and hybrid architectures. Private Cloud employs in-house data and computing components running behind corporate firewalls. Public Cloud offers services over the Internet with data and computing resources available on publicly accessible servers. Hybrid environments have a mixture of components running as both in-house and public services. Cloud analytics is a service model, in which elements of the data analytics process, e.g. data sets, analytics components, computing components, are provided through a public, private or hybrid Cloud.

It is important to have a choice of cloud deployments because location is one of the first architectural decisions in a Cloud analytics project. For some analytics projects in large enterprises, the existing enterprise data sets are very large or highly volatile. It would be both expensive and time consuming to move these data, so the analytics computing component may need to access these data from their current storage location. In addition, in many public sector and finance sector projects, legal and regulatory requirements may also impact where data can be located since many countries have data sovereignty laws that prevent data about individuals, financial, and healthcare data from travelling across country borders.

On the other hand, for the analytics projects in small and medium enterprises (SMEs), the enterprise data sets are usually not very large, and not as sensitive as the ones in large enterprises in terms of government regulation. In order to derive better insights from these data, we often need to combine these SME data sets with large amount of public available data, e.g. social network data, industry public available data, market research data, etc. When combining the enterprise data sets with public available data, the analytics need high performance computing power which is often too expensive for SMEs to afford.

Therefore, where should the data set be located and where should the analytics and computing components be located relative to the location of the data set are critical for a Cloud analytics projects.

Pattern 1

Context: Enterprise data sets are too huge to move, or data cannot be moved due to legal and regulatory requirements.

Solution

The analytics and computing components can be deployed near to the enterprise data sets to optimize processing as well as to address any compliance or regulatory requirements. A common solution is to have the analytics application and computing components be completely deployed and managed in the local enterprise environment either on a private Cloud infrastructure or a traditional on-premise infrastructure environment.

Recently, another innovative solution built on top of hybrid Cloud is proposed. In this solution, agent software can be deployed on-premise that pulls the right analytics application component from the public Cloud, runs it on the local computing component with on-premise data, while communicating with off-premise data sources, if required. In this case, the analytics applications can be managed centrally in a remote public Cloud environment efficiently, and rapidly deployed to the local location on-demand.

Benefits

There are a number of benefits in running analytics close to the data:

- Avoid the movement of large volume of data, which can be both expensive and time consuming
- Address any compliance, legal and regulatory requirements
- Deploy analytics applications on the local computing environment rapidly

Offerings

- **Local Deployment and Management:** Many companies such as IBM, HP and Microsoft provide private Cloud or traditional on-premise legacy infrastructure to support local deployment and management of analytics components. The analytics applications and computing components can be deployed in the private Cloud or on-premise legacy infrastructure which also stores enterprise data. Usually local deployment and management solution requires one copy of analytics per location and a manual aggregation of the analytics results centrally. The analytics may be of different versions or may operate in a different environment, leading to inconsistent risk assessments. Also, there is a huge risk of human error leading to a violation in doing all of this manually. Lastly, in each such location, IT skills are required in maintaining the local analytics components leading to higher operational costs.
- **IBM Micro Cloud Solution:** Micro Cloud can be viewed as a mobile device for the enterprise. Just like the mobile device provides a controlled environment in which apps can be seamlessly deployed and used, Micro Cloud takes existing enterprise applications, puts them in the central Cloud environment, and allows them to be downloaded and run on an on-premises appliance. Compared to the current remote deployment solutions on private Cloud or on-premise legacy infrastructure, Micro Cloud reduces management complexity, and lets on-premises IT operate at costs and speeds comparable to the public Cloud.

Pattern 2

Context: Small and Medium Enterprise (SME) need to combine its own limit enterprise data with public data sets to derive deeper business insights, and leverage on public Cloud to provision high performance computing environment with low cost affordable by SME.

Solution

The enterprise data sets can be moved to a public Cloud environment, which contains a number of public available relevant data sets and can provision high performance computing power for running the analytics with low cost.

Benefits

There are a number of benefits of running analytics in a public Cloud:

- By combination with publically available data sets on public Cloud, SMEs can augment their limited enterprise data sets to derive better business insights.
- By leveraging a public Cloud for infrastructure, SMEs do not need to build and maintain the high performance computing infrastructure, which is too expensive for many SMEs.

Offerings

- **Amazon Web Services (AWS):** AWS provides a centralized repository of public data sets that can be seamlessly integrated into AWS cloud-based applications. The public data sets are hosted in two possible formats: Amazon Elastic Block Store (Amazon EBS) snapshots and/or Amazon Simple Storage Service (Amazon S3) buckets. Currently there are near to 100 public data sets available in AWS, and the number of data sets keeps increasing. AWS Elastic Compute Cloud (EC2) provides resizable compute capacity in the cloud, and it is designed to make web-scale Cloud Computing easier for developers. SMEs can access these public data sets via the AWS centralized data repository and analyze them using the analytics applications running on Amazon EC2 instances or Amazon EMR (Hosted Hadoop) clusters.
- **Oracle Data as a Service (DaaS) for Marketing:** Oracle DaaS for Marketing is part of Oracle Data Cloud and provides a comprehensive Business-to-Business (B2B) data set to power smarter marketing decisions. This B2B data set is developed in collaboration with some of the biggest B2B data providers, including Dun & Bradstreet and Madison Logic. By adopting Oracle DaaS solution, SMEs are able to combine their own marketing data with 300 million anonymous business profiles from Oracle Marketing Cloud, and run the analytics applications on Oracle public Cloud infrastructure. Using this the SMEs can create a more complete profile of target customers and develop better marketing strategy.

CONCLUSION

The patterns presented in this chapter showcase various cloud deployment use cases beyond the typical Infrastructure-as-a-Service (IaaS) usage of cloud. These use cases provide alternate approaches to addressing a number of enterprise requirements such as augmenting compute and storage capacity, implementing disaster recovery and data center migration and consolidation. Each of the use cases does not prescribe a particular offering or product to address the requirements, but instead describes a pattern-based approach that can be leveraged to put together a solution.

While the list of patterns is not exhaustive, the described patterns in this chapter can be considered as some of the most common patterns that can be leveraged to tap into the benefits provided by Cloud Computing.

REFERENCES

Alexander, C. (1979). *The Timeless Way of Building*. Oxford University Press.

Bergin, J. (2012). *Pedagogical Patterns: Advice For Educators*. CreateSpace Independent Publishing Platform.

Buschmann, F., Meunier, R., Rohnert, H., Sommerlad, P., & Stal, M. (1996). *Pattern Oriented Software Architecture: A System of Patterns*. Wiley.

KEY TERMS AND DEFINITIONS

Architectural Pattern: A general, reusable solution to a commonly occurring problem in system architecture within a given context.

Infrastructure as a Service (IaaS): A form of cloud computing that provides physical or virtualized computing, storage, or network resources over a network.

IT Architecture: Structure of the system, which comprise software and hardware elements, the externally manifested properties of those elements, and the relationships among them.

Platform as a Service (PaaS): A cloud computing model that allows customers to develop, run, and manage applications without the complexity of building and maintaining the infrastructure.

Software as a SERVICE (SaaS): A software licensing and delivery model in which software applications are hosted by a vendor or service provider and made available to customers over a network.

Use Case: A set of possible sequences of interactions between systems and actors in a particular environment to achieve a particular goal.

Chapter 5
Industrial Patterns on Cloud

Sreekrishnan Venkateswaran
IBM Corporation, India

ABSTRACT

Cloud Computing is rapidly gaining traction today as the preferred platform for deploying both development and production workloads. Every industry has started adopting hybrid hosting models to leverage benefits that accrue from a convergence of technologies; Cloud is being used as a flexible springboard to mount a defense against disruptive digital trends. The use cases and associated gains are industry specific, ranging from leveraging auto-scaling to assuage seasonal spikes in Retail, and creating software-defined network functions in Telecom, to aggregating and analyzing sensor data in Automotive, and deploying multi-site disaster recovery in Government. In this chapter, we will embark on an expedition spanning ten industries, searching for patterns where Cloud enables advantageous solutions to business-specific categories of use cases. The observations are based on actual case studies chosen from hundreds of real Cloud deals across industries.

INTRODUCTION

Cloud computing, along with the transformative triumvirate of analytics, social and mobile, is disrupting industries. Cloud solution architects often encounter requirements and workload behaviors specific to business groupings, which translate to developing an ensemble of industry-specific assets and reference architectures. Many of them qualify as reusable patterns of solution blueprint. If an architect engages customers with industry-specific insights, it is easier to establish credibility and collaboratively agree on the Cloud adoption roadmap.

In this chapter, we look at major industries through the Cloud hosting lens. The terms *industry* and *sector* are used interchangeably, the assumed semantic being a segment of the economy where business activities share common characteristics. We look at ten major industries and see why they have affinity to Cloud Computing. Under each head, we lay out basic technology use cases and map them to Cloud-enablement patterns. Note that a pattern listed under one industry can (and often will) be applicable to other industries as well, because of intersection between use case groupings.

DOI: 10.4018/978-1-5225-0759-8.ch005

CLOUD SOLUTION ARCHITECTURES FOR INDUSTRIES

Some business drivers for Cloud adoption are common across industries. Standardization, for example, is a "true Cloud" benefit that attracts companies from across the industry spectrum to Cloud. Standardization is a lever to achieve several gains: reduced complexity, volume optimized delivery, increased speed of adoption, and reduced total cost of ownership. Self-service from a catalogue is another such common driver that offers fast, reliable, simple, and low-touch control to the consumer. Cloud is a powerful vehicle to introduce automation in many spheres, for example, post-provisioning workflows to eliminate an array of manual tasks performed by administrators after a server is commissioned.

However, there also are industry-specific benefits that accrue from Cloud; use cases and associated solution architectures that have come to be associated with different sectors of the economy. Let's take an industrial tour and see how Cloud can help businesses surmount modern day challenges that stand in the way of surviving and thriving in an ultra-competitive economic environment.

RETAIL AND E-COMMERCE

With the advent of the digital economy, the retail sector is being hit by disruptive forces. The first of these forces is the new age model of consumption and marketing based on technology, the Internet, and software code. A second is the deluge of data coupled with the explosion of social media. Brick and mortar has decisively given way to e-commerce.

The retail sector, in general, has not only leveraged Cloud to overcome these disruptive forces; it is in fact at the forefront of shaping the very evolution of Cloud computing. Amazon, the biggest retailer in the world by market value (Pettypiece, 2015), is also the largest provider of Cloud computing services in the planet. Walmart, the world's largest company by revenue ("List of Largest Companies", n.d.) is one of the biggest adopters of OpenStack for mission critical workloads; the company regularly shares experiences from its Cloud journey during OpenStack summits.

DRIVERS AND USE CASES

The retail industry, by its very nature, seeks many Cloud benefits. The seasonal spikes that it suffers can be assuaged by automatic expansion and contraction of compute footprint. The demand for zero-downtime translates to affinity for redundant components that have geographic spread. The need to serve thousands of simultaneous users is answered with elastic load balancing. Auxiliary requirements such as data analytics are cast into Big Data operations that are more optimal if they run off-premise.

In a recent survey ("Online Retailers", 2015), 26 percent of large scale retailers claimed that Cloud technology is critical to their company's future growth. Let's consider how:

1. With Cloud, the ability to procure and run sophisticated IT is no longer a prerequisite to get ahead in retail business. Retailers want to shift capital investment to operational expenses and divert dollars to innovation that will expand their core business.
2. Cloud allows easy scaling of IT as commercial activity waxes and wanes across seasons. In tandem with elasticity that matches purchase cycles, Cloud also allows the possibility of dynamic SLA

penalties (slippage during the "golden quarter" could be considered a heavier breach than a lapse during other months), and dynamic choice of managed services from a catalogue of tiered service definitions.

3. Cloud, in tandem with technologies for Content Delivery Networking (CDN), allows global reach, important for retailers.

4. Retailers exploit Cloud to create new business models. Some businesses bring out new applications by the week, instrument feedback based on customer behavior, and respond quickly to change in requirements.

5. Cloud is a friendly vehicle for analytics, which is becoming an inseparable part of retail business. Given the intense competition in the retail space, analytics is not merely an auxiliary piece when it comes to e-commerce; it is a core component that helps personalize shopping experiences, predict market behavior, determine prices, and even read the customer's mind in real time by observing user sessions and determining why a purchase was made or not made.

6. Business continuity is critical for the retail industry as it is for many other industries. Downtime directly translates into loss of revenue and credibility. Cloud offers a cost-effective way to architecturally minimize downtime.

ARCHITECTURAL PATTERNS

Hybrid Deployment

Retail workloads can be classified into two categories:

1. Front-end transactions before potential customers populate an item in the shopping cart. This includes operations on the retailer's catalogue, and analytics to derive purchase recommendations.

2. Back-end processing after an item has been added to the shopping cart. This includes order management, billing, and fulfillment.

Processing "above the shopping cart" has to be production-grade, but action "below the shopping cart" is super-critical. The former includes the stage when customers browse and search the retailer's catalogue, evaluate personalized recommendations, and manage accounts. The latter commences after the shopping cart has been populated and encompasses payment and delivery. Big retailers are reluctant to move "below the cart" processing off-premise to a public Cloud because this portion is built in a highly redundant fashion with clustered dedicated components without single points of failure. This is difficult to replicate on many public Clouds, but possible on private Clouds. For example, a clustering solution that needs a dedicated network link to carry heartbeats is hard to realize on a multi-tenant Cloud. Or if workloads are sensitive to regulation – such as Payment Card Industry (PCI) in this case – it is easier to host them on a private Cloud over which the retailer can retain architectural control.

Many retailers are, however, eager to move "above the cart" processing to public Clouds. In addition to being less mission critical, these functions fall under a category known as Systems of Engagement (Moore, 2011). Users of Systems of Engagement (SoE) interact with the IT environment in real time. Creating a client-focused enterprise is the success mantra in every industry, especially in the face of modern day challenges and competition. In the context of the retail industry, SoE will provide users a personalized shopping experience, typically by leveraging social media and mobile. SoE are usually "Cloud native" or born-on-the-Cloud, so they are more comfortable living off-premise. Structured static data known as Systems of Record (SoR), on the other hand, tend to reside as close to on-premise as possible. Systems of Insight (SoI) leverage both SoE and SoR to come up with innovation and improvement – for example, sales forecasts, type and timing of promotions, and optimal pricing. SoE and SoI thrive on public Clouds because of the nature of tools they rely on - Map Reduce algorithms, the API economy[1] and such.

Figure 1 depicts a deployment that reflects the strategy described above.

Multi-Tiered Networking and Load Balanced Auto-Scaling

A retail deployment is often multi-tiered across Virtual Local Area Networks[2] (VLANs) for applications, databases and Web serving. Each tier resides on a separate VLAN as shown in Figure 2. Assume that all three tiers are running on an off-premise public Cloud. The compute capacity of each tier needs to be proportional to the load. Imagine the Web and application tiers as arrays of homogenous compute nodes. During holiday season, when access spikes, the Cloud can be configured to automatically scale this array horizontally. A load balancer distributes incoming requests across the dynamically scaled Web array. The database tier, assuming it is relational, will need to scale vertically. This is done by adding or subtracting CPU cores or RAM and is relatively easy to achieve on the Cloud as well.

Figure 1. A hybrid cloud deployment pattern for the retail industry

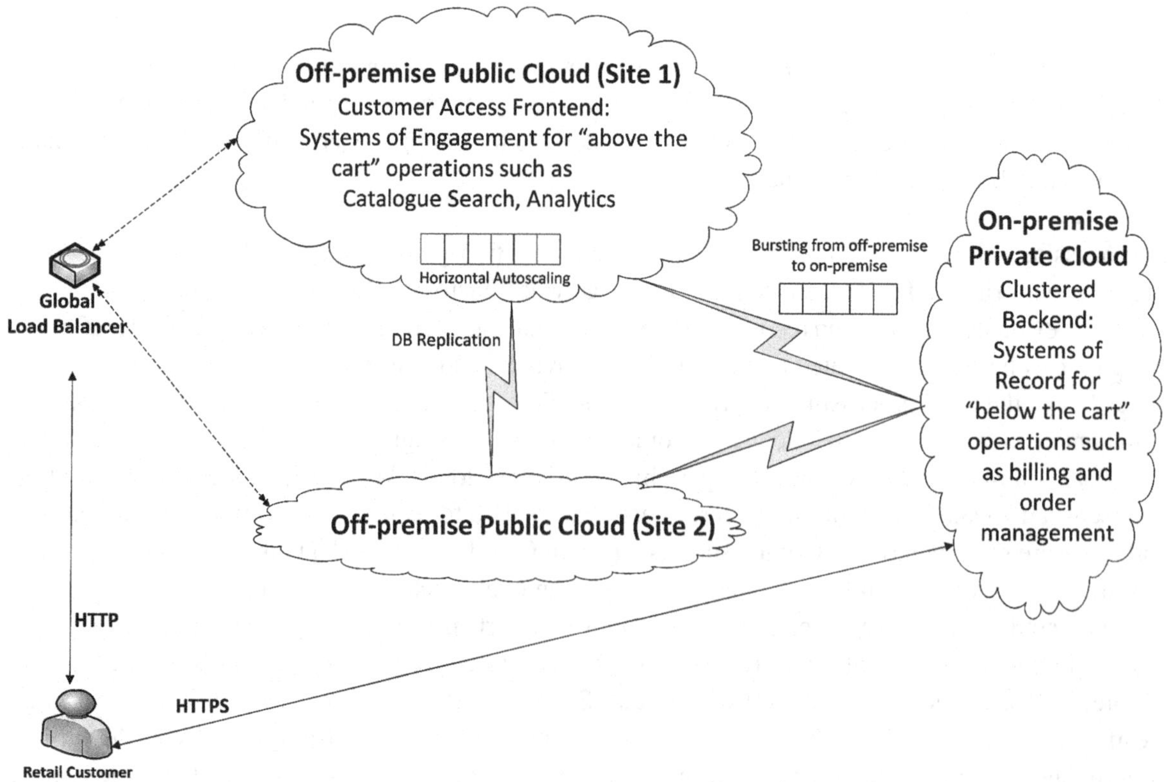

Figure 2. A 3-tier e-commerce deployment

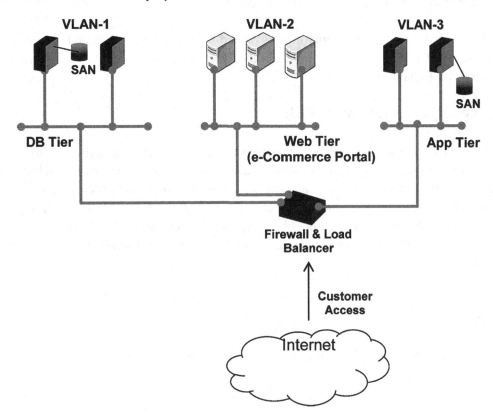

The above deployment can also be hosted on a private Cloud, and set to burst horizontally from on-premise to a public Cloud, or rather from any base Cloud to a more economical Cloud - and vice versa. There are vendors who support dynamic bursting capability on and across mainstream Clouds in an easily consumable fashion; or you could optionally implement it using a body of code that leverages APIs exposed by the source and target Clouds.

Business Continuity and Global Load Balancing

High Availability (HA) and Disaster Recovery (DR) are important in the retail sector because even a short downtime can translate to steep losses. Putting a Global Load Balancer (GLB) in front of a multi-datacenter Web tier is a common strategy to achieve business continuity in tandem with load sharing. The GLB transparently routes customer requests to the optimal available location as depicted in Figure 1. The database tier needs special attention in order to support this, but most commercial databases have built-in deployment modes that support HA and DR. We will discuss HA and DR in more depth when we talk about the financial sector.

Global Reach with Content Delivery Networks

Retailers need global reach without compromising on end-user experience. Content Delivery Networks, in tandem with the Cloud, help establish this ability. We will explore content delivery when we talk about the Media & Entertainment sector.

Omni-Channel Retailing and the Cloud

Omni-channel retailing is about offering a uniform shopping experience regardless of the channel of purchase, physical or digital. Irrespective of whether the sale was transacted via a brick-and-mortar outlet or over phone or the Internet, customers can view store-wise inventory and personalized recommendations, browse full purchase history, and specify any pickup location. Omni-channel retailing works by integrating systems and processes of all possible purchase routes at the backend, and that task is easier if the backend systems are hosted on Cloud over a standard technology framework and a common governance mechanism.

SUMMARY

Table 1. summarizes prominent Cloud use cases specific to the retail sector.

FINANCE

Financial services encompass a range of businesses such as commercial banking, insurance, credit card operations, and stock brokerages. Large financial houses often have thousands of branches in dozens of countries serving millions of customers; their IT spans multiple data centers across geographies.

Because of security and regulatory pressures, financial businesses often deem it a risky proposition to relinquish control over their IT infrastructure, so they predominantly take the private Cloud route to transform their datacenters into a software defined environment (SDE). They seek to push the Cloud

Table 1. Cloud and retail

Retail Use Cases	Challenges	Cloud Brings
Shopping Portal	Seasonal Spikes	Auto-scaling
	Performance	Load Balancing
Inventory Management	Disaster Recovery	Global Load Balancing
Customer Analytics	HPC Analytics	Compute-intensive servers at hourly rental
Warehouse Management	Content Distribution	Content Delivery Networking
Digital Marketing	Global Access	High Speed private back bone & CDN
Security	Three-tier deployment of workloads	Router/Firewall Appliance as a Service
Omni-channel retailing	Uniform shopping experience regardless of the route of purchase	Easier integration of backend systems and processes across channels

lever to enhance the triumvirate of customer experience, service effectiveness, and operational efficiency in the face of a shrinking technology budget.

Because of the large size and complexity of their existing environments, financial businesses – like large enterprises in other sectors such as telecom – transform to Cloud in phases. A time-lined roadmap is developed to the move existing legacy environments to the Cloud. In general, Cloud-enablement occurs in two broad phases:

1. A stabilization phase when virtualization is introduced, development-test and non-critical production workloads are expanded to Cloud, hardware and software are consolidated and standardized, non-standard systems are reduced or eliminated, service and delivery models are established for workloads categories, and a governance mechanism is instituted.
2. A modernization phase where more workloads including mission-critical ones move to the Cloud, the IaaS becomes more advanced with the help of technologies such as SDN[3], Cloud hosting gets aligned with business strategy, full security certifications are achieved, developer productivity is increased by introducing Platform-as-a-Service, the Cloud becomes more hybrid, DevOps[4] is leveraged to bridge the gap between development and production, pattern-based deployment of middleware components is introduced, economies of scale are realized by leveraging technologies such as Dynamic Automation[5], and services are exposed via the API economy.

USE CASES AND ARCHITECTURAL PATTERNS

Security

Regulatory and security compulsions on the financial sector were originally viewed as Cloud unfriendly, but times have changed. Cloud benefits such as agility, cost savings and faster provisioning times have increased Cloud adoption in capital and financial markets. Security architectures have also evolved such that hybrid Clouds can cost-effectively comply with a wide array of regulation.

Security in the financial sector has two dimensions:

1. **Functional Requirements Related to Security:** Data security is for the financial industry, what safety is to the airline industry. A breach can break a company; a business is only as good as its last failure.

Both data at rest and in motion need to be secured. The scope of this task starts from physical security and surveillance of the data center. Portal access security via password protection, multi-factor authentication, and API security comes next. At the infrastructure level, this could translate to architectural elimination of noisy neighboring hypervisors or virtual machines (VMs), adequate network isolation, encryption, deployment of intrusion prevention and detection devices, mechanisms for protection from DDoS (Distributed Denial of Service) attacks, and monitoring. Application security and governance completes the security wheel: usage of SSL (Secure Socket Layer) certificates to ensure confidentiality of data in transit, SAML (Security Assertion Markup Language) tokens for authentication and authorization, and such.

There are enterprise-grade tools in the market to achieve any or all of the above, but the tooling needs to be used in tandem with well-designed processes. Mandating periodic vulnerability scans on applications and the operating system, enforcing recurrent password changes, auto-scheduling malware and antivirus scans, and continuous monitoring of the infrastructure fall under this head. Finally, employees with the right skills complete the people-processes-tools triad required to set up a hard security ring.

Internal security standards of the financial organization might stipulate controls and safe guards as well. It may, for example, ask for the right to audit suppliers (including the Cloud provider's data center, if off-premise) at regular intervals via an audit organization of its choice.

2. **Regulatory Requirements Related to Security:** Data has to be managed in conformance to in-country laws that regulate activities and behavior of the financial industry (e.g., FFIEC in the US). Many big banks operate in multiple geographies, so multiple sets of laws could be at play while managing the IT of a financial services company. Such laws cover many of the aspects referred to earlier; stipulations may range from enforcing data sovereignty[6] and lengthy retention of backups and logs, to demanding hooks for lawful interception.

High Availability

Systems that host financial transactions are mission-critical and are expected to be always up. Availability of a system refers to its uptime guarantee. A highly available (HA) system is designed to continuously operate with negligible downtime.

Consider the system on the left of Figure 3 comprising of three components X, Y and Z, each of which is a potential point of failure. Assume that the uptime probability of each component is p. The overall availability of the system in native mode is p^3, provided the probabilities of failure of the components are mutually exclusive.

The deployment on the right depicts the same system in HA mode. Components X, Y and Z are clustered and have 3, 2 and 2 levels of redundancies respectively; the system continues to possess three potential points of failure. In this mode of deployment, the overall availability of the system translates to $(1-(1-p)^3)*(1-(1-p)^2)*(1-(1-p)^2)$.

Figure 3. Modeling high availability

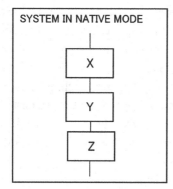
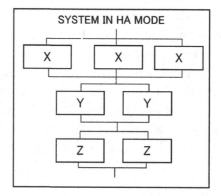

Thus, if p, the probabilistic uptime of each component of the system, is 98%, the overall availability of the system is 94% in native mode and 99.9% in HA mode.

The HA mode depicted above can be implemented at various levels:

1. At the hypervisor level, you can enable *live migration* that will move a VM (and optionally storage) across hosts based on server load. You can also enable *dead migration*, which will restart VMs on another server if the primary server goes down, but you would see some delay as the second instance boots up[7].
2. OS-level clustering protects from hardware and OS-level failures. A warm secondary OS instance can immediately take over if the primary server fails. The systems can be active-passive, with the secondary taking over the IP address of the primary if the latter goes down, or active-active where a load-balancer dynamically directs traffic across the clustered environment[8].
3. Application clustering designs applications and middleware components such as databases to be redundant and distributed. The clustered pieces will co-ordinate via control mechanisms such as "heartbeat" signals and failover on the fly.

Disaster Recovery

Financial services are not tolerant to data loss or service disruption, so they usually have stringent demands on Recovery Point Objectives (RPO) and Recovery Time Objectives (RTO). RPO dictates allowable data loss, whereas RTO specifies how long a business can go without a particular service. In the finance industry, it is not uncommon to see requirements for near-zero RTO and RPO.

Like with High Availability, architectural patterns to achieve disaster recovery also work at different levels:

1. **At the Infrastructure Layer:** Hypervisor-level replication keeps virtual machines and virtual disks replicated across two sites. With storage-level replication, the storage array replicates each byte across a network to a target device in real time.
2. **At the Application Layer:** DR can also be at the OS plane, where file systems are periodically replicated via a utility such as *rsync*[9], and databases leverage built-in deployment modes that allow clustering across the network between primary and secondary instances.

Replication can be synchronous or asynchronous. When replication is synchronous, each write transaction completes only after modifying both copies. This requires a network that has low latency, often less than a millisecond, possible under a 300-kilometer distance with dark fiber connectivity. An active-active configuration with low RTO/RPO is tough to achieve and may need synchronous infrastructure-level replication. Asynchronous replication, on the other hand, can take place over a slower Wide Area Network (WAN) at RPO frequency, and is used in cases where the deployment can tolerate relatively large RTOs.

There are also two dimensions to Disaster Recovery on the Cloud: protection of the managing environment and that of the managed environment. If the former is not rendered DR-safe, the latter will not have a Cloud management system and a self-service portal after failover. However, in many cases, there may be no specified requirements on the RTO within which the Cloud stack needs to be up at the failover site.

Hybrid Deployment

The financial industry has a natural affinity to hybrid Clouds. Enterprises prefer mission critical and regulation sensitive workloads to run on private Clouds where the business can exercise architectural control. Less critical production workloads and Systems of Engagement are migrated to public Clouds. Components of the hybrid IT need to interact with each other, but service management across the different infrastructure pieces should preferably be single-pane and uniform. Figure 4 shows a hybrid Cloud deployment pattern for a banking workload.

SUMMARY

Table 2. summarizes prominent Cloud use cases specific to the finance sector.

Figure 4. A hybrid cloud deployment pattern for the banking industry

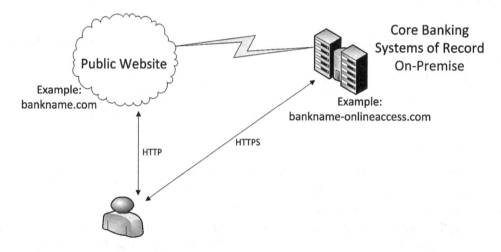

Table 2. Cloud and finance

Financial Use Cases	Challenges	Cloud Brings
Security and regulation	Security of data at rest and in motion, data sovereignty, long retention of backups and logs	Standard ways to deploy security tools, processes and people. Automation-friendly platform.
Business Continuity	Stringent recovery targets in the face of disaster	Multi-site replication at hypervisor, storage, OS or application levels
High Availability	Near-zero downtimes and absence of single points of failure	Virtualized infrastructure is HA-friendly
Wide range of workload categories	Continuum of SLA, latency and security requirements	Ability to setup hybrid deployments dynamically

TELCOMMUNICATIONS

The telecom industry is the one with the largest reach, hurrying on its way to directly impact every citizen on the planet. Over the past decade, it has advanced rapidly, evolving in higher value, quality, speed and cost-effectiveness, every year.

Telecom is synonymous with technology, so it is no surprise that this industry is a major consumer and provider of Cloud computing services.

USE CASES AND ARCHITECTURAL PATTERNS

Broadly, there are two categories of use cases in the telecom industry: generating revenue by selling Cloud services; and driving efficiency improvements by adopting Cloud technologies for internal workloads.

Service Provider Cloud

Telecoms today, want to generate a revenue stream from Cloud. To achieve this, they bundle Cloud along with services such as voice, data, and email, for which they already enjoy high penetration and market share. There are two ways for telecoms to become Cloud Service Providers (CSPs):

1. Build a Private Cloud in "Service Provider Context" and offer Cloud services to end-customers. The Cloud needs to support the notion of a service provider in terms of hardened and holistic separation across on-boarded tenants, as well as portal roles that allow super-administrator operations. An aggregation layer is also required above the service provider Cloud in order to manage multiple customers, partners, and commerce.
2. White-label services from Cloud vendors and resell them from third party data centers. This is achieved by deploying a "storefront", offered by companies that specialize in Cloud services broker enablement[10]. The storefront has a centralized catalogue that provides access to a pre-negotiated set of public and private Cloud services. The telecom provider can control the features of the underlying service offerings that are to be exposed to end-customers, and also integrate new services into the catalogue. White-labeling can be limited to changing the skin of the storefront, or can go deeper and disguise the identity of the underlying Cloud service that is being resold.

Network Function Virtualization

Network Function Virtualization (NFV) moves network functions such as firewalls from dedicated and specialized hardware to soft appliances hosted on virtual machines running on commodity servers. Such virtual appliances implementing NFV are natural workloads for the Cloud. Telecom companies have started selling network functions as a service, via the NFV-on-Cloud route. Common NFV offerings include Firewall-as-a-Service, Load-Balancer-as-a-Service, IDPS[11]-as-a-Service, and VPN[12]-as-a-Service.

Cloud-Enabling a Large Brownfield Deployment

To host their IT, telecom providers are often compelled to set up dedicated datacenters to comply with government regulation. Data residency in-country (often on-premise) is often a statutory requirement that the industry has to adhere to. It is not merely customer data that needs to be in dedicated space, but also management data such as incident tickets and monitoring alerts. Moreover, the IT inventory is often Brownfield – the sheer quantum of the subscriber base (in hundreds of millions) would have necessitated large investments in technology over the years; naturally, telecom providers want to leverage their existing estate to realize benefits that accrue from adopting Cloud.

Legacy Brownfield IT deployments become heterogeneous – and hence unwieldy - over time, with diverse server and hypervisor technologies, large number of processor cores, an assorted storage environment, and a hierarchical network. There could be hundreds of applications and middleware components extending across multiple geographically separated data centers; some of the applications –such as billing - could be deemed super-critical and out of bounds of virtualization and Cloud. The IT estate could be conforming to ITIL[13]-like processes that need to continue after the Cloud management stack is introduced. All this make Cloud-enablement a complex proposition. This holds not only for telecom, but for large business in other industries as well.

Service Management Integration

When you transform an existing environment, the resulting Cloud management system cannot live as an island. It has to integrate with existing processes and tools in the shop floor. This is one part of the standard Cloud that is necessarily bespoke.

The existing service paradigm might be following a defined process flow for server build. This could include creating a configuration item in a ticketing system to track the life cycle of the new server, getting it discovered by an asset management tool, checking for licensing entitlements, verifying if the server's configuration conforms to internal security policies, installing agent software for monitoring, and such. These tasks are accomplished by leveraging automation tools that come with the Cloud management stack for stitching together post-provisioning work flows. Business Process Management (BPM) engines come out of the box with most enterprise Cloud stacks for this reason. You can programmatically reshape and adapt the Cloud, so that it not only integrates with existing processes and tools, but also introduces automation into the environment wherever possible.

Service management integration holds for any large enterprise with complex internal IT, but is especially relevant for legacy sectors such as telecom and finance.

Intelligent Capacity Planning: Mobile Number Portability Example

Capacity Planning is a necessary facet of running any data center, but more so if it is Cloud-enabled. This is because of the increased flexibility of placement, movement, and optimization that come with Cloud. Capacity management of virtual environments allows administrators to create sizing plans and reports based on analytics of past utilization fluctuations. It helps to arrive at decisions on when to expand capacity and by how much, and how to repurpose existing hardware, repartition servers, and redo allocations. Capacity planning tools will also allow insertion of fictitious servers in the environment and obtain a projection of resulting performance and sizing plans.

Capacity Planning is also influenced by the workload. Consider that a new colossal workload arrives in a telecom provider's data center, for example, a national roll-out of Mobile Number Portability (MNP). This service can trigger massive but volatile load on the IT that will touch aspects such as middleware and resource auto-scaling, in addition to conventional capacity management. The demands on IT will also ripple across DevTest/DevOps[14], staging, and production environments. The integrated capacity planning algorithm has to be smart enough to handle such intricacies.

Dynamic Expansion to Public Clouds

Many internal telecom workloads, such as MNP that we discussed, are unpredictable. They need to grow or shrink based on demand. These workloads are developed in a Cloud native fashion with built-in awareness of APIs exported by the Cloud, such that they are not affected by failure as traditional workloads are. While the telecom Cloud is primarily running on-premise, these workloads want the ability to leverage off-premise public Clouds on a need basis. Most enterprise Cloud stacks offer a "gateway" to enable this. An application deployment pattern created atop the Cloud stack will be realizable on any Cloud supported by this gateway such as on-premise OpenStack or an in-country (and regulation-compliant) Cloud service of say, Amazon, Azure or Softlayer.

Savings versus Investment

When a private Cloud is proposed to transform a large traditional environment, one of the first questions posed is the financial viability. Will savings be greater than expenses, and if yes, by how much?

The savings case comprises aspects such as:

1. The cost takeout resulting from core consolidation due to virtualization and resource over-commit. This would be the monetary equivalent of freed physical servers as well as associated licensing contraction.
2. Cost reduction accruing from reduction in labor needed to manage a Cloud-enabled data center vis-à-vis a traditional IT shop floor.
3. Savings from reduction in the number of Layer-3 devices and labor to manage an environment enabled with an SDN overlay[15].
4. Cost reduction from storage virtualization due to capabilities such as real time compression and thin provisioning that converge to a decreased cost per Gigabyte.

Some of these items, especially the labor takeout accruing from the effects of automation are not easy to calculate. To figure out an estimate, one has to understand the tasks and subtasks of each category of work, and then agree on which aspects can be automated with Cloud. For example, the ability to auto-scale the Cloud based on movement of characteristics such as CPU or memory utilization can result in a system that auto-stabilizes itself at optimal cost, and this can reduce the number of incident tickets. Similar are the effects of run-time load balancing, which will automatically move virtual machines out of overloaded physical servers on to idle ones. Tasks such as patching can be semi-automated with Cloud and rendered less labor intensive. Standardizing the catalogue reduces heterogeneity, and is another area that is inversely proportional to cost. Cloud also introduces abstractions that reduce labor in a transformational fashion. For example, the concept of projects and resource quotas tied to Cloud, nudge out the practice of triggering approval flows to change entitlements, as long as they fall within predefined thresholds.

The expense case lays out items such as:

1. Software license cost of the Cloud stack;
2. Hardware Bill of Material (BoM) to deploy the Cloud managing environment;
3. Labor to deploy the Cloud stack and manage it during steady state operation;
4. Cost of migrating the current environment to the Cloud;
5. Cost of network virtualization; Software Defined Network (SDN) if applicable; and
6. Cost of storage virtualization.

In the final analysis, a case for Cloud-enablement might translate to proving that the savings potential is greater than the cost case. This is not always true - certain enterprises, regardless of the apparent savings case, might be willing to invest in Cloud for benefits such as agility, automation, standardization, and the granular control associated with having a modern programmable self-serviceable software-defined data center.

SUMMARY

Table 3. summarizes prominent Cloud use cases specific to the telecommunications sector.

MEDIA AND ENTERTAINMENT

The Media & Entertainment (M&E) industry has crossed the trillion dollar mark and is in the limelight, thanks to advances in technology and recovery of the global economy. The three main components of the

Table 3. Cloud and telecom

Telecom Use Cases	Challenges	Cloud Brings
Cloud hosting of internal IT – Telco BSS/OSS (DevTest and Production)	Large multi-site data centers hosting hundreds of middleware components and applications; IT systems integrated with ITIL-type processes	Automation and workflows to integrate with existing processes and tools. Pattern-based deployment; orchestration via workflow engines.
B2B & B2C Cloud Service Provider	Reselling & White labeling of IaaS & PaaS	Clouds such as OpenStack support multi-tenancy, and hence service provider context. Easy to integrate standard public Clouds with a store front for reselling.
Security	Regulatory Compliance	Regulation-sensitive workloads that need architectural control go to on-premise Clouds; others including Systems of Engagement, move to cost-effective public Clouds
DevOps enabled development-test environments	Large scale development of complex applications across multiple versions and releases	Many DevOps tools integrate with Cloud; the "Ops" of DevOps can be realized via Clouds
Network Function Virtualization (NFV) provider	Virtualize traditional services such as firewalls and load balancers	NFV services are easily realizable via appliances on Clouds

M&E business - content creation, processing, and distribution - are all being transformed by technology. Traditional methods need heavy investment in compute-intensive hardware and blazing-fast networks. Such capital is no longer a prerequisite with the advent of Cloud-based M&E development and distribution platforms. Let's take a look at some interesting facets of this industry that call for Cloud-enablement.

USE CASES AND ARCHITETURAL PATTERNS

Media & Entertainment (M&E) businesses have some unique use cases:

Rendering

Image rendering, the process of creating images from models, is a common task in the M&E space. This needs on-demand high performance compute that is cost effective, in the face of fluctuating demands and seasonal spikes. Public Clouds such as Amazon, offer GPU-optimized[16] or compute-optimized virtual machines in their catalogue. Others such as SoftLayer offer high horsepower bare metal servers ideal for high performance computing (HPC). Two related requirements are low network bandwidth cost and accelerated delivery of the rendered streams to the points of consumption. Different Cloud vendors, along with their partners, have different ways to offer this enablement.

Content Delivery

A Content Delivery Network (CDN) is a fleet of global servers that stream data from a node near to the point of consumption, rather than from origin servers hosted on the Cloud or elsewhere.

Transcoding is a CDN capability. It detects the user's CPU capacity and bandwidth in real time and dynamically adjusts the quality of the media stream. The user receives a different bit rate depending on whether he accesses a video stream from a cell phone versus a web browser on a laptop. The CDN service achieves this with the help of encoders. You could also use the CDN service to configure and control caching of categories of data objects via programmable workflows. A news feed, for example, can be cached for several hours, whereas a tennis score cannot be cached for more than a minute.

Some public Cloud providers partner with CDN vendors. SoftLayer, for example, provides easy integration with Vodafone Edgecast. Amazon has a home brewed CDN offering called CloudFront. However, there is no hard coupling between Clouds and CDN providers. You could, for example, leverage Akamai's CDN service regardless of your hosting Cloud.

Digital Archiving

The M&E industry often needs to archive vast quantities of large data in a cost effective way. Conventional block storage and file systems do not easily scale out; it is Object Storage that comes to the rescue in this requirement space. The unit of storage is an Object, which can be a photo, a video, a thumbnail or an image snapshot. Each Object is associated with a URL handle and can be operated on via APIs.

Most Public Clouds offer support for cheap Object Store containers through which media (and other) files can be stored, indexed, searched, and retrieved. Amazon comes with S3; SoftLayer comes with an offering that complies with OpenStack Swift[17].

Digital Video Recording (DVR)

DVR on the Cloud is starting to change the face of media, entertainment and advertising. This technology allows subscribers to stream video to any Internet-enabled device without compromising on Quality of Service. Because cable companies have personalized knowledge about their subscribers, they will be able to virtually tailor the individual experience for each subscriber with off-premise DVR.

SUMMARY

Table 4. summarizes prominent Cloud use cases specific to the Media & Entertainment sector.

GOVERNMENT AND PUBLIC SECTOR

Governments around the world are embracing technology to provide better citizen services. Cloud is taking center stage in government IT data centers since it brings tools and processes to cost-effectively address challenges in e-governance: delivery of innovative services, creating ecosystems of stakeholders, a service delivery platform that is transparent and accountable, and conformance to regulation atop a standardized environment. The importance of the latter in government often translates to a preference for private on-premise Clouds that allow control over platform architecture and data residency.

Governments seek an infrastructure consumption model that will let them cut IT budget and channel accrued savings to public services. Given the size of federal and state government budgets, this can run into billions of dollars.

USE CASES AND ARCHITECTURAL PATTERNS

Regulation

Government business is large; the contracts are often high-value and multi-year. Data has to be in-country; often there has to be isolation at the data center level. Each government department is considered a separate tenant and they operate in a shared nothing mode.

Table 4. Cloud and media and entertainment

M&E Use Cases	Challenges	Cloud Brings
Rendering	Cost effective high-performance compute in the face of seasonal spikes	Multi-core multi-processor bare metal servers on rent
Content Delivery	Stream data from a node near to the consumer for low latency user experience	CDN coupled with trans-coding and programmable workflows
Digital Archiving	Large media streams to be stored cost effectively	Object Storage services

An umbrella of compliance requirements could be at play. A health department might need to comply with regulations laid out by the U.S. Food and Drug Administration (FDA) and Health Insurance Portability and Accountability Act (HIPAA); the ministry of finance may need to adhere to PCI; most departments will need archiving and audit trails. Financial data will need to be made available to citizens to maintain transparency.

Cloud renders the IT infrastructure standardized and amenable to automation, and that eases compliance implementation. The concept of a Continuous Compliance framework is gaining ground in the Cloud managed services business today, and aims to transform compliance in regulation sensitive sectors.

Application Ecosystems via Platform-as-a-Service

Ecosystem enablement is a common theme in government. An example is a community Cloud that a department of education can leverage to connect teachers, students and parents. Another is where a tax department creates a platform for vendors to develop tax filing applications for categories of businesses such as real estate or banking.

Platform-as-a-Service (PaaS) platforms are tailor-made to support such requirements. They offer a composition environment for the modern application developer. Runtimes are available ready-made, as are a tool box of services in a catalogue. Examples of services are NoSQL and relational databases, messaging primitives, mobile application frameworks, and natural language processing functions. All catalogued services are managed by the PaaS provider; they are monitored, patched, backed up, and rendered DR-safe. Applications being composed can also leverage platform features such as auto-scaling and DevOps[18].

Government Solutions via Software-as-a-Service

Innovative citizen services such as property tax filing and navigating an employment exchange are better consumed online. With a Software-as-a-Service (SaaS) model, applications can easily move from dated legacy to state of the art. And the skills needed to run and manage the application can be outsourced to specialist vendors.

Scalability and Resilience

The Government sector needs to serve large numbers of simultaneous users, often in the millions. The services hence need to be tolerant to heavy fluctuations. A tax department will see bursts near deadlines; an emergency response division will experience huge number of hits during disasters. Intelligent and robust auto-scaling features are a must-have expectation from the Cloud to contend with the lofty scalability requirements. Because of these aspects, and also due to the critical nature of Government data (e.g., financial transactions while paying taxes) and the sensitive nature of stored information (e.g., citizen health records), Disaster Recovery requirements are stringent and often call for near-zero data loss and instant failover. We discussed High Availability and Disaster Recovery within a Cloud framework while exploring the Financial Sector.

Analytics and Systems-of-Insight

Crunching past data to reveal hidden patterns and subtle correlations are relevant in most industries, even though the use cases are different. Prevention of crime and terrorism by police departments is an example where insights (SoI) can be drawn via a combination of crawling social media in real time (SoE) and analyzing citizen data (SoR).

SUMMARY

Table 5. summarizes prominent Cloud use cases specific to the Government sector.

HEALTHCARE

Technology is transforming healthcare, one of the fastest growing industries. From IBM's Watson supercomputer that can help physicians make better treatment decisions based on crunching a patient's past history in real time, to mobile applications that track calories and heart rate, the horizons of medical care have expanded.

USE CASES AND ARCHITECTURAL PATTERNS

The following are the major demands on the next-generation medical industry that attract it to the Cloud.

Table 5. Cloud and the government

Government Use Cases	Challenges	Cloud Brings
Central IT governance across departments	Multiple departments and autonomous data centers	Centralized and uniform IT governance. Ability to manage hybrid IT from a single pane of glass.
Scalability & Resilience	Failure of some government services can be life threatening, so their DR-safety is critical	DR-safe solution that spans multiple Cloud regions
Regulation	Regulatory compliance is expansive since it can encompass arenas such as finance (PCI), healthcare (HIPAA, GxP), and defense (ITAR)	Regulation-sensitive workloads that need architectural control go to on-premise Clouds; others go into cost-effective public Clouds
Faster Provisioning and Deployment	Time to stand up IT infrastructure should be shortened, as is the time to provision	Self Service UI and automated provisioning
Smart citizen services	Drive intelligent decisions with Big Data, Social Media and Communities	Insights derived from analytics and Systems-of-Engagement hosted on Cloud

Collaborative Care

Modern-day medical care is delivered without spatial boundaries. Providers connect specialists with patients, and share patient records securely, digitally and rapidly. Healthcare needs to be collaborative across patients, care givers, insurance providers and social media. Technology is leveraged to create and manage support ecosystems of patient communities.

Cloud-based collaboration platforms allow participants to be in the same virtual meeting room. They can securely share media, and exchange ideas on the fly. Easy-to-use collaborative tools deliver a quality user experience and can increase productivity and efficiency. Cisco's *Webex Cloud* is an example of a Cloud-based collaboration solution.

Remote Patient Monitoring

Sensor Clouds can facilitate hosting and delivery of intelligent networks that monitor patient parameters such as cardiac data captured by pacemakers. Back-end systems hosted on Cloud will automatically analyze data received from smart sensors attached to patients or hospital beds, and alert the care giver when change patterns are observed in monitored parameters. We discuss more on Sensor Clouds under the Automotive Industry.

Medical Imaging and Cloud Storage

Vast amounts of diagnostic multimedia such as patient medical images are generated by the healthcare industry every day. Such data needs to be archived in a cost-effective fashion in a regulatory compliant manner. Cloud based Object Storage offers guaranteed durability of data at low cost using commodity hardware. The data is rated to be safe, secure and untouched, literally for hundreds of years. Object Storage can be interconnected with Content Delivery Networks to reduce network latencies.

Object Stores are meant to be secondary cold storage – retrieval is slow, but easy, via standard APIs. There are restrictions on access, the primary use being long-term storage of static data as discussed under the Digital Imaging use case of the Media & Entertainment Industry. However, storage of medical images and media streams is a natural fit for Object Store containers.

Hospital Management Systems and the Cloud

Sophisticated and standardized hospital management systems can be hosted on a Cloud framework to derive service efficiency and cost reduction. Mobile-enabled healthcare platforms commonly have a Cloud-hosted backend.

Regulatory Compliance

Security needs are stringent in healthcare, given regulatory and privacy laws. An example is the U.S. Government's HIPAA that we alluded to earlier. While there are challenges to comply with certain regulations on multi-tenant public Clouds, private Clouds can be cost-effective hosting frameworks for compliance.

Analytics and Systems-of-Insight

Systems of Insight built around analytics drive innovative decision making in healthcare like in many other industries. The intersection between Systems of Engagement (relationships and interactions between care givers, patients and larger communities via social and mobile) and Systems of Records (history of patient data and internal hospital transactions) is significant in health care, and this is what leads to Systems of Insight such as:

1. Personalized care via disease prediction and prevention based on past diagnostic data
2. Improved outcomes by measuring clinical results based on patient responses to treatment, and
3. Modeling expected outcomes if the patient embarks on a new course of treatment

As we discussed in the section devoted to the Retail Industry, Cloud is an ideal vehicle to host Systems of Engagement and Insight because of the unpredictable characteristics of those workloads.

SUMMARY

Table 6. summarizes prominent Cloud use cases specific to the Healthcare sector.

TRANSPORTATION, AVIATION, LOGISTICS, AND SUPPLY CHAIN

Transportation and logistics are the pillars that support supply chains. This sector of the economy touches shipping, airlines, railroads, postal, and logistics providers. From an IT perspective, the foundational system for this industry is Supply Chain Management (SCM) software.

Table 6. Cloud and healthcare

Healthcare Use Cases	Challenges	Cloud Brings
Collaboration	Geographically separated stake holders need to digitally, securely and rapidly communicate	Cloud-based collaboration platforms enable participants to be in the same virtual room
Remote Patient Monitoring Systems	Massive amounts of sensor data collected from a large number of medical devices	Sensor Clouds can aggregate and analyze vast quantities of patient data
Systems of Engagement used to glean intelligence that can translate to personalized insights	Large combination of secure patient records and Web based social ecosystems	Analytics and Big Data crunching have affinity to the elasticity that comes with Cloud
Regulatory Compliance	Architectural control necessary to comply with laws	Private Clouds can provide automation and cost-effectiveness while building adherence to regulation
Archiving diagnostic medical images	Extensive media streams to be stored in a cost-effective fashion	Object Storage and other cold storage containers on the Cloud

USE CASES AND ARCHITECTURAL PATTERNS

SCM on the Cloud

Supply Chain Management (SCM) software controls and manages the flow of materials from production to consumption. SCM products from SAP and Oracle are popular with enterprises. Businesses want to run SAP and Oracle workloads on the Cloud, and consume those platforms as a service. With managed SAP systems, for example, the customer relinquishes control over the underlying infrastructure architecture and merely talks in terms of hardware-independent SAPS (SAP Application Performance Standard) metrics.

When SCM applications are hosted on a managed SAP or Oracle offering on the Cloud, enterprises can realize benefits such as the following, not seen if these systems were to be hosted on conventional IaaS Clouds:

1. SLAs at the platform level
2. Ease of requesting new services from a catalogue
3. Rapid provisioning of the underpinning SAP/Oracle systems
4. Cost effectiveness due to Cloud economics and progressive automation of the platform.

Hybrid Deployment

Aviation is a part of the transportation industry that benefits from hybrid Cloud deployments. Figure 5 describes a scenario where a mission critical airline reservation system is hosted on a secure dedicated private Cloud, and the customer-engaging front-end is running on a public Cloud.

SUMMARY

Table 7. summarizes prominent Cloud use cases specific to the Transportation sector.

Figure 5. A hybrid cloud deployment pattern for the airline industry

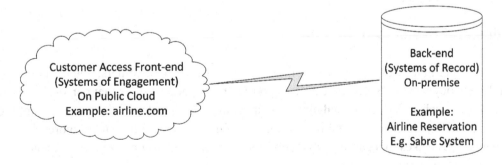

Table 7. Cloud and transportation

Transportation Use Cases	Challenges	Cloud Brings
Supply Chain Management software based on SAP or equivalent middleware, is often the IT brain of logistics and transportation companies	SAP and Oracle applications are examples of complex workloads that needs specialized skills and infrastructure to deploy and manage	SAP and Oracle SCM applications hosted on a managed Cloud in PaaS mode bring benefits such as rapid provisioning and reduced cost

AUTOMOTIVE

Studies estimate that there are over a billion motor vehicles on the road world-wide. New vehicle sales are about 100 million per year; a sizable percentage of those are "smart" vehicles connected via embedded telematics.

Google's self-driving cars have elevated in-car intelligence and sensing systems to the plane of vehicles that think. As of 2015, Google says their autonomous cars have driven over a million test miles on United States roads. With this, artificial intelligence and robotics have entered the automotive domain.

Automotive is an example of an industry being transformed by CAMSS, an acronym for the intersection of Cloud, Analytics, Mobile, Social and Security. CAMSS technology enables intuitive and personalized services to be accessed securely via mobile or in-car.

USE CASES AND ARCHITECTURAL PATTERN

Embedded Telematics → Internet of Things → Sensor Clouds

Internet of Things (IoT) is about networking everyday objects to bring about a better quality of life. In the context of implementing IoT on intelligent cars, embedded electronics coupled with telematics can capture and transport sensor data from connected vehicles to backend systems in real time.

Cloud can be leveraged as a powerful platform to receive and store this sensor data, which can be accessed from anywhere via any device. Visualization and analysis tools can be run on this data in-Cloud. The "Sensor Cloud" exports REST-ful APIs[19] that can be programmatically manipulated to transport, process, and draw insight from the sensed data.

Analytics and Systems-of-Insight

Like in many other industries, automotive sellers need to know their customers, understand their preferences and how they behave. Social platforms supported by Cloud can offer that personalized insight.

Technologies such as Warranty Analytics are helping the auto industry manage costs. Insights derived from past data help predict future trends on what parts fail repeatedly and who is more likely to claim replacements. This makes root cause analysis possible that enables isolation and subsequent elimination of bottlenecks in components or processes.

SUMMARY

Table 8. summarizes prominent Cloud use cases specific to the Automotive sector.

MANUFACTURING

The manufacturing sector covers wide ground. Its scope ranges from engineering equipment, machines, steel, marine, metal, mining and military electronics, to food, apparel, chemicals and home appliances. Businesses in this sector want to become global suppliers while optimizing manufacturing costs. They want to rapidly deploy new infrastructure in the face of aging IT assets. They desire to reduce capital expenditure, control operational costs, and increase overall automation. And Cloud is one of the vehicles to help achieve these goals.

USE CASES AND ARCHITETURAL PATTERNS

ERP on the Cloud

Enterprise Resource Planning (ERP) solutions are commonly seen in industries such as manufacturing and finance. ERP spans product planning, manufacturing, sales, marketing, finance and Human Resources (HR). When ERP is hosted on a managed platform on the Cloud, enterprises can realize benefits that we discussed under the section *SCM on the Cloud*.

Hybrid Deployment

Like with several other industries, the manufacturing sector often needs a hybrid deployment across on-premise and off-premise infrastructure. Some drivers are unique to this industry, however. Business applications that embed manufacturing trade secrets and intellectual property are sought to be hosted on-premise on a private dedicated Cloud. Even network access out of the on-premise infrastructure could be restricted to rule out leakage of assets. Another example of the need for a private dedicated Cloud piece is in the case of a military electronics business that is governed by laws such as U.S. Government International Traffic in Arms Regulation (ITAR). The private Cloud could optionally be outsourced and consumed in an expanded pay-as-you-go model.

Table 8. Cloud and automotive

Automotive Use Cases	Challenges	Cloud Brings
An IoT framework is the vehicle to ferry data from smart automotives to points of compute	Extensive data from large numbers of devices	Sensor Clouds can help aggregate and analyze data arriving from embedded electronics. Cloud, with its elasticity is Big Data friendly.
Personalized insights delivered to automotive customers	Rapidly analyze social media based on data emitted by in-car telematics	The intersection of Cloud, analytics, mobile, and social is a formidable enabler of insightful collaboration

On the other hand, most businesses in this sector do have workloads that are comfortable living off-premise on public Clouds. Development-and-Test is at the top of the list; non-critical production workloads may also fall under this category.

Business Continuity

The ability to continue manufacturing operations in the face of disaster or component failure is important for the manufacturing sector. The hosting design needs to be highly available to protect against system downtime arising out of single component failures. Disaster Recovery processes guard against lengthy down times due to loss of the entire site. Backup and archiving mechanisms are also sought to be in place to protect against data loss in a cost effective manner. We discussed HA and DR mechanisms under the Financial Industry.

SUMMARY

Table 9. summarizes prominent Cloud use cases specific to the Manufacturing sector.

ENERGY AND UTILITIES

Like several other industries we talked about, the Energy and Utilities industry also seeks to become smarter, operationally more efficient, obtain better returns on its assets, and draw on intelligence gleaned from social media analytics to reach better business decisions. Modern technology centered on Cloud can be the vehicle to acquire these capabilities.

Table 9. Cloud and manufacturing

Industrial Use Cases	Challenges	Cloud Brings
Hosting highly secure workloads along with non-critical ones	Leakage of trade secrets in business applications, intellectual property preservation, compliance to regulation such as ITAR	Smart orchestration across hybrid IT components on and off premise
Enterprise Resource Planning based on SAP or equivalent middleware provides the intelligence framework for the manufacturing industry	SAP and Oracle applications are examples of complex workloads that need specialized skills and infrastructure to deploy and manage	SAP and Oracle ERP applications hosted on a managed Cloud in PaaS mode bring benefits such as rapid provisioning and reduced cost
Business Continuity	DR, HA, Backup and Archival	Automated, cost-effective and managed Disaster Recovery, High Availability, Cost-effective Backup and Archiving

USE CASES AND ARCHITETURAL PATTERNS

Smart Metering

Smart metering services are deployed on the Cloud by energy companies either as hosted applications or in a SaaS mode. Smart meters transmit data from customer homes to collectors of the energy provider over a cellular or radio link, from where a secure VPN connection ferries it to the smart metering application on the Cloud. An architectural decision needs to be arrived at for the scaling policy associated with the infrastructure that hosts the smart metering application: Should scaling be dynamically determined based on connected users or statically deduced based on the number of smart meters being serviced? At what point should the number of hosting VMs be scaled up or down? Such versatile scaling policies are easier to implement on the Cloud compared to traditional infrastructure.

Billing in Service Provider Context

There can potentially be multiple levels of service providers in the smart metering chain. The smart metering application could be owned by a vendor, who offers it as a service to energy companies. The vendor in turn hosts the metering application with a Cloud provider. The smart meters themselves are connected to end-customers of the energy company.

The Cloud provider likely sees a single account on-boarded by the metering service vendor, and will invoice this account based on infrastructure consumption in terms of provisioned servers and storage. The vendor, on the other hand, will need to bill energy companies in a pay-as-you-go fashion linked to real service consumption, for example, the number of meters being served. A model for this upstream to downstream billing translation needs to be determined. Cloud helps in this endeavor via automation to collect metering data in different models and generate appropriate invoices.

Tax Laws and Cloud Architecture

In some countries, because of the way government subsidies are applied, Energy & Utility companies want to have capital on their books. A Capital Expense model is more attractive than an Operational Expense model in such scenarios. Such customers desire to build their infrastructure with on-premise private Clouds rather than public Clouds.

The Energy & Utility sector often sees big Mergers and Acquisitions. In some of these M&A scenarios, in-country tax laws may allow restructuring costs to be written off. Cloud is a way to establish a fast IT delivery path; the less the time taken to deploy infrastructure, the more the money that can be written off in restructuring.

SUMMARY

Table 10. summarizes prominent Cloud use cases specific to the Energy & Utilities sector.

Table 10. Cloud and energy

E&U Use Cases	Challenges	Cloud Brings
Scaling the infrastructure that hosts Smart Metering applications	Determining the scaling policy: When to scale the VMs hosting the smart metering application?	Quick provisioning and auto-scaling
Metering and billing suited to service provider context	Usage-based billing downstream (to the energy company) in terms of number of users/meters, whereas the upstream invoice (from the Cloud provider) is based on infrastructure consumption	Facilitates automation to collect metering data in different models and generate appropriate invoices
M&A tax laws may allow write-offs of restructuring costs	Establish an IT delivery path quickly in order to obtain benefits faster	Agile and rapid provisioning of infrastructure

INTERSECTION OF INDUSTRIES

Several businesses play in cross-industrial spaces. Many e-commerce vendors, for example, offer payment options in equated monthly installment (EMIs) at specified interest rates. Such transactions would fall under the ambit of laws governing the financial industry, and are necessarily both retail and financial.

Telecom companies today are operating in the area of payment banking that offers payment and remittance services using mobile-phone based money. The entire economies of some African nations are dependent on this mode of money transfer. Telecom companies can bring financial inclusion to rural areas where many people do not have bank accounts. Telecom providers with their wide reach and network of outlets, are often better equipped than banks to play in this space in a cost effective manner. This is at the crossroads of telecom and financial industries.

Most large automotive companies also have finance wings that operate auto leasing. This is a space where the automotive and finance industries meet with the help of compliant ERP systems that are hosted on the Cloud.

The Media & Entertainment industry touches many other industries via targeted advertisements. In evolved markets, cable television advertising performs demographic and geographic targeting. If you own a Mercedes, you get an upgrade offer from a local Mercedes dealer; your neighbor who owns a Toyota gets an offer from a dealer of that brand.

The Government is representative of a sector than spans industries. Government IT needs to serve departments touching the breadth of the economic spectrum ranging from finance and health, to telecom and manufacturing.

Workloads that span industries will be governed by multiple sets of regulation and can be subjected to a continuum of associated non-functional requirements. Cloud transformation of such applications needs to be mindful of the necessity to map the managed hosting solution to the full complement of cross-industrial requirements.

INDUSTRY-AGNOSTIC PATTERNS

In this section, let us look at hosting patterns that are of interest across the industries that we toured.

Development-and-Test

Development and Test (DevTest) is a recurring theme across industries. DevTest is a separate grouping because requirements such as infrastructure uptime SLAs, service-level availability and disaster recovery are often not important for these workloads. The life time of a DevTest deployment topology is also typically short and witnesses rapid change.

Progression from DevTest to Production is an important consideration while designing development or test environments on the Cloud. A mismatch between test and production environments can impact progression from test to release. Cloud can help developers easily migrate from DevTest to Staging to Production by enabling rapid creation of matching hosting topologies via technologies such as cloning.

DevTest environments offered as a service have been gaining ground in recent years. The focus here is three-fold:

1. An environment that can perform development-friendly activities such as full cloning of the entire setup with the push of a button.
2. An envelope of REST-ful APIs that can be used to extend the environment and integrate it with DevOps tools. Out-of-the-box integration with standard DevOps software is usually provided as part of the environment.
3. Cost efficiency of the platform. DevTest servers can usually be hosted on multi-tenant environments, so DevTest-as-a-Service providers virtualize physical servers on the Cloud and stand up a multi-tenant Cloud stack (see Section 3.3, "Cloud-on-Cloud") to host workloads across customers.

DevOps

When Cloud centric applications are being developed, the aim is to exploit Cloud at a business level and not merely to increase IaaS utilization. The goal is to change the way that applications are developed over time, introduced in the market, and maintained. The DevTest model needs to adapt to change in business requirements in a fast and agile fashion. Companies such as Netflix bring out applications by the week; they instrument customer feedback and behavior in the field and quickly respond to changes in functional and non-functional requirements. To achieve this, their DevTest environment is a loosely coupled fabric where components can be plugged, played, and unplugged. Open Source is commonly part of the equation since new components, if Open Source, can be easily introduced and discarded to maintain best fit. Additionally, the development-test cycle needs to be integrated with IT and Operations departments, and that is where DevOps comes in.

Cloud is not a prerequisite for DevOps, but the latter is more powerful when Cloud is the vehicle to realize the "Ops" part. DevOps uses the concept of "Infrastructure as Code", the idea of capturing environments as templates of blueprint. These templates are more versatile if they are in an industry standard format, for example OpenStack HEAT or TOSCA (Topology and Orchestration Specification for Cloud Applications).

DevOps tools talk with main stream Clouds in order to deploy these blueprint templates. Each instance of the template can hold a different mode of the "Dev" environment (for example, Production, System Testing, Quality Assurance, and User Acceptability Testing) and realize it on different "Ops" targets (for example, OpenStack private Cloud, Amazon Web Services, or SoftLayer). Different deployments can hold different versions of constituent software components, as well as variant topologies such as components in highly available mode.

DevOps also often implies continuous integration, which is a tool-driven pipeline of automation across build, deployment, test, and release. It also marries with modern development philosophies such as Agile Programming and acceptance-test driven development where the developer thinks of test cases before thinking of writing code.

DevTest may or may not imply DevOps. Depending on the enterprise in question, the environment destined to the Cloud could be DevTest sans DevOps.

Cloud-on-Cloud: Private Cloud Hosted on Public Cloud

"Cloud on Cloud" is becoming a common solution pattern across industries. This refers to the ability to carve out and stand up a single-tenant private Cloud environment on a public Cloud. A pre-requisite is that the Cloud provider has to offer bare metal servers on rent. Customers can virtualize this bare metal farm using a hypervisor of their choice and bring in the Cloud stack they are comfortable with, for example, OpenStack. The following are uses cases when this is an attractive option:

1.   The business needs architectural control of the hypervisor and Cloud managing environment, but there are no regulatory or latency requirements that mandate a dedicated on-premise deployment.
2.   The business wants a public Cloud consumption model, but wants to run workloads on an open, mainstream Cloud platform such as OpenStack.
3.   An on-premise Cloud needs to be deployed, one (or more) of whose regions is sought to be extended off-premise to cater to bursting or SoE workloads.

Software Defined Network (SDN) Enablement

Software Defined Networking has arrived both in private data centers and in public Clouds. Drivers for SDN are several. SDN decouples the network control plane of a data center from the data plane, and centralizes the former inside a controller node. This brings immense power of dynamic configurability to the network environment and reduces the labor required for network management.

An important use case for SDN in public Clouds is to circumvent the problem of overlapping IP addresses between a customer's on-premise and off-premise environments. It is difficult to allow customers to bring their own IP addresses to the Cloud without SDN enablement. With Clouds such as SoftLayer that allow customers to rent bare metal, enterprises can build an SDN-enabled private Cloud on top of virtualized physical servers. SDN provides each tenant of this private Cloud with a separate IP address space.

OpenStack Neutron provides a vendor agnostic layer to manage an SDN-enabled network. It natively brings SDN support via Open vSwitch (OVS) technology and also enables integration of OEM offerings such as VMware NSX.

Migrating to the Cloud

Migration is one of the two major hurdles to Cloud adoption across industries, the other being the perception that security is not hard on shared Clouds. Migration is expensive – and can potentially even break Cloud deals - since there are manual aspects to its implementation. The apparent solution is to inject automation into migration and render it as rapid and cost-effective as possible. There are several companies that specialize in the migration niche today.

The four major phases of a complex migration project are the discovery of the source environment, identifying the closest matching infrastructure on the target environment, putting together the stages of implementation (called wave planning), and remediating the migrated target so that it mirrors the source.

During wave planning, the migration architect has to finalize which servers would move to the Cloud and when, and estimate the velocity of migration along with the rate of ramping up to the determined velocity. Depending on the discovered characteristics of the source IT inventory, the migration architect will pose and reach answers to questions such as:

1. How much of the estate is Cloud friendly? What percentage of workloads need to be excluded because of say, the critical nature of specific applications, or the risk of migrating certain databases from high-performance physical servers to the Cloud?
2. How many OS images are already virtualized? How many virtualized OS images can be moved to Cloud as-is, with only data migration to be performed?
3. How many servers need a reinstall? How many can be upgraded? And how many can be upgraded in-place?
4. How complex is the storage migration? What is the average size of the data disks? Is a change in storage technology necessitated as a result of Cloud-enablement?
5. Are there dependencies on the roadmap of the Cloud stack that will influence the planning of migration waves?
6. What is the skill level of the available team that will run the migration project?

Cloud Brokerage

As discussed earlier, IT in sectors such as retail, finance and telecom, is becoming substantially hybrid. As an offshoot, IT departments in those businesses have environments hosted on multiple Clouds. A Cloud broker is an intermediate layer between Cloud providers and consumers. The broker eases cross-Cloud consumption across providers by offering a single fulfillment engine, often called a marketplace.

The customer needs only a single subscription with the Cloud broker to purchase services across providers. Provisioning of cross-Cloud services can be accomplished through a common portal interface via a single shopping cart and payment mechanism. Brokers may also offer a common management platform, which is a uniform dashboard through which customers can perform operations such as start/stop/monitor/patch/audit of servers across participating Clouds, in addition to rendering graphical views of cost aggregation and consumption metrics derived with Cloud analytics.

Some Cloud brokers also provide server templates to easily deploy applications on a supported Cloud of your choice. A template specifies how to build an application pattern, for example, using a scalable application tier, a DB tier, and a load balancer. The created template could then be deployed on the least expensive Cloud that matches requirements, thus achieving a form of workload arbitrage.

FUTURE RESEARCH DIRECTIONS

Cloud-enabling a data center is no longer about merely deploying a Cloud stack to automate provisioning of virtual servers and middleware from a self-service catalogue. The lay of the Cloud land is rapidly evolving, and along with that, customer expectations across industries.

The infrastructure-as-a-service layer is increasingly being assumed as a given, abstracted by standard north-bound Application Programming Interfaces (APIs) exposed by technologies such as OpenStack. Future work in this area will be around new-age hosting models that can automatically and intelligently deploy workloads. This translates to the ability to work with middleware and application patterns without the need to bother about the vagaries of the underlying infrastructure or even the Cloud Stack (Brandle et al., 2014), but also rendered industry-aware; it is about the ability to marry powerful workflows, often industry-specific, that can granularly control underlying deployment engines.

The foundation of these capabilities will include an industry-savvy fulcrum that enables hybrid IT integration. This hybrid harness will provide a fabric into which private and public Clouds, along with traditional infrastructure, can plug in and out at will in an industry-conscious fashion, allowing movement of workloads across hosting platforms depending on the degree of their Cloud-nativity and the economics of workload arbitrage. Further research, thus, will focus on bringing customers the ability to programmatically orchestrate such a Cloud-enabled data center in a model-driven and industry-cognizant fashion using non-proprietary APIs that conform to open or *de facto* standards without vendor lock-in.

CONCLUSION

This brings us to the end of the industry Cloud tour. We discussed use cases and challenges commonly observed in ten selected industries and mapped solutions to macro patterns.

Each customer is different, so there is no canned approach to designing a Cloud solution. Assets created out of lessons learned, however, increase the quality of the architecture while decreasing design time and cost. While proposing a transformative solution, keep in mind that there is no magic wand that instantly carries existing IT infrastructure to Cloud land. The adoption has to be phased; there has to be a timeline and a progression. Reference architectures gleaned from industry-specific insights can help ease this journey.

REFERENCES

Brandel, C., Grose, V., Hong, M., Imholz, J., Kaggali, P., & Mantegazza, M. (n.d.). *Cloud Computing Patterns of Expertise*. IBM Redbooks.

List of Largest Companies by Revenue. (n.d.). In *Wikipedia*. Retrieved from https://en.wikipedia.org/wiki/List_of_largest_companies_by_revenue

Moore, G. (2011). *Systems of Engagement and the Future of Enterprise IT: A Sea Change in Enterprise IT*. Retrieved 2011, from http://www.aiim.org/

Online Retailers Expect to Increase Revenue. (2015). Retrieved from http://www.ebayenterprise.com/press-room/press-releases/online-retailers-expect-increase-revenue-17-percent-2015

Pettypiece, S. (2015). *Amazon Passes Wal-Mart as Biggest Retailer by Market Value.* Retrieved July 2015, from http://www.bloomberg.com/news/articles/2015-07-23/amazon-surpasses-wal-mart-as-biggest-retailer-by-market-value

ENDNOTES

[1] A framework where application services are written and consumed via APIs

[2] A VLAN is an isolated and virtual broadcast domain. A physical LAN can carry multiple VLANs.

[3] SDN is discussed in Section Software Defined Network (SDN) Enablement

[4] DevOps is discussed in Section *DevOps*

[5] Dynamic Automation is an Expert System that attempts to auto-remediate incidents with the help of solver robots (or virtual engineers). The system uses machine learning to improve its effectiveness, so the number of automatically resolved tickets increase over time.

[6] On customer data and/or operational meta-data

[7] VMware VMotion and VMware HA are examples of live and dead migrations respectively, at the hypervisor level

[8] Windows Server Failover Clustering (WSFC) is an example of clustering of the Windows Server platform

[9] A common tool in UNIX-like systems used to keep two copies of a file system in sync

[10] See section *Cloud Brokerage*

[11] Intrusion Detection and Prevention Systems (IPDS) are security devices that guard against illegal network access

[12] VPN or Virtual Private Networks allow private Intranets to span locations by drilling secure tunnels through the public Internet

[13] Information Technology Infrastructure Library (ITIL) is a standard for service management operations

[14] See sections Development-and-Test and DevOps

[15] See section Software Defined Network (SDN) Enablement

[16] GPU or Graphics Processing Units are processors optimized for workloads such as image processing and gaming

[17] Swift is the component of OpenStack that implements Object Storage. The Swift API is becoming a de facto standard for Object Storage access

[18] See section *DevOps*

[19] REST or Representational State Transfer is an API-based mode of service access carried in XML (eXtensible Markup Language) over HTTP

Section 2

Chapter 6
Cloud Build Methodology

Richard Ehrhardt
IBM, Australia

ABSTRACT

The cloud build methodology chapter provides an introduction to the build methods for hybrid clouds. It does this by first introducing the concept of a hybrid cloud and the different types of services provides by clouds. It then overviews the components of hybrid clouds and how these components get incorporated into the design. It takes a brief look at the cost drivers with building a cloud to provide background with design decisions to be made. With the background on the design, it takes the reader through the build of a hybrid cloud and how automation can be used to reduce the cost. Lastly, it takes a brief look at a possible direction of cloud builds.

INTRODUCTION

The idea of computing being viewed as a utility is not new, the fact we now call it cloud is symptomatic of the maturity level the idea has now reached. As with any new technology, with greater uptake comes maturity and with maturity comes the beginnings of standardisation of design. This was seen with the electrical supply industry. In that industry's early days, there were no standards around type of current, connector or even voltage. Companies and households - collectively referred to as consumers - saw the benefit of electricity over gas or in house coal burning to drive manufacturing engines, but they had to decide which electricity company to follow. This meant picking a voltage, current type - Alternating or Direct - and if they were offered it at all, a connector for their lights and machines. At the time, lights and electrical based equipment was comparatively more expensive than it is now largely due to the different standards employed by the various suppliers. Even now, light bulb manufacturers still need to account for many different connector options. Slowly, the consumers and the machinery suppliers to those consumers, moved to Alternating Current (mainly because of the electrocution risk with direct current – if a person grasps a cable that is carrying direct current there is the risk that the muscles will contract and not release) and on standard voltages and connectors - at least at a country level. So that today the electric industry has standardised on current and voltage. Although variances with voltage still occur between countries.

DOI: 10.4018/978-1-5225-0759-8.ch006

Cloud is still in the phase of consumers needing to make a decision about the type of cloud technology to use with the very real risk that they will need to change in the near future as the industry moves down a different tack. Fear not though, a modular approach to design and build can reduce the risk.

An example where significant variances still exist in our electrical supply are with connectors. Whilst household and commercial power connectors are standardised within each country, light bulb connectors or sockets vary. There is the Edison screw, the bayonet fitting and then there are different sizes of each. This has driven a modular approach to light bulbs with manufacturers building bulbs in two parts, the top being the light emitting part and different bases for connection to different types of sockets.

Like the electrical supply industry, it is based upon, clouds can also be carefully designed in a modular fashion to allow for changes to be made without complete re-designs. This chapter will give you the tools you need to make the decisions about what design is right for your requirements and how you can safely ride the current of cloud to its future standard.

BACKGROUND

There are several different types of cloud. Each type has its own design requirements.

Public Cloud

As with most new technologies, they evolve and change as new uses become available. The initial concept of cloud computing was along the lines of a power supply model. At it's most fundamental, a power supply model has one or more power generators, a distribution network and a means of measuring a user's usage. This is not dissimilar to the model initially conceived for cloud computing. One or more central data centres housing all the compute power, a distribution network (the internet) to allow users to access the compute power and user access controls with metering to measure user usage. This is what we today call Public Cloud computing.

Private Cloud

With a Public Cloud model, users log in through the internet to a computing environment that is shared with other users. The extent of sharing being in part a factor of the supplying company and also the amount of segmentation the user requests (and is willing and able to pay extra for). Although Public Clouds were the original vision of cloud computing, other models have evolved for specific requirements. The first of these is what is referred to as a Private Cloud. This is like having your own generator in the power supply analogy. Like its analogy, this requires the owning party to provide all the infrastructure to provide this capability. It is typically used by large enterprises who have requirements that fall in to one of more of the following areas:

- Dedicated infrastructure,
- Security requirements or concerns,
- Data sovereignty requirements and no available public cloud in country or state,
- Legacy systems requiring cloud systems to be physically co-located due to latency or bandwidth issues, and

- Existing virtualised infrastructure that is to be leveraged for the cloud systems.

Typically (although not always), a private cloud is charged out to other business units within the company like a public cloud is charged out to other companies or individuals. This is important to drive the behaviour that reduces cost due to a cloud implementation.

Hybrid Cloud

The other type of cloud is a combination of public and private clouds, referred to as a Hybrid cloud. This is the newest cloud type and consists of as the name suggests a mix of clouds on private infrastructure and on public infrastructure. This is viewed as the direction that clouds are heading in. Rather than single disparate clouds, a collection of clouds all managed through the same console providing governance over which cloud is best for each type of workload. It is the ultimate goal for many enterprises as it provides:

- Ability to keep legacy and private data protected on a company's own infrastructure.
- Ability to have a pay as needed compute capacity in the public cloud for public facing workload.
- Ability to have a development environment in the public cloud which can be stood up and taken down on a project by project basis.

From an enterprise perspective, hybrid clouds are, currently at least, mostly used for either development or for web front ends. This is mostly due to company, industry or government regulations or standards on the storage of sensitive data on shared environments and technology challenges in making it happen.

Virtualization versus Orchestrated

A common misconception is that a virtualised environment is the same as a private cloud. This is not the case. A virtualised environment is typically (although not always, for instance in the case of bare metal cloud provisioning) used by the cloud services to host workload, but it lacks the consumer interface, automation and other essential services to be called a cloud. Clouds provide "as a Service" functionality to consumers.

Infrastructure as a Service (IaaS)

To understand the differences between virtualisation and cloud, we need to explore the services provided by cloud. At its simplest, a cloud provides "Infrastructure As A Service" or IaaS for short. The scope of the service various between clouds, but they all have one thing in common - they all provide a means of access to provision infrastructure as needed through a service portal. The infrastructure includes a minimum of compute and storage options.

Compute including both central processing unit (CPU) and random access memory (RAM). A consumer can request compute capacity to suit their needs like selecting between single phase or three phase power from an electrical company. There may or may not be a base charge to the consumer for the allocation of this capacity. Alternately, a service provider may only charge for the allocation and not the usage.

In addition to, or sometimes instead of, a base charge for the resource allocation, most IaaS providers will charge consumers for the amount of compute, memory, storage and network resources used. There are a number of different methods of doing this at present and typically vary by cloud provider and cloud software vendor. Included for compute are megahertz (MHz) billing where the CPU usage is measured in terms of the physical CPU cycles consumed, virtual CPU (vCPU) allocation which measures how much of a physical CPU is allocated, not necessarily utilised. Compute allocation is often based upon over-allocation where a virtual CPU may be only a portion of a physical CPU, so the amount of over-allocation or over-commitment is important in these models. Memory and disk storage is typically billed on an allocation model and as with compute, over-allocation also exists. Storage may also be billed out on a utilised storage method rather than allocation. Network usage is typically how many virtual local area networks (VLANs) have been allocated to an account or how many IP addresses are used, but may also include bandwidth charges for internet facing accounts / providers.

Bare Metal as a Service

Bare Metal as a Service or Metal as a Service (MaaS) is similar to IaaS except that instead of providing virtualized infrastructure, it provisions and manages physical infrastructure.

Platform as a Service (PaaS)

Platform as a Service (PaaS) is an extension on IaaS in that it adds the middleware and database software to the supplied resources. This can be very valuable for software development where the application is being developed on a standard set of software products. The ability to stand up the same platform means the development or testing can be done without needing to first build the platform each time. Depending upon the platform, this can be either a dedicated platform per consumer, or a shared platform per consumer. Charging for Platform as a Service is similar to IaaS, but includes the software charges for the platform, including any operating system, database or middleware software included. Sometimes this may be a rolled up cost including all elements in to a single charge.

Software as a Service (SaaS)

Whereas IaaS and PaaS are based upon dedicated compute and storage resources, with Software as a Service (SaaS) the application is shared among a number of different consumers. Therefore, the metering and accounting needs to be managed by the application and not the cloud. Although it is common for the software platform to still need to be metered by an IaaS supplier and this is an example of where a reseller business model comes in. A company buys IaaS from a cloud provider. That company then builds the software one that IaaS and sells it as SaaS. Unlike IaaS and PaaS, Software as a Service is typically charged back in terms of the software being provided. This is a cost model that aligns to the specific software being provided and includes all the underlying infrastructure and software costs. Examples include per user or time usage. A whole chapter could be written on how to construct pricing for these models.

Desktop as a Service (DaaS)

Desktop as a Service (DaaS) can be viewed as a subset of SaaS except that the application software being provided is a remote desktop application.

Anything as a Service (XaaS)

Anything as a Service (XaaS) is a newer term to refer to the extension of cloud services outside of purely infrastructure or software based services. Examples of XaaS are service requests for data centre floor space or even a network cable. The possibilities for XaaS are endless providing they can all be order through a services portal.

Operational Support

Operational support describes the functions needs to support the cloud services. As the name implies, it covers any service to do with the operational aspects of providing a cloud. This includes services such as event monitoring, performance management, capacity management, patching, backup and restore. These are typically performed by the service provider in the case of a public cloud and the IT department or an external IT provider in the case of a private cloud.

Business Support

Whereas the operational support covers the operation of a cloud, the business support covers the business aspects of a cloud. Essentially, client management, metering and billing. These are services typically performed by a service provider or in the case of a private cloud, the IT department for internal chargeback and other account management functions.

COMPONENTS OF A HYBRID CLOUD

There are many ways to define the components of a cloud (Fang Liu. et al. 2011) and each is valid in its own right. For the purposes of this narrative, the following components will be used.

- Data Centre,
- Infrastructure Layer,
- Virtualization Layer,
- Orchestration and Automation,
- Authentication,
- Interface,
- Operational Support Services, and
- Business Support Services.

Orchestration and Automation

The orchestration and automation layer (Behrendt. 2014) is where the cloud services start to be added. These provide services to the consumers and administrators including the ability to deploy new virtual instances, add storage or even configure new networks with firewalling and routing. The orchestration layer itself is broken into two areas. The pattern engine which defines what is to be built and the business orchestration area which defines the business processes which need to be followed in order to perform the build or change. This can include integration with service management systems or approval steps.

The orchestration and automation layer is often split between central services and regional services in a multi-site deployment. Under this arrangement, the services common to all sites like authentication, registrar of available services and orchestration are centralized. The services which are infrastructure specific are moved to the region. This includes services like the abstraction layer and software deployment.

In every cloud there is an authentication and authorization service. It keeps track of the credentials (authorization) for every human and non-human (system) user. It also tracks what elements each of these users has access to (authorization). This system can be solely contained within the cloud, or it can be linked to enterprise authentication and authorization systems. This is typically implemented with a Light Directory Access Protocol (LDAP). The external service may also be used for authentication and authorization of deployed virtual services.

The interface layer, as would be expected, provides the interface for the consumer and administration of the cloud. It provides the user interface to the other cloud services. It also includes connectivity to external services that are consumed by the cloud such as domain name services, network time protocol or mail transport systems.

Data Centre

The type of data centre used to provide a cloud (Pietro Iannucci. 2013) depends upon the importance of the cloud. The private cloud for a small single business could be housed on a handful of servers in a computer cupboard. However, for larger deployments, installation in to a hardened data centre with multiple levels of redundancy is essential to providing the level of availability expected for a cloud implementation. The tier of a data centre is a measure of the built-in redundancy. The following is a brief overview of the different tiers of data centre only. A tier 1 data centre has no redundancy of any components. It has no power redundancy and a single network path to the outside world. The failure of any element will stop the service.

Tier 2 data centres add redundant site infrastructure capacity components such as network and power. Note that this does not constitute dual power to all IT equipment, just the ability to fail over to an alternative power source.

Tier 3 data centre includes dual power paths on all equipment and multiple network paths in and out of the premise.

A tier 4 data centre is the most redundant and secure data centre type available. It has redundancy on all systems including power, cooling, fire protection, servers, network paths and so forth. In addition, it has the highest level of physical security for the site.

Infrastructure

There are three basic types of physical resources needed to provide cloud services - compute, storage and network. Each comes in different types, sizes and reliability.

Compute is the processing power for the cloud services and provisioned virtual servers. It consists of one or more physical servers.

Physical servers are sometimes referred to as "bare metal" as they are the raw hardware with no operating system installed. Each physical server is often referred to as a node. So a cloud environment would consist of multiple compute nodes.

Storage is where all the virtual server instances, software binaries, server images and data is stored. Depending upon the type of cloud software there may be dedicated storage servers which are often referred to as storage nodes. Different types of storage are used for different purposes in a cloud. Block storage provides raw disk capacity that an operating system partitions and formats. File storage is provided to a server as an already formatted file system that files can be read from and/or written to. Object storage does not have the same level of file structure as file storage, but instead stores collections of objects in containers. The stored objects are accessed by means of GET and PUT commands through an HTTP service.

Typically block storage is used by the virtualization layer and formatted as a file system to store virtual server instances. It is also used as the basis for raw disk storage provided for virtual servers as additional disk space.

File storage is becoming less popular although still used when a shared file space is required.

In consumer environments object storage can be seen in the online "cloud" photo and file storage options. In an enterprise cloud environment, object storage is typically used for storage of virtual server images that can be used to launch new virtual servers, keeping clones of virtual servers and backup of block storage file systems.

Network

The network is critical to the function of the cloud. It provides the communication between all the physical and virtual servers together (East – West communication) with the connection to the world outside of the cloud (North – South communication). Being the front door to the virtual servers running in the cloud, it is responsible for the security of the cloud environment. The security can be handled at the North – South connection, at each virtual server or a combination depending upon the software used and the configuration required.

Virtualization

The virtualization layer (IBM. 2015) provides an abstraction layer between the physical infrastructure and the virtual resources provided in the cloud. It does this by emulating physical infrastructure in software. The virtualization layer consists of compute, network and storage virtualization. These may be provided through one or multiple virtualization software products.

Examples of the different flavours of virtualization software or hypervisors are, VMware ESXi, Microsoft Hyper-V, IBM Power VIO, Citrix XenServer and the Kernel-based Virtual Machines (KVM) software.

Virtualization Management

As the virtualization layer grows, tools are needed to manage the nodes. To help with these, a number of vendors have released management software that allows for groups of nodes to be managed from a single console. Examples are VMware vCenter for ESXi/vSphere, RedHat Enterprise Virtualization – Management (RHEV-M) for KVM and IBM PowerVC (Blanchard. et al. 2014) for VIO. This is the virtualization management layer.

Operations Support

The operation support layer provides the functions responsible for ensuring the availability of the cloud. This includes systems for monitoring, performance management, capacity management, software patching, backup, restore, security, license management. Monitoring provides the ability to provide feedback on the status of a physical or virtual server, network, storage or software. Performance management (The Open Group. 2013) ensures that the performance of a server, network, storage or other infrastructure element is meeting the required levels. Capacity management is similar to performance, only it is not real time. It focuses on the planning of the capacity for infrastructure elements. Enabling the growth of the environment to be planned to avoid future issues. Software patching provides the management of applying patches to any software, including operating systems. Backup and restore provide the ability to recovery should the worst happen. Security management provides both intrusion detection and intrusion prevention services. License management provides management of deployed licenses in either the cloud management suite or the consumer deployed virtual resources or both. It is often used with PaaS or SaaS or where the vendor licensing agreement requires monitoring the usage of cloud software.

Business Support

The business support layer provides functions responsible for managing consumers of the cloud. This includes account management, together with chargeback, invoicing and payment functions. Account management provides on-boarding new users, modifying existing users (like password resets or updating a billing requirement) and deletion of user accounts. Chargeback provides the capability to meter (it is sometimes referred to as "Metering and Chargeback") the usage of virtual resources by user and provide this as input to either a billing report or to an invoicing system. Invoicing as would be expected manages issues invoices to users. Payment functions manage the processing of payments for invoices. These are sometimes included in the same software as the orchestration layer, but often it is separate, especially if a public cloud is required.

DESIGN OF A HYBRID CLOUD

Before commencing any ordering or build of a cloud, the time should be spent developing the detailed design of what the final cloud should be. This detailed design needs to include such things as the physical specifications of what is to be ordered, the software products required and what the configuration of each item should be. It is not uncommon for complex cloud solutions to have a team of designers working on the various elements of a cloud design due to the different technologies that all need to work together to provide the cloud services. This includes, data centre design, physical compute and storage infrastructure design, network design, virtualization software design, cloud services design, operational services design, business services design and so forth.

When building the detailed design many considerations and choices need to be made. These should be linked back to requirements of the cloud. Compromises on the services to be provided are not uncommon when determining the software that can be used.

Although it is tempting to jump straight to designing the physical infrastructure, it is better to start with the services which the cloud will need to provide and then look at the non-functional requirements to determine the physical aspects from requirements like availability, scale and performance.

Using the required services, or use cases, as the starting point it is possible to narrow down the software products available through vendor selection techniques. Not all software products support all the required use cases and, in most instances, a cloud design will need multiple software products to be able to meet all the required use cases.

Firstly, what type of cloud is required – public or private? What services will be provided – Infrastructure, platform or software services? Each of these decisions will affect the software products that are available and the build approach.

The simplest cloud is a private cloud that only offers Infrastructure as a Service. When looking at a private cloud, there are often existing virtualized or non-virtualized workload that needs to be taken into account. What operating systems are in use? Looking at the existing virtualized workload, what hypervisor technologies are in use? Is any consolidation of hypervisor technologies possible? For instance, by migrating from one x86 virtualization platform to another. Are the non-virtualized workloads able to be migrated into the virtualized environment or are there constraints to this occurring? The answers to these questions will give a view as to the hypervisor technologies that need to be supported. This will affect the choice of software products able to support the environment.

Then how many sites need to be included in the cloud? How are physically apart are the sites? What network connectivity exists between the sites? This will affect the physical placement of the cloud components in the design.

Infrastructure as a Services can include compute, network and storage virtualization services. Are all these going to be provided or only a subset like compute and storage? If storage virtualization is provided, which type will be available to consumers – block, file or object? If network virtualization is required, it is important to look at what physical network components are already in place.

The services available from network virtualization include the ability to provision, modify or delete virtual networks, subnets, firewalls, routing and load balancers. Network virtualization is one of the areas of clouds that is the furthest from having a standard solution in place. Each software type has its own approach to achieve the same or similar results. There are two approaches to network virtualization.

The first approach requires links in to the physical network fabric to be able to provision additional networks and other network elements. This is typically vendor specific. In this approach, the hypervisor requests a new network element which is created in the network fabric and presented back to the hypervisor as a new capability. This approach can often result in higher performance networks as the hypervisor does not need to handle the network functions in addition to the compute and storage functions it provides. It does however, typically require a network vendor to be locked in. The interface between the hypervisor and network virtualization needs to be considered when choosing software products.

In the second approach, the network fabric is constant and the changes occur above the hypervisor. All the network elements required are emulated by the hypervisor. This typically requires less software as all the required network functions are virtualized by the same software that also provides the compute and storage virtualization. This approach also requires design considerations on the physical specifications of the hypervisor nodes to minimise performance impact from the addition of network virtualization. Not all cloud software supports network virtualization. And those that do have varying degrees of supported services.

As previously described, Metal as a Service (MaaS) is similar to IaaS except it provisions and manages physical infrastructure rather than virtual. This means that the software requirements for it vary from IaaS. In particular, the hypervisor is not required for MaaS, but software is needed to be able to build the operating system on bare metal. OpenStack Ironic or a custom workflow for PXE boot are examples of methods to implement bare metal provisioning. Depending upon the hardware it may also be possible to make calls from the orchestration layer to the system management controller to install an image on to bare metal as in the case of a blade server configuration. For network virtualization, the vendor specific network fabric layer virtualization is a good fit for MaaS requirements.

For a platform as a service (PaaS) on private cloud, additional components are needed to support adding and managing the software on top of the infrastructure. Often this is done with additional software to the cloud services. If this is determined to be the case, then the integration between the two needs to be considered. A typical use case around platform as a service is,

Step 1: Consumer requests a new platform.
Step 2: IaaS provisions the infrastructure for the platform.
Step 3: Another cloud software product then implements and configures the middleware and database software required for the platform.

The platform details are provided to the consumer who can then implement their application for development testing or production purposes.

Where more than one virtual server is involved with the required platform, the PaaS software needs to be have knowledge of all the servers to be able to correctly configure the software. For instance, where middleware software on one server needs to be configured to communicate with database software on a different server.

PaaS needs to also take into account the management of the provisioned platform as a single entity for the consumer. The consumer needs to be able to shutdown, modify or delete the whole platform, not just individual infrastructure elements. As such, there may need to be cloud service interface elements that need to have the capability to manage the PaaS.

Since PaaS is providing an entire platform to a cloud consumer, all elements of that platform need to be managed. Consequently, PaaS requires managing the software licenses and cost recovery of those licenses. Other services that may be provided under a PaaS model are the capacity management of the platform, the performance of the platform, backup and restore of the platform and patching of the platform (or at least keeping the images and/or build scripts updated to the required patch level). These elements are covered in the operational support and business support service components.

Like PaaS, Software as a Service (SaaS) requires a custom interface with the ability for consumers to track software rather than infrastructure elements. Unlike PaaS, the operational and business elements of the service are mandatory as the cloud consumer expects the software to work as required. The service provider is responsible for all aspects of the service from the infrastructure right through the middleware, database and application. The consumer accesses the SaaS directly and typically does not utilise the cloud interface. Often the provider of SaaS is a consumer of the cloud service. From a cloud design and build perspective, the software to provide SaaS is a combination of IaaS and PaaS. The user management, metering, chargeback and other such services are managed by the SaaS solution and not typically included in the cloud design, other than the infrastructure requirements to run the software of course.

Since the users of Desktop as a Service (DaaS) have not visibility to the underlying cloud infrastructure, it is treated the same as SaaS. Besides needing to take in to account the infrastructure build and manage functions for DaaS, the user and business functions are typically handled within the DaaS software.

Then there are the requirements which are combinations of the above. IaaS with MaaS, Iaas with PaaS, IaaS with MaaS and PaaS are all common combinations. Combining these services means considering overlapping services and whether a single software product or multiple products meet the requirements. If multiple products are chosen, then the integration of these needs to be considered to ensure a seamless presentation of the services to the consumer.

A requirement for a public cloud adds the need for software able to handle the automated customer management, partner management, payment handling and product catalogue. The automated customer management allows for new users to access a web site and request a new account. This account then needs to be able to manage their own account for actions like password resets. It may also include the ability to create additional accounts by an administrator, retailer or agent. Partner management is similar to the customer management, but allows for additional functions like metering data across multiple accounts. Customer and partner management functions are usually managed by an LDAP backend (which must be shared with the other cloud services software), an orchestration function (which is often the same as the cloud services implemented one) and portal front-end which is usually a custom web site. These can even be extended with Customer Relationship Management (CRM) software to allow for profile tracking and the like. On boarding actions can be handled by the orchestration software. And once the account is created, the user will typically log in to either a front end to or the orchestration interface directly for provisioning and managing virtual resources.

Payment handling functions require software able to handle automated processing of credit cards and the like. This is typically implemented with dedicated payment processing that are able to securely interface with financial institutions. It may be necessary to have multiple payment processing software in place for different financial institutions and/or payment methods. For instance, a credit card versus direct debit capabilities.

The product catalogue is normally implemented with separate software again. The software needs to handle product/offering definition and pricing as well as the ability to publish offerings, withdraw offerings or delete offerings. Since the cloud is going to be providing offerings to users, it is important to consider what happens to the existing provisioned offerings when the offering is deleted or withdrawn.

Other optional software may include subscription management to allow customers to buy up to a pre-agreed amount of resources. This is commonly implemented with the same software that manages the metering and chargeback, but may need extensions. It may also include software for managing brokers, agents or resellers.

Another aspect of a public cloud implementation is whether the deployed virtual servers will be managed by the provider, the consumer or a third party. Management can include service management type functions such as monitoring, event management, backup, restore, patching, security, capacity management or performance management. If it is the consumer or third party, then no additional software is needed other than ensuring any firewall gateways support user software for the functions.

If the virtual servers are to be managed by the cloud service provider, then additional design considerations need to be made as to what software will provide the services and how the software will connect to the virtual servers it is managing.

Connectivity from the support tools to the virtual servers can need careful planning, particularly in the case of a cloud with software defined networking (SDN). In an SDN cloud, the client can choose the subnet addresses and security between the external networking and the virtual servers. As the support tools are typically located in a dedicated network, there is a real possibility that there will be overlapping network addresses between clients and the potential that firewall rules for connection may not exist. A solution to this is the use of network address translation (NAT) for every deployed virtual server. It is possible to assign every client virtual server with another IP address that is used by the support tools to access the client. The reverse connectivity is also required – from the virtual server back to the support tools. This is usually implemented with a default route pre-defined for the virtual routers and firewall rules pre-defined in the default security groups.

In order to provide the management of either the cloud services or deployed virtual resources, a group of services is required to be included in the design – operational support services. As with the management of deployed virtual resources, this includes functions for Management can include service management type functions such as monitoring, event management, backup, restore, patching, security, capacity management or performance management. Each of these typically need their own software products or at a minimum the functional requirements for each of these services needs to be aligned to one or more software products. Each of these services also needs connectivity from or to the cloud services that they are supporting. This requires network planning.

In addition to the operational support services, business support services need to be planned for, even for a private cloud. This includes services such as metering, chargeback and account management. Metering and chargeback are often covered by the same software products. This software may be included with the cloud services software or can be separate. The account management software will vary depending upon the extend of account management needed. The most basic provides the ability to register new users and change passwords. The more advanced account management software also handles on-boarding, reporting and multiple account roles such as consumer, tenant administrator or service broker. AS with the operational services, these products need connectivity to the virtualization layer as well as connectivity to the users.

A consideration, particularly for multi-region or pubic clouds is the language that is to be used by users. This affects not only the portal interface, which may need to support multiple languages, but also the handling and management of any provisioned virtual resources. The virtual resources may be in different languages which could affect the choice of software that is to be installed for monitoring and other management functions. This is particularly true if there are any double or triple-byte character set languages to be supported by Chinese or Korean as the software needs to be able to support the associated operating systems.

Although it may not be called out by any specific functional requirement, there is a need to consider some external services that are required for the cloud to function. One of these is the network time protocol (NTP). NTP is used to keep all the services in the cloud synchronised to the same clock. There are several internet NTP services available or a dedicated one can be built for the cloud.

Another required external service is the Simple Mail Transport Protocol (SMTP). This is important for the notification of cloud consumers and others as to actions that have occurred or will occur to their virtual resources or providing details on requests like the details of a virtual server that has been provisioned (or for notification of approval/action requests). The orchestration layer will typically connect to this to provide this service. Depending upon the size of the cloud, it may be necessary to create a relay service within the cloud that then connects to an external service.

A further is an external domain name service (DNS) if the cloud (and it is unusual if not) connected to an external network. This provides a reference service for hostnames and associated IP addresses to be stored. This allows users and other services to locate servers or web sites based upon their human friendly hostname rather than an IP address. It is usually wise to include a child DNS within the cloud services to cache requests from within the cloud to the external service. This can be on it's own dedicated server (or servers) or be shared on one of the other cloud servers. If the design requires multiple sites, it is also worth considering having a service at each site.

The last external service to consider is a connection to an external authentication system. Although it is possible to have a purely internal authentication system (for instance in a public cloud), it is more common particularly in private clouds to have a connection to an enterprise LDAP service. This enables enterprise users to access the cloud services using their corporate credentials rather than a separate set of credentials for the cloud services. The same service can also be used for the virtual resources that are provisioned through the cloud services. The cloud services typically include an internal authentication system that also handles authorization and connects to an external (enterprise) authentication system if the user is not defined within itself. If this service is being provided to the virtual resources being provisioned and is a multi-site configuration, then an LDAP client should be considered at each location to cache the credentials.

It is important to review each of the functional requirements, including use cases, back through the one or more software products that will support it. Once the software products are defined, the non-functional requirements should be used to determine the physical aspects of the design.

The first obvious non-functional requirement design driver is the size of the cloud to be supported. The more virtual servers and virtual workload that needs to be hosted in the cloud, the more infrastructure is needed. However, even here there are decisions to be made about the amount of over-commit that will be provided to the workload. Over-commit or sometimes referred to as over-subscription is supported by most hypervisor technologies. It permits multiple virtual servers to run on the same virtual resources at the same time. An example is running 5 virtual servers on the same CPU core. Each virtual server thinks it has the entire CPU core, however, the hypervisor will time-slice each virtual server just like an operating system kernel running multiple processes at the same time. Just like running multiple processes on the same CPU, if each is requiring the majority of the CPU time at the same time then this leads to conflict and the performance of the individual virtual servers is impacted. The amount of over-commit possible depends upon the type of hypervisor software – some are better at this than others – and the type of workload to be hosted.

During the design phase, thought needs to be put in to the types of workload that will be run on the cloud. An analysis of the workload should look at the average resource requirements the workloads that are expected to be hosted in the cloud. It may be necessary to group like workloads into different areas of the cloud to avoid contention.

It is not uncommon to have a one-to-one mapping between virtual and physical resources in the cloud in the event that the workload has high performance requirements.

In addition to the physical resources required for the virtual workload to be supported, the physical servers also need to be able to run the hypervisor software itself. The amount of overhead physical resources necessary to run the hypervisor varies by software vendor and the types of workload being hosted. As a rule of thumb, the more virtual servers that need to be hosted on a physical server at the same time, the higher the amount of CPU and memory overhead needed. This is because each of the virtual servers still needs a base amount of compute regardless of the amount of virtual resources it is consuming.

The availability requirements for the cloud will affect how many virtual and physical servers are required. The higher the expected availability, the more infrastructure is needed to ensure redundancy. This applies to the physical hardware which may need multiple power supplies, multiple Input / Output (I/O) cards, multiple network devices and multiple storage devices to allow for redundancy in the case of physical failure in addition to needing multiple physical servers in case one of them fails. It also applies to the virtual servers which may need to be duplicated into clusters to enable a single virtual server to fail (for instance due to the physical server on which it is hosted failing).

In the case of a multiple site solution, the availability requirements may call for the replication of virtual servers or storage between the sites in order to meet the recovery time objective (RTO) or recovery point objective (RPO). There are several solutions for disk replication, but they come down two types, storage level or file level. The storage level will replicate an entire storage pool between the sites. It is typically implemented using vendor software linked to the storage hardware. File level replication is done at a software level and replicates specific files. These files could be virtual servers or storage objects.

Performance is another design driver that affects all aspects of the design. From the physical infrastructure through to the choice of software products, the performance requirements need to be considered. Software needs to be able to support the required response times. The placement of each service needs to be considered and how it will impact on the responsiveness of the cloud services. This is particularly impact when building a cloud that is at diverse physical locations. Even if the network is able to handle the data throughput, often the physical distance between the sites is enough to impact performance. For this, the cloud services should be placed as close as possible to workload to avoid the need to pass large quantities of data between the sites. An example here is the image store. Having a central image store may make the management easier, but it is going to impact performance if an image needs to be copied from a one physical location to another in order to provision a new virtual server.

The physical compute infrastructure needs to have enough capacity to execute all the physical and virtual processes within the required performance requirement. The network needs to have enough bandwidth to allow the volume of data to be transferred within the required performance requirement. The physical storage infrastructure needs to support the number of reads, writes and throughput expected by the performance requirement.

COST

The cost of building a cloud can be broken in to floor space, hardware, software and the build services. This does not include the cost of running the cloud.

Floor space is a factor of resource density and size of the cloud. The denser the compute, storage and network resources can be made, the less space is required to provide the same capacity. The bigger the expected size of cloud for the same resource density, the more space it will take up. Ways of increasing density are, blade servers, better cooling to allow more in each rack and using compute nodes of high specification. For instance, the use of compute nodes with 12 core CPUs instead of 4 core.

The cost of the hardware is mostly attributable to the size, performance and availability requirements of the cloud. The size being driven by the number and size of virtual resources that are needed. The performance of the cloud drives the hardware requirement through the needing higher specification hardware to achieve the higher performance. The availability requirements of the cloud drives the cost of the hardware by needing additional redundant hardware to support the availability needs.

Software costs vary depending upon the vendor. Unfortunately, there is no common method for software license or maintenance charging. Methods include by the number of physical resources like CPU that the software will run on through to the number of virtual resources to be supported by the software. In general, though, the larger the cloud, the more the cost of the software will be.

The services cost to build a cloud is less about the size of the cloud and more about the complexity. Drivers include the number of physical sites, the number of different hypervisor technologies required and the amount of third party integration required.

Third party integration is required where a cloud needs to interact with existing systems. The existing systems can be existing virtualization or service management systems that need to be interacted with as part of a business process workflow. The more complex the workflow or automation and the more third party integration that is required, the higher the cost.

BUILDING A HYBRID CLOUD

As would be expected, the project schedule depends upon the size and complexity of the environment. A simple cloud implementation built on existing physical infrastructure could take as little as a few days, whereas a complex cloud solution consisting of many compute nodes, different virtualization technologies and multiple sites can take several months to implement.

There are several different types of human resource needed to build based upon the layers of the cloud that are required. Of course, a project manager is needed to keep the schedule, scope and cost under control for the construction. Before construction is started, an IT architect should put together a detailed design of what needs to be built.

Infrastructure specialists will be needed for the physical infrastructure builds. This includes server, storage and network specialists. It is not uncommon to have this function provided by a third party such as a business partner to the infrastructure supplier.

Once the infrastructure is built, virtualization specialists are required to implement the virtualization layer. Often software specific skills are needed such as a certified VMware practitioner. This may be the same person who will implement the orchestration layer, or a separate resource with specific skills on the orchestration software may be needed.

Other resources that may be used include:

- A security specialist may be brought in to provide advice, guidance and design input on various aspects of the cloud to ensure it meets or exceeds the security standards required.
- An image specialist may be used to develop the virtual server images that will be templates for virtual servers.

- A network specialist may be needed to design and build the networking if it is complex, such as with Software Defined Networking or Network Function Virtualization.
- A storage specialised may be needed for the storage elements either physical or virtual.
- Tools specialists may be needed to implement and configure any operational or business support tooling that is required.
- An automation or workflow specialist may be needed for provide the development of any automation needed to provide one or more services.

The project should start with a kick off meeting in which all delivery participants are present. This is typically chaired by the project manager. The agenda needs to include a walk-through of the detailed design by the architect and a walk-through of project schedule by the project manager. The project manager needs to obtain agreement from each of the participants on their responsibilities for the build.

The project is broken up in the same manor as the cloud components with an over-arching project management function. The project management function includes oversight on the scope, schedule and cost of the project plus managing stakeholders.

Data centre preparation gets the site ready for the infrastructure and includes ensuring power, cooling, physical security and networking from the data centre to the outside world is in place.

The infrastructure build involves the installation of racks, building servers, building the storage system, building the network devices and cabling the whole lot up. The installation of racks involves wiring power in to these racks and ensuring they have cooling from under floor or other method in place. Building the servers requires the servers to be unboxed and installed in to the racks. Depending upon the type of hardware and the manufacturing, they may also need internal components such as additional Input / Output (I/O) cards installed and configured. Once implemented in the rack, the servers are cabled for the IO options such as storage or networking and power from the rack.

For blade type servers, the steps involve implementation of the blade chassis in to the rack as described above and then the implementation of each blade server in to the chassis.

The storage systems are built in a similar fashion to the servers. The build will depend upon the type of storage system. A storage cluster is basically a serious of servers each with internal disk so the build is identical to that for servers. A traditional Storage Area Network (SAN) system consists of SAN switches, disk controllers and disk arrays. Each of these are built along the same lines as the servers with either fibre or high speed Ethernet cabling between the components and to the servers.

Network components may consist of switches, routers and/or firewalls depending upon the design choices made. Each require implementation into a rack and cabling to the other components. As with the server builds, it is not uncommon to require additional components such as interface modules to be added either before or after a network frame is installed in a rack.

The virtualization build is commenced once the physical infrastructure has been implemented. It consists of powering on each of the units and implementing the virtualization software. If network virtualization is being provided, the order of implementation may need to be varied to build the network virtualization before other functions. Depending upon the type of virtualization software, this can be an all-in-one operating system build (for a VMware ESXi solution as an example) or a build of an operating system and then the implementation of virtualization software (as is the case for a KVM solution). In each case, there are several methods for performing this build from an image of the operating system and software. One method is to have the software on a CD-ROM and boot the server from the CD-ROM. Along the same lines is to use a USB stick with software to boot from. Another option is to have a server in the network which allows for network booting. Using this method, called Pre-eXecution Environment (PXE) the server searches the network for a server to provide it with a boot image. The server has the network MAC address of the server and provides the server with the relevant software image to boot from. The server which supplies the software may often be a pre-configured laptop that is plugged in to the environment. This is useful as the network can be isolated from anything outside the cloud during the build. Not all the virtualization layer needs to be built initially, only enough for the cloud services to be built and tested. The remainder of the environment is typically built either in parallel to the cloud services build, or afterwards. Depending upon the cloud software chosen, it can even be performed by the cloud services themselves.

The orchestration, or cloud services, build is added once the initial virtualization is in place. The orchestration software implementation typically takes the longest time and planning here makes all the difference. The layer requires the implementation software on either bare metal or virtual server operating systems depending upon the type of software chosen. There is also in some cases the option of installation using virtual appliances. These are pre-packaged operating system, middleware and application virtual images that can be deployed as a single device. The operating system build on a bare metal server occurs in the same manor as the virtualization software. It can be achieved by either booting from a CD/DVD, USB or network server.

The operating system build in a virtual environment is similar, but not the same as there are additional tools available to get the operating system binaries to the server. This includes, the ability to mount a virtual CD/DVD or USB, together with the network boot as before, but it also has the option of using virtual images as the base. A virtual image is a template of a complete virtual server and may be copied to a new virtual machine with no software loaded where it may be customized to create a virtual server. Typical customization items include IP address, hostname, Domain Name Service (DNS) settings and static routing settings.

Having loaded the operating system, it may need the latest patches loaded together with pre-requisite software packages for the main software items. Software pre-requisites include middleware items such as a python programming language client used by some software. The binaries for the installation can be downloaded on to the machine from the internet if a connection is available, or as internet connectivity is not always available, can be copied from a local source such as a USB, object store or file system store in the build environment. An example of the latter would be the use of a web service on the installation device to allow files to be retrieved through a GET command.

As previously stated, the orchestration layer consists of two areas, the pattern and business orchestration areas. The pattern area interfaces to the virtualization and virtualization management layers. It provides the build service for virtual infrastructure solutions. The build of this layer requires the software implementation and the configuration of the interface to the virtualization infrastructure.

The business orchestration layer interfaces with the portal, the pattern area, the business support services layer and the operational support services layer for service management functions.

The operational support services build is done similar to the cloud services, although often by different personnel. The monitoring, patching, license management, capacity management and performance management are typically services that run on virtual machines and require no further physical infrastructure. The number and configuration of the virtual machines required to run the operational support services varies depending upon the choice of vendor and the size and complexity of the environment.

Depending upon the choice of solution, backup and restore software can require additional physical infrastructure in the form of slow speed disk or tape storage solutions. The build for the physical infrastructure is similar to that described earlier for server and storage infrastructure. Once the physical infrastructure is in place, the software for backup and restore is implemented on to a physical or virtual machine as before.

Business Support Services (BSS) consists of the software to run the client management side of the cloud. The software which provides these services typically run on one or more servers which may be virtual or physical. The implementation of BSS typically involves creating the operating system layer on either the virtual or physical server, mounting a drive with the software binaries or downloading the binaries, installing the software, then configuring the software. Often there is more than one server involved as the software is usually multi-tier (web front-end, application server and database server), and/or clustered.

Having built out the software for the cloud services and associated systems, it is necessary to build the services that will be provided to the users.

WORKFLOWS AND AUTOMATION

The workflows in cloud align to the functional use cases that the cloud needs to perform. These allow for complex business and operational processes to be automatically carried out by the cloud during provisioning, modifying or deleting cloud resources.

The use cases that can be leveraged by an automated workflow include:

- Provision a virtual server and configure the backend systems to provide operational support for it
- De-provision a virtual server and also decouple from the backend systems
- Provision virtual resources and ask for approval from a third party to proceed
- Provision virtual resources, including a virtual network and configure the firewalls outside the cloud to allow access to services on the network.
- Modify virtual resources at a scheduled time after raising a change, then having it scheduled and approved.
- Review the time since a virtual server has been provisioned and either shutdown or destroy the virtual server after a pre-defined timeframe.

An example of a business process workflow that addresses the first use case to provision a new virtual server is as follows:

Step 1: User logs in to the portal.
Step 2: User requests a new virtual server.
Step 3: Orchestration tool requests details of virtual server from user, excluding hostname which it calculates based upon the enterprise's standard naming convention.
Step 4: Orchestration tool raises a change request in the service management tool.
Step 5: Orchestration tool calls the cloud region to provision the virtual server.
Step 6: Cloud region calls the infrastructure management layer to create a virtual machine
Step 7: Cloud region calls the infrastructure management layer to copy the image on to the virtual server.
Step 8: Cloud region calls the infrastructure management layer to power on the virtual server.
Step 9: Virtual server obtains configuration information from the cloud region.

Step 10: Cloud region confirms virtual server is running and confirms status to orchestration tool.

Step 11: Orchestration tool calls software deployment engine to install support agents.

Step 12: Software deployment tool installs agent software on target virtual machines and confirms when done.

Step 13: Orchestration tool connects to backend monitoring, patching and backup systems to configure new virtual server in systems.

Step 14: Orchestration tool updates the domain name service (DNS) with the hostname and IP details of the new virtual server to allow users to connect to the virtual server using the hostname.

Step 15: Orchestration tool updates the authentication and authorisation system with the details of the new virtual server to allow user access to the virtual server.

Step 16: Orchestration tool updates change record in service management tool to confirm successful implementation.

Step 17: Orchestration tool updates configuration management database with details of the new virtual server.

Step 18: Orchestration tool emails details of the new server to the user.

If the deployment were unsuccessful, the use case might look like:

Step 1: User logs in to the portal.

Step 2: User requests a new virtual server.

Step 3: Orchestration tool requests details of virtual server from user.

Step 4: Orchestration tool raises a change request in the service management tool.

Step 5: Orchestration tool calls the cloud region to provision the virtual server.

Step 6: Cloud region calls the infrastructure management layer to create a virtual machine.

Step 7: Cloud region calls the infrastructure management layer to copy the image on to the virtual server.

Step 8: Cloud region calls the infrastructure management layer to power on the virtual server.

Step 9: Virtual server fails to power on correctly, or fails to obtain correct configuration.

Step 10: Cloud region advises orchestration tool that deployment has failed.

Step 11: Orchestration tool raises a problem ticket in service management tool.

Step 12: Orchestration tool updates change in service management tool with unsuccessful result.

Step 13: Orchestration tool notifies user of unsuccessful result and details of problem ticket.

During the build, these use cases need to be programmed in to the respective tools to enable the end to end workflow to occur.

Many of these steps require integration between different systems such as from the orchestration tool to the service management tool. This integration requires a common language for the two systems to both authenticate with each other and also to make requests of each other. Unfortunately, this is another area where the standards have not entirely come to cloud. The most common Application Programming Interfaces (API's) are Representational State Transfer (REST) and Simple Object Access Protocol (SOAP). Both of these are used, although REST is the more common.

The REST protocol uses standard HyperText Transfer Protocol (HTTP) for communication. Communications are secured with Secure Socket Layer (SSL) encryption or its successor, Transport Layer Security (TLS). SSL and TLS are frequently both called SSL. Since REST is used for machine to machine communications, data transfers are required. The origin of HTTP is a means of formatting human readable content. As such, the data types that can be transferred are usually in alphanumeric format. Although it is possible to pass data objects embedded as binary data, it is more common to send the data in a text format. EXtensible Markup Language (XML) or JavaScript Object Notation (JSON) are common protocols used by REST to send the data in text format.

SOAP uses its own communication protocol. This makes it more difficult to implement, however, it does allow for greater flexibility with security and reliability. SOAP can use SSL/TLS for security like REST, but it can support Web-Services Security (WSS or WS-Security) as well. WSS allows for authentication via an intermediary unlike SSL/TLS which is only point-to-point. The down-side of this security is significantly slower transmission speeds.

Whilst REST is dependent upon a client retrying if a communication attempt fails, SOAP has additional controls in place to check that the communication was successful. Like REST, data transfer occurs using text formatted mark-up. In the case of SOAP, this has to be done via XML.

At the end of the day, for clouds the choice of communication protocol often comes down to the protocols used by the cloud software that best meets the requirements and any third party backend systems that the cloud services need to connect with.

It is also possible to build these workflows as entirely process driven actions where each step is performed by a human rather than a machine. This is often the approach used when introducing new automation into a previously manually process. It helps to confirm the process is not missing any steps, makes the enterprise comfortable as it is low risk and allows for lower cost implementations up front.

Once the workflow is fully automated, enterprises are seeing reduced costs to perform the previously manual processes and the more rapid deployment, modification and removal of virtual resources. Automation also allows for software to be deployed on to virtual resources. This allows for custom environments to be deployed and ready without the need for a human to log in and install any software.

Software automation is accomplished by an additional step in the workflow to call a software engine that installs and configures the software on to each virtual server. An example of the steps involved are,

Step 1: Retrieve software binaries or mount drive with software binaries.
Step 2: Execute a script to run install the software with the specified parameters.
Step 3: Confirm successful implementation.
Step 4: Remove or unmount software binaries.
Step 5: Remove installation script.

The script that installs and configures the software is sometimes a customized shell script or may be through tools such as Chef Server, Puppet, Ansible or Salt Stack. They all provide an abstraction capability to install software on to different platforms. This abstraction removes the need of the install steps to know items like the package management tool. Each also provides additional features such as infrastructure management on top of software implementation. Each of these tools performs the same actions slightly differently with the same result. These products perform software implementation in two ways.

The first method is to have a client that runs on the target server. This client connects to the server and pulls down the required software and configuration. It then executes using the client the commands to install and configure the software. Within this method, the configuration of the software needs to be configured on the server before the execution of the client software on the target server or the client software needs to know the configuration. It has the advantage that the software deployment server need not know the credentials of the target server. The disadvantage is the need to configure the deployment server first or pass all the parameters to the client for the configuration.

The other method is a push approach. This method has the software implementation initiated from the server. The server connects to the target server using supplied credentials. It then executes the commands to download, install and configure the software.

Together with the instructions on how to build the software, a repository for the software binaries is needed. This can either be included within the cloud itself or, if external connectivity is possible, it may exist on an external server (for instance a public software repository).

Part of the software deployment may require license updates. Software license keys can be provided by a workflow that allocates the next available key, by the use of a "golden key" which is usable for an unlimited number of uses or by a having the virtual server connect to an external entity to register for a license.

Although it is possible to implement the software without the cloud services in place, there are advantages of doing so. Significantly the use of cloud services to perform the software implementation steps has the advantage that the parameters for the software implementation can be calculated in the pattern or workflow or obtained from the consumer when requesting the service. Examples of the parameters that may be passed to a software installation script are,

- Installation location,
- User names and passwords to configure,
- IP address or hostnames of other servers the software needs to connect to,
- Credentials for other servers the software will connect to, and
- Database instance names (for database software implementation).

The other key advantage to using the cloud services for this is the option to connect to systems outside of what is being created to configure those for the new software. For example, the implementation may require a new node to be registered with a backend system. The orchestration tool is able to handle this as part the workflow. An example of this is an update to the domain name service (DNS) when a new virtual server is deployed. The orchestration tool is able to pass the hostname and IP address to the DNS as an update to allow consumers to log in to their new server using the hostname rather than the IP address.

The same process automation can also apply to business processes not directly related to cloud services. Take the below example of a request for a new workstation.

Step 1: Consumer requests new workstation through portal.
Step 2: Orchestration tool asks for details from consumer from a list of pre-defined options.
Step 3: Orchestration tool sends request to consumer's manager asking for approval.
Step 4: Manager approvals in orchestration tool.
Step 5: Orchestration tool raises a support ticket in service management tool to request workstation per the approved requirements.
Step 6: Support ticket is actioned by the supply personnel and new workstation provided to the consumer.
Step 7: Orchestration tool determines the completion of the support ticket and notifies consumer.

Whilst this example could equally be performed by the service management tool itself, it does give a view of the types of non-cloud services that are possible through the orchestration tool.

This leads to another area where clouds have a huge impact on enterprise and one that needs to be considered when building a cloud. The success of a cloud in enterprise is in part the success of the design and build. It is just as much in the uptake of the services by the enterprise. By enabling a single portal for service requests, the cloud consumers are having to go through a single portal for their requests. This allows the process to be standardised. So if in the past, there were two different processes in an organisation to order a new server, the introduction of a cloud can reduce that down to a single one, even if it includes non-cloud infrastructure requests using XaaS.

Since the processes are automated, the cost to run the process can be significantly reduced over a manual process. This applies to both the operational and business areas of the enterprise. If previously someone had to manually create a billing spreadsheet for other business units, the collection and formatting of that data can be automated within the cloud. If someone had to manually create a change record in order to make modify a server, that process can be automated in the cloud. It is not uncommon to see the time to deploy a new server drop from weeks to minutes when a cloud is fully configured and automated.

Given that the development platforms can be re-defined, as described earlier, it also provides enterprises with the opportunity to standardise on a platform across business units. This can lead to reduced development and software costs. Reduced development costs as the development teams only need to be trained in the standard platform. Reduced software costs as the number of software products required can be kept to just those in the development platform.

Building Cloud Services with Automation

The automation technique described above to the provisioning of virtual resources within a cloud can also be applied to the build of the cloud services themselves. In this way, the software build portion can be partially or fully automated.

An example of the steps involved with an automated cloud deployment are:

Step 1: Network boot bare metal.
Step 2: Install hypervisor software.
Step 3: Create initial virtual server for hypervisor management software.
Step 4: Network boot the virtual server.
Step 5: Install the operating system on the server.
Step 6: Create a virtual server for the hypervisor management database software.
Step 7: Install the operating system on the server.
Step 8: Implement and configure the hypervisor management software and database software on the two provisioned virtual servers.
Step 9: Create the virtual servers for the cloud software.
Step 10: Install the operating system on these servers.
Step 11: Implement the cloud services software and configure to use the hypervisor management software.
Step 12: Create virtual servers for the operational support services.
Step 13: Install the operating system on these servers.
Step 14: Implement the operational support services and configure to interface with the other components.
Step 15: Create the virtual servers for the business support services.
Step 16: Install the operating system on these services.
Step 17: Implement the business support services and integrate with the other components.

Step 18: Configure the cloud software with the required consumers.

Step 19: Configure the cloud software with the required services that the consumer will access. These could be workflows or just enablement of out of the box functionality.

As can be seen from the above, the steps involved closely resemble those of provisioning a new virtual environment from the cloud services themselves. It is such that may of the same technologies are used for both building the cloud and then building the services within that cloud.

The method to install an operating system (or hypervisor in this case) on a virtual or physical server is the same and the PXE boot can be automated. This is typical for the implementation onto bare metal. It can also be used to install the operating system on to a virtual server. Alternately, the base operating systems can be virtual images themselves.

The same software deployment software used to automate the deployment of software onto provisioned operating systems can also be used to deploy the cloud services software on to its operating systems prior to the cloud being in place. In fact, with careful planning, the implementation of this software first can enable the same install of this software to be used to both build the cloud services and then deploy software on to the provisioned operating system during cloud run-time.

Depending upon the orchestration software, it is possible to automate the import of workflows and other automation using custom scripts. For a one off cloud build this is not a cost feasible option and it is typically by by hand once the cloud is built. However, if building multiple clouds that share the same design and software it may be an option to be considered to reduce the risk and cost of the build

FUTURE OF CLOUD BUILDS

The design and build methodology of clouds continues to evolve. Designs are becoming more standard across multiple software and services vendors. With the standardization of design, it allows for automation to be used more commonly to deploy the cloud environments.

There are two major players in cloud software at present, VMware vSphere and OpenStack. OpenStack (OpenStack Foundation. 2014) is being widely used by itself as publically available software and within several distributions including Ubuntu OpenStack, and Red Hat Enterprise Linux OpenStack Platform. OpenStack is also behind some of the public cloud vendors such as Rackspace. The development and usage of OpenStack is similar to what was seen with another significant open source product from a couple of decades ago – Linux. Each OpenStack release has brought more features and with this more uptake. VMware vSphere continues to be the favoured product for private clouds by enterprises who value the robustness, security and performance of the product line that started enterprise server virtualization over a decade ago.

The good news is that the majority of cloud vendors are seeing the advantage of collaborating with other vendors to produce a standard interface. The release of VMware Integrated OpenStack (VIO) (VMware. 2015) as an OpenStack distribution by VMware for management of vSphere hypervisors is an example of the direction the industry is taking. Since OpenStack allows for plugins of different technologies, this allows for a common cloud interface to be used across multiple cloud technologies – an abstraction layer. In this way, multiple hypervisor technologies can be hosted under the same central cloud services.

There is still a way to go. For instance, you cannot easily move workload from one virtualization technology to another. However, these are possible features in the foreseeable future as the platforms continue to standardise.

One approach being taken today to the migration of workload between cloud technologies is to use software solutions to create an image of an existing physical of virtual server on the new location, then synchronise the processes so that the old and new server are exact copies running in parallel. The old version is then stopped and the new one continues where it left off.

Whichever way cloud technology heads it is going to be more standardized. There will always be a need for cloud design and builds offering new functionality to cloud consumers.

CONCLUSION

Clouds are evolving quickly as are the methods to build them. Different services and different technologies all contribute to the complexity of building a cloud. Standards are needed to make the build more consistent. Automation is critical to reduce the cost of implementing the core cloud services and when adding components to the cloud.

REFERENCES

Behrendt, M. (2014). *CCRA 4.0 Overview Deck*. Retrieved March 2015, from, https://www.ibm.com/developerworks/community/files/form/anonymous/api/library/e1e5df30-d839-4965-97bb-b3f05fbe7dee/document/56af12bb-6259-4cc6-bf6d-2776682bd232/media/CCRA%204.0%20Overview_20140918_non_conf.pdf

Blanchard, B., Corti, G., Delaware, S., Kim, H. J., Plachy, A., Quezada, M., & Santos, G. (2014). *IBM PowerVC Introduction and Configuration*. Retrieved September 2014 from, http://www.redbooks.ibm.com/redpieces/pdfs/sg248199.pdf

Iannucci, P., & Gupta, M. (2013). *IBM Smartcloud: Building a Cloud Enabled Data Centre*. Retrieved from: http://www.redbooks.ibm.com/redpapers/pdfs/redp4893.pdf

IBM. (2015). *Implementing IBM Power Virtualisation Center in Your Data Center*. Retrieved September 2014 from, http://www.redbooks.ibm.com/technotes/tips1136.pdf

Liu, F., Tong, J., Mao, J., Bonn, R., Messina, J., Badger, L., & Leaf, D. (2011). *NIST Cloud Computing Reference Architecture*. Retrieved August 2015 from http://www.nist.gov/customcf/get_pdf.cfm?pub_id=909505

OpenStack Foundation. (2014a). *OpenStack Configuration Reference, icehouse*. Retrieved December 2014, from http://docs.openstack.org/icehouse/config-reference/config-reference-icehouse.pdf

OpenStack Foundation. (2014b). *OpenStack Operations Guide*. Retrieved from: http://docs.openstack.org/ops/

OpenStack Foundation. (2014c). *OpenStack Installation Guide for Ubuntu 12.04/14.04 (LTS), icehouse.* Retrieved September 2014 from, http://docs.openstack.org/icehouse/install-guide/install/apt/openstack-install-guide-apt-icehouse.pdf

The Open Group. (2013). Cloud Performance Metrics: Performance Metrics for Evaluating Cloud Computing. Draft. Author.

VMware. (2015). *VMware Integrated OpenStack 1.0 Documentation.* Retrieved July 2015, from http://pubs.vmware.com/integrated-openstack-1/index.jsp

KEY TERMS AND DEFINITIONS

Business Support: A component of a cloud responsible for providing business services such as customer management and chargeback.

Cloud: An IT framework that provides "as a service" computing. This could be infrastructure as a service through to software as a service and anything in between.

Hybrid Cloud: A cloud that consists of multiple virtualization technologies and locations. This can include a private cloud and a public cloud. It also extends to a cloud that encompasses a platform like VMware vSphere under the same services as a KVM region.

Managed From: The area of a cloud responsible for providing the services to cloud consumers.

Managed To: The area of a cloud where a consumer's compute, network and storage resources are hosted.

Operational Support: A component of a cloud which provides the services that maintain the cloud management platform (managed from). Included are services such as monitoring, problem management, change management and backup/recovery. This may also extent to managing the "managed to" environment in the case of a managed cloud service.

Orchestration: The logic behind the cloud that provides the services. Typically broken into Brokerage or cross cloud orchestration, service orchestration (or workflow orchestration), software orchestration (which coordinates the build of software on a platform) and infrastructure orchestration (which coordinates the build of the cloud resources for compute, network and storage that provides the platform).

Virtualization: A base component of the cloud that consists of software that emulates physical infrastructure.

Virtualization Management: A component of the cloud that manages the placement, movement and allocation of the virtual resources.

Chapter 7
Virtual Machine Placement in IaaS Cloud

Prateek Khandelwal
BITS – Pilani, India

Gaurav Somani
Central University of Rajasthan, India

ABSTRACT

A crucial component of providing services over virtual machines to users is how the provider places those virtual machines on physical servers. While one strategy can offer an increased performance for the virtual machine, and hence customer satisfaction, another can offer increased savings for the cloud operator. Both have their trade-offs. Also, with increasing costs of electricity, and given the fact that the major component of the operational cost of a data center is that of powering it, green strategies also offer an attractive alternative. In this chapter, the authors will look into what kind of different placement strategies have been developed, and the kind of advantages they purport to offer.

INTRODUCTION

The advantages that cloud computing has to offer must be quite evident at this stage. The computational flexibility that a cloud user can get becomes an enabling factor to provide a better return on investment. However, for the cloud provider the same computational flexibility becomes an engineering challenge that needs to be addressed to.

It is important, from the point of view of a cloud operator, to make an optimum use of the infrastructure so as to maximize one's revenue. On a very abstract level, intuitively one knows that the only way to maximize revenues, or, make profit to keep the expenditures as much low as possible when compared to the income.

In the context of cloud computing, how one places a virtual machine on a physical machine is a very critical question, as all the costs that are associated with a cloud infrastructure are affected by it. How does one achieve this s what are the costs involved ? and how to optimize the placement, and this minimize these costs are some of the questions that we'll be answering in this chapter.

DOI: 10.4018/978-1-5225-0759-8.ch007

FORMAL DESCRIPTION OF VM PLACEMENT PROBLEM

On a theoretical level, the problem of Virtual Machine placement can be modeled as the problem of packing balls into bins, where the instead of single scalar weight and capacity associated with the bins and balls respectively, one has to deal with a vector, where each component can me mapped to multiple resources.

Formally, given that we have different resources,,, ..., in our system, one can represent each *physical machine* (PM), with in the vector notations as,

where each of, represent the individual capacity a physical node has for each the resources.

Similarly, a *virtual machine* (VM) can be represented as

where each of, represent the individual resource requirement of the virtual machine.

Considering the problem of placing VMs such that the total number of PMs is minimized can be thus modeled as a multi-dimensional bin packing problem, which can be proved as NP-Complete, since if the problem for dimensions is tractable, then the simple bin packing problem can be solved by assigning the value of to components, and the respective weights and capacity to the single dimension.

The assignment of virtual machines to physical machines is called placement, and the mapping that represents it is called a VM Placement Schedule.

Since the problem is *NP-Complete*, *heuristics* and *approximation algorithms* are used to produce sub-optimal and near optimal placement schedules according to different components of the vector and the objectives that the algorithm is trying to optimize on.

We'll discuss the different costs involved next.

COSTS IN A CLOUD

Setting up a data center is a capital intensive undertaking, as there are a lot costs involved including the cost of procuring the infrastructure, both technological and real-estate, and the costs associated with running a data center, which include the costs for electricity for cooling purposes and powering the servers and network components, and the costs for human resource required to ensure an efficient running of the systems.

Also, since a cloud provider is offering the cloud service commercially, there is also an angle of performance guarantees (called *SLA*, or, *Service Level Agreement*), and the associated penalties, involved.

From the perspective of VM Placement algorithms, we would like to take into account some of these costs to as to make placement decisions that are frugal on one or more of these costs. Any Virtual Machine placement strategy tries to optimize either one or more of these costs. The costs that one chooses to save on varies from case to case, as we shall see in the following sections. A general structure of data center is provided in Figure 1

These costs can be divided into the following broad categories:

- **Power Costs:** Power cost is the cost that is associated with electricity to run a particular physical server. A sizable chunk of the running costs related to operating a data center comprises this, therefore, any optimization here can have a huge impact on overall costs.

Figure 1. General structure of a data center

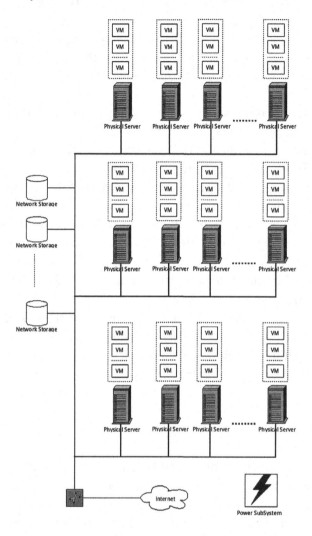

- Cooling Costs: Cooling cost is the cost involved with cooling the data center. As data centers are generally huge and expansive, the heat generated by them is also considerable, and therefore, optimum management of heat becomes highly crucial to the functioning of machines itself.
- **Network Costs:** Network Cost is the cost associated with providing the networking infrastructure for the data center. Lately, the trends have started showing an increase in the share of costs related to network in the overall operational costs. If the virtual machines hosted on the data center have a considerable amount of inter VM communication, the architecture of the underlying network and the placement of virtual machines can significantly effect the performance of virtual machines, and hence, effect the *performance costs* (discussed next).
- **Performance Costs:** Performance Cost is the cost associated with placing a virtual machine at a location where its performance may suffer. If this decrease in performance violates *SLA*, this then translates into the penalty that the service provider may have to pay to the consumer of its service.

Performance may suffer because of the virtual machines it is co-located with, and/or, because of the communication it does with other virtual machines.

It is important to note that since cloud basically stands on the ability of virtual machines to share common physical hardware using virtualization, a bad/non-optimal placement of a VM can not only lead to a deteriorated performance for that particular VM, but also the VMs that are co-located with it, and thus, it becomes even more important to place the VMs in an optimal fashion.

VM PLACEMENT: WHEN, HOW, AND WHAT

Dynamic Placement of VMs can enable a cloud service provider to efficiently deliver on the promise of elasticity they make to the user. However, the way in which this tool of dynamic placement is used is also a critical question, and just like any other tool, dynamic placement all by itself cannot give performance benefits. The questions that one must address are that of *when*, i.e., How frequently and in what conditions dynamic placement should be used, *How*, i.e., what all factors should be considered while making a decision to dynamically place a virtual machine, and *what*, i.e., what kind of schedule is to be generated, and how exactly is it supposed to be executed so that the overall process of dynamic placement is efficient too.

We'll take a look at these three questions first and how they play a role in efficient data center performance.

When to Go for Dynamic Placement

This question asks when should the dynamic placement process should be called, should a cloud provider wait for Utilization to increase beyond a threshold, or observe explicit performance drop and then call the placement module, i.e., a *reactive* strategy, or predict an approaching spike and take the decision, i.e., a *proactive* strategy. In fact, a single strategy might not suffice at all, as Gmach et al. (2009) show.

How to Gather the Required Data

How is one going to gather performance metrics related to the physical and virtual machines ? What kind and level of access to the internal status of virtual machine is available to the cloud operator? It is important to address these questions before choosing a particular placement strategy. Certain situations might allow for an access to the internal usage statistics of a VM, i.e., a *GrayBox* strategy might be viable, while it might not be possible to make such inferences in other settings, calling for a *BlackBox* approach Wood et al. (2009).

What data has to be captured and how frequently it is to be captured is an important engineering decision too, as a wrong choice might increase the overhead of the Placement Manger or decrease its effectiveness completely.

What Is to Be Optimized

Once we have collected the data about the resource usage, a placement manager needs to decide what is the metric it is going to optimize, what kind of heuristics exist for such problem formulations, and is the approach scalable for a large problem instances? This point will be addressed in the coming section with more details. Gmach et al. (2009) investigate the efficiency of the combinations of Migration Controller and Workload Placement Controller in different operational modes to identify the optimum combination and whether it should be reactive or proactive.

CLASSIFICATION OF PLACEMENT STRATEGIES

Different VM placement strategies try to save on different costs, or even combination of them, and thus we can have a broad classification of what are the different classes of such strategies based on the costs they try to save. These classes are:

Performance Oriented Strategies

The focus of these types of strategies is to maximize the performance of the virtual machine. Typical use case scenarios include High Performance Computing workloads, where HPC applications, which traditionally run on dedicated physical clusters, are ported to cloud, with virtual clusters. In such scenarios, delivering high performance on a workload which is utilizes CPU resources quite lavishly, and might or might not come with deadline sensitivities becomes a challenge to address.

Another kind of objective that one can have here is to guarantee high availability of the services, that is, a cloud user might want to build a fault tolerant service leveraging the cloud infrastructure. Such kind of use cases entails maintaining, that is guaranteeing relocation of a VM to a working host in event of its current host's failure, when addition hosts have also failed. These objectives become important when one is trying to build a robust service on top of cloud, and if specified in the *SLA*, becomes a factor cloud operator cannot overlook.

Power Aware Strategies

Power costs are a major component to the operational expenditure of a data center, and the biggest two fractions of this expenditure goes to operating the servers themselves and towards running the cooling system to ensure efficient functioning of the virtual machines.

With the increasing costs of electricity, and the rising awareness about the effects of greenhouse gases, cloud operators use such strategies to both bring down the costs of operations and to reduce the carbon footprint of the data center. These strategies rely on power management functionality that the new servers provide like *DVFS*, and *idle states* where one can reduce the power consumption of a physical server dynamically (of course, this might affect the performance too). Experimental results show that such strategies can lead to significant savings for the cloud operators, while a marginally reduced performance for the cloud user.

Network Aware Strategies

Generally, the cloud users prefer cloud services for their ability to scale *on-demand*, which ultimately enables a service running on cloud to cater to the increase or decrease in the demand of the service. Generally, such services are comprised of virtual machines that communicate among each other too. Also, one might deploy a static virtual machine set of which perform some task that involves heavy inter VM communication. In such scenarios, a placement strategy that is oblivious to such situation can place the different virtual machines quite far (*topologically*) away, which would then lead to a degraded performance, and also, an increased traffic on the network infrastructure of the data center. Since the network infrastructure is a shared resource too, this can in turn effect performance of other VMs.

Network aware strategies try to minimize the distance between the communicating virtual machines by placing them close to each other, which increases the performance of the VMs.

Co-Location Aware Strategies

Virtual machines, unlike physical systems, might share the same hardware, that is, two VMs can be located on the same PM (termed *co-location*), where they share the same CPU, or other network & I/O interfaces. Since these resources are shared, one VMs extensive use of a particular resource can have an effect on the other system's performance too, in case of CPU this can arise from a shared cache, while in case of network from the point of a shared network interface card and so on. This competition among VMs for the shared resource is called *resource contention*.

A placement strategy which aims at exploiting these co-location behavior tries to place a mix of virtual machines which do not extensively use the same type of resources together, which in turn increase the performance of the entire set.

Federation and Hybrid Cloud Oriented Strategies

With the expansion of the public cloud market, and the availability of solution to create private cloud, often one can get better performance and return on investment if one adopts a hybrid approach, i.e., using a mix of both public and private cloud services.

These strategies try to exploit the price differential that exists between different cloud providers to schedule the VMs in such a way that the overall cost of running the services is minimized. There is one difference though, while the other strategy classes we've discussed so far are used by the cloud providers, this strategy however, is used by the cloud service consumer who is using a mix of public and private cloud.

Again, one can go for a combination of these strategies too, as long as one can maintain a *viable* trade-off. For example, one might use a mix of power aware and performance oriented strategies, wherein one's primary objective remains to deliver the guaranteed performance, however, if there is room for power saving, one can optimize that as a secondary objective too.

We'll discuss each of these strategies in detail next, along with the researches that introduced them.

Power Aware Placement Strategies

As discussed above, the objective of the strategies of this class is to minimize the data center costs associated with powering and cooling the data center.

A direct method to achieve power efficiency in a data center is to minimize the number of physical servers required to host the VMs, and by switching off (or switching to idle states) the servers which are unused. Further savings can be made by effectively using Dynamic Voltage & Frequency Scaling functionality, *DVFS* with the supported servers.

The direct applicability of the bin packing model becomes quite apparent here, where the physical servers can be modeled as bins and the VMs can be modeled as balls. Since this problem itself is *NP-Complete*, we'll see what kind of heuristics and metric are used to create *near-optimal placement schedules*.

The naive approach to avoid *SLA* violations is to provision services on the basis of the peak demand. This however, might not be the most economically optimum provisioning, as it may lead to wasted, or, unused resources, as generally in many of the business applications, the peak demands are transient and for most of the time the servers experience only a small fraction of load as compared to the peak demand.

Virtualization technology allows the cloud manager to move virtual machines from one physical server to another on the go, with only a marginal affect on their performance. This is done using a technique called, where in a virtual machine is migrated *live* without stopping it to a different physical server with only a momentary stoppage in service (100ms). *Live Migration* and dynamic placement can in turn be employed to achieve and this called.

In Bobroff, Kochut, and Beaty (2007), the authors try to exploit of dynamic placement to perform dynamic consolidation while maintaining SLA fulfillment which is offered on a statistical guarantee. The resource usage patterns are analyzed to first understand to what extent an energy-cost gain is possible, as different workload may exhibit different kind of variation in the resource usage and only some of them might be viable for dynamic consolidation. This is captured using a formula which approximates the level of gain that is possible is one uses dynamic consolidation over that workload, and also if the utilization level of that VM is predictable or not. A demand forecasting module is then built which predicts the workload on the basis of observed past workloads in a confined time window. The proposed algorithm runs a loop, which then repetitively measures the current resource utilization (only *CPU Utilization* in this case), forecasts the expected utilization values and performs dynamic consolidation.

pMapper Verma, Ahuja, and Neogi (2008a) , which is a power aware application placement framework, is another such work that tries to save on energy usage. Along with the energy usage, it factors in the migration costs too. The placement middleware is composed *Arbitrator, Performance Manager, Power Manager* and *Migration Manager* modules, which then generates a placement schedule. Here, *Performance Manager* handles the actions of VM-re-sizing and idling, *Power Manager* handles power management at the hardware level and *Migration Manager* deals with consolidation related activities. The *Arbitrator* module searches for the best possible placement and VM sizes based on the estimates received from the three above mentioned modules. All the three *Performance, Migration & Power Manager* modules rely on a separate module, *Knowledge Base*, to determine and estimate their respective metrics like performance, power and migration costs based on the different possible configurations. The framework uses a number of constraints that represent various trade-offs that one has to work with, namely, *Cost Performance Trade-off, Cost Minimization with performance trade-off* and *Performance Benefit Maximization with Power Constraints*.

The placement strategies exploits these properties and constructs variants of *First Fit Decreasing* heuristic, *mPPH & PMaP* to produce a near-optimal placement schedule. It is important to note that this approach can factor in the heterogeneity using different power models too.

Verma, Ahuja, and Neogi (2008b) addresses the issue of scheduling HPC applications in a Power Aware scenario. HPC workload traces are first analyzed for the feasibility of consolidation, as without sufficient variability in the workload, consolidation might not give the desired benefits. Another aspect of HPC workload that cannot be ignored is the interference with the co-located virtual machines. The authors investigate the impact on performance depending on the workload mix a physical server hosts and conclude that placing applications with small memory footprint together with each other, and placing applications with large memory foot print together can lead to an acceptable degree of isolation, however, mixing applications with large and small memory footprint might lead to adverse effect for the VM with small footprint. Using this knowledge, the *pMapper* frame work is modified to take placement decisions with factoring in working set information too.

In *GreenCloud* Liu et al. (2009), the problem of finding an energy efficient placement is constructed such that it minimizes the cost associated with the physical machine, i.e., the energy cost and cost incurred during the live migration to take the placement decision. The heuristic itself is presented as a search algorithm where it searches for an optimal placement in placement space, while ruling out unfeasible placements and their neighbors to search efficiently.

In situations where a cloud provider has multiple data centers, which are spread across various geographical locations, one can exploit the heterogeneity this situation offers to save on energy costs Garg et al. (2009). The energy consumption, energy cost and profit is formalized as a function of *required resources, deadlines, CPU's operating frequency, CPU boundness, etc.*, which is then used in the *meta-scheduler* to produce a placement which minimized emissions while maximizing the revenues. The meta-scheduler assigns application to different cloud sites, where again they are scheduled over individual servers with the objective of either maximization of profit or minimize carbon emissions. Moreover, each cloud site uses a DVS based scheduler to gain further power savings. Greedy Strategies are employed for making the placement decisions taking into account the carbon emission v/s profit trade-off. .

Generally the approach towards solving such problem is to use variants of First Fit Decreasing approximation, as the application of constraint programming can be very expensive, however, Entropy Hermenier et al. (2009), shows that with factoring in the migration costs involved the constraint based approach efficiently solves the problem of dynamic consolidation while minimizing the migration time in the cluster too.

A multi-objective approach is presented in Beloglazov and Buyya (2010), where continuous dynamic consolidation is employed while factoring in the system resources like *CPU, RAM* and *Network I/O*, the *Inter-VM Network Communication* and the *Thermal State* of the physical servers. The data center is assumed to be made of up heterogeneous physical nodes, each having a local manager module in the virtual machine monitor to observe the utilization levels and the thermal states. Local managers are complemented by global managers that take as input from each of local managers the utilization levels and the VMs that have been identified for migration. The global manager module then applies distributed semi-online bin-packing heuristic to generate the placement and allocation schedule, which is then executed using live migrations and/or VM resizing as per the requirement. The physical nodes that are idle are switched off to save power. This approach has an advantage of being free of *Single Point of Failure (SPOF)*, since it is a distributed algorithm. The advantage of having a heterogeneous set of physical nodes is that one has access to different price-performance trade-offs and hence can assist in an efficient placement decision.

Younge et al. (2010) proposes energy aware scheduling policies along with efficient virtual machine images that provide a better performance by optimizing over the unnecessary components of the virtual image, while on the scheduling front, the approach tries to pack as many VMs on a physical host as possible, which then translates into power savings on the scale of entire data center.

In threshold based approaches, where the placement module is called if certain resource utilization level exceeds a threshold, one limitation that arises is that one cannot assume a constant threshold level if the workload is unpredictable, also, one cannot use the same threshold levels across different applications. This issue can be tackled using an approach where the threshold levels are adaptive Beloglazov and Buyya (2011). In the proposed approach the dynamic consolidation is triggered with the objective of minimizing energy consumption. The power model that this approach consider suggests that the energy consumed by a server is a function of its CPU utilization, and thus the objective becomes to improve on CPU utilization. The approach describes each VM's CPU utilization as a random variable with a persistent distribution in a given window of time, and for the host, the corresponding utilization can be represented as a sum of the utilization distribution of the virtual machine it hosts. One can calculate the sample mean and the standard deviation over the current time window. The inverse cumulative probability function then calculated can be used to create the threshold levels, both upper and lower. For the placement decisions, the approach uses a bin-packing heuristic, *Best-Fit-Decreasing* algorithm to generate near-optimal approximations with relatively simple complexity. Since the threshold levels here adapt dynamically, the approach is able to save on a SLA violations while delivering good energy savings, and further savings are possible if one chooses to relax the SLA guarantees.

The go-to solution for energy efficiency in a data center is to consolidate the servers. M. Chen et al. (2011) formulates the problem of efficient virtual machine consolidation as a *stochastic bin packing* problem where the objective is to place the virtual machines on as few physical servers as possible while ensuring that the probability that the aggregated load of the virtual machines on a server exceeds the capacity is bounded by, which is a given parameter. The approach builds on the concept of *effective sizing*, where each virtual machine's demand for resource is represented as a random variable. Estimation of the physical server's load can be done in two parts, it first calculates the *intrinsic demand* which is a function of a VMs own demand and the server's capacity, and the *correlation aware demand* which captures the effect of VMs demand in presence of the *co-located* virtual machines.

Although Dynamic voltage and Frequency scaling (DVFS) capabilities enables a server to save energy, it also impacts the performance of the applications running on that server. Similarly, *Dynamic Server Consolidation* can also lead to a drop in performance due to resource contention. Predicting the drop in the system performance can act as a crucial input while going for power scaling and VM capacity resizing. S. Chen et al. (2011) proposes an alternative measurement based approach that relies on the metric of *CPU Gradients* to predict the drop in system performance with variation in power savings. The metric of CPU Gradient consists of two other gradient metrics, namely, *frequency gradient*, which represents the rate of change of performance with respect to the change in CPU frequency, and the *capacity gradient*, which is the rate of change of application's performance with respect to the change in the fraction of allotted CPU capacity. The CPU gradient can be then used to build a performance-aware energy controller such that the energy consumption is reduced while maintaining the application's performance.

One striking feature of most of the optimization algorithms we've seen till now is that they are *centralized algorithms* running on a central node. *Centralized Algorithms* have a serious limitation when it comes to using them for large scale and distributed systems. A failure of the central node lead to stoppage of the entire system. This problem is called *Single Point of Failure (SPOF)*. An *Ant Colony Optimization* approach is presented in Feller, Rilling, and Morin (2011) where the problem of dynamic consolidation is formulated as a multi-dimensional bin packing problem solved using *ACO* in a fully distributed environments to produce near-optimal solutions. The *ACO* approach relies on creation of *artificial ants* (a *multi-agent* system), which then starts to search for the optimal solutions using indirect low-level communications. Initially, each ant receives the set of all VMs, each opens a single bin and tries to pack it. In doing so, it picks an item using a probabilistic decision rule, which is based on the *pheromone* concentration on the particular *item-bin* pair and heuristic information associated with that *item-bin* pair, which favors those items more which uses a bin better, i.e., leaves the maximum residual capacity on the bin. The autonomous nature of the algorithm eliminates the Single Point of Failure completely and ensures scalability too.

A cloud user might want to host a real time application using the cloud infrastructure. Provisioning such applications such that the power efficiency of the cloud is maintained is another problem with practical implications. Kim, Beloglazov, and Buyya (2011) present an approach for the same, where they model the real time application service to a service model that can be hosted using virtual machines and then use a provisioning scheme which utilizes DVFS scaling to optimize power consumption. Both Hard Real time and Soft Real time virtual machine models have been proposed, and the *Real-Time* virtual machine request can ask for either a Hard Real time VM or a Soft Real Time VM. These Real Time virtual machines are them mapped to physical servers by taking power aware provisioning decisions.

Reduction in power costs in a data center adds to the objective of profit maximization. In Shi, W., and Hong, B. (2011) a profit maximization approach has been proposed which uses a *linear power model* to estimate the cost for powering a server in relation to the VM load level. This optimization problem is then solved using a *First-Fit* heuristic based algorithm.

Beloglazov, Abawajy, and Buyya (2012) proposes heuristic for energy aware resource allocation with the objective of increasing the energy-efficiency. Here too, the power model has been assumed to be a linear function of the CPU utilization on the server, and the energy consumption for a particular server can be calculated by integrating this function with the respective time boundaries. In addition to the power consumed by the servers, this approach also proposes a policy which saves on migration costs by minimizing the number of migrations required.

Adaptive heuristics have been proposed by Beloglazov and Buyya (2012), which enables an optimized online placement of virtual machines. For both Single VM migration and dynamic VM consolidation problems, competitive analysis and proof for the competitive ratios for the optimal online deterministic algorithms have been provided. A novel adaptive heuristic has been introduced which perform well in dynamic and unpredictable environment. The proposed adaptive utilization threshold adjusts the upper utilization threshold level on the basis of the *median absolute deviation* over CPU utilization levels, a second adaptive threshold for the utilization bound has also been proposed which is based on the *interquartile range* of CPU utilization values. A local regression based algorithm has been employed for the prediction of future values on the basis of historical data. The placement is then performed using a modified version of *Best-Fit-Decreasing* algorithm, the *Power Aware Best Fit Decreasing Algorithm*, which places the overloaded virtual machines efficiently on the physical servers. The advantage that adaptive heuristics offer is that they can recognize the changes in the workload and enable the reduction in SLA violation and in the number of virtual machine migrations.

Besides the approaches mentioned above, there are many other approaches existing in literature too, we'll briefly mention a few of them. Yang et al. (2011) presents *Green Power Management* which enables green load balancing on cloud infrastructures, and can be integrated with OpenNebula. Dupont et al. (2012) presents an approach for energy-aware resource allocation using constraint programming technique. The power model for the data center is represented as an aggregate of power consumption of individual servers, while also accounting for the changes in the power consumption of individual server in case of VM *movements*. Feller et al. (2012) presents an energy aware VM management framework which takes a holistic approach with providing monitoring, estimation, detection, consolidation and power management, towards achieve efficient energy management. The architecture defines a hierarchical structure composed of three layer, the client layer, Hierarchical layer and the physical layer. Multi objective ant-colony based algorithm has been used in Gao et al. (2013) to obtain a set of *non-dominated* solutions which can be used for minimizing resource wastage and energy consumption simultaneously. Katsaros et al. (2013) presents a framework for assessing the energy efficiency of the cloud entities. A model has been presented that enables forecasting of future values of energy efficiency based on the entity's behavior. The forecasting is based on a linear regression model. A placement algorithm has been presented which employs the energy model for energy efficient placement. A framework for energy modeling in cloud context is also presented by Castañé et al. (2013). The proposed model considers the energy consumed by memory devices by considering the individual *state-wise* consumption in the pre-charge activate state, the *read state*, the *write state* and the *refresh state*. In addition to the energy consumed by the CPU and memory, the energy consumed by the disk drives and the NICs and the power supply units have been factored in too.

PERFORMANCE CENTERED PLACEMENT STRATEGIES

Placement strategies that are centered towards delivering high performance try to create a placement schedule which maximizes the performance for the virtual machines. It is important to keep in mind that virtualization is a technology which leverages sharing of hardware resources, and thus, the neighbors of a virtual machine can have an effect on performance too. An intelligent management of such situation can have a favorable impact on performance, while ignoring it can lead to adverse effect.

The naive approach to ensure high performance of a virtual machine is to provision according to its peak resource requirements. This, as mentioned before, leads to significant resource wastage. Therefore, identifying an optimal allocation such that the quality of service doesn't suffer, while ensuring that the capacity of the physical server is efficiently utilized becomes an important subject. Gmach et al. (2009) presents a case study where they discuss the trade-offs between the required capacity for a service v/s the power usage, resource access quality of service v/s memory resources and the number of migrations. They present a set of 10 *Pareto-optimal* combinations of lower and upper CPU and memory thresholds, which can be used by the data center operator according to the *capacity v/s quality* trade-off one is willing to opt.

A *utility* based approach is considered in Van, Tran, and Menaud (2009), where each application's state is mapped to a scalar value reflecting the level of satisfaction with respect to its performance goal. The approach tries allocate virtual machines such that the *Global Utility* is maximized. With the *utility function*, the level of application satisfaction with respect to its SLA can be captured, and although it is a high level abstraction, it can act as a valuable input for the efficient allocation. While in *VM Provision-*

ing stage, VM allocation vectors are generated for applications such that the global utility is maximized, the packing and migration is handled in the *VM Packing stage*. Here the VM allocation vectors for each application are used to generate a placement schedule that minimizes the total number of physical machines used. Both of the stages are expressed as *constraint satisfaction problems*, and iteratively search for optimal solutions, however, certain time bounds can be applied for acceptable, but quick solutions.

Sandpiper Wood et al. (2009) framework aims at mitigating hotspots in a data center effectively. The framework focuses on CPU and memory hotspots, however, the approach can be extended to accommodate other resources too. The resource utilization is captured using either a *GrayBox* or *BlackBox* approach. Also, a prediction module can predict future levels which can be taken as an input while making the placement decisions. The metric that *Sandpiper* uses is the *Volume-Size Ratio (VSR)*, where the *Volume* is a scalar value that captures the load on a physical and individual virtual machine, the size is the amount of memory reserved by the virtual machine. The hotspots are then mitigated by moving the virtual machines with the highest load from the overloaded servers to lightly loaded physical machines. The new provisioning is done using the predicted load values. The provisioning is accomplished using a variant of *First Fit Decreasing* Heuristic. The mitigation process first goes for a migration approach to bring the utilization levels below an acceptable threshold, and still if there are certain unmitigated hotspots remaining, swapping is used to swap a set of *low Volume* VMs with the *high volume* VM. As far as the approach to capture statistics is concerned, *Sandpiper* shows that *GrayBox* approach can enable one to take *proactive* actions, hence delivering better performance as compared to the *reactive* mitigation triggered under a *BlackBox* approach. The observations made in *Sandpiper* can be used in other approaches which account for other resource utilization and/or employ different heuristics.

Andreolini et al. (2010) adopts a *sans* utilization-threshold based approach by considering the trend of usage rather than instantaneous observations. The physical hosts are divided into *sender*, *receiver* and *neutral* sets. Here the selection of the sender hosts is done using a *Cumulative Sum (CUSUM)* algorithm, which takes into consideration both the *intensity* of the load a physical machine experiences, and the *extent* to which it persists. This is followed by the selection of the guests from the selected hosts to be migrated on the basis of their *behavioral trend*. From each of the identified sender host, the virtual machines exhibiting the highest load are selected for migration.

Resource usage patterns are also used in Gong and Gu (2010), where the application's resource (*CPU*, *memory & I/O*) usage *signatures* are used along with the utilization signatures from the hosts over a *sliding window* of time to obtain an efficient consolidation scheme. For the physical machines, the approach calculates *residual signatures*, which give a better picture of the available resources on a physical machine and minimizes the negative sharing impact among the co-located virtual machines. The approach uses *Fast Fourier Transform* to extract repeating patterns in the demand series, along with *Dynamic Time Wrapping* algorithm to account for the possible shift in time (As the system doesn't employ a globally synchronized clock). It also employs *multidimensional time series indexing scheme* to filter out the dissimilar signatures and use DTW based matching on the signatures that may be a potential match. The time series is split into multiple segments, over which bounding envelopes are crated, which is followed by a pre-filtering process and then the DTW to find the best match. A threshold can be used to select a matching, and to select the virtual machines that qualify for the approach. In case a significant pattern is not observed the algorithm can fallback to traditional placement logic. Also, one can use predictive techniques here to predict future demand signatures, going for latest usage data extraction only if there are too many mispredictions. The approach provides for a global VM allocation process which is employs a *greedy* heuristic running periodically, along with an *on-demand* VM relocation process that can be called if hotspots are detected.

In scenarios where multiple virtual machines are co-located, as is generally the case in cloud, one cannot rely on CPU utilization of the virtual machines to estimate the actual demand if they are not using the same physical resources Isci et al. (2010). The actual demand can be captured on the basis of the time a virtual machine waits for the CPU v/s the time it actually spends on the CPU. This can be expressed as a ratio of *fruitful time* over CPU v/s the *total time* it spent on the CPU and while waiting for it. Any virtual machine can be assumed to be in one of the three states at any instance, namely, *used* - when the VM is executing on the CPU, *waiting* - when the VM is waiting for a resource and *ready* - when the VM is waiting to be executed on the CPU. In case there's no *resource contention*, the time a VM spends while waiting for a CPU, that is, in the *ready* state, can be safely assumed to be zero, and thus, the *CPU Demand* can be estimated using the simple ratio mentioned above. However, in situations where resource contention is present, which is more likely to happen in real use case scenarios, one has to factor in the *ready time* too to get a better estimate of real demand. This estimate can then be used to take placement decisions.

A user of cloud service might want to create a fault tolerant system. One way to achieve fault tolerance would be to have redundant virtual machines running in the cloud, where one VM can take over if the other fails. In such scenarios, a placement approach that is oblivious to such requirement might place the virtual machines in a non-optimal way, or, in the worst case, might render the system highly susceptible to hardware or power failure, where one such fault might bring down the entire service, completely defeating the purpose of the user.

Machida, Masahiro Kawato, and Maeno (2010) proposes a placement scheme which can provide fault tolerant configuration of consolidated virtual machines. The objective is to achieve a *k-redundancy* level, where even in case of host failures, a minimum configuration virtual machine should still be available to serve the requests. This involves estimation of the required number of virtual machines with respect to the performance goals, and then to place them over hosts while meeting the *k-redundancy* criteria. Assuming that the application exists in the its desired redundant configuration, the problem boils down to efficient, fault tolerant placement of these images. The problem is formulated as a combinatorial optimization problem, assuming a homogeneous data center, and homogeneous application requirements. The approach first identifies the minimum number of physical servers required according to the factors like *number of application classes, maximum number of virtual machine a physical server can host*, the *desired redundancy level* and the *average response time required* (a quality metric). This has to be decided while also considering the lower bound over the number of hosts, which is imposed by the performance requirements, which dictate the minimum number of virtual machines required per application. The Virtual Machine Placement module then takes the calculated minimum hosts and minimum guests per application to generate a placement schedule while ensuring redundancy. The heuristic aims at distributing the same application instances to different hosting server, hence ensuring that the virtual machines instances running the same application do not reside on the same physical server. Evaluation against naive *FFD* heuristics make a strong case for customized placement strategies when the goal is High Availability, as the naive heuristics are not *Fault-tolerance aware*.

Jayasinghe, Pu, and Eilam (2011) formulate the placement problem to provide a schedule which improves *availability* and *performance* of a cloud service. The problem is formulated as a *constraint satisfaction problem* which factors in three constraints, namely, the *Demand* constraint which is a lower bound on the resources that a virtual machine requires to meet the SLA, the *Availability* Constraint, which is expressed as the collocations constraints (so that the application doesn't experience resource contention), and the *Communication* constraints, which represents the significance of communication between two virtual machines, which basically expresses the quality of network connection required. The placement plan is generated using two sub-planners in a divide and conquer based algorithm, where first the VM groups are created such that the *intra-group* communication is maximized along with the minimized *inter-group* communication. This is followed by assigning the each group on suitable servers racks such that the total communication cost is minimized while respecting the satisfaction of *anti-collocation constraints*, and then this is further refined by assigning VMs to the individual physical servers. This approach reduces the communication costs by dividing the VMs into groups with heavy intra-group communication and also ensure that the performance of the virtual machine doesn't suffer by using the anti-collocation constraints.

In private cloud environments, delivering a maintained performance requires efficient *load balancing*. Ni et al. (2011) proposes a *multi-resource load balancing* policy with *self-adaptive weights*, which is used with a probabilistic selection of target physical node for mapping while also avoiding the problem of *load crowding* that might occur in case of many concurrent users.

One of the main attraction that a cloud user has towards a public cloud is the feature of *on-demand* resources, where the user can dynamically *scale up* and *scale down* the resources its service uses, and thus, pay only for what it consumes. Providing on-demand resources is not that difficult for large scale cloud providers, where due to the scale and heterogeneity of the kind of services deployed, one can easily find the desired resource bracket. However, for small and medium scale cloud service providers, addressing this issue is quite difficult. Keeping this in view an advanced reservation based allocation policy is presented in Lu et al. (2011) based on the QoS specified by the SLA, which allows increased utilization of resources while also meeting customer demands. It should be noted that this approach basically is taken during the SLA negotiation phase, hence acts as an aid for the cloud provider to better utilize its resources, along with the counter offer where a potential un-availability can be flagged in advance and appropriate alternatives can be adopted.

Bin et al. (2011) suggests another approach towards ensuring high availability goals of virtual machines. They define a virtual machine to be *k-resilient* if it is required that the virtual machine should be relocated to a healthy host as long as there are no more than k host node failures. The proposed approach transforms the placement problem to one which involves *shadow virtual machines* and the generated solution can be then used for placement in the original problem space. The idea is to create and place at least shadow virtual machines per *original* virtual machine, while ensuring that they do not share the same physical host. Shadow virtual machines basically ensures that in case of a re-allocation, the constraints for migrating the virtual machine will not be violated (since shadow VMs act as placeholders for the original VMs) An advantage that shadow virtual machines offer is that multiple shadows can overlap, hence reducing the physical space that the schedule might have consumed. The constraint satisfaction problem then generates the placement schedule on the basis of the resource requirements of the virtual machines, the available resource capacities, the *anti-location* and *anti-co-location* constraints.

There is always a trade-off involved between the profit of a cloud service provider v/s the quality of service one can provide, in this context J. Chen et al. (2011) proposes a new utility based models to measure the customer's satisfaction, which can be then used for creating *utility-based SLAs*. Utility is modeled as linear function of *service response time* and the *service price*, where the slopes associated with both of these variables are negative, that is, if either of response time or service price increases, the utility drops. This model is used to capture the customer satisfaction level in a metric, which, along with the metric representing the profit of the cloud provider, is used inputs to the proposed scheduling algorithms, one which aims to maximize the profit while maintaining customer satisfaction (the *First-Fit-Profit* algorithm), and the other which aims to maximize customer satisfaction while maintaining a bound on the service profit (the *FirstFit-Satisfaction* algorithm). The customer satisfaction and the profit of the provider have negative correlation, hence, flexible satisfaction levels in scenarios where the workload or the prices of the VM instances are heavy might allow the cloud provider to optimize the profit dynamically.

A few of the other approaches are discussed as follows. A *Rule Based Mapping* is proposed by Kleineweber et al. (2011), which can have dynamic mappings to adapt the mappings between virtual machines and physical machines, where the mapping can be taken as a weighted combination of different target function. Also, the approach allows for *run-time* changes in the weights and the functions too, which allows the system to dynamically adapt. Marshall, Keahey, and Freeman (2011) proposes a technique where a shared infrastructure between among HTC application users and IaaS cloud providers allows for an opportunistic provisioning of CPU cycles from idle nodes for other processes, hence enabling better utilization of the resources. Mihailescu, Rodriguez, and Amza (2011) attempts at increasing robustness of the application in an IaaS cloud environment using availability and network communication optimization. The application-level availability constraints are specified by the tenants, which are enforced using an *online topology graphs* which is partitioned according to the application availability constraints and the communication patterns. The system can capture the *inter-VM* communication during run-time, which allows it to provide a dynamic optimization, rather than just a static allocation. The *operating cost v/s performance trade-off* is again analyzed in Minarolli and Freisleben (2011), where a *two-tier resource manager* has been proposed that uses *local node utility* function which is the aggregate of the individual utilities of the VMs hosted on that system, and a *global system utility* function which is the sum of all the local node utilities. This two tier approach can allow for a better control over the cost-performance trade-off by varying the individual VM utilities and the costs associated with the nodes. Probabilistic approach to ameliorate load in case of load crowding due to concurrent users has been discussed in Ni et al. (2011) too. This approach considers multiple resources for making the placement decision rather than considering only a single resource. Here, the initial placement of virtual machines is done such that the placement is robust against load crowding, and VM live migration then enables handling of dynamic conditions. In certain scenarios, placement of virtual machines can be tailored specifically to support a particular distributed application. *Purlieus* Palanisamy et al. (2011) is a resource allocation system geared towards improving the performance of MapReduce jobs. The approach exploits data locality in a coupled data and VM placement scheme. The placement approach factors in MapReduce Job characteristics along with the load on physical systems to generate a placement schedule which achieves high data locality. A cloud provider can increase its revenue by leasing out its resources on basis of market driven prices, and for that it can run an auction-based market for the VM instance types. Qi Zhang, Quanyan Zhu, and Boutaba (2011) addresses this problem for a single cloud provider scenario where the is to price and allocate these *Spot Instances* in such a way that the revenues are maximized, while the energy cost is minimized. Tsakalozos, Roussopoulos, and Delis (2011) considers a scenario where the cloud site consists of non-homogeneous hardware infrastructure. Since the hardware is different, one cannot use generalized power, performance models across the site. To address these scenarios, the authors propose a two-phase placement scheme, where in first phase, a *cohort* of physical machines is selected, and in the second phase the low-level constraints are considered to map the virtual machines to the physical servers. A parallel genetic based approach has been proposed by Zhongni Zheng et al. (2011) where the objective is utilize the resource as much as possible. The problem is formulated as an *Unbalance Assignment Problem*, and offers better performance as compared to greedy algorithms. Breitgand, Dubitzky, and Epstein (2012) proposes an approach where the *probability of SLA violation* with respect to the level of *over commitment* can be made explicitly known, and a novel method for planning cloud capacity with significant increase in over-commit ratio while still maintaining SLA satisfaction. The approach defines *nominal demand*, *effective nominal demand*, and then uses as estimator to generate the effective nominal demand from the momentary nominal demand values. The current nominal demand is been treated as the future demand too. A *Backward Speculative Placement* approach has been proposed by Calcavecchia et al. (2012) which optimizes virtual machine placement under a continuous stream of deploy requests. The placement approach projects the past demand trend of a VM, captured from the historical traces, to a candidate target host and captures the VM's correlation aspects in an efficient way. The placement decision is taken in two phases, where in the first phase, the manager disallows migrations and serves the deployment request optimally, and the second phase where the current placement is re-optimized using migrations. Chaisiri, Lee, and Niyato (2012) presents optimal cloud resource provisioning algorithm which helps a cloud user to reduce the on-demand cost associated with *under-provisioning* of cloud service and the *over-subscribed costs* associated with the over-provisioning. This problem is formulated using a *stochastic programming model*, which is solved with a *multi-staged recourse*. The objective of stochastic integer formulation is to minimize the cloud user's total provisioning cost. An analytical performance model has been formulated for a server farm by Do and Rotter (2012) which factors in the QoS guarantees and the operational energy consumption for the farm. Three allocation schemes have been investigated, namely, The *Most-Free Capacity*, The *Least-Free Capacity* and the *Priority scheme* which allows user specific ordering to decide the selection. Using the analytical model, it is possible to obtain performance measures like *average energy consumption*, *heat emissions* and *blocking probabilities* for requests. Also, the study identifies that in certain load conditions, least-free and priority schemes can lead to savings on energy consumption. Ghosh and Naik (2012) presents a mechanism for estimation of the risks associated with over commitment of resources. The mechanism is based on statistical analysis of the aggregate resource usage of a group of workloads. The approach allows for computation of bounds on the probability of exceeding the utilization thresholds. Malawski et al. (2012) maximizes the number of user prioritized workflows that can be completed under the given cost and deadline constraints. The approach is formulated as a maximization problem where the number of *prioritized workflows* is to be maximized. Jeyarani, Nagaveni, and Vasanth Ram (2012) proposes an Adaptive Power Aware Virtual Machine provisioner which uses *swarm intelligence* to efficiently map virtual machine instances on servers from a highly dynamic resource pool such that the maximum number of workload request are satisfied. The approach minimizes the incremental power drawn due to the placement of a VM while maintaining the performance. The approach is self adaptive. Goudarzi and Pedram (2012) presents an approach where in multiple copies of a VM are created and placed across datacenter such that the requests are distributed across all copies and hence, the resource required per VM copy is reduced, leading to efficient utilization of servers while increasing the availability of the service too. Nathani, Chaudhary, and Somani (2012) focuses on scheduling *deadline sensitive leases*, where it finds multiple slots in addition to finding single slot for the workload. It uses the concepts of *swapping* and *backfilling* to optimize the scheduling and reducing the number of rejected leases. Halder, Bellur, and Kulkarni (2012) proposes a VM packing scheme which considers the *correlation* among VMs while deciding on the VM to PM mapping. A risk metric has been proposed which incorporates the degree of resource unavailability. Luo and Qian

(2013) proposes a VM provisioning scheme that takes into account *burstiness* of the server requests during the consolidation process. A two state Markov chain has been used to represent the burstiness and the reservation strategy applied is based on queuing theory. Deadline-constrained work flow scheduling algorithms based on *Partial critical paths* have been proposed by Abrishami, Naghibzadeh, and Epema (2013). The authors have proposed two scheduling schemes, which are, the one-phase IaaS Cloud Partial Critical Path algorithm, and the two phased IaaS Cloud Partial Critical Path with Deadline Distribution algorithm. The objective of the approaches is to schedule workflows on IaaS clouds so as to maximize cost savings. An approach towards Dynamic cloud resource reservation using cloud brokerage has been presented by Wang et al. (2013) where the broker exploits the price differential between on-demand and reserved instances of virtual machines. Beloglazov and Buyya (2013) proposes a workload independent QoS metric, *Overload Time Fraction* using which the SLA goals can be specified. A Markov chain model based approach is then proposed that optimally solves host overload detection by maximizing the mean of the time between two migrations under the specified QoS goals. A multisize Sliding Window workload estimation technique allows the algorithm to heuristically adapt to handle unknown non-stationary workloads. For the purpose of scheduling deadline-constrained bag-of-task type of applications over hybrid cloud, Van Den Bossche, Vanmechelen, and Broeckhove (2013) have proposed an approach which uses linear programming formulations. The factors that are considered are the *deadlines met*, *cost-efficiency*, *computational efficiency*, application *turn around times* and *robustness* with regard to the *errors in runtime estimates*. Lloyd et al. (2013) investigate the performance implications of multi-tier application deployment on IaaS cloud by considering the following factors, *component placement across VMs*, the *VM memory size*, the *type of hypervisor* and the *VM placement*. They discover that component based deployment didn't provide the fastest performance, Increasing VM memory allocation didn't guarantee improved application, service isolation has a performance overhead involved with it which has to factored in the hosting costs. For soft real-time applications, An et al. (2014) presents a cloud middleware framework for ensuring high availability and performance. The middleware uses an *online VM replica* placement algorithm which is formulated as an ILP problem and leaves room for the user to specify deployment algorithms. Garg et al. (2014) presents a SLA-based virtual machine management approach for *heterogeneous workloads* in a data center which uses an *Artificial Neural Network* based forecasting model to predict the CPU utilization in an *offline* mode.

NETWORK AWARE PLACEMENT STRATEGIES

Generally, the virtual machines that a cloud user requests also involve some *inter-VM communication*, and thus, there is generation of *network traffic* among themselves. Since the network is a shared resource, a non-optimized placement of this set might lead to increased network traffic, affecting the performance of other VMs too.

Efficient placement of such VMs can enable a cloud to scale efficiently Meng, Pappas, and Zhang (2010), and thus the requirement of a Traffic Aware Virtual Machine Placement *(TVMPP)*. The problem is shown to be *NP-Hard*, and hence a heuristic is proposed. The solution is generated using a two-tier approach, where first the VMs and hosts into clusters and them matches the VMs and the hosts first at the cluster level, followed by matching at the individual machine level. The general problem itself is an NP-Hard problem belonging to the class of *Quadratic Assignment Problem*, however, the proposed heuristics work efficiently to deliver improved network traffic. *.

There is also a possibility that a virtual machine might be accessing some data that is placed on some other virtual machine (in contrast to simple communications), in such scenarios too, optimizing the placement of the source and receiver of the data affects the network costs. Piao and Yan (2010) addresses this problem using a constraint satisfaction approach to minimize the data transfer time between the virtual machines by taking into account the *distribution of data* over the topology. Such an approach ultimately leads to reduced network traffic, also if the application's execution time depends critically on the transferred data, the application's performance increases too. The algorithm takes as an input the quality of different links available in the network and the distribution of data required by a virtual machine over the nodes in network. The approach can be dynamically applied when the execution time for an application increases beyond a specified threshold according to the SLA.

Jayaram et al. (2011) studies the similarity in virtual machine images in order to create an efficient virtual machine distribution network, which can efficiently deliver the virtual machine instance demands. Also, this can be exploited to provide an approach that optimizes the data transfer during virtual machine provisioning and execution stages. If one can efficiently reduce the VM image data that is stored and transferred across network, the overall performance of the cloud management system can increase, also, reduced network traffic always help the performance of overall cloud too. One can have hypervisor level caches that enables sharing of image portions among the instances it hosts, which will again improve the performance of the cloud.

Maintaining a network has an associated power cost too, hence, one can also develop network-aware placement strategy with the objective of reducing the cost of powering the network. Mann et al. (2011) present an approach which takes into account both the network traffic and the topology for VM placement and migration decisions. The approach uses *dynamic virtual machine placement* and *programmable flow based routing* to achieve its power minimization objective. The optimization problem is NP-Complete, and hence a greedy heuristic has been proposed for the placement decision. The network is modeled using graph where the nodes represent the switches, the physical hosts and the external clients that connect to the data center (represented by a single vertex). The nodes are joined by edges which represent the network links and have associated capacity with them. The virtual machines can then be placed on physical nodes, with restriction that at-most one VM can be placed on a single host. The source or the destination can be either one of the virtual machine, or the external client node. A set of demand requests is also given which specifies the requested network rate between two source and destination of network traffic. With each switch and physical node, there is a power cost associated. The objective of the placement engine is to generate a mapping of virtual machine to physical host, such that the constraints of edge capacity, flow conservation and demand satisfaction are met. If for an assignment, all the demand requests are satisfied, it is called feasible. The greedy algorithm that is presented iterates over the demands and for each demand picks a physical node assignment and flow which consumes minimum power.

By factoring in dependencies among virtual machine in a data center and the underlying network topology, the network traffic can be reduced drastically Shrivastava et al. (2011). Here *AppAware* proposes an approach focused on multi-tier applications where the application itself spans across multiple virtual machines, and thus might involve data-dependencies among the virtual machines too.

Few of the other approaches are as follows. *Markov approximation* have been employed by Jiang et al. (2012) to optimize the *Joint VM placement* and *routing* of data center traffic. Modeling of CPU usage has been presented in relation to co-location and the dispersion of the communicating virtual machines in Sudevalayam and Kulkarni (2013). This model can then be used to predict the impacts of co-location and VM dispersion in case of communicating VMs for making efficient placement decisions. Guo, Stolyar and Walid (2013) proposes a shadow-routing based approach for adaptive placement of VMs in large datacenters within in a network cloud to deliver performance, robustness and adaptability. VMPlanner Fang et al. (2013) exploits VM Migration along with programmable flow based routing to reduce the network power costs in the data center. The optimization process is split into three sub-problems. This approach jointly optimizes VM placement and Traffic routing in the data center.

CO-LOCATION AWARE PLACEMENT STRATEGIES

In cloud environment many factors drive the consolidation of virtual machines. In fact, it becomes critical for a cost-optimal functioning of a cloud that the virtual machine instances are consolidated, so that as few physical servers are used as possible, and deliver as much power saving as possible. However, we have also observed how performance of co-located virtual machines gets affected if there is resource contention. In cases where the adherence to SLA fulfillment has higher priority, one needs to take into consideration the co-location interference too, else there is a chance of generating a performance wise sub-optimal placement schedule, and the potential penalties associated with it.

A study is presented in Kousiouris, Cucinotta, and Varvarigou (2011) which looks into the effects of factors like real time scheduling decisions, the type of workload and deployment scenarios that may arise due to consolidation on performance and QoS satisfaction of virtual machines. The authors present a prediction model based on *Genetically Optimized Artificial Neural Networks*. This model can assist the placement controller to generate optimal placement strategies by allowing it to have accurate predictions over the performance loss the application may suffer due to the interference, or the performance benefit an application might achieve in certain other placement scenarios.

A few of the other approaches are as follows. In Gupta et al. (2013), concepts of Cross-Application interference, Topology awareness, Hardware awareness have been covered to allow an optimal VM consolidation in HPC cloud. The applications are characterized along two dimension, *cache intensiveness* and *parallel synchronization & Network sensitivity*. It has been discovered that the *smart co-location* can in fact lead to improvement in the performance, and placement techniques taking benefit of it can deliver improved performance of the cloud. Tchana et al. (2013) proposes a resource management approach in for the master-slave applications, where the consolidation along with dynamic application sizing to avoid needless co-locations.

SCHEDULING FOR HYBRID AND FEDERATED CLOUDS

A cloud user can use a mix deployment of public and private cloud for deploying a service, i.e., use a *hybrid cloud*. Even multiple cloud providers can use each others services for providing their own services, i.e., a *federated cloud*. The reason to go for such an approach is to get a better return on the services. In hybrid cloud environment, one might choose to temporarily off-load the load on its private infrastructure using the services provided by some public cloud provider, in doing so, one can maintain the desired performance levels while saving on the costs involved in expanding the private cloud infrastructure. Other reason can be to ensure the security level of some core business logic, i.e., while a business can use a public cloud to provide a scalable front end, it might still chose to rely on in-house private infrastructure to deliver a secure service. A public cloud provider's motivation can be similar too, only that the scale at which a public cloud operator exploits this *price differential* can be huge as it abstracts a lot of costs involved with operating a data center.

From the point of *off-loading* certain workload to a public cloud provider in order to maintain the SLA (called *surge-computing*), Van den Bossche, Vanmechelen, and Broeckhove (2010) provides a cost optimal solution for VM scheduling. The workload is characterized as deadline constrained and pre-emptible workloads which cannot be migrated across different providers or instance types. The problem is formulated as a *Binary Integer Program*. *Application Processing Requests* describe the workload along with the desired level of *quality*. The objective of the scheduler is to take these requests into account while scheduling to find a minimum-cost solution. For each instance type of a virtual machine, we associate a CPU and a memory resource parameter, while each application provides their strict-deadlines and the set of tasks associated with it. These are then used to formulate a *binary decision program* which generates a placement minimizing the overall costs of the configuration.

As discussed above, federated cloud environments include multiple clouds partnering together for cost benefits. Breitgand, Marashini, and Tordsson (2011) considers a federated cloud paradigm where a cloud can *sub-contract* its workload to a different cloud to meet peak demands, where they design a placement model which aims at maintaining QoS while maximizing profit. The approach uses the concept of *Virtualized Execution Environment, VEE*, which can be then used by the service providers to supply the service to end user, and the placement problem then becomes an optimization problem of mapping these VEEs to physical hosts, within or outside the cloud to maximize profit. They also define a *Federated VEE Placement Optimization Meta-Problem, FVMP*, where each cloud maximizes the utility of VEE placement exploiting both the local and remote resources autonomously. FVMP as a framework can incorporate different local placement policies. The problem is formulated as an ILP problem, with two proposed policies, one of which optimizes power saving, while the other for load balancing, and can be used to minimize the cost of outsourcing workload to external clouds.

An advantage that having a multiple site cloud which spreads over multiple geographical locations is the *electricity price differential* that exits in such scenarios. Also, in certain geographical location, the external temperature might itself further lower down the cooling costs. A cloud provider can exploit this to save on energy costs and thus, maximize its profits. For such scenarios Le et al. (2011) propose an approach which takes into account the energy price across the sites including the *peak power charge*, and the *energy* that the cooling system for the data center consumes to create an efficient placement schedule to minimize the energy costs. The power associated with the cooling system is modeled as a function of the outside temperature, base power demand of the server, and the average dynamic power demand for a server. The approach uses estimations for running a job on a data center, which are modeled as the additional power consumed for running that job accounting for the required cooling, base, dynamic and peak power usage for that server. The approach proposes two greedy policies, *Cost-Aware Distribution* and *Cost-aware Distribution with Migration,* where the second policies allow for migrations between site at the end of each epoch to minimize the overall costs too.

Cloud Scheduling deals with efficient scheduling of a service over multiple clouds, and it may/may not involve a *cloud brokering system*. Static cloud scheduling cannot adapt to the change in pricing and requirement of the user. In such scenarios, a *Dynamic Cloud Scheduling* approach can increase the return and optimize the performance for the cloud user. A cloud user might also choose to interact with a cloud brokering system, which in-turn implements dynamic cloud scheduling for it.

A linear programming model for dynamic cloud scheduling is proposed by Li, Tordsson, and Elmroth (2011) which uses VM Migrations to implement the schedule. The model identifies three objectives, *maximization of Total Infrastructure Capacity, minimization of Total Infrastructure Price*, and *Minimization of the cost associated with the restructuring* of the service, so as to maintain the service quality. Using these three models can be framed, which can optimize infrastructure capacity while considering the migration costs, minimize the price while maintaining lower bound on threshold, and to minimize the restructuring costs due to migrations while maintaining performance and price bounds.

Van den Bossche, Vanmechelen, and Broeckhove (2011) consider the scenarios where deadline constrained batch type jobs are scheduled over a hybrid cloud. Here, the objective again is to maximize the profit while accounting for *data transfer costs*, along with the data transfer time, and factoring in the potential impact that the application might suffer when the application is scheduled in such a setting. The scheduler itself leaves room for varying the conservativeness of the placement so as to deliver certain bounded performance, or to maximize the profits in case of a relaxed deadline.

A few of the other approaches are as follows. Tordsson et al. (2012) presents a *cloud brokering mechanism* which tries to optimize the placement of virtual machines across multiple clouds. The scheduling algorithm is formulated as an integer Linear Program. Lucas-Simarro et al. (2013) proposes scheduling strategies for federated cloud in the scenario where the pricing is *dynamic*. It allows the users to specify their minimum performance expectations and the available budget, using which the scheduler tries to optimize the placement.

ROLE OF LIVE MIGRATION

Live migration of virtual machines is an indispensable tool for efficient management of data center. In fact, it won't be an exaggeration to say that one of the cloud's main feature, that of on-demand scalability of resources will be rendered impractical without it, with heavy downtime associated with migrations. A graphical overview of the live migration process is provided in Figure. 2. Live migrations acts as an enabler of the entire placement optimization process, whether it be to save energy, or to enable high availability, or to deliver high performance. However, one must not take this enabler for granted, as it is an expensive process, involving copying of virtual machine's memory image from one system to other,

Figure 2. Live migration process

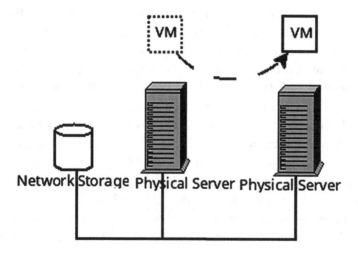

which creates a lot of network traffic, also, there is a down time associated, even though negligible when compared to other migration techniques, that leads to performance drop. Another thing is that even though a single live migration's cost might not appear that significant, on the scale of data center with huge number of virtual machines involved, optimizing and saving on live-migrations becomes critical too. Generally, the approach is to avoid live migration with *VM Resizing* in situations whenever it is possible Wood et al. (2009).

Ferreto et al. (2011) proposes an approach aimed towards server consolidation with migration control, in that the virtual machine with steady capacity are prioritized, such that their performance is not effected by unnecessary migrations. The problem of dynamic consolidation is formulated as an integer linear program, and extra constraints are added to avoid moving virtual machines with steady capacity. The constraints capture if there has been any change in virtual machine's capacity, and the original hosts of the virtual machines, hence for such virtual machines, migration is triggered only if a change in capacity is required.

In the context of federated clouds too, even though there might a flexibility of moving virtual machines across the providers, still the performance deterioration is heavy, as live migration might not be possible (different cloud providers are likely to maintain separate SAN for hosting the VM images), and thus optimizing the migrations becomes an even bigger challenge in such setting.

CONCLUSION

We have seen how virtual machine placement plays a crucial role in the performance of a data center, on both scales, financial and technical, and the services they offer. Also, how the performance of a data center and that of the services it offers might present conflicting goals to achieve. We began with presenting a rough categorization of the existing placement algorithms with a brief description of each approach and their goals. We then investigated the existing approaches from literature and *placed them in different bins* by categorizing them on the basis of the primary cost they try to optimize on.

We started with *Power-Aware* placement strategies, and how the different strategies try to use *dynamic consolidation* to construct an *energy-efficient* placement, and how different *power models* can be constructed and then employed with *prediction* algorithms to improve the efficiency of the placements. Dynamic workloads can also benefit from adaptive strategies which can adapt the conservativeness of the strategy with change in workload in the cloud.

We then covered the *Performance-Centered* strategies where the placement of virtual machines is driven to achieve high performance goals for the virtual machine instances. We saw how one can save on *over-commitment* for virtual machines, and how to use *Live-Migration* enable smooth scaling of the virtual machine instances, and how to detect if the performance of a virtual machine is in deteriorated state. We also covered a few strategies which enable efficient hosting of virtual machine instances with *high availability goals,* such as ensuring that a VM placement configuration with *k-redundancy*.

We then investigated the placement strategies that optimize the *network traffic* in a data center. Since a cloud site can consist of a huge number of virtual machine instances, the communication involved in their running and management can lead to significant cost, and deterioration in the performance of the cloud as a whole. We saw some strategies which saves this cost by placing communicating virtual machines as close to each other as possible. We also covered a few strategies which use *programmable flow based routing* to mould the network flow for an optimized performance.

After covering these areas, we shifted our focus towards *Co-location Aware* placement strategies, which takes into account the co-location behavior of virtual machines while making the placement decisions too. Many of the strategies discussed in previous categories also qualify for this class, as in any placement scenario, resource contention can affect the performance of the virtual machine instances. Lastly, we investigated a placement scenario where the cloud covers multiple sites, or is a combination of private and physical cloud. The unique advantages that this kind of situation has to offer, and the unique challenges were covered.

The aim of this categorization, although on a broad level, is to provide a clear demarcation with regard to the primary objective of the data center provider, and thus enable one to engineer the cloud to provide maximum benefit over that objective. By this point in chapter, it would be safe to say that in case of VM Placement too, *one cannot have his cake, and eat it too*. The VM placement scenario consists of conflicting objectives, and trade-off will always have to be made for any practical scenario.

REFERENCES

Abrishami, Naghibzadeh, & Epema. (2013). Deadline-constrained workflow scheduling algorithms for Infrastructure as a Service Clouds. *Futur. Gener. Comput. Syst., 29*(1), 158–69. doi:10.1016/j.future.2012.05.004

An, Shekhar, Caglar, Gokhale, & Sastry. (2014). A cloud middleware for assuring performance and high availability of soft real-time applications. *J. Syst. Archit., 60*(9), 757–69. doi:10.1016/j.sysarc.2014.01.009

Andreolini, M., Casolari, S., Colajanni, M., & Messori, M. (2010). Dynamic Load Management of Virtual Machines in a Cloud Architectures. In *Lect. Notes Inst. Comput. Sci. Soc. Telecommun. Eng.* doi:10.1007/978-3-642-12636-9_14

Beloglazov, Abawajy, & Buyya. (2012). Energy-aware resource allocation heuristics for efficient management of data centers for Cloud computing. *Futur. Gener. Comput. Syst., 28*(5), 755–68. doi:10.1016/j.future.2011.04.017

Beloglazov, A., & Buyya, R. (2010). Energy Efficient Resource Management in Virtualized Cloud Data Centers. *Clust. Cloud Grid Comput. (CCGrid), 2010 10th IEEE/ACM Int. Conf.* IEEE. doi:10.1109/CCGRID.2010.46

Beloglazov, A., & Buyya, R. (2010, November). Adaptive Threshold-Based Approach for Energy-Efficient Consolidation of Virtual Machines in Cloud Data Centers. In *Proc. 8th Int. Work. Middlew. Grids, Clouds E-Science.* doi:10.1145/1890799.1890803

Beloglazov, A., & Buyya, R. (2012). Optimal online deterministic algorithms and adaptive heuristics for energy and performance efficient dynamic consolidation of virtual machines in Cloud data centers. In Concurr. Comput. Pract. Exp., 24, 1397–1420. doi:10.1002/cpe.1867

Beloglazov, A., & Buyya, R. (2013). Managing overloaded hosts for dynamic consolidation of virtual machines in cloud data centers under quality of service constraints. *IEEE Transactions on Parallel and Distributed Systems, 24*(7), 1366–1379. doi:10.1109/TPDS.2012.240

Bin, E., Biran, O., Boni, O., Hadad, E., Kolodner, E. K., Moatti, Y., & Lorenz, D. H. (2011). Guaranteeing high availability goals for virtual machine placement. In *Proc. - Int. Conf. Distrib. Comput. Syst.* IEEE. doi:10.1109/ICDCS.2011.72

Bobroff, N., Kochut, A., & Beaty, K. (2007). Placement of Virtual Machines for Managing SLA Violations. *2007 10th IFIP/IEEE Int. Symp. Integr. Netw. Manag.* IEEE. doi:10.1109/INM.2007.374776

Van Den Bossche, Vanmechelen, & Broeckhove. (2013). Online cost-efficient scheduling of deadline-constrained workloads on hybrid clouds. *Futur. Gener. Comput. Syst., 29*(4), 973–85. doi:10.1016/j.future.2012.12.012

Breitgand, D., Dubitzky, & Epstein. (2012). Sla-aware resource over-commit in an iaas cloud. *Proc. 8th Int. Conf. Netw. Serv. Manag.* Retrieved from http://dl.acm.org/citation.cfm?id=2499406.2499415

Breitgand, D. Marashini, & Tordsson. (2011). Policy-driven service placement optimization in federated clouds. Academic Press.

Calcavecchia, N. M., Biran, O., Hadad, E., & Moatti, Y. (2012). VM Placement Strategies for Cloud Scenarios. In *2012 IEEE Fifth Int. Conf. Cloud Comput.* IEEE. doi:10.1109/CLOUD.2012.113

Castañé, Núñez, Llopis, & Carretero. (2013). E-mc2: A formal framework for energy modelling in cloud computing. *Simul. Model. Pract. Theory, 39*, 56–75. doi:10.1016/j.simpat.2013.05.002

Chaisiri, S., Lee, B.-S., & Niyato, D. (2012). Optimization of Resource Provisioning Cost in Cloud Computing. *IEEE Trans. Serv. Comput., 5*(2), 164–177. doi:10.1109/TSC.2011.7

Chen, Joshi, Hiltunen, Schlichting, & Sanders. (2011). Using CPU gradients for performance-aware energy conservation in multitier systems. *Sustain. Comput. Informatics Syst., 1*(2), 113–33. doi:10.1016/j.suscom.2011.02.002

Chen, J., Wang, C., Zhou, B. B., Sun, L., & Lee, Y. C. (2011). Tradeoffs Between Profit and Customer Satisfaction for Service Provisioning in the Cloud. In *Proc. 20th Int. Symp. High Perform. Distrib. Comput. - HPDC '11.* New York: ACM Press. doi:10.1145/1996130.1996161

Chen, M., Zhang, H., Su, Y. Y., Wang, X., Jiang, G., & Yoshihira, K. (2011). Effective VM sizing in virtualized data centers. In *Proc. 12th IFIP/IEEE Int. Symp. Integr. Netw. Manag. IM 2011.* IEEE. doi:10.1109/INM.2011.5990564

Do & Rotter. (2012). Comparison of scheduling schemes for on-demand IaaS requests. *J. Syst. Softw., 85*(6), 1400–1408. doi:10.1016/j.jss.2012.01.019

Dupont, C., Schulze, T., Giuliani, G., Somov, A., & Hermenier, F. (2012). An energy aware framework for virtual machine placement in cloud federated data centres. In *Proc. 3rd Int. Conf. Futur. Energy Syst. Where Energy, Comput. Commun. Meet - E-Energy '12.* New York: ACM Press. doi:10.1145/2208828.2208832

Fang, Liang, Li, Chiaraviglio, & Xiong. (2013). VMPlanner: Optimizing virtual machine placement and traffic flow routing to reduce network power costs in cloud data centers. *Comput. Networks, 57*(1), 179–96. doi:10.1016/j.comnet.2012.09.008

Feller, E., Rilling, L., & Morin, C. (2011). Energy-Aware Ant Colony Based Workload Placement in Clouds. In *2011 IEEE/ACM 12th Int.Conf. Grid Comput.* IEEE. doi:10.1109/Grid.2011.13

Feller, E., Rohr, C., Margery, D., & Morin, C. (2012). Energy management in IaaS clouds: A holistic approach. In *Proc. - 2012 IEEE 5th Int.Conf. Cloud Comput. CLOUD 2012*. IEEE. doi:10.1109/CLOUD.2012.50

Ferreto, Netto, Calheiros, & De Rose. (2011). Server consolidation with migration control for virtualized data centers. *Futur. Gener. Comput. Syst., 27*(8), 1027–34. doi:10.1016/j.future.2011.04.016

Gao, Y., Guan, H., Qi, Z., Hou, Y., & Liu, L. (2013). A multi-objective ant colony system algorithm for virtual machine placement in cloud computing. J. Comput. *Syst. Sci., 79, 1230–42*. doi:10.1016/j.jcss.2013.02.004

Garg, Toosi, Gopalaiyengar, & Buyya. (2014). SLA-based virtual machine management for heterogeneous workloads in a cloud datacenter. *J. Netw. Comput. Appl., 45*, 108–20. doi:10.1016/j.jnca.2014.07.030

Garg, S. K., Yeo, C. S., Anandasivam, A., & Buyya, R. (2009). *Energy-Efficient Scheduling of HPC Applications in Cloud Computing Environments*. Retrieved from http://arxiv.org/abs/0909.1146

Ghosh, R., & Naik, V. K. (2012). Biting Off Safely More Than You Can Chew: Predictive Analytics for Resource Over-Commit in IaaS Cloud. In *2012 IEEE Fifth Int. Conf. Cloud Comput*. IEEE. doi:10.1109/CLOUD.2012.131

Gmach, Rolia, Cherkasova, & Kemper. (2009). Resource pool management: Reactive versus proactive or let's be friends. *Comput. Networks, 53*(17), 2905–22. doi:10.1016/j.comnet.2009.08.011

Gong, Z., & Gu, X. (2010). PAC: Pattern-driven application consolidation for efficient cloud computing. *Proc. - 18th Annu. IEEE/ACM Int. Symp. Model. Anal. Simul. Comput. Telecommun. Syst. MASCOTS 2010*. IEEE. doi:10.1109/MASCOTS.2010.12

Goudarzi, H., & Pedram, M. (2012). Energy-efficient virtual machine replication and placement in a cloud computing system. *Proc. - 2012 IEEE 5th Int. Conf. Cloud Comput. CLOUD 2012*. doi:10.1109/CLOUD.2012.107

Guo, Y., Stolyar, A. L., & Walid, A. (2013). Shadow-Routing Based Dynamic Algorithms for Virtual Machine Placement in a Network Cloud. In *INFOCOM, 2013. 32nd IEEE Int. Conf. Comput. Commun.* doi:10.1109/INFCOM.2013.6566847

Gupta, A., Kalé, L. V., Milojicic, D., Faraboschi, P., & Balle, S. M. (2013). HPC-aware VM placement in infrastructure clouds. In *Proc. IEEE Int. Conf. Cloud Eng. IC2E 2013*. IEEE. doi:10.1109/IC2E.2013.38

Halder, K., Bellur, U., & Kulkarni, P. (2012). Risk Aware Provisioning and Resource Aggregation Based Consolidation of Virtual Machines. In *2012 IEEE Fifth Int. Conf. Cloud Comput*. IEEE. doi:10.1109/CLOUD.2012.86

Hermenier, F., Lorca, X., Menaud, J.-M., Muller, G., & Lawall, J. (2009). Entropy: a Consolidation Manager for Clusters.*Proc. 2009 ACM SIGPLAN/SIGOPS Int. Conf. Virtual Exec. Environ. - VEE '09*. doi:10.1145/1508293.1508300

Isci, Hanson, Whalley, Steinder, & Kephart. (2010). Runtime Demand Estimation for effective dynamic resource management. In 2010 IEEE Netw. Oper. Manag. Symp. - NOMS 2010. doi:10.1109/NOMS.2010.5488495

Jayaram, Peng, Zhang, Kim, Chen, & Lei. (2011). An empirical analysis of similarity in virtual machine images. In Proc. Middlew. 2011 Ind. Track Work. - Middlew. '11. New York: ACM Press. doi:10.1145/2090181.2090187

Jayasinghe, Pu, & Eilam. (2011). Improving performance and availability of services hosted on iaas clouds with structural constraint-aware virtual machine placement. *Serv. Comput.*, 72–79. doi:10.1109/SCC.2011.28

Jeyarani, R., Nagaveni, & Vasanth Ram. (2012). Design and implementation of adaptive power-aware virtual machine provisioner (APA-VMP) using swarm intelligence. *Futur. Gener. Comput. Syst.*, *28*(5), 811–21. doi:10.1016/j.future.2011.06.002

Jiang, J. W., Lan, T., Ha, S., Chen, M., & Chiang, M. (2012). Joint VM placement and routing for data center traffic engineering. In Proc. - IEEE INFOCOM. IEEE. doi:10.1109/INFCOM.2012.6195719

Katsaros, Subirats, Fitó, Guitart, Gilet, & Espling. (2013). A service framework for energy-aware monitoring and VM management in Clouds. *Futur. Gener. Comput. Syst.*, *29*(8), 2077–91. doi:10.1016/j.future.2012.12.006

Kim, Beloglazov, & Buyya. (2011). Power-aware provisioning of virtual machines for real-time Cloud services. *Concurr. Comput. Pract. Exp.*, *23*(13), 1491–1505. doi:10.1002/cpe.1712

Kleineweber, C., Keller, A., Niehorster, O., & Brinkmann, A. (2011). Rule-Based Mapping of Virtual Machines in Clouds. In *Parallel, Distrib. Network-Based Process. (PDP), 2011 19th Euromicro Int. Conf.* IEEE. doi:10.1109/PDP.2011.69

Kousiouris, Cucinotta, & Varvarigou. (2011). The effects of scheduling, workload type and consolidation scenarios on virtual machine performance and their prediction through optimized artificial neural networks. *J. Syst. Softw.*, *84*(8), 1270–91. doi:10.1016/j.jss.2011.04.013

Le, K., Bianchini, R., Zhang, J., Jaluria, Y., Meng, J., & Nguyen, T. D. (2011). Reducing electricity cost through virtual machine placement in high performance computing clouds.*2011 Int. Conf. High Perform. Comput. Networking, Storage Anal.* doi:10.1145/2063384.2063413

Li, W., Tordsson, J., & Elmroth, E. (2011). Modeling for dynamic cloud scheduling via migration of virtual machines. In *Proc. - 2011 3rd IEEE Int. Conf. Cloud Comput. Technol. Sci. CloudCom 2011.* doi:10.1109/CloudCom.2011.31

Liu, L., Wang, H., Liu, X., Jin, X., He, W. B., Wang, Q. B., & Chen, Y. (2009). GreenCloud: A New Architecture for Green Data Center. In *Proc. 6th Int. Conf. Ind. Sess. Auton. Comput. Commun. Ind. Sess.* doi:10.1145/1555312.1555319

Lloyd, Pallickara, David, Lyon, Arabi, & Rojas. (2013). Performance implications of multi-tier application deployments on Infrastructure-as-a-Service clouds: Towards performance modeling. *Futur. Gener. Comput. Syst.*, *29*(5), 1254–64. doi:10.1016/j.future.2012.12.007

Lu, K., Roblitz, T., Yahyapour, R., Yaqub, E., & Kotsokalis, C. (2011). QoS-aware SLA-based Advanced Reservation of Infrastructure as a Service. In *2011 IEEE Third Int. Conf. Cloud Comput. Technol. Sci.* IEEE. doi:10.1109/CloudCom.2011.46

Lucas-Simarro, Moreno-Vozmediano, Montero, & Llorente. (2013). Scheduling strategies for optimal service deployment across multiple clouds. *Futur. Gener. Comput. Syst., 29*(6), 1431–41. doi:10.1016/j.future.2012.01.007

Luo, Z., & Qian, Z. (2013). Burstiness-aware server consolidation via queuing theory approach in a computing cloud. *Proc. - IEEE 27th Int.Parallel Distrib. Process. Symp. IPDPS 2013*. doi:10.1109/IPDPS.2013.62

Machida, F., Kawato, M., & Maeno, Y. (2010). Redundant virtual machine placement for fault-tolerant consolidated server clusters. In *2010 IEEE Netw. Oper. Manag. Symp. - NOMS 2010*. IEEE. doi:10.1109/NOMS.2010.5488431

Malawski, M., Juve, G., Deelman, E., & Nabrzyski, J. (2012). Cost- and deadline-constrained provisioning for scientific workflow ensembles in IaaS clouds. In *2012 Int. Conf. High Perform. Comput. Networking, Storage Anal.*. IEEE. doi:10.1109/SC.2012.38

Mann, V., Kumar, A., Dutta, P., & Kalyanaraman, S. (2011). VMFlow: Leveraging VM mobility to reduce network power costs in data centers.Lect. Notes Comput. Sci., 6640, 198–211. doi:10.1007/978-3-642-20757-0_16

Marshall, P., Keahey, K., & Freeman, T. (2011). Improving utilization of infrastructure clouds. In *Proc. - 11th IEEE/ACM Int. Symp. Clust. Cloud Grid Comput. CCGrid 2011*. IEEE. doi:10.1109/CCGrid.2011.56

Meng, X., Pappas, V., & Zhang, L. (2010). Improving the scalability of data center networks with traffic-aware virtual machine placement. In Proc. - IEEE INFOCOM. IEEE. doi:10.1109/INFCOM.2010.5461930

Mihailescu, M., Rodriguez, A., & Amza, C. (2011). Enhancing application robustness in Infrastructure-as-a-Service clouds. In *2011 IEEE/IFIP 41st Int. Conf. Dependable Syst. Networks Work*. IEEE. doi:10.1109/DSNW.2011.5958801

Minarolli, D., & Freisleben, B. (2011). Utility-based resource allocation for virtual machines in cloud computing. In *Proc. - IEEE Symp. Comput. Commun*. IEEE. doi:10.1109/ISCC.2011.5983872

Nathani, Chaudhary, & Somani. (2012). Policy based resource allocation in IaaS cloud. *Futur. Gener. Comput. Syst., 28*(1), 94–103. doi:10.1016/j.future.2011.05.016

Ni, J., Huang, Y., Luan, Z., Zhang, J., & Qian, D. (2011). Virtual machine mapping policy based on load balancing in private cloud environment. In *2011 Int. Conf. Cloud Serv. Comput*. IEEE. doi:10.1109/CSC.2011.6138536

Palanisamy, B., Singh, A., Liu, L., & Jain, B. (2011). Purlieus. In *Proc. 2011 Int. Conf. High Perform. Comput. Networking, Storage Anal. - SC '11*. New York: ACM Press. doi:10.1145/2063384.2063462

Piao, J. T., & Yan, J. (2010). A Network-aware Virtual Machine Placement and Migration Approach in Cloud Computing.*2010 Ninth Int. Conf. Grid Cloud Comput*. IEEE. doi:10.1109/GCC.2010.29

Shi, W., & Hong, B. (2011, December). Towards profitable virtual machine placement in the data center. In *Utility and Cloud Computing (UCC), 2011 Fourth IEEE International Conference on* (pp. 138-145). IEEE.

Shrivastava, V., Zerfos, P., Kang-won, L., Jamjoom, H., Liu, Y.-H., & Banerjee, S. (2011). Application-aware virtual machine migration in data centers. In 2011 Proc. IEEE INFOCOM. IEEE. doi:10.1109/INFCOM.2011.5935247

Sudevalayam & Kulkarni. (2013). Affinity-aware modeling of CPU usage with communicating virtual machines. *J. Syst. Softw., 86*(10), 2627–38. doi:10.1016/j.jss.2013.04.085

Tchana, Tran, Broto, DePalma, & Hagimont. (2013). Two levels autonomic resource management in virtualized IaaS. *Futur. Gener. Comput. Syst., 29*(6), 1319–32. doi:10.1016/j.future.2013.02.002

Tordsson, Montero, Moreno-Vozmediano, & Llorente. (2012). Cloud brokering mechanisms for optimized placement of virtual machines across multiple providers. *Futur. Gener. Comput. Syst., 28*(2), 358–67. doi:10.1016/j.future.2011.07.003

Tsakalozos, K., Roussopoulos, M., & Delis, A. (2011). VM placement in non-homogeneous IaaS-clouds. Lect. Notes Comput. Sci., 7084, 172–87. doi:10.1007/978-3-642-25535-9_12

Van, H. N., Tran, F. D., & Menaud, J.-M. (2009). SLA-Aware Virtual Resource Management for Cloud Infrastructures. In *2009 Ninth IEEE Int. Conf. Comput. Inf. Technol.*. IEEE. doi:10.1109/CIT.2009.109

Van den Bossche, R., Vanmechelen, K., & Broeckhove, J. (2010). Cost-Optimal Scheduling in Hybrid IaaS Clouds for Deadline Constrained Workloads. In *2010 IEEE 3rd Int.Conf. Cloud Comput.* IEEE. doi:10.1109/CLOUD.2010.58

Van den Bossche, R., Vanmechelen, K., & Broeckhove, J. (2011). Cost-Efficient Scheduling Heuristics for Deadline Constrained Workloads on Hybrid Clouds. In *2011 IEEE Third Int. Conf. Cloud Comput. Technol. Sci.* IEEE. doi:10.1109/CloudCom.2011.50

Verma, A., Ahuja, P., & Neogi, A. (2008a). pMapper: Power and Migration Cost Aware Application Placement in Virtualized Systems. In Middlew. 2008 (LNCS), (vol. 5346, pp. 243–64). Berlin: Springer Berlin Heidelberg. doi:10.1007/978-3-540-89856-6_13

Verma, A., Ahuja, P., & Neogi, A. (2008b). Power-aware dynamic placement of HPC applications.*Proc. 22nd Annu. Int. Conf. Supercomput. ICS 08.* New York: ACM Press. doi:10.1145/1375527.1375555

Wang, Niu, Li, & Liang. (2013). Dynamic Cloud Resource Reservation via Cloud Brokerage. In *2013 IEEE 33rd Int. Conf. Distrib. Comput. Syst.* IEEE. doi:10.1109/ICDCS.2013.20

Wood, Shenoy, Venkataramani, & Yousif. (2009). Sandpiper: Black-box and gray-box resource management for virtual machines. *Comput. Networks, 53*(17), 2923–38. doi:10.1016/j.comnet.2009.04.014

Yang, Wang, Cheng, Kuo, & Chu. (2011). Green Power Management with Dynamic Resource Allocation for Cloud Virtual Machines. In *2011 IEEE Int. Conf. High Perform. Comput. Commun.* IEEE. doi:10.1109/HPCC.2011.103

Younge, A. J., von Laszewski, G., Wang, L., Lopez-Alarcon, S., & Carithers, W. (2010). Efficient resource management for Cloud computing environments. In *Int. Conf. Green Comput.* IEEE. doi:10.1109/GREENCOMP.2010.5598294

Zhang, Q., Zhu, Q., & Boutaba, R. (2011). Dynamic Resource Allocation for Spot Markets in Cloud Computing Environments. In *2011 Fourth IEEE Int. Conf. Util. Cloud Comput.* IEEE. doi:10.1109/UCC.2011.33

Zheng, Z., Wang, R., Zhong, H., & Zhang, X. (2011). An approach for cloud resource scheduling based on Parallel Genetic Algorithm. In *2011 3rd Int. Conf. Comput. Res. Dev.* IEEE. doi:10.1109/ICCRD.2011.5764170

Chapter 8
Security and Compliance:
IaaS, PaaS, and Hybrid Cloud

Heather Hinton
IBM Corporation, USA

ABSTRACT

Despite a rocky start in terms of perceived security, cloud adoption continues to grow. Users are more comfortable with the notion that cloud can be secure but there is still a lack of understanding of what changes when moving to cloud, how to secure a cloud environment, and most importantly, how to demonstrate compliance of these cloud environment for regulatory purposes. This chapter reviews the basics of cloud security and compliance, including the split of security responsibility across Cloud provider and Client, considerations for the integration of cloud deployed workloads with on-premises systems and most importantly, how to demonstrate compliance with existing internal policies and workload required regulatory standards.

INTRODUCTION

Despite a rocky start in terms of perceived security, cloud adoption continues to grow. Users are growing more comfortable with the notion that cloud can be secure. A recent study by the Economist Intelligence Unit found that "the most mature enterprises are now turning to cloud strategies as a strategic platform for growing client demand and expanding sales." (Columbus, 2015; Economist Intelligence Unit, 2015). While initial fears of would-be-cloud-adopters focused on the security of the Cloud provider's environment, most analysts have now moved beyond that to focus on governance of the client's cloud-hosted workload.

Charting the change in viewpoint, in 2013, typical articles all cited cloud as insecure and not safe for data and workloads:

The biggest risk when it comes to cloud computing is that you never know what is up ahead. Hackers have been around from the start and they are not going anywhere any time soon. And as technology advances, so do the risks that come with adopting them..."The cloud is not for everyone," [Neil] Rerup

DOI: 10.4018/978-1-5225-0759-8.ch008

said. "Like with all solutions, you have to weigh what level of risk you are comfortable dealing with."
(Angeles, 2013)

By late 2014, the overall tone was changing to recognize that while breaches will still occur when using cloud, it is not going to be the cloud provider's fault:

Cloud data breaches are a sure thing. Forrester doesn't mince words with this one, saying that CIOs should expect to encounter a breach in the cloud – and that it will be their fault, not the SaaS provider. "The culprits will likely be common process and governance failures such as poor key management or lack of training or perimeter-based thinking by your security department," the report states. (Gagliordi, 2014)

And by 2015, analysts such as Jay Heiser of Gartner, were articulating the need for clients to move beyond security and embrace oversight and governance, in particular for the client's own use of the cloud:

The ongoing concern about cloud 'security' is distracting from what is ultimately the more significant concern "how are you going to ensure that your employees make appropriate, safe and secure use of applications that you are not running in house?" The biggest 'security' problem isn't that SaaS vendors are being hacked, its that your users are putting sensitive data into SaaS without recognizing that they need to control access and usage. Its time for the cloud risk community to evolve beyond superficial concepts of 'cloud security' and start strategizing 'cloud governance' approaches. (Heiser, 2015)

Despite this encouraging move to cloud, and the need for cloud governance, there is still a lack of understanding of what changes when moving to cloud, how to secure a cloud environment, and most important, how to demonstrate compliance of these cloud environment for regulatory purposes. This chapter introduces the basics of understanding the roles and responsibilities for Cloud security, how to secure a cloud-hosted workload, how to integrate this with in-house, or on premises systems, and most importantly, how to approach governance through compliance with existing internal policies and workload required regulatory standards.

BACKGROUND

IaaS – Infrastructure as a Service - is the most basic of Cloud offerings. IaaS platforms provide physical and virtual servers in a consumptive, on-demand manner. These resources are deployed by the provider's orchestration and automation tools; they use the provider's network infrastructure to interconnect the servers to each other and to the Internet and/or the client's internal, on-premises network. IaaS services are typically "self-serve" where the client has complete control over their deployed environment. Well-known IaaS providers include Amazon Web Services (AWS), Microsoft Azure, Google, and IBM SoftLayer. Some providers also include a "managed services" option, by which the provider will handle the operational management (configuring, maintaining) of a cloud environment, such as with IBM's Managed Services for Cloud.

PaaS – Platform as a Service - "is a category of cloud computing services that provides a platform allowing customers to develop, run, and manage applications without the complexity of building and maintaining the infrastructure typically associated with developing and launching an app" (Wikipedia,

2016). This type of offering allows a client to select and control software deployment from a set menu of offerings that are managed by the PaaS provider. PaaS offerings are available as public cloud offerings and in many cases as dedicated offerings (hosted on IaaS but dedicated to a client). Many PaaS offerings are built up on a cloud provider's existing IaaS offering and so blur the lines between PaaS and IaaS for discussion purposes.

PaaS offerings are also available as privately deployed offerings, more like traditional software that is deployed on-premises and managed by internal IT departments. This latter type of on-premises PaaS, with infrastructure managed by the client, typically mirrors a traditional on-premises environment for management purposes and so is beyond the scope of this discussion.

SaaS – Software as a Service - is the most familiar of cloud offerings. SaaS offerings are a cloud-like environment where a complete software application is provided for a client's use. These services are available to the client in an on-demand, consumptive manner. The SaaS provider is responsible for the complete management of a software application. SaaS applications are quite familiar to clients – examples of SaaS applications include consumer-targeted applications such as mail (gmail, Yahoo!), chat (WeChat, Weibo, Snapchat) and storage (icloud, Instagram) and business targeted applications such as sales and client management tools (Salesforce, Sugar) and storage (box, dropbox).

We do not include SaaS offerings in this chapter as they represent the "cleanest" of the security and compliance separation-of-duty scenarios – the complete security and compliance responsibility of the offering rests with the provider, who has responsibility for the management of the SaaS environment, including the client's data. Clients can evaluate the provider's security, typically through compliance assertions and contractual and SLA terms, and chose to use the SaaS offering or not. The client's role in this scenario is limited to the control of the user lifecycle for those users authorized to use the SaaS offering, and the collection and oversight of evidence (logs, audit reports) from the SaaS provider to support the client's broader compliance requirements (typically more an issue for business-focused SaaS as opposed to consumer-facing SaaS).

Hybrid Cloud "refers to a combination of a public cloud service and a private cloud on-premises; however, hybrid clouds could also consist of two public clouds provided by different providers or even a combination of a cloud and traditional IT" (Erber, 2014). Many early adopters of IaaS and PaaS cloud are now becoming early adopters of hybrid cloud as they seek to leverage the benefits of cloud while retaining control over resources that cannot be moved to cloud (for latency, porting, data residency or security reasons). Prior to this IaaS/PaaS-hybrid cloud, however, adopters of SaaS have also been engaged in hybrid cloud deployments, as they use on-premises service management tools to invoke SaaS-based solutions, and as they have integrated SaaS-provided information on usage (user management and general usage logs) with on-premises systems including log stores and security-information event management (SIEM) systems.

For the purposes of this chapter, we will focus on the hybrid model resulting from the extension of an on-premises environment to include the cloud-hosted workloads. In all cases, IaaS, PaaS, SaaS and Hybrid cloud, clients have two categories of security concerns: the security of the cloud offering itself, and how to secure the workloads that are deployed on the cloud offering. Included with both categories is the requirement to secure the access to the offering and workload (as required) and to ensure the appropriate logging and monitoring of the use of the offering and workload to ensure compliance with security requirements and regulatory requirements. As part of a focus on governance, the client's internal security and compliance tools and practices should be extended to include the client's responsibility in the overall shared responsibility model.

In the rest of this chapter we focus first on how to evaluate the security (and compliance) of the IaaS and PaaS offering and then the workload that is deployed on the cloud offering. As the most overlooked part of these evaluations is a focus on the roles and responsibilities of the Client and the Cloud provider, we conclude this chapter with discussion of how to evaluate security and compliance for a hybrid cloud example.

Security, Compliance, Audit in the Cloud

While security and compliance are often referred at the same time, they are not the same thing. In the context of Information Technology, we talk about systems that are secure, meaning that there are controls in place to protect systems and networks, and their hosted applications and data. The "goodness" of these controls is typically assumed or asserted based on a risk-based assessment of the required controls. The effectiveness of these controls is demonstrated by audits that check if and how these controls are actually used, demonstrating compliance with the stated security policy and its controls.

Security controls are (or should be) defined by security policies, and the procedures that define how to implement, or operationalize, these policies. These policies may be good or not-so-good, such as:

- All passwords must be at least four (4) characters long (not so good), or,
- Passwords must be at least 12 characters long, including at least one UPPER, lower, alpha, numeric and special character (good)

An audit of policies and controls typically involves an examination of an entity's security policies and the controls that are in place to enforce these policies. The appropriateness of security policies is evaluated in the context of the defined risks to the system; do the policies provide protect against identified risks to the system? Policies are typically implemented by operational procedures (instructions on what to do and when) and tools to support these procedures. The effectiveness of controls is evaluated by examining the overall system, including system logs, looking for evidence that policies are implemented or instances where they were not properly enforced.

As an example, a commonly implemented policy states that an employee who has left the company is removed from access systems in a timely manner. The purpose of this policy is to reduce the risk that this employee can come back after their employment has terminated and access the company's systems and resources, possibly with bad intentions. Operational procedures will require that this employee's manager notify Human Resources to change their employment status and otherwise notify/remove any access rights they may have. Removing access rights includes both logical (account privileges) and actual (receiving the employee's badges, key fobs and other company issued systems) and may be accomplished by the employee's managed, by HR, or yet another party. Audits will look for evidence that the employee's rights have been removed (their status was disabled in the HR systems, their permissions and accounts were disabled in access control systems, and employee badges were properly returned and deactivated). Evidence that says that these actions did not take place indicates a gap between policy and implementation of the policy.

Any system involving humans is likely to have gaps; if this process finds evidence of gaps or failures of controls, the next step is to look for evidence that these failures led to compromise of the system. Common follow on questions include: Are there compensating controls in place that further minimize the risk of compromise? Are these one-time gaps or systemic failures? This is in many cases where the real evaluation of security effectiveness comes in – are there single points of failure or a suitably "defense-in-depth" based approach to protect the system? The assessment of these risks, if any, provides a view on the overall maturity of the environment and its suitability for different types of workloads.

Security Policies and Frameworks

In the world before Cloud, clients often defined their security policies as needed, building them up based on experiences both good and bad. As these policies are relevant to that client only, these policies are (and remain) private and thus difficult for outsiders to evaluate. However, as there was typically never a need for an outsider to review or assess these policies, this was not an issue.

As clients move from entirely self-managed environments to strategic outsourcing (SO) and data-center co-location (CoLo), a split of responsibility for these controls is introduced. The physical and environmental security of the facility hosting an IT infrastructure lies with the data center facility provider but the client retains all other responsibility. The SO/CoLo provider is now a separate entity, not just a separate division within a company; their policies and procedures are now subject to scrutiny by their clients.

Moving to a Cloud model extends the split of responsibility as the Cloud provider manages the Cloud infrastructure and tools that are exposed to clients to allow the client order and manage servers and services. The Cloud infrastructure includes the virtualization infrastructure that supports the virtual machine aspects of a cloud and the physical networks over which each client's virtual network(s).

The Cloud provider now has a more intimate role in the security of a client's environment. This in turn means that clients are far more interested in the details of the provider's security policies and procedures. Clients moving to Cloud require that the Cloud provider can provide assurance the infrastructure is managed to standards that are at least as rigorous as the client's on-premises environment. Typically this is provided through audit reports and compliance certificates and assertions that are made available to the client on request.

Evaluating Provider Security Policies

Having to rely on Cloud providers as the responsible party for increasing aspects of a workload's security leads to the strong desire by clients to evaluate the details of a Cloud provider's security policies. The use of published standards and frameworks as the basis of a Cloud provider's security policies allows high level discussion of security best practices and implementations, without disclosing the intimate details of those policies. This also provides a framework for the discussion of roles and responsibilities of both the Cloud provider and the client.

In our experience, client policies are typically derived from one of two frameworks; NIST 800-53 (http://csrc.nist.gov) or ISO27001 (http://www.iso.org/iso/iso27001). The NIST 800-53 security controls "are designed to be technology-neutral such that the focus is on the fundamental countermeasures needed to protect organizational information during processing, storage, or transmission" (Dempsey, 2014). An ISO27001 approach is based on the definition of a risk-based management model that is assessed through a quality program audit. The control families of each are shown in Table 1. Both are widely used, to the end that NIST provides an Appendix with a mapping of one to the other (one mapping in each direction).

Table 1. Listing of NIST 800-53 and ISO / IEC 27001: 2013 Control Families

NIST 800-53	NIST Control Family	ISO / IEC 27001: 2013	ISO 27001
AC	Access Control	A.5	Information Security Policy
AT	Awareness and Training	A.6	Organization of Info Security
AU	Audit and Accountability	A.7	Asset Management
CA	Security Assessment and Authorization	A.8	Human Resources Security
CM	Configuration Management	A.9	Access Control
CP	Contingency Planning	A.10	Cryptography
IA	Identity and Authentication	A.11	Physical and environmental Security
IR	Incident Response	A.12	Operations Security
MA	Maintenance	A.13	Communications Security
MP	Media Protection	A.14	Systems Acquisition, Development and Maintenance
PE	Physical and Environmental Protection	A.15	Supplier Relationships
PL	Planning	A.16	Information Security Incident Management
PS	Personnel Security	A.17	Info Security aspects of Business Continuity Management
RA	Risk Assessment	A.18	Compliance
SA	Systems and Services Acquisition		
SC	Systems and Communications Protection		
SI	Systems and Information Integrity		

We will use NIST as the basis for discussion because of its focus on well-defined controls areas. The NIST Computer Security Division has issued an excellent white paper that provides an excellent summary of the updates to NIST 800-53 as part of the v4 release in 2014 (Dempsey, 2014).

Adherence to Security Policies: Demonstrating Compliance

Cloud providers engage independent, third-party auditors to assess the effectiveness of their controls against various standards. Most audits are performed on a bi-yearly or yearly basis, and most providers are audited against multiple standards. It is not uncommon for a Cloud provider to be in a perpetual state of audit. Against this background of perpetual state of audit, requests for client-driven audits are not scalable and are almost always rejected by a Cloud provider.

To compensate for this inability to support client-driven audit, Cloud providers will make their audit reports available to clients, usually under a Non-Disclosure Agreement. The two most common audit and compliance standards claimed by Cloud providers are ISO/IEC 27001 compliance certificates and the associated statements (Statement of Applicability) and AICPA-based (www.aicpa.org) based Statement of Controls (SOC) SOC1 and SOC2 audit reports (typically provided a "Type II" format, issued as detailed, auditor-to-auditor report).

Cloud provider audit reports should be provided in sufficient detail to allow clients to use them as evidence when auditing their cloud hosted workloads. These reports should be provided in an un-edited format, including findings and notes by the auditor and what remediation, if any, have been put in place by the Cloud provider. It is the experience of the authors, having lived through too many audits, that there is no such thing as a "clean" audit – a diligent auditor will always find something to comment on, just as a suitably motivated penetration test will always find a way to break a system. The trick for the reader of the report is to put the findings into context in terms of risk to the information system.

Compliance with clearly defined, publicly available, international standards provides clients with the evidence needed to forgo client-led audits of the Cloud provider itself. This together with visibility and transparency of a cloud environment allows clients to successfully move past this change in thinking. Proactively engaging internal risk assessment teams during the cloud evaluation process, and working closely with the Cloud provider to understand the controls in place and their evaluation in the context of the Cloud provider's audit and compliance assertions is a key part of this overall transition and migration to cloud.

Cloud Stack Roles and Responsibilities

Unfortunately a Cloud provider's audit report alone is insufficient to assert that a deployed Cloud-hosted workload is secure. Put another way, it is still very easy for a client to deploy an insecure, or poorly secured, workload on a secure infrastructure. The client, as the Cloud adopter, must have a clear understanding of their roles and responsibilities in the management of the environment, over and above the Cloud provider's responsibilities. There must also be a clear understanding of how any required communication with the Cloud provider will take place. Without this, gaps based on assumptions "but I thought they were responsible for that" or "but I wasn't told about this (quickly enough)" will introduce vulnerabilities into the operational management and use of the deployed Cloud workload.

Figure 1. shows the end-to-end application stack and the commonly accepted division of responsibility between the Cloud provider and the client for IaaS, PaaS, and SaaS models. For comparison, in the client on-premises model, the client has complete responsibility of the stack as shown in Figure 1.

Unfortunately Figure 1 does not allow us to easily separate out the primary role and responsibility (R&R) within each layer for those layers where both the Cloud provider manages the infrastructure and the client uses the infrastructure. We need a means to visualize the separation of responsibility for the management for the cloud infrastructure. As an example, within the network layer, the Cloud provider will retain responsibility for the physical network connecting all the cloud servers and the client will use this physical network in a virtual construct. Figure 1 is further thus refined in Figure 2 to separate the use and management of the stack by the client (use) and by the Cloud provider (management).

The separation of "use" and "management," is shown in Figure 2 for an IaaS specific model. This allows us to introduce the concept of sole responsibility and shared responsibility. Sole responsibility actions are implemented by tools, policies and procedures that are under the complete control of one party, either the client or the Cloud provider. This one party has the sole responsibility for providing the inputs necessary to perform the required actions, performing those actions and for the security controls required to support those actions. Shared responsibility actions involve both the client and the Cloud provider. Typically the client is responsible for providing the proper inputs as part of a request for an action, while the Cloud provider is responsible for validating the inputs, performing the request and ensuring that the appropriate evidence is in place to support the assertion of correct completion of the request.

Figure 3 shows the further breakdown of shared responsibility, or use and management, for an IaaS stack

Figure 1. End-to-end stack and responsibility for IaaS, PaaS, SaaS

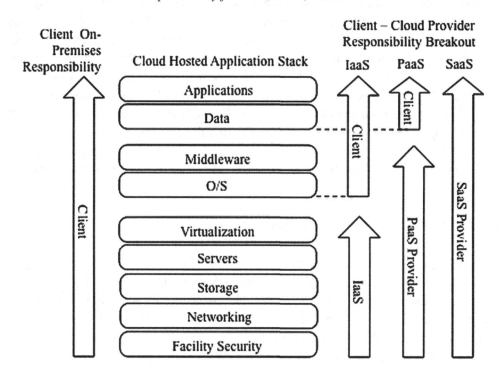

Figure 2. IaaS: Use and management for shared application stack layers

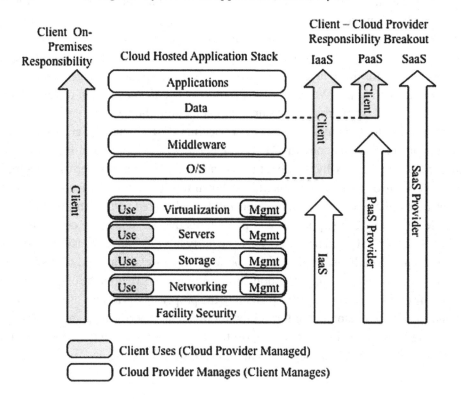

The Cloud provider's exposed management tools are the mechanisms that introduce shared responsibility actions: the client uses the tools to request actions and the Cloud provider performs the actions. An example of this is process to request the provisioning of virtual machines. The client is responsible for providing the Cloud provider with all necessary information to allow the Cloud provider to authenticate, authorize and complete the request. The Cloud provider, in turn, performs the action and provides the Client with the necessary evidence that the action has been properly performed.

Understanding when and how shared and sole responsibility actions are in place is necessary to ensure both proper evaluation of the Cloud provider's security and the proper implementation of client side controls and communications. The Request, Perform, Inform, Evidence (RPIE) model introduced in the next section allows the clear identification of who does what in a shared responsibility model and thus provides the basis of the evaluation of security and compliance for a cloud hosted workload.

Cloud "RPIE" Responsibility Model

In the Project Management world, the Responsibility Assignment Matrix, also known as the RACI model (Responsible, Accountable, Consult, Inform), is used to define roles and responsibilities across stakeholders in an organization (Table 2). This model assumes that the stakeholders (participants) in the RACI model are all part of a single organization, working towards a single project and a single goal, even if they have different roles.

To support a separation of roles in a multi-organization model, we introduce an analogous model, broken down the roles into a "RPIE" model (Request, Perform, Info, Evidence), shown in Table 3. The RPIE model is built on the natural separation of "who does what" in a Cloud model modeled as a closed loop process, shown in in Figure 4.

Figure 3. IaaS model: Client, cloud provider shared, sole responsibility model

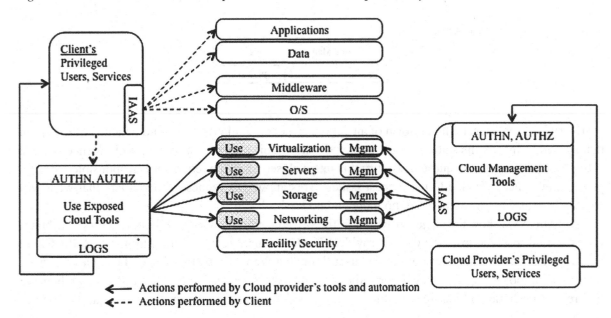

Table 2. RACI model for project management

	Project Management	
	Stakeholder	**Responsibility**
R	Responsible	Who is responsible?
A	Accountable	Who is accountable?
C	Consulted	Who is consulted?
I	Informed	Who is informed?

Table 3. Cloud request, perform, inform, monitor (RPIE): roles and responsibilities

	Cloud Role and Responsibility Model	
	Action	**Responsibility**
R	Request	Create request to perform
P	Perform	Perform requested action
I	Inform	Information for status of request, statistics, events, system behavior, notification
E	Evidence	Evidence including action completion status, statistics, events, system behavior, notification

Figure 4. RPIE closed loop model

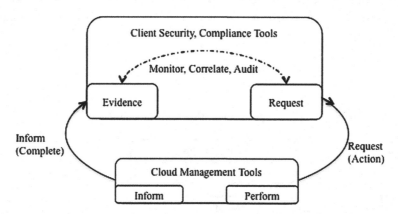

Every Request triggers the Perform of an action. Every action Perform should generate information that is used to Inform the status of the completed action. This information is used as Evidence that the action was performed as requested. To turn this into a closed loop, the requestor is responsible for mapping the evidence provided to the request issued. This allows the requestor to validate that what was performed was what was requested, no more and no less.

In Figure 5 we show the stages of RPIE for the shared action by which a Client requests an Ubuntu Linux virtual machine from the Cloud provider. The Client uses requests the action against the Cloud provider. This may be done by a privileged user through a Web API, by the client's ITIL-based service management tools using an API call, or some other means, as represented by R_C (request by Client) in Figure 5. The Cloud provider receives the request, validates it and then performs the request, as repre-

Figure 5. RPIE for shared responsibility, request a virtual machine

PROVISION VIRTUAL MACHINE
R_C –Request by Client to provision virtual machine with Linux
P_{CP} – Perform by Cloud provider of provisioning of VM and install of O/S
I_{CP} – Inform by Cloud Provider to Client that action is complete
E_C – Evidence-monitor by Client

WORKLOAD
P_C – Perform by Client of additional config and virtual server configuration and management including install of patches

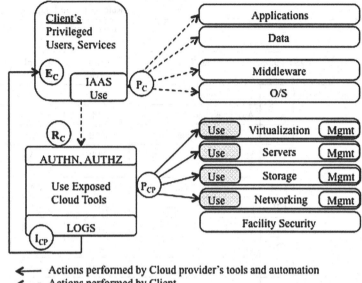

sented by P_{CP} (perform by Cloud provider). Once completed, the Cloud provider will inform the Client, through closure of a Cloud provider service ticket, system notification, email or other mechanisms, as presented by I_{CP}. The Client is then responsible for taking this information, together with any additional evidence, and using it for evidence-based monitoring of the system. This may be accomplished by closing out a service ticket that created the request, by ingest into an SIEM system or other mechanisms, as represented by E_C.

We can now use this break down of roles and responsibilities to break down of responsibility for individual controls (and evidence required for shared controls) in the context of control families such as NIST 800-53.

THE RPIE MODEL AND NIST 800-53 CONTROL FRAMEWORK

Table 4 shows the RPIE model in the context of the NIST 800-53 control family, broken out across the three categories of responsibility: the Cloud infrastructure, the Client's use of the Cloud infrastructure (including the Cloud management tools made available by the Cloud provider), and the Client's workload as deployed on the Cloud infrastructure. Roles and responsibilities can now be easily identified: if the cell at the intersection of a role (column) and responsibility (row) has the full "RPIE" responsibilities, then that role has that sole responsibility for that control. For example, the Cloud provider has full responsibility for Contingency Planning for the Cloud infrastructure (intersection of Contingency Planning row and Cloud provider sub-column for Cloud Infrastructure), but the Client has full responsibility for Contingency Planning for the Client's use of the Cloud infrastructure and the Client's deployed workload.

As part of the clear definition of roles and responsibilities, the sum of the individual RPIE-assigned responsibilities across the Cloud provider and the client for any cloud view should provide one and only

Table 4. RPIE roles and responsibility assessment with NIST 800-53 control families

			Role by Cloud Usage					
			Cloud Infrastructure		Client's Use of Cloud Management		Client's Deployed Workload	
NIST 800-53 Control Family			Cloud Provider	Client	Cloud Provider	Client	Cloud Provider	Client
Responsibility	AC	Access Control	RPIE	N/A	PI	RE	N/A	RPIE
	AT	Awareness and Training	RPIE	N/A	N/A	RPIE	N/A	RPIE
	AU	Audit and Accountability	RPIE	N/A	PI	RE	N/A	RPIE
	CA	Security Assessment and Authorization	RPIE	N/A	N/A	RPIE	N/A	RPIE
	CM	Configuration Management	RPIE	N/A	PI	RE	N/A	RPIE
	CP	Contingency Planning	RPIE	N/A	N/A	RPIE	N/A	RPIE
	IA	Identity and Authentication	RPIE	N/A	PI	RE	N/A	RPIE
	IR	Incident Response	RPIE	[I]	[I]	RPIE	[I]	RPIE
	MA	Maintenance	RPIE	N/A	PI	RE	N/A	RPIE
	MP	Media Protection	RPIE	N/A	N/A	N/A	N/A	RPIE
	PE	Physical and Environmental Protection	RPIE	N/A	N/A	N/A	N/A	N/A
	PL	Planning	RPIE	[I]	[I]	RPIE	[I]	RPIE
	PS	Personnel Security	RPIE	N/A	N/A	RPIE	N/A	RPIE
	RA	Risk Assessment	RPIE	N/A	N/A	RPIE	N/A	RPIE
	SA	Systems and Services Acquisition	RPIE	N/A	N/A	RPIE	N/A	RPIE
	SC	Systems and Communications Protection	RPIE	N/A	N/A	RPIE	N/A	RPIE
	SI	Systems and Information Integrity	RPIE	N/A	N/A	RPIE	N/A	RPIE

one responsible owner for each role. So it should not be possible for both the Cloud provider and the Client to have the "Perform" role for a given responsibility: if this does happen, we have identified a scenario where overlapping responsibilities may lead to missed actions and vulnerabilities. There is one minor exception to this, for Inform actions, where each participant has Inform responsibilities across all areas of responsibility.

The added benefit of this layout is that we can now discuss who does what for the Client's use of the Cloud infrastructure so that we can evaluate the impact of actions and the effectiveness of associated controls across each control family for the different stakeholders in a Cloud environment.

RPIE for Cloud Infrastructure

Table 4 clearly highlights what we should already know and intuit: the Cloud provider has sole responsibility for the management of the Cloud infrastructure. Client's who are evaluating Cloud providers will require evidence of the effectiveness of the Cloud provider's sole controls.

Clients and their auditors are interested in how a Cloud provider manages their employees for control families such as "Awareness and Training" and "Access Control." Clients do not need to rely on "Trust Me" statements from the Cloud provider but can use the evidence from the Cloud provider's audit reports and compliance statements.

There are two control families that have special requirements on the Inform action that may not be included in a Cloud provider's audits: Incident Response and Planning. These are areas where Cloud provider actions may impact the Client and are areas where a special emphasis on clear lines of communication is required.

Incident Response (IR)

Incident response (IR) requires a clear line of communication, including notification and response between Cloud provider and Client. This is not new. And while neither party would normally never inform the details of their internal environment, each does have a duty to inform the other if there are actions or events that may impact the other.

For example, the Cloud provider has a duty to inform the client if there is an incident that may impact the client, such as suspected unauthorized access to the Client's environment. Similarly, if the Client experiences a security incident on its Cloud deployed workload, such as theft of privileged user passwords, including those passwords used to access the Cloud management tools, they should notify the Cloud provider; this allows the Cloud provider to take whatever actions it believes are necessary, including supporting the Client during the client's incident response process.

It is strongly recommended that the Cloud provider and client clearly identify means of communication to support incident management and response included name "first responders" who can be contacted at any time day or night as part of an incident response agreement between the two.

Planning (PL)

Planning (PL) includes security related activities, such as "*security assessments, audits, hardware and software maintenance, patch management, and contingency plan testing. Advance planning and coordination includes emergency and nonemergency (i.e., planned or non-urgent unplanned) situations.*" (National Institute of Science and Technology, 2015)

From the Cloud provider's side, most planned security-related activities will be invisible to the client. There are scenarios, often associated with vulnerability management and the broader topic of patch management, in which notification should be provided to the client (remember that while most vulnerabilities will require a patch, most patches are not associated with vulnerabilities). The Cloud provider should provide advanced warning of operational management events that may impact the client. As an example, even if configured in redundant pairs for high availability purposes, if a Cloud provider is going to perform maintenance on its routers that may involve even momentary downtime, the Cloud provider should notify the client. This is where the lines of communication established as part of a broader relationship, including Incident Response process will be put into use.

As a reminder, the client has no say in when the Cloud provider will patch their infrastructure for normal patches or vulnerability-driven patches. This has the impact of forcing clients to live with aggressive patch schedules that they may otherwise chose to extend; for this reason, client workload should be designed with resiliency in mind when considering the impact of Cloud provider management. For those cases where the client must have complete control over the configuration and management (patch) of the infrastructure, the client should consider Bring-Your-Own-Virtualization deployment models with a physical server based cloud.

In context of Planned events, the client should inform the Cloud provider of certain events, in particular, security assessments including penetration tests, against the client's Cloud hosted workload. This may be required as a contractual item to allow the Cloud provider to respond properly should a client's penetration testing tools "misbehave" and duplicate an attack against the client that also threatens the broader Cloud environment such as the overall Cloud network and available bandwidth. In the absence of notification, a Cloud provider may shut down such an account, as part of the protection of the Cloud infrastructure for all other clients. With the knowledge that this may be a client test gone wrong, the Cloud provider can work with the client to restore services.

RPIE for Client Use of Cloud Infrastructure (Shared Responsibilities)

In a Cloud, a client uses the Cloud provider's tools and automation to order and customize servers, storage and networks. The Cloud provider will make available Web and API based tools and services to the client and the client's privileged users but will retain operational control for these tools and services.

The Cloud provider will expose supporting functionality or services, such as authentication of users, to support the proper use of its Cloud services and tools. These supporting functions are where the shared RPIE responsibilities are most clearly identified. Repeating Table 4 with just the shared controls of the Cloud Infrastructure in Table 5 we can see the shared roles and responsibilities called out for the Cloud Provider (Perform, Inform) and the Client (Request, Evidence).

While every control family deserves its own lengthy discussion, in this section we provide a brief overview of the implications, by control family, of the shared responsibility controls, Access Control, Audit and Accountability, Configuration Management, Identity and Authentication, and Maintenance.

Access Control (AC), Identity, and Authentication (IA)

The overall user lifecycle management functionality, also known as UAM or IAM, crosses two control families in the NIST control family: Identity and Authentication, Access Control. This set of control families is worth special mention because of the additional complications from the many types of and privileges of Client side users. By separating the Client's use of the Cloud infrastructure from the Client's deployed Cloud workload, we can limit the focus to the subset of Client-side user types who have permission to use the Cloud provider's tools and automation.

Recall that as part of the Perform of an action in response to a Client request, the Cloud provider relies on the Client to provide accurate, correct requests, ones that can be authenticated and authorized. The Cloud provider retains responsibility for the implementation of the identification, authentication and authorization (access control) for requests, including users making the requests, received from the Client.

When we introduced the RPIE model, we showed the RPIE actions as part of a client's request to provision a virtual machine in Figure 4. This is repeated here, Figure 6, to allow us to focus on the details of the Request and Perform interaction. The Request from the Client will trigger several actions for the Cloud provider to Perform. Before the Request itself can be fulfilled, the Cloud provider must authenticate and authorize both the request and the requestor.

Table 5. RPIE in NIST control family for client's user of cloud infrastructure

Client's Use of Cloud Management Tools				
NIST 800-53 Control Family			**Cloud Provider**	**Client**
Responsibility	AC	Access Control	PI	RE
	AT	Awareness and Training	N/A	RPIE
	AU	Audit and Accountability	PI	RE
	CA	Security Assessment and Authorization	N/A	RPIE
	CM	Configuration Management	PI	RE
	CP	Contingency Planning	N/A	RPIE
	IA	Identity and Authentication	PI	RE
	IR	Incident Response	[I]	RPIE
	MA	Maintenance	PI	RE
	MP	Media Protection	N/A	N/A
	PE	Physical and Environmental Protection	N/A	N/A
	PL	Planning	[I]	RPIE
	PS	Personnel Security	N/A	RPIE
	RA	Risk Assessment	N/A	RPIE
	SA	Systems and Services Acquisition	N/A	RPIE
	SC	Systems and Communications Protection	N/A	RPIE
	SI	Systems and Information Integrity	N/A	RPIE

Figure 6. RPIE details for shared responsibility

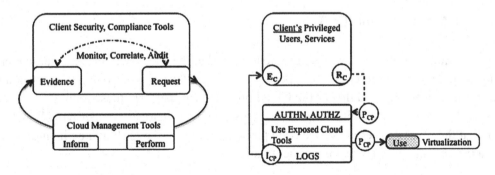

Clients will need to extend their user lifecycle management tools and procedures for those privileged users who have permission to Request actions against the Cloud provider's management tools. Areas that we have seen as requiring extra attention include privilege management and account off-boarding, for those user accounts that are maintained at the Cloud provider side, and the ingest of data from the Inform step into the client's local logging and monitoring tools and processes.

Note that the Cloud provider has no role or responsibility for those actions that are at the Client's responsibility (operating system and above) or for those client users who have direct access to the Client's deployed environment. The Cloud provider has Perform and Inform scope only for those Client users who use the Cloud provider's tools and interfaces to manage the Client's environment.

Audit and Accountability (AU)

Audit and Accountability (AU) controls align with the Inform and Evidence actions in the RPIE model. That is, the Cloud provider makes available the evidence needed for the Client's AU controls. The Cloud provider will (should) make available logs of corresponding actions, including actions associated with user account management, login attempts, login failures, changes to a user's permissions and profile and actions taken by the user. The Client is responsible for using this evidence to provide its own audit and accountability steps – for example, to make sure that one of the Client's privileged users has not somehow been able to present valid credentials as part of a request of which the Client itself has no knowledge.

In addition to audit and accountability for user actions, the Cloud provider will also be responsible for providing log evidence for actions against devices and services. This allows the Client to correlate events – logs from the Cloud provider show that a server is rebooted at 2:04pm on Monday and from the Client's ITIL-based service management tool show that the tool requested this server shutdown at 2:01pm on Monday. The correlation of event (server shutdown) to action (service management request) provides the Client with visibility into their environment and further provides assurance that the Cloud provider, or a rogue user, cannot take actions against the environment without evidence being provided to the Client.

These logs and evidence are often made available through API calls in formats that can be ingested into existing log store, monitoring and analytics tools. The Client is responsible for including logs in the Client's preferred monitoring and analytics activities. If the Client choses to not use this evidence, this is the Client's decision and responsibility.

Configuration Management (CM)

As part of the requesting of services from the Cloud provider, the Client will provide parameters (such as the number of cores for a server, or the expected size of a database) that govern the configuration of requested services. It is expected that as the Cloud provider will perform these requests, including the configuration that is in scope. Again, the evidence provided by the Cloud provider will allow the Client to confirm that the requested services have been properly configured and should be included as part of the Audit and Accountability control implementation.

Maintenance (MA)

While the majority of NIST's Maintenance controls relate to physical infrastructure and information systems, there is explicit reference to the sanitization of media prior to removal as part of a broader focus on data deletion and to prevent the leakage of residual data when devices are removed from service.

Cloud providers have robust procedures for the deletion of data and decommissioning of servers. In a Cloud environment, however, Clients may stop using a server or service long before it is removed from service, and thus before it is subject to data wipe or sanitization by the Cloud provider. Consider a Client provisioned virtual server that is used for a period of time then de-provisioned. The underlying host will continue to host and remove virtual machines until the host itself is decommissioned. There is no guarantee that a host server will be physical wiped between virtual server provisioning and de-provisioning activities.

This means that clients will have to rely on Client-implemented primary controls for the deletion of data at the workload level and use audit reports from their Cloud providers as evidence of the secondary controls of media sanitization and data deletion as implemented by the Cloud provider on out-of-service and decommissioned hardware.

Systems and Communication Protection (SC)

The systems and communication protection (SC) control family does not represent a shared control. We include it in this discussion however as many Clients believe that this is a service that is by default performed by the Cloud provider, even if not explicitly requested by the Client. The SC control explicitly identifies the need and role for gateways, routers, firewalls, and guards to protect the network.

Clients are responsible for the use of their virtual network provided, including its configuration and the deployment of (virtual) devices for the configuration and protection their virtual network. Clients may order and use Cloud provider services for this functionality, but the actual responsibility for this remains with the Client.

RPIE and Client's Cloud Deployed Workload

Just as the Cloud provider is solely responsible for the management of the Cloud infrastructure, the Client is solely responsible for the management of their Cloud deployed workload. Referring back to Table 4, the mirror image nature of responsibilities for the Cloud infrastructure and the Client's deployed workload is seen by comparing the Cloud Infrastructure and Client Deployed Workload columns.

RPIE and Hybrid Cloud Models

Table 6. extends previous tables to include a column for On Premises workload, showing the RPIE model for a hybrid cloud environment. For those controls that are the sole responsibility of the Client across an entire row (such as Awareness and Training for On Premises Workload, Client's Use of Cloud Management Tools and Client's Cloud Deployed Workload, no changes are required to the Client's existing policies and procedures. For those controls that include a Perform and Inform responsibility by the Cloud provider, however, the Client should review their existing procedures and tools to ensure that the appropriate information is flowing back and forth to allow the Client to ensure the appropriate controls are in place. Note that when looking at Table 6 a reasonable conclusion is that these changes and Client-side reviews are required, whether the Client is engaged in a hybrid cloud model or not.

Impact of Shared Responsibility on a Client's Security Policies

While many clients will simply apply their existing security policies to their Cloud deployed workload, a good number will also define a Cloud specific policy. Cloud specific policies should be designed to reflect the changing responsibility for primary and secondary controls of the Cloud environment and the risks associated with different types of workload and their suitability for Cloud.

Table 6. NIST controls for on-premises and cloud deployed (hybrid) workloads

Responsibility			On Premises Workload		Client's Use of Cloud Management Tools		Cloud Deployed Workload	
	NIST 800-53 Control Family		Cloud Provider	Client	Cloud Provider	Client	Cloud Provider	Client
	AC	Access Control	N/A	RPIE	PI	RE	N/A	RPIE
	AT	Awareness and Training	N/A	RPIE	N/A	RPIE	N/A	RPIE
	AU	Audit and Accountability	N/A	RPIE	PI	RE	N/A	RPIE
	CA	Security Assessment and Authorization	N/A	RPIE	N/A	RPIE	N/A	RPIE
	CM	Configuration Management	N/A	RPIE	PI	RE	N/A	RPIE
	CP	Contingency Planning	N/A	RPIE	N/A	RPIE	N/A	RPIE
	IA	Identity and Authentication	N/A	RPIE	PI	RE	N/A	RPIE
	IR	Incident Response	N/A	RPIE	[I]	RPIE	[I]	RPIE
	MA	Maintenance	N/A	RPIE	PI	RE	N/A	RPIE
	MP	Media Protection	N/A	RPIE	N/A	N/A	N/A	RPIE
	PE	Physical and Environmental Protection	N/A	RPIE	N/A	N/A	N/A	N/A
	PL	Planning	N/A	RPIE	[I]	RPIE	[I]	RPIE
	PS	Personnel Security	N/A	RPIE	N/A	RPIE	N/A	RPIE
	RA	Risk Assessment	N/A	RPIE	N/A	RPIE	N/A	RPIE
	SA	Systems and Services Acquisition	N/A	RPIE	N/A	RPIE	N/A	RPIE
	SC	Systems and Communications Protection	N/A	RPIE	N/A	RPIE	N/A	RPIE
	SI	Systems and Information Integrity	N/A	RPIE	N/A	RPIE	N/A	RPIE

Our experience, as laid out in the Hybrid Cloud use case scenario below, is that the real area of focus is ensuring that the Client's existing tools and processes are extended to the Cloud, resulting in a "hybrid tooling" model to support the hybrid cloud.

SECURITY CONTROLS WITH A SIMPLE HYBRID CLOUD APPLICATION

Having worked through how to approach cloud in terms of roles and responsibilities, we put this into context with for a simple hybrid cloud application where we will focus on how to secure our cloud deployed workload and environments. This use case is based on our client experience and draws best (and not-so-best) practices from many different scenarios across all industries, but primarily focused within the Financial Services space (global and regional banks and insurance companies).

The use case we will consider addresses an internal application for a financial institution. The client, "Investing4You" (I4U) has an in-house application used to provide Monte Carlo simulations of market risk profiles. They are currently maintaining a large server infrastructure to support the peak loads of this application. Due to budget constraints and executive mandate, this application is a candidate for moving to cloud.

I4U's due diligence has included an analysis of the performance and network connectivity and architecture implications for a cloud deployment. They have identified the controls that must be extended to the Cloud environment to ensure compliance with the financial institution's internal policies and risk management assessments. At the same time, I4U is using this cloud migration as an opportunity to bring additional operational efficiencies to the environment through automation.

As result of I4U risk assessments, they have made several technology choices, including the use of IBM SoftLayer for their Cloud hosting platform. This will allow them to leverage physical servers (also known as bare metal servers), including the Intel TxT functionality. These servers can be ordered to I4U's specification so that they match what I4U has already profiled and scoped with their in-house environment, and can provisioned in hours, with complete transparency down to the server sub-component level. I4U will also adopt new use tools and services from the IBM Marketplace, including Cloud Raxak's Raxak Protect to provide the infrastructure components and management tools identified for their cloud hosted application.

[NOTE: We have chosen to identify IBM SoftLayer as the basis of this example as this use case is drawn from several real-world scenarios of financial institution clients hosting workloads on IBM SoftLayer, using Softlayer's physical server options and IBM Marketplace hosted tools].

I4U Application Cloud Architecture and Requirement Details

Key areas that I4U's architecture team focused on with their cloud architecture included network connectivity, physical and virtual servers, and local versus on-premises versus SaaS tools. During application reviews and proof of concept exercises, and in response to functional and non-functional requirements, I4U's team made several up-front technology choices and decisions. These are listed below and are reflected in the overall application architecture shown in Figure 7:

- **IaaS Platform:** IBM SoftLayer with bare metal servers with Intel TxT and dedicated virtual servers. CloudRaxak's RaxakProtect will be used for initial configuration and continuous compliance management.
- **Hybrid Cloud Tools:** I4U will extend its on-premises solutions for AntiVirus (A/V), Security, Incident Event Monitoring (SIEM), and Encryption and Key Management (KM) to the cloud deployed environment.
- **User IAM:** I4U will extend its existing Active Directory (AD) integration to support server login on the cloud deployed environment for tools and privileged users who manage the environment. There will be a small set of users (approximately five) and two service accounts who will be set up with accounts against the SoftLayer control panel, allowing them to manage the environment.
  - For now, these users will be managed through a simple set of directory-federation scripts that will ensure that I4U's AD remains the authoritative source of user information and is used to sync to the SoftLayer side.
  - I4U may chose to use SoftLayer's SAML-push abilities in the future, but have decided that they prefer the control that comes with directory federation and the SLAPI.

Figure 7. I4U's IaaS hosted, hybrid cloud application

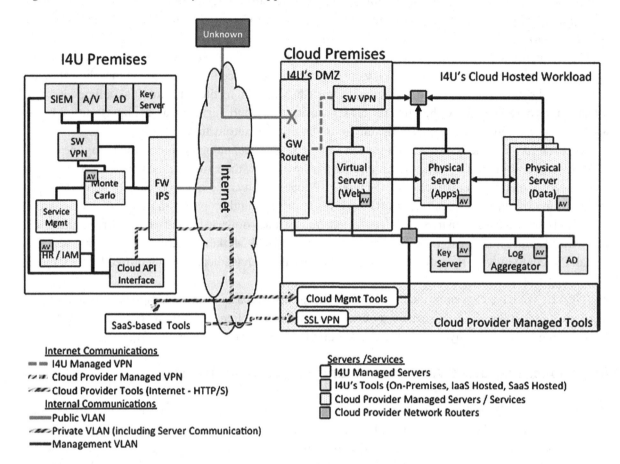

- **Applications Network Connectivity:** I4U's existing application is internal only. The Cloud-hosted aspects of this application will remain internal (they will not be Internet facing).
  - I4U will deploy a gateway router at the network edge that will be configured to whitelist only known I4U locations and IP addresses. This will block all other locations from input to the I4U environment.
  - To support future enablement of this environment as a SaaS offering for I4U's clients, I4U will design the Cloud-hosted workload to support a Web front end but all servers will be configured for zero-bandwidth on their public facing network.
- **Administration Network Connectivity:** I4U will use an Internet-facing server hosting an IPSEC VPN to provide connectivity to the Cloud environment for administrative purposes.
  - I4U's clients and administrators will use this VPN to access and manage the provisioned servers and applications for operational management purposes.
  - I4U will also use this VPN for bulk data transfer to and from cloud environment.
  - The IPESC VPN will be deployed as the exception to the "No Internet Facing" rule and as such is hardened to prevent compromise and closely monitored to detect attempts at compromise.

- ○ I4U will enable their third-party SaaS tools to use the IBM SoftLayer VPN to access their environment (third-party SaaS tools will not use the IPSEC VPN).
- **Server (Physical) Configuration:** Bare metal/physical servers will be used for data storage and for hosting high I/O processing in the cloud environment, mirroring the I4U on-premises environment.
  - ○ I4U will duplicate the configuration of their on-premises physical servers which are configured with 1 TB RAM, two 1.2 TB SSD drives, and four 6 TB SATA drives each.
- **Operating Systems Configuration:** I4U will adopt automation and processes to ensure both initial and ongoing configuration of servers and applications in accordance with I4U's security policies and configuration specifications.
  - ○ I4U will implement ongoing configuration monitoring and compliance using Cloud Raxak's RaxakProtect tool. This will allow I4U to run configuration checks, with automated remediation, on a schedule and on-demand, with full evidence of findings and remediation actions.
- **Autoscaling:** I4U knows how big a given run will be and so can accurately forecast the capacity required. I4U's service management tool (which is used to trigger runs of the Monte Carlo app) will be extended to spin up the required Cloud servers using the IBM SoftLayer API (SLAPI).

These requirements, both functional and non-functional, are the basis of the architecture that is shown in Figure 7.

I4U's Hybrid Application and Security Policy: Shared Controls

Identification and Authentication (IA), Access Control (AC)

I4U has identified a small set of I4U privileged users and tools that will require access to the Cloud provider's tools and the Cloud hosted servers. These will require new roles and privileges that must be managed within the context of I4U's policy framework.

I4U will extend their account management to include the use of the Cloud. This will allow them to retain responsibility for user management, including aspects of their security policy that require periodic revalidation of user status. By comparing information from the Cloud provider (user's account is disabled) together with information from the HR system (user was terminated 3 months prior, all accounts were disabled), I4U will have the evidence needed to demonstrate continued compliance with their IA, AC policies.

I4U's Cloud Infrastructure Management Privileged Users

All I4U users will continue to be managed by I4U within their existing HR and IAM systems. A new role will be created, for "Cloud Infrastructure Management" privileged users (CIM privileged users). The small set of users with this role will have defined permissions that will allow them to manage the Cloud environment.

I4U will create a simple tool to listen to the on-premises IAM systems for changes that are relevant to these privileged users. The tool will then update the user's required account information, including permissions and account status, using the Cloud provider's published API. This will allow these users to login to the Cloud provider's tools with a username and password defined by I4U, managed to the

I4U's password and authentication policy and will allow I4U to retain authoritative, non-circumventable control over the user's status and ability to log in at the Cloud provider.

I4U's risk assessment team has approved this IAM implementation as they are confident that they retain full user account control and have the evidence to demonstrate everything that happens against a user account.

I4U's Cloud Infrastructure Privileged Management Tools

I4U's simulation scheduler and the IAM synchronization tools require accounts at the Cloud provider, Each tool will have a unique account with a unique API key for authentication purposes, where each account is set up with only the permissions needed for that service account. These will be set up by hand initially and then managed by the same automation used for user account management. The service accounts will be configured to prevent interactive login. Further, this account will be configured so that use of the account's API key is authorized only for the static IP address(es) associated with the service management tool(s).

I4U's risk assessors have accepted this usage of an API key, even though the key is not created by the I4U, because of the IP address lockdown and the control over the setting, resetting and disabling of the API key provided to the client, combined with the full transparency into actions taken against I4U's account.

I4U's Account Privileges and Access Management

I4U's policies require both separation of duties and least privilege principles to be part of the privileges assigned to users and roles. I4U will use the granular privilege structure exposed by the Cloud provider to define I4U-specific roles for users and tools.

The risk assessment team has reviewed the privileges for the I4U's accounts and explicitly required that human (interactive) users are not given the privilege to provision or de-provision servers; this privilege will be provided for the service management account only. This will ensure that no user can order a new service or device at the Cloud provider outside of the I4U's service management tools and associated workflow approvals.

I4U's Cloud Deployed Workload Privileged Users

Just as with an on-premises servers and applications, I4U will have a set of privileged users responsible for server and application management. These users will be managed using the same tools and processes as on-premises environments. In this respect, I4U's cloud hosted servers are no different from their on-premises servers.

In I4U's on-premises environment, Active Directory is used to control access to all servers. This will be extended to the Cloud environment with an AD instance deployed in the Cloud environment and federated with the Client's on-premises AD forest.

This will allow I4U to keep its existing processes for server access and management, and will support requirements from I4U's risk assessment team. I4U's risk assessment team requires that server and application administrators will not have accounts or privileges against the Cloud provider's tools. This enforces separation of duty whereby a server administrator is not able to order or provision a server in the Cloud environment.

All servers will be part of the I4U's Active Directory network; this allows the I4U to manage all of the server administrators within their Human Resources (HR) systems. This means that the only changes to the I4U's procedures will be to add the deployed servers to their AD infrastructure (as is common with many environments, the I4U's HR systems provide direct feeds to Active Directory). Server administrators will log in to servers through AD and so their access will be limited to their permissions and status as maintained in AD, including their employment status as maintained by HR.

I4U's Future IAM Direction

I4U investigated using a federated single-sign-on approach (such as SAML) to support federation of their users across both I4U and the IBM SoftLayer. They determined that the set of users that need to be enabled is small enough that the SLAPI directory federation approach satisfied their requirements. I4U will pilot SoftLayer's SAML-based single sign-on as they increase their Cloud deployment.

Audit and Accountability (AU)

One reason that I4U's risk assessment team has become comfortable with Cloud is the ability to have comprehensive logging that feeds into I4U's on-premises systems. This allows I4U to use and extend their analytics and monitoring to the Cloud environment and the hybrid of Cloud and on-premises.

While I4U will extend their monitoring to look for actions that are unique to the transient nature of their Cloud environment (atypical provisioning or de-provisioning of servers, for example). As this will be done with tools that the I4U team is already familiar with, I4U's risk assessors are comfortable that once they have demonstrated the correct integration (information pull from I4U) that I4U will have complete visibility into their Cloud hosted environment.

I4U's Privileged Management Tool Logs

I4U will use the Cloud provider's API to import log information and usage statistics into their on-premises log aggregation tools for use by their monitoring and analytics tools. This will include log information such as login attempts by users and changes to servers as requested using the API or through a chat with a Cloud provider support person.

I4U's Cloud Deployed Workload Logs

I4U will have a Cloud-hosted log aggregator used to collect log information (such as syslog) from the Cloud-hosted servers. This information will be subject to the same analyses as information gathered into on-premises log aggregators from on-premises servers. Once initial analysis has been performed, high-level results will be forwarded to I4U's on-premises security event and incident management (SIEM) tools over the VPN tunnel between I4U's on-premises and cloud environments.

Configuration Management (CM), Maintenance (MA)

I4U's security team initially wanted to do a "lift and shift" of their tools and procedures to their Cloud hosted environment. As not all of their tools easily extended into the Cloud / Software as a Service model (where their in-house tools would appear to be SaaS tools for their cloud environment), they have found a SaaS-based alternative.

Automation for Configuration and Compliance

System configuration (operating system and application) is an area where I4U plans on leveraging new approaches to configuration management. Currently this is done through agent-based tools and subsequent manual checks for validation. Using automation based configuration management will allow I4U to configure, check and continually maintain their servers with the require configuration settings, including patch currency.

I4U initially planned on implementing their own Chef-script based automation for configuration and remediation of server settings but have opted to go with a SaaS-based tool (Raxak Protect) from the IBM Marketplace. Raxak allows I4U to harden to NIST and DISA configuration guidelines. Raxak Protect was easily integrated into I4U's on-premises service management tool and set up to run configuration checks with automated remediation on a daily basis.

RaxakProtect will also be a part of I4U's cloud-aware patching strategy. I4U has decided to jettison their existing approach to patching in favor of cloud-based agility. In response to notification that a web or app tier server is out-of-date with respect to patches, I4U's team will provision new, patched servers, test these servers and then migrate to new, patched servers, shutting down the unpatched servers.

When demonstrating this tool to their risk assessment team, the server management team was able to show a real-time run of configuration checks together with an automated remediation of any variations; both the risk assessment and internal audit teams have made use of this tool mandatory for all Cloud deployments within I4U and are further investigating its use internally. Further, as a result of this demonstration, I4U had no resistance to its change in patching policy for their cloud hosted servers. Their policy now reads that servers are patched, or replaced, within the appropriate timeframe based on patch sensitivity.

Incident Response (IR)

Information Security Incident Management

I4U has an internal Computer Security Incident Response Team (CSIRT) that will extend their responsibility to include the Cloud deployed environment. This team will be the interface with Cloud provider's SOC and incident response teams. They have set up lines of communication with the SOC team and established a set of guidelines to ensure that they receive all notifications from Cloud provider. Internally I4U's CSIRT team has identified a set of situations that may require them to notify the Cloud provider of issues and have clearly documented how that communication will be initiated.

I4U's risk assessors have asked for a table top exercise to test this process; I4U is working with the Cloud provider to put this in place once the initial deployment is complete.

I4U's Hybrid Application and Security Policy: I4U Sole Controls

Contingency Planning (CP)

As part of their move to cloud, I4U's project managers had initially sized the migration effort based on a "lift-and-shift" approach – that is, one where the existing application is exactly duplicated and replicated in the cloud environment. Happily, several of I4U's lead architects with experience with virtualization environments were involved in the initial risk assessment reviews. When discussing controls within the Contingency Planning framework, the move from (in-house) physical servers to (cloud-hosted) virtual servers, required a change in thinking about the underlying architecture itself. A result of this was a requirement, driven by Disaster Recovery and Business Continuity, but also applicable to High Availability, that all servers that are to be hosted in virtual machines at the Cloud side will have at least two instances running on separate hosts to provide a level of resiliency against virtual machine failure. Note that the in-house/in-cloud is a red herring here; what matters is the move from physical servers to virtual servers.

Systems and Communications Protection (SC)

Just as with their on-premises environment, I4U must protect the boundary to their Cloud-hosted application as if it was on-premise. The wrinkle is that they can't necessarily rely on existing on-premises tools such as in-house firewalls. I4U has to deploy additional boundary protection for their Cloud-hosted application, to protect the application from Internet-based traffic and threats, and to protect their on-premises environment from any compromise that may be experienced at their Cloud-hosted application.

Boundary Protection, Access Points

An I4U managed IPSEC VPN tunnel will be put in place to support "always on" connectivity for I4U's on-premises services and tools. Because of the always-on nature of the IPSEC VPN, I4U will deploy a firewall (gateway router) between their premises and the Cloud provider. This will be configured to allow only authorized communications between the two environments, for the purposes of I4U management of the SoftLayer hosted servers (physical and virtual) and data transfer as part of the scheduler operation. In particular, the firewall will block any unauthorized or unexpected traffic from the Cloud environment back the I4U's premises.

SaaS tools will use the Cloud-provider managed SSL VPN functionality. This will allow the SaaS tool to directly access I4U's private network without having to come through I4U's Internet-facing gateway. This will allow the SaaS tool to set up a temporary SSL VPN session for the purposes of managing the environment and provides I4U with complete control over the SaaS tool connectivity – they can turn off the tool's access at any time. If a SaaS tool requires an always-on option, they will be migrated to I4U's IPSEC tunnel.

IA, AC, AU Implications

Because of the way that IBM SoftLayer manages this VPN connectivity, each of the SaaS tools will have a SoftLayer user (service) account; I4U will need to ensure that they properly manage the lifecycle of these accounts including permission management and on-going account revalidation. This may require additions to their in-house security policies and procedures related to the management of business partners (viewing the SaaS provider as a business partner). These accounts will be managed by hand and not by I4U's service management tools.

I4U's risk assessors are comfortable with this approach as I4U has demonstrated that they will include the log information associated with these service accounts in their overall SIEM monitoring, adding rules to look for suspicious activity around SaaS account creation and privilege escalation.

IR Implications

In case I4U's monitoring turns up suspicious behavior by a SaaS partner, they have implemented a procedure to validate the type of expected activity and steps to temporarily or permanently disable the associated user accounts until the investigation is complete.

Application Security, Data Security, and Privacy

While I4U is confident that the data that is hosted at the Cloud side has been suitably masked in terms of client-identifying and proprietary information, their risk management team has put in place a requirement that all of the data used for the Monte Carlo simulation be encrypted at rest at the Cloud side. Because the I4U has complete control of their workload, that includes the ability to deploy both the encryption and key management solutions of their choice and to retain complete control of their encryption keys at all times.

I4U has a preferred in-house solution for key management that they will extend to their cloud-hosted environment (remember that encryption is the easy part, key management, including rollover, is the hard part). This will allow I4U to deploy the necessary agents on their servers (as part of their Golden Master image) configured to use the I4U's on-premises key management server.

I4U's risk assessors like this approach as it means that I4U will continue to use its existing, tested, key management procedures. As these have been subject to many (clean) audits, the risk assessors are confident that as long as the required encryption agents are deployed for the cloud-hosted servers, the required encryption and key management procedures will be in place. Thus the risk assessor's focus will be on the logs of each deployed server to ensure that they require encryption agents are deployed and in use.

Overall Audit and Compliance

Cloud Workload Audit

As a financial institution, I4U is federally regulated. This means that they need to apply extra rigor to their operational management procedures. For this application, I4U determined that an assessment by their internal risk management team, together with the audit reports provided by the Cloud provider, and independent audits of the client-controlled portion of the environment, was required prior to their deployment to cloud. This was deemed necessary to satisfy both internal I4U business owners and I4U's their regulators.

I4U's risk assessment was conducted in several steps. I4U provided a copy of their risk assessment questionnaire to the Cloud provider. On completion, I4U set up a series of meetings to go through the answers and drill down on any additional questions. As part of this assessment, I4U and the Cloud provider discussed questions or concerns with the Cloud provider's audit reports as well as reviewed requirements such as communications paths as part of their joint Incident Response responsibilities. This allowed I4U to fully and accurately represent the entire environment in and on which their application is hosted.

Regulator Review and Audit

As part of a yearly visit and review by the I4U's regulatory body, the Financial Review Team (FRT, a fictitious financial regulatory body drawn from our experience with multiple different regulatory bodies), I4U worked with the FRT to demonstrate the appropriate control and oversight for their cloud hosted workload. During this review, I4U provided the FRT with copies of I4U's audit reports, the Cloud provider's audit reports (both produced by an independent third-party) together with I4U's internal business controls teams reviews and the I4U-Cloud Provider risk assessment.

During this review the FRT had some questions about the Cloud Provider's environment. In response, the I4U, FRT and Cloud Provider set up a joint conference call where the Cloud Provider reviewed their audit reports with the FRT, and answered the outstanding FRT questions.

As a result of this review and information sharing, the FRT is satisfied that the I4U has adequate control over their environment and that the Cloud Provider is providing adequate controls over the Cloud infrastructure.

IMPLICATIONS FOR SECURITY POLICIES IN A HYBRID CLOUD DEPLOYMENT

Conclusion and Recap

This chapter has focused on the implications of moving to cloud on overall workload security and compliance. Cloud providers retain control of the Cloud infrastructure operational management; likewise the Client will have operational responsibility for their deployed workload. To deploy a Cloud environment, that is, for a client to use the Cloud provider's exposed tools, introduces a separation of Requesting an action (typically by the Client) that is Performed (by the Cloud provider). This separation of Request and Perform is the basis of a shared responsibility model that requires insight into the other parties operations, security controls, evidence and compliance information.

The Bad

The bad news is that moving to cloud when one does not have good or best practices already in place can compromise a workload. This is especially true if not-so-best practices are repeated and extended to the cloud. It is not uncommon for a review of Cloud provider's compliance against a Client's internal policies and regulatory standards to highlight scenarios where not-so-best practices are in place at the Client and their on-premises environment.

The Ugly

Clients who do not pay attention to security, or who believe that they have "good enough" security, may be unpleasantly surprised when their "good enough" for on-premises is not good enough for Cloud. Unfortunately, this realization often comes after a compromise of their Cloud environment.

The net result: Moving to cloud will expose the security maturity of an organization. A Client not already adopting security best practices (one that has survived with "good enough" security) should use the move to Cloud as the opportunity to driven security best practices across the organization and thus strengthen overall security for on-premises and Cloud environments.

The Good

Moving to cloud does not require a brand new approach to security. One key to success is to clearly understand the breakdown of responsibility, between Request and Perform, between the client and the Cloud Provider. From there, clearly understanding, and using, the Evidence provided as part of Cloud Provider Inform(ation) should provide complete visibility into a Cloud hosted environment – often more visibility that a client will have of their on-premises environment.

Security tools can be extended to work in a hybrid environment and a wide variety of tools are now available as SaaS- or Cloud-deployed options, making it easier to add and extend tooling based practices to both on-premises and cloud-deployed environments.

Securing a cloud environment requires the same policies, processes, tools, and overall logging and monitoring as a non-cloud environment. There are areas requiring special attention, in particular, in the extension of best practices for Identity and Authentication (IA), Access Control (AC) and Audit and Accountability (AC) to support user lifecycle management and logging and audit, to support the approved and appropriate use of the Cloud and the collection of evidence necessary to demonstrate compliance with policies.

In the meantime, clients gain the benefit of the Cloud provider's implementation of physical and environmental security and the audits and compliance. When coupled with all the other promise of business benefit, security is now part of the compelling draw to cloud for client's world wide.

REFERENCES

Angeles, S. (2013, October 17). *8 Reasons to Fear Cloud Computing*. Retrieved March 07, 2016, from Business News Daily: http://www.businessnewsdaily.com/5215-dangers-cloud-computing.html

Columbus, L. (2015, September 27). *Forbes.com*. Retrieved March 07, 2016, from http://www.forbes.com/sites/louiscolumbus/2015/09/27/roundup-of-cloud-computing-forecasts-and-market-estimates-q3-update-2015/#2b64aed56c7a

Dempsey, K. (2014). *NIST Computer Security Division*csrc.nist.gov*Summary of NIST SP 800 - 53 Revision 4, Security and Privacy Controls for Federal Information Systems and Organizations.* NIST, NIST Computer Security Division csrc.nist.gov Summary of NIST SP 800 - 53 Revision 4, Security and Privacy Controls for Federal Information Systems and Organizations Kelley Dempsey. NIST.

Economist Intelligence Unit. (2015, May 14). *Economist Insights.* Retrieved March 07, 2016, from http://www.economistinsights.com/analysis/mapping-cloud-maturity-curve

Erber, M. (2014, January 13). *Thoughts on Cloud.* Retrieved March 07, 2016, from http://www.thoughtsoncloud.com/2014/01/what-is-hybrid-cloud/

Gagliordi, N. (2014, November 13). *ZDNET.* Retrieved March 07, 2016, from http://www.zdnet.com/article/forresters-2015-cloud-predictions-docker-rises-storage-pricing-war-claims-lives/

Heiser, J. (2015, June 4). *Gartner Blogs.* Retrieved March 08, 2016, from http://blogs.gartner.com/jay-heiser/2015/06/04/saas-puppy/

National Institute of Science and Technology. (2015). *NIST 800-53 Controls.* Washington, DC: NIST.

Wikipedia. (2016, March 7). *Wikipedia.* Retrieved March 07, 2016, from https://en.wikipedia.org/wiki/Platform_as_a_service

KEY TERMS AND DEFINITIONS

Audit: The process of examining evidence of actions, such as system logs, status messages and other system information, to validate that actions defined by governing policies and procedures are in effect.

Client: In this context, the entity that has signed up for and is a paid customer of a provider.

Cloud Provider: In this context, the entity that is providing services in a cloud-consumptive fashion.

Compliance: The state of adherence to policies and procedures by tools and actions within a system.

Control(s): The tools and procedures in place to implement a policy. Controls may be implemented with tools (including services, programs and other automation based means), for example, an access control system. Controls may be implemented by human or manual action, for example, checking a user's driver's license to ensure their identity.

Framework: In this context, framework, also known as a security framework, or policy framework, refers to the high level grouping of similar controls designed to address a given risk family.

Governance: The process of ensuring that policies are followed (that the required controls are in place an operational). Unlike an audit, which is typically a short exercise conducted over a short period of time, governance as a whole is on-going and intended to ensure continued compliance with required policies.

RPIE (Request, Perform, Inform, Evidence): The lifecycle of an action to be performed, from its initial invocation of the action (Request) to the validation and completion of the action (Perform) to the completion of the action with including the action's status (Inform) and the use of information on the request's completion (Evidence). Intended to be a closed loop, in that the Requestor uses Evidence to ensure the request was properly fulfilled, and the Perform(er) produces Inform(ation) to demonstrate that they have properly completed the action.

Responsibility (for a Control): The entity that is expected and required to correctly implement a control without input from any other entity.

Shared Responsibility Control: A control that requires input and action from more than one entity to complete. In such a model, it is critical that each entity understands the limits of its role and how to interact with the other entity to provide a model that correctly implements a given control.

Sole Responsibility Control: A control that is request, completed, logged and monitored for correctness by a single entity with no input from any other entity.

Chapter 9
Cloud Computing Data Storage Security Based on Different Encryption Schemes

Hicham Hamidine
University of Bridgeport, USA

Ausif Mahmood
University of Bridgeport, USA

ABSTRACT

Cloud Computing (CC) became one of the prominent solutions that organizations do consider to minimize and lean their information technology infrastructure cost by fully utilizing their resources. However, with all the benefits that CC promises, there are many security issues that discourage clients from making the necessary decision to easily embrace the cloud. To encourage the use of CC, clients need to be able to strategically plan their future investments without the uncertainties of security issues that come with hosting their data in the cloud. This chapter will discuss different mitigation techniques and the common proposed security algorithm schemes for data storage encryption based on classical "symmetric and asymmetric" and with an emphasis on fully homomorphic encryption schemes.

INTRODUCTION

Globalization has forced organizations to accomplish a lot with far less technical, personnel and budget resources. Therefore, when the cloud model was introduced and started to mature it became an obvious choice to many corporations regardless of size. This new model promises that clients can have as many hardware, and software resources as they wish and when it's most needed, which made scalability an issue of the past and at a much less cost. Today, most of the cloud services are in the nature of Infrastructure as a Service (IaaS), Platform as a Service (PaaS), and Software as a Service (SaaS). These services revolutionized the way information technology decision makers assess projects and their related risks versus return on investments. However, the looming security risks and issues an organization may face

DOI: 10.4018/978-1-5225-0759-8.ch009

still are the biggest obstacles that refrain clients from fully harnessing the benefits of the cloud; especially for those whom their data security is an essential component of their daily business.

Many solutions have been identified to achieve security in the cloud and protect data either by using access control, data storage encryption, or a combination of the two. This paper presents a comprehensive survey of different encryption schemes used or are proposed to protect data in the cloud including the algorithm(s) the scheme uses to achieve the sought after level of confidentiality, integrity, and authenticity.

Storing and accessing data in the cloud has its own challenges that compounded the classical issues of security. Today, an organization may choose to host its sensitive data in the cloud to harness the benefits of cloud computing and compete in the respective domain of business it relies on for day to day operations. However, when the data is sensitive its stewards need to implement the most rigorous security scheme that not only should provide them with the appropriate access level but makes sure that no data is compromised or leaked. The classical scenarios of security schemes may still be used. However, there is a limitation that comes with them. For instance, if the data need to only be accessed by the internal staff then a symmetric encryption scheme may be used and the key management is less of a concern but a key management control must be in place. On the other hand, if the data must be accessible to internal and external users, then an asymmetric scheme will be more preferable. In both scenarios, the cloud provider need to gain access to the key to perform usable functionalities against the encrypted data. This exposure of the key may not be acceptable due to the fact that the CP itself may be curious to know the nature of the sensitive data stored on its premises. To accommodate clients' security requirements, researchers are turning to the mathematical characteristics of fully homomorphic algorithms which enables search to be performed against encrypted data without the need of decrypting it.

In the rest of this paper we will examine different secure proposed solutions for accessing and transferring data in the cloud using different schemes that are based on the classical symmetric or asymmetric algorithms. Then, state the new solutions that are based on fully homomorphic schemes. These schemes are trying to solve the same problem which is securing data while enabling arbitrary calculation to be performed against it, except introducing asymptotically better performance in time and space. Finally, analyze these solutions in the paper conclusion based on the need of cloud computing in a multi-tenant environment and secure delegation computation.

Literature Review

Dent (2006) Cryptography is the branch of information security which covers the study of algorithms, protocols that secure data, and addresses several security properties mostly what's known as CIA. One of cryptography's goal is masking the plaintext to an unreadable format using a key to create a cipher text. Diffie and Hellman (1976) stated that classical cryptography systems are based on the NP-hardness of a mathematical problems, such as factoring two large primes or discrete logarithm. Authors also mentioned that these problems are said to be trapdoor functions because it is easy to compute the function one way, but extremely taxing to compute the reverse without some special information, known as the trapdoor. Diffie and Hellman (1976) classified cryptography schemes into two main categories: symmetric and asymmetric. Symmetric cryptography, uses one secret key for both encryption and decryption. Asymmetric cryptography "or public key cryptography" uses two different keys known as public and a private key, either of which can be used for encryption or decryption. The most widely used public key system is RSA, which relies on the factorization of two large prime numbers. In addition to the classical cryptosystems, scientists are researching homomorphic cryptography schemes to ensure privacy of data in communication, storage or in use by processes with mechanisms similar to conventional cryptography, but with added capabilities of computing over encrypted data. Homomorphism is a property by which a problem in one algebraic system can be converted to a problem in another algebraic system, be solved and the solution later can also be translated back effectively. Thus, homomorphism makes secure delegation of computation to a third party possible. Many conventional encryption schemes possess either multiplicative or additive homomorphic property and are currently in use for respective applications. However, on based on Gupta, and Sharma, (2013) a scheme that contains a special functions that form an arbitrary encryption system and capable of performing any arbitrary computation over encrypted data only became feasible in 2009 due to Gentry's work.

Chapter 1: Data Storage Security Based on Symmetric Encryption Schemes

Sharma, Chugh, and Kumar (2013), proposed a solution to the data storage security issues in the cloud. This solution relies on DES to construct the security component which is one of many components proposed to achieve secure working system in the cloud. For users, the system proposed a scheme for data support which includes block update, delete, and appended operations. For administrators, the system guarantees dependability and storage correctness by relying on DES and erasure-correcting code in the file distribution preparation to provide redundancy parity vector. Moreover, it uses homomorphic token with distributed verification of erasure coded data to achieve the integration of storage correctness insurance and data error localization. The scheme consists of seven components that are:

1. **Client Authentication Component:** Client initiates communication with the server by sending the query to the cloud server as a request. The server then sends the corresponding file back to the client as a response. However, before sending the response to the client the server initiates the authorization step and either finalize the response or mark as an intruder.

2. **System Component:**
   a. **User:** Either individual or an organization and rely on the cloud for data computation.
   b. **Cloud Service Provider (CSP):** It's the central entity of the cloud and whom has significant resources and expertise in building and managing distributed cloud storage servers, owns and operates live Cloud Computing systems.

Figure 1. Cryptography diagram
Source: Khan, Hussain, & Imran, 2013

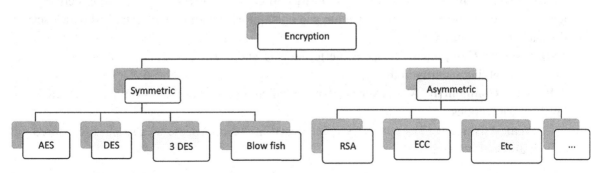

Figure 2. Client authentication
Source: Sharma et al., 2013

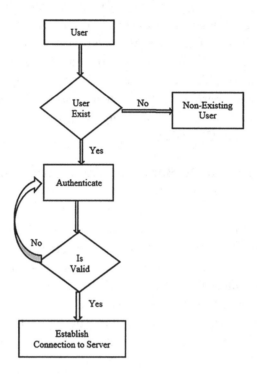

c.   **Third Party Auditor (TPA):** Optional but who has expertise and capabilities that users may not have, is trusted to assess and expose risk of cloud storage services on behalf of the users upon request.

3.   **Cloud Data Storage Component:** This component refers to the actual process of data storing, retrieving, and interaction with the cloud servers via CSP.

4.   **Cloud Authentication Server Component:** Cloud Authentication Server (CAS) functions are as any authentication server (AS) but with a few additional behaviors added to the typical client-authentication protocol such as behaving as a ticketing authority, and controlling permissions on the application network:

a.   Sending of the client authentication information to the masquerading router.

b.   Updating of client lists, causing a reduction in authentication time or even the removal of the client as a valid client depending upon the request.

5.   **Unauthorized Data Modification and Corruption Component:** Responsible of effectively detecting any unauthorized data modification and corruption including tracing to find which server the data error lies in.

6.   **Data Security Component:** Responsible for storing and retrieving secure data using DES and therefore enabling security in the system.

7.   **Adversary Component:** Any adversary source which are classified to two types with different levels of capabilities:

a.   **Weak Adversary:** The adversary is interested in corrupting the user's data files stored on individual servers.

Figure 3. Working architecture of system
Source: Sharma et al., 2013

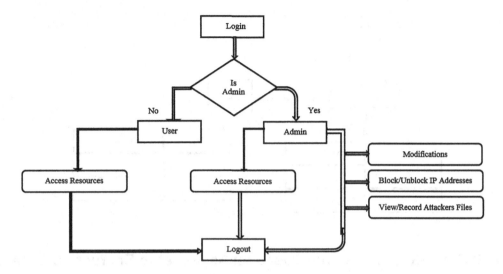

b. **Strong Adversary:** Worst case scenario, in which assumed that the adversary can compromise all the storage servers to the level that they all are conspiring together to hide a data loss or corruption incident.

In the Security Model proposed in Nafi, Shekha, Hoque, and Hashem (2012) which deals with the security system of the entire cloud environment, the encryption key for a particular file system of a particular user is only known to the main system server. The communication from the main system server to the storage server is fully encrypted and therefore there is no need for channel security. Moreover, the model is proposing a hardware encryption to make databases fully secure from attackers and unauthorized users. Kawser et al, proposed the use of these security algorithms: RSA algorithm for secure communication, AES for secure file encryption, and MD5 hashing for cover the tables from user. Moreover, there is an enforcement of using a onetime password for authentication. This model of authentication is cumbersome as users get a onetime pass for the future every time they log in to the system.

The algorithm for generating the hash table which is used for inserting a file in the database table of the storage server is described below:

Step 1: Select a seed for generating the hash table which is equal to the block size of the table. Block size means with how many positions of files will be taken from a series of execution

Step 2: Compute the position where to insert a file. Position = N2 mod S. Where N represents the no. of file and S represents the seed value.

Step 3: A - If Position is empty, then insert the file in that Position. B - Else, increment the Position and set Offset. Repeat step 3.

The analysis of the simulation results of this model showed that the proposed solution works smoothly and ensures higher security than the current running models in the cloud computing environment.

Figure 4. Proposed security model/ structure
Source: Nafi et al., 2012

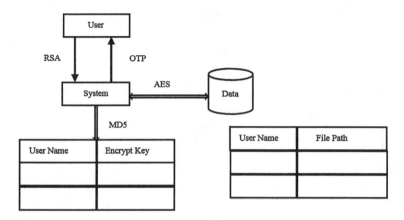

Chapter 2: Data Storage Security Based on Asymmetric Encryption Schemes

In Tirthani, and Ganesan (2014), the authors proposed a solution for designing cloud architectures that ensures secure movement of data at the client and server ends. The solution is based on the notion of the non-breakability of Elliptic Curve Cryptography for data encryption and Diffie Hellman key exchange mechanism which uses a combination of linear and elliptical cryptography methods to establish connections.

1. **Connection Establishment:** The connection is secured using the HTTPS and SSL protocols to enable users to create an account.
2. Account Creation
3. Authentication
4. Data Exchange

In Tirthani, and Ganesan (2014), authors proposed architecture, the key generation takes place at two levels, Elliptic Curve Cryptography (ECC) and Diffie Hellman. In ECC, The public key is a point on the curve which get generated by multiplying the private key with the generator point of the used function here the private key is a random number. One of the ECC algorithm properties is its ability to get a new point on the curve given by computing the product of two points. The general equation of an elliptic curve is given as: $y^2 = x^3 + ax + b$

Key generation step in Tirthani, and Ganesan (2014) is responsible for producing both public and private key and can be achieved as follows:

1. Choose a number d where $d \in \{1, n-1\}$
2. Public key: $Q = d * P$, where P is a point on curve.
3. **Private Key:** d

Figure 5. Account creation process

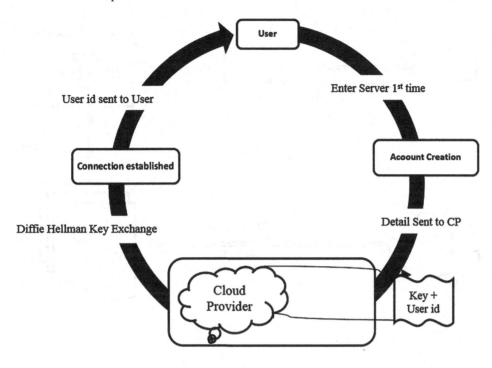

Figure 6. Account authentication process

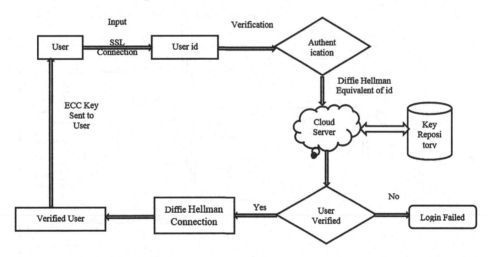

For encrypting user's message m which has point M on the curve E. the algorithm randomly select a value $K \in [1, n-1]$ which will result in two cipher texts C_1 and C_2. Where: $C_1 = K * P$ and $C_2 = M + (K * P)$. To decryption m we simply compute: $m = C_2 - d * B$.

Figure 7. Data processing view of client

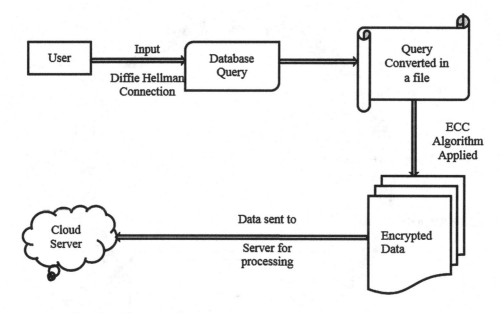

Figure 8. Data processing view of server

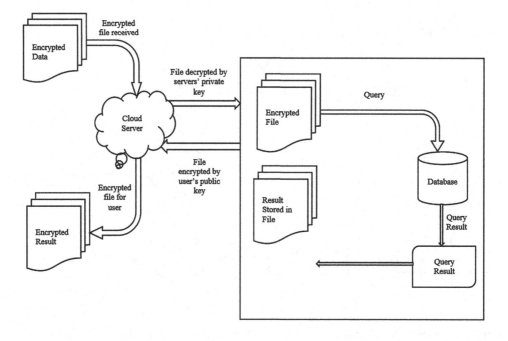

Data Storage Security in the Cloud Using RSA

In Yellamma, Narasimham, and Sreenivas (2013), authors proposed a security scheme for providing data storage and security in cloud using the widely used public key cryptosystem RSA. In the proposed solution by Yellamma et al. (2013)'s Cloud environment, Pubic-Key is known to all, whereas Private-Key is known only to the original data owner. This architecture implies that encryption is done by the cloud service provider and decryption is done by the cloud user. However, this implementation is identical to the current RSA regardless of the environment.

RSA Based Storage Security (RSASS)

In Venkatesh, Sumalatha, and SelvaKumar (2012) scheme RSA based storage security (RSASS) which uses public auditing of the remote data by improving existing RSA based signature generation which support large and different size of files and provide better security in storing the file data. There are three entities involved to carry out the overall process flow in the system.

The client stores data in the remote cloud server and continuously monitors it using the third party auditor (TPA) which is a monitoring tool that analysis the integrity of the stored file in the server using the RSA based signature generation algorithm and report. Based on the analysis results of the TPA, the user is notified if there is any sign of misbehavior on the data files. These analysis are done using RSA algorithm and are described as follows:

1. **Methodology:** In the RSASS, data is continuously monitored using RSA based signature algorithm by having the user challenging the server using the provable data possession (PDP) model which is a challenge and response protocol.
2. **Setup Phase:**
    a. Client generates a file $F = \{m_1, m_2, ..., m_n\}$, which is a finite ordered collection of n blocks.
    b. Generates public key 'rpk' and secrete key 'rsk' using the key generation of RSA algorithm.
    c. Five step process illustrated in Figure 10.

        i. Client generates the signature (tag) for each file block using the secret key rsk and hash algorithm as $T_i = (H(m_i).g^{m_i})^{rsk}$
        ii. A signature set $\phi = \{T_i\}$ is generated which is the collection of signature of file blocks.
        iii. A Merkle Hash Tree (MHT) is constructed for each file block using hash algorithm.

Figure 9. RSASS data flow architecture

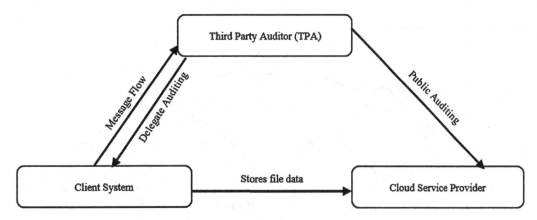

Figure 10. Preprocessing of file blocks

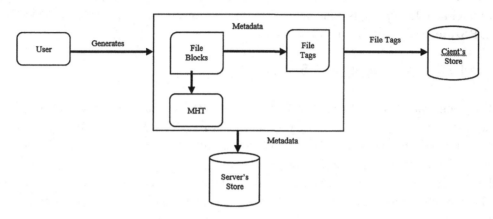

iv. The root R of the MHT is signed using the secret key as $sig_{rsk}\left(H\left(R\right)\right) = H\left(R\right)^{rsk}$.

v. The generated client advertise $\left\{F,\ \Phi,\ sig_{rsk}\left(H\left(R\right)\right)\right\}$ to the server and deletes Φ and $sig_{rsk}\left(H\left(R\right)\right)$ from its local storage. The client delivers the public key to the third party auditor (TPA) to monitor the remote files.

3. **Integrity Phase:**

a. Selecting a subset of file blocks as $I = \left\{s_1, s_2, ..., s_c\right\}$ of set $[1, n]$ such that $s_1 \leq s_2 \leq ... \leq s_c$ and random coefficient $a_i = f_k\left(s_i\right)$ for $i \in I$ and k is the security parameter.

b. Client sends the challenge $\left\{i, a_i\right\}$ to the server.

c. The server generates the proof based upon the challenge it receives. Proof P contains $\left\{T,\ M,\ \left\{H\left(m_i\right),\ \Omega_i\right\}\ s_1 \leq i \leq s_c,\ sig_{rsk}\left(H\left(R\right)\right)\right\}$ where

i. Tag Blocks: $T = \Pi\ T_i^{ai} mod\ N\ \left(for\ i = s_1 to\ s_c\right)$

ii. Data Blocks: $M = \Sigma a_i m_i mod\ N \left(for\ i = s_1 to\ s_c\right)$

iii. Auxiliary Authenticate Information: $\left\{\Omega_i\right\}\ s_1 \leq\ i \leq\ s_c$

Figure 11. Merkle hash tree (8 blocks)

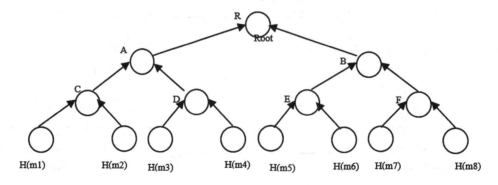

d.   The server sends the generated Proof P to the client as a response.

e.   Validates proof by generating the root R using $\left\{\Omega_i, H\left(m_i\right)\right\}$ $s_1 \leq i \leq s_c$ and authenticates by checking its secret key rsk.

f.   Send final response based on verification process flow.

RSASS Scheme Algorithms

The Proposed RSASS system generates the signature using RSA algorithm which supports large and different size of files and provides much security in storing the file data. This system ensures the possession of the file stored in the remote server using frequent integrity checking. This system is applicable to large public databases such as digital libraries, astronomy, medical archives, etc. In future, this RSASS system will be incorporated in a dynamic real time application to have much more effective data storage security in cloud computing .

Figure 12. Integrity checking process flow

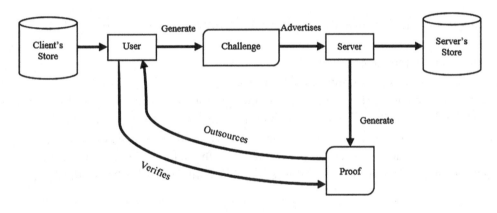

Figure 13. RSASS scheme

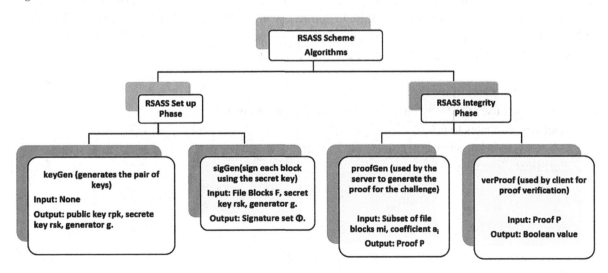

Secure Cloud Storage Framework (SCSF)

In Xiao, Zeng, and Hoon (2014) authors proposed a scheme to securely store and access data via internet. The authors designed a secure cloud storage framework (SCSF) that relies on ECC based PKI for certificate procedure instead of RSA to reduce computation cost and overhead due to that fact that ECC 160 bit key size provides equal security level complexity as RSA 1024 bit key size. This framework promised to enable users to store and access data through an unsecure channels in a secure manner ensuring the security and privacy of the data in the cloud. This scheme works by encrypting data on the client promises before uploading it to the cloud and decrypting it on the client promises after downloading it from the cloud. Moreover, the authors provided a way to share data with more than one authenticated user by encrypting it with the owner's private key and therefore have it available for download and decrypting with the owners public key in the certificate.

SCSF consists of two parts for every user's data:

- Private where users can store sensitive data, and
- Public where users can share data with multiple authenticated users.

There are four steps that users must follow to successfully gain access to the system:

- First, user must authenticate to the CA.
- Second, user authenticates to the Cloud interface.
- Third, for private data part user first need to encrypt the data at its side with the help of the PKI Enabled Application (PEA) before uploading it to the private data part of the cloud. Then downloads and decrypts the data with his session key when needs to operate on it.
- Finally, for shared data part user can share data with other authenticated users by first encrypting it using their session key then encrypts the session key with the private key of the key pair provided by CA.

Second, uploads the concatenation data to the shared data part of the cloud. SCSF Scheme utilizes symmetric encryption algorithm to encrypt data with different session keys. However, for shared data, the scheme encrypt the session key using ECC public key algorithm with their private key and decrypt with public key. Finally, all CA and cloud interface operations are managed through PEA.

PKI Certificate Management Procedure consist of five steps:

1. User sends request message to CA.
2. CA verifies user's identity and sends request message to user.
3. User authenticates to CA.
4. CA sends to acknowledgement message to user.
5. Certificate Issuance.

Figure 14. Secured cloud storage framework (SCSF)

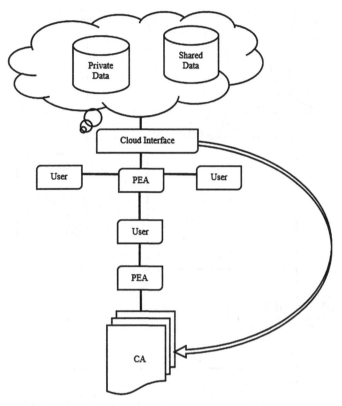

Table 1. Notations

Symbol	Definition
h(.)	One way hash function
ID_{USER}	Identity of the user
ID_{CA}	Identity of the CA
E	An elliptic curve defined on F_p with prime order n
P	A point on elliptic curve E with order n
(s_1, V_1)	Private/public key pair of user, where $V_1 = s_1 P$
(s_2, V_2)	Private/public key pair of CA, where $V_2 = s_2 P$
p, n	Two large prime numbers
M	Requested Message M
||	Concatenate
K	ECDH Session Key
H′	Hash digest H′ of received M. H′ = h (M)

Figure 15. SCSF PKI certificate management procedure

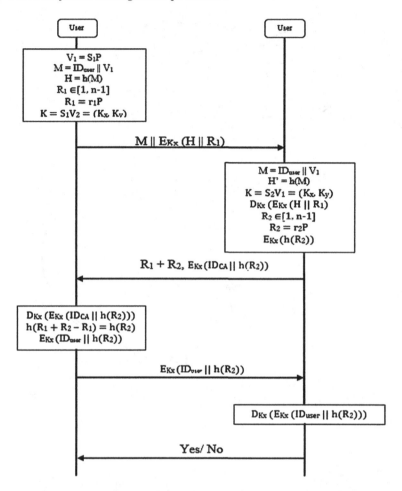

Chapter 3: Data Storage Security Using "Fully" Homomorphic Encryption Scheme

Homomorphic Encryption Cryptosystems

Fully Homomorphic cryptosystems can be used to securely search clients' encrypted data on the CP premises without the need to share the private key with the Cloud Provider and therefore eliminating the concern of non-secure or curious cloud providers.

Additive Homomorphic Encryption

An additively homomorphic scheme is one with a cipher text operation that results in the sum of the plaintexts. That is: $Encrypt\left(m1\right).Encrypt\left(m2\right) = Encrypt\left(m1 + m2\right)$ where the decryption of both sides yields the sum of the plaintexts.

$$Decrypt\ (Encrypt\ (m1).Encrypt\ (m2))\ =\ Decrypt\ (Encrypt\ (m1\ +\ m2))\ =\ m1\ +\ m2$$

Example: Additively homomorphic Paillier by Coron, Mandal, Naccache, and Tibouchi (2011)

$$c_1\ =\ g^{m_1}r^N mod\ N^2,\ and\ c_2 = g^{m_2}s^N mod\ N^2,\ Then\ c_1 \cdot c_2\ =\ g^{m_1+m_2} \cdot\ (rs)^N mod\ N^2$$

Multiplicative Homomorphic Encryption

A multiplicatively homomorphic scheme is one that has an operation on two cipher texts that results in the product of the plaintexts. That is: $Encrypt\ (m_1).Encrypt\ (m_2)\ =\ Encrypt\ (m_1.\ m_2)$ where the decryption of both sides yields the product of the plaintexts.

$$Decrypt\ (Encrypt\ (m_1).Encrypt\ (m_2))\ =\ Decrypt\ (Encrypt\ (m_1.\ m_2))\ =\ m_1.\ m_2$$

Example: Multiplicatively Homomorphic of RSA by Coron et al. (2011)

$$c_1\ =\ m^e_1 mod\ N,\ and\ c_2\ =\ m^e_2 mod\ N,\ Then\ (c_1 \cdot c_2)\ =\ (m_1 \cdot m_2)^e mod\ N$$

Half Homomorphic Encryption

Half, partial, or somewhat homomorphic is an encryption scheme that allows a limited number of operations due to the growth of the error rate that prevents the proper decryption of the message to its original form. Therefore, an additive homomorphic scheme is a scheme that allows an unlimited number of additions with the plaintext message such as Pailler and Goldwasser-Micalli cryptosystems. Similarly, a multiplicative homomorphic scheme is a scheme that allows an unlimited number of multiplications with the plaintext message such as RSA and El Gamal cryptosystems.

Full Homomorphic Encryption

A Full Homomorphic Encryption (FHE) is a scheme that allows an unlimited number of operations (addition, and multiplication) on the plaintext message without the risk of preventing the decryption of the cipher text due to error growth such as Craig Gentry's. In another word, authors of Tebaa, El Hajji, and El Ghazi (2012) describe it as it is a scheme that allows unlimited number of addition and multiplication operations. Algebraically, it's the mapping ∂ between two groups (G, $\Diamond$) and (H, *) such that:

$$\partial\ (X \Diamond Y)\ =\ \partial\ (X)\ *\ \partial\ (Y)\ for\ X,\ Y G\ and\ \partial\ (X),\ \partial\ (Y) H.$$

With Gentry's work and discovery that a feasible fully homomorphic scheme is possible, many subsequent proposals have been introduced that made improvements to the original proposal including new protocols from Gentry himself.

Gentry's Homomorphic Scheme

During Gentry's PhD dissertation research he was able come up with an alternative approach to the fully homomorphic encryption scheme by constructing it first from a somewhat homomorphic, then refreshing the cipher message periodically instead of relying on the structure of the encryption scheme. However, Gentry (2009) author's proposed scheme uses a key that grows substantially in length as the number of operations grow. This scheme uses of hard problems on ideal lattices and must allow an unlimited number of addition and multiplication operations on the ciphertext. However, the exponential error growth prevents the scheme from executing unlimited number of additions and multiplications on the message after a threshold number of operations that makes it difficult to decrypt the message to its original form. In particular, suppose that there is an "error" associated with each ciphertext, that ciphertext's output by $Encrypt_e$ have a small error, but have larger error that increases with the depth of the circuit being evaluated after receiving the ciphertext output of $Evaluate_e$, and that eventually results in a decryption error when applying $Decrypt_e$ to the ciphertext. Aguilar, Bettaieb, Gaborit, and Herranz (2011) stated that this is due to the fact that in lattice based schemes, the number of homomorphic operations that can be performed had a direct impact on the ciphertext size. These facts is what pushed researchers including Gentry himself to either rethink Gentry's initial scheme and produce techniques to refresh the ciphertext or move from algorithms that are based on the hardness of lattices to ones over integers. In Gentry (2009), author constructed a FHE scheme based on ideal lattices with three main steps starting from initial construction using ideal lattices, bootstrapping, then squashing technique to permit bootstrapping. All schemes that were introduced based on ideal lattices the ciphertext takes the form of a $C = V + X$, where V is an ideal lattice and X is an error vector that encodes a plaintext m. Moreover, the ciphertext vectors are intercepted as coefficient vectors of elements in a polynomial ring $Z_{[x]} / f(x)$ where ciphertext are added and multiplied using ring operations. Compared to previous work especially Boneh-Goh-Nissim, Gentry (2009) work is an improvement as it allows greater depth for multiplication. Yet, the scheme is only homomorphic for a threshold number of addition and multiplication operations as the errors vector grows beyond the level that allows the ciphertext to be correctly decrypted to its original plaintext. To overcome this issue, refreshing the ciphertext technique was introduced. This technique enables the algorithm to obtain a new ciphertext with a shorter error vector and therefore, making it bootstrappable. Finally, Gentry (2009) stated that the scheme's security is based on the natural decisional version of the closest vector of ideal lattices for ideal in a fixed ring and therefore makes it semantically secure.

DGHV Scheme

Dijk, Gentry, Halevi, and Vaikuntanathan (2010) stated that DGHV scheme that was introduced in 2009 included many of Gentry's constructions but didn't require the use of ideal lattices. In Jian, Danjie, Sicong, and Xiaofeng (2012) proposal, the authors show that the component which uses the ideal lattices can be replaced by a simpler one that uses integers instead for the somewhat homomorphic scheme introduced in Gentry (2009) and keeps similar properties with regards to homomorphic operations and efficiency.

van Dijk, Gentry, Halevi, and Vaikuntanathan (2010) authors stated in Def 3.7 that to overcome the limitation imposed on the scheme due to the growth of noise, Gentry introduces two techniques: Bootstrapping: encryption of the secret-key bits. And Squashing: a method for reducing the decryption complexity at the expense of making an additional and fairly strong assumption, namely the sparse subset sum assumption. These techniques are used to truly make the scheme fully homomorphic with unlimited number of additions and multiplications on the ciphertext. Finally, the Jian et al. (2012) scheme can be converted from a symmetric as described above to asymmetric by introducing "The public key consists of many "encryptions of zero", namely integers $x_i = q_i p + 2r_i$ where q_i, r_i are chosen from the same prescribed intervals as above. Then to encrypt a bit m, the ciphertext is essentially set as m plus a subset sum of the x_i's .

Gentry (2010) scheme implies that ciphertext is: $c = pq + m$ where c is the ciphertext, m is the plaintext, p is the key, and q is a random number. This encryption function is homomorphic with respect to addition, subtraction, and multiplication.

1. **KeyGen:** produces a P-bit odd integer p.
2. **Encrypt**$_\varepsilon$ (p,m) where m $\in$ {0,1} and m' is a n-bit random number where

$m' = m \ mod \ 2$. $C \leftarrow m' + pq$, where q is a random Q-bit number.

Figure 16. DGHV

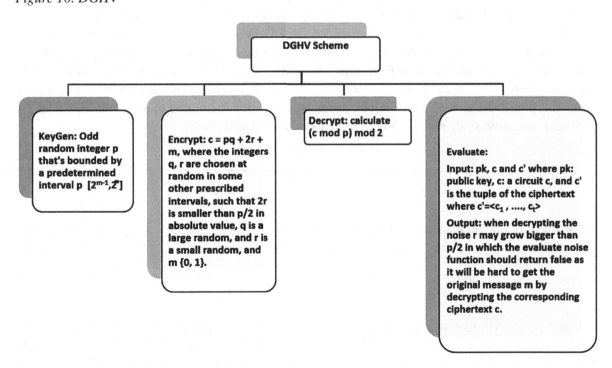

3. **Decrypt**$_\bullet$ $\left(p,c\right)$ $=$ $c\ mod\ p\ where\ p \in \left(-p\,/\,2,\ p\,/\,2\right)$

4. **Homomorphic Operations:**

1. $Add_\varepsilon\left(c_1,c_2\right)$ $=$ $c_1 + c_2$
2. $Sub_\varepsilon\left(c_1,c_2\right)$ $=$ $c_1 - c_2$
3. $Mult_\varepsilon\left(c_1,c_2\right)$ $=$ $c_1 * c_2$

Evaluate$_\varepsilon\left(f,\ c_1,\ ...,\ c_t\right)$ which expresses the boolean function f as a circuit C with XOR and AND gates.

Coron et al (2011) introduced an improvement to Dijk et al. (2010) DGHV scheme by showing how to reduce the somewhat homomorphic public key from its original complexity of $O\left(\lambda^{10}log\lambda^{10}loglog\lambda^{10}\right)$ to $O\left(\lambda^{7}log\lambda^{7}loglog\lambda^{7}\right)$ by storing only a smaller subset of the public key. In addition, authors describe how to implement a fully homomorphic DGHV scheme under new variant, using some of the optimizations from Gentry, and Halevi (2011) and proved that the scheme still semantically secure and of same asymptotic performance as of Gentry-Halevi implementation in Gentry, and Halevi (2011). However, with the work of Chunsheng (2012) which showed the possibility of a heuristic attack using lattice reduction algorithm on fully homomorphic encryption schemes constructed over the integers, there is a concern that an attacker in case of not carefully choosing the parameter may derive the plaintext from a ciphertext and the public key without need to the secret key. Moreover, Chunsheng (2012) author showed that an attack can be avoided by setting parameter $\gamma=\lambda^6$ but with the concern that performance will be greatly hindered. Finally, they provided an improvement to the scheme while keeping it semantically secure by replacing the secret key from large integer to a matrix.

Coron, Lepoint, and Tibouchi (2012) extended the DGHV scheme to support encrypting and homomorphically processing a vector of plaintext bits as a single ciphertext. Yet, keeping the variants semantically secure under the Error-Free Approximate-GCD problem. In addition, Coron et al. (2012) proposed scheme homomorphically evaluates a full AES circuit with close efficiency as Graig et al "Homomorphic evaluation of AES Circuit" paper. However, for encrypting multiple bits into a single ciphertext, the authors rely on the Chinese Remainder Theorem to obtain:

$$C\ =\ q.\prod_{i=0}^{l-1}p_i\ +\ CRT_{p0,...,pl-1}\left(2r_0\ +\ m_0,...,2r_{l-1}+m_{l-1}\right)$$

and produce the correct plaintext bit vector

$$m_i\ =\ \left[c\ mod\ p_i\right]_2\ for\ all\ 0\ \leq\ i\ \leq\ l^{CRT^{(a0,...,al-1)}_{p0,...,pl-1}}$$

Finally, authors proved the proposed scheme semantic security by proving that ciphertext is independently randomized modulo each pf the p_i's by first proving that the batch DGHV scheme is semantically secure under new assumptions, then showed that these assumptions are applied by the Error-Free

Cloud Computing Data Storage Security Based on Different Encryption Schemes

Approximate-GCD. In the same context and by using the Chinese Remainder Theorem (CRT), the authors of Kim, Lee, Yun, and Cheon (2012) paper revisited Rivest, Adleman, and Dertouzos old proposal from 1978 that is based on the CRT and is a ring homomorphic. In Kim et al. (2012), authors presented a secure modification of their proposal by showing that the proposed scheme is fully homomorphic and secure against the chosen plaintext attacks under approximate GCD and the sparse subset sum assumptions when the message space is restricted to the Z_2^k. This scheme can be seen as a generalization of the DGHV scheme with larger plaintext with support for SIMD operations. Yet, its overhead is reduced to $O\left(\lambda^5 log\lambda^5 loglog\lambda^5\right)$ compared with DGHV's $O\left(\lambda^8 log\lambda^8 loglog\lambda^8\right)$ for the security parameter λ. Moreover, this scheme can have an $O\left(\lambda\right)$ if restricted to a depth of $O\left(log\ \lambda\right)$.

In Jian et al. (2012), authors proposed a practical and simple fully homomorphic encryption scheme called SDC which only used elementary modular arithmetic based on Gentry's cryptosystem but more secure and feasible when it comes to the aspect of ciphertext retrieval. This paper compared SDC algorithm to those proposed by Gentry (2009) and Dijk et al. (2010) where the retrieval algorithm of DGHV needs to transfer the private key P to server and retrieval algorithm for Gentry (2009) have to submit the constant number q to server. In addition, the authors claim that SDC is much secure as it doesn't provide the private key P and merely share random number q with the server and therefore no opportunity to leak out any valuable information during the application of ciphertext retrieval. Moreover, due to its nature of utilizing elementary modular arithmetic its performance evaluation proved that SDC is practical but I'll argue what the authors claim that its security analysis proved its validity as the same need that their statement used for labeling Gentry's retrieval algorithm as unsecure is also needed by SDC to compute R.

SDC Scheme

SDC Scheme of Jian et al. (2012), which is derived from Gentry's cryptosystem defined as followed as supports the following homomorphic operations:

- **Homomorphic Operations:**

$$c_1 = m_1 + p + r_1 * p * q$$

$$c_2 = m_2 + p + r_2 * p * q$$

  ○ **Additive Property:**

$$c_3 = c_1 + c_2 = \left(m_1 + m_2\right) + \left(r_1 + r_2\right) * p * q + 2p$$

$$m_3 = c_3 mod\ p = m_1 + m_2$$

  ○ **Multiplicative Property:**

Figure 17. SDC scheme

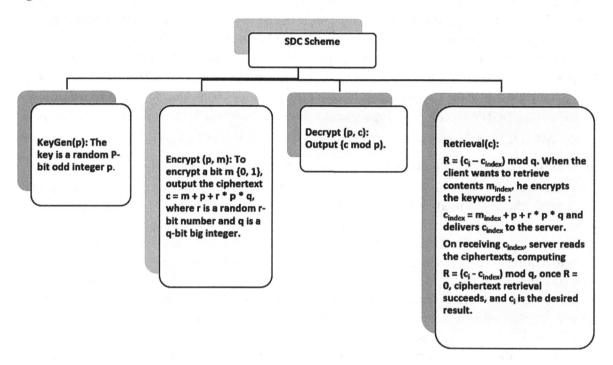

$$c_4 = c_1 {}^* c_2 = m_1 {}^* m_2 + \left(m_1 + m_2 + p\right) p + r_1\left(p + m_2 + r_2\right) pq + r_2\left(p + m_1\right) pq$$

$$m_4 = c_4 \bmod p = m_1 {}^* m_2$$

Single Instruction Multiple Data (SIMD)

In Smart, and Vercauteren (2011), authors presented a variant of Gentry's fully homomorphic public key encryption scheme with support to SIMD operations. The paper showed how to select parameters to enable SIMD operations while keeping the practicality of the key generation technique addressed by Gentry and Halevi where they used an efficient key generation procedure based on Fast Fourier Transform (FFT) and a simpler decryption circuit. This is achieved by obtaining a somewhat homomorphic scheme supporting both SIMD operations and operations on large finite fields of characteristic two. Then, converting the SHE to a FHE scheme by recrypting all data elements separately. The bootstrapping process requires a "dirty" ciphertext to be publicly reencrypted into a "cleaner" ciphertext. Based on Smart, and Vercauteren (2011), this implies that the SHE scheme must implement its own decryption circuit homomorphically to a certain threshold depth. Gentry and Halevi (2011), presented an optimized version of Smart and Vercauteren variant by introducing efficiency in the Key Generation procedure based on the FFT and simpler decryption circuit. These changes allowed the implementation of the FHE including the ciphertext cleaning operation.

Yet, Smart and Vercauteren scheme can support SIMD operations on non-trivial finite fields of characters two instead of operations on a single bit under certain conditions when it comes to choosing the parameters, the proposed parameters in these schemes do not allow SIMD operations to be realized. The method used to generate keys efficiently precludes the use of parameters that support SIMD. The goal is to allow any FHE scheme to embed a number of small plaintext within large ciphertexts independently and therefore enabling more efficient use of both space and computational resources. This paper, investigate SIMD operations in FHE schemes and show that by adapting the parameter settings from Gentry, and Halevi (2011) and Smart, and Vercauteren (2010) we can realize the benefits SIMD operations yet, continue to support the efficiency improvement from Gentry and Halevi (2011) work. Moreover, authors' show how we can benefit from FHE scheme with enabled SIMD operations to perform AES encryption homomorphically and searching an encrypted database on a remote server. Finally, the main contribution of this paper is a recryption procedure that makes use of the SIMD operations to improve the overall computational cost of the scheme by reducing the cost of recryption which was described in Chapter 5 and stated how to use SIMD operations to recrypt the r bits embedded copies of F2 in parallel.

- Recrypt Ciphertext Algorithm without SIMD

$C' \leftarrow 0$

$For \ i_1 \ from \ 0 \ to \ n-1 \ do$

$\quad For \ i_2 \ from \ 0 \ to \ l-1 \ do$

$\quad\quad C'i_1,i_2 \leftarrow BitRecrypt\left(\left[C.V \ i_1,i_2\right]d \ , \ pk\right)$

$\quad\quad\quad C' \leftarrow C' \oplus C'i_1, i_2 \odot (Tn,l \ (0,...,0, \overset{\Psi}{i1}, \ 0,...,0)) \ | \ \alpha$

$Return \ \left(C'\right)$

- Recrypt Ciphertext Algorithm with SIMD: Parallel recryption

$C' \leftarrow 0$

$\quad For \ i_1 \ from \ 0 \ to \ n-1 \ do$

$\quad Sum \leftarrow 0$

$\quad A \leftarrow 0, \ where \ A \ \epsilon \ Ms \ x \ \left(p \ + \ 1\right) \ \left(Z \ / \ dZ\right)$

$\quad\quad For \ i_2 \ from \ 0 \ to \ l \ - \ 1 \ do$

$\quad\quad\quad Ci_1,i_2 \leftarrow C \ . \ V \ i_1,i_2\left(mod \ d\right)$

$\quad\quad\quad\quad For \ j \ from \ 0 \ to \ s \ do$

$$y \leftarrow Ci_1, i_2 \ . \ x_j \ \left(mod \ d\right)$$

$$For \ k \ from \ 0 \ to \ s \ - \ 1 \ do$$

$$If \ y \ is \ odd \ then$$

$$Sum \leftarrow sum^{\oplus} e_j, k, i_2$$

$$b \leftarrow compute\_bits\left(y\right)$$

$$For \ u \ from \ 0 \ to \ p \ do$$

$$A_{j,u} \leftarrow A_{j,u} \oplus \left(b_u \ . \ c_j, k, i_2\right)$$

$$y \leftarrow y \ . \ R\left(mod \ d\right)$$

$$a \leftarrow school\_book\_add\left(A\right)$$

$$C'' \leftarrow sum \oplus a_0$$

$$C' \leftarrow C' \ C'' \ _{i_1} \odot (T_{n,l}(0, ..., 0, \Psi^1, \ 0, ..., 0)) \ \Big|_\alpha$$

$$Return \ \left(C'\right)$$

FHE-LWE

Brakerski, and Vaikuntanathan (2010) presented a FHE scheme based on learning with error (LWE) assumption which uses lattices and its security is based on the worst case hardness of the shorth vector problem. Yet the scheme deviates from Gentry's squashing technique and showed that SHE can be based on LWE by using a new re-linearilization technique. This scheme has a very short ciphertext and therefore it was used to construct an asymptatically efficient LWE based on using private information retrieval protocol for the public key model with a complexity of:

$$K.PolyLog\left(K\right) \ + \ Log\big|DB\big|$$

bits per single bits query. Where K is a security parameter.

- **Encryption:** $\left(a, b \ = \ <a, b> \ + \ 2e \ + \ m\right)$
- **Decryption:** $\left(b \ - \ <a, s> \ mod \ q\right) \ mod \ 2$

Instead of using squashing which is a method for reducing the decryption complexity at the expense of making an additional and fairly strong assumptions namely the sparse subset sum assumption this paper used as dimension modulus reduction which will transform a cyphertext with parameters(n, log q) into a cyphertext of the same message m but with parameters (k, log p) which are much smaller. This achievement enabled the LWE scheme to become a bootstrappable and the combination of all mentioned techniques in the paper resulted in a very short cyphertext of $(k+1) log\ p\ =\ O(k\ log\ k)$ bits. Moreover, the paper analyses the PIR protocol in the public key model and therefore ignoring the public key when calclating the communication complexity which yields to $LogN.\ PolyLogLogN$ compared to Gentry's $O(Log^3 N)$ bit communication.

Xiao, Bastani, and Yen

In Xiao, Bastani, and Yen (2012) authors developed a non-circuit based symmetric key homomorphic encryption scheme with security that is equivalent to the large integer factorization problem and can withstand an attack up to ($m\ ln\ poly(\lambda)$) chosen plaintexts for any predetermined m where λ is the security parameter. The scheme analysis showed that its multiplication, encryption, and decryption are linear in mλ, and that its performance is much faster compared to Gentry's original homomorphic scheme. However, to achieve efficiency the scheme downgrades the security requirements especially the encryption algorithm which encrypts plaintexts over Z_N into the matrix ring $M_4(Z_N)$ by applying a similarity transformation by the key $K \in M_4(Z_N)$ to a diagonal matrix with two entries equal to the plaintext where m is the product of $2m$ prime numbers and is of size nm bits. m is any predetermined constant that is polynomial in the security parameter λ. And the decryption is performed by applying the inverse similarity transformation. This scheme implemented a diferent aproach to construct homomorphic encryption algorithms with plaintexts over a finite domain such as finite field and therefore eliminating the circuit based computation overhead. However, authors claimed that all previous schemes that were constructed using non-circuit based either have been attached or luck securit evidence. Thus, homomorphic encryption scheme of Xiao et al. (2012) can be used in applications where semantic security is not required and one-wayness security is sufficient. A further consideration in Xiao et al. (2012) is practical multiple-user data-centric applications. To allow multiple users to retrieve data from a server all users need to have the same key. In Xiao et al. (2012) the master encryption key is transformed into different user keys to develop a protocol to support correct and secure communication between the users and the server using different user keys. The data in the data center are encrypted using homomorphic encryption with a master key. Different keys are assigned to different users which are actually transformations of master key k. This proposed multi-user system can withstand an adversary with up to m ln $poly(\lambda)$ plaintext ciphertext pairs.

Design Concept of Xiao et al. (2012) were based on Rabin's encryption algorithm which is a multiplicative homomorphic encryption then generalizing the ciphertext domain from Z_N to ring of matrices over Z_N. Given a plaintext x, the encryption algorithm is $E(x)\ =\ x^2 mod\ N,\ where\ N\ =\ f\ =\ pq$.

To a new transformation:

$$E_1(x)\ =\ \begin{pmatrix} x & 0 \\ 0 & r \end{pmatrix} mod\ N$$

where x is the eigenvalue of the vector $V_{1,0} = (1,0)^t$. However, an adversary can reverse x gevin the ciphertext by solving the linear equation $E_1(x)\overrightarrow{v_{1,0}} = x\overrightarrow{v_{1,0}}$. Therefore, the encryption algorithm applied a randomly selected similarity transform k to $\begin{pmatrix} x & 0 \\ 0 & r \end{pmatrix}$ which becomes:

$$E_2(x,k) = k^{-1}\begin{pmatrix} x & 0 \\ 0 & r \end{pmatrix}k \ mod \ N$$

where k is a randomly selected 2 x 2 invertible matrix. With this similarity transformation that transforms the eigenvector of x from $V_{1,0}$ to $k^{-1}V_{1,0}$, and since the adversary has no knowledge of the value of the key k it can't know the transformed eigenvector and therfore can't establish the linear equation system to optain the plaintext. Yet, E_2 is not resistant to the chosen plaintext attack and therefore the scheme associated the eigenvalue x with two eigenvectors V_1 and V_2 instead of only one eigenvector V. To maintain the homomorphic addition and multiplication of the scheme all plaintext must use one eigenvector V_1 but randomly choose V_2 with property distribution D.

Kipnis and Hibshoosh

FSERF is a fully homomorphic symmetric key encryption and randomization function presented in Kipnis, and Hibshoosh (2012) and it's a set of methods for practical randomization of data over commutative ring, and symetric key encryption of random mod N data over ring Z_N. These methods provide security to the multivariate input of the coefficients of a polynomial function. Beacuse the scheme is based on non deterministic linear transformations, the authors show that FSERF scheme only requires a randon plaintext to be secure and therfore enable the algorithm to run on any untrusted cloud while keeping the data secure. This means that the scheme security semantics is based on contraining the plaintext to have random large numbers in Z_N. Moreover, the paper showed how to take advantage of the scheme methods to provide enhanced protection against certain attacks such as enhancing security of Ong, Schnorr, and Shamir (OSS) public key signature agaist Pollard attack, and protection for AES key agaist side channel attacks. Finally, FSERF methods provide fault detection and verification of computed data integrity.

FSERF methods are imviariant under encryption or randomization where each of the two isomorphic methods the authors defined a domain for secure encryption and another one for randomization. The schemes defined two isomorphic methodes, Matrix Operation for Randomization or Encryption (MORE), and Polynomial Operation for Randomization or Encryption (PORE).

Zhou and Wornell

In Zhou, and Wornell (2014), the authors showed that a more efficient FHE is practical when only supporting those encryption computation needed by the target application. This scheme was developed based on the constrain that it's for signal processing applications and operates directly on integer vectors that supports three operations. The approch was different from the main stream previousely proposed papers

Figure 18. FSERF scheme

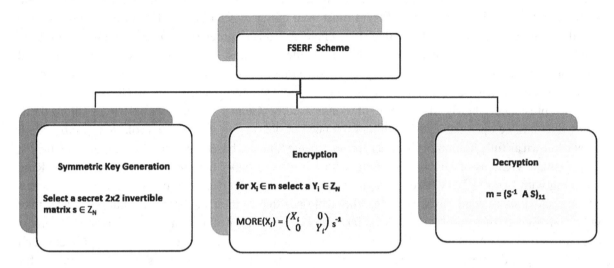

about FHE, where the authors concentrated on efficiency not by introducing a new technique that will make the encryption, decryption, or the evaluation algorithms have a smaller complexity but rather by examining the need of the applications and the tasks each needs to perform.

In Zhou, and Wornell (2014) mentioned proposal above, the sever has the processing algorithm which can't be leaked to the users. Therefore, the server computes $f(x)$ and returns the result to the user. All computation take place in the encrypted domain. This scheme is an extension of a pereviously proposed scheme by operating on integer vectors instead of binary vectors. Moreover, it support three operations on the encrypted data: Addition, Multiplication, and Weighted Inner products.

CONCLUSION

In this paper, we have surveyed cloud data storage security based on the classical symmetric / asymmetric cryptography and the newly discovered fully homomorphic schemes starting with Gentry's work.

Figure 19. Traditional proposals vs. proposed solution

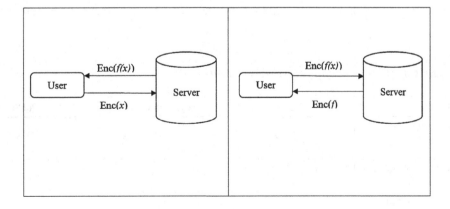

We have presented samples of the latest papers with related work showing their solution to ensure data security in the cloud by relying on old and most used classical security algorithms and those that are based on either Half or Fully homomorphic schemes. Both Chapter one and two solutions are very feasible and implementable as they are built on schemes that most organizations are already using and familiar with and have a fair decryption performance that can be tolerated even when dealing with big data, especially when the solution is implemented using symmetric algorithm. In Chapter three, however, we presented a newly discovered solutions based on Gentry's work in 2009 which allowed encrypted data to be operated against without the need of decrypting it first. This solutions are based on what's known as fully homomorphic encryption schemes and are based on either Lattices as of Gentry's, Approximate GCD as of DGHV, Learning with Error as in paper by van Dijk et al. (2010), or Ring Learning with Error as BGV. Even though, these are a very powerful solutions that have proven security complexities as equal or close to the classical ones due to their mathematical nature of how they were constructed, their implementation is far from being ideal for real business applications or against big data due to the complexity of their algorithms that requires intensive computational resources such as: refreshing and squashing with Gentry's initial work and size of the used keys or the error growth for others. Since Gentry's proposal for a FHE scheme, many new proposals have tried to reduce his initial work complexity including Gentry himself. The reduction was based on introducing new techniques such as ciphertext combining or packing which combines multiple ciphertext into a single one like Smart and Vercauteren's that was based on the Chinese Remainder Theorem (CRT). Or based on lattices, encrypt and process based on a binary vector instead of a single bit, based on ring learning with error, applying a technique to support SIMD operations by encrypting multiple bits within the same ciphertext and perform the same operation on them. Using SIMD made the FHE scheme faster and reduces the ciphertext space. Gentry's initial scheme complexity bound for the approximate shortest vector problem (SVP) in lattices and ideal lattices bounded distance decoding problem (BDD). In Dijk et al. (2010) paper, the scheme's semantic security is based on the hardness of the approximate greatest common divisor problem as well as the hardness of the sparse subset sum problem (SSSP) for the squashed scheme. For the FHE LWE scheme presented in van Dijk et al. (2010) paper, the security is based on the $LWE_{n,q,e}$ with the note of the bigger the noise e, the more secure the scheme becomes however it must be within a predefined constraint. This scheme also accomplish a poly-logarithmic overhead for wide enough arithmetic circuits on Z_p for $p = poly(\lambda)$. For the asymptotic time complexity when it comes to computation, constructing a scheme over integers rather than lattices prove to be faster. For Kim et al. (2012), which is a generalization of the DGHV scheme but with larger plaintext space. In Gupta, and Sharma (2013), the authors presented a solution based on the hardness of factorization of large integers and support operation based on matrices. This scheme has a constant plaintext expansion and better time space.

Table 2. Comparison of key and ciphertext sizes (in bits)

Scheme	Secret key size	Ciphertext size	Public key size
LWE (Brakerski, and Vaikuntanathan(2011))	$n \log q$	$(n + 1) \log q$	$O(n^2 \log^2 q)$
LWE/RLWE (Brakerski, Gentry, and Vaikuntanathan(2011))	$2d \log q$	$2d \log q$	$2dn \log q$

based on van Dijk et al. (2010)

Finally, both symmetric and asymmetric classical cryptography schemes provide semantic security with asymptotically linear time and space complexities. In contrast, FHE schemes have an asymptotic complexity that is far greater in time and space "at least as of now" than its classical ones and uses larger security keys that makes the computation complexity also greater. However, FHE schemes provide the ability to query encrypted data without the need of sharing any keys and protects against security leaks or curious servers and therefore have far more security semantics especially when computation is done on the cloud or in a multi-tenant environment.

REFERENCES

Aguilar, M. C., Bettaieb, S., Gaborit, P., & Herranz, J. (2011). *Improving Additive and Multiplicative Homomorphic Encryption Schemes based on Worst-Case Hardness Assumption.* Cryptology ePrint Archive Report 2011/607.

Brakerski, Z., Gentry, G., & Vaikuntanathan, V. (2011). *Fully homomorphic encryption without boot-strapping.* Cryptology ePrint Archive, Report 2011/277.

Brakerski, Z., & Vaikuntanathan, V. (2011). *Efficient Fully Homomorphic Encryption from (Standard) LWE.* Electronic Colloquium on Computational Complexity, Report No. 109 (2011).

Chunsheng, G. (2012). *Attack on fully homomorphic encryption over the integers.* Cryptology ePrint Archive Report 2012/157.

Coron, J., S., Lepoint, T., & Tibouchi, M. (2012). *Batch fully homomorphic encryption over the integers.* Cryptology ePrint Archive Report 2013/036.

Coron, J. S., Mandal, A., Naccache, D., & Tibouchi, M. (2011). Fully homomorphic encryption over the integers with shorter public-keys. *Advances in Cryptology - Proc. CRYPTO 2011,* (LNCS), (vol. 6841). Springer. doi:10.1007/978-3-642-22792-9_28

Dent, W., A. (2006). *Fundamental problems in provable security and cryptography.* Royal Society. Cryptology ePrint Archive Report 2006/278.

Diffie, W., & Hellman, M. E. (1976). New Directions in Cryptography. *IEEE Transactions on Information Theory, 22*(6), 644–654. doi:10.1109/TIT.1976.1055638

Dijk, M. V., Gentry, C., Halevi, S., & Vaikuntanathan, V. (2010). Fully homomorphic encryption over the integers. *LNCS, 6110,* 24–43.

Gentry, G. (2009). *A Fully Homomorphic Encryption Scheme* (PhD thesis). Stanford University. Retrieved from https://crypto.stanford.edu/craig/craig-thesis.pdf

Gentry, G. (2009). *Fully homomorphic encryption using ideal lattices.* ACM. doi:10.1145/1536414.1536440

Gentry, G. (2010). Computing arbitrary functions of encrypted data. *Communications of the ACM, 53*(3), 97–105. doi:10.1145/1666420.1666444

Gentry, G., & Halevi, S. (2011). Implementing Gentry's fully homomorphic encryption scheme. EURO-CRYPT 2011, (LNCS). Springer. doi:10.1007/978-3-642-20465-4_9

Gupta, C. P., & Sharma, I. (2013). *Fully Homomorphic Encryption Scheme with Symmetric Keys*. University College of Engineering, Rajasthan Technical University. Retrieved from http://arxiv.org/abs/1310.2452

Jian, L., Danjie, S., Sicong, C., & Xiaofeng, L. (2012). A Simple Fully Homomorphic Encryption Scheme Available in Cloud Computing. *Proceedings of IEEE CCIS2012*.

Khan, M., Hussain, S., & Imran, M. (2013). Performance Evaluation of Symmetric Cryptography Algorithms: A Survey. *ITEE Journal of Information Technology & Electrical Engineering, 2*(2).

Kim, J., Lee, M., S., Yun, A., & Cheon, J., H. (2012). *CRT-based fully homomorphic encryption over the integers*. Cryptology ePrint Archive Report 2013/057.

Kipnis, A., & Hibshoosh, E. (2012). *Efficient Methods for Practical Fully-Homomorphic Symmetric-key Encryption, Randomization, and Verification*. Cryptology ePrint Archive, Report 2012/637.

Landau, S. (n.d.). *Standing the Test of Time: The Data Encryption Standard*. Academic Press.

Nafi, K. W., Shekha, K. T., Hoque, S. A., & Hashem, M. M. A. (2012). A Newer User Authentication, File encryption and Distributed Server Based Cloud Computing security architecture. *International Journal of Advanced Computer Science and Applications, 3*.

Sharma, S., Chugh, A., & Kumar, A. (2013). Enhancing Data Security in Cloud Storage. *International Journal of Advanced Research in Computer and Communication Engineering, 2*(5).

Smart, N. P., & Vercauteren, F. (2010). Fully homomorphic encryption with relatively small key and ciphertext sizes. Public Key Cryptography – PKC 2010. doi:10.1007/978-3-642-13013-7_25

Smart, N., P., & Vercauteren, F. (2011). *Fully homomorphic SIMD operations*. IACR Cryptology ePrint Archive, Report 2011/133.

Tebaa, M., El Hajji, S., & El Ghazi, A. (2012). Homomorphic Encryption Applied to the Cloud Computing Security. *Proceedings of the World Congress on Engineering*.

Tirthani, N., & Ganesan, R. (2014). *Data Security in Cloud Architecture Based on Diffie Hellman and Elliptical Curve Cryptography*. School of computing Sciences and Engineering, M. tech. – Computer Science, VIT, Chennai Campus.

Venkatesh, M., & Sumalatha, M. (2012). *Improving Public Auditability, Data Possession in Data Storage Security for Cloud Computing*. ICRTIT.

Xiao, C. Y., Zeng, G. L., & Hoon, J. L. (2014). *An Efficient and Secured Data Storage Scheme in Cloud Computing Using ECC-based PKI*. ICACT.

Xiao, L., Bastani, O., & Yen, I. L. (2012). *An efficient homographic encryption protocol for multiuser systems, 2012*. Cryptology ePrint Archive Report 2012/193.

Yellamma, P., Narasimham, C., & Sreenivas, V. (2013). Data Security in the Cloud Using RSA. *IEEE - 31661*. ICCCNT.

Zhou, H., & Wornell, G. (2014). *Efficient Homomorphic Encryption on Integer Vectors and Its Applications*. Dept. Electrical Engineering and Computer Science, Massachusetts Institute of Technology. Retrieved from http://www.mit.edu/~hongchao/papers/Conference/ITA2014_HomomorphicEncryption.pdf

APPENDIX

RSA Algorithm (Tebaa et al. (2012))

Key Generation Algorithm

1.   Randomly and secretly choose two large primes: p, q.
2.   Compute $n = p.q$.
3.   Compute $\phi(n) = (p - 1)(q - 1)$.
4.   Select Random Integer e where e $\in]1, n[$ and $gcd(e, \phi) = 1$.
5.   Compute d such as $e.d \equiv 1 \bmod \phi(n)$ and $d \in]1, \phi(n)[$.
6.   Public Key: (e, n)   and   Private Key: (d, n)

Encryption Process

1.   Suppose entity A needs to send message m to entity B where $m \in]0, n[$.
2.   Entity A will encrypt m using B's public Key:
$c = m^e \bmod n$, then sends encrypted text $c \in]0, n[$ to entity B.

Decryption Process

1.   Entity B decrypts the received encrypted message to obtain the plaintext message:

$$m = c^d \bmod n$$

Paillier Algorithm (Tebaa et al. (2012))

Key Generation Algorithm

1.   Randomly and secretly choose two large primes:
p, q *where* $gcd\left(pq, (p-1)(q-1)\right) = 1$
2.   Compute $n = p.q$ *and* $\lambda = lcm(p - 1, q - 1)$
3.   Select Random Integer g where $g \in Z *_{n}^{2}$
4.   Must satisfy: $\mu = \left(L\left(g^{\lambda} \bmod n^2\right)\right)^{-1} \bmod n$, where function L is:

$$L(u) = \frac{(u-1)}{n}$$

5.   Public Key: (n, g)
6.   Private Key: (λ, μ)

Encryption Process

1.   Suppose entity A needs to send message m to entity B where $m \in]0, n[$
2.   Select random r where $r \in Z^*_n$. Then compute:
       $c = g^m . r^n mod \ n^2$, then sends encrypted text c to entity B.

Decryption Process

1.   Entity B decrypts the received encrypted message $c \in Z^{*2}_n$ to obtain the plaintext message: $m = L\left(c^\lambda mod \ n^2\right) . \mu \ mod \ n$

Data Encryption Standard (Landau)

The Data Encryption Standard (DES) is a symmetric- key block cipher published as FIPS-46 in the Federal Register in January 1977 by the National Institute of Standards and Technology (NIST). At the encryption site, DES takes a 64-bit plaintext and creates a 64-bit ciphertext, at the encryption site, it takes a 64-bit ciphertext and creates a 64-bit plaintext, and same 56 bit cipher key is used for both encryption and decryption. The encryption process is made of two permutations (P-boxes), which we call initial and final permutation, and sixteen Feistel rounds. Each round uses a different 48-bit round key generated from the cipher key according to a predefined algorithm as shown in Figure 20.

The function f is made up of four Chapters: 1. Expansion P-box, 2. A whitener (that adds key), 3. A group of S-boxes, 4. A straight P-box.

Diffie Hellman (Tirthani & Ganesan, 2014)

Diffie Hellman key exchange mechanism is one of the traditional protocols used to obtain a public key.

       Input: Consider G as an abelian group where $g \in G$ and m is a prime multiplicative order.
       Output: A secret $s \in G$ which will be shared by both the sides.

   Steps:

- Sender generates random $d_A \in \{2..., m-1\}$ and compute $e_A = g^d_A$.
- Sender sends e_A to receiver.
- Receiver generates a random $d_B \in \{2..., m-1\}$ and computes $e_B = g^d_B$.
- Receiver sends e_B to receiver.
- Sender calculates $s = \left(e_B\right)^d A = g^d A^d B$
- Receiver calculates $s = \left(e_A\right)^d B = g^d A^d B$

Figure 20. DES

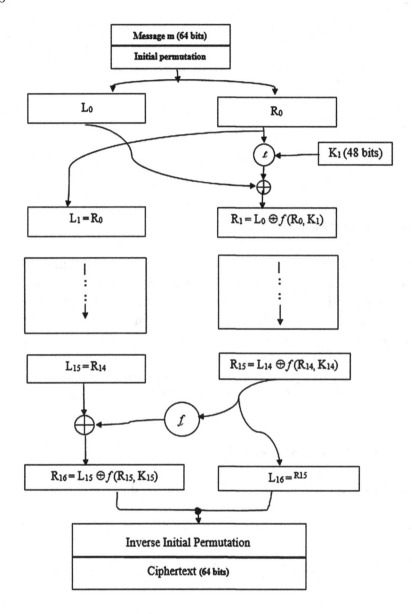

Elliptic Curve Cryptography (ECC) (Tirthani & Ganesan, 2014)

Implementing Group Operations

```
1.       Main operations - point addition and point multiplication
2.       Adding two points that lie on an Elliptic Curve - results in a third
point on the curve
3.       Point multiplication is repeated addition
4.       If P is a known point on the curve (aka Base point; part of domain
```

parameters) and it is multiplied by a scalar k,

$Q = k * P$ is the operation of adding P (k times)

5.   Q is the resulting public key and k is the private key in the public-private key pair

Adding Two Points on the Curve

1.   P and Q are added to obtain $P + Q$ which is a reflection of R along the X axis

2.   A tangent at P is extended to cut the curve at a point; its reflection is 2P

3.   Adding P and 2P gives 3P

4.   These operations can be performed as many times as desired to obtain $Q = k * P$

Chapter 10
Multi–Aspect DDOS Detection System for Securing Cloud Network

Pourya Shamsolmoali
Advanced Scientific Computing, CMCC, Italy

Masoumeh Zareapoor
Shanghai Jiao Tong University, China

M.Afshar Alam
Jamia Hamdard University, India

ABSTRACT

Distributed Denial of Service (DDoS) attacks have become a serious attack for internet security and Cloud Computing environment. This kind of attacks is the most complex form of DoS (Denial of Service) attacks. This type of attack can simply duplicate its source address, such as spoofing attack, which defending methods do not able to disguises the real location of the attack. Therefore, DDoS attack is the most significant challenge for network. In this chapter we present different aspect of security in Cloud Computing, mostly we concentrated on DDOS Attacks. The Authors illustrated all types of Dos Attacks and discussed the most effective detection methods.

INTRODUCTION

Cloud computing according to National Institute of Standards and Technology (NIST) is "a service that is provided in two forms. Computing power and data storage, remotely over the internet with negligible efforts for resource allocation, management, and release" (Mell and Grance, 2011). The US National Institute of Standards and Technology (NIST) have captured five essential cloud characteristics which are (Mell & Grance, 2011). "Ubiquitous network access, Rapid elasticity, Resource pooling, on-demand self-service, measured service".

DOI: 10.4018/978-1-5225-0759-8.ch010

With Cloud Computing, users use a range of devices, including PCs, laptops, smartphones and PDAs to access programs, storage, and application development platforms over the Internet, via services offered by cloud computing providers Cloud computing provides three major services to its users at various layers of computing. These include as follow: "software as a service, platform as a service and infrastructure as a service". Advantages of the cloud computing technology consist of cost savings, high availability and easy scalability (Man & Huh, 2011). Cloud computing has three basic abstraction layers i.e. "system layer (which is a virtual machine abstraction of a server), the platform layer (a virtualized operating system of a server) and application layer (that includes web applications)" (Shelke et al., 2012).

While switching from traditional local computing paradigm to the cloud computing paradigm, new security and privacy challenges come out because of the distributed nature of cloud computing. A number of these security vulnerabilities leave open doors, which stem from the existing computing models; and some of them, inherent from cloud-based models. Therefore, Attacker force these doors to attack the system, and they attack end-users' private data; processing power, bandwidth or storage capacity of the cloud network.

Armbrust et al. (2010), noted, the cloud has the ability to change a large part of the IT industry. Currently, it is rising as a computing key platform for distributing infrastructure resources, software resources and application resources (Doua et al., 2013). "DDOS attacks prevents the legitimate access the server, exhaust their resources and accrues large financial loss and have become one of the most important security threats to the Net". It is simple to start an attack with few tools but at the victim side, it is not easy to stop it (Du and Nakao, 2010; Doua et al., 2013). Therefore, these critical services need some advanced protection system. "Network Performance degradation, revenue loss, and service unavailability is an issue that motivated us to offer protection for these collaborative applications.

Since Cloud infrastructure has massive network traffic, the traditional Intrusion Detection Systems are not competent enough to handle such a large data flow. Most known Intrusion Detection Systems are single threaded and due to prosperous dataset flow, there is a need of multi-threaded Intrusion Detection Systems in Cloud computing environment.

In this chapter, it is aimed to offer definitions and properties of several attack types in cloud network and to introduce DDOS detection and prevention models to resist these types of attacks. The Proposed model has a high accuracy, very simple to set up and requires very small storage.

BACKGROUND

The increased incidences of security threats and increased harm by DDoS attacks have motivated the development of multiple types of attack detection mechanisms. These approaches differ depending on the purpose of detection and set of rules required for operation. Most of these methods are based on identifying anomalies in network traffic.

Specht and Lee (2004) , Shamsolmoali et al. (2014) mentioned "DDOS attack is generally classified into bandwidth depletion and resource depletion attack. In bandwidth depletion attack, attackers flood the target with huge packet traffic that avoids the legitimate traffic and intensifies the attack by sending messages to broadcast IP address." In resources reduction attack, attackers aim to tie up the significant resources (processor and memory) then trying to enable the victim to process the services.

Karimazad and Faraahi (2011) introduced an anomaly based DDoS detection system based on features of attack packets. For evaluation, the author used Radial Basis Function (RBF) neural networks. Vectors with seven features are used to activate an RBF neural network and classify traffic into normal or DDoS attack traffic. They evaluated the approach by using UCLA Datasets. Their system can be classified either normal or attack, but the system can't classify and identified which form of attacks has been targeted the network. Dou et al. (2013) "proposed a method for filtering a DDOS attack called CBF. This system calculates the score of a particular packet at the attack time and decides whether to discard it or not."

In Basheer Nayef (2005), the correlation between the outgoing and incoming traffic of a network is discussed and the changes in the correlation are the metrics to detect DDoS attack. Fuzzy classification is used in order to guarantee the accuracy. Their method is evaluated by using DARPA datasets.

In Chen et al. (2006), "a multiple data mining approaches is used to classify the traffic pattern and diverse attacks. Decision Tree has been used in this model to select important attributes and neural networks are exploited to analyze the selected attributes".

Oktay and Sahingoz (2013) presented a "review on the different attack types, which affect the availability, confidentiality and integrity of resources and services in cloud computing environment. Additionally, the chapter also introduces related intrusion detection models to identify and prevent these types of attacks".

Raj Kumar and Selvakumar (2012) have done research work on DDOS attack detection systems. "They evaluate the performance of a comprehensive set of machine learning algorithms for choosing the best classifier. They note that single classifier creates an error on different training samples. So, by creating an ensemble of classifiers and combination of their outputs, the total error can be much reduced and the detection accuracy can be significantly improved".

Limwiwatkul and Rungsawang (2006) proposed a model to discover DDoS attack against well- defined rules and conditions, and distinguishing the difference between legitimate and attack traffic. The authors significantly focus on ICMP, TCP, and UDP flooding attacks. In (Thwe and Phyu, 2013), this approach is a statistical approach based on multiple features values. The proposed system only showed features extraction module and saved these features into the database to identify normal and attack packets.

(Varalakshmi and Selvi, 2013), proposed "a multiple level DDOS defense mechanisms by using an information divergence method that detects the attacker and rejects the packets in a fixed amount of time in an organized way". Du and Nakao (2010), Shamsolmoali et al. (2014) "proposed architecture to mitigate DDOS attacks by introducing a credit-based accounting mechanism, where a machine can send packets based on its credit points".

In Thwe and Thandar (2013) the proposed system has a combination of data mining technique to detect protocol anomaly against DDoS attack. In this work, traffic features are extracted from network traffic and then it clustered into legal and attack traffic by using a data mining classification algorithm. Chonka et al. (2011) noted "HTTP Denial of service and XML Denial of service attacks are the most serious threats to cloud computing. They offer a scheme called as Cloud Trace Back (CTB) to locate the source of these attacks". Li and Li (2010) introduced an adaptive system, which is used for defending against DDOS attacks. Lu et al. (2007) "proposed a novel framework to robustly detect DDOS attacks and recognizes attack packets." Kim and Reddy (2008) "Proposed a traffic detector, which can be worked in real time by monitoring the packet headers".

Man and Huh (2011), proposed a model called as Collaborative Intrusion Detection System. "The proposed system could reduce the impact of these kinds of attacks through providing timely notifications about new intrusions to Cloud users' systems. To provide such ability, IDSs in the cloud computing regions both correlate alerts from multiple elementary detectors and exchange knowledge of interconnected Clouds with each other".

CLOUD COMPUTING SECURITY

Cloud Computing

Cloud Computing is getting extensive in the worldwide business and IT industry. Clouds computing can be distinct as an Internet-based computing which Virtual shared servers provide all the required resources to the Cloud customer (CAIDA, 2007). The most advantage of Cloud Computing is that the customers can able to select what they want at any location. It also aims to diminish the maintenance and operational cost. The third party provider commonly known as Cloud provider provides any kind of physical infrastructure for rent. Hence, Cloud customers do not need to own the physical infrastructure, therefore, reduces the cost of physical infrastructure. There are three layers in the Cloud computing these three layers are discussed as follow:

1. **Cloud Application:** This is the first layer of the Cloud. The remote clients get access to all applications and data provided by a web browser. So it is not required to install the applications on customer's computer and thereby it decline the maintenance cost and operational cost of a Companies.
2. **Cloud Platform:** This is the second layer in the Cloud. The computational service is supplied by this layer to the customer. This Computational service enables customers to make modification in the server's configuration and settings according to the demand of a customer.
3. **Cloud Infrastructure:** The last layer of the Cloud provides a Cloud Infrastructure. The conception of Virtualization is provided by this Cloud layer. Virtualization enables customers to share a range of software and hardware components and supply platform by means of splitting a single piece of hardware and independent components. Virtualization is the establishment of a near version of software and hardware components. These are then interconnected with others for flexibility and additional storage (CAIDA, 2007).

The cloud computing layers are described in architecture diagram as following (see Figure 1).

The main benefits for all the small scale and large scale organizations using Cloud Computing are mentioned below:

1. **Cost Reduction:** By shifting to Cloud environment Customers avoid the heavy expenditure of spending a large amount of cost for establishing set-up. This also decreases the operational cost. The customers may pay for only what they use.
2. **Scalable and Flexible:** Companies are able to start a business from the simpler model and can create the complex model and if required can again get back to the previous model. Verity enables Customers to use more resources at peak time in order to satisfy the requirements of clients.
3. **Quick and Easy Implementation:** A Company can get the Cloud service in a short period and easy to implement without any software licenses or implementation services.
4. **Reduced Maintenance Cost:** The Cloud service provider provides any maintenance to the customer and maintenance of application is done by APIs, thus reducing maintenance cost.
5. **Quality of Service:** Cloud service provider provides 24*7 support and immediate service in case of faults.
6. **Mobility:** Cloud customer can able to access the data and application from any location at any time by just having an internet connection. So it is idle for increasing productivity by a mobile user.

Figure 1. Cloud architecture

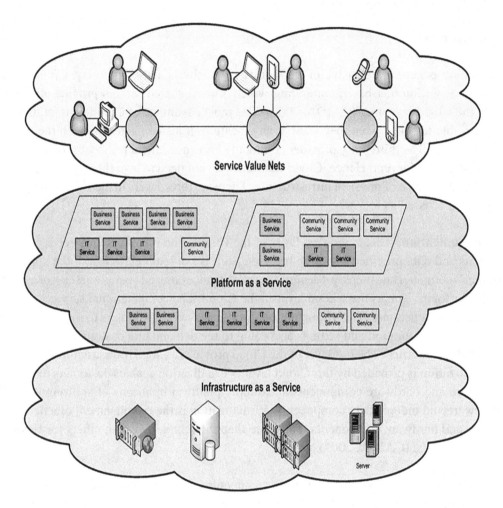

Virtual Machines

Virtualization is a vital component in cloud computing. "It is a key element which simplifies the service delivery of a set of animatedly scalable resources such as storage, software, processing power and other computing resources to the cloud users which can be accessed over the Internet on demand. A user needs only a browser and an Internet connection to use these resources. Virtual machines (VMs) are created within a virtualization layer" (Jin et al., 2011). A cloud is built upon numerous host machines these physical machines then run multiple virtual machines, which is accessible to the end-users. Moreover, virtualization software existing that can imitate entire computer, for an instant, a single computer can perform as though it were actually 50 computers. With the use of such kind of software, one might be able to migrate from a datacenter with thousands of servers to very few numbers.

"Virtual machines are only limited in the way that their stipulation cannot exceed their host machine."

A virtual machine is a software execution of a computing environment in which an operating system (OS) or program can be installed and run. "The virtual machine normally emulates a physical computing environment but asks for CPU, memory, hard disk, network and other hardware resources from the host machine that is handled by a virtualization layer which translates these requests to the underlying physical hardware. Researchers have the right to test applications, their deployments, and upgrades more efficiently by using VMs." They do not need several OS and installation configurations.

Cloud Security Issues

Cloud computing security is one significant issue in the practice of cloud services. Cyber-attacks to the large internet ventures keep on rising and they directly affect the cloud users. Cloud customers (organizations) are questioning the security of moving their computational resources to the cloud. "These improper operations are generally conducted due to a number of reasons. Financial gain also can motivate to steal valuable information from sensitive organizations such banking sector. Cyber surveillance operations in general conducted to compile the information about financial or industrial adversaries are some of the new trends over the internet". Current network security mechanisms encounter new challenges in the cloud such as DDOS attacks (Monowar et al., 2013), "virtual machine intrusion attacks and malicious user activities. Thus, new security methods" (Chuan et al., 2012), (Subashini and Kavitha, 2011) are required to raise users' level of trust to cloud computing.

At the present era, cloud service providers implement data encryption for the data centers, virtual firewalls, and access control lists. (Cloud Security Alliance, 2010) identify the following threats in the initial document:

- Abuse and Nefarious Use of Cloud Computing,
- Insecure Application Programming Interfaces,
- Malicious Insiders,
- Shared Technology Vulnerabilities,
- Data Loss/Leakage, and
- Account, Service & Traffic Hijacking.

DDOS Attack

A DDOS attack is a malicious effort to do not let the resources (a server or a network resource) be available for the end users, usually by blocking or interrupting the services of a host machine. DDOS attack took place by using a number of computers and Internet connections often distributed globally. Figure 2 shows a simple DDOS attack scenario (Weiler, 2002), (Bhadauria et al., 2011) in which multiple attacker computers are sending streams of malicious packets to the victim machine.

DDoS Attacks in Past

DDoS attacks are commenced by a network of remotely controlled, well structured, and widely dispersed nodes called Zombies. The attacker launches the attack with the help of zombies. These zombies are called as secondary victims. "The recent attacks in 2013 take in the attack in China's websites, Bitcoin, largest cyber-attack by Cyber Bunker, NASDAQ trading market, Iranian Cyber-attacks on FBI and so. From the above survey, most of the victims of DDoS attacks are distributed and shared. Apart from the list illustrated there are numerous anonymous tools emerging day by day".

Figure 2. Distributed denial-of-service attack scenario

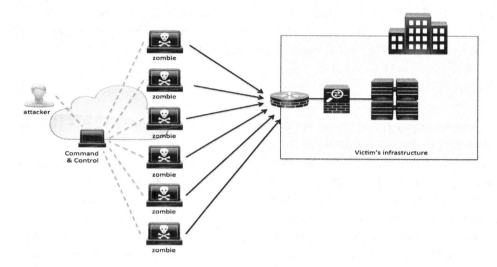

Table 1 lists the DDoS attacks occurred over years and how it evolved (DDOS attack tool, 2000; History of ddos, 2012; Denial of service, 2012).

DDOS attacks try to carry out the following malicious operations:

1. Control legitimate network traffic by flooding the network with malicious traffic.
2. Deny access to a service by way of disrupting communication between legitimate sender and receiver,
3. Block the right to use a particular service or an individual.

Table 1. DDoS attacks in past

Year	Details
1998	First, DDoS tools were discovered. These tools were not used widely but point-to-point DoS attacks and Smurf amplification attacks continued.
1999	Trinoo network was used to flood a single system at the University of Minnessota, which made the network unusable for more than 2 days. And massive attack using Shaft was detected. The Data gathered during the attack was then analyzed in early 2000 by Sven Dietrich and presented in a paper at the USENIX LISA 2000 conference.
2000	• 15 year old boy Michael Calce (Mafiaboy) launched attack on Yahoo's website. He was then sentenced in juvenile detention center for 8 months. He also went forward to degrade the servers of CNN, eBay, Dell, and Amazon, showing how easy it was to damage such major websites. • One of the first major DDOS flooding on Yahoo
2001	• The attack size grows from Mbps to Gbps. Efnet was affected by a 3 Gbps DDoS attack. • DNS servers attack as reflectors. DOS attack on Irish Government's Department of Finance server. The target was Register.com
2002	• It was reported that 9 of the 13 root internet servers were under serious threat of DDoS attack. Congestion due to attack made few rootname servers were not reachable from many parts of the global Internet, which made many valid queries unanswered. • DDOS flooding attack thru Domain Name System (DNS) service.

continued on next page

Table 1. Continued

Year	Details
2003	• Mydoom was used to shut down the service of SCO group's website. Thousands of PC's were infected to send the data to target server. • Attack on SCO and Microsoft.
2004	• Authorize-IT and 2Checkout were Online payment processing firms attacked by DDoS in April targeted. It was later known that the attackers extorted and threatened to shut down there sites. • Attack on SCO Group website to make it inaccessible to valid users.
2005	In August of 2005, jaxx.de, a gambling site was under DDoS attack and to stop this attack, the attacker demanded 40,000 euros.
2006	• A number of DDoS attacks targeted the blog of Michelle Malkin. The attacks started on Feb. 15, and continued till Feb. 23. • Target US Banks for financial gain.
2007	• In December 2007 during the riots in Russia, government sites suffered severe DDoS attacks. Access to IP addresses outside Estonia was removed by many of them for several days. • Estonia Cyber Attack
2008	• In November 2008, the Conficker worm used vulnerabilities found in Microsoft OS. It uses vulnerable machine and other machines are unwillingly connected to it, to make a large botnet. • DDOS Attack on BBC, Amazon.com and eBuy.
2009	• On 4th July (Independence Day in the US) 27 websites of White House, Federal Trade Commission, Department of Transportation, and the Department of the Treasury were attacked. On 1st august, Blogging pages of many social networking sites (Twitter, Facebook etc.) were affected by DDoS attack, aimed at "Cyxymu" Georgian blogger. • DDOS flooding attacks on South Korea and the United States in July 2009 against government news media and financial websites.
2010	• Operation Payback: DDoS attacks launched on websites of MasterCard, PayPal and Visa, as they decide to stop giving service to WikiLeaks.
2011	• LulzSec hacktivist group attacked website of CIA (cia.gov). • DDOS attack on Sony.
2012	• Many attacks at us banks involve use of itsoknoproblembro DDoS tool. Many such do-it-yourself toolkits are available. • DDOS Attack on Canadian Political Party Elections and on US and UK Government Sites
2013	• DDOS attack on stock exchange websites in London. • 150 Gbps DDoS attacks are increasing.
2014	114 percent increase in average peak bandwidth of DDOS attacks in Q1 vs. Q4 2013. The Media and Entertainment industry was the target of the majority of malicious attacks. (Retrieved December 05, 2014 from http://www.akamai.com/html/about/press/releases/2014/press-041714.html)

DDOS attacks guide to interruption of services in the cloud and is considered as one of the significant intrusions in cloud computing. Intrusion detection and prevention systems taxonomy attacks are classified as outside and inside attacks (Specht and Lee, 2004), (Vasanthi and Chandrasekar, 2011). The attacks that enter from external origins are called outsider attacks. Insider attacks involve unauthorized internal users attempting to expand and misuse non-authorized access privileges. Intrusion detection is the mechanism of monitoring computers or networks for unauthorized entry, activity or file variation. Attacks may be treated as incidents. "Although many incidents are malicious naturally, many others are not; for example, a person might mistype the IP address of a computer and by coincidence attempt to connect to a different system without authorization.

There is an established underground cybercriminal economy which works to attain their private individual goals best known for their keen interest in spying or for competitive monetary gains, motives that are possible by the use of disruptive technologies like DDOS attack". Thus creating the science of DDOS attacks ever evolving and growing in the current context in such a method that a continuous monitoring with sophisticated watchdog capabilities is required as these attacks continue to generate online outrages, "customer inconvenience and reputation damages across all industries and geographies". The best-known victims of recent moves of these DDOS attacks (Udhayan and Anitha, 2009), (Chuiyi et al., 2011) and "those who have been successfully being able to mitigate such attacks can never get a sound sleep as it is apparent from current incidences of this attack globally".

Types of DDOS Attacks

Distributed Denial of Service (DDoS attack) is a customized form of DoS attack. DoS attack is triggered to make unavailable the targeted system to its intended users by flooding the targeted system with malicious traffic using a single node. While DDoS attack is initiated by gaining illegal remote access to some compromised machine known as Zombies.

"DDOS attacks uses zombies, to send infinite requests to a target system on command from the attacker. generally DOS attacks involve spoofing of the attackers' IP addresses as the victims' IP addresses, making it complex to recognize the attackers" (Chonka et al., 2012), (Kim et al., 2011), (Shamsolmoali et al., 2014) "have done systematic review on the dark side of the internet. The authors summarized the most important type of DOS attacks". The main forms of DOS attacks are as follow.

1. **Network Depletion Attack:** In network depletion attack, the attacker tried to consume all the targeted network bandwidth by flooding targeted network with malicious traffic which will eventually avoid the legitimate traffic from approaching the targeted network. Network depletion attack can further classify into two types.
   a. Flood Attack.
   b. Amplification Attack.
2. **Ping Flood:** "A ping flood is the basic form of DOS attack. In this type of attack, the attacker simply sends a large number of ping packets to the victim node. If the target sends replies, the effect is amplified".
3. **Smurf Attack:** "It is very similar to the ping flood attack; a smurf attack uses ping packets. The attacker sends ping packets, with the spoofed source IP address to be the victim's IP address, in the direction of computers that keep a broadcast address. All computers in the broadcast address that get the ping packet send responds to the victims' IP address. A packet that sent to the broadcast address is amplified by the number of computers that send reply packets".
4. **UDP Flood:** "In a UDP flood attack, the attacker sends a large number of UDP packets to random ports to the target. As the UDP does not have a congestion control system, the attacker can potentially send infinitive packets. This attack is generally used with IP address spoofing so that the attacker can stay away from detection".
5. **Mail Bomb Attack:** "In a mail bomb attack, the attacker sends a lot of e-mails to a target e-mail address to overflow the victim's mailbox or slow down the mail server. The attacker may command zombies to send e-mails to the victim e-mail address simultaneously. An attacker may create each e-mail with a different message to pass the spam filters".
6. **Resource Depletion Attack:** In this kind of attack, attacker goal is to exhaust server's processing capabilities or memory. two types of attack which target Server resources are as follows:

a. **Protocol Exploit Attack:** "The idea behind this kind of attack is to find an exploit in a specific feature of the protocol used by the victim and then consume the excess amount of resources from it" (Mell and Grance, 2011). The best example of this kind of attack is TCP SYN attacks.

b. **Malformed Packet Attack:** Data Packet is wrapped with the malicious information. "This kind of packet is sent to the victim's server by an attacker to crash it. IP Address attack and IP Packet options attack are the best example for this kind of attack" (Mell and Grance, 2011).

7. **TCP SYN Flood:** "TCP SYN flood is a type of attack which the attacker sends a large number of SYN packets (connection requests) to the target, and fills up the connection queues on the target, so the victim cannot launch connections for legitimate clients".

8. **Peer-to-Peer Attack:** "Conventional DDOS attacks use zombie computers to send a large number of requests to the victim.P2P attacks to use clients linked to P2P file sharing hubs".

9. **Application Attack:** In this kind of attack, the attacker finds an exploit in the application protocol. An attacker can target any of the application protocol such as HTTP, HTTPS, DNS, SMTP, FTP, VOIP, and other application protocols which hold exploitable weakness.

10. **Protocol Attacks:** Protocol Attacks take advantage of a specific feature or implementation bug of some protocol installed at the victim for the function of consuming the maximum amount of its resources to take benefit of protocol intrinsic design. "All these attacks require a lot of attackers

Figure 3. Taxonomy of DDoS attacks

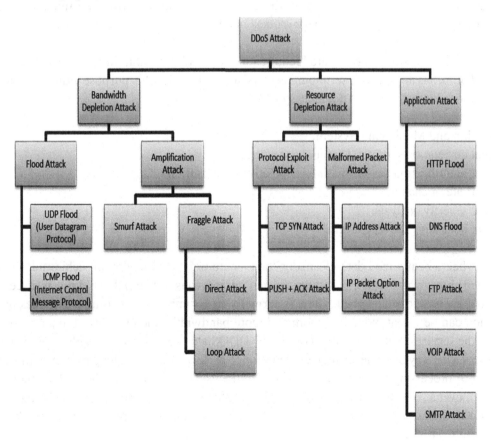

(zombies) and are mitigated by changing the protocol features. Some examples of popular protocol attacks Smurf Attack, UDP Attack, ICMP Attack, SYN attack, Attack using DNS systems", CGI request attack, Attack using spoofed address in ping, Authentication server attack etc.

11. **Software Vulnerability Attacks:** Software Vulnerability Attacks allows an attacker to take advantage of a software program design flaw that may be a Land attack, Ping of Death or Fragmentation etc. Vulnerability in software means a weakness which permits an attacker to lessen a system's information assurance.

DDOS Attack Statistics

Attackers are getting complicated. "They are changing their tools and techniques to intrude into the network of others and attack intentionally". Following are the factors that show light on attack sophistication of the intruders:

- Intruders are doing their best to apply multi-vulnerability attack mechanism to target all layers of the victim's IT infrastructure. The layers namely the network, servers, and application layers.
- Intruders are more concentrating on DDoS tools to focus on applications rather than distributed denial of service (DDoS) attack tools that focused on networks.
- Intruders are using "low & slow" attack mechanism keeping in mind to misuse the application resource rather than resources in the network stacks.
- Intruders are more focusing on evasion techniques to avoid detection and mitigation including SSL based attacks, changing the page request in a HTTP page flood attacks etc.

Following components/processes are "required to ensure high availability of services for the cloud customers that means appropriate scrubbing centers are required for this purpose either at cloud service provider end or user end which is not an easy task."

- Detection and Monitoring System.
- Threat correlation services.Threat alert system.
- Threat identification service with false positives recognition.
- Threat rate of change.
- Threat severity analysis.
- Threat heuristics at every layer.

Hence, when a centralized data cleansing stations are organized having all achievable capabilities as mentioned above where traffic is scrutinized and mischievous traffic (DDOS, known susceptibilities and exploits) are moved or absorbed. There is normally an assumption that volumetric attack bandwidth consumption can be defeat by adding more and more bandwidth, and swallow all data traffic thereby continuing the services. Since "the target of the any DDOS attackers is normal to block or oversubscribe resources in such a way that it leads to degraded service performance time, long response time matching the demand of processing the incoming workload remains a constant headache." Many methods have been evolved over a considerable time now and all these methods or technologies that claim to safeguard us from DDOS attacks also consider the various possible correlations which might be working for the advantage of the attackers.

Existing Techniques for Detecting DDoS Attacks

In this part, we present a review of existing literature on DDoS attack detection methods. These methods are based on the structural design discussed above namely, victim-end, source-end, and in-network. We discuss these schemes without taking into consideration their practical deploys ability in real networks. Current trends illustrate that soft computing approaches have been used heavily for DDoS attack detection:

1. **Statistical Methods:** In Muda et al. (2011) authors proposed "network detection solution by combining supervised learning technique and unsupervised learning technique. They used K-Means algorithm for unsupervised learning and Naive Bayes algorithm for supervised learning". The first step of the algorithm is "using K-Means algorithm to group data to normal or attack. Then, use Naïve Bayes algorithm to classify the obtained result into attack type. The KDD 99 dataset was used to evaluate the performance of this algorithm. The detection rate was improved to 99.6 percent. However, this solution is not practical for the real network because K-Means algorithm requires" other time to process vast data in real networks which could lead to bottleneck trouble and system crash.

2. **Intrusion Detection System:** The majority standard feature of IDS is that it consistent for each virtual machine in a cloud environment. This is the method is used for detecting the DDoS attacks in (Lonea and Popescu, 2013). In IDS system, the IDS are used at the cluster controller. And it is "applied to each virtual machine and in this way cloud computing platform avoids the overloading problem that could be caused by DDoS attack. And the furthermore advantage of this strategy as described by Roschke et al. (2009)" is the advantage of decreasing the impact of the probable attacks by the IDS Sensor VMs.

3. **IDS Based DempsterShafer Theory:** This technique generally focuses on detecting and analyzing the Distributed Denial of Service (DDoS) attacks in cloud computing environments. The DDoS attacks mostly target on cloud service disruptions. The "solution is imposed to combine the previous work of Intrusion Detection Systems (IDSs) deployed in the virtual machines of the cloud environment along with a data fusion methodology in the front-end. So when the attacker attacks cloud system, the VM-based IDS will get a warning, which will be stored in the Mysql database" or any database that is joined to the cloud system placed within the (CFU) i.e. Cloud Fusion Unit of the front-end server. "A quantitative solution is proposed for analyzing alerts generated by the IDSs, using the Dempster-Shafer theory (DST) operations in 3-valued logic and the fault-tree analysis (FTA) for the mentioned flooding attacks". At the final step, the solution uses the Dempsters combination rule to fuse evidence from several independent sources.

4. **Packet Information Gathering and Pre-Processing:** DDOS attacks have various categories like Zombie Cloud Client, correlated to virtual machines like hypervisor attack of the virtual machine. In (Modi et al., 2013) authors concentrated on distinguishing the hypervisor attack. While this attack took place it causes the resource imbalance and data loss. "The detection procedure is done with packet analysis that consists a packet loader and packet collector. Packet loader stores the files about collected packets using packet capture tool in HDFS". Packet collector performs packet information gathering through Libcap and Jpcap module from the live interface.

5. **Host Based Intrusion Detection Systems:** In (Modi et al., 2013) author explained a "host-based intrusion detection system i.e. HIDS which monitors and analyzes the information collected from a host machine. And the detection procedure follows in which the different type of the informa-

tion such as system files used, calls of system, type of data etc". Afterward, this detection system observes the modification in the host kernel and moreover checks for program's behavior. If any deviation is observed from the default behavior then the report of the attack is generated.

6. **Network-Based Detection System:** In (Muda et al., 2011) author proposed "network detection solution by combining supervised learning technique and unsupervised learning technique. They used K-Means algorithm for unsupervised learning and Naive Bayes algorithm for supervised learning". The first step of the algorithm is "using K-Means algorithm to group data to normal or attack. Then, use Naïve Bayes algorithm to classify the obtained result into attack type. The KDD 99 dataset was used to evaluate the performance of this algorithm. The detection rate was improved to 99.6 percent. However, this solution is not practical for the real network because K-Means algorithm requires" other time to process vast data in real networks which could lead to bottleneck trouble and system crash.

7. **Real-Time Detection System:** In (Komviriyavut et al., 2009) authors proposed a real-time detection approach. "They used a packet sniffer to sniff network packets in every 2 seconds and pre-processed it into 12 features and used decision tree algorithm to classify the network data. The output can be categorized into 3 types which are DDoS, Probe and normal. The result shows that this algorithm as 97.5 percent of detection rate. This technique is fast and able to use in the real network. However, it was not designed to detect unknown attacks".

Although there are many techniques are developed so far to detect and mitigate the DDoS attacks in the cloud environment but none an ideal technique has been developed yet.

DDOS Attack in Cloud Environment

Recently cloud computing has been greatly increased equally in academic research and industry technology. DDoS are one of the security threats that challenge the availability. According to Cloud Security Alliance, DDoS is one of the main nine threats to cloud computing environment. Out of many attacks in

Table 2. Comparative analysis of different DDoS detection techniques

Name of Techniques	Throughput	Fault Tolerance	Performance	Overheads	Response Time	Detection Rate (%)
Statistical Method	NO	NO	YES	NO	NO	NA
Ids	YES	NO	YES	YES	YES	NA
Ids based dempster-Shafer theory	NO	YES	YES	NO	NO	NA
Packet information gathering and pre-processing	NO	NO	NO	NO	NO	NA
Host-based Intrusion Detection Systems	NO	NO	YES	NO	YES	NA
Network Detection System	NO	YES	NO	NO	NO	99.6
Real-time Detection System	YES	NO	YES	YES	YES	97.5

Figure 4. DDoS defense mechanisms

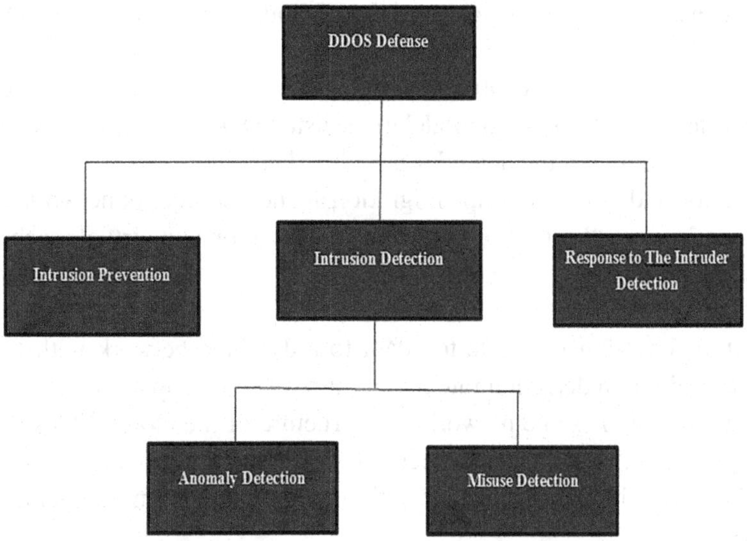

cloud environment 14% are DoS attacks. Many recognized websites like yahoo were affected by DDoS in early 2000. Website of grc.com was hit by huge DDoS in May 2001 (Ferguson and Senie, 2001). The company was dependent on the internet for their creation work and business was seriously impacted. Forrester Consulting was contracted by VeriSign in March 2009 to carry out a study on DDoS threats and protection. The survey was performed among 400 respondents from the US and Europe (Cert advisory, 1998). 74% had experienced one or more DDoS attacks in their organizations. Out of this 74%, according to 31%, the attacks caused service disruption, according to 43% attacks does not result in services disruption. The survey of DoS attacks in cloud says that as the use of cloud increases the rate of DDoS attacks will also grow at a fast pace. In Cloud environment when the workload increases on a service, it will start providing computational power to endure the extra load. Which means Cloud system works not in favor of the attacker, but to some extent it supports the attacker by enabling him to do most possible harm to the availability of service, starting from single attack entry point.

Cloud service consists of other services provided on the same hardware servers, which may suffer by workload caused by flooding. Thus, if a service tries to run on the same server with another flooded service, this can affect its own accessibility. Another effect of a flooding is raising the bills for Cloud usage drastically. The problem is that there is no "upper limit" to the usage (Jensen et al., 2009). And one of the potential attacks to a cloud environment is neighbor attacks i.e. VM can attack its neighbor in same physical infrastructures and thus avoid it from providing its services. These attacks can affect cloud performance and can cause financial losses and can cause a destructive effect on other servers in same cloud infrastructure.

Impact of Cloud Computing on DDoS Attack Defense

Currently, attackers can launch a range of DDoS attacks including resource-focused ones (e.g. network bandwidth, memory, and CPU) and application-focused ones (e.g. web applications, database service) from approximately everywhere.

To be realistic, 'we have to assume attackers can reside either in a private network, in a public network, or in both. To this end, we find the following properties of cloud computing affect DDoS attack defense".

1. Instead of users, cloud providers control network and computation resources, i.e., physical servers. This property differs from the system model in the usual DDoS attack defense, where the protected application servers are within the defender prohibited network.
2. Resource allocation and virtual machine migration are new sources of network topological changes from the defender's view. "Moreover, the resource allocation and virtual machine migrations processes are fast-paced.

The DDoS attack defense must be able to adapt to a dynamic network with frequent topological modifies and still maintain high detection rate and prompt reaction capability".

All cloud users distribute the same network infrastructure of the cloud. "This raises a reliable network separation requirement, which has not been considered in traditional DDoS attack defense. The enterprise must make certain its DDoS attack detection/defense operations neither affect nor be affected by other cloud users".

HOW CLOUD COMPUTING CAN IMPROVE EXISTING DDOS SECURITY TECHNIQUES

DDoS attacks can probably affect every layer of the OSI model, but the mitigation of large-scale DDoS attacks take place over layers 3, 4 and 7. Our discussion focuses on attacks performed over layer 4 and 7, because of their current rise in reputation and complexity at defending and mitigating their effects. A DDoS attack originating from malware infected SG devices that are executed over these layers could have major impacts on the operations of the SG (Goel, 2015).

There are several different techniques to defend against DDoS attacks (Darwish et al., 2013), but our analysis is limited to the DDoS defense techniques that can be enhanced by operating the inherent attributes of CC. "We are also accepting that CC is a fully included component of SG, to the extent that CC is not just being used for data storage, but also data processing, virtualizing software for energy suppliers, utility companies, consumers, and integrating corporate networks and industrial control systems." (Peng et al., 2007) DDoS defense techniques categorized into four major types:

*   Attack prevention,
*   Attack detection,
*   Attack source identification, and
*   Attack reaction.

Attack Prevention Defense Mechanisms

Attack prevention mechanisms try to stop DDoS attacks earlier than they can approach their target, typically through the use of a variety of packet filtering techniques (Mirkovic & Reiher, 2004; Park & Lee, 2001). "Methods such as ingress/egress filtering and router-based packet filtering are effective for small scale attacks, but in large, commonly distributed DDoS attacks; they are ineffective even when the source of the attack is known" (Swaprava et al., 2012). As the efficiency of filtering techniques is questionable, particularly for OSI layer 7 attacks, energy suppliers, and utility companies could utilize honey pots and honeynets to gain intelligence of potential DDoS attacks. Honeypots are systems configured with partial security to trick would-be attackers to target them as an alternative to the actual system (Spitzner, 2002). Honeypots could take benefit of CCs ability to virtualize servers and duplicate services (Biedermann et al., 2012).

Traditionally, high-interaction honeypots have been costly to maintain, "Especially when virtualization is unavailable. The design of an array of honeypots with different configurations, to detect vulnerabilities from malware, replication vectors, and databases could be implemented economically, be less resource intensive, and be restored more quickly if compromised". In combination with a robust network intrusion detection system (IDS), honeypots could be dynamically distributed across VMs to moderate computational overload, and play an integral role in a coordinated DDoS defense strategy (Biedermann et al., 2012; Bakshi & Yogesh, 2010).

Attack Detection

Attack detection techniques should be able to detect attacks in real-time plus post incident. Detection of DoS attacks is largely based on network data analysis (e.g. connection requests, packet headers, etc.) to distinguish anomalies in traffic patterns and imbalances in traffic rates (Carl et al., 2006). The detection system must be able to differentiate between legitimate and malicious traffic, keeping false positives outcome low down so that genuine users are not affected. Furthermore, these systems must have good system coverage and a short recognition time (Mahajan et al., 2002). Moreover, if verification schemes for SG attached devices are cooperation, attack source identification schemes may verify very useful at detecting malicious action (Fadlullah et al., 2011).

DoS-Attack-Specific Detection is used to identify attacks that "utilize the Transmission Control Protocol (TCP) over OSI layer 4 (e.g., SYN Flooding). DoS-Attack-Specific detection methods try to identify when incoming traffic is not proportional to outgoing traffic, the traffic is statistically unstable, or the attack flow does not have periodic behavior" (Gil and Poletto, 2001). These forms of detection techniques have had limited success against DDoS attacks (Peng et al., 2007), as each compromised host can closely mimic a legal user since there is no need to control the traffic pattern of a single host. Pretentious that the natural features of the attack are able to be detected early, elastic computing resources could make stronger SYN flood defense methods (Ghanti & Naik, 2014), and hypothetically be used to initiate an intentional increase in attack strength. "The geographic diversity of cloud resources could be leveraged, use of data from both the first mile and last mile routers throughout a CSPs network to pinpoint the attack source and aid ingress or egress filtering. This, coupled with redundant resources able to execute packet state investigation, would decrease the amount of time needed to shut out illegitimate traffic" (Choi et al., 2012).

Anomaly-Based Detection plans at detecting irregularities in traffic patterns on OSI layer 7 that do not match common traffic patterns collected from training data. This detection method has seen partial success against DDoS attacks because of the size and perceived legitimacy of BOTNETs. "Anomalies are not detected when traffic seems to observe with normal traffic patterns. This technique may only be effective if irregularities can be detected concerning the geographical location of IP addresses or percentage of new IP addresses seen by the victim (Peng et al., 2007). Historical data from across geographic diverse CSP resources may make anomaly detection techniques more effective by providing a more robust data set for analysis". The agile and elastic concert capabilities of CC may permit more resilient mitigation algorithms, such as an adaptive system for detecting XML and HTTP application layer attacks (Vissers et al., 2014), and SOTA (Chonka et al., 2011) to further mitigate X-DoS and DX-DoS attacks.

Attack Source Identification

Attack source recognition attempts to place where DDoS attacks are originating from. These techniques are extremely reliant on the Internet router infrastructure, and because DDoS attacks begin from the different geographical locality, many Traceback schemes are not successful against DDoS attacks. The hash-based IP Traceback system is worth mentioning as it has been shown to be successful against DDoS attacks, with some caveats (Snoeren et al., 2001). The network topology promise offered by SG and CC (Hahn et al., 2013) may possible new attack source identification schemes that succeed where usual Traceback schemes have fallen short (Park and Lee, 2001). "For hash-based IP Traceback to be effective there needs to be a wide geographic sharing of modern Traceback routers and an abundance of computing overhead to analyze packet data, especially over long periods of time (Snoeren et al., 2001). Assuming that CSPs have a large distribution of Traceback routers throughout their network and that cloud resources are spread out geographically, IP Traceback could take advantage of the agile and redundant resources available in CC. The agile and redundant computational capabilities could be leveraged for packet filtering techniques working in conjunction with other DDoS defense mechanisms" (Vasanthi & Chandrasekar, 2011), to maintain SG services, and achieve data analysis from Traceback routers on the CSP network to aid ingress and egress filtering.

Attack Reaction

Attack reaction techniques try to mitigate or eliminate the effects of a DDoS attack. For the prospect SG, this is an essential feature to avoid the SG from being completely paralyzed by an attack (Hahn et al., 2013). "Techniques consist of but are not limited to filtering out bad traffic, duplicating network resources, or even assigning costs to certain processes or transactions to limit the abuse of computational resources. CC offers many opportunities to enhance these capabilities, increasing their capacity and endurance."

History-based IP filtering (HIP) is a mechanism where routers permit arriving packets when they are verified against a pre-populated IP address database (Mitrokosa & Douligeris, 2007). "This defensive process is deemed meaningless if devices with a rightful reason on the SG are compromised and being used as part of a BOTNET (Mitrokotsa & Douligeris, 2007). "HIP filtering defense could leverage the geographic diversity, agility, and elastic performance of CC, but additional detail would be needed about how CSPs would implement the authentication process for IPs to know how and when this would be a benefit."

Load balancing is come to picture when there is a need to amplify the available server functions for vital systems to avoid them from shutting down in the event of a DDoS attack (Mitrokotsa and Douligeris, 2007). Load balancing has the ability to utilize computational resources across distributed networks (Randles et al., 2010), readily utilizing inherent abilities of CC, such as agility and redundancy, real-time response and elastic act, and virtualization and automation services (Randles et al., 2010; Begum & Prashanth, 2013). There are challenges to defeat, such as the cost of the distributed computational load (Khiyaita et al., 2012), latency, and computational bottlenecks (Hu et al., 2010), but if accurately implemented, the benefits of load balancing could be used by CSPs to help mitigate the effects of a DDoS attack made in opposition to the SG.

Discriminating pushback attempts to filter the data stream close to the DDoS attack source by finding the source of the attack and transfer the location data to all upstream routers (Mahajan et al., 2002). When attack traffic is normally distributed, or the attack basis IP is spoofed, tries of filtering attack traffic become difficult (Peng et al., 2007). Regardless of the exact technique used to monitor network congestion and packets legitimacy, the goal of the pushback technique is to filter the bad traffic as near to the source of the attack as possible. CC would be deployed indirectly, much like with DoS-Attack-Specific Detection and IP Traceback, taking benefit of agility, geographic diversity, and elastic performance to enhance the effectiveness of pushback schemes such as the cooperative pushback mechanism proposed by (Mahajan et al., 2002).

Source-end response schemes, such as D-WARD, attempt to catalog data flow statistics by continually monitoring the two-way traffic between the source network and the rest of the Internet (Mirkovic et al., 2002). "Statistics are collected such as the ratio of in-traffic and out traffic, and a number of connections per destination. The system periodically compares collected data against normal flow data models for each type of traffic that the source network receives, and if a mismatch occurs, traffic is either filtered or rate-limited" (Mirkovic et al., 2002). with the exception of privacy issues, the ability of CC could be leveraged with virtualization and automation services to catalog the traffic between SG infrastructure, CSP resources, utility companies, and infrastructure control networks, managing a robust dataset that could be used to look after the SG infrastructure. Furthermore, the elastic concert of CC could be leveraged to swiftly and efficiently compare historically and new data to detect irregularities and create quicker attack responses.

Fault Tolerance methods believe that it is impossible to prevent or stop DDoS attacks fully and to a certain extent focus on mitigating the effects of attacks so the affected network can remain operational. The line of attack is based on duplicating network services and diversifying points of the right of entry to the network. In the event of an attack, the blocking caused by attack traffic will not take down the entire affected network.

Similar to that of load balancing, "fault tolerance methods could leverage CC attributes, such as agility and redundancy, real-time response and elastic performance, and virtualization and automation services to duplicate services and keep the SG network responsive for legitimate traffic."

Resource Pricing is a mitigation move toward that utilizes a distributed gateway architecture and payment protocol to set up a dynamically changing cost, or computational burden, for initiating different forms of network services (Cert Advisory, 1998). "This technique favors users who perform well and discriminates against users who abuse system resources, by partitioning services into pricing tiers to avoid malicious users from flooding the system with false requests to attempt price operation. The high agility and elastic performance inherent in CC would alleviate the computational burden of Resource Pricing techniques" (Lonea and Popescu, 2013).

As the order of assigning prices to users grows, the computational demand would be simply mitigated by the ability of CSPs to insert extra computing resources. Expenditure levels could easily be allotted to put users into a cost hierarchy, and virtualization capabilities could be used to duplicate network resources and infrastructure capabilities, partitioning users spending dissimilar cost levels into separate processing areas. Unlawful traffic would be sectioned off from the lawful traffic, sinking the impact of an attack, and if desirable, be geographically independent.

Response to Detection

In the case when DDoS attack is detected, the next issue to do is the attack should be blocked and attacker should be traced for discovery out attacker's identity and location. This can be done in two days, firstly manually using ACL or automatically. Certain schemes used for tracing and identifying the attacker as shown in Table 4. Besides various techniques used to stop DDoS attacks but not all of the can be detected and prevented. All that can be done is to decrease the impact of the attack.

Table 3. Defense techniques and beneficial cloud computing attribute

Type of Defense	Type of Attack	Defense Technique	Beneficial CC Attributes*
Attack Prevention	SYN Flood (TCP), Smurf Attack, PDF GET, HTTP GET, HTTP POST	Honeypots	AR, SH, V
Attack Detection	SYN Flood, Smurf Attack	DoS-Attack-Specific Detection	AR, DLI, RPP
	PDF GET, HTTP GET, HTTP POST	Anomaly-Based Detection	AR, DLI, RPP
Attack Source Identification	SYN Flood, Smurf Attack; PDF GET, HTTP GET, HTTP POST	Hash-Based IP Traceback	AR, DLI
Attack Reaction	SYN Flood, Smurf Attack; PDF GET, HTTP GET, HTTP POST	HIP Filtering	AR, DLI, RPP
		Load Balancing	AR, RPP
		Selective Pushback	AR, DLI, RPP
		Source-End Reaction	AR, RPP
		Analysis of Traffic Data	AR, RPP, SH, V
		Fault Tolerance	AR, DLI, RPP, SH, V
		Resource Pricing	AR, DLI, RPP, V

*AR: Agility & Redundancy, SH: Self-healing, V: Virtualization, DLI: Device & Location Independence, RPP: Real-time Response & Elastic Performance

Table 4. Traceback Methods

Method	Description
ICMP traceback	The mechanism deals with forwarding low probability packets to each router and also sends an ICMP traceback message to the destination. With major no of ICMP messages which used to identify the attacker, faces issues like additional traffic, also the validation of these packets is difficult and moreover path detection overhead of information from route map.
IP traceback	This method traces back the attacker's path to find the origin of the attack. In this technique, the path of the attacker is followed back to find its source. But this becomes difficult if source accountability in TCP/IP protocol is disabled and also internet is stateless.
Link-testing traceback	This mechanism tests each of incoming links to check the probability of it being an attack. This is done by flooding large traffic and testing if it causes any network disruption. But the precondition to do this would be a system that will be able to flood traffic and information about the topology of the network.
Probabilistic packet marking	This technique overcomes drawbacks of link-testing traceback as it does not require previous knowledge of network topology, large traffic etc. This advantage also overheads the systems but there are many methods to avoid this overhead as proposed in.

Architecture of Proposed System

We have proposed a novel architecture for securing cloud towards network based attacks based on the previous research gaps that we have identified. Our proposed DDOS detection system is a novel architecture for detecting and mitigating DDOS from virtual machines and external entities on a cloud network. Our work focuses on offering robust security to cloud with reasonable cost. This section describes proposed model. The overall architecture of proposed model showed in Figure 5.

The proposed model consists of three main phrases as follow:

Firstly, the most important features are extracted from packets. Most effective features are extracted from the packet. Detection system extract features such as source IP, TTL, destination IP, ports and protocol flags as basic features. Karimazad et al. (2011) declared some parameters to identify the DDoS attack packets in traffic data. We also use these features because the analysis of traffic based on these features can improve the detection accuracy (Reyhaneh & Ahmad, 2011). Seven traffic features are used to detect the packets as legitimate or attack traffic. In the proposed model, only the Source port, Destina-

Figure 5. Overall architecture of proposed model

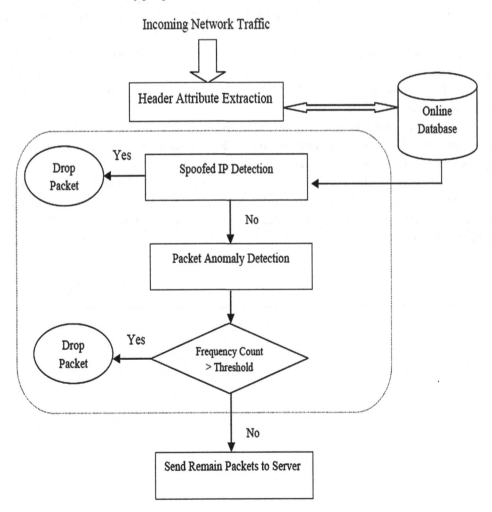

tion port, TTL, Total length, Protocol type, Window size and Flag of the packet are extracted. Secondly, the system "extracts the TTL value for all incoming packet and calculate the number of hops the packet has traveled. The attacker is able to spoof the packet header but cannot manipulate the number of Hop that each packet traveled to reach the destination count" (Varalakshmi & Thamarai, 2013). By comparing TTL's value with IP to hop count value. If exact matches do not found, so the packet is spoofed and the system discards it directly (Swaprava et al., 2012). The rest of the packets are passed to the next level.

At the end, the system clusters the traffics into ordinary or attack traffics by using deviation or anomaly behavior detection. In modern level the header information compares with the profile information which is previously trained in the database, to determine the information divergence between the two profiles. The packets are considered at this point for any anomaly behavior in the Header of the packets. The extracted attributes and their possibility for each field are considered for a certain time span. The trained profile of each attribute updates regularly to ensure negligible changes in the behavior of genuine users. We used the concept of Jensen-Shannon Divergence. The following Equations were used to compute Information Divergence (D).

By comparing the profile of already trained traffic with the new incoming traffic, the system can distinguish the legitimate traffic from the attack traffic. Information divergence is a non-commutative measure of the difference between two probability distributions P and Q. P typically represents the True distribution of data, or a precise calculation theoretical distribution. The measure Q usually represents a theory, model, or approximation of P. By referring to (1) this system firstly compute divergence for (P ∥ M) and (Q ∥ M) then by using (2) we can get the total divergence for the (*i*th) IP. If for the (*i*th) IP Information Divergence is more than learned profile (D$i \succ \gamma$) so the two probabilities have divergence. Therefore, P and Q denote the behavior of different entities. But if Di is equal to 0.0 then it indicates that there is a possibility of attack.

We analyze the packets which are stored in an intermediate buffer for attack use the frequency counter. The system, campers each packet with the blacklisted IP for similarity. If an exact match identified the frequency count of the packet is incremented by 1. There is a very high possibility that the attacker sends similar packet continuously which almost happens in a flooding attack. The frequency count of each packet is checked. If it exceeds the threshold value for a particular IP, the system indicates the packet as an attack and that IP is identified as the attacker. Then the system discards the packet and adds the attacker IP to the blacklist.

$$Di = \sum P(i) \times \log \frac{P(i)}{Q(i)} \tag{1}$$

$$Di = \frac{1}{2} D(Pi \parallel Mi) + \frac{1}{2} D(Qi \parallel Mi) \tag{2}$$

$$M = \frac{1}{2} - (P + Q) \tag{3}$$

In the proposed model, two algorithms are developed; Hope-count Algorithm and deviation or anomaly detector algorithm to distinguish attack packets from legitimate packets.

Algorithm 1. Hope-count

```
Algorithm Input: Network
Packet
 Output: Detect spoofed packets
  Start
   For each packet:
    Extract the TTL and the source IP address; Retrieve
    the initial TTL (Tij);
    Estimate the hope-count Hci=Tij-Tfi;
     Obtain the stored hope-count (Hsi)
             for the indexed Si; If
             (Hci≠Hsi)
            Packet is manipulated, "so it
               spoofed" drop it;
            Else
            The packet is
              legitimate to pass
              it;
            End If
          End
  For
 End
```

Algorithm 2. Packet Anomaly Detection

```
Algorithm Input: packet Header
Attributes
Output: Detect Attack Packet
Start
  For each section (t)
  If learning period
   classify probabilities of each
 value for header Attributes;
   Else
         identify probabilities of each
         value for the header Attributes for
         every IP;
         Define the Difor IPi; If Di≈0.0
chance of flooding
attack Use
```

```
frequency counter;
  If flooding attack "(frequency
  counter > threshold)" DDOS attack
  detected
  Drop matching
 packets;
      Else
 Pass the
packet; End
 If
      Else
 Add the Attacker IP to
 Blacklist; End If
End
If End
For
End
```

Evaluation of the System

An effective detection system should be able to overcome all the existing issues of cloud computing to could detect all the known and unknown DDOS attack to the cloud environment.

The proposed model is evaluated with respect to implementation. For generating network traffic and DOS attack we created a cloud Lab. We have chosen a HP proliant DL 180 Gen9 server with following features: Intel Xeon E5606, 8 GB RAM, 2×500 GB SCSI Hard Drives, we also selected VMware ESXI 5.0.0 Hypervisor as virtual machine manager (VMM) and windows 7 as guest operating system. We also have 5 clients with following features: Intel core 2 duo (2.53 GHZ), 2GB RAM.

On each client machine, we installed virtual machines with the random IP addresses for generating traffic. Three client machines are generating Normal traffic consist of FTP access, Web page access, e-mail access and UDP traffic. 2 of the client machines generate attack traffic. The performance of server at the time of attack traffic is shown in Figure 6.

This work used Netwag tool to generate DDOS attacks. "For capturing the packets and access to header information, a packet capturing tool JPCap is used. JPCap is an open source java Library tool for capturing network packets And devolve applications to capture packets from a network interface and explore them in java" (Varalakshmi & Thamarai, 2013). In the beginning, all non-spoofed packets are allowed in the training period and once profiled are trained, the deviation can recognize the result in rules being framed and therefore DDOS attack packets which match the rules are discarded. Once an attack is detected, rules are framed in order to stop similar packets from entering the system" (Varalak-shmi & Thamarai, 2013). This might decline the number of false positive to a small extent. In our first experiment, we used 2000 data points randomly from our lab dataset to check the detection rate and the false alarm rate of proposed system.

For evaluation of proposed system, we compared our proposed model with the Some Classifiers. From the presented list we have selected PART, Random Forester, Ripper and NaiveBayes to classify attack type. We used two datasets to ensure the performance of our model against the existing algorithms.

Figure 6. Server Performance

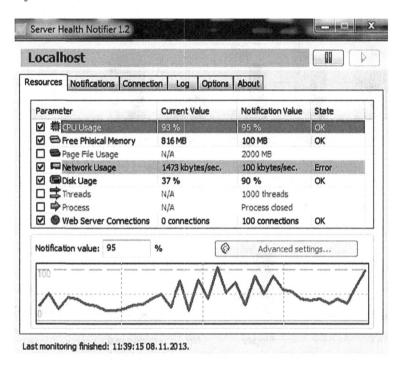

Our synthetic Lab dataset and CAIDA dataset "DDoS Attack 2007". On the other hand to check the performance of proposed system with the balance and imbalance dataset as well. The dataset contains approximately one hour of anonymized traffic traces from a DDoS attack on August 4, 2007. The details of performances are showed in Figure 7, 8 and 9. "The classification accuracy shows the amount of attacks which are classified correctly, the number of unclassified instances measures the technique's limitations, which means failures in classifying a number of attacks" (Khorshed et al., 2012).

As it is evident in Figure 3 and 4 the detection accuracy of proposed model by used of Lab dataset is above 97% and the false alarm rate is 0.6%. On the other hand, Random Forester detection rate and False Alarm rate are 98% and 0.7% respectively. Furthermore, Ripper classification algorithm has more than 99% of detection nevertheless the false alarm rate is 0.7%. NaiveBayes has above 96% of detection and the false alarm rate is around 0.5%. The part algorithm has the detection rate of 97%; moreover, the false alarm rate is 0.8%. By this comparison, there is no doubt that PART, Ripper and Random Forester

Figure 7. Detection accuracy

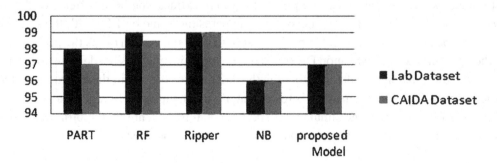

Figure 8. False alarm rate

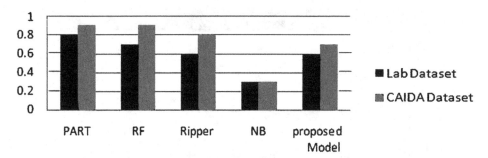

Figure 9. Detection processing time

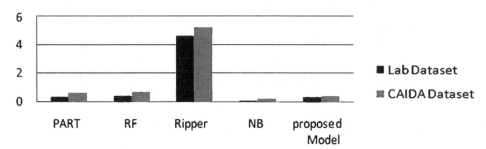

Classifiers in detection accuracy and False Alarm Rate have negligible better performance in comparison with our proposed model. The results show that our proposed system has an insignificant problem in the detection rate of attack traffic. This indicates that the DDOS defense system setting required to be adjusted for improving the efficiency. In Figure 5 the time processing of different classifiers showed. By comparing the time processing of different classifiers we observed. Ripper, PART, and Random Forester have significant consumption time than the proposed model. From the overall result, it is evident that the proposed model has better performance in compare to the State of Art Classifiers.

CONCLUSION

DDoS attack is one of the most significant security threats on the Internet. Detection of DDoS attack is considered to be one of the main phases in overcoming the DDoS problem. In this system, the packet features which exhibit the DDoS attack in traffic are discussed and we proposed two level of filtering to detect the attack. At the beginning, the proposed system extracts the header fields of the incoming packet to the system. In the next level, the system compares the value of TTL with the stored value of IP2HC. If there be no exact matching, the packet is spoofed and the system drops the packet. At the end, we used the concept of Jensen-Shannon Divergence. The incoming packets header information compare with the profile information that already stored in the database, to figure out the information divergence among the profiles. The core of our work is to present a system with an efficient reduce the false alarm rate and processing time. From the simulation experiments, it is evident that the proposed model in the overall has better performance in comparison to the state of art classifiers.

REFERENCES

Advisory, C. E. R. T. CA-1998-01, Smurf IP Denial-of-Service Attacks. (1998). Available: http://www.cert.org/advisories/CA-1998-01.html

Armbrust, Fox, Griffith, Joseph, Katz, Konwinski, Lee, Patterson … Zaharia. (2010). A view of cloud computing. ACM, 53(4), 50–58.

Bakshi, A., & Yogesh, B. (2010). Securing cloud from ddos attacks using intrusion detection system in virtual machine, in Communication Software and Networks, 2010. ICCSN'10. Second International Conference on. IEEE.

Basheer Nayef, A. D. (2005). *Mitigation and traceback countermeasures for DDoS attacks*. Iowa State University.

Begum, S., & Prashanth, C. (2013). Review of load balancing in cloud computing. *International Journal of Computer Science Issues*, *10*(1), 343–352.

Bellovin, S. (2000). The ICMP traceback message. Network Working Group, Internet Draft. Available at http://lasr.cs.ucla.edu/save/rfc/draft-bellovin-itrace-00.txt

Bhadauria, R. C. R., Chaki, N., & Sanyal, S. (2011). A survey on security issues in cloud computing. Retrieved from http://arxiv.org/abs/1109.5388

Bhuyan, K., Kashyap, H. J., Bhattacharyya, D. K., & Kalita, J. K. (2013). Detecting Distributed Denial of Service Attacks: Methods, Tools and Future Directions. *The Computer Journal*, *57*(4), 537–556. doi:10.1093/comjnl/bxt031

Bhuyan, M. H., Kashyap, H. J., Bhattacharyya, D. K., & Kalita, J. K. (2014). Detecting distributed denial of service attacks: Methods, tools and future directions. *The Computer Journal*, *57*(4), 537–556. doi:10.1093/comjnl/bxt031

Biedermann, S., Mink, M., & Katzenbeisser, S. (2012). Fast dynamic extracted honeypots in cloud computing. In *Proceedings of the ACM Workshop on Cloud computing security workshop*. doi:10.1145/2381913.2381916

Brody, A. (2013). History of DDoS. Retrieved from: http://www.timetoast.com/timelines/history-of-ddos

Brown, R. E. (2008). Impact of smart grid on distribution system design, in Power and Energy Society General Meeting-Conversion and Delivery of Electrical Energy.*2008 IEEE International conference*.

Burch, H., & Cheswick, H. (2000). Tracing anonymous packets to their approximate source. Proceedings of USENIX LISA (New Orleans) Conference.

Carl, G., Kesidis, G., Brooks, R. R., & Rai, S. (2006). Denial-of-service attack detection techniques. *IEEE Internet Computing*, *10*(1), 82–89. doi:10.1109/MIC.2006.5

Chen, Y., Hwang, K., & Ku, W. S. (2006). Distributed change-point detection of DDoS attacks over multiple network domains.*Proceedings of the IEEE International Symposium on Collaborative Technologies and Systems*, (pp. 543–550). IEEE.

Choi, K., Chen, X., Li, S., Kim, M., Chae, K., & Na, J. (2012). Intrusion detection of nsm based dos attacks using data mining in smart grid. *Energies*, *5*(10), 4091–4109. doi:10.3390/en5104091

Chonka, A., Xiang, Y., Zhou, W., & Bonti, A. (2011). Cloud security defense to protect cloud computing against HTTP-DOS and XML-DOS attacks. *Journal of Network and Computer Applications*, *34*(4), 1097–1107. doi:10.1016/j.jnca.2010.06.004

Chonka, A., Xiang, Y., Zhou, W., & Bonti, A. (2011). Cloud security defence to protect cloud computing against http-dos and xml-dos attacks. *Journal of Network and Computer Applications*, *34*(4), 1097–1107. doi:10.1016/j.jnca.2010.06.004

Chonka, A., Xiang, Y., Zhou, W., & Huang, X. (2012). Protecting Cloud Web Services from HX-DoS attacks using Decision Theory. IEEE International conference on communications in china: advanced internet and cloud (AIC). IEEE.

Cloud Security Alliance. (2010). Top Threats to Cloud Computing. Retrieved from http://www.cloudsecurityalliance.org/topthreats/csathreats.v1.0.pdf

Darwish, M., Ouda, A., & Capretz, L. F. (2013) Cloud-based ddos attacks and defenses. In Information Society (i-Society), IEEE International Conference. Retrieved from http://staff.washington.edu/dittrich/talks/sec2000/timeline.html

Doan, M. N., & Eui-Nam, H. (2011). A Collaborative Intrusion Detection System Framework for Cloud Computing.*Proceedings of the International Conference on IT Convergence and Security*, (pp. 91-109).

DoS and DDoS Evolution. (n.d.). Retrieved from http://users.atw.hu/denialofservice/ch03lev1sec3.html

Doua, W., Chen, Q., & Chen, J. (2013). A confidence-based filtering method for DDoS attack defence in cloud environment. *Future Generation Computer Systems*, *29*(7), 1838–1850. doi:10.1016/j.future.2012.12.011

Douligeris, C., & Mitrokotsa, A. (2004). Ddos attacks and defense mechanisms: Classification and state-of-the-art. *Computer Networks*, *44*(5), 643–666. doi:10.1016/j.comnet.2003.10.003

Du, P., & Nakao, A. (2010). OverCourt: DDoS mitigation through credit-based traffic segregation and path migration. *Computer Communications*, *33*(18), 2164–2175. doi:10.1016/j.comcom.2010.09.009

Fadlullah, Z. M., Fouda, M. M., Kato, N., Shen, X., & Nozaki, Y. (2011). An early warning system against malicious activities for smart grid communications. *IEEE Network*, *25*(5), 50–55. doi:10.1109/MNET.2011.6033036

Feng, Y., Guo, R., Wang, D., & Zhang, B. (2009). *A comparative study of distributed denial of service attacks, intrusion tolerance and mitigation techniques, intrusion tolerance and mitigation techniques.* Academic Press.

Ferguson, P., & Senie, D. (2001). Network ingress filtering: defeating Denial of Service attacks which employ IP source address spoofing. RFC 2827.

Ghanti, S. R., & Naik, G. (2014). Protection of server from syn flood attack. *International Journal of Electronics and Communication Engineering & Technology*, *5*(11), 37–46.

Gibbens, R. J., & Kelly, F. P. (1999). Resource pricing and the evolution of congestion control. *Automatica*, *35*(12), 1969–1985. doi:10.1016/S0005-1098(99)00135-1

Gil, T. M., & Poletto, M. (2001). Multops: a data-structure for bandwidth attack detection. In *USENIX Security Symposium*.

Goel, S. (2015). Anonymity vs. security: The right balance for the smart grid. *Communications of the Association for Information Systems*, *36*(1).

Hahn, A., Ashok, A., Sridhar, S., & Govindarasu, M. (2013). Cyber-physical security testbeds: Architecture, application, and evaluation for smart grid. Smart Grid. *IEEE Transactions on*, *4*(2), 847–855.

Hu, J., Gu, J., Sun, G., & Zhao, T. (2010). A scheduling strategy on load balancing of virtual machine resources in cloud computing environment.*International Symposium on Parallel Architectures, Algorithms and Programming (PAAP)*.

Jin, H., Xiang, G., & Zou, D. (2011). A VMM-based intrusion prevention system in cloud computing environment. *The Journal of Supercomputing*, 1–19.

Karimazad, R., & Faraahi, A. (2011). An anomaly based method for DDoS attacks detection using rbf neural networks. In *Proceedings of the International Conference on Network and Electronics Engineering*.

Khiyaita, A., Zbakh, M., Bakkali, H., & Kettani, D. (2012). Load balancing cloud computing: state of art. In *Network Security and Systems (JNS2), National Days of*. IEEE. doi:10.1109/JNS2.2012.6249253

Khorshed, M., Ali, A. B. M. S., & Wasimi, S. A. (2012). A survey on gaps, threat remediation challenges and some thoughts for proactive attack detection in cloud computing. *Future Generation Computer Systems*, *6*(28), 833–851. doi:10.1016/j.future.2012.01.006

Kim, S., & Narasimha Reddy, A. L. (2008). Statistical techniques for detecting traffic anomalies through packet header data. *IEEE/ACM Transactions on Networking*, *16*(3), 562–575. doi:10.1109/TNET.2007.902685

Kim, W., Jeong, O.-R., Kim, C., & So, J. (2011). The dark side of the Internet: Attacks, costs and responses. *Information Systems*, *36*(3), 675–705. doi:10.1016/j.is.2010.11.003

Komviriyavut, T., Sangkatsanee, P., Wattanapongsakorn, N., & Charnsripinyo, C. (2009). Network intrusion detection and classification with decision tree and rule based approaches.*International Symposium on Communications and Information Technology (ISCIT)*, (pp. 1046-1050). doi:10.1109/ISCIT.2009.5341005

Li, M., & Li, M. (2010). An Adaptive Approach for Defending against DDoS Attacks. *Mathematical Problems in Engineering*, 1–15.

Limwiwatkul, L., & Rungsawang, A. (2006). Distributed denial of service detection using TCP/IP header and traffic measurement analysis.*Proceedings of the IEEE International Symposium Communications and Information Technology*, (pp. 605–610).

Lo, C. C., Huang, C. C., & Ku, J. (2010). A Cooperative Intrusion Detection System Framework for Cloud Computing Networks. In *39th International Conference on Parallel ProcessingWorkshops*, (pp. 280-284). doi:10.1109/ICPPW.2010.46

Lonea, A. M., & Popescu, D. E. (2013). TianfieldDetecting DDoS Attacks in Cloud Computing Environment. Int J Comput Commun, (1), 70-78.

Lu, K., Wu, D., Fan, J., Todorovic, S., & Nucci, A. (2007). Robust and efficient detection of DDoS attacks for large-scale internet. *Computer Networks*, *51*(18), 5036–5056. doi:10.1016/j.comnet.2007.08.008

Mahajan, R., Bellovin, S. M., Floyd, S., Ioannidis, J., Paxson, V., & Shenker, S. (2002). Controlling high bandwidth aggregates in the network. *Computer Communication Review*, *32*(3), 62–73. doi:10.1145/571697.571724

Meiko, J., Jorg, S., & Nil, G. (2009). On technical issues in cloud computing. *IEEE International Conference on Cloud Computing*. IEEE.

Mell, P., & Grance, T. (2009). *Effectively and Securely Using the Cloud Computing Paradigm*. US National Institute of Standards and Technology.

Mell, P., & Grance, T. (2011). The NIST Definition of cloud computing. National Institute of Standards and Technology Special Publication, 800-145. doi:10.6028/NIST.SP.800-145

Mihailescu, M., & Teo, Y. M. (2010). Dynamic resource pricing on federated clouds. In Cluster, Cloud and Grid Computing (CCGrid), IEEE/ACM International Conference, (pp. 513–517).

Mirkovic, J., Prier, G., & Reiher, P. (2002). Attacking ddos at the source. *IEEE International Conference*, (pp. 312–321). IEEE.

Mirkovic, J., & Reiher, P. (2004). A taxonomy of ddos attack and ddos defense mechanisms. *Computer Communication Review*, *34*(2), 39–53. doi:10.1145/997150.997156

Mitrokotsa, A., & Douligeris, C. (2007). Denial-of-service attacks. Network Security: Current Status and Future Directions, 117–134.

Modi, C., Patel, D., Borisaniya, B., Patel, H., Patel, A., Rajarajan, M., & Gujarat, N. S. (2013). A survey of intrusion detection techniques in Cloud. *Journal of Network and Computer Applications*, *36*(1), 42–57. doi:10.1016/j.jnca.2012.05.003

Muda, Z., Yassin, W., Sulaiman, M.N., & Udzir, N.I. (2011). Intrusion detection based on K-Means clustering and Naïve Bayes classification. Emerging Convergences and Singularity of Forms, 1-6.

Oktay, U., & Sahingoz, O. K. (2013). Attack types and intrusion detection systems in cloud computing. 6th international information security & cryptology conference, (pp. 71-76).

Parag, K., Shelke, S. S., & Gawande, A. D. (2012). Intrusion Detection System for Cloud Computing. *International Journal of Scientific & Technology Research*, *1*(4), 67–71.

Park, K., & Lee, H. (2001). On the effectiveness of route-based packet filtering for distributed dos attack prevention in power-law internets. *Computer Communication Review*, *31*(4), 15–26. doi:10.1145/964723.383061

Peng, T., Leckie, C., & Ramamohanarao, K. (2007). Survey of network-based defense mechanisms countering the dos and ddos problems. *ACM Computing Surveys*, *39*(1), 1–42. doi:10.1145/1216370.1216373

Pourya, S. (2014). C2DF: High Rate DDOS filtering method in Cloud Computing. *Computer Network and Information Security*, 6(9), 43–50. doi:10.5815/ijcnis.2014.09.06

Raj Kumar, P. A., & Selvakumar, S. (2011). Distributed denial of service attack detection using an ensemble of neural classifier. *Computer Communications*, 34(11), 1328–1341. doi:10.1016/j.comcom.2011.01.012

Raj Kumar, P. A., & Selvakumar, S. (2012). M2KMIX: Identifying the Type of High Rate Flooding Attacks using a Mixture of Expert Systems. *Computer Network and Information Security*, 1, 1–16.

Raj Kumar, P. A., & Selvakumar, S. (2013). Detection of distributed denial of service attacks using an ensemble of adaptive and hybrid neuro-fuzzy systems. *Computer Communications*, 36(3), 303–319. doi:10.1016/j.comcom.2012.09.010

Randles, M., Lamb, D., & Taleb-Bendiab, A. (2010). A comparative study into distributed load balancing algorithms for cloud computing. In Advanced Information Networking and Applications Workshops (WAINA), IEEE International Conference on. doi:10.1109/WAINA.2010.85

Reyhaneh, K., & Ahmad, F. (2011). An Anomaly-Based Method for DDoS Attacks Detection using RBF Neural Networks.*International Conference on Network and Electronics Engineering IPCST*.

Roschke, S., Cheng, F., & Meinel, C. (2009). Intrusion Detection in the Cloud. In *Eighth IEEE International Conference on Dependable, Autonomic and Secure Computing*, (pp. 729-734).

Savage, S., Wetherall, D., Karlin, A., & Anderson, T. (2001). Network support for IP traceback. IEEE/ACM Transaction on Networking, 9(3), 226-237.

Snoeren, A. C., Partridge, C., Sanchez, L. A., Jones, C. E., Tchakountio, F., Kent, S. T., & Strayer, W. T. (2001). Hash-based ip traceback. *Computer Communication Review*, 31(4), 3–14. doi:10.1145/964723.383060

Specht, S. M., & Lee, R. B. (2004). Distributed Denial of Service: Taxonomies of Attacks, Tools, and Countermeasures.*Proceedings of the International Workshop on Security in Parallel and Distributed Systems*, (pp. 543-550).

Specht, S. M., & Lee, R. B. (2004). Distributed Denial of Service: Taxonomies of Attacks, Tools, and Countermeasures. International Conference on parallel and Distributed computing Systems, International Workshop on Security in Parallel and Distributed Systems, (pp. 543–550).

Spitzner, L. (2002). *Honeypots: tracking hackers* (Vol. 1). Addison-Wesley Reading.

Subashini, S., & Kavitha, V. (2011). A survey on security issues in service delivery models of cloud computing. *Journal of Network and Computer Applications*, 34(1), 1–11. doi:10.1016/j.jnca.2010.07.006

Swaprava, N., Ekambaram, V. N., Anurag, K., & Vijay, K. P. (2012). Theory and Algorithms for Hop-Count-Based Localization with Random Geometric Graph Models of Dense Sensor Networks. *ACM Transactions on Sensor Networks*, 8(4), 111–149.

The CAIDA UCSD. (2007). DDoS Attack 2007 Dataset. Retrieved from: http://www.caida.org/data/passive/ddos-20070804_dataset.xml

Thwe, O. T., & Thandar, P. (2013). A Statistical Approach to Classify and Identify DDoS Attacks using UCLA Dataset. *International Journal of Advanced Research in Computer Engineering & Technology*, *2*(5), 1766–1770.

Thwe & Thandar. (2013). DDoS Detection System based on a Combined Data mining Approach.*4th International Conference on Science and Engineering*.

Tool, N. (n.d.). Retrieved from: http://ntwag.sourceforge.net/

Udhayan, J., & Anitha, R. (2009). Demystifying and Rate Limiting ICMP hosted DoS/DDOS Flooding Attacks with Attack Productivity Analysis.*Advance Computing Conference. IACC 2009*, (pp. 558-564). doi:10.1109/IADCC.2009.4809072

Varalakshmi, P., & Thamarai Selvi, S. (2013). Thwarting DDoS attacks in grid using information divergence. *Future Generation Computer Systems*, *29*(1), 429–441. doi:10.1016/j.future.2011.10.012

Vasanthi, S., & Chandrasekar, S. (2011). A study on network intrusion detection and prevention system current status and challenging issues. Advances in Recent Technologies in Communication and Computing, 181-183.

Vissers, T., Somasundaram, T. S., Pieters, L., Govindarajan, K., & Hellinckx, P. (2014). DDOS defense system for web services in a cloud environment. *Future Generation Computer Systems*, *37*, 37–45. doi:10.1016/j.future.2014.03.003

Weiler. (2002). Honeypots for Distributed Denial of Service Attacks. International Workshops on Enabling Technologies: Infrastructure for Collaborative Enterprises (WETICE'02).

Xia, Du, Cao, & Chen. (2012). An Algorithm of Detecting and Defending CC Attack in Real Time. Industrial Control and Electronics Engineering (ICICEE), (pp. 1804-1806).

Xie, Zhang, Bai, Luo, & Xu. (2011). A Distributed Intrusion Detection System against flooding Denial of Services attacks. Advanced Communication Technology, 878-881.

KEY TERMS AND DEFINITIONS

DDoS: A distributed denial-of-service (DDoS) attack occurs when multiple systems flood the bandwidth or resources of a targeted system, usually one or more web servers.

Information Divergence: Is a measure of the difference between two probability distributions.

Virtualization: In computing, virtualization refers to the act of creating a virtual (rather than actual) version of something, including virtual computer hardware platforms, operating systems, storage devices, and computer network resources.

Section 3

Chapter 11
Transition and Transformation into a Cloud Environment

Clea Zolotow
IBM Corporation, USA

Rebecca Huber
IBM Corporation, Germany

Florian Graf
IBM Corporation, Switzerland

Marcel Schlatter
IBM Corporation, The Netherlands

Birgit Pfitzmann
IBM Corporation, Switzerland

Claus Schrøder-Hansen
IBM Corporation, Denmark

Anthony Hunt
IBM Corporation, USA

ABSTRACT

It is a challenge to migrate and transform existing workloads into the cloud, especially those requiring the higher standardization of managed services. Covered here are the various types of transition and transformation into the cloud from lift and shift to automated migration; the tooling and automation for the cloud environment; and the migration services via wave planning and check-pointing to the cloud for customers. Transition and Transformation is an integral part of cloud services, and creating a repeatable, reusable, factory model for a customer ensures a successful cloud migration.

INTRODUCTION

The cloud journey starts with building a private or signing up for a public cloud offering. Cloud offers many opportunities and advantages for enterprise customers, but also reveals challenges migrating existing workload into a cloud. Current workload is the majority of the workload when a large enterprise adopts cloud and new, greenfield, developments are usually an exception. Managed cloud services, such as IBM's Cloud Managed Services (CMS) offer services and Service Level Agreements (SLAs) above the hypervisor (IBM, 2015b), but impose additional requirements for migrations, compared to an unmanaged cloud (such as IBM's SoftLayer, (IBM, 2015c) or Amazon's Web Services (AWS) (Varia & Sajee, 2013) .

DOI: 10.4018/978-1-5225-0759-8.ch011

Note that larger customers will tend towards managed services. "Customers that need resilient infrastructure and the ability to scale up to large databases with many users will gain the most benefit from managed services. With managed services, the vendor will builds and manages the infrastructure including Operating System (OS) management, patching, backup, security, and compliance with SLA's at the VM level. IBM's CMS is the only fully managed cloud with a choice of x86 or AIX managed application services for SAP, SAP HANA and Oracle workloads" (IBM, 2015b).

One of the reasons customers desire the managed capabilities of a fully managed service like CMS is that this capability relieves them from that responsibility allowing them more time to focus on their applications and core business. We have observed that many large IT shops do not keep up with even minimally required care of key IT components such as OS and security compliance. Application owners are often under pressure to provide business functionality and defer or ignore the maintenance as long as things are still working. Additionally we have observed that some customers are more advanced than others in the implementation of ITIL compliant service management. This is another benefit as you have the option not only to leverage the infrastructure provided by cloud, but managed offerings allow the client to continue to move up the capability stack of managed services and improve operation capabilities in many areas.

Some customers will opt for a hybrid environment, utilizing AWS or SoftLayer with the larger managed services for servers that do not require the higher management options available.

The goal for many customers includes providing remote managed operations, shared services, and regional services for data center services to reduce business operational risks related to Disaster Recovery (DR) and Business Continuity Program (BCP) capabilities. Cloud can also enable business growth through the usage of common shared services via the service catalog, providing increased operational effectiveness and efficiency. Cloud services are characterized by secure multi-tenant services, standardization and cloud features such as auto-provisioning and metered chargeback. They include services for virtual and physical servers, selected databases and middleware, and a few application services as defined by the service catalog, and orderable through a common services portal.

Figure 1. Migrations into the cloud

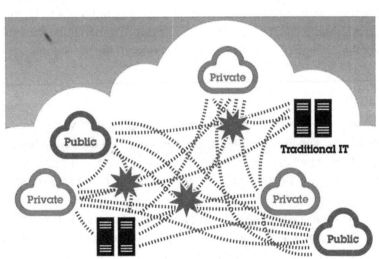

Migration is a key phase in getting from the traditional IT into a public, private, managed, or non-managed cloud. The task of migration includes moving applications to a cloud environment that can be shared or private, and on-premise (thus not requiring a lot of physical movement) or off-premise (requiring a larger transition).

Data Centre Migration: Terminology

Since the following terms are used interchangeably, here's a definition on how they are used in this paper:

- **Data Centre Migration (DCM) and Data Centre Relocation (DCR):** Fundamentally the same thing and represent the physical or logical relocation of IT services from one hosting location to another. This relocation could consist of no physical hardware moves at all, or it could consist of everything being loaded into a truck and driven to the new location, or anything in between. Sometimes "relocation" is associated with pure moves without many changes to the software and management, while "migration" is used for stronger transformations, such as to a managed cloud.
- **Data Centre Consolidation (DCC):** A DCM or DCR from multiple hosting locations into fewer hosting locations.
- **Data Centre Transformation (DCT):** The process of bringing maximum technical, operational and cost efficiency to the Data Centre through a formal program of review and technology change.
- **Data Migration (DM):** The migration of data from one application, database or service to another, and a far simpler task, with many data replication technologies available to support such data movement. Data Migration is likely to be a component of a DCM, DCR or DCC program (Dagley, 2011).

ENGAGING THE ENTERPRISE

A migration to cloud has to bring benefits to the application owners not just by reducing the cost after the migration but also by minimizing resource and downtime impact during migration. At the same time the capability to leverage standardized cloud offerings after migration has to be enabled. As with any large, complex project (Mindtools, 2015), the enterprise has to generate a momentum and engage all stakeholders to make this change of IT delivery model across all business units.

Wave Planning

This figure shows an example of wave planning across multiple sites. A wave is a group of servers or applications migrated in the same time period. Each site is denoted by a color and the connectivity between the servers is indicated by lines. Note that this would be a very difficult group of servers to break into waves as all the servers seem to be connected to each other in one form or another; however, this is not a rare situation.

IBM has developed an industry-leading, patented migration process and tooling to address these challenges during migration to a cloud. This article provides practical insight from many architects explaining their multi-year experience working with customers during their cloud journey, especially with larger customers migrating to CMS, and shows how we have innovated migrations to Cloud.

Besides determining the post-migration state of applications and services and the migration methods to reach that state, planning and scheduling is a critical topic. One way to ensure planned migrations is to determine major waves for the migrations with set milestones. This can ensure that source data centers are emptied at the required time, assuming the data centers and the services in them are ready in time for the planned migrations. This can also ensure that localized waves (i.e., on-premise) are thought about so that migrations do not traverse the same LAN or arrive at the same hardware concurrently. In the figure above, note that three datacenters are migrating into a new datacenter, either on- or off-premise. The DC1, DC2, and DC3 waves have been planned to arrive at differently zoned areas within the new datacenter, as not to overstress the LAN utilization as well as the storage.

Within each wave, a detailed plan composed of move groups is created jointly with the application owners. A move group is a set of servers and software components to be migrated together, typically during a low utilization period such as a weekend for critical applications. Typically, a move group consists of one or more related business applications, to ensure consistency of the business applications during migration and to minimize the need for downtime and testing of each business application. The move groups are distributed as uniformly as possible over time to ensure there are sufficient resources, both human and technical, to perform the migration process with minimized risk.

Figure 2. Wave planning across multiple sites

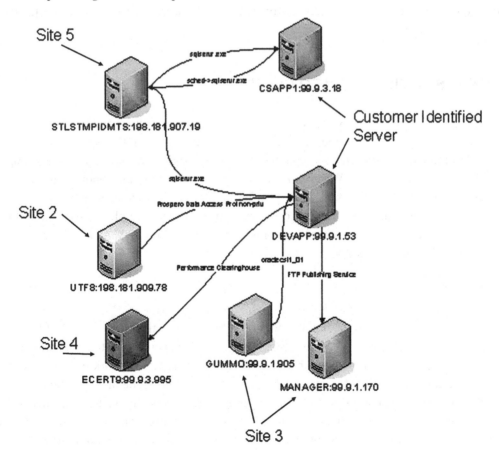

257

Business Application Owners

Business applications provide a functionality that supports business departments with business workflows. Each business application has an application owner who is responsible for providing the application functionality, determining the business criticality and thus determining the service levels and any disaster recovery requirements for the application. It's important to note that cloud migration is not a server migration; it is an application migration. The application owner must be involved early in the migration process for interviews, where application information from automated discovery is verified and various service aspects are determined. During the migration planning, the application owner also provides potential change windows for the migration and validates the migration design and plan.

The business application owner is also responsible for all changes that are planned on application components to ensure compliance, and to provide and execute the tests that are used for baseline testing before migration of the application and for User Acceptance Testing (UAT) of the application in the target environment. These can be the normal tests for the business application, or for simple migrations without real application changes, a suitable subset. Also the necessary setup for the tests, e.g., using the "test" environment of the business application, possibly with simulations of other business applications, is to be provided and typically reusable from other tests of the application.

Similarly, cut-over and roll-back plans for the business application are to come from the business application owner. It is essential that the business applications are identified with the corresponding application owners and are associated with the servers that host the various application components. These are then registered in the data center Configuration Management DataBase (CMDB) for each migrated server and service.

CHALLENGES IN MIGRATION TO CLOUD

Challenges in migration can be many. One of the initial challenges is how to handle security and sensitive data. When doing a physical migration, steps need to be taken to ensure that special data (i.e., HIPPA or financial data) remains whole and encrypted. Choosing the right vendor is another challenge. Cloud computing is not a one-size-fits-all. When choosing a migration strategy, it is important to fit that strategy with the vendor's strength, weaknesses, and specifically how the particular vendor needs or supports the application to be migrated. For example, one vendor may only take applications migrated via a predefined telecommunications path, another may only allow reinstall for disk, and another is flexible and will support any migration method,

Physical Layer

When a decision for one or multiple cloud vendors has been taken, the challenges start by moving the workload to the cloud datacenter (i.e., the physical movement). This involves the relocation of the servers onto a different physical computer, storage and network layer. The network becomes the backbone of the cloud solution. Most migration activities go through a network channel into the new cloud data center (excluding the rare lift and shift and reinstall of applications with no data movement). This pipe has to be reliable and provide enough bandwidth for the migration itself plus the subsequent production operation. Note that the transition network should be different from the production network, whenever possible. Further, note that many large transitions require primary and backup pipes from different vendors in order to ensure redundancy.

The compute block is based on a hypervisor, like VMware ESX or KVM. The conversion from physical to virtual or the change of the virtualization hypervisor can influence the workload in different ways. The performance of the new hardware needs to be at least equal to the source system. Benchmarks like rPerf (Cler, 2013) or RPE2 (Temple, 2012) can help in that area. Physical servers may also be included in the cloud.

Another impact which is often overlooked is the licensing aspect. Licenses from business applications (such as Oracle Database Management System) can be based on the count of CPU or other compute parameters. The number of CPUs often change with cloud migration by adding more virtual CPUs or having a higher virtual compute unit (vCU) based on the newer hardware in the Cloud. The cloud architecture licenses have to be assessed for each middleware in advance of the migration, because when the workload has been moved to the Cloud it's often too late to start the license procurement process and too late to reroute exorbitant license charges (Foran, 2015). For example, if the Oracle license is a per engine license, and Oracle databases reside across the multiple VMs that are not stacked on a physical device, the software licenses would not be cost optimized compared to dedicating one, for example, xSeries machine to Oracle and sharing the virtual CPUs for Oracle only.

Figure 3. Common orchestration services

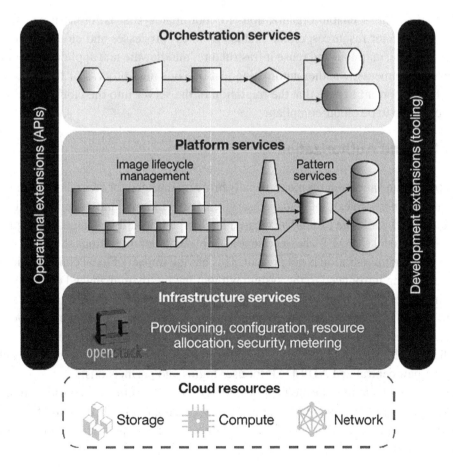

System Management Stack of MIaaS

Managed Cloud or Managed Infrastructure as a Service (MIaaS) come with their own system management toolset to provide backup, monitoring, patching, security compliance and many other services. These tools have to be deployed onto the migrated systems, which can be challenging for image-based migrations due to the heterogeneous structure of the migration candidates. Each of the managed services to be deployed has its own pre-conditions which have to be fulfilled to successfully install the software. These can range from a minimum operating system patch level to the availability of specific libraries. The migration process has to ensure that these preconditions are met or even better that the managed services deployments are robust enough to fulfill their preconditions themselves. For that to take place the scope of the managed services development has to be extended to not only cover freshly provisioned but also migrated workload.

The migration candidates already contain a set of tools that were used to manage the workload in the source data center. These tools have to be assessed prior to the migration to see if their functionality is now provided by cloud-managed service or if they have to be reconfigured to work properly in the new environment. The most important part is to minimize conflicts in the system management landscape. For example multiple different patching or backup services on the same system often don't make sense and can even lead to system outages. However, two different monitoring solutions may make sense, although not optimal, if they monitor different parts of the stack. Practical experiences show that application monitoring is not the same tool as for the infrastructure.

"Orchestration solutions enable organizations to coordinate—that is, orchestrate—the automated deployment of data center resources, cloud-enabled business processes and cloud services. They empower IT staff to create, maintain and reuse infrastructure, middleware and application templates across heterogeneous environments, whether automating just one business process or the entire data center" (IBM, 2014). It is important to note that the migration of the server into the cloud contains the "washing" of the application to be cloud-compliant.

Authentication and Authorization

Security, compliance and audit requirements usually bring up the need for centralized authentication and authorization mechanisms. In case of managed services, the Windows landscape is usually managed by Active Directory (AD) while the Linux/Unix-based landscape is usually managed through Lightweight Directory Access Protocol (LDAP). The experiences from customer migrations show that a strict change control in the system administration is not present. This has the impact of local configurations, including application users, being introduced to the system without having them managed correctly.

During a migration to the managed Cloud, the system is attached to the centralized authentication system and all local unmanaged users are revoked unless specific exceptions are approved. Therefore, it is important to assess the user set-up of each application in advance to lower the risk of breaking the business application. Furthermore the business application often requires a configuration change to be able to query the new centralized AD/LDAP for user logins and permissions.

Some companies prefer to migrate their applications first and then enforce security compliance (Hosting, 2015). While this approach will ensure less breakage during the UAT, it should be recognized that this step will happen and must be planned for accordingly with a fast-path post-migration to update the AD/LDAP environment.

Architectural and Technological Governance and Quality Gates

Large enterprise customers often lack global architectural and technological governance for many reasons, such as growth through acquisition. In many cases the migration teams encounter incomplete system landscape maps to miss migration-relevant information such as current operating system level, used and allocated (virtual) resources, installed system management tooling or user setup. Not knowing the source of the migration makes a transition project very difficult to do correctly. Therefore, source systems are usually scanned for their current information and network affinities. Only that way it is possible to decide on the suitable target cloud environment, ensure correct prior remediation activities, and ensure migration success.

The same is not only true for the operating system platform but also for the middleware layer. MIaaS often offer a set of higher value Platforms as a Service (PaaS) such as database or application servers. In case it is wished to consume the PaaS service as well, the middleware has to be on a supported level and a set of standard industry-wide best practices are applied to the configuration. In the worst case this can negatively influence the operation of the business application, but has to be done to ensure a homogenous landscape.

In Figure 4 we show a generic governance for managed service clouds covering the roles and activities for service delivery between the strategic, tactical, and organizational lines. No governance is complete without including quality gates. The wave lifecycle contains quality checkpoints at the end of

Figure 4. Governance

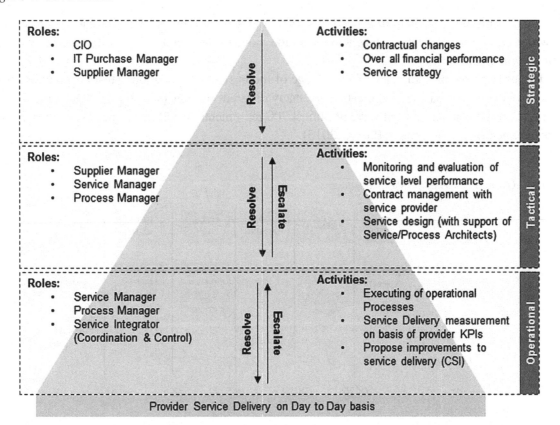

each phase (as in the figure below), e.g., to ensure that relevant application and middleware discovery has been completed before final plans are made, and that plans are final with all relevant aspects before migration starts. Phases that have a critical milestone as part of their process have a checkpoint within the phase, e.g. detailed design contains a financial checkpoint, and migration contains a migration Go/ No Go checkpoint.

Checkpoints are formal mandatory meetings in which a review of evidence required by the checkpoint's checklist will take place. The requirements of so called "hard" checkpoints must be met for the wave or application group activity to continue beyond the checkpoint, while requirements of a "soft" checkpoint allow wave or application group activity to continue but not beyond the following checkpoint.

Since some of the phases are iterative, there will be checkpoints that occur multiple times during a wave. As a minimum, the number of checkpoint meetings that occur for each wave will be driven by the number of application groups.

Lack of Priority and Knowledge

The application owners are under pressure to provide business functionality and ignore the need for IT to move to a new delivery model. Cost driven departments where IT is not the core business are constantly asked to do more with less. Cloud can be one of the differentiating factors in becoming more agile as services can be consumed instantly and charged on a pay per usage base. In order for the IT department to move to this new cloud-based delivery model, the application owner has to support the migration of the workload. The same application owner is asked to provide new application features at the same time and the developer team is under large pressure to constantly deliver new releases. These contradictory requirements make it very hard to generate momentum for the migration. The mitigation is to engage the whole enterprise as primary stakeholders, so the move to the cloud is a priority together with the business functionality.

Another large pitfall is the lack of knowledge of the business application. Most corporations have lost knowledge of the business application for many different reasons (see above). "One organization reported that the next anticipated wave of almost 700 retirements would mean the loss of over 27,000 years of experience" (Dorothy & Barton, 2015).

Figure 5. Quality delivery gates example

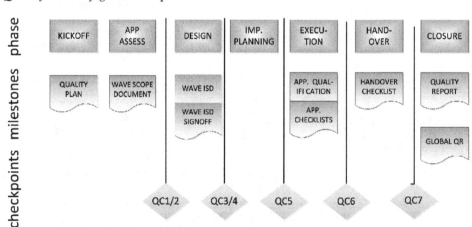

The development teams, especially in the agile style, are constantly re-assigned to different scrum teams. Those with the most urgent need receive personnel. If a business application has not undergone a large development effort in the recent past, usually the knowledge about the application is lost. During migration it becomes really difficult to understand the application and decide on the critical factors to make the migration a success. Practical experiences show that the configuration and the affinities are not always documented and change-controlled. Adaption to the new cloud environment is additional effort often overlooked.

Customized Tailored Services Out of the Standardized Cloud

In the traditional IT shop the IT services are tailored to the organization units or departments needs. By moving to a highly standardized delivery model, like the cloud, these customizations are limited. Business application owners often keep asking for customized services out of the standardized cloud as they are used to customized service from their local IT providers – usually in-house. In contrast a global IT department wants to keep a homogenous service landscape and provide all departments with the same service.

Practical experiences show that application standardization has not been the case in the past years as application owners do not want to standardize. However, the IT department still wants to use the migration to cloud to drive the standardization in the enterprise. Application owners will persistently ask for customized tailored service. Although the cloud service catalog is readily available, the owners still want additional platforms or middleware supported or even ask for their own unique managed service as they have been provided in the past. This is completely legitimate but comes with a longer timeline, and a higher price tag, not only to establish, but also maintain these customized services.

It is important that the expectations are managed and the need for IT to move to a new delivery model is clearly expressed and some benefits are shared with the application owners. The introduction of company-wide standards can be a painful process at the beginning, but will turn out as a positive return on investment.

Testing Effort and Acceptance of Migration Window

Service disruption during migration is unavoidable. Before the execution of the migration an agreement has to be reached with the business owners of the application for when and for how long it is acceptable to be unavailable. A set of migration activities, like data transfer, can happen in parallel to the production operation of the application but at a certain point in time the migration window for the cut-over has to be started. Practical experiences show that it is challenging to find an agreement with the business for one or more migration windows.

In order to validate that the migration has been performed successfully and the application has stabilized in the target environment, a user acceptance test is conducted. Depending on the application complexity and the level of changes during migration, the user acceptance test may be a subset of test cases to ensure the application is ready for production and non-functional requirements are fulfilled. During a migration to cloud the workload can be relocated to a different geographical location, which influences the network latency, both for the LAN and the WAN. The availability of knowledgeable application testers and the definition of test cases is key to the success of the migration. The test cases should be build based upon areas of risk identified as a result of the migration. The risk is a result of change. In most cases, the application code is not changing, but the external interfaces may be. There is not need to do a full regression test as the application team would normally do as part of an application change, but instead define a test plan that focuses upon the elements of change, such as access validation and external interfaces as an example. The agreement on the migration window(s) is influenced not only by the business decision of having the application unavailable but also on the availability of the testers (typically during weekends). The same tests should be performed before migration as "baseline test" to compare the post-migration results with.

Once the application is ready and an external write-transaction (proving the application works) with another productive system has been executed, the "point of no return" for the migration has been reached. "Write-transactions" mean any transactions where other productive systems change state based on the fact that they interacted with the newly migrated applications. Subsequent problems will be fixed in a "fix-forward" way, i.e., maintaining the migrated state of the application. The reason to use fix-forward is that the production servers may have had side effects not only on directly connected servers, but also indirectly on other servers in the enterprise.

Migration to cloud needs extensive planning for correct execution. As always, when the challenges are clearly understood the solution to them is usually quite straightforward. IBM has developed a large set of assets and learning via Migration Master Classes in order to plan and execute the migrations smoothly.

Transition and transformation into a cloud environment can be very difficult as transition (physical migration) and transformation (change of any compute system, i.e., OS, application, etc.) into cloud requires standardization.

CLOUD AND TRANSITION TYPES

There exist many transition and transformation tools to ensure that applications migrated into the cloud meet the cloud standards. For example, many cloud customers will have legacy environments that need to be upgraded to be cloud-ready, such as operating systems, system management tooling, business application, and/or middleware. Further, the patching of servers in the cloud environment is consistent, much different than legacy datacenters today where security and operating system patching can be customized for the individual application.

Transition and transformation complexity also depends on the type of cloud environment. Specific workloads will go into public clouds, such as test and development as datacenters start their cloud journey. Many times these environments will be migrated from the cloud production application, then replicated as a test or development workload.

Private clouds are utilized when a more secure environment on a customer premise is desired. These environments can be migrated in a usual manner (i.e., image migration) if these image components (operating system or application) meet the cloud standards. Many times the private cloud environment may be more flexible and non-conforming images will be placed into the legacy datacenter and remain non-clouded .

Hybrid clouds are interesting as the images can go into either the public or private cloud space depending on the customer's needs. Migration into the public cloud may be more difficult as the rules for the application will usually not be customizable (e.g., allowing Windows 2008 Standard Edition in the private cloud but only allowing Windows 2008 Enterprise Edition in the public cloud).

Software As A Service (SaaS) will require that the customization of the application (such as SAP) follows standard rules, such as user modifications placed in a specific, named directory, rather than modifying standard application code; data files placed on the SAN in a specific format and of a specific, standard size, and standardization of the application infrastructure following the public cloud rules (e.g., only 5-tier SAP systems, only Oracle RAC, etc.).

TOOLING AND AUTOMATION

There are many different types of tooling to perform cloud migrations. It is important to note that standard datacenter migration tools (both image- and SAN-based) can work for the cloud environment. Usually, when utilizing image-based migration tools and SAN based tools (utilizing tools such as IBM's Global Mirror), the image goes into to a pre-cloud zone, where the image can be washed for the cloud. Other cloud tools add orchestration to the process and can wash the image as well (either pre- or post-migration) for relatively minor operating system and tooling changes. IBM offers a low-risk and highly automated image migration process into IBM's Cloud Managed Service. The tooling imports the migrated workload into CMS (obeying the capacity and asset management as well as network constraints), adjusts the workload to Cloud standards and makes it manageable for IBM by installing all system management tools.

Additional tooling is also found in discovery modules. IBM Services teams use a discovery toolset deployed as an appliance. At the core of the tooling is a discovery tool such as IBM's Tivoli Application Dependancy Discovery Manager (TADDM). This tooling produces reporting to show what applications are connected to other applications for distance migrations. For example, when migrating over a long distance, separating a database from the middleware component and the web-facing component is not recommended as response time will elongate. The toolset will perform the discovery and the analytics in order to produce the wave and affinity reporting to ensure linked applications, databases, and middleware move together. More details are shown in the following picture. In addition, IBM's InterCloud Storage toolkit or ICStore can migrate workloads across multiple clouds by storing data redundantly on object storage (Darryl K. Taft, 2013).

"IBM Cloud Automated Modular Management (AMM) – migration service is designed to streamline the time and costs of image migrations onto SoftLayer. The offering provides a self-service dashboard to migrate both single and group physical/virtual image workloads onto the SoftLayer platform, and

Figure 6. Migration to cloud: factory model

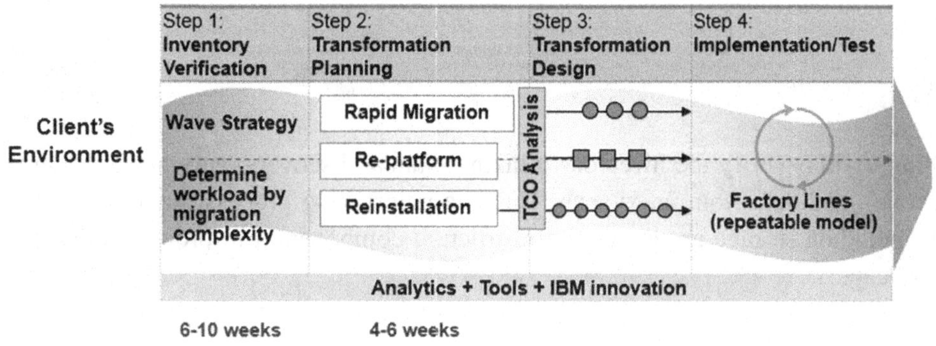

Figure 7. Use of discovery and planning

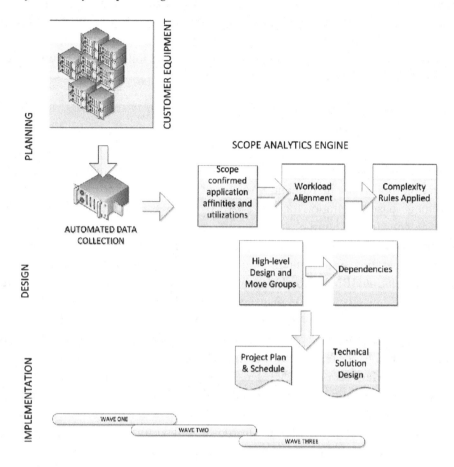

monitor the migration. The service also virtually eliminates manual steps, such as determining server sizes, provisioning migration servers, installing migration software, and configuring VMware and virtual machines. Through our offering, you can perform these steps via one user-friendly portal" (IBM, 2015a).

STEPS FOR TRANSITION AND TRANSFORMATION

IBM utilizes a factory approach for migration into the cloud. Below are the major steps that encompass this approach.

Discovery

The first thing to do is verify the inventory utilizing manual discovery, automated discovery (such as TADDM above), and data from interviews. This is a painstaking process that defines the datacenter end-to-end (including storage groups and infrastructure components) in order to fully determine the compute landscape.

- **Discovery:** The sub phases are discovery scope and authorization, and then the actual automated discovery.

    ○ Discovery scope and authorization. The preliminary sub phase of providing the scope for the discovery, authorizing it for this scope, and assigning the actual access credentials often takes much longer than the actual discovery. Furthermore discovery tooling has to be installed in the source datacenter. It is a task for the security teams responsible for the source data centers and the business applications there.

    ○ Automated discovery is a predictable, rather short-term activity, dominated by the time agreed on for affinity and utilization discovery, e.g., 35 days.

Planning takes place at several levels of granularity. Many of the activities are based on the discovery results, as well as on knowledge of the as-is state. Each plan has to be signed off by authorized signers of all involved parties.

- Customer readiness planning plans everything that is central for the customer in its future sites, such as security zones and systems, services, and identity management integration. It takes place mainly with the teams governing and managing the infrastructure in the source data centers.
- Per-application planning happens mainly with the individual business application owners. Within it, there is per-service planning, in particular analyzing current operating systems and software for cloud compliance and planning corresponding migration methods. Overall planning for a business application includes non-functional requirements, affinities to other business applications, test cases and setup, and cut-over and potential roll-back plans.
- Move-group planning means deciding on the move groups. A key input are the dependencies among business applications and the business application sizes, but also possible change windows and availability of key personnel. There is some feedback from move-group planning to per-application planning, because testing, cut-over, and roll-back depend on whether entire connectivity components can be used as move groups or how they are cut.

Certain results of the planning feed the central capacity management process so that any additional purchases can be made in time. Customer readiness is split into the minimum tasks for the use of Cloud services, and extra tasks requested by the customer because of their existing environment. Both follow the results of customer readiness planning, and have data center readiness as a precondition.

- *DC Readiness* (data center readiness) is a precondition for customer readiness. This means that all cross-customer infrastructure and components have to be available, and cloud service requests can be fulfilled.
- *Customer onboarding execution* is the minimum tasks. E.g., security zones must actually be realized by VLANs, subnets, and firewall contexts; directory domains have to be configured, and the customer has to be on boarded into the service management and systems management tools.
- *Customer readiness execution* contains all other tasks at the overall customer level that have been planned, e.g., establishing special services agreed with the customer, or integrating existing service or identity management tools of the customer.

- **"Customer Ready" Gate:** Only the customer onboarding execution needs to be finished for suitable first migrations to start.

Migration of a move group can start when customer onboarding execution is ready, any planned application remediation has been finished, and any customer-specific services that this move group requires have been finalized in customer readiness execution. The reason to treat these tasks, in particular application remediation, as separate preliminary tasks is that the migration factory phase is to consist only of standard tasks with a fixed timeline.

- **Move-Group Tasks:** By definition, a move group consists of business applications (or parts) that have important dependencies. Hence tasks that require consistency, such as the last backup on the source side, cut-over, sign-off, and potential roll-back, are done for the entire move group together.
- **Business Application Tasks:** Any planned application-level adjustments, such as changing IP addresses in applications that hardcode them, belong to the business application. Tests are typically owned by the business application owners, although some may need the presence of the entire move group for their execution. The same UATs have to be applied before migration as a baseline as after migration, so that no pre-existing problems prevent the successful conclusion of the migration.
- **Per-Server Tasks:** At least in the factory style migrations, complex application remediation is already done, and thus servers and services are migrated one by one. This can happen in parallel; "per-server" means that there are run books and tracking per server, and more servers require more resources.
- **Cutover to Production:** A key point at the end of the migration of a move group is the cutover to production, i.e., when the migrated applications replace those on the source side for their business use. From this point on, any new problems should, if at all possible, be fixed in the new data center, because rolling back to the last backups in the old data center can have ripple effects via external dependencies and user beliefs. However, a roll-back plan as a last resort was to be provided in the planning phase.

Early-life support and steady-state. In these phases, the business applications and the underlying services are taken over by the normal cloud delivery teams. During early-life support, the migration team is still on call in case of problems, and the steady-state team observes the application with particular care.

The gates are largely decided by the application owner, but the other parties have a veto right if the management of a migrated application seems not possible.

There are checklists for what has to be achieved in a certain phase for a corresponding entity (customer, move group, business application, or server, respectively). These checklists are to be checked off, and where a decision is to be made, the result is to be documented. In particular, the checklists of the planning phase lead to a Solution document. More precisely it is a document tree, with an overall customer part from customer readiness planning, and business-application parts from the business application planning etc.

The checklists are also extended into project plans by the addition of dependencies, durations, timings, and exact people to carry out the tasks with the desired results. Results of the planning phase lead to customization of the project plans for the migration execution.

Run books (also called workbooks) are at a more detailed level than checklists and project plans. They are step-by-step descriptions for the human executors for certain tasks, and not tracked by the overall project managers.

Wave Planning

The discovery information is fed into an analytics engine holding the discovery results, in order to determine the wave and affinity planning. The database of server affinity and application dependency data gathered from IBM's automated data collection tools makes such analysis possible.

Once waves have been defined, the database can be interrogated to see how/if they are connected to other waves. This becomes a specific point to pursue on during application assessment (in the detailed Solution Design phase) to determine migration impact management. This may change the grouping (combination/recombination) of servers & apps in each wave and may determine the scheduling of waves in relation to one another (either to occur at the same time or in sequence).

As the key unit for migration is a business application, the most important element in such a graphic (which will be produced in the planning phase for the real applications) is dependencies across business applications. Dependencies materialize as communication, and are partially discovered in the Discovery phase (those that are present at one of the query points in the discovery interval).

If a connectivity component contains too many servers, it has to be broken into several move groups. This situation requires more planning with the business application owners, e.g., which dependencies are the least critical to cut, how the communication during the (if possible short) interval between the moves is done and changed testing requirements. The planning effort becomes even larger for a business application that is so large that it cannot be moved at the same time at all.

Note that different, separated environments of a business application can be treated as different business applications in move-group planning. It is even recommended to migrate the test environment first, because – assuming it is indeed representative – any problems that might arise from the new cloud management are already discovered during the test move. Thus the risk of migration failure and the need to roll back is significantly reduced, and testing on the production environment can be minimized.

Another complication is communication with applications external to this customer, or applications that must, for some legal or technical reasons, stay behind in the old data center. Besides the fact that the distance between the internal and external applications changes, the tests need particularly careful planning, because the owners of the external applications may not even be aware of the cloud migration program initially.

Besides dependencies by communication, there may also be components jointly used by multiple business applications, e.g., a server and database installation hosting a database farm. These dependencies are particularly strong, because assigning the business applications to different move groups means breaking up at least one of them internally.

Transformation Planning

Transformation planning is the phase where the type of migration is considered, such as Image Migration, Re-platform, and Re-installation. The type of transformation is determined both from the type of cloud and from the customer requirements. Some customers have legacy workloads that require major uplift to be cloud-enabled and sometimes those applications are reinstalled by the customer. Image Migration

Figure 8. Example wave planning with migration units

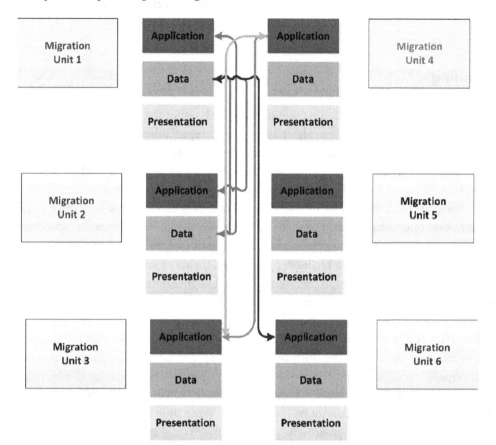

as a migration type can be chosen if the target cloud supports the migrated operating system platform, reinstall is applicable to redeploy the application on the OS platform of the same family (Windows 2008 to Windows 2012) and re-platform covers the remaining migration types where major parts of the architecture are being changed (e.g., Solaris to Linux).

Then, the next action is to design the actual transformation, i.e., how the applications will be transformed and tested post-implementation. This activity includes tasks such as describing outage windows, security, DR, and change freezes for the business. The end result is a technical solution document showing how the servers, images, data and applications within the source data centers can be migrated to target data center(s).

Migration Methods for Transformation

Within a business application, the actual migration is typically executed and tracked per server. (The exception is major logical application changes, but those should rather be in the application remediation phase; they are not part of the repeatable migration process.)

Servers in the same business application can be migrated with different methods. Recall that UAT, cut-over, roll-back etc. are performed only for the entire business application. For the per-server migration, there are four key methods:

- **Image Migration:** This moves an entire OS image with everything on it, and subsequently adjusts it ("washing") to cloud standards.
- **Re-Install:** A new operating system according to cloud standards is provisioned, and applications and all other necessary components from the source system are newly installed on it. For re-install, the old and new operating systems must be from the same vendor and only differ in the version. Changes to middleware, code and data may be needed, but are moderate.
- **Re-Platform (e.g., from Solaris or Mainframe to Linux on X):** Applications typically have to be re-compiled, or rewritten, or even require a new application architecture design.
- **Lift and Shift:** An entire physical server is relocated. Some washing may take place.

In addition to the key migration methods listed above, other methods are:

- *"Leave As Is"*, also called "stay behind", where the evaluation of technical and business requirements yields that the system cannot be migrated to the cloud and will remain in a location of the customer
- *Sunsetting*, e.g., infrastructure applications from legacy datacenters that are no longer needed in the cloud
- *Specific methods* for data-less or clustered servers

The resulting roadmap is then reused for further transitions/transformation for the customer.

Lift and shift migration are usually only allowed in a private cloud environment, as they require provisioning from bare metal (as in a non-virtualized environment).

GENERAL TRANSITION AND TRANSFORMATION

There are many concerns that apply not only to cloud migration, but also standard transition and transformation projects. Below, we discuss some of the more common concerns around IP and DNS addressability, networking, security, disaster recovery, and capacity and performance and tuning.

Networking Considerations for Transition and Transformation

Re-IP and Networking Settings

It is usually considered a value-add to the datacenter migration to receive a new IP address in the target security zone in the cloud data center, in order to avoid conflicts and collisions on the network as well as clean up the existing networking IP in the current datacenter. Many times, the datacenter network has been around for so long that it is undocumented and doesn't have the resiliency of a new network, with separate VLANS for administration, production, and backup.

Figure 9. Migration types

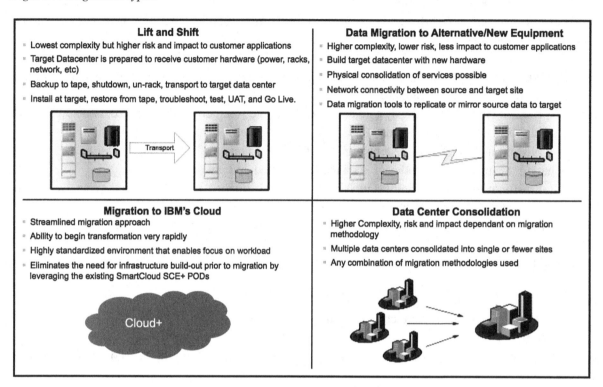

For image migrations that are congruent with the new cloud, IP addresses and related network settings are automatically adjusted on the OS instances during normal washing, utilizing tooling. For reinstall and re-platform migrations, the migrated servers get new IP addresses as part of the normal provisioning process as automated by the cloud.

Applications using IP addresses directly (rather than DNS names) need to be reconfigured by their owners to use the corresponding DNS name during the application remediation phase as direct IP addressability is not usually allowed into the cloud due to inflexibility. This direct-IP to DNS conversion should before the actual migration. Where that is not possible (e.g., in certain clusters or mainframe communication), the migration plan for the business application has to contain a step where the owners of the affected components make the IP address changes while the application is migrating.

It is important to note that many application owners will not know if they have hardcoded IP addresses and the discovery phase should look for these artifacts. For example, to detect whether an application uses a particular IP address to communicate to other systems would require a custom way to read the specific configurations, read the embedded configurations, etc. This is not a trivial task as it is variable for custom applications and is typically dealt with as risk during a migration event. Testing can be performed prior to a migrated system being turned on into production. However, that can be costly upfront, costly to mitigate at the time of migration or missed completely due to the existence of legacy systems still successfully responding to requests (Perpetua, 2015).

The approach to gather this information, without having to perform system scans, is to compare name resolution caches to server communication attempts. This can be done using a layer 2 to layer 3 mapping (MAC address to IP address mapping) or it can be done directly using layer 3 operating system commands (Perpetua, 2015).

Software licenses may also be affected by the change in IP addresses; if this requires procurement or other interaction with the software vendor, this has to be planned for the application remediation phase.

In some migration programs the hosts will also get new hostnames. The application owner is responsible to change all addressing in their application (including in workstations and as known to users) to the new DNS names. Such migrations require extended testing.

Image migration is an accepted alternative where the hostname is retained, because it is a fast migration methods without application changes. During cut-over, DNS alias changes are required to point the DNS aliases to the new IP addresses.

Networking Considerations for Migration

This section describes strategy aspects related to the DC LAN and WAN during the migration to the cloud or other new data centers. A precondition for migration is that the network is capable of handling the productive network traffic load. Note that bypassing the LAN and utilizing WAN-only transfer methods is highly recommended with large migration loads due to over-weighing the LAN as well as uplink problems on the production network core.

During the migration, additional network bandwidth is needed between and within the source and target data centers. The exact capacity amount needed depends on the planned move groups and schedule. If all data are transferred while the applications are down, the bandwidth can be computed as the storage used by the move group, divided by the length of the change window, plus the typical network overhead. If data are transferred while the applications are running, a more complex computation based on the change rate is needed, because resynchronization is then the limiting factor. If the bandwidth has to be ordered earlier than the move groups are available, an estimate has to be made based on the overall storage and the expected available time for change windows.

Figure 10. Sample WAN-only storage migration with Vicom

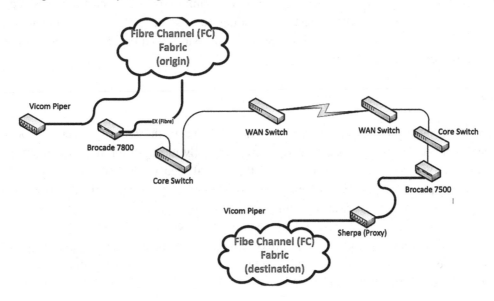

Note that latency is generally accepted to be 10 ms per 1000 miles. In some cases, WAN accelerators may be utilized to decrease latency. WAN Accelerators (WANX) encapsulate the TCP/IP packet to ensure that the short acknowledgement required by native TCP/IP is overridden. Some examples of WAN accelerators are Riverbed devices such as Steelhead and Cisco's Wide Area Application Services (WAAS). IBM's standard is Riverbed. The latency needs to be taken into account when doing the wave planning as some business applications can be split as the effect of latency on application interoperability is low, while others may require additional scrutiny because they do not tolerate high latency. This may result in a higher number of servers moving during a wave in order to ensure we do not split such applications.

Lines such as OC-3 and 1 GB/E have a stated payload (maximum of the line) as well as an assumed effective rate which is considered to be anywhere from 60-80% of line capacity depending on the overhead of the line. When calculating datacenter migration line speeds it is also important to note that lines do not run at capacity for a 24-hour period. There are starts and stops inherent in the wave planning, therefore effective daily throughput is estimated based on a 15-hour day. Firewall settings for the migrated applications have to be planned beforehand, based on dependency discovery and application questionnaires or on existing firewall rules.

For the testing of the migrated applications, special care must be given to interfaces external to the move group to ensure that data is not transferred inadvertently with external systems or other productive business applications. An example of a particularly critical impact would be outgoing connections triggering financial booking, or incoming connections from external parties that might entail erasing files that have been transferred and thus not transferring them to the productive systems. The process of ensuring that any migrated application in test does not inadvertently send or receive messages or use external interfaces is referred to as ring-fencing. The reason to select the move group as the unit to isolate together is that the move groups were initially planned as a unit to migrate and test together. It will often be a business application, but it may also be a group of several smaller, closely interacting business applications. Then their test versions can all interact safely within the same isolated environment.

As a general rule, all external network connections (inbound and outbound) will be blocked during tests, except the protocols required for the actual migration and, in a later stage, for the UAT. One key mechanism for this blocking is firewall rules. The firewall rules for both the ring fencing period and the final state have to be planned in advance during the planning phase for each business application. If firewall protection is not feasible for the ring fencing because of specific communication patterns, careful detailed design of another approach is needed. Similarly, load balancer configurations have to be performed before or in migrations.

Security

This section describes rules, definitions and practices related to the security. Security tools such as security health checkers and virus scanners are treated usually in migration like systems management tools (patching, monitoring etc.). This means that the central security components are present prior to migration, freshly provisioned services come with all necessary agents and configurations, and that in an image migration, washing with these agents and configurations is executed. Quarantine zones for non-compliant servers may be required, at least separate VLANs surrounded by strict firewall rules.

The application owner is responsible for providing any compliance requirements of their business application on the underlying IT services and components, and for comparing them with the security policies offered by the cloud. In a private cloud, the policies may be adjustable by particular customer requirements. The policy selection will be stored in the CMDB of the cloud. Systems with certain high compliance requirements may not be migrated to certain clouds, e.g., data that have to stay within one country cannot be migrated to a cloud where the data or their backups may be stored in another country. The application owner is also responsible for achieving and maintaining compliance for all application components not managed by the cloud provider, and for the application as a whole.

Data transfer may require encryption. As the high-volume migration is necessarily done with a fixed tool set and processes, and will require a high bandwidth, it has to be calculated how sufficiently fast encryption can be provided. Note that the WANX products discussed above as well as the SAN migration devices provide encryption at little to no bandwidth degradation.

Disaster Recovery

The application owner is responsible for deciding on the various Disaster Recovery (DR) options of those services that are freshly ordered in the selected migration scenario. In some cases DR options can be changed after the provisioning, but in other cases, they are fixed for a specific provisioned instance in the cloud, so this decision should not be taken lightly.

The application owner should ensure that the application components automatically restart when the underlying cloud services do. Typically such mechanisms were already in place before migration because they are also useful for maintenance and high availability. In an image migration, the mechanisms are typically preserved, but it is recommended to verify.

For components that are migrated as a whole that had their own disaster recovery mechanisms, e.g., database log shipping or an application-level active/active setup, it must be validated whether these measures are viable in the new cloud environment. For example, if the database log shipping was synchronous and the database is heavily used, then the same setup may lead to intolerable database delays with an out-of-region DR site. In such cases, the best-suited solution has to be selected together with the application owner during migration planning. It may require a selection of both high-availability and disaster recovery mechanisms in the cloud, while in the old data centers, some clusters were used for both HA and DR.

If application owners decide to introduce an application-level DR capability, they are responsible to transform the application to support the required capabilities. This application transformation is not part of the migration and needs to be completed beforehand in the application remediation phase, or started in the cloud after the migration.

Migration planning is also a good opportunity for application owners to extend or change their disaster recovery plans, i.e., the human procedures needed in the case of a disaster. If they rely on the DR of the cloud service, and have appropriate startup mechanisms already, the application will usually recover automatically even without such a plan, if the cloud vendor has thought through the DR services.

If a disaster occurs during the migration, the DR is still upheld, because disaster recovery is always made from a replica on one side, not mixed. This is shown in the figure below. This figure shows three states of the migration, depending on where the business application (or entire move group) is currently running in production. Whenever it is in production in one data center (in the figure "Old DC1" and "New E1"), the disaster recovery for that datacenter is naturally used if a disaster happens there, while a disaster in another data center does not matter. In an intermediate phase where the application is down in the old data center, and not yet up in the new one, the disaster recovery state in the partner of the old data center, here "Old DC2" is correct (within the RPO) with respect to the latest state of the business

Figure 11. Disaster recovery during migration

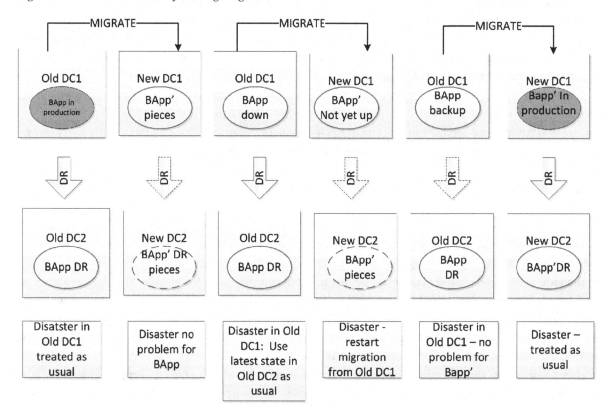

application in Old DC1. BApp' is the possibly changed version of BApp in the new data center, e.g., by use of Cloud services.

More precisely, the figure holds for move groups rather than business applications: If multiple business applications are in one move group, they are consistently recovered as a whole. If one business application has to be broken across several move groups, then BApp in the figure is such a part of the business application, say together with BApp*. As a precondition for this situation, it was decided in move group planning that BApp and BApp* can be migrated separately, say BApp first. This means that BApp' can work together with BApp* in the interim phase, as if they were separate, dependent business applications. Hence again all states that we can reach with disaster recovery are states that also occur without disaster recovery.

Capacity and Performance Considerations

The target performance configuration for compute, memory, and storage (including the tier if known in the planning phase) will be determined according to the sizing of the source system. The default choice is usually the standard cloud configuration offering closest higher performance to the source system. This reduces later operational risks related to performance or throughput of the associated services.

Industry benchmark data is used to map the source configuration to the target configuration, along with utilization data and data collected during discovery and application owner interviews. The application owner can request a different configuration during the per-business-application planning.

Note that for the most loved applications, it is usually better to have an end-to-end performance and capacity analysis done. In many cases, performance problems that have always existed in multi-tier applications will be highlighted when the migration is done, giving rise to the "you touch it, you own it." Having benchmarks and response times from the applications before they were migrated can mitigate a lot of free consulting.

SUMMARY

The cloud environment promises managed operations, shared services, and regional services to enable business growth through an efficient, secure standard services. Corporations are challenged to bring existing workloads into the cloud, especially those requiring the higher standardization of managed services. Here, we have discussed the various types of transition and transformation into the cloud from lift and shift to automated migration; the tooling and automation for the cloud environment; and the migration services via wave planning and check-pointing to the cloud for customers. Transition and Transformation is an integral part of cloud services, and creating a repeatable, reusable, factory model for a customer ensures a successful cloud migration.

REFERENCES

Cler, C. (2013). *How to Use rPerfs for Workload Migration and Server Consolidation*. Retrieved September 22, 2015, from http://www.ibmsystemsmag.com/aix/tipstechniques/Migration/rperf_metric/

Dagley, R. (2011). *Data Centre Migration: Managing hidden business risks*. IBM. Retrieved from: https://www-935.ibm.com/services/uk/gts/pdf/GTW03030_GBEN_00.pdf

Dorothy, G. L., & Barton, S. W. (2015). *What's Lost When Experts Retire*. Retrieved September 23, 2015, from https://hbr.org/2014/12/whats-lost-when-experts-retire

Foran, J. (2015). *Cloud computing licensing: Buyer beware*. Retrieved September 23, 2015, from http://searchcloudcomputing.techtarget.com/feature/Cloud-computing-licensing-Buyer-beware

Hosting. (2015). *Security Challenges Involved with Cloud Migration - HOSTING*. Retrieved September 23, 2015, from http://www.hosting.com/security-challenges-involved-with-cloud-migration/

IBM. (2014). *Simplifying cloud management and data center automation*. Retrieved from: https://www.viftech.com.pk/wp-content/uploads/2015/05/White-Paper-Simplifying-cloud-management-and-data-center-automation.pdf

IBM. (2015a). *IBM Cloud AMM - migration service by IBM Cloud - Automated Modular Management | IBM*. Retrieved September 22, 2015, from https://marketplace.ibmcloud.com/apps/3933?restoreSearch=true#!overview

IBM. (2015b). *Managed Cloud: IBM Cloud Managed Services.* Retrieved September 22, 2015, from http://www.ibm.com/marketplace/cloud/managed-cloud/us/en-us

IBM. (2015c). *Softlayer: An IBM Company.* Retrieved September 22, 2015, from http://www.soft-layer.com/info/transparency?utm_source=google&utm_medium=cpc&utm_content=Brand_-_IBM_Softlayer&utm_campaign=PPC-AMS-Region-Brand&utm_term=ibmsoftlayer&matchtype=e

Mindtools. (2015). *Stakeholder Management - Project Management Tools from MindTools.com.* Retrieved September 22, 2015, from https://www.mindtools.com/pages/article/newPPM_08.htm

Taft. (2013). *IBM Secure Cloud Migration Tool Released.* Retrieved September 22, 2015, from http://www.eweek.com/cloud/ibm-secure-cloud-migration-tool-released.html

Temple, J. (2012). *A More Effective Comparison Starts With Relative Capacity.* Retrieved September 22, 2015, from http://ibmsystemsmag.com/mainframe/administrator/performance/relative_capacity/

Varia, J., & Sajee, M. (2013). *Overview of AWS.* Retrieved September 28, 2015, from https://d36cz9bu-wru1tt.cloudfront.net/AWS_Overview.pdf

Chapter 12
Workload Migration to Cloud

Choong Thio
IBM Corporation, USA

Jim Cook
IBM Corporation, USA

ABSTRACT

Workload migration to cloud is a critical area in increasing the adoption of cloud. In order to fully lever-age the power of cloud computing, clients need to determine what workloads and applications are good candidates in the cloud and migrate them quickly and in an efficient manner into the cloud. The main goal of this chapter is to explore and study how workloads can be migrated into cloud. In addition, this chapter will also describe the overall end-to-end process for cloud migration and its resulting benefits.

INTRODUCTION

Many applications in the cloud are new green field applications developed specifically for the cloud. What about the existing application landscape? How can these existing application workloads take advantage of the cloud-computing environment? How can these existing applications be migrated seamlessly into the cloud environment? How can these existing applications continue to function and connect back to their Systems of Record in traditional computing environments? These are typical questions facing many clients today about their existing application portfolio. One common approach is to reinstall their application in the cloud environment and customize it to ensure it operates correctly in the cloud environment. This can be a time consuming and pain-staking event as numerous changes and customization to the Operating System and application environments may be required for the application to function correctly in the cloud environment.

DOI: 10.4018/978-1-5225-0759-8.ch012

BACKGROUND

One particular model for cloud migration provides a modular approach of migrating cloud-enabled workloads to cloud more quickly and cost effectively. It is an end-to-end migration consisting of multiple phases, including data collection, analysis, wave planning, migration planning, project governance, cloud environment setup, actual migration, application testing, etc. These phases can be utilized in a modular fashion, allowing organizations to opt for just the migration component of the end-to-end process. The creation of an overall business case is also critical to clearly show the financial benefits, both hard and soft benefits, of a cloud migration. This model of a cloud migration comes with a very flexible delivery model as these modules can be delivered using the appropriate resources.

MIGRATION MODEL

The migration model transformation and migration process of existing customer workloads into cloud consist of four steps.

Steps 1 and 2 are part of the 'due diligence' phase. Step 1 is about "data discovery and assessment." To be able to define the best migration path, it is important to gather key data on the existing customer server and workload environment. Some of the key data to be collected are as follows:

Number of Servers

It is critical to discover all of the servers that are in scope for the migration up front so that the baseline for the migration can be established clearly. This baseline information is necessary to facilitate discussions with the stakeholders on what servers should be included in the scope of migration and what servers should be excluded from the scope of migration. It will also drive the scope and benefits of the business case for migration to cloud.

Figure 1. The migration model

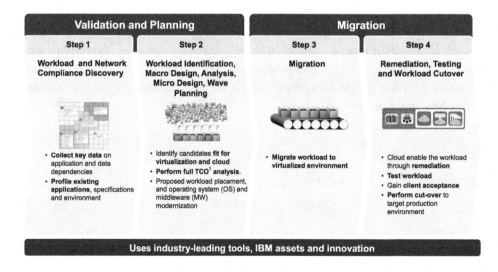

Operating Systems and Levels

Some operating systems are easier to migrate than others. For example, the labor it takes to migrate Unix workloads is typically higher than the labor it takes to migrate Intel workloads. In addition, the operating system versions will alter the migration techniques and labor used to possibly upgrade them to the latest version. Therefore knowledge of the operating system types and versions are key to drive the migration techniques to be used and the development of the associated business case.

- **Server Configuration, Including Number and Type of CPU, Storage, Network Interfaces Cards (NICs):** Server configuration information is important during the planning of migration as it influences how to migrate the workload to cloud and what specific configuration remediation is required after the migration is completed to ensure the application remains functional. For example, there may be situations where the network interfaces will need to be repurposed for different functions, such as backup or administration.
- **Server Utilization:** This information is needed to determine which specific workloads can be hosted together on the same hypervisor. Typically, the analysis will determine which workloads are a good fit to be hosted on the same hypervisor based on the workload utilization characteristics. For example, an application that runs batch jobs at night will fit well with another application that runs primarily during the daytime. This will ensure both applications are not contending for the same server resources at the same time. Instead each application will be heavily using the shared server resources while the other application is more dormant. Typically, a minimum of 35 days of data collection is required to capture the utilization of any applications that may only be executed on a monthly basis. The application owners need to be polled to see if there are any seasonal or special quarter-end or year-end processing that could influence utilization considerations.
- **Network Configuration, Including VLANs, IP Addresses:** For the application to continue to function correctly in the new environment, the network configuration including VLAN topology configuration will need to be setup correctly in the new cloud environment. This has a dependency on the discovery phase to discover the current network configuration and VLAN topology so that we can replicate the same environment or improve in the new environment to ensure the application can still communicate to other systems of records that may continue to reside in the existing environment.

Understanding the IP addresses scheme is also critical as it identifies what application remediation may need to be done for any potential IP addresses changes. For example, a well-designed application typically does not hardcode the IP address in its code. So changes in the IP address as part of the migration would only require the Domain Name Server hostname to be changed. However, a poorly designed application with hardcoded IP addresses in its code will require changes or redesigns in its code to accommodate the IP address change.

- **Firewall Rules Configuration:** For any applications that need to communicate with other applications in another demilitarized zone (DMZ), an understanding of the protocol they use and the associated firewall ports they communicate over, will be crucial. Knowledge of the firewall ports usage will help drive the design and planning on what firewall rules are needed to be configured in the firewall to enable application communications. In addition, knowledge of the firewall rules is necessary to be able to setup the correct security zones in a Software Defined Network environment.

- **Applications:** An understanding of what applications are running on the server or virtual machine is key to determine if these applications can be migrated to the cloud. For example, there may be regulatory constraints for the application or software licensing prohibition that may rule out the migration of the application into a cloud environment. Or it may identify certain cloud remediation that is required to ensure that these applications can be migrated to the cloud and run in a cloud environment. This information is typically captured through an interview with the application owner using standard application questionnaire templates.

- **Data Dependencies/Affinities between Applications:** The application affinities are information about what other applications a specific application is communicating with. For example, a front-end web server communicating with a back end database server has an affinity with each other. In order to ensure unnecessary network latency is not introduced to the application communications, the migration planning process needs to take this affinity information into consideration to migrate both applications together in the same wave group. This information can be discovered in a static or dynamic approach; from a static approach, the affinity discovery tool will scan the application configuration files and determine what other applications this specific application may be communicating with; from a dynamic approach, the affinity discovery tool will sniff and monitor the network link for all communications in and out of the specific application dynamically. The monitoring needs to be done over a sufficient period of time to capture any communication affinities that are irregular.

All this data needs to be collected in a non-intrusive and secure manner. Typically this is done through the deployment of a standalone appliance in the network environment (e.g. Riverbed SteelCentral, Risc Networks Cloudscape, RackWare. etc.). This does not require any agents to be installed on each of the source servers. However, it does require the appropriate credentials to be enabled for the discovery appliance to be able to poll each of the servers to collect all of the information it requires. This appliance-based approach reduces the performance impact on the current environment including network and server impacts. The time required to collect the data needs to be determined by consulting the application owners to get their perspective on variability in their applications throughout the business cycle. Sometimes this requires using historical data and educated assessments and predictive analysis on future utilization across the applications. After collection, they have to be analysed and assessed—and sorted by certain criteria to be able to move into the second step, which is the planning phase.

Step 2 is the "transformation planning and design" phase. In this step, analytics tools are used to qualify the data and identify optimally suitable transformation and migration candidates (and of course those that are not suitable are also identified), as a migration plan is being built. For those applications that are fit for migration to the cloud, an application assessment report, architecture for the target deployment and a recommendation for how the appropriate migration strategy might be scheduled, are typical outputs of this phase. In this step, not only do technical and architectural data get analysed, a second key input is the financial validity of the transformation and migration, which are the best candidates from a total cost of ownership perspective, and which migration plan is optimal from a financial perspective:

1. The first key aspect that the analytics tool will consider is the application affinity. The tool will have to analyse the application affinity information that was collected in the previous phase to determine what applications have an affinity with other applications. It will then group the applications that have affinity with each other into the same migration wave group. This will ensure after the migration that the applications can continue to communicate with each other without any increase in network latency. If an application cannot be migrated to a cloud, then typically all other applications that have an affinity with this specific application should not be migrated to the cloud, for the primary concern of increased network latency. Additionally, an application performance test may be planned, scheduled and conducted to determine if the resulting network latency is acceptable to the application after migration.

2. The analytics tool will assess the server utilization information to determine what specific applications should be migrated on the same hypervisor in the cloud environment. This analysis may be impacted and negated depending on the characteristics of the target cloud environment; if the cloud performs automatic workload movement based on capacity management, then the initial placement of the workload in the cloud environment is not as critical.

3. The analytics tool will determine what is the best migration technique to migrate the workload into the cloud environment. Some of the various migration techniques are:
   a. Image based migration,
   b. Pattern based migration,
   c. Application based migration,
   d. Reinstallation, and
   e. Replatform.

4. The analytics tool will also assess what remediation tasks and steps are required for the application, network and OS environment. Depending on the migration technique used, the remediation tasks will vary. Some amount of remediation tasks will be required to ensure the migrated application can continue to function correctly and be able to communicate with other applications in an efficient manner.

5. The analytics tool will assess and create a detailed business case to document clearly what the appropriate cost savings are for migration of the workload to a cloud environment. The business case will need to identify clearly the resulting steady state management cost, the added agility in the cloud environment and the migration cost it would take to transform the application in a cloud environment. The business is critical for business owners to assess and determine the value proposition of the workload migration to cloud.

Step 3 is the "migration" phase, where the selected workloads are migrated to the cloud environment. Typically, a dry run or pilot is planned before the full migration. Development and test workloads are usually planned to be migrated first in the pilot to ensure minimal impacts to the production landscape.

There are 5 ways of moving workloads into the cloud:

1. **Reinstallation**
   a. The workload is installed from scratch on a cloud server. In this scenario, a new VM is provisioned in the cloud environment. The latest OS version is provisioned to execute within the VM. The application is then installed on the OS within the VM. This can include the installation of a new version of the application. If the version of the application remains the

same, the application remediation activities required will be minimal. However, if the version of the applications changes, for example an upgrade to the latest version, then the application remediation activities required may be substantial to replicate the application configuration.

    b.   The steady state management costs of the newly reinstalled application (including both the management of the OS, middleware and applications) will be lower if the application is upgraded to the latest version as part of the reinstallation.

    c.   Many customers are leveraging this approach as part of their refresh program to reinstall the latest version of the application in a cloud environment.

2.   **Image Migration**

    a.   In this technique, the server image (operating system and applications) is captured and replicated (cloned) onto a server in the cloud. All of the configuration for the operating system, middleware and applications are also included as part of the server image capture.

    b.   This technique is the least intrusive to the application as all of the existing configurations are replicated as part of the migration. The amount of application remediation required will be minimal. Some application remediation may include changes to the IP address and so on.

    c.   The cost of migration for this technique will also be the lowest.

    d.   The steady state management costs of the migrated application (including both the management of the OS, middleware and applications) will be approximately the same as it was before the migration, as the OS, middleware and applications have not changed significantly during the image migration process.

    e.   Some solutions that leverage this technique include RackWare, Platespin, Double Take and so on.

3.   **Application Migration**

    a.   This is a unique solution for selected applications (not the operating system) and associated data that are migrated to a server in the cloud in a Microsoft Windows environment. This approach leverages technology such as AppZero where it will monitor the execution of the application and copies the appropriate files over to the cloud environment.

    b.   This technique does not require the operating system version of the source and target server to be the same.

    c.   One typical use case of this technique is to migrate an application running on a Windows 2003 operating system to a target environment running Windows 2012 operating system. In other words, this allows for an application to be migrated to the cloud with an operating system upgrade.

    d.   The steady state management costs of the underlying OS will be lower since the OS will typically be the latest version. However, the steady state management costs of the migrated application itself will be approximately the same as it was before the migration, as the application has not changed significantly during the migration process.

4.   **Patten Based Migration**

    a.   In this approach, the workload is migrated using a pattern-based approach. The application pattern is discovered and mapped to a standard pattern that has been deployed in a cloud environment. The configuration of the application is then migrated over to the standard application in the cloud that has been deployed using a pattern.

    b.   In this scenario, a new VM is provisioned in the cloud environment. The latest OS version is provisioned to execute within the VM. The application pattern from the pattern library is provisioned on top of the OS within the VM, typically using tools such as IBM Cloud Orchestrator. After which, the configuration of the application is applied to the newly provisioned application in the cloud environment. Tools such as IBM UrbanCode Deploy (IBM Corporation, 2013) can be used to replicate the application configuration in an automatic fashion. This approach introduces an upgrade to the application leveraging a standard best of breed pattern deployed in the cloud.

    c.   The leverage of a standard application pattern in the cloud will result in a substantial decrease of application or middleware steady state management costs.

5.   **Replatform**

    a.   This approach is similar to the reinstallation approach, except in this case, the operating system is changed as part of the replatform. For example, an application running on HP/UX will be reinstalled on a Linux operating system. This approach will have the most impact to the application, in other words, the amount of application remediation required will be significant and will have to be planned accordingly.

There are benefits to each migration method and this chapter will explore each technique in more detail. Migration technology is evolving and self-service migration portals are being deployed that reduces the time and effort to perform migrations while also lowering the skill level required by the person doing the migration.

Step 4 is the last step in the process—"remediation, testing and workload cutover." The migrated image, now boarded in the cloud environment, goes through some initial start-up tests (smoke tests) and additional more extensive tests, and—if successful—gets handed over to the client.

- A basic 'smoke' test is typically done to ensure the operating system is functional, the network connectivity is in place among all of the applications and that the migrated application can be executed.
- Application remediation is performed by the application owners to potentially reconfigure the application to ensure it can run in the new environment.
- Functional testing is the next level of testing and it is typically performed by the application owner to ensure that the application is functional.
- Customer acceptance testing is the final testing that is executed by the application owner to ensure if the migrated application is satisfactory and can now be maintained by the steady state team.

Finally, the last two weeks after cutover to the client, the image is '"formally deployed" in the cloud environment.

In summary, cloud migration is a critical component and process as part of the cloud adoption strategy. It enables existing applications and workloads to be migrated in a seamless and cost effective fashion into a cloud environment, allowing the applications to take advantage of the cloud resources and functionality.

MIGRATION PROJECT ACTIVITIES

Moving a few servers into the cloud tends to be easy to understand and execute. However, the complexity of migrating servers into a cloud environment grows rapidly based on the number of servers because there are more moving parts and interactions between the parts that need to be coordinated and tracked. In addition, the interconnection of servers grows which increases the complexity of the up front discovery and analysis. To provide better context around the complexities involved we will go into the typical activities required to perform a successful migration project for a non-trivial number of servers.

Project Planning and Project Kick-off Phase

Like any complex project, the role of a project manager is needed to drive the project and mitigate risk. The project manager needs to develop a project baseline, which includes defining the project scope (number of servers to be considered for migration, time frame for migration, project constraints, staffing plan, ballpark project cost, identify the project stakeholders and their desired outcome, etc.). The project manager will review project criteria with the stakeholders for approval and funding. Once approved, the staff required to do the migration needs to be acquired and boarded. Typical project boarding activities include procurement of ID's for the staff, team rooms, travel planning, office space acquisition, etc.

Discovery Phase

Once the team is in place, the next phase for the migration project is the discovery process. The purpose of the discovery is to do a thorough inspection of the source environment servers, networking and possible constraints so that a proper analysis can be performed in the next phase. A list of servers and their attributes (Operating System, Utilization, Memory Size, Storage Size, Physical or Virtual, etc.) is required. Sever affinities (which server communicates with which server), is required. This information can be obtained from an existing source, such as an inventory spread sheet, application documentation, and interviews with application owners. However, usually some of this information is not available, is missing data points, or is of questionable validity. This requires installing and configuring data collection tools in the source environment. These tools can produce a server inventory and also monitor the environment to determine server communication patterns. They also measure resource utilization. Typically these tools are run for weeks or months in order to get an accurate picture of the environment... especially to detect infrequent server affinity patterns. The observation of the workloads during this period should be sufficient to be representative of the average and peak workloads throughout a typical business cycle.

A part of the discovery phase is to provide validation that the original scope of the project is accurate and to determine disposition of new servers or applications that have been discovered that was not in the original scope of the project. If a large set of new servers is discovered, then the discovery of those servers will need to be performed. This can cause the discovery phase to iterate and take longer than initially planned.

During the discovery process other activities include performing a regulatory assessment, identifying relocation constraints and insuring that there are no restrictions of migrating workloads into the cloud. One typical regulatory constraint that is found is data locality. The data needs to reside in the country of origin. Data locality can eliminate the possibility of a cloud migration if the cloud provider does not have a location that is congruent with data locality constraints, or increase the complexity with a hybrid cloud solution. There are also usually relocation constraints for when a server can be migrated, such as off-hours during a maintenance window and compatible with the business calendar, that needs to be taken into account.

An output from the discovery phase is a business and technical risk model. It identifies all the complexities that need to be taken into consideration during the analysis phase so that they can be accounted for.

The final step in the discovery process is to revisit the project scope document and make any adjustments as needed following the project change control and stakeholder sign off processes. Usually these changes are in the scope of the project as either new servers are identified, or servers that were identified are excluded based on a constraint.

The discovery phase may identify serves that need to be remediated... for example... they are running on an unsupported operating system or hardware. For those servers, a transformation or modernization plan for that server needs to be developed and executed prior to the migration to make the server fit for working properly in the cloud. This is especially prevalent when operating systems or middleware reach end of life.

Analysis Phase

Once all of the data has been collected, the analysis phase begins. The output of this phase is a detailed project plan of which servers are going to move when and what the end-state targe environment will look like. Migration plans may also include server consolidation. By server consolidation, we mean that multiple servers may be consolidated on the same physical server, but as separate VM's on that server. Merging multiple applications across multiple servers into one sever, is a transformation project and should be typically performed either before the migration, or after the migration as a separate project.

The first step of the analysis phase is to do a macro design. The macro design has what the end-state target platform will look like and what storage patterns are needed. The construction of a baseline for the target environment provides an overall architecture for the end-state environment. In order to develop this, the dependencies discovered in the discovery phase needs to be analysed to insure that the end-state environment will support the source servers being migrated.

The macro design creation process includes performing application affinity workshops that delves into the topology of how applications communicate with each other and the communication latency requirements. The final design will include sections on application data flows, the network architecture and the operational model. The operation model is formulated and articulated as part of the analysis phase.

For large-scale migrations, it is usually impossible to migrate all of the servers together in one change window. Large projects are broken up into sets of servers who logically need to move together. These sets of servers are called dependency groups. From the discovery input, these logical application dependency groups can be created. These dependency groups are a key component in the next analysis step, wave planning. The macro design not only takes into account technical and logical requirements, but must be congruent with business needs as well.

Other deliverables may include a system context model and component model.

Once the macro design architecture has been defined, it needs to go through a review process to with the stakeholders and for signoff and possible project scope adjustment.

The last major step of the Analysis phase is the detailed wave planning. The complete migration process is broken up into logical groupings of servers and each group is migrated in what is known as a wave. For small projects, one wave is sufficient, and discovery and analysis is altogether trivial. For large projects, multiple waves are required as just one wave is too big, complex, and has a risk profile that is undesirable. Based on the application dependency groupings identified earlier in the process, waves are defined. There are many factors that go into which server is in each wave and the size of the wave other than just the affinity analysis. These factors include the manpower on the project, the business constraints on the server, network capacity, and level of acceptable risk. If data is too large to be migrated electronically, either data accelerators need to be considered or external storage and courier transport method needs to be used. For courier transport, the service needs to be identified, engaged, and portable media needs to be acquired.

The wave plan will serve as a baseline and it needs to ensure that the migration activities are achievable across all waves.

When the macro wave plan has been developed, the project scope document needs to be reviewed and make any adjustments as needed following the project change control and stakeholder sign off processes.

Once the wave planning has been completed, a detailed (micro level) project plan can be developed that will be the blue print for the migration phase of the project. This plan needs to be congruent with the business calendar and to insure that the servers can be migrated when they are scheduled. When a group of servers are migrated, there is usually a particular start-up sequence required, for example, a database server may need to be started before an application server. This start-up sequence will be defined as part of the planning. As part of the micro level planning is the test plan, success criteria, and back out plan should issues occur with this wave. Repeatable activities across the waves, such as entering change records, should be automated or reduce labor via use of templates or other labor saving activities. All of the steps required to migrate a server will be detailed in a step-by-step runbook that the migration engineers will use to perform the migration process for a particular server.

The output of the wave planning phases is a complete overall solution implantation plan that will guide the actual migration process.

Migration Phase

Once all of the up front discovery, analysis, project plan development activities and appropriate sign offs have been completed, the migration phase can commence. In this phase the workloads are migrated from their source environment to their cloud target environment, tested and the source images are decommissioned.

The migration phase is repeated for each wave defined for the project.

The first step in the migration is the target environment build out. In some cases this is a manual process, and in others, it could be automated as part of the migration software automatically provisioning the appropriate sized servers in the cloud environment. It could be a hybrid between the two approaches; for example, manually provision a hypervisor on a physical server in the cloud and the migration software automatically provisions the VM's. For the manual process, the server build requirements gathered in the analysis phase are used to provision servers according to the wave plan and build requirements. These servers are customized as needed. As with any good project plan, a communication plan (conference call numbers, status meetings, chat rooms, etc.) is required along with a remediation plan for each migration wave.

A set of quality assurance tasks is performed to confirm that the source environment is operating properly as well as the target environment is ready to accept the workload. These tasks include items like obtaining license keys, confirm backups have been completed, confirm the network is working, confirm firewalls have been opened, insure extranets are accessible in the new environment, check load balancers are operational, storage is appropriately allocated and any cluster or high availability configurations are operational. When the target environment has been confirmed as ready for migration and the change control process of submitting change records and getting approval has been completed, the workload can me moved based on the migration schedule.

With proper planning and up front analysis, the migration process should be uneventful. The first step is to perform any pre-migration activities including installing the necessary agents (if required) on the source servers. The source servers will then need to be quiesced so that the server image can be captured and transferred to the target server. Many migration tools support the concept of a final sync so that the bulk of the data can be transferred while the source server is running. The final sync just copies only the changes from the initial copy and the current state, which greatly reduces the final migration time.

Once the data has been migrated, the new target server is ready to be used. An initial server and application health check is performed followed by more extensive customer acceptance testing to verify that the server is operating properly. Of course, if this server has dependencies on other servers being migrated, the testing is delayed until all dependent servers are migrated and active. During customer acceptance testing, should issues arise they should be triaged to determine if they are solvable or if the migration wave should be backed out. Once customer acceptance testing has been completed successfully and the customer has signed off that the new environment is working properly, any final "cutover to production" steps should be initiated.

The migration does not need to be a one-time event. Best practices suggest that migrations will have a dry run and testing while the production systems are running and then once the stakeholders are satisfied, the real migration will take place. With the data sync capabilities of migration tools, the initial dry run will take the longest, but the follow on migrations will be much shorter. These dry runs can be repeated as necessary to insure an uneventful production migration is achievable.

Once the stakeholders as satisfied that the new cloud environment is meeting objectives, the disposal or repurposing of the retired hardware will be performed.

When this wave has been completed, a "lessons learned" exercise is applied to refine and improve (in terms of both quality and time to execute) the follow on waves.

Project Completion

Once all the migration waves have been completed, some final steps should be performed including verification with the stake holders that the project had met exit criteria, consolidate the lessons learned from each wave, final assessment of the project, and disengagement activities.

IMAGE MIGRATION

Image migration is the technique where the source server image (bytes) is captured and then replicated to the target server. You can think of this technique as being a non-disruptive backup and restore (to a different computer).

The main benefit to this type of migration is that you are copying everything on the server so the potential for intra server related issues (e.g. missing software or data) are eliminated. This works well when the current technology stack on the source server is desirable. If the current technology stack is not desirable (e.g. down level version of the operating system or middleware), then other migration techniques (e.g. Application or Pattern Based migrations) may be more desirable.

While there are a variety of image migration software solutions on the market today, they all have a similar process:

1. **Discovery:** The source server is interrogated to discover metadata about the source server. This data includes things like the operating system, hardware configuration (processor, memory, devices, etc.), networking, and attached storage.
2. **Capture:** The source image, operating system, applications, and data is captured in a consistent state.
3. **Transmission:** The data is transmitted to the target server destination. Transmission is either across the wire or manually using a removable media device.
4. **Restore:** The data is restored on the target server in a consistent state.
5. **Remediate:** The target server image is configured properly to operate in the new hardware environment that typically includes injection of drivers for the particular hypervisor environment.

How the various software vendors can achieve each of these steps vary greatly. For example, some vendors install an agent on the source server and some operate agentless, some transfer the data directly from the source to the target server and others use an intermediary server to orchestrate the process.

Image migration software has become very sophisticated and continues to mature from their original form of a basic backup and restore software. As migration software continues to mature, it can handle more migration scenarios and the skill level required to perform a migration is greatly reduced. This maturation of migration technology is what is making it possible for service providers to offer migration-as-a-service offerings using a self-service portal where low skilled people can be reasonably expected to be able to perform successful migrations.

The current state of the art has the following characteristics:

- **Discovery:** The ability for the software to discover the source server hardware and software configuration.
- **Non-Disruptive:** Ability to capture an image while the source server is active. This requires taking a snapshot of the images (e.g. Shadow Copy) so that the disks are in a consistent state.
- **Transformative:** Ability to detect differences from source and target environments and make automatic changes to the image to insure a successful migration. For example, migrating an OS from a physical server to virtual server running under a hypervisor may require injection or removal of drivers in order for the server image to run properly in the target environment. Even going from one version of a hypervisor to another version of a hypervisor (e.g. from Xen 6.0 to Xen 6.2) requires old drivers to be removed and new ones injected.
- **Cloud Aware:** Ability of the software to interface with the cloud infrastructure API's (e.g. OpenStack) to automate the provisioning of an appropriately sized target server as determined by the discovery process.
- **Synchronization:** The ability to synchronize the changed data on the source server to the target server. Once an initial capture of the image has been deployed on the target server, it is advantageous to be able to just replicate changes. A good use case is where prior to a production cutover, the source server image can be migrated to a target server. When it is time for a production cutover, the data can be synchronized more quickly than coping the whole image, which leads to less down time. A best practice is to initially migrate the server, do a data sync shortly before the

production cut-over to get the bulk of the changes and then do a quick final sync during production cutover which gets the final changes. Since synchronization is non-disruptive, it can be performed while the source server applications are up. It is best practice to have the source server applications down when doing the final sync.

- **Transport:** The ability to transfer the captured image from the source to the target system.
- **Encryption:** The ability for captured image data to be transmitted using a secure protocol and if the captured image is every at rest, stored in an encrypted manner.
- **Automation:** The ability to define automation steps during the migration process to eliminate any manual steps like changing IP address or other configuration changes once the server has been moved.
- **Agentless:** The ability to migrate a server without having to manually install an agent or any pre-requisite software on the servers you want to migrate.

Synchronization Techniques

Synchronization techniques for keeping the target and source data in sync can be split into two classes; snapshot and continuous:

- **Snapshot:** The snapshot technique is when periodically image sync is performed. There are numerous technical ways of accomplishing this, but one way is the source file system is compared against the target file system and differences are replicated from the source to the target. This includes adding new files, deleting old files, and sending update packets to changed files. The snapshot techniques can be scheduled during off peak periods to lessen any impact on the production server or network. The best practice is to do a snapshot sync shortly before the final production cutover so that the delta between the source and target are minimized to doing a final sync during cutover is minimized.
- **Continuous:** The continuous synchronization technique is that every write to the disk on the source server is captured and immediately replicated to the target server. This keeps the source and target in lockstep. During network disruptions, the updates are queued and transmitted once the network is restored. It is possible to pause this process and the updates are queued up until the replication process is restarted. The main benefit of this technique is that since the data is always in sync, there is no need for doing a final sync during production cutover.

RackWare

To help drive these points home, let's explore one particular image migration vendor, RackWare, as a functional example. RackWare is a mature image migration software solution that is cloud aware and is highly automated (Maja & Jinho, 2016). It supports both Windows and Linux image migrations. RackWare can be manually installed in a customer's environment or for migrations to the cloud environment; there is a self-service portal that completely automates the migration process. In either case, the migration process is similar. The migration server that RackWare is installed on requires access to the source and target servers and holds the captured server images as an intermediate location during the migration process. The user only needs to interface with the RackWare software to perform the migration, which is very convenient.

RackWare is an agentless system. The user provides RackWare with the IP address and administrative (root) credentials and it will interrogate (discover) the system without the need of an agent install. Once the server discovery is completed and the server is verified as suitable for migration (for example it has a supported operating system), RackWare will then capture the server image and store it on the migration server. Once the image has been captured, it can be assigned to the target server. The assign process takes the captured source server image from the migration server and loads it on the target server. The target server can be already provisioned, or if the target server is cloud based, it can be automatically provisioned based on the characteristics of the source server. During the assign process, if there are operating system changes needed, such as driver injection when moving to a new hypervisor, RackWare will automatically inject the drivers. RackWare also has a post migration scripting capability to perform any custom changes required during the migration process (e.g. IP Address changes). RackWare also has a sophisticated scheduled data synchronization mechanism so that the source and target can be kept in sync for quick migration cutover.

While not migration specifically, the more mature migration software, including RackWare, can provide Disaster Recovery protection and cloud scaling and bursting capabilities. As image migration software matures, they are morphing into a workload portability engine that can move workload across disparate hardware environments and providers.

APPLICATION MIGRATION

Application migration is the process of migrating only the application and its associated data from a source server to a target server. The operating system, other applications, and associated data are not migrated. There are several use cases for using application migration:

1. **Operating System Modernization:** When the application is running on a down level or unsupported operating system, it is advantageous to migrate only the application(s) to a new appropriate system.
2. **Application Subset:** When only a subset of the applications on a server needs to be migrated.
3. **Gold Image:** When the operating system is a non-standard build, you can migrate the applications to a standard build. This is typical when a company acquires another company and wants to standardize their IT infrastructure.

A side benefit to using application migration is that the time to perform the migration can be shortened since only the application and its data is being migrated.

While both image and application migration techniques can achieve the same goal, depending on the requirements of the particular server to be migrated, a particular migration technique to use is usually apparent.

AppZero

A functional example of an application migration solution is AppZero. AppZero performs windows application migrations. AppZero provides a user interface that totally automates the application process so that users do not need to leave the tool to perform a migration. The process is as follows:

1. The user specifies the source server IP address and administrator credentials.
2. The AppZero software interrogates the source server and provides the user with a list of applications that it discovered.
3. The user can select from the list of applications that should be migrated.
4. The applications are migrated to the target server.

The technology to do the migration is very sophisticated. AppZero interrogates the source server to find applications. It discovers are the registry entries and the executable files for applications. It will copy those over to the target server and put it into an AppZero proprietary container. The purpose of the container is to monitor the execution of the application and automatically remediate issues. For example, if the application while running in the container opens a file that has not been migrated, AppZero will automatically migrate the file to the target server. The container provides real-time remediation of application dependency issues. The application can run in this container indefinitely, or if the user prefers, after a suitable period of time, the container can be dissolved and the application will run natively on the target server. Once dissolved, the ability to remediate missing data will no longer be available.

PATTERN BASED MIGRATION

Patten based migration is a relatively new migration technique that is being explored that does not rely on lifting and shifting code or operating system images from the source to the target, but instead is based on discovering topology patterns on the source server and deploying them on the target server.

The pattern base migration software interrogates the source environment to determine what information technology topology is deployed. An example of a topology would be a three-tier (web server, application server, database server) application environment. The migration software would then deploy in the target environment a standards based three tier topology and then import/migrate the applications, data, and settings from the source environment to the new target environment.

The potential benefits to pattern based migration, especially in a cloud environment, is to abstract the deployed applications into standardized components and result in a consistent cloud environment that is easy to comply with corporate IT standards. Not only do you get the benefits that cloud computing has to offer, but you also "clean up" the atrophied original environment.

DATA MIGRATION

Traditional migration of large amounts of data has been typically done using hardware WAN accelerator solutions. While that works well when you have control of the source and target infrastructure, typical cloud providers have not heretofore provided acceleration hardware in their environment. This makes hardware acceleration solutions not viable for migration projects into the cloud.

Software based acceleration tools are coming to the forefront, which just requires normal cloud commodity servers to be used. This vastly increases the applicability of these tools, especially when migrating into the cloud. These acceleration servers are placed at the source and destination locations and all data traffic flows between the two servers. Data acceleration solutions improve transfer speed by using multiple connection channels, utilizing more efficient protocols, compressing the data being sent, and removing duplicate blocks so the amount of data transferred across the wire is reduced. Depending on the data being sent, a speed up factor of 100 or more is achievable. Example tools in this space are Aspera or TransferSoft.

REFERENCES

IBM Corporation. (2013). *IBM UrbanCode Deploy.* Retrieved from http://public.dhe.ibm.com/common/ssi/ecm/en/rad14132usen/RAD14132USEN.PDF

Maja, V., & Jinho, H. (2016, April). Cloud migration using automated planning. *NOMS 2016 - 2016 IEEE/IFIP Network Operations and Management Symposium* (pp. 96-103).

APPENDIX: SAMPLE MIGRATION PROJECT PLAN

This is a high level sample migration plan that can be used as a good starting point for developing your own migration project plan.

Migration Project Planning and Kick-Off

- Complete Transition from Engagement Process
  - ○ Engage PM (program started and this step is assigning program manager)
  - ○ Deliver Baseline & Inventories Documentation to PM
  - ○ Deliver Contract/SOW to RackWare PM
  - ○ Deliver/Provide Overview of Final Solution Document to RackWare PM
  - ○ Deliver Baseline Requirements Specification (Business & Technical Requirements) to RackWare PM
  - ○ Analyze Engagement Materials (Requirements, Inventories, Plans) and identify migration project risks
- Establish PM Office & Start Phase Work for Project Planning & Kick-off Phase
  - ○ Start staffing processes
  - ○ Begin ID Admin process (establish ids for all technical teams)
- Establish PM Office Operations, Transformation Procedures, & Governance
- Establish Migration Project Plan Baseline for Transformation
- Project Kick-off
  - ○ Prepare and Conduct Project Orientation Kick-off Meeting

Discovery

- Automated Data Collection Setup for Client Environment Discovery
  - ○ Install/Configure Data Collection Tools (in source environment)
- Client Environment Discovery for Network/Security/Compliance
  - ○ Analyze current network environment and requirements for target network
  - ○ Regulatory Assessment (Regulations that they would must adhere to, i.e. PCI, HIPPA, FDA, Data can't leave the country, European Union)
  - ○ Understand Network design to determine impact on migration speeds
- Client Environment Discovery for Applications
  - ○ Confirm Applications for Client Environment Discovery
- Establish Relocation Constraints
  - ○ Review any current in flight projects which might conflict with relocation activities or need to be monitored
  - ○ Review schedule of events - outage and maintenance windows, business calendar
- Establish Business & Technical Risk Model for Wave Planning,
- Prepare for Applications Discovery,
- Discover Applications
  - ○ Perform Source Environment Inventory (Hardware / Logical / Virtual / Software)

    ◦   Understand server groups and migration windows

    ◦   Map target environment (disks & partitions)- understand differences from source

    ◦   Determine storage requirements and staging (temporary storage required)

- Validate Client Environment Discovery for Applications
  - Establish the Environment configuration Baselines
- Determine whether SOW adjustment needed
  - Reconcile Source Environment inventory with engagement documents
  - Review and Approve contract updates from baseline result, determine cost difference, create PCR and modify Project Definition if required

Analysis and Macro Design

- Establish In-Scope Target Platform & Storage Patterns
- Construct Baseline for Target Environment Macro Design
- Prepare for Target Environment Macro Design
- Create Macro Design for Target Environment
  - Develop the integration solution to ensure the solution meets the architecture and critical business requirements
  - Deliver Architectural Overview
  - Deliver Network Architecture Document
  - Application Data Flow Diagrams reviewed
  - Architectural Readiness Review
  - Review Logical Network Architecture Strategy
  - Architecture Signoff
- Create Application Dependency Groups
  - Define migration approach and oversight to technology selection
- Determine whether SOW adjustment needed
  - Review and Approve contract updates from baseline result, determine cost difference, create PCR and modify Project Definition if required

Wave Planning

- Establish Project Plan Baseline for Migration
  - Validate application test plans are in place
  - Work with application owners to validate outage windows and migration timeframes
  - Verify wave plans with customer
  - Deliver Implementation Plan (for overall solution)
  - Develop Wave migration plan based on Application Affinities and consolidation plan
  - Review application development schedules through project lifecycle - add to business schedule
  - Deliver Wave Technical Solution Design
  - Establish Wave Baseline Plan
  - Ensure the migration activities are achievable across all waves

- ○ Wave Plan signoff
- Determine whether SOW adjustment needed
  - ○ Review and Approve contract updates from baseline result, determine cost difference, create PCR and modify Project Definition if required
- Target Environment
  - ○ Acquire/Obtain Transportable Storage (e.g. External Hard Drive) for data migrations using Courier Transport method
- Analysis & Micro Design for Migration Waves,
  - ○ Migration Waves Analysis & Micro Design
    - ▪ Client provides approval for Cloud Portal Access
    - ▪ Create Change Ticket Templates
    - ▪ Communicate test cases and results

Migration

- Target Build Out
  - ○ Install migration tools for migration work
  - ○ Provide server build requirements
  - ○ Provision servers according to Wave Plan and build requirements and customize as needed - (SL Cloud)
  - ○ Create Wave Project Plan (Runbook)
  - ○ Create Migration Wave Communication Plan (conference call numbers, status meetings, chats, etc...)
  - ○ Define and review remediation tasks and confirm everyone's responsibility
- QA built servers
  - ○ Source Server Checkout (Sending DC) - set migration window
  - ○ QA built servers (Target)
    - ▪ License Keys obtained
    - ▪ Destination Server Checkout
    - ▪ Confirm Backup requirements
    - ▪ Confirm Network
    - ▪ Confirm Firewall ports open
    - ▪ Confirm Extranets
    - ▪ Confirm Network Load Balancers operational
    - ▪ Storage available
    - ▪ Clustering operational
- Signoff Target Center is ready for Wave
  - ○ Input Change Records and obtain approval
  - ○ Complete Configuration tools and begin pre-migration checklist
- Migrate
  - ○ Generate Migration Workbook
  - ○ Execute Server Migration/Consolidation Activities
  - ○ V to V / P to V

- Stop necessary source server services
- Execute Data Migration
- Perform post migration server health check
  - Execute Break/fix, QA Testing, and final checkout before UAT
  - Execute Industry Specific Testing, e.g. FDA or GXP as appropriate
  - Execute Customer/User Acceptance Testing
  - Approve Wave - Acceptance / Customer Sign-off
  - Cut-over to Production
  - Coordinate System Outage Windows for Dry Runs and Move
  - Data Synchronization
  - Restore at Target Data Center
    - Obtain Software Application Keys for Target Host
    - Perform initial system and infrastructure verification
    - Perform UAT Testing
    - Perform Dry Runs
    - Customer Signoff
    - Perform Cutover
    - Final Customer Signoff / Go Live
- Decommissioning
  - Disposal / Removal of Retired Hardware

Project Close

- Consolidate Lessons Learned from Phases,
- Confirm Project Exit Criteria have been met,
- Close Transformation Management Systems for Project
  - Complete Closeout activities - Formal close out, release resource, lessons learned out, close out finances

Section 4

Chapter 13

Establishing Governance for Hybrid Cloud and the Internet of Things

Martin Wolfe
IBM Corporation, USA

ABSTRACT

This chapter is focused on the current and future state of operating a Hybrid Cloud or Internet of Things (IoT) environment. This includes tools, data, and processes which allow an organization to use these assets to serve business goals. Examining governance in this context shows how it works today and how it should change, using some real-world examples to show the impacts and advantages of these changes. It is a high level overview of those important topics with prescriptive detail left for a future and follow-on analysis. Finally, all of the lessons learned, when combined together form a governance fabric, resulting in a set of techniques and actions which tie together into a supporting framework and set of processes. The important questions include: Why does governance matter in the deployment and operation of Hybrid Cloud and IoT? If governance already exists how must it change? What are the important and salient characteristics of governance which need special focus? Thus, this analysis gives a context of how today's governance approach should change when moving to a Hybrid Cloud or IoT model.

INTRODUCTION

The focus of this chapter is a review on the unique perspective of governance when deploying, operating or using a Hybrid Cloud or Internet of Things (IoT) technical infrastructure. This type of governance has many unique considerations, but understanding the similarities with traditional ITIL-style governance ensures the most important foundations are not ignored. It is the combination of new and existing techniques which are key to the success of governance in this rapidly changing style of technology deployment. It is these similarities and differences which are key guiding principles in how to establish a governance process when working with different service providers, in different locations, all with different approaches to security, deployment and operations. The need for technical integration, for the

DOI: 10.4018/978-1-5225-0759-8.ch013

sharing of data and resources, is the typical and seemingly obvious entry being the first thing considered for change or update. The more important and vital need is to establish a set of processes where it is *well understood* how services interact, how they are chosen, how they are secured, how they are deployed, how they are updated and how they are operated.

Throughout this chapter, the various stages of governance as it applies to Hybrid Cloud or the IoT will be covered. It is important to understand how governance may change and is applied when deploying an infrastructure versus when it is being operated or updated. In addition, in this chapter the terms *infrastructure* or *environment* are used interchangeably throughout the text. The broader relationship between the key governance stages is shown in Figure 1.

Many organizations and companies, small and large, are using services from various providers, and they are doing it now, either with the blessing of their Information Technology (IT) staff and just as often without IT knowing that it is happening, a common phenomenon called Shadow IT (Raden, 2005). For those companies which are relatively new, say less than 5 years old and around 100-1000 employees, this is likely how they are currently opperating. Their base assumption is focused on the idea that IT infrastructure is not something they need to own, but just use as needed, much like power and water. Everything treated as a utility. For existing organizations, who have legacy assets with stricter data and compliance protocols, there is a mix of these existing assets (data, servers, policies, and processes) and the need and desire to use new capabilities, often provided by outside vendors and in fact managed by those vendors. They want to use and experiment in an agile fashion, with new business models while keeping the cost of this experimentation as low as possible. While it always depends on the size and type

Figure 1. The important stages of hybrid governance

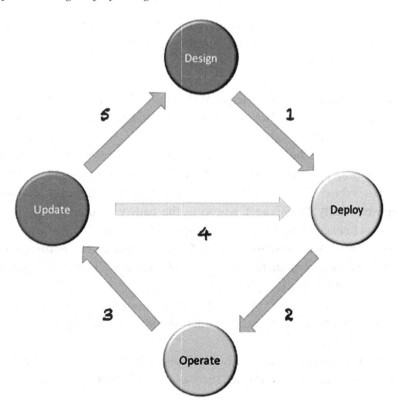

of company, the mindset of the IT team is often different from those focused on business goals. Thus, governance, rules, and policies on how technology is used to meet business goals are going to have a different focus in each of these groups.

The application of governance for these new deployment models, such as Hybrid Cloud and IoT, requires special consideration of the audience or constituency which will create the model and who will be the users impacted by the processes and model when put into practice. Furthermore, the creation of this model needs to take into account whether it is applied differently for different situations or events. In a similar fashion to standard ITIL based governance, when applying to Hybrid Cloud and IoT, the application of incident, problem, and change management processes will need to be applied in a way that matches the event being governed. For example, if there is a network outage this is handled primarily through incident management with problem and change management being invoked to prevent this from occurring in the future. It's a linear progression and application of core governance processes. However for those events such continual data assurance and security perimeter control, just two of many types of examples, the application of incident management should be considered to be in parallel with problem and change management. These two types of events require that the governance processes have a different *temporal applicability*, once being linear and one being in parallel. Thus the event type and audience applying the governance processes need to be considered. Given this, there are some really important guiding principles when it comes to governance and the relationship to Hybrid Cloud and IoT. This is not just about governance but why it is important and what should be done to get started and keep the momentum going into steady state operations.

Guiding Principles

While this might be obvious in some cases, in nearly every Hybrid deployment, governance turns out to be overlooked and is the missing key component. Agreeing on these early on, makes it all much easier, and less expensive in the long run:

- **The Basics are the Same:** The governance processes and model for both Hybrid Cloud and the Internet of Things are the same. How incident, problem, and change management are handled is not fundamentally different.
- **Hybrid Cloud is the Foundation:** It's easier to leverage or deploy IoT resources, tools and components if you start by using Hybrid Cloud. An IoT hosting platform and the "things" it connects can only run in a Hybrid Cloud hosting environment. IoT needs Hybrid Cloud to work properly.
- **Data Lineage is Vitally Important:** Knowing the path your data travels is really important. Knowing the data lineage is the basis for both Hybrid Cloud and IoT Security.
- **Different Deployment Makes Sense:** Hybrid Cloud and IoT can be entirely "off-premises", entirely "on-premises" or a combination of on and off premises. There are many different deployment patterns where governance applies.
- **The Network is Key:** Net-centric operating principles (such as synchronous and asynchronous integration), including complex connectivity across physical and logical locations, form the core of the governance model.
- **Governance May Change:** Depending on the phase in which governance is being used, governance may be applied differently. Phases such as initial design, deployment to the end user, or

operation of the environment, plus the management disciplines such as incident, problem, change, and security management disciplines can be applied differently

Which Characteristics Are Impacted?

Understanding the impacts of a Hybrid Cloud or Internet of Things style of technology deployment is important in determining the right governance model to put in place. There are some key impacts to consider both when there is some type of governance in place as well as when there is not any governance in place. In both situations, determining where and how to apply governance processes is important to ensure it can be effective in these new deployment models. More detail is provided throughout this chapter describing how real-world experiences are influenced and how those change how governance is applied.

Design and Deployment

One of the most important aspects of deploying or using a Hybrid Cloud technology infrastructure and, for that matter, using an Internet of Things platform to connect devices is overlooked and typically handled reactively instead of proactively. The ability for these types of technology environments to just work is not enough, they must be something that can be actually deployed and operated once deployment is complete. Understanding the integration between the processes needed to operate a Hybrid Cloud or IoT environment and those processes used to run the rest of IT while aligning with key governance processes used by the business is important in defining a Hybrid governance model. Governing both the design and deployment is important, but if it cannot be effectively operated, then all the work to design the model is merely academic. It is also important to note one of the important factors in governance of this type of complex deployment is tracking and management of the assets or "bill or materials" of those services and platforms being used in runtime environment. This is all part of the governance of a runtime system.

Security

The massive growth, both predicted and realized, in the deployment of devices and sensors creates an integrated web of connected "instances" both physical and logical. Given this growth, in both the number of devices and the number of service providers, all supporting the same solution, the movement of data and the number of possible entry points increases dramatically (Meulen, 2015). With each new connection and each new device, these become a new "door" or entry point for a hacker to try and penetrate. The key aspects of incident management are important in responding to breaches rapidly, where problem and change management need to be in place to prevent or mitigate the likelihood of future security incursions. Ensuring the feedback loop between operating an environment, updating, and then re-deploying that environment to handle security issues is something that needs to be addressed in these three areas of governance.

Operations

Data Quality and Assurance

In an environment with a heterogeneous set of service providers, data sources, integration points and different approaches to security and incident, problem, and change management, the lineage of data as it moves throughout a system of services and components needs to be both well understood and monitored. This is one of the most important foundations for assuring the quality and integrity of the data, in line with some of the precepts of Defense in Depth ("Defense in Depth", 2015). Furthermore, data lineage is key to root cause analysis (RCA). Determining where problems arise in these types of complex systems, where many providers and "things" are being integrated takes on additional complexity. Knowing where and how data moves is important in getting to root cause quickly, ultimately increasing availability and reducing operational expense.

Reusability

In part, this analysis focuses on the important aspects of governance and how it should be used and possibly adjusted to support a Hybrid Cloud or IoT deployment. However, one of the key guiding principles is that existing ITIL style governance does not have to be re-written but can be modified in some cases and used "as-is" in other cases. Some of the client examples, elsewhere in this chapter, discuss these type of examples. Thus, reusing an existing governance model with, what in the larger scheme of impacts are minor adjustments to support a service bureau and elastic consumption model, saves significant time and money for an organization. This is especially true for existing organizations, but it also has real value for new organizations. For new organizations, their ability to take an existing governance model and adapt it to their goals and needs, also has significant savings in time and money. It really makes sense to use an existing governance model, while making adjustments to the model, in specific ways, supporting this ability to consume technology resources in an elastic model, like a utility, and to support multiple technology deployment models. These types of deployments include on-premises, off-premises and multiple combinations of these models as needed for a particular organization or company. One of the key assumptions in this chapter is the ability to reuse an existing governance model, leveraging ITIL techniques as a guide and making modifications to it to support the service bureau and service broker style of delivery between IT to the business in an organization.

BACKGROUND

In deploying and using a Hybrid Cloud model, there are several important concepts and assumptions which are typically applied when talking about the design, deployment and operation of this type of technical infrastructure. As described elsewhere in this chapter, many of these key concepts apply not only to Hybrid Cloud but also to using and deploying devices and data to an Internet of Things platform. This topic of governance is more important than is typically understood. Without some kind of governance in place, and the needed updates and enhancements in order to support Hybrid Cloud and IoT, these types of environments and technical infrastructures will not be able to operate. In the worst cases, determining the root cause of problems and ensuring data integrity across the connective fabric of these systems will be nearly impossible to determine and mitigate. Thus, the inspiration for this chapter and this topic is to help assure that when dealing with the highly complex nature of these integrated physical and logical systems, there is a foundation and set of processes in place to help operate and maintain the availability, resiliency and reliability of these environments. This work is inspired not by analysts reports or presentations but by real-world implementation experience through anecdotal evidence from many types of engagements and deployments.

Moreover, this chapter contains a focus on how an IT organization would operate a Hybrid Cloud style infrastructure or how it would leverage IoT technology to connect devices and objects both physical and logical. While reviewing the content here, it is important to understand there is both explicit and implied bias towards IT. However, governance is equally valuable to both an IT organization and the business entities it supports. Governance is the fabric to tie together the ability of IT and the business to successfully deliver capability in support of the organization's goals and measurements.

Where and How Does Governance Apply?

Think about the two types of organizations and the most important questions to address when applying governance in this Hybrid world:

1. For existing organizations, how do they have a common "management" and "governance" set of steps, which responds at the speed of their business, both for existing assets and these new capabilities, which they want to rapidly integrate into their toolset?
2. For new organizations, what is the path of evolution from their combined model of operating to separation of concerns in their organization and yet leverage a common operating model (instead of just yelling across the office when there's a problem, college dorm room style)?

Furthermore, examining Figure 1, the application of governance will be slightly different in each phase of a governance lifecycle.

Design

During the design phase, this is where the deployment specifications are created, including a definition of the functionality provided, such as cloud services from a Hybrid Cloud or the connection of devices and systems through an IoT deployment. In addition to the functionality, the question of "how well" the system will work is specified through Service Level Agreements (SLA) and Service Level Objectives (SLO) in line with the ITIL model of governance. The design phase is key since this sets the tone for how much governance will be needed to deploy, update, and operate a Hybrid Cloud environment. The transition from designing to deployment is dependent on a sufficient level of design, and specifying these different service levels drives how much monitoring will be required for the Operate phase. Also covered during the design phase are the services, versus service levels, provided. Services such as infrastructure, connectivity or specific business functions are candidates for inclusion in a catalog of services. The design phase defines the initial set of these services which drive the SLA and SLO definitions for the deployed Hybrid Cloud or IoT environment.

Deploy

The deploy phase is where the actual implementation, installation, and configuration start. The result should be a running environment in support of the initial set of services in the catalog with the ability to extend in support of future services. The first instances of incident, problem, and change management will be encountered during this phase, as they apply typically to a runtime environment.

Operate

Once deployment is complete, transition into the Operate phase is next. The focus will be on incident and Problem Management specifically. Incident and Problem management are in flight considerations.

Update

Change management will be the key process during any updates to a deployed Hybrid Cloud or IoT environment. During the Update phase, change management is key especially given the complexity of multiple on-premises and off-premises systems. Any change to a single component will have a potential ripple effect across multiple systems. This is the same issues encountered when migrating from a traditional environment to a Hybrid Cloud environment, the affinity between systems must be understood. It is this affinity and inter-dependence between systems which requires an effective change management process to ensure that these cross-system effects are well understood. Once the update phase is complete, and there has been effective Change Management, re-deployment can occur ensuring all the right steps are in place and initial testing can take place.

Multiple Systems, Processes, and Integrations

What happens when we take the model of multiple components and multiple integrations to it's logical evolution? Having a combination of systems of record, systems of insight and systems of engagement both on premise and off premise is the typical pattern of complexity in this heterogeneous deployment. The key questions are how this be effectively managed and governed, and why is that important?

In fact, if you think about it, everyone is using this Hybrid model. We pay someone to collect our trash, pay the water company for just the amount of water we use and the power company for just the power we use. The utility model. It's a pay per use model in much of our daily lives and it is this Hybrid environment, comprising many components, systems, rules, laws, policies, and processes that we live in every day.

When it comes to consuming IT assets and technology imagine the issues when trying to use a utility style of consumption every day. Changes in how budgets are appropriated (from pre-defined to just-in-time), a different set of roles in IT, expectations from the business side of the house that more flexibility and speed of deployment are not only possible but are now an assumed minimum capability. In this new delivery model, and this is especially important with the increasing complexity of this truly distributed system of "pieces", management, governance, data integrity, and problem determination are more complex than ever. It is increasingly, and even exponentially difficult, to just "talk to the server team" or "talk to the network team" or "talk to the web server team" to figure out why the website is down, or SAP is not available. It's challenging to use this approach since it requires finding and bringing together just the right personnel to know the status of resources or the sources of problems in the runtime environment. For example, what happens when an organization's payroll does not get distributed on time. Since this is probably the most important business function in any organization, the entire IT staff typically organizes a series of root cause analysis and recovery sessions. Thus, governance is key. The ability to rapidly identify an event or incident, feed that into a problem management process, and leverage an effective change management method allows for the ability to learn from previous mistakes and problems and work to prevent them in the future.

In this review of Hybrid Cloud and IoT Governance, some fairly deep analysis is included, conclusions are provided, and some examples are provided in order to understand the context of where a Hybrid Governance Fabric should and would be applied.

How can we track the movement of data and track down the various issues that arise when these types of heterogeneous systems are used to build applications for the business? In this heterogeneous deployment, the data used by various applications is moving back and forth, on and off-premise, and the number of integrations between systems are significantly higher than a single system. This increases the complexity in trying to provide a governance framework, end to end, for these systems. Moreover, each point of integration between components and data sources has its own service level, support structure, and technology stack. The *composite nature* of these applications makes it much harder and more complex to manage changes, updates to releases, incidents and issues as well as ensuring security and compliance.

Regardless of the name applied to this governance approach, the truth about using this utility "cloud" model for delivering functionality, in support of the business is there will always be some "systems" which remain on-premises and some that are off-premises. All of these will likely be based on a variable set of technologies. It can be argued there are some organizations and enterprises which will use only those capabilities which they do not own. In this case everything will be consumed as a utility. However, for every case where there are no on-premises IT systems or on-premises data, there is at least one scenario where some piece of enterprise collateral will remain on their premise, at their site and/or in their possession. The "ground truth" is there will always be data sources and "business and technology assets" on premise which may or may not be core to the business. It is vital to bring these together in the proper order and in the proper context.

All enterprises and organizations, regardless of size, will retain some data or technical component "on their premise" and thus governance is needed to track, check, and maintain this cross-premise deployment of data, business logic, and applications. They will build more and more of these applications which integrate various components and data sources, both on and off-premise.

Bringing all of these aspects together is a model called the Hybrid Governance Fabric. This fabric is a compilation of important components. These include processes, existing and modified support models, data lineage and security, root cause analysis and multi-location deployment. Brought together these components form a tapestry which needs to be correctly and properly woven together.

Comparing Hybrid Governance to Your Life

This idea of the Hybrid Cloud and the Internet of Things (IoT) models being both similar to each other and essentially the same theme as how people live their daily lives, is illustrated in these views. In Figure 1, the deployment models of on and off-premise are mapped to ownership, incorporating also management as it applies to ownership and locality. The important factor is to understand the differences between each sector of the picture, which could easily be open for debate, and how they relate to the way utilities are consumed, such as power, water, food, etc. In Figure 2, you can see how the typical utilities which power society's infrastructure have a relationship to the various technology and IT related services consumed in an enterprise. In both scenarios, the connectivity between various systems, the location of those systems, and the importance of how data and information moves between them is key. Just as it is important that the power company properly meter the usage of power, it's important that the usage of compute, storage, network, data and applications be metered in manner that supports the ability to consume these resources in an elastic model.

The ability to apply policies and to actually meter and monitor the usage of different systems is the vital element in ensuring that you can actually ensure security, compliance, and reliability of interconnected, heterogeneous, and location independent components. This interconnected and dispersed model is the foundation and key assumption in the deployment of a Hybrid Cloud infrastructure and an Internet of Things system of devices and data.

Hybrid Cloud and IoT can Use the Same Governance

The Internet of Things and Hybrid Cloud have emerged as commonly agreed upon models of deployment, they are typically considered different especially in the use cases they support. Experience in real-world deployments has shown that an IoT deployment is dependent on a Hybrid Cloud model and thus they are actually complimentary deployment models with many key similarities when it comes to governance, management, and operations. Thus, deploying governance in this type of heterogeneous mode, the steps and lifecycle of governance in support of *Connected Things* and in support of a Hybrid Cloud or IoT operating model share many of the same characteristics.

Figure 2. The hybrid and IoT operational model

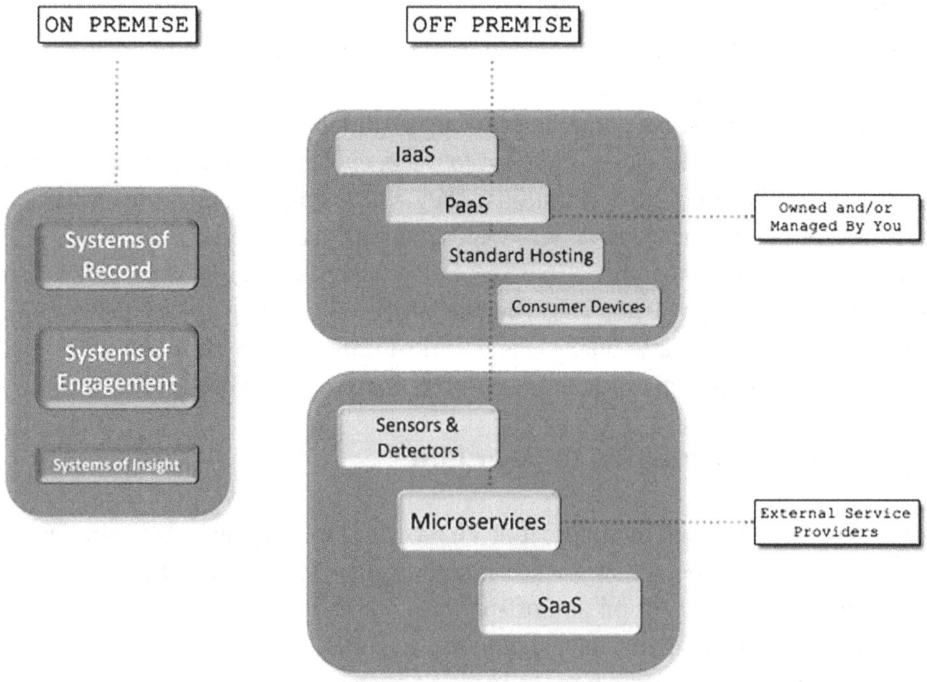

Figure 3. Your life follows the integrated and interdependency model

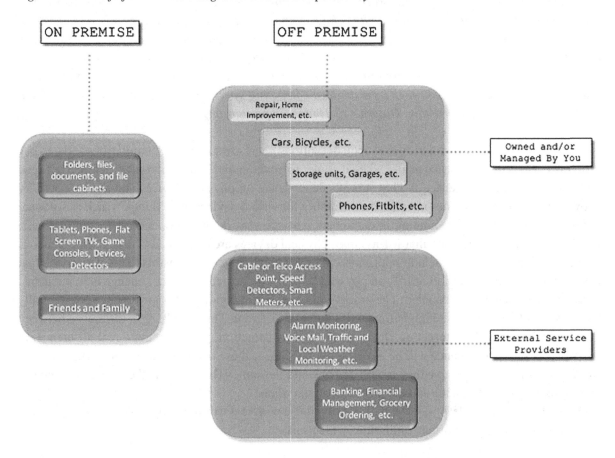

What are the key similarities between the Hybrid Cloud (sometimes called Hybrid IT) and Internet of Things (IoT) models? Let's take a look at the generic definitions of each, using Wikipedia, typically a generic enough source:

Hybrid cloud is a composition of two or more clouds (private, community or public) that remain distinct entities but are bound together, offering the benefits of multiple deployment models. Hybrid cloud can also mean the ability to connect collocation, managed and/or dedicated services with cloud resources. Gartner, Inc. defines a hybrid cloud service as a cloud computing service that is composed of some combination of private, public and community cloud services, from different service providers. A hybrid cloud service crosses isolation and provider boundaries so that it can't be simply put in one category of private, public, or community cloud service. It allows one to extend either the capacity or the capability of a cloud service, by aggregation, integration or customization with another cloud service (Cloud Computing, Hybrid Cloud section).

and

The Internet of Things (IoT) is the network of physical objects or "things" embedded with electronics, software, sensors, and network connectivity, which enables these objects to collect and exchange data. [1] The Internet of Things allows objects to be sensed and controlled remotely across existing network infrastructure,[2] creating opportunities for more direct integration between the physical world and computer-based systems, and resulting in improved efficiency, accuracy and economic benefit. Each thing is uniquely identifiable through its embedded computing system but is able to interoperate within the existing Internet infrastructure. (Internet of Things, 1ˢᵗ paragraph)

Evaluating the two commonly agreed upon definitions, there are a number of similarities and one key difference. Does this difference matter when it comes to governance? The important difference between Hybrid Cloud and the Internet of Things is it's dependence on physical devices and the connectivity between those devices. It does not rule out the ability for virtual devices and "things" (such as software defined radios, applications running in containers, virtual network switches, and other "appliances"), but there is a clear expectation that IoT assumes physical devices are connected across a heterogeneous network fabric, which can include both physical and logical devices and assets. This dependence, at least in terms of the definition of IoT, on physical sensors and devices, does not change how incidents, problems, and changes are handled. The process and method for handling this governance is essentially the same, while the tools used might (and will likely) be different. Thus, the biggest difference between a Hybrid Cloud and the Internet of Things is more of a distinction without being a real difference, in the broadest sense governance will be the same. What's key is these being two different definitions, but from a governance perspective they are treated one and the same. The model is the same. The impacts are the same. The governance and management are the same.

When looking at the definitions and comparing those with real world deployment experiences, there are a number of really important similarities which surface.

1. **Heterogeneous Interconnectivity:** Both IoT and the Hybrid model are based on connecting and running different components, systems, data sources, Application Programming Interfaces (API), and networks
2. **Location Independence:** The various components, assets, and functionality of a system can be located in different places, on or off-premise, in different countries or regions. Net-Centricity (Net-centric, 1ˢᵗ Section)
3. **Data Lineage:** While security is really important, the integrity and security of data is the core

Thus, one of the most of important shared aspects is the combination of incorporating a heterogeneous set of assets and functionality, and the need to interconnect these in a single operating environment to ensure data integrity, reliability and resilience.

In a Hybrid and IoT Connected Model, Governance is Important and Vital

It's important to note that this is IT governance versus just generic governance, so it's not as broad in scope as governance needed by formal governments or across an entire enterprise. However, it's scope is cross-enterprise in the sense of where technology assets are used, thus there are specific and numerous integrations between IT governance and corporate governance. While these integration points deserve their own detailed treatment, when establishing a governance model, the commonalities become clear.

Thus, there are many similarities, but what's important for the context of the Hybrid Governance Fabric, is a focus on how this affects the operating model when using IT in support of providing business functionality. The IT governance Institute's definition is:

"... leadership, organizational structures and processes to ensure that the organization's IT sustains and extends the organization's strategies and objectives." (IT Governance Institute, p. 6)

HYBRID CLOUD AND IoT REQUIRE ADHERENCE TO GOVERNANCE

The set of Hybrid Cloud use cases is useful in understanding where and how governance may or may not apply. The really interesting observation is how close Hybrid Cloud and the Internet of Things are when it comes to governance and management of these environments.

When evaluating how to define a special governance model for Hybrid Cloud and IoT, understanding where there is overlap is important in determining where to focus. Notice that Hybrid Cloud is appropriate in nearly every use case, and this makes sense as the Internet of Things require a Hybrid Cloud style deployment foundation in order for it to effectively tie together all the various physical and logical devices and end points.

In evaluating how to define the more optimized governance model, specifying how many aspects of governance are affected provides a good foundation for establishing the best processes and role definitions.

Incident, Problem, and Change Management

While there are standardized definitions for incident, problem, and change management, typically spoken of as "ICP", the view used in this chapter will be one based on real-world and anecdotal experience from across a good number of organizations.

Figure 4. Mapping hybrid cloud and IoT to the key use cases

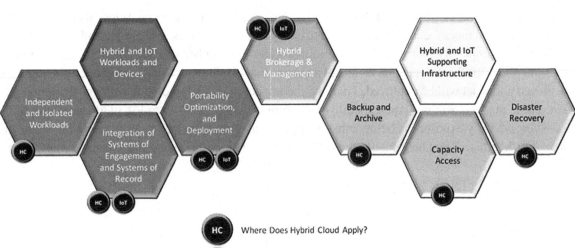

Incident Management is focused on the tracking and monitoring events which occur, typically, when some kind of technology based outage or error occurs in the use of a technology infrastructure. Sometimes this also includes reports of unofficial functionality which, while not an error, are unexpected.

Consider this representative list of important considerations for incident, problem, and change management:

1. Does the incident cross the boundaries of more than one environment? This is important in Hybrid Cloud, sincere there are multiple providers in multiple locations however it is even more important when it comes to IoT. Security is key and is at higher risk with IoT so understanding the root cause of an incident in a multi-environment and multi-device world is fundamentally important.

2. Once the problem has been identified, how can it be remediated? There is a key dependency on have good cross-site, cross-environment and cross-device incident management, so the root cause can be identified and documented. Now that the event has been documented, going through the full root cause analysis and remediation process is important so that this can be prevented in the future, if possible. Quite often, dealing with a problem is managed through the "fire drill phone call" or meeting where everyone who might be involved gets together and tries to figure out if this is the real problem, if the cause is known and how it could be fixed or remediated. This will not scale in a world where there are numerous end points, devices, cloud environments and technical platforms with an exponentially larger number of interconnections between systems and components. Problem Management must be modified in order to more rapidly determine root cause and remediation. This can be achieved through more pro-active monitoring, asset tracking for interconnections, devices, and components, and well defined services which have well specified interfaces.

3. How can an existing problem be prevented from happening again? Change management is the final step in ensuring that future problems are less likely through making sure changes go through a well understood and documented process. Change management does not have to change to make this happen, it just needs to be applied.

Security

The challenge with security, in this Hybrid Cloud and IoT deployment approach, is less about the number of components and more focused on being able to easily add new services, end points, and devices nearly at will. Thus, complexity increases but more importantly the number of end points offering potential access into the overall system increases and at an unpredictable rate. Security is all about knowing what is deployed and what will be deployed. Tracking the impact of this unpredictable change in complexity is key. Asset management is a core capability to ensure is included. Modern IoT platforms, at least the ones where security exposure is being considered, have asset management and tracking built into the system. Further this asset management needs to focus on both the components and their interconnections.

SOLUTIONS AND RECOMMENDATIONS

Creating a Fabric for Hybrid Cloud and IoT Governance (HGF)

In terms of computing, IT, technology and applications, the idea of *fabrics* are a fundamental deployment concept. This interconnected set of processes is something called a "governance fabric". It is a single approach to managing the movement of data between service providers, different services, data sources, and heterogeneous infrastructures. The definition of a fabric is a really important foundation for the governance fabric. The definition has some important characteristics:

Fabric computing or unified computing involves constructing a computing fabric consisting of interconnected nodes ... Usually the phrase refers to a consolidated high-performance computing system consisting of loosely coupled storage, networking and parallel processing functions linked by high bandwidth interconnects ... but the term has also been used .. to describe platforms ... where the common theme is interconnected nodes that appear as a single logical unit ... The fundamental components of fabrics are "nodes" ... and "links". While the term "fabric" has also been used in association with storage area networks and switched fabric networking, the introduction of compute resources provides a complete "unified" computing system. Other terms used to describe such fabrics include "unified fabric", "data center fabric" and "unified data center fabric". (Fabric Computing, 1ˢᵗ paragraph)

Governance needs to be treated as its own fabric since it is the glue and the unifying approach to ensuring a Hybrid Cloud or IoT deployment can be effectively managed and operated. Furthermore, governance is much more challenging to effectively implement given the different types of integration between data sources, services, components, and service providers. Ensuring data integrity and determining the lineage of data are more challenge as is the determination of the root cause of incidents and problems that arise in the deployment and operation of these complex systems.

The Most Important Hybrid and IoT Deployment Considerations

Governance is focused on many different aspects of ensuring the Hybrid Cloud and IoT deployment models will effectively meet the goals set for the functionality needed, either by the business, IT organizations, or customers of an enterprise. One the most important phases is the actual deployment which includes both initial deployment and iterative re-deployment and updating of functionality. To prepare for deployment, there are a number of important focus areas that need to be addressed. Not surprisingly, this list is the same for both Hybrid, IoT, or more legacy deployment models. The details are key.

When evaluating each important consideration, there are some fundamental topics to cover and question to ensure all of the core characteristics are covered. In this table, many of the guiding principles and considerations are covered and some evaluation criteria are provided to ensure the governance model is being structured properly:

Real Client Examples

Figuring out how best to implement governance, and just the right amount of governance, is best understood through some examples. These are from real-world experiences, in different industries. These

Table 1. The most important design, deployment, and operational considerations

Characteristic	Criteria
Security and Compliance	Focused on topics such as encryption, key management, regulatory compliance, compensating controls, intrusion detection, and auditing • Does the data need to be encrypted in flight or at rest (or both)? Do the transactions need to be encrypted? • Who will own management of encryption keys? • What types of auditing (e.g. level of detail or specific compliance) need to be supported once the workload is deployed? • What level of monitoring needs to be recorded and stored? • Will special intrusion detection (at the network, storage, and compute layers) be required? • What are the regulatory and/or compliance requirements (including FDA, HIPPA, PCI, FFIEC, etc.)? • Does the data need to stay within country and/or locale and does this include both application data and management system data? • Now that we are moving into the Cloud, are there compensating controls and/or reporting that can be put in place to achieve same result?
Capacity	Capacity requirements (the initial capacity needs) and capacity management (the needs during steady state) are some of the first things to understand including how much compute, storage, and network capacity is required • What initial capacity is needed to get the system initially up and running (understanding that you can scale up later) ? • What is the steady state capacity needed? • If the workload is re-engineered / re-architected when moving into a Cloud environment, how do the capacity requirements change? • What are the different levels of capacity needed for development, test, QA, and production?
Connectivity	The method for connecting from the existing enterprise network to a Cloud provider needs to be defined • What amount of bandwidth will be required for development, test, QA, and production deployments? • Are clients on the current network allowed direct workstation VPN client connectivity to an off-premise Cloud or must they go through a corporate VPN? • Is an IPSEC VPN required between the client and the cloud network? • Will the current environment and the target (cloud) environment be co-located in the same data center? • Will parts of the workload/application be located in different cloud data centers and across different Cloud providers? (e.g. leading to Hybrid Cloud)
Services Management (ITSM)	Defining how incidents, problems, and changes (requests) are handled now that the workload will be running in the Cloud • What is the process/workflow needed to support incident, problem, and change management once a workload is deployed into a Cloud environment? • How do these processes need to change in development, test, QA, and Production contexts? (Experience tells us there will surely be changes needed especially in a "Hybrid Cloud" scenario • Monitoring – How will monitoring be performed and who will have access to the monitoring data?
Managed Services	This topic is focused on providing management and oversight and is tightly linked to services management • Does corporate IT want full management from a vendor or partial "a la carte" management? (e.g. such as software patch management for a specific set of Cloud workloads, etc.) • Will the vendor's managed services (outsourcing) team be managing deployment of workloads to a single Cloud vendor or multiple service providers? • Metering – How will the use of the Cloud be measured? How does the client wanted to be charged? Will there be a need for an internal chargeback within the client's environment? • Will the managed services vendor have visibility to the data or only ping, power, and pipe?

continued on next page

Table 1. Continued

Characteristic	Criteria
Performance	Determining the level of performance (scalability, reliability, availability, etc.) required once in the Cloud will guide many other decisions • When moved to the Cloud, will the same level of performance be required in development, test, QA, and/or production use cases? • How is performance measured? • Who will execute performance testing and will the same scripts and use cases be used once the workload is moved to the Cloud?
Roles and Access	Focused on the ability to consume and access of the workload once it's deployed into a Cloud environment • Who will be accessing the workload? business users? IT administrators? Developers? Third party vendors? • How will each user group access the workload? via API? via UI? via Reporting? via status provided by an outsourcing team? • How will access and status of the workload be determined? Who will have access to monitoring data and how will they access it? • How will ID's and the management of user IDs be managed and governed?
Data	The ownership and location of data is vitally important • Data Integrity - What is the location of data and how is that different as it relates to development, test, QA, and production? • Will the data be located separately from the application? (if yes, does that require its own secure connection?) • Is the data in scope of any specific compliance and/or regulatory requirements? • Who will own the data? • Data Lineage - What is lineage of the data? What is the golden master version?
Deployment Model	Where will the workload be deployed? • Is off-premise or on-premises required? • Does the workload map to existing items in the Cloud catalog? • Will this be Bring Your Own License (BYOL)? • Is cross-site, cross-geo and/or multi-provider required? • Will the deployment model be determined by the service levels of the providers or a centralized governance model? • Will it be deployed to a single or multiple environment(s)? • What is the bill of materials and/or list of assets to be deployed, integrated and managed
Workload Architecture and Integration	The architecture of the workload and its external dependencies are important to know up front • Does the workload require integrations/connections to systems or data sources in other cloud or non-cloud environments? • Is the architecture of the workload 'cloud ready', 'cloud native', or requiring dedicated hardware, network, and storage resources? • Will the application and data be separated or co-located?

should hold up in pretty much any geography. I will cover compliance and security concerns where applicable, but mostly this will focus on incident, problem and change management.

EXAMPLE 1: GLOBAL MANUFACTURER

Organization Summary

This enterprise is a global manufacturing company, with revenue between $50B and $100B, selling and manufacturing their products in all major geographies including North America, Europe, Middle East,

Africa, and Asia-Pacific. They have and continue to acquire smaller manufacturers primarily to grow their presence in a particular geography. The challenges of evolving their current IT governance model while integrating with the governance that their acquisitions already have in place coupled with local and global compliance and security requirements leaves them in a state where most incidents, problems, and changes are handled through *heroic* work. Given this environment let's focus on a particular pattern of components and processes that IT is having to deploy, with the help of vendors, all in this fluid and changing environment.

Scenario

In this scenario, the client is upgrading core SAP 'basis' components and migrating from DB2 and Oracle to use SAP's HANA environment, deployed globally, each location has its own applications and some are shared across all regions. They leverage a managed services vendor to operate their systems which include traditional assets such as mainframes, dedicated Linux and windows servers, as well virtualized environments using VMWare. Further, there is an Analytics environment used to collate the data from appliances connected via an IoT platform and an IoT platform, both of which are off-premise. Taking a look at the environment, you can see it's a mix of on and off-premise with some assets owned by the client and some by third party vendors.

For this enterprise, they will continue to need both on and off-premise capabilities and thus the ability to have connectivity between heterogeneous components is key. Moreover, the need to not be tied to location and knowing the flow and lineage of their data is vitally important. The key technologies and workstreams include: SAP HANA, Managed Services, Internet of Things, Mainframe, Analytics, and ServiceNow

Current Approach

Incidents are handled, typically, through a combination of manual processes, recent use of ServiceNow to track incidents, and "Crisis conference calls" to determine the scope of the incident. Identification of incidents is a manual process. Since there is little match between the servers and physical IT assets and the running applications, determining root cause of an issue is a complex effort requiring the time of many technical experts from both corporate IT, regional IT groups and any 3rd party vendors.

Tools and technologies are used in the typical fashion. The managed services, outsourcing, managed operations provider uses their own set of tools to both meter usage and track operational issues. Manual integration (e.g. phone calls and e-mails) between the 3rd party managed operations team and corporate IT (using ServiceNow). This includes no centralized CMDB, essentially "spreadsheet based" change management.

When an incident occurs, typically there's a ticket submitted and all the relevant resources (people) are gathered together. Typically, the outsourced operations team, which has a good track record of responding to issues, does not have visibility to all incidents, especially if they are not submitted into the ServiceNow system (which many are not). So the main challenge for this organization in handling incidents is understanding:

1. The root cause of the incident,
2. Having predictive insights into potential issues and

3.   Well defined and rapid processes to respond and remediate the cause of the incident.

Hybrid Governance Enhancements

Some of the recent enhancements made to address improvements supporting multi-site, heterogeneous integration, and improved data linage management include:

- Recent inclusion of automation tools used by the outsourcing team has sped up and added more standardization
- The process is still handled, for the most part, manually.
- The organization has initiated the creation of a common services catalog
- The organization wants common visibility across all applications and server to server connectivity to understand the root cause of the incidents
- Recently an assessment was completed of their major data centers to understand how servers (both physical and logical) are interconnected as a source of information for root cause analysis (RCA)
- Response times are marginally faster than before, overall the number of incidents has decreased through more monitoring and more automation.
- The impact on operations is still determined through a largely manual process and restoration leveraging either backups or a DR process is still far too time consuming
- Traceability of the incident is partially available via the ServiceNow system and tools used by the managed operations team
- There's more of a need to secure in flight data as it moves from on-premises to off-premise

Next Steps

The next phases of improvements include:

- Traceability of an incident from initiation/discovery through the problem management and change management processes.
- The combination of SAP HANA + Managed Services + Internet of Things + Mainframe + Analytics + ServiceNow adds cross-site governance complexity to both the movement of data and to ensure that when incidents occur in one system the cascade effects of those incidents are known.

EXAMPLE 2: GLOBAL RETAILER

Organization Summary

A retailer with a recently deployed e-commerce online presence and over 1000 brick and mortar stores in North America supported by a global supply chain and various global product manufacturers. They have over $50B in annual revenue and a fairly large IT budget as it relates to overall enterprise revenue and profit. Their IT department is run in a fairly traditional centralized and project based manner, as overall IT budget is largely determined and allocated through project definition. Thus, the total number of projects is combined to make up the overall budget allocated. Each project leverages a common infrastructure but can request additional physical or logical infrastructure for just their project.

Scenario

Currently, they have deployed a global e-commerce solution but the supporting services in only a small portion of their locations. The solution comprises many different components including order management, e-commerce and payment solutions, as well as delivery and fulfillment. Integration with supply chain and purchasing is not yet implemented directly, but there are asynchronous connections with these systems through queuing, thus they are indirect. The Hybrid Cloud characteristics include connectivity between on and off-premise systems with integration to both systems owned by this organization as well as those of external service and functionality providers.

Current Approach

Governance, including operations, development, and testing processes are driven by this organization but actually executed by several service providers. These external providers cover both application and infrastructure management, and have their own management and governance processes. The integration of governance and management between these providers and the main organization is largely manual requiring constant preparation but using little or no automation when an incident occurs. The overall change management process is project focused and thus does not have the context of shared services, thus lessons learned are not well integrated into future enhancements.

Hybrid Governance Enhancements

No enhancements to the processes have been implemented. However, one of the key service providers has implemented a rigorous preparation scheduled for major events ensuring that if an incident does occur, there's a clear escalation and ownership process in place. This is one of the key foundational steps to ensure the eventual use of policy based automation will be effective in deploying incident, problem, and change management in a cross-site and multi-vendor deployment.

Next Steps

Automation is the theme.

1. Establishing automation when incidents occur and to take lessons learned and incorporate them into the broader change management process is key
2. Allowing for better portability of the components of a Hybrid Deployment through the use of container technology will support the deployment a governance fabric since this will be a more loosely coupled deployment.

In both of these examples there are several important themes which are common and which are typically found in many organizations.

- Visibility across all components is important in understand where problems occur (incident management), how to repair and remediate problems (problem management), and how to lessen the likelihood these issues will happen in the future (change management)
- Understanding the escalation and ownership process when trying to operate this type of complex environment
- Establishing an effective Backup and DR strategy is both important and much more complex given the unpredictable nature of adding new services (Hybrid Cloud) and devices (Internet of Things)

CONCLUSION

The Importance of Net-Centric Operating Principles in a Hybrid Governance Fabric

In defining the most important characteristics of an HGF, using aspects of the ITIL governance framework is valuable, but the core tenants of net-centricity have equally or more important applicability. When looking at the definition of the "net-centric" operating model:

Net-centric, or "network-centric", refers to participating as a part of a continuously-evolving, complex community of people, devices, information and services interconnected by a communications network to optimize resource management and provide superior information on events and conditions needed to empower decision makers. Many experts believe the terms "information-centric" or "knowledge-centric" would capture the concepts more aptly because the objective is to find and exploit information, the network itself is only one of several enabling factors along with sensors, data processing and storage, expert analysis systems and intelligent agents, and information distribution. (Net-centric, 1ˢᵗ paragraph)

Heterogeneous Integration is a Core Guiding Principle

The importance of governance becomes clear, usually in hindsight, when integrating many different components and data sources. Typically, there is a large deployment of some monolithic application or "system" and it is assumed, since there is a typically an available set of API functions, that integration is fairly straight forward. This *technical* integration, while important and sometime fraught with difficulty, is actually not the major challenge. The ability to determine where the root cause of a flaw in that integration, especially when dealing with things like security breaches, data corruption, or performance issues, is where a large amount of OpEx is spent.

This net-centric integration of different devices and components affects incident, problem, and change management. When dealing with an incident, essentially and event that occurs, typically there is a gathering of as many of the people and information available to determine the current state of the incident and the initial steps to take in order to resolve the incident moving it into the problem management phase. The manual approach to dealing with incidents simply does not scale when addressing events in a heterogeneous integration scenario especially when there are different technologies in place, each potentially with their own support models and paths to resolve problems. Automation and policy based resolution are key to dealing with incidents. Policies are really important here. Leveraging a policy and template based approach to handling incidents allows for a set of tools to automatically respond to incidents, gather the core supporting data and to bring together those personnel who may have supporting information in addressing the incident and preparing for a root cause analysis.

It is important to address the results of identifying an incident throughout it's entire lifecycle, bringing the resulting problem to resolution. Moreover, preventing the problem in the future is key. In a Hybrid and IoT environment, dealing with an initial incident and determining the root cause are hard enough, however when there are a multitude of integrations between both physical and logical components, services, and assets, the ability to manage the resolution to a problem and to further prevent future occurrences of that problem are much more complex. Thus, the problem management process, needs the ability to track the changes needed across the many different components and different locations, the order of these changes in order to support a Hybrid style of change management.

Location Independence is Typical

In both the Hybrid Cloud and Internet of Things deployment models, net-centricity is one of the important governing principles, and is the reason why cross-site and multi-location deployment is not only possible but actually the most likely and typical scenario. Given the regularity of using multiple locations in a Hybrid model, applying incident, problem, and change management requires accounting for multiple locations, but interestingly these locations can change rapidly and regularly. This is what is atypical about the Hybrid and IoT models. Not only is cross-site typical, the addition and removal of new services, devices, and assets to the overall working system or operating environment happens both rapidly but also quite unexpectedly. These services can come from any provider that meets the basic service levels needed, and this clearly implies that services came come from different locations and thus different locations are typical.

Dealing with incidents in an environment where locations can change frequently, rapidly, and unexpectedly, means that automation could be limited. This is where the importance of using policy based control is key. Policies can be created to reduce the response time when an incident occurs, even if automation is not readily available. Of course, when automation can be used it definitely accelerates the ability to respond. Responding to incidents in a distributed and multi-site deployment does not require changes to a typical ITIL style incident management process, but it does require a better feedback loop from problem and change management lessons learned. In addition to this feedback loop, a multi-site deployment supporting Hybrid or IoT environments requires the ability to incorporate many different service levels, service definitions, and support models from many different providers in order to more rapidly get to root cause.

Data Lineage is Vital for Reliability, Security, and Resiliency

The one aspect of changing to a new operating model is the ability to trace and track the movement and storage of data. Data is, in reality, the most important possibly the only important asset for any organization. It is the reason that an organization has a mission or it's the result of their mission. It is the core. In the Hybrid and IoT models, ensuring that data, as it moves through the network and is both accessed and affected by the various services and service levels, is a much more complicated task. The typical terminology for following the flow of data is called Data Lineage. Data Lineage (Harreis, 2015) is not specifically the tracking of data but it is ensuring that the integrity and security of the data is maintained at the level required by the owning organization. In the Hybrid and IoT models, dealing with incidents and the incident management process, is unique due to the multi-location, heterogeneous integration, and of course data lineage expectations.

When an incident occurs, typically these are not just generic events but typically something that is not supposed to happen. The loss of access to data, the loss of data, the unplanned distribution of data or the corruption of data quality and accuracy are often the root causes of an incident. The typical incident management process needs to be amended to not only identify that an atypical event has occurred but it needs to prevent further affect on the lineage of data. The process needs to stop any further impact to the data, while beginning to analyze the root cause of the incident and as a preparation for the problem management process.

Governance is Complicated in a Hybrid and Connected Things Operating Environment

Applying governance is more than just looking up definitions in the most recent version of the ITIL standard or installing a tool that "implements governance" or defining patterns of architectures. The purpose of governance, and this comes out in the definition, is to ensure that the assets and tools being used to run the organization are in fact effectively ensuring the organization is achieving its business goals. Both the journey and the destination are important when it comes to deploying governance.

FUTURE DIRECTIONS AND CONSIDERATIONS

How Do You Know If You Need Hybrid Governance?

There are a set of important questions and topics that must be addressed when defining how governance a Hybrid Cloud or IoT deployment should be formulated.

1. Is there existing, *documented*, governance in place?
2. If there is existing governance is it tracked, metered, and *measured*?
3. How much governance is needed? Is it needed just for compute, storage, and/or network?
4. How many providers of services will need to be tied or integrated together in governance model?
5. Do all services, systems, or components need the same level of governance?
6. How should governance be handled before, during and post migration of workloads from on-premises to off-premise.
7. Does data lineage tracking and metering already exist?
8. Is deployment to multiple locations required or already in place?

In addition to these important topics, one of the rapidly emerging use cases, especially for those enterprises with fairly complex IT topologies, is using services from various external providers in conjunction with their existing systems.

A good example of this is with the Internet of Things (IoT) where various sensors, devices, mobile apps (systems of engagement) and legacy information sources (systems of record) are combined. Many of the key characteristics of Services Oriented Architecture (SOA) apply here, but now in a geographically distributed and cross-provider model.

Integrated Services Management

In this Hybrid model, whether it's Hybrid Cloud or the Internet of Things, it is important to take a look at the most common governance processes and examine if these need to be changed, when they need to changed, and if they need to be changed. With the assumption that Hybrid Cloud and IoT really expect and leverage the same style of governance, the Incident, Problem, and Change Management models can be looked at as one set of processes in this same context. Moreover, updates to these processes are needed, but those modifications are specific and do not result in a fundamental re-engineering of these foundational governance processes.

Handling Data Provenance: Data Lineage and Traceability (DLT)

Governance is not just about dealing with problems but also focused on best practices for monitoring and securing various parts of a system. When an organization uses a combination of components and systems, deploying in various sites with many different interconnections and service levels, ensuring data integrity is key and surely more complex.

- The lineage of data, as it passes and has passed through the various components of a Hybrid Cloud or IoT deployment, is important in determining root cause of an issue. It is important to isolate the cause and the various components of a system using a forensic style approach. Understanding the original source of the data and knowing the form of the golden master version is vital to understand how it has changed and if that change matters. Managing the incident and bringing it to resolution through a problem management process are almost entirely dependent on knowing the original source. Incident and Problem Management processes need to be adjusted to ensure that both data integrity and the lineage of the original source of the data are well understood before a proper root cause can be determined.
- Change Management is focused on managing the process for implementing changes but, just as importantly, this process is used to clarify those changes that are needed and especially when changes are not required. The Change Management process should be modified to include steps to ensure that the results of incidents and problems result in well managed instead of haphazard changes to the golden master versions of data. Thus, changes will happen but they must be done in way that ensures the integrity of the original form of the data so the incident management process has the necessary foundation to compare original versus current forms, as these will show where and how changes occur and their impacts on the overall system. Understanding both data lineage and it's impacts on data integrity are key guiding principles.

Hybrid Root Cause Analysis (HRCA)

One of the most challenging aspects of Hybrid Cloud, where many different components, systems, and data sources are stitched together to form a single business function is to determine how to resolve functional and delivery issues as they arise. Hopefully good design of each "service" lessens the possibility of functional or operational problems.

The key aspect is to create incident, problem, and change management processes that take into account having a heterogeneous set of functionality, service providers and methods of connectivity (APIs,

Middleware, and Network infrastructure). There are early aspects of this described in early work done in the SOA Governance and Maturity Model (SGMM), but here are the main points:

- Incident and Problem Management need to take into account not just functional issues but the interconnections between those systems, the various APIs being used, and the movement of data and how it may have changed as it moves between services and service providers. Handling and identifying an incident that likely spans multiple components in multiple locations is the key here.
- Change Management is the place where leveraging DevOps and Continuous Integration techniques are really valuable. It's vitally important that both building services and the integration of those services is merged into the overall process of operations governance.

The most important IT capability is not servers, networks, services or databases, but it's the data that is most important. This is the most interesting and the most cutting edge aspect of establishing common governance. The ability to know the location, status, and security of data is vital as it moves between services and components especially from on-premises to off-premise locations. To assure the integrity of the data is key and thus knowing the linage of the data and have the ability to trace and track its movement across systems is key to being able to adequately govern data which is, above and beyond all other things, the most important asset an enterprise or organization owns.

Establishing common governance in a Hybrid Cloud model has turned out to be the most important aspect to going beyond just deploying tools for Hybrid Cloud and consuming Cloud services. Being able to assure the integrity of data as it moves between the components in a Hybrid deployment and integrating with a process to determine the root cause of problems and manage changes is key to successful deployment.

Blockchain

Blockchain is essentially a secure ledger supporting the combination of specific blocks (events and entries) into chains where the blocks are tied together to show a complete lineage of a transaction. This allows for there to be no single owner of the chain and is fully transparent to all those participating in the chain. This makes it perfect for digital currencies, tracking a physical or logical supply chain, and it can be applied to the manufacturing and distribution industries to ensure all needed components are in place. When it comes to Hybrid Cloud and IoT, the integration and interconnectivity of services is a key requirement. One of the challenges is to ensure the lineage of data, described in other sections, and the other is to allow for the elasticity of connections between services. The ability to connect, disconnect, and re-connect services into the whole system is required to make Hybrid Cloud and IoT function and for these types of system to allow for some type of governance mechanism to work effectively. The Blockchain model can be applied to the interconnectivity of services and devices in a Hybrid Cloud or Internet of Things composite system of components. As these two models evolve, Blockchain techniques make sense in tying together the various components and devices in a way that assures connectivity and the lineage of data as it moves between systems. Given this evolution, the techniques and examples for Hybrid and IoT governance covered in this analysis can be applied to ensure the "chain" of components in these systems stay tied together.

REFERENCES

Cloud Computing and Hybrid Cloud. (n.d.). Retrieved May 09, 2016 from https://en.wikipedia.org/wiki/Cloud_computing#Hybrid_cloud

Corporate Governance of Information Technology. (n.d.). Retrieved May 09, 2016 from https://en.m.wikipedia.org/wiki/Corporate_governance_of_information_technology

Create, W.The Project? (n.d.). Retrieved on May 10, 2016 from https://www.hyperledger.org/

Fabric Computing. (n.d.). Retrieved May 09, 2016 from https://en.wikipedia.org/wiki/Fabric_Computing

Harreis, H., Lange, M., Machado, J., Rowshankish, K., & Schraa, D. (2015). *A marathon, not a sprint: Capturing value from BCBS 239 and beyond.* McKinsey & Company. Retrieved May 09, 2016 from http://www.mckinsey.com/~/media/mckinsey/business%20functions/risk/our%20insights/a%20marathon%20not%20a%20sprint%20capturing%20value%20from%20bcbs%20239%20and%20beyond/a_marathon_%20not_a_sprint_capturing_value_from_bcbs_239_and_beyond.ashx

Internet of Things. (n.d.). Retrieved May 09, 2016 from https://en.wikipedia.org/wiki/Internet_of_Things

IT Governance Institute. (2003). *Board Briefing on IT Governance* (2nd ed.). Rolling Meadows, IL: IT Governance Institute. Retrieved May 09, 2016 from http://www.isaca.org/restricted/Documents/26904_Board_Briefing_final.pdf

Meulen, R. V. (2015, November 10). *Gartner Says 6.4 Billion Connected.* Retrieved May 05, 2016 from http://www.gartner.com/newsroom/id/3165317

National Security Agency. (2015). *Defense in Depth, A practical strategy for achieving Information Assurance in today's highly networked environments.* Ft. Meade, MD: National Security Agency, Information Assurance Solutions Group – STE 6737. Retrieved May 09, 2016 from http://www.iad.gov/iad/library/reports/defense-in-depth.cfm

Net-centric. (n.d.). Retrieved May 09, 2016 from https://en.wikipedia.org/wiki/Net-centric

Raden, N. (2005). Shadow IT: A Lesson for BI. *BI Review Magazine.*

What is ITIL® Best Practice ? (n.d.). Retrieved on May 10, 2016 from https://www.axelos.com/best-practice-solutions/itil/what-is-itil

KEY TERMS AND DEFINITIONS

Blockchain: Blockchain is a peer-to-peer distributed ledger technology for a new generation of transactional applications that establishes trust, accountability and transparency while streamlining business processes. Think of it as an operating system for interactions. It has the potential to vastly reduce the cost and complexity of getting things done. The key to Blockchain is assuring data integrity and data lineage (Why Create The Project, 1st paragraph).

Defense in Depth: Originally a military a strategy for ensuring redundancy when systems and procedures fail, this is typically applied to technology deployments. Focused on both security "at the edge"

and the redundancy of each component in a system of systems context, this approach ensures that any one component will not reduce the reliability of the whole system.

Governance: Generically governance is a set of processes and models that define roles and how people and technology are used to both influence and control the design, delivery and operation of a system. This view on governance has a technology bias, but is generally applicable to most any context.

Hybrid Cloud: This a cloud deployment model that combines several cloud environments, typically more than one. These remain separate environments but are connected together, combining on-premises collocation, managed services and off-premises cloud-native services. All of this can be presented to the consumer as a single service providing a specific functionality. Furthermore, the intent of a Hybrid Cloud is to allow for simple services to be enhanced through the combination with other services in a single pool of capability (Cloud Computing, Hybrid Cloud section).

Internet of Things (IoT): This is a connected network of physical and logical objects, devices, and structures. It combines both physical and logical objects where logical objects could include specific data sources, all interconnected and sharing information in a chain of connectivity. It relies on a Hybrid Cloud model in order to function effectively (Internet of Things, 1st paragraph).

ITIL: This is an acronym for Information Technology Infrastructure Library and is intended as a guide for describing the processes and procedures used to govern a technology environment, especially infrastructure and data centers. Included in this are the roles and delivery plans focused on topics such as incident, problem, and change management. ITIL advocates that IT services are aligned to the needs of the business and support its core processes. It provides guidance to organizations and individuals on how to use IT as a tool to facilitate business change, transformation and growth (What is ITIL Best Practice?, 2016). A large number of processes are addressed both for pre-delivery, runtime, operations, and post-delivery. This is not specific to an organization but is intended as a foundation for an organization to define their specific processes, procedures, roles, and delivery plans.

Net-Centric / Net-Centricity: A continuously-evolving, complex community of people, devices, information and services interconnected by a communications network to achieve optimal benefit of resources and better synchronization of events and their consequences (Net-centric, 1st paragraph).

Chapter 14
Design and Implementation of Service Management in DevOps Enabled Cloud Computing Models

Shelbee Eigenbrode
IBM, USA

Suheil Nassar
IBM Cloud, USA

ABSTRACT

This chapter examines the importance of including value-add service management practices early in the Continuous Integration/Continuous Delivery (CI/CD) pipeline. The authors will also address the importance of establishing a balance between the development and delivery of features with the development and delivery of practices that support overall infrastructure and service management capabilities. Without fully encompassing all of these practices, the DevOps benefits of reducing time-to-market for a set of features can be negated by a potential increase in security exposures as well as overall quality issues. Within this chapter, several key service management practices are identified as well as the importance of fully incorporating those practices into a DevOps adoption.

INTRODUCTION

According to a recent Gartner study, 25% of Global 2000 companies are expected to adopt DevOps by 2016 (Gartner Inc., 2015). Cloud computing has proven to be an ideal platform for enabling DevOps practices due to the inherent speed and agility cloud computing provides. Companies and enterprises of all sizes are rapidly embracing DevOps practices due to the recognized benefits including:

- Increased agility,
- Decreased time-to-market,

DOI: 10.4018/978-1-5225-0759-8.ch014

- Improved quality, and
- Ability to respond quickly to the customer.

The benefits of delivering new features and functions utilizing DevOps practices is resulting in all of the benefits above for many companies; however, isolating the use of DevOps practices to only features and functions can drastically limit the overall benefits that can be gained by adopting DevOps practices to the underlying infrastructure, platform and service management activities.

BACKGROUND

This chapter is not intended to provide a detailed description of all DevOps practices. There are many other resources available that speak at length about the various key practices included in the DevOps methodology. However, this chapter will focus on the practices of Continuous Integration and Continuous Delivery so those two practices will be defined for clarity within this chapter. Continuous Integration is the practice of frequently integrating code into a common automated build process that automatically validates the build then executes layers of automated testing and validation. An essential outcome of Continuous Integration is that source code changes from multiple team members are continuously being merged into a common code stream, or branch. Continuous Delivery is the practice of ensuring that the merged, tested, and validated code base can be automatically and reliably delivered at any time. Continuous Integration is a prerequisite for Continuous Delivery.

The adoption of Continuous Integration through Agile and DevOps practices allows Developers to frequently commit code and integrate it into a common automated build process including varying degrees of validation. The label of Developer in this case includes anyone that contributes code, which could potentially be someone from traditional functional roles such as operations or security. The label of code in this case should also not be limited to code providing a specific feature or function. Code can, and should, include infrastructure, service management and operational components.

Excluding service management and operational considerations early in the DevOps delivery pipeline can quickly negate all of the benefits gained through adopting DevOps practices. Service management and operational considerations includes all practices related to delivering and operating a given solution. This includes a broad variety of practices including but not limited to: patch management, configuration management, security, monitoring, change and incident management, and capacity management. This also includes the automation of day-to-day operational activities within these practices such as self-healing capabilities, automatic scaling, and automatic security remediation. The DevOps delivery pipeline essentially defines how code will move from development to production utilizing continuous integration and continuous delivery practices. A standard delivery pipeline will identify the activities and tools that enable Continuous Integration (CI) and Continuous Delivery (CD) practices. The detailed pipeline will also typically include identified practices such as: automated provisioning, configuration management, orchestration, quality gates and feedback loops. Within the pipeline, it's key to understand that all of these activities are being integrated in small batches to optimize the ability to deliver frequent updates quickly. The common DevOps practices included in a CI/CD delivery pipeline provide the ideal mechanism for including and automating operational aspects quickly and early.

Figure 1. High level DevOps continuous integration and continuous delivery pipeline

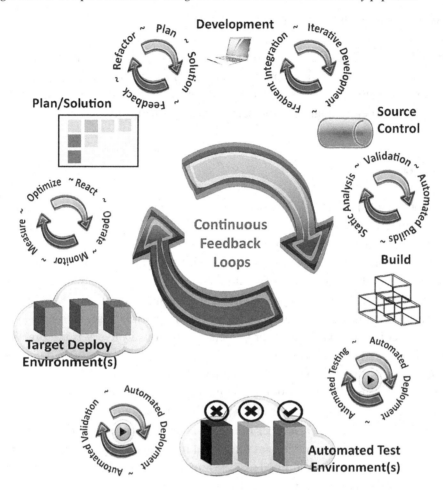

A Delivery Pipeline that focuses on a full-stack deployment will allow an organization to take advantage of all of the benefits provided by DevOps adoption. This means that not only should an organization be concerned with developing features/functions of a solution but it's also critical to ensure service management practices such as security and patch management are developed and included early in that overall delivery pipeline. This practice of including operational assets, such as required security configuration settings, early requires increased collaboration across functions to understand the end-to-end needs of delivery a solution. This requires expertise and knowledge across functional areas such as: Business Owners, Architects, Developers, Testers, Security Experts and Operations.

Another area to consider when defining a strategy to automate service management practices is to note that the goal of DevOps is not to simply automate existing process that may be archaic, ineffective, or insufficient. As components are being automated and delivered through a CI/CD pipeline, the task or process should be evaluated to make sure it's a value-add activity. Before automation is developed an evaluation should also be conducted to ensure the task, process or solution is still meeting the overall intent and objective of the solution as well as service management requirements specific to a solution or organization. Value stream mapping is a method that can be utilized in this case to analyze the current end-to-end process flow before defining the future process flow. The method allows a team to quickly identify and target existing bottlenecks and inefficiencies. It also helps ensure that teams aren't just automating existing inefficiencies but finding more streamlined ways to solution a specific process flow.

Traditionally project teams are defining the solution architecture as well as identifying the appropriate DevOps delivery pipeline and service management practices are often minimal or excluded from the initial design. Many DevOps solutions lack the end-to-end design that incorporates operational assets and procedures early in the delivery pipeline. Many factors contribute to the lack of service management and operational readiness early in the delivery pipeline including: lack of collaboration and knowledge sharing across stakeholders, not considering full stack implementations within Continuous Integration/ Continuous Delivery (CI/CD) pipelines, and not utilizing repeatable deployment patterns. A frequently seen anti-pattern in this area includes not incorporating security configurations early. For example, a lot of internal security policies state that all logs have permissions set so they are inaccessible by unauthorized identities or groups. If this configuration is not included in the development and test environments during testing, it's very possible that once those files are locked down in production it will break processes or applications that were relying on a broader access to those files. This results in code changes, additional testing and then deployment of the updated security configuration that would have been a simple fix if included early in the development process.

Excluding service management considerations early in the pipeline leads to a reduction in quality, increased re-work, increased costs, and increased time-to-market. As an example, if the design of a Continuous Integration solution is not explicitly designed to include and systematically build in automated security tests and quality gates that solution will very likely be deployed with exposed security vulnerabilities as well as compliance issues. Those vulnerabilities will then need to be fixed either late in the lifecycle or post-deployment which requires additional re-work with associated costs. This includes monetary cost that is easy to quantify such as human labor to remediate and test as well as missed Service Level Agreements due to downtime. However, the costs can also be more difficult to quantify but equally impacting such as brand image if a vulnerability is exploited. DevOps Continuous Integration practices provide the methodology as well as a wide variety of tooling to include and automate service management tasks such as security early in the development lifecycle.

The following topics will be covered in detail within this chapter:

1. **Cross-Functional Collaboration:** The key to enabling an effective end-to-end Continuous Integration/Continuous Delivery (CI/CD) pipeline.
2. **Balancing Requirements:** The importance of balancing features/functions with operational considerations.
3. **Key Practices:** Identifying key service management practices to include early in the DevOps delivery pipeline.
4. **Impact Analysis:** Impact analysis of including vs. excluding service management practices within a DevOps delivery pipeline.
5. **Design Patterns:** Identifying design patterns and solutions to enable service management early in the DevOps delivery pipeline.

Automating operational aspects, such as security, allows solutions to be deployed reliably without sacrificing the speed that is gained through DevOps and agile methodologies. While the intent of the chapter is to provide information related to all aspects of including service management within a DevOps delivery pipeline, a lot of detailed focus will be targeted on the area of security for illustrative purposes. As cloud computing projects continue to become more agile with the goal of rapid releases, the ability to include and automate security becomes critical. In addition, security breaches are occurring at an alarming rate across platforms as attackers become more sophisticated. As a result, increased emphasis on including security early within the DevOps delivery pipeline is becoming critical.

In summary, this chapter will focus on optimizing the DevOps delivery pipeline by including service management practices early to fully gain the recognized benefits of DevOps Continuous Integration and Continuous Delivery practices within a cloud-computing environment.

CROSS-FUNCTIONAL COLLABORATION

It's impossible to embrace DevOps and fully realize the benefits to be gained without recognizing the need for cross-functional collaboration. The most difficult aspect of adopting DevOps practices is the change in traditional technology cultures. Traditional methodologies often include a set of practices with very defined functional boundaries. A Developer develops application code. An operations team member supports that solution in production. DevOps is intended to blur or eliminate those functional boundaries. The blurring of those boundaries allows for a higher level of quality and quicker delivery by aligning both development and operations on the common goal of delivering value to the user. The resulting collaboration allows key practices to shift left in the development lifecycle. As companies begin to adopt DevOps practices or mature an existing adoption, the key to being successful in this area is to ensure the solution is not a "No-Ops" or a "No-Dev" solution. The expertise across functions can be utilized to ensure practices are shifting left and being automatically integrated and verified as opposed to being eliminated.

When organizations begin to adopt DevOps practices, the tendency is to begin those efforts with members from the Development organizations or to create a "DevOps Team". A lot of debate is centered on the validity in forming DevOps teams and whether that is counter-intuitive to DevOps in general. Regardless of the team label or naming, the real key is to ensure the project team includes a cross-functional representation with common goals, responsibilities, and objectives.

DevOps relies heavily on collaboration and feedback loops throughout the pipeline. A cross-functional team ensures a necessary level of expertise across the software lifecycle. Collaboration should include not only the standard development of features but also the business and operational objectives. A developer may understand the application in depth from a technical functional perspective while an operations person may better understand the application's impact on security, compliance, backup, monitoring and logging solutions. On the other side, a product owner may have a better understanding of the detailed customer requirements related to functionality but also uptime, resiliency and stability. If any of the stakeholders are excluded from the initial solution design and collaboration efforts, there will be a gap in the solution that is not addressed early in the delivery pipeline. Working in small batches enables the team to frequently exercise these feedback loops, and gives many opportunities to practice whole-team collaboration.

Collaboration and organizational silos tend to be the biggest barrier to adopting DevOps practices in many organizations today. There are many different ways to address the issues surrounding a lack of collaboration and a solution that works for one organization may not necessarily work for another. However, there are some common practices to help enable collaboration across teams including but not limited to:

- Ensuring all teams are accountable for the same business, functional, and operational objectives and goals,
- Balancing cross-functional representation on solution teams,
- Forming cross-functional squad teams,
- Providing visible dashboards that make discussions, decisions and assumptions visible to all team members,
- Encouraging cross training and job rotation,
- Promote the practice of taking risks and failing fast, and
- Integrating small batch changes and new code frequently as iterative collaboration progresses.

When the organizational barriers are removed, this allows teams to more effectively include operational considerations early in the lifecycle. Developers tend to be really effective at working with new technologies and the ability to implement new features/functions very quickly. Operations teams tend to be really good at understanding resiliency, security, scalability, and other operational considerations. Enabling the teams to collaborate without barriers allows for the development and coding of operational assets early in the CI/CD pipeline by utilizing the cross-functional experts most efficiently.

BALANCING REQUIREMENTS

In the previous section, the idea of working towards common business objectives and goals was mentioned as a way to increase collaboration. Part of working towards common objectives and goals must include balancing requirements across the entire needs of the solution, which includes not only feature/function but also operational requirements. When the balance is not proportionate, technical debt continues to accrue in the areas of quality, security, reliability and maintainability.

To ensure requirements are balanced, it's critical to identify all stakeholders that provide requirements as well as the overall Product Owner that manages & prioritizes those requirements. Often requirements come from several stakeholder groups such as offering teams, development teams, operations teams, sales teams, and client services teams. If each of those teams has a different business objective or goal, the task of balancing requirements will be exponentially difficult. If all of the stakeholder teams are working towards the same business objectives, then the task of prioritizing requirements becomes less of a struggle between stakeholders driven by varying goals.

While clearly identifying common business objectives and goals is critical, it's equally important to understand and provide a balance between the types of requirements that get prioritized. The Product Owner needs to make a concerted effort to not only prioritize and rank features/functions but also to prioritize and rank requirements that may make a solution less costly to operate, increase time-to-market, improve security posture or improve the overall quality. The person that is prioritizing the backlog needs to be held accountable for all aspects of the system including functionality as well as reliability, quality, and security.

In Figure 2, a dashboard illustrates the incoming requirements and the theme area addressed by those requirements. The key is to keep a balance among the requirements to ensure that the solution is providing necessary features with positive customer feedback but is also operationally efficient. Utilizing DevOps dashboards for visibility into the overall health of a CI/CD pipeline can be a valuable resource in identifying when the balance in requirements is not optimal. For example, including visibility into

Figure 2. Balancing functionality with non-functional considerations

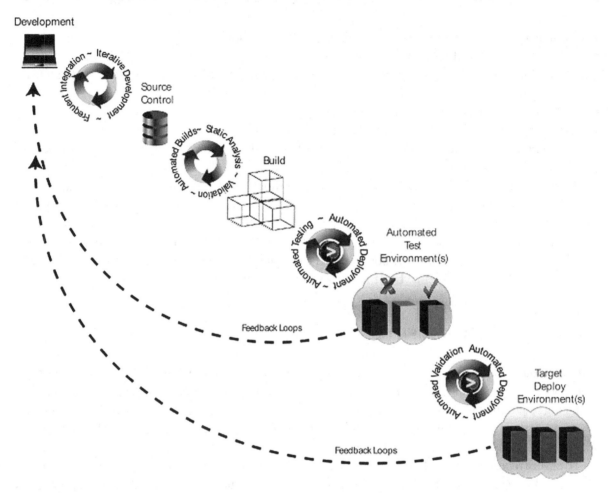

metrics such as failed deployments or increased customer tickets could signal the requirements balance may need adjusted to prioritize requirements improving stability or specific issues in the CI/CD process higher than a new feature. Although the above diagram shows a categorization of incoming requirements to better understand the types of requirements being worked, it's still key to prioritize and rank all incoming work within a single rank ordered backlog for the solution overall.

Balancing requirements can be difficult and finding the balance is always going to be dependent upon a specific solution and overall product goals. In the end the Product Owner is responsible for maintaining that balance within active work as well as within the backlog prioritization to ensure the solution is achieving goals in terms of functionality, quality, security, and agility.

KEY PRACTICES

One of the key tenants of DevOps is to automate tasks that are painful or costly. This includes not only automating but also ensuring they are included within the CI/CD pipeline. The cost of delivering and supporting a solution can quickly reduce any potential profit related to a solution if service management capabilities aren't automated and built into the solution. This means shifting tasks that are traditionally performed later in the solution lifecycle to the left so they are occurring during the development & automated test cycles.

Although it is always important to include service management aspects within any end-to-end methodology, utilizing DevOps practices and tools allows these aspects to be automated and included even earlier within the Software Development Life Cycle (SDLC). Automating the operational aspects of a solution as well as including those practices within a Continuous Integration solution allows those service management practices to be consistently utilized and deployed across environments. This limits the risk of introducing operational considerations in late phase environments such as staging or production.

When considering service management early it's key to not only identify the service management practices that should be included but also to ensure the solutions and components to support those practices are treated the same as standard feature or function code. This means treating infrastructure as code so the code that is written to provision, configure, test, and deliver a full stack solution must also flow through the CI/CD pipeline. For example, when identifying a solution for configuration management it's important that the configuration management infrastructure solution itself is deployed using CI/CD practices but also the configuration management scripts or recipes are also treated as code flowing through

Figure 3. Shift operational aspects left in the development lifecycle

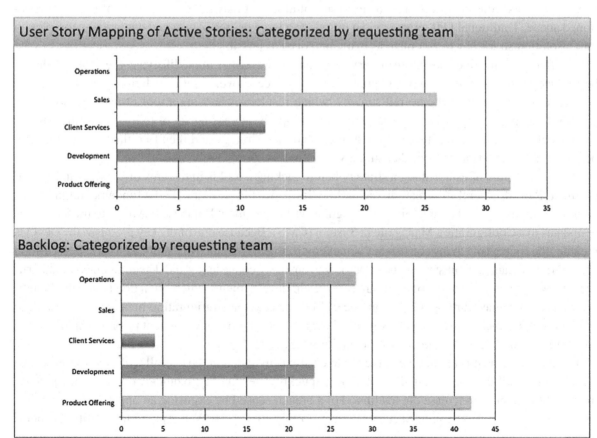

the same CI/CD process. This ensures all code used to provision, configure, test and deliver that complete configuration management solution is also using an automated consistent repeatable delivery method.

The service management practices discussed in this section include:

- **Configuration Management:** The ability to provide visibility for system attributes as well as consistency across components through the lifecycle.
- **Patch Management**: The ability to acquire, test, and deploy vulnerability updates to a given solution.
- **Monitoring and Logging:** The act of proactively and reactively applying probes to the system to collect information that can be utilized to not only fixed current issues but also proactively avoid issues.
- **Security:** The ability to protect a system against threats and vulnerabilities by identifying how a system should be secured.
- **Compliance:** The ability to demonstrate that a system is secured according to an identified security standard.
- **Incident, Problem, and Change Management:** The practice of managing issues and changes within an environment.

Each of the practices above includes areas of depth that will not be covered in this chapter; however, the intent is to identify and illustrate key concepts and potential areas to consider when designing a new DevOps enabled solution or updating an existing solution that may be missing some of the areas mentioned above. Traditional ITIL practices can introduce a large degree of cost and operational complexity into a solution so it's key to automate as many practices as possible.

To effectively include and automate service management earlier in the lifecycle, the solution should be focused on the overall strategy and goal of each practice above. A lot of solutions tend to focus on a specific tool rather than the overall strategy, which results in choosing a tool instead of choosing a solution. The popularity of DevOps has generated a rapidly increasing set of tools supporting various DevOps practices; however, it's key to first understand the strategy and then find the tool or tools that best facilitates the enablement of that strategy.

A good example of establishing a strategy before picking a tool is in the area of configuration management. Part of general Information Technology Infrastructure Library (ITIL) fundamental practices includes establishing and maintaining a Configuration Management Database (CMDB) to track changes to updates in a Configuration Management System (CMS). Because one of the key premises for DevOps includes the concept of having consistency across environments obtained through CI/CD practices, a good configuration management strategy becomes key in ensuring consistency and detecting unexpected drift across environments. A lot of solutions are brownfield development, which often don't have the benefit of consistency gained through CI/CD practices. In these cases, a configuration management system to establish environmental parity can be key to gain consistency across environment prior to implementing automation that is dependent on a specific environment state.

Patch management is another key practice to ensure is included in the overall CI/CD solution so that critical vulnerabilities can be tested and deployed quickly. The inability to quickly deploy tested patches in an environment can increase the likelihood of a breach caused by exposing an unpatched vulnerability. The Open Web Application Security Project (OWASP) Top 10 Web App Vulnerability list notes Security Misconfiguration as the fifth leading cause of security exposures (The Open Web Application

Security Project, 2013). One of the common causes of this specific exposure is due to missing patches on a system. DevOps practices enable teams to quickly deploy patches through a CI/CD pipeline that includes automatic regression testing and automatic deployment. The CMS tools that exist also facilitate the ability to push patches out to multiple systems using a reliable deployment mechanism.

Security is arguably the most critical service management practice to ensure is being integrated into an overall automated CI/CD pipeline. The number of data breaches in 2014 was nearly 25 percent higher than in 2013 (IBM, 2015). Hackers are becoming more and more sophisticated every year which means companies need to ensure they are continually updating and securing technical solutions. The degree of security included in a product can have an enormous impact on the overall success of a project because it has the potential to impact so many areas including: quality, cost, brand image, compliance, and time-to-market. Many organizations adopting DevOps are still not adopting the practice of automating and integrating security early in the CI/CD pipeline. Keeping a system secure is an expensive process especially if issues are not being found until later stage environments as well as still being identified and remediated manually. DevOps practices inherently provide several enabling practices that makes early integration of security easier than ever through practices such as: frequent integration to catch defects early, automated validation and testing, consistent deployment patterns, configuration management systems to enforce configuration across environments, and metrics needed to manage your technical debt related to security issues.

Monitoring and logging are also key service management practices that are critical to include in a DevOps strategy. The ability to openly monitor systems as well as provide general dashboards across processes and environments allows for continuous feedback to all stakeholders. This means everyone on the team is able to quickly identify and react to the status of things such as but not limited to: environments, components, applications, builds, technical debt, backlog work, change status and work in progress. Including the ability to monitor almost anything allows for the ability to start quantifying progress across varying metrics. This allows everyone to identify and react to opportunities for improvement quickly. Another benefit of comprehensive monitoring at the system level is that it allows for comprehensive logging. This is critical because it provides the ability to analyze logs to proactively perform automated administrative activities to proactively prevent an outage or alert.

Several key tasks should be performed when evaluating the appropriate service management practices and solutions to include in the CI/CD Pipeline including:

- **Talk to the Experts:** There is a reason DevOps relies heavily on collaboration. Each functional area has deep expertise in specific areas so utilizing a cross-functional team is critical. For example, to implement security early it's important to talk to security experts to better understand what coding practices and automated security tests should be included early. Having cross-functional squad teams that are fully accountable for the end-to-end solution also encourages collaboration across topics and ensures adequate representation and participation from discipline experts.
- **Assess Current Strategies and Policies:** Evaluate existing policies and practices that may be in place at a business or organization level to identify opportunities to streamline. For example, many organizations have outdated security policies that may need to be re-evaluated for newer technologies such as cloud as well as new potential vulnerabilities. In many cases, re-evaluating some of these old policies can help streamline the end-to-end solution. For the policies that are still valid, access which can be automated as well as which can be included in the CI/CD pipeline.

- **Automate Consistently:** Ensure that all practices that should be in place at production are included and automated within the CI/CD pipeline. In DevOps environments, all of the environments will ideally look the same, which allows for repeatable deployments across environments. As an example, the patching solution that is planned for production should be planned and executed the same way for all environments.
- **Evaluate Service Management Layers:** Identify the level of service management that is appropriate at different layers in the pipeline. As an example, implementing security within the pipeline may initially include a degree of automated unit testing & static code analysis before moving to a more comprehensive automated integrated test, which will continue building additional security test layers into the test framework.
- **Ensure Infrastructure is Code:** Too often infrastructure is still not being considered as part of the code base for a new solution. Infrastructure is the core to building a repeatable deployment, which means the code required to implement new infrastructure needs to also go through a CI/CD pipeline as functional code. Engineers from both development and operations should be able to easily contribute changes to the source code repositories used for functional code and for infrastructure. Again, cross-functional squads ensure there is expertise in infrastructure to facilitate the creation of this code.

The tasks above will help facilitate the overall strategy when defining the practices and solutions to include in the CI/CD pipeline. It's also important to understand the impact of choosing to include or exclude a specific practice from the overall DevOps strategy.

IMPACT ANALYSIS

The impact of not including service management practices early can be both quantitative and qualitative. The concept of including operational aspects early is not necessarily a new topic nor is it a DevOps specific topic; however, this chapter focuses on DevOps because the methodology itself enables the inclusion and automation of service management practices early. The ability to deliver a quality solution quickly depends on having service management practices included in that solution. The ability to deliver quality quickly cannot be achieved if operational aspects are continually left out or separated from the overall CI/CD solution.

One key way to gauge impact related to quality is by maintaining metrics as well as providing visibility on those metrics to all stakeholders. Those metrics can provide immediate feedback and become a key factor into a continuous improvement program. Without metrics there is no quantifiable method to indicate whether there is any degradation or improvement in the delivery pipeline. Several metrics can be specifically collected and evaluated that can tie to the impact of missing service management practices throughout the end-to-end pipeline. Below are just some the potential of metrics that could potentially identify an issue related to the DevOps service management strategy:

1. Security Metrics
    a. **Number of Breaches:** If security breaches are occurring, this is a key indication that there is a major security flaw in the overall solution. A thorough analysis of all attack vectors needs to be conducted immediately. As a result of the analysis, new security changes in support of

hardening the solution should be pushed through the CI/CD pipeline. This ensures the hardening is executed consistently as well as quickly. When there is a known security threat, this is when the process of accessing the risk and potentially re-prioritizing operational issues over a specific feature/function becomes critical.

b. **Time to Remediate Vulnerabilities:** A critical practice in keeping systems secure is having the ability to rapidly deploy patches across environments quickly. Monitoring the time to patch or deploy updates to systems is a key metric in ensuring systems stay secure when there are vulnerabilities identified in specific code levels. In 2013, 79% of vulnerabilities had patches available on the day of disclosure (Net-Security, 2014). Having an automated patch deployment strategy is critical within a DevOps strategy to deploy patches quicker and successfully.

c. **Number of Vulnerabilities:** Having visibility into identified vulnerabilities is especially key to the development and operations stakeholders. The identification and remediation of these vulnerabilities needs to occur during automated testing cycles. Choosing to run security tests and security scans when code is pushed to staging or production is too late. The changes to remediate a vulnerability can often be disruptive to multiple development components so catching these dependencies and vulnerabilities early is key to ensure limited re-work as well as a secure system.

2. Configuration Management Metrics

a. **Degree of Drift:** Even with a configuration management strategy, drift often occurs. Drift can occur for multiple reasons such as: automation gaps, human error, or change gaps. There are some metrics that can be collected regarding drift as well as perform some potential correlation of drift impact. For example, an environment may be experiencing an increase in the number of incidents as well as an increase in the meant time to resolution (MTTR). If environmental drift is also increasing at the same time it could indicate the degree of drift is leading to maintenance and quality issues in the environment and give an early indicator of action required.

3. Incident, Problem, and Change Management Metrics

a. **Number of Tickets Manually Opened:** Tracking the number of manually opened tickets may be an indication of automation gaps. For example, if supports teams are manually opening a large number of problem tickets it could be an indication of a larger issues such as: lack of monitoring in a specific area or lack of automated workflows.

b. **Standard Ticket Metrics:** Providing visibility to standard ticket metrics provides a tangible indication of the degree of change and problems an environment is capable of performing at. As automation increases, the number of changes that can be performed on the system should be increasing while the number of problems/incidents should ideally be declining due to automation and less manual intervention. Basic metrics also allow for the ability to trace root causes as needed when changes introduce issues in the environment. These metrics are important not only for the technical teams but for management to be able to clearly identify tangible benefits to increase DevOps adoption.

c. **Mean Time to Recovery (MTTR):** This metric provides visibility into the time it takes to recover from a failure. This can be a good indication of potential issues with maintainability and operational effectiveness.

The metrics above are only samples of a vast array of metrics related to service management that projects should be collecting, monitoring, and providing visibility to in support of continuous improvement. Monitoring and logging solutions have become very sophisticated and are now enabling further degrees of automation and analytics. The ability to monitor and parse verbose logging information real-time allows for teams to continually identify the need for and inject automated solutions. A simple example may include a probe to monitor the up/down status of a specific process. An automated re-start process can be implemented to run in the event of a down status in the logs. The concept of self-healing systems can greatly reduce the manual labor spent doing routine and often tedious steady state maintenance tasks.

Due to the low cost of storage, many organizations are following a "monitor everything" philosophy. This ensures that as new data points and key indicators are identified, there is enough historical data to benchmark as well as perform analysis. DevOps continuous monitoring practices provide the ability to monitor and actively utilize data to improve a solution, system, or business process. Due to the enormous amounts of data, DevOps dashboards provide a method to aggregate and visually identify key metrics from various systems and sources into a single source of data. DevOps dashboards should be available across all stakeholders to encourage transparency and amplify internal feedback loops. The various views on a dashboard can be tailored across various user groups such as management teams and development teams. This allows the whole team to quickly identify potential issues, key successes, and provide focus on continuous improvement. A DevOps dashboard can include metrics from various sources and should be tailored to include the data that is most meaningful to the specific squad and/or organization.

Metrics are critical regardless of whether they are targeted at service management practices or utilized to continuously improve the overall solution and supporting processes. Ensuring service management specific metrics are included in the overall metrics strategy will allow a team to quickly identify and quantify the value of automating service management processes.

DESIGN PATTERNS

Because each service management practice contains a lot of detailed aspects that could each be a separate book to cover the topic in any degree of depth, the design patterns chosen within this section are intended to be high level and will include a narrow focus for illustrative purposes and an introduction into key concepts.

Monitoring and Logging

Monitoring & logging can be applied across a variety of aspects within a solution. This can include but it not limited to monitoring of everything from business processes, development status, deployment status, test status, as well as system and application status. This section will focus specifically on the topic of building continuous monitoring into deployed technical environments to improve overall quality of a solution.

The figure below shows a basic iterative deployment pipeline across several standard environments with monitoring built in across environments. Monitoring should be included in early stage environments to allow teams to identify and remediate issues prior to production. The iterative nature of agile and DevOps combined with continuous monitoring allows issues to be identified and fixed early. The monitoring data that is collected needs to be visible across all teams so that everyone is able to clearly visualize the impact of a specific piece of code and take action accordingly.

Figure 4. shows several types of monitoring are occurring in the early stage environments such as test and staging. This allows developers to receive immediate feedback on code so they can provide a fix quickly. In traditional methodologies, developers may not have visibility into monitoring information once the code is handed off to test and operations teams. Providing immediate feedback and visibility to all stakeholders not only allows for issues to be addressed quickly but for developers to learn more about operational considerations. Many of the items noted in the feedback loop data above should be available via a readily available in a dashboard visible by all stakeholders.

Including comprehensive monitoring across environments ensures a variety of issues are caught early in the pipeline. This includes catching operational and service management issues early. Table 1. shows common types of monitoring as well as the impact on the overall end-to-end pipeline effectiveness.

Regardless of the monitoring strategy that is chosen for a specific solution, the key is ensuring the monitoring gets put in place early enough to identify and fix potential issues early in the pipeline. It's also important to ensure metrics are maintained and everyone has visibility into the monitored information to enable continuous improvement activities.

Security

Security is perhaps the most critical service management practice to ensure is being integrated into an overall automated CI/CD pipeline. DevOps practices are an ideal methodology to automate and integrate security considerations early into a solution. This can be accomplished by coding security into the system, including automated security tests, enforcing consistency and repeatable configurations, providing the ability to automatically re-build to a non-compromised system state if needed, and providing visibility into technical debt specifically related to security. Automating security and log collection also feeds into

Figure 4. Continuous monitoring and feedback cycle

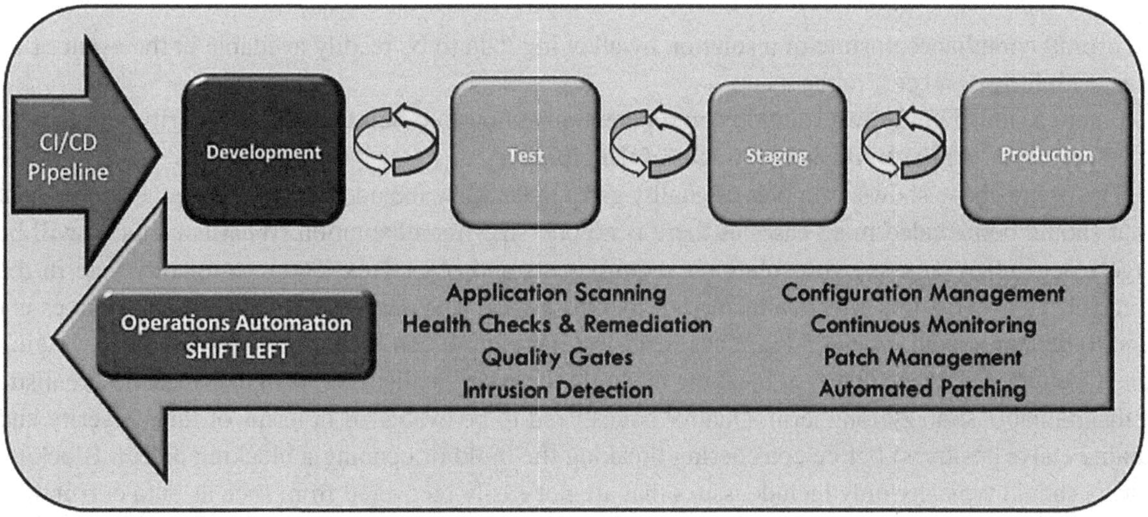

Table 1. Monitoring types and impact correlation

Monitor Type	Description	Impact
Test Monitoring	Test monitoring includes monitoring all of the detailed automated tests and test result data	Automated testing is a key practice in ensuring a successful DevOps adoption. Successfully monitoring the tests across environments is critical to identifying and fixing issues early.
Configuration Monitoring	Configuration monitoring includes monitoring the degree of consistency across environments and identifying configuration drift	Inconsistencies between environments can lead to system outages, non-compliance issues and automated delivery and deployment issues.
Application Monitoring	Application monitoring allows for a very detailed analysis of code at runtime with the abilities to identify performance impact of specific pieces of code.	The sophistication of current tools allows applications to be monitored down to the code level providing a level of granularity that enables quick troubleshooting.
System Monitoring	For simplicity, this category combines monitoring of both infrastructure and platform. This category includes standard system monitoring that provides visibility into the state of components such as infrastructure, network, storage, servers and operating systems.	Because DevOps practices support full-stack automated deployments, the code that is used to create and configure the automated deployments needs to be tested as well as monitored across environments to identify any gaps in automation, design, coding, or operations.
Log Monitoring	Log monitoring solutions provide real-time monitoring, correlation and analysis of logs to aid in identify issues quickly.	Utilizing tools to monitor and perform analysis on active logs enables teams to be notified quickly not only when an issue is occurring but also predict when an issue may occur. This allows teams to react quicker and proactively avoid problems and outages.
Orchestration Monitoring	Monitoring orchestration solutions includes monitoring tools that are utilized to provide continuous delivery/deployment to target environments.	Monitoring success and failure rates for automated deployments allows teams to identify gaps in automation or orchestration across deployment patterns being used.
End-User Monitoring	This level of monitoring can be deployed into a UAT environment or a production environment to gain valuable insights from the end-user such as how the users are utilizing various aspects of a solution by capturing and analyzing information about every transaction from every user.	One of the key success points of DevOps is ensuring customer feedback is a driving force to ensure changes are quickly introduced into the system based on identified feedback. Without understanding customer usage of a system, it's difficult to truly measure the customer experience. This monitoring helps gauge features that may be more popular or features that are seldom used.

the overall compliance posture of a solution by allowing data to be readily available in the event of an audit with little or no cost to the team.

Figure 5. illustrates how a solution could potentially choose to build and layer security into the CI/CD pipeline during the Build & Test stages of the pipeline.

The figure above shows examples of quality gates that can be included but is not meant to represent what should be included in all cases as there is no one-size-fits-all solution. What is included will be largely dependent on a specific solution's requirements and objectives. The term quality gate in the context used above refers only to a method of identifying varying degrees of quality. The gate does not need to be, nor should it be in a lot of cases, a blocking gate. It can be thought of more as a swinging gate. Opening a blocking defect or breaking the build for every quality issue will likely not be a realistic or maintainable strategy long term. Quality issues need to be evaluated in terms of their severity and validity (false positives) before considering breaking the build or opening a blocking defect. Blocking defects should typically only include issues that are not easily recovered from such as data corruption.

Figure 5. Building in incremental security quality gates

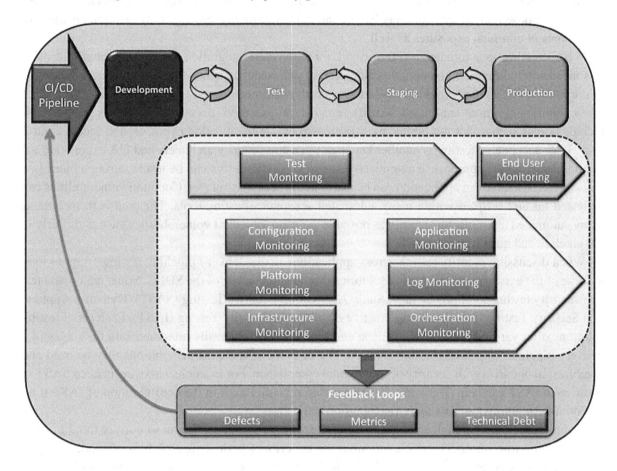

The primary benefit is providing visibility into quality issues that can contribute to technical debt and should not be allowed to continually accrue.

The expectation is that embedded security logic and automated security tests are coded during development. With the practice of Test Driven Development (TDD) the development of automated tests and code are performed simultaneously. The key is to ensure those automated tests include security tests as well. There is a limited scope that a unit test can effectively cover; however, things such as boundary testing can be included at this stage. Input validation is another simple but key coding practice. According to the Open Web Application Security Project (OWASP), the number one security vulnerability for web applications is injection flaws (The Open Web Application Security Project, 2013). Although several bad coding practices can contribute to exposing injections flaws in code, one simple coding practice that can be performed to protect against injection includes input validation. Input validation can easily be coded and validated very early in the development process. Unit testing alone does not provide sufficient testing primarily because a lot of security functionality and controls are typically embedded into the infrastructure, servers, and network components. This means it's important to layer and build on your levels of testing as code is moved across the pipeline.

As an added layer of qualification and validation, the practice of layered quality gates ensures that if the code is not written to appropriately handle input, the automated browser tests can quickly identify these types of common exposures as well.

When creating an automated test framework for automated integration and user acceptance testing, it is increasingly important to continue collaboration with security teams to understand new exposures or corporate policies that should be embedded into the automated tests. Integrated testing is the point when significantly more automated security tests can be executed. Security tests at this point should include threats such as but not limited to: injections flaws, authentication bypasses, and access control tests. User acceptance testing is another key area to ensure security architects and QA experts are assisting in writing the appropriate automated test cases. Anything that can be tested during a black box security assessment of an application can be tested at the acceptance layer. Common vulnerabilities can be tested for and scripted within many automated acceptance-testing tools. The goal is to include as many automated test cases for security as possible to ensure potential vulnerabilities are caught early in the pipeline and quickly remediated.

When discussing security testing across applications in the delivery pipeline, it's important to look at some of the existing security testing solutions that span the scope of the SDLC. Some major penetration security testing solutions include: Static Application Security Testing (SAST), Dynamic Application Security Testing (DAST), and Interactive Application Security Testing (IAST). Each set of testing solutions offer varying degrees of coverage and functionality and easily integrates into the stages of a delivery pipeline. Depending on the solution, one or more of the existing solutions may be used and combined to obtain overall security objectives and compliance. For example, choosing to keep SAST in addition to IAST can help overcome challenges with potential gaps in the configuration of IAST if all potential permutations are not identified appropriately.

Figure 6. represents a high level overview of the various solutions. The most current trend in Info-Sec is moving towards IAST, which combines the benefits of both static and dynamic code analysis. It also addresses some of the common issues with existing static and dynamic analysis tools such as false positives. Gartner identified IAST as one of the Top 10 Technologies for Information Security in 2014 (Gartner, 2014). However, some IAST solutions are not fully mature yet and can be complex to implement depending on the chosen tool so a combination of solutions may be needed to obtain desired level of security.

Each of the solutions above can be integrated into the overall delivery pipeline to identify and address security issues early in the process. Identifying which solutions to use will largely depend on the overall solutions security requirements.

If a security breach does happen, CI/CD enables the ability to either immediately deploy a fix and/or re-build to a previous compliant state due to reliable version control. Because DevOps practices enable the ability to automatically build, test, and deploy a new full stack environment it's now possible to recover in minutes or hours instead of days. Without DevOps CI/CD practices, the time to get a system back online after a breach is greatly increased.

Patching

A key part of securing any solution includes the ability to deploy patches to an environment quickly in order to avoid the exploitation of identified vulnerabilities in various code levels. Patching can include

Figure 6. Comparison of security test methods

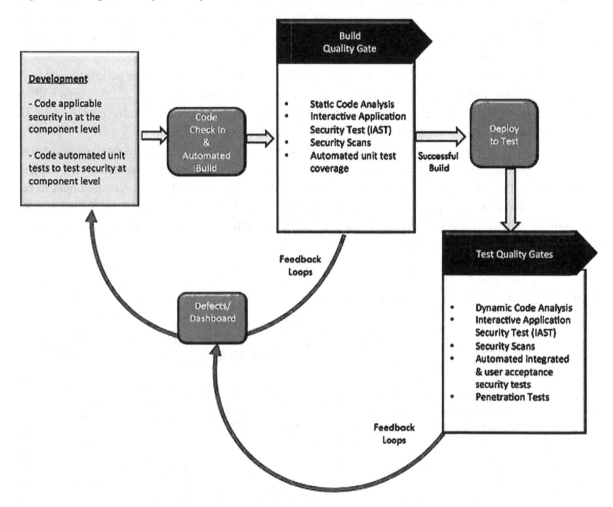

the changes required to secure any layer of the stack. Automated patch management is critical to any solution for many reasons including:

- Manual patching is expensive,
- Manual patching is error prone, and
- Delays in patching can lead to breaches.

Manually applying patches to multiple servers can be extremely expensive not only in the cost to deploy but also in the cost to test the patch. Ensuring patches go through a CI/CD pipeline allows patches to be automatically tested as well as automatically deployed using a reliable repeatable deployment process. The automation of the testing and deployment of patches also significantly reduces the number of errors that are possible under a manual patching strategy. When patches deploy through a CI/CD pipeline, the deployment of patches can be accomplished quicker and more reliably than via traditional methods.

In the case of patching the platform as well as software components, the existing tools in this space have become increasingly sophisticated and provide a solid framework to manage patches across environments. By codifying the infrastructure and configuration of a system, it becomes easy to integrate these changes into an existing CI/CD pipeline process.

Figure 7. shows the previously depicted delivery pipeline and how patches can be introduced and managed within the CI/CD pipeline to drive patch automation. Patch automation is another area within service management that can greatly benefit from being included and coded directly into the CI/CD pipeline to maximize the benefits of utilizes DevOps practices.

A newer practice used for installing new updates includes the concept of immutable infrastructure meaning that patches are not applied to existing servers but are deployed as new instances or containers that replace the old versions. DevOps practices again allow the new instances and containers to be thoroughly tested as well as automatically deployed. Immutable infrastructure for Cloud Computing is becoming an increasingly popular way to deploy and CI/CD practices are enabling those newer methods especially for more mature DevOps adoptions.

Figure 7. Including patching in the CI/CD pipeline

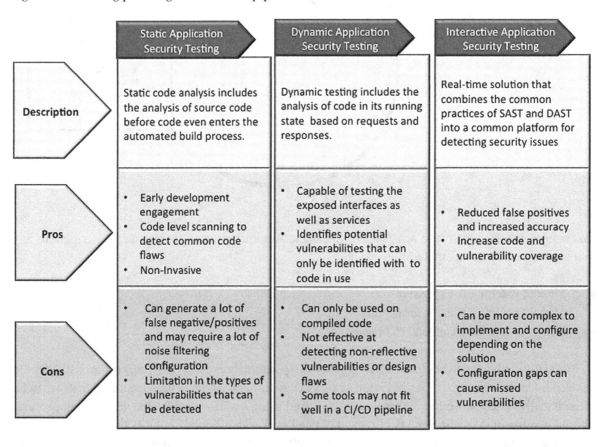

Compliance

As previous described compliance is the ability to demonstrate that a system is secured according to an identified security standard. There are many security policy and regulatory standards that may be applicable to a given solution; however, for simplicity this section will discuss the automation of compliance for company specific security policies.

As companies drive towards DevOps practices, it's important to start engaging the security experts in the company and work with them to start identifying security standards in a way that can translate directly to code. Specifying security standards in this way allows for the automation of these compliance activities across the pipeline. When policies become embedded in automated code it takes the guess work out of interpreting the policy and provides quick visibility to non-compliant items.

Maintaining a compliant posture in the event of a security audit takes a lot of manpower and get be an extremely tedious and timely activity if automation is not embedded into at least some aspects of the compliance process. During a security audit, a detailed analysis of a solution's ability to conform to an established set of security policies is evaluated. A security audit can be conducted for a number of reasons whether it's an internal audit or an audit performed to determine regulatory compliance. Security audits are looking for consistency with policies as well as audit trails and activity logging. Several practices can be automated and introduced into a CI/CD pipeline DevOps practices to assist with compliance activities such as:

- **Release Management Automation:** Many release automation tools provide governance over workflow, which is often a component of a security policy. Release automation allows for code to be packaged, updated, and deployed through a consistent repeatable process. The process typically includes a workflow that identifies approvals and checkpoints across the delivery of a package.
- **Automated Configuration Management:** Configuration management systems can allow teams to identify and enforce compliant settings across environments as well as provide a record of compliance when needed during an audit.
- **Health Checking Automation:** Many security policies require the routine practice of health checking at an identified time interval. The health checks are intended to monitor the system against specific security settings and provide proof of compliance. Given current DevOps tools and practices, health checks can easily be conducted and retained utilizing existing configuration management systems combined with continuous monitoring techniques.

Automating each of the practices above into a consistent repeatable CI/CD process enables teams to effective produce proof of controls across the system for auditors. It also enables the ability to collect evidence automatically. This reduces the labor cost commonly associated with preparing for an audit caused by manually collecting evidence across various systems. Also, automatically tracking compliance metrics on a continual basis ensures audit readiness and reduces the last minute scramble that often happens when trying to identify and find the correct evidence during an audit.

CONCLUSION

The purpose of this chapter was to demonstrate the concepts, purpose, and benefits of including service management practices and operational considerations early within a CI/CD pipeline. The focus on utilizing cross-functional teams or squads to ensure the necessary expertise is included and utilized in the end-to-end coding and solution was also identified as a key practice. Having cross-functional teams leads to an architecture that is more resilient. Developers who architect without understanding the operating environment tend to design solutions that are difficult to operate. Giving teams the balance in expertise ensures the solution can be developed and delivered in small batches that avoid continuous re-work. If service management is only being considered or applied when a solution is delivered to production, there will be re-work and issues. Utilizing the CI/CD pipeline to automatically build, validate and deliver service management and operational solutions allows those assets to be integrated into a repeatable consistent process. That process allows solutions to not only be delivered with built-in operational considerations but also delivered quicker, more reliably and with increased quality.

The ability to effectively deliver and operate a solution at scale in production is a large topic that could be covered in a book in itself. The intent of this chapter was to introduce key aspects that need to be addressed in the overall solution from the enablement of collaboration to the technical aspects of CI/CD and infrastructure-as-code. The cost of operating a system using traditional manual methods can quickly make a solution unprofitable to operate. By assessing current service management solutions and mapping a strategy to automate the relevant practices into the CI/CD pipeline, solutions can fully recognize the complete benefits of an end-to-end DevOps delivery pipeline.

REFERENCES

Gartner. (2014). *Gartner Identifies the Top 10 Technologies for Information Security in 2014*. Retrieved from http://www.gartner.com/newsroom/id/2778417

Gartner Inc. (2015, March 5). *Gartner Says By 2016, DevOps Will Evolve From a Niche to a Mainstream Strategy Employed by 25 Percent of Global 2000 Organizations*. Retrieved from www.gartner.com: http://www.gartner.com/newsroom/id/2999017

IBM. (2015, Jan 1). *IBM X-Force Threat Intelligence Quarterly, 1Q2015*. Retrieved Sep 30, 2015, from http://www-01.ibm.com/common/ssi/cgi-bin/ssialias?subtype=WH&infotype=SA&appname=SCTE_WG_WG_USEN&htmlfid=WGL03073USEN&attachment=WGL03073USEN.PDF#loaded

Leigh, D. (2015, October 5). *Contributions and Peer Review*. IBM Senior Technical Staff Member, IBM Transformation and Operations Division.

Luke, M. (2015, October 5). *Contributions and Peer Review*. IBM Senior Technical Staff Member, Cloud Data Services DevOps Practice Lead in IBM Analytics.

Net-Security. (2014, Feb 27). *Third-party programs responsible for 76% of vulnerabilities in popular software*. Retrieved Oct 1, 2015, from Help Net Security: www.net-security.org

The Open Web Application Security Project. (2013). *OWASP Top Ten Project*. Retrieved 09 28, 2015, from www.owasp.org: https://www.owasp.org/index.php/Category:OWASP_Top_Ten_Project

KEY TERMS AND DEFINITIONS

Cross-Functional: A collective set of stakeholders with skills representing the necessary skills required to delivery a system, feature, or function from initiation to completion.

Service Management: The practices surrounding the overall abilities to support and manage a set of functionality provided via a system, service, or application.

Chapter 15
Enterprise IT Transformation Using Cloud Service Broker

Rajesh Jaluka
IBM Corporation, USA

ABSTRACT

Cloud is significantly changing the economics as well as delivery and support model for Information Technology. Every enterprise needs to come up with a plan to transform their current IT and embrace cloud. The road to transformation poses many challenges and there is no one right answer. The objective of this chapter is to describe some of the key challenges and provide a methodology based on IBM Design Thinking to address the challenges. The author will also enlighten the readers on how a Cloud Service Broker can help smoothen the journey.

INTRODUCTION

Large and medium enterprises have developed a large number of IT systems over several decades. Many of these systems are complex and involve many components. These systems support mission critical functions. Uprooting these systems from the current on-premises datacenter and moving them to a cloud environment is complicated and involved. For example, a survey found 48% of businesses and government organizations continue to rely heavily on COBOL and many of these applications are two decades old (Fiscutean, 2015). The application owners need to take into account factors like migration cost, differences in technology stack, the skills of its technical staff, software licensing, security, supportability, availability, recoverability, and total cost of ownership. Furthermore, the enterprises are building new services on cloud that will need to work seamlessly with their existing systems.

Security and data privacy remain the biggest barriers to the adoption of cloud. On the commercial front, any extended downtime or security breach can severely impact customer satisfaction, lead to customer attrition, affect revenue or even tarnish a company's reputation. One such recent (May 21, 2015) example is Apple iCloud outage that affected 200 million users (Kelly, 2015). The outage lasted seven hours and affected 11 services including email, calendar, and reminders. A similar outage in March

DOI: 10.4018/978-1-5225-0759-8.ch015

Figure 1. Tweets following iCloud outage
Source: Kelly, 2015

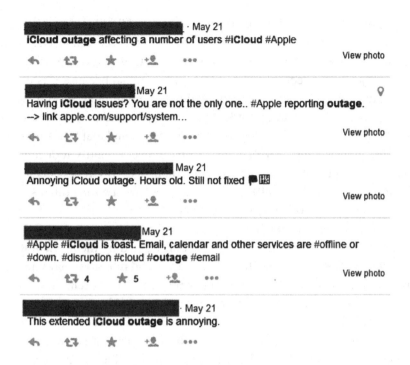

2015 cost Apple $9.12 million (Geier, 2015). However, when the breaches happen on the social front the impact is much wider.

The attack on Anthem, a U.S. health insurance provider, in February 2015 potentially exposed social security numbers, addresses, phone numbers, email addresses, employment data and income data of 80 million patients and employees (Terhune, 2015). Another such attack on the U.S. Office of Personnel Management compromised data of 21.5 million federal workers (Scuitto, 2015). These attacks can lead to citizens' call for stricter laws and regulations. These laws and regulations can severely restrict what services can be consumed from cloud and how they are consumed. For example, data residency laws will limit enterprises and agencies to only those service providers that have presence in the country or the region. Similarly, these attacks can also lead to geopolitical tensions between countries. In the U.S. Office of Personnel Management case, the initial reports have tied the attacks to China-based hackers. Such instances can lead to new laws and regulations that may require enterprises to react quickly to comply with these laws and regulations. Service providers, too, can impose self-regulations to promote an underserved social cause or take a moral stand.

To address such concerns, service providers have come up various designs to implement cloud e.g. public cloud, private cloud, and hybrid cloud. A hybrid cloud uses private cloud infrastructure in combination with public cloud services. It is possible for very small businesses to have all its IT needs completely served through public cloud service providers. However, most medium and large enterprises will continue to have compute resources in its traditional data centers for many years to come and will combine it with private and public clouds from multiple service providers. According to IBM (n.d. a),

"The reality is a private cloud can't exist in isolation from the rest of a company's IT resources and the public cloud."

One of the disruptive forces cloud has enabled is "shadow IT." Cloud and Software-as-a-Service (SaaS) have made technology more accessible and usable for non-technical users. Shadow IT is a term used to describe the phenomena where Lines of Businesses (LOBs) are bypassing the central IT and leading technology projects and decisions. The LOBs are doing so because it is enabling them to get directly involved in the assessment and evaluation without going through several layers of IT. Further, it is offering businesses a faster route to market and realize business benefits quicker. A CEB CIO Leadership Council (2014c) survey of 181 business executives found that 80% of these executives have experience with technology projects and 74% are willing to lead [identify tool capabilities, select and procure tools, manage projects, and manage vendors]. Another CEB CIO Leadership Council (2014a) survey of 934 IT employees found that 94% of IT employees have a wrong mind set – 87% are process centric, 68% are risk averse, and 40% have silo mind-set.

Shadow IT is not a new phenomenon. In the pre personal computer era, the LOBs had to go through the central IT for all its computing needs. LOBs were constrained by the availability of resources and priorities of the central IT. They, often, had to wait for weeks and months to have their needs addressed. The advent of personal computers (PCs) empowered the LOBs to decentralize the processing. The LOBs started getting PCs into their department, buying off-the-shelf software, and hiring professionals to build custom applications. This ad-hoc and rapid expansion led to security, backup, and maintenance headaches. Central IT was able to bring things under control with client-server technology. The control has shifted back and forth between Central IT and LOBs many times with access to better software, improved connectivity, and increase in processing capabilities in the hands of the users.

In order to avoid the repeat of similar mistakes, Central IT will have a very important role in creating guidelines, setting standards, and governing which cloud services and cloud service providers meets the enterprise needs. Central IT has used several forms of governance like architecture control and review boards, security reviews, design authorities, programming standards and so on. However, the majority of these governance require extensive documentation and are time consuming. Implementing similar form of governance will frustrate LOBs and force them to bypass Central IT.

To navigate through these minefields, a carefully planned transformation strategy is critical for success. The following sections will propose a lifecycle approach to the cloud journey. The first four phases of the lifecycle are inspired from the Design Thinking methodology. The phases do not imply a waterfall sequence for the entire transformation, but an iterative approach – taking each area of transformation and then iterating through these phases.

UNDERSTAND

One of the most important aspects of this journey is goal setting – what problems is the enterprise solving and what outcomes are its users expecting. While the central IT could be focusing on reducing cost by virtualizing their infrastructure, LOBs could be looking for new capabilities to address the business challenges they are facing from their competitors. Similarly, the development team could be focusing on optimizing the DevOps process while the LOBs are considering a Software-as-a-Service (SaaS) application that offers far more superior capabilities compared to in-house software.

Figure 2. Cloud transformation lifecycle

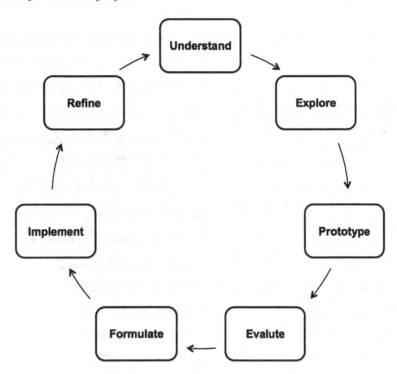

To illustrate the need to understand the pain points further, let us look at Gartner's insight from 169 online surveys (Decker & Iervolino, 2015). It clearly shows that reducing enterprise's operating cost is important but Business Intelligence, analytics, and performance management are on top of the list. Therefore, instead of migrating existing systems to cloud, the priority could be to invest in new cloud services that address the CFO's priorities.

The central IT of an enterprise needs to collaborate with the LOBs to identify and prioritize business problems. IBM Design Thinking is one such powerful tool to define user-centric market outcomes. The next few sections will use this methodology and show how it can be applied to navigate through the transition to cloud. The sections will only touch upon parts of the methodology relevant for this discussion. For more details, go to IBM's website at http://www.ibm.com/design.

So, what is Design Thinking? According to Don Norman (n.d.), designers "don't try to search for a solution until they have determined the real problem, and even then, instead of solving that problem, they stop to consider a wide range of potential solutions. Only then will they finally converge upon their proposal." Don further explains, "We need to question the obvious, to reformulate our beliefs, and to redefine existing solutions, approaches, and beliefs." This entire process is "Design Thinking." All the steps discussed in Understand and Explore phases are best done in a face-to-face collaboration with all the stakeholders.

Step 1: With IBM Design Thinking, you start with personas. A persona represents a group of users with similar goals, pain points and motivations. Build a persona by observing and interviewing several people that fit the group.

Figure 3. Top areas needing support
Source: *Decker & Iervolino, 2015*

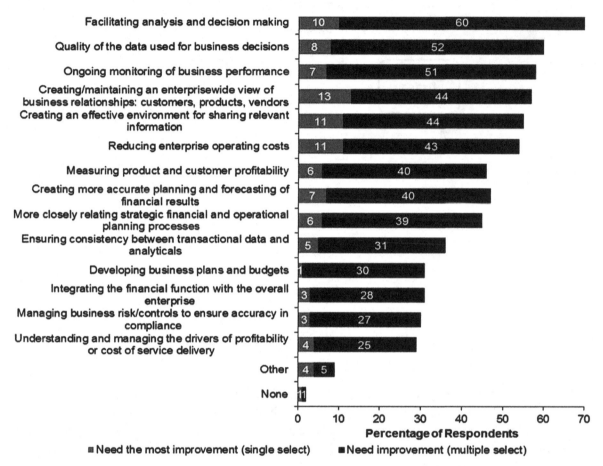

Step 2: Next, aggregate and synthesize the information into Empathy Maps and As-Is Scenario Maps similar to the ones shown below. An Empathy Map helps uncover the frustrations, obstacles, and desires of a persona. An As-Is Scenario Map captures a persona's current workflow and maps the pain points to the steps in the workflow. This mapping provides insight into the specific steps that cause the frustration and dissatisfaction. It will also help the business quantify the business value of optimizing that step.

As you can see in the Empathy Map (below), users are unhappy with the current travel reservation system. Further, mapping these point points to the As-Is Scenario Map shows that "too many tools," "repetitive data entry," and "too many restrictions" keep appearing at various stages of the travel process. This clearly demonstrates that simply moving the current application to cloud will not address any of the concerns with the users within the enterprise. Instead changes in policies in combination with a modern SaaS might provide a cheaper and superior solution.

You will need to keep iterating between Personas, Empathy Maps, and As-Is Scenario Maps to establish a good understanding of the pain points. The success of these steps depends on two things. First, make sure everyone's voice is being heard. Any negative attitude or attempt to suppress or only hearing the loudest voice will kill ideas with big potential. Second, make sure the voices are being captured. These steps are best done with everyone writing his or her thoughts on sticky notes, posting on a wall, and then discussing and distilling them. This approach promotes inclusion and collaboration so voices from all corners are heard and understood without any fear of being cut-off. For teams with no experience in this methodology, it is a good idea to have a Design Thinking facilitator initiate and lead these activities.

EXPLORE

Step 1: In the exploration phase, the team collaborates to brainstorm some big picture ideas on how to solve the pain points. It is very important that all stakeholders express their ideas instead of simply being led by technical leaders. The ideas must be broad and conceptual focusing on user needs and not feature centric. Further, it should only take a sentence or two to express the idea. For example, for one of the clients, the users complained that it took more than a week for them to get new software on their desktop. This was impacting their productivity. Saying "we need a software distribution tool to automate the desktop software installation," would have constrained the solution options to a software distribution tool only. An idea that states "we need a Netflix like experience where a user can choose from a list of software titles similar to movie titles and the

Figure 4. Empathy map
Source: IBM, n.d.

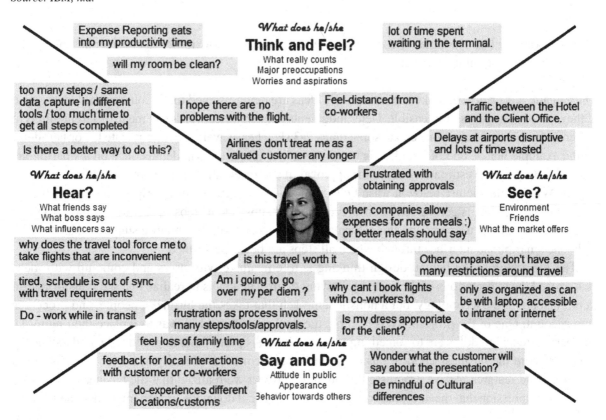

Figure 5. As-is scenario map
Source: IBM, n.d.

Steps / Phases	Gather Details	Obtain Approval	Make Reservations	Travel	Prepare and Submit Expense Report
Doing ☞	Gather dates, location, purpose, urgency. / Prepare estimates / Assess impact on current professional and personal commitments	Create a Travel Request with details, business justification, and estimates. / Respond to queries explaining the details / Adjust and resubmit when rejected	Reserve car, hotel, air. / Prepare directions / Make dinner plans / Purchase supplies	Pick up car / Drive to airport / Fill gas / Check-in, Security..... / Pickup luggage / Drive to hotel / Check-in at hotel / Check-out	Pick up car / Drive to airport / Fill gas / Check-in, Security Check, Board, Travel / Drive to hotel / Check-in at hotel
Thinking ☁	is this travel worth it / Is there a better way to do this?	Other companies don't have as many restrictions around travel	Other companies don't have as many restrictions around travel / do-experiences different locations/customs	Am i going to go over my per diem? / Is my dress appropriate for the client?	Other companies don't have as many restrictions around travel
Feeling ♡	too many steps / same data capture in different tools / too much time to get all steps completed / why does the travel tool force me to take flights that are inconvenient	too many steps / same data capture in different tools / too much time to get all steps completed / Frustrated with obtaining approvals	too many steps / same data capture in different tools / too much time to get all steps completed / why can't I book flights with co-workers to	Airlines don't treat me as a valued customer any longer / tired, schedule is out of sync with travel requirements	too many steps / same data capture in different tools / too much time to get all steps completed

software will be available for use within one hour" gives the flexibility to consider an option like using SaaS or online app store.

Once again, it is critical to make sure everyone's ideas are being listened to. Encourage wild ideas, even if they sound outrageous or infeasible. Defer judgments to later. Since words can mean different things to different people, have everyone create some quick 2-3 sketches as well to communicate his or her ideas. In the example below, one of the ideas is to have user only enter the trip details once on a smartphone and use it to generate estimates, submit for approval, make reservations, check-in, and submit expense report. Without the picture below it wasn't clear how the steps after entering trip details were happening – are the trip details getting fed to different tools and subsequent steps happening on those tools or some mechanism for user to copy this information into every tool. The picture suggests that there be only one smartphone interface through which all steps are being performed.

The main philosophy behind design thinking is to empathize with users and come up with ideas that exceed the expectations of the users by wowing them. The key is to realize that the transformation is not just about the technology, but a holistic approach that takes the business, people, and processes into account. One of the projects I was leading, the goal from central IT was to replace their aging IT infrastructure and middleware to something more modern. As part of this migration, the understanding was to rewrite the business applications on the new platform as-is without any major changes to the functions and features. As we progressed through the project we realized that the business users were under the impression that the new platform will significantly cut down the time to implement new report

Figure 6. Idea sketch

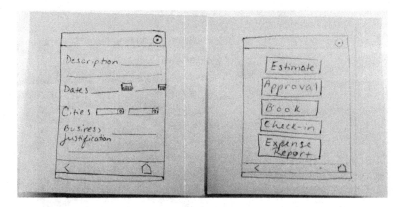

requests. A large part of writing reports was requirement gathering, availability of developers to write, test, fix defects, and promote code from development to test to production. None of these were going to be eliminated with just porting over to the new platform. Through a series of interviews and discussions I found that a large majority of these reports were being requested from the Finance department and involved complex calculations. I developed a new module that allowed business users to specify the logic through a series of drop downs. The module automatically generated the reporting using this information. This wowed the business users as it completely eliminated the need to interact with developers. The users were able to design, test and finalize their own reports on the fly within an hour. In this example, I exceeded the users' expectations and completely changed their experience for requesting new reports.

Step 2: Next, cluster similar ideas together into master ideas. For example, if two participants have come up with an idea to have a single mobile app to manage the entire travel experience, cluster them into one even though they may have some differences in implementation or user experience.

Step 3: Next, have each member vote every [master] idea on feasibility (e.g. cost, technical feasibility) and importance (e.g. market differentiating, cost saving, revenue opportunities, strategic advantage).

Step 4: Arrange the ideas into a prioritization grid, like the one shown in Figure 7.

Ideas that get voted high on both feasibility and importance are obvious choices. Avoid the trap of only picking ones that are feasible. Ideas that have low feasibility or low importance are not worth pursuing. Avoid spending too much time on these "unwise" categories. Ideas that fall in between are tough choices and require some additional refinement.

Step 5: Once you have narrowed down the choice of ideas, validate that the ideas have not drifted away from the original goal. The can be done by expressing the idea into a sentence structure composed of a "Who" (a specific user or a group of users), a "What" (a specific action or enablement), and a "Wow" (a measureable market differentiator) e.g. *The user* needs a way to *do something that addresses their need* so that *they benefit directly.*

Step 6: Create storyboards to visually tell a user-centric story of how his or her pain points will be addressed. While building the storyboard make sure to choose the best parts of each of the ideas that were clustered into this master idea. This is to further emphasize the need to build a solution

Figure 7. Prioritization grid
Source: IBM, n.d.

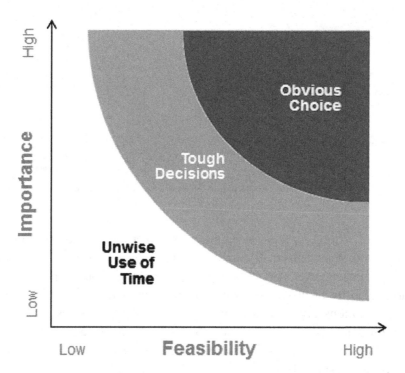

that represents the entire team's thinking as opposed to just one person. Avoid drawing too many screens because this is not a user interface mockup. The storyboards need to focus on the personas and their actions, thoughts, goals, emotions, and relationships.

Step 7: Give the storyboard a reality check by documenting the assumptions. Assign risk and uncertainty level to these assumptions. Any assumption with high risk and high level of uncertainty must be resolved sooner. Again, it is important that the team is honest and open. If the solution is full of uncertainties and risks, it is time to move to the next idea. The goal of this exercise is to fail fast and cheaply. You may have to iterate through the steps in the exploration stage to find ideas that are going to work.

Step 8: The final step in the exploration phase it to identify the Minimum Viable Product (MVP). This concept has originated from Agile and Lean. What is the minimum bare-bone product that would give value to the users? The idea is to build the solution in small increments iteratively and get feedback from the users early. Often people make the mistake of too much emphasis on "minimum" and "viable" but very little on "product." It is important that you do no produce something that provides no value to your users. Otherwise, it will turn them off early. The following cake analogy is a good way to explain (see Figure 8). Take your big wedding cake idea and distill it down to birthday cake and further into a cup cake. The cup cake is simple, easy, and cheap to make but it still gives the user an idea of the taste, flavors, and creativity you are going to deliver with the wedding cake.

Figure 8. Minimum viable product
Source: IBM, n.d.

PROTOTYPE

Evaluation Criteria

Once the team has shortlisted the ideas, it is time to prototype or build the cupcake. As you prototype, establish a clear set of evaluation criteria to align with your business objectives. This is important because when dealing with cloud service providers, many have predefined and fixed Terms and Conditions with very little room to change. The providers may promise a very high level of service but the penalties and liabilities for not meeting them might be frail. Here are some major areas to watch out for:

- **Security:** The evaluation criteria need to cover how the provider manages the physical as well as logical security. For the logical security assess all layers – network, system, middleware and application. Security along with privacy concerns, as per Gartner, is the top adoption inhibitors for all industries (Anderson & Mazzucca, 2015). It is very important to be pragmatic. People tend to make false assumptions and generalize too much. For example, many assume that everything related to government or financial requires highest level of security and must be kept in a private cloud. It is very important to clearly classify your data so you can determine the level of risk you can tolerate and the type of security you need. Typically, data can be classified as regulatory, confidential, internal, and public. There are many examples of government data that lives in public domain e.g. property records, labor statistics, and trade data. The risk tolerance for such categories of data is very high and would not warrant a high degree of security.
- **Privacy:** Many tend to treat security and privacy the same way. While security is about who is authorized to access the data, privacy is about appropriate usage of the data you have access to. It is easier to control access to data but more difficult to control how the data gets used. Most enterprises implement processes and procedures to enforce privacy. This poses a unique challenge when dealing with cloud because the compute resources are distributed. Similar to security, it is important to classify your data from privacy perspective as well. The regulatory requirements and control mechanism when dealing with financial data versus health data will be completely different. The evaluation criterion needs to take into your regulatory and compliance requirements, data residency laws, privacy policies of the service providers and its partners, and your enterprise policy.

- **Affordable:** Overall cost reduction was number one reason for adopting public cloud according to a Garner survey (Ng, Anderson, & Anderson, 2015). The ease at which you can request new Virtual Machines (VMs) from an Infrastructure-as-a-Service (IaaS) is both a positive and negative. While it brings agility and speed, it also implies that things can easily go out of control. The monthly cost of individual VMs may seem cheap but it quickly adds up when you have hundreds of them. Further, there can be many line items of charges – storage, redundancy, number of CPUs, amount of memory, number of images, bandwidth and so on. The evaluation criterion needs to include some usage scenarios to calculate total cost of ownership to compare between different options instead of simply looking at a line item. In addition, favor a service that offers a simple pricing structure against one that has a very complicated pricing structure that would takes hours every month to reconcile the charges.
- **Level of Automation:** In the same survey, agility and scalability was the number one priority for CIOs. For the business problem you are trying to solve, assess how critical is speed and factor this into your evaluation criteria. Too many manual steps during the provisioning or onboarding process will frustrate the users.
- **Scalable and Elastic:** Unlike a traditional data center where you relied on fixed sized servers with capacity planning and forecasting to adjust the environment, cloud offers the ability to scale up and down dynamically as the need changes. For the specific problem you are trying to solve, assess if workload is highly elastic. For example, e-commerce applications in North America will have to deal with high demand during Thanksgiving and Christmas. Ensure that the service provider you select can cater to those needs.
- **Reliable:** Similar to scalability, assess whether high availability is critical for your workload. Availability of 99% implies a maximum of 87.6 hours of downtime in a year. This could mean around 1 hour 40 minutes every weekend. While 5 9s (99.999%) implies only a little over five minutes of downtime in a year. Higher availability comes at a price. No all applications require 5 9s or even 2 9s. The cost difference between 95% and 99% can be very high. Not all applications need to be available all night or all weekend. The IaaS or Platform-as-a-Service (PaaS) provider may guarantee five 9s (99.999%) but if you are building your own application achieving the same level of availability might be very expensive. A SaaS provider offering a similar guarantee might be a better choice in that scenario. The exact Terms and Conditions of these guarantees must be examined to ensure it meets your needs.
- **Modular:** Due to the fast pace at which technology is evolving, enterprises do not want to lock-in multi year contracts with service providers. It is difficult to foresee whether a service provider will provide the capabilities needed in the near future. Further, as the existing application portfolios are replaced, enterprises will combine multiple SaaS and Business-Process-as-a-Service (BPaaS) offerings together into composite applications. This is because they want to leverage the best of breed to build a solution. In your evaluation criteria, make sure that the options you are evaluating are not bundled and tightly coupled. It should allow you to consume only the module that best serves your need.
- **Composable:** Composable implies the ability to integrate different modules together from different providers to build a solution. Modular does not guarantee composability. Only services that offer Application Programming Interfaces (APIs) and are based on open standards are composable. In your evaluation criteria ensure that the service you select has APIs to support your current integration needs. For example, if you are building a warehouse management system, it should

provide an API for receiving, shipping and fulfillment functions instead of assuming that these steps are performed through its own user interface. The APIs will enable you to integrate the warehouse management system with other Enterprise Resource Planning (ERP) systems. Without APIs, you will have to build complex mechanics to get data in and out of the warehouse system.

- **Hybrid Integration Support:** Cloud-to-cloud integration is relatively easy because the chances are high that both source and target support the standard cloud technologies like Representational State Transfer (ReST) and JavaScript Object Notation (JSON). Hybrid integration is about the ability to integrate the cloud services with on-premises systems. Many on-premises systems still do not have APIs and need to rely on methods like File Transfer Protocol (FTP), Structured Query Language (SQL), flat files, email, Java Message Service (JMS), and Message Queuing (MQ). To assess the ease of integration with on-premises systems make sure to compile a list of current integrations in place and technologies used to realize these integrations.

- **Self-Service:** A digital experience that allows you to discover, learn, and try on your own can expedite prototyping and evaluation. Any high touch service that requires engaging with sales and technical teams may not provide the detailed insight you need. Similarly, the ability to buy, activate, deactivate, and modify subscription on your own will give you immediate access to capacity, expand, change class of service, and shrink as you need instead of relying on sales and support teams.

- **Ease of Use:** There are several aspects of ease of use – ease of signing up, ease of setting up and configuring the service, and easy of operating the service. For example, if the sign up process for each user is lengthy, requiring them to fill out many details, it will distract the users. A simple sign up process that starts with the bare minimum details and gives the flexibility to finish rest of the details later is a better approach. For example, LinkedIn allows you to sign up without filling out all the details about education and work history. It has reminders inserted in various places keeping you aware of addition information you need to enter but they are optional and only enforced when you want to perform a specific action that needs this information.

- **Configurable:** In case of Commercial Off The Shelf (COTS) software, enterprises had the ability to customize the software to suit their business processes and needs. In cloud, the systems are closed and provide no access to the internal structure and code. Further, the code for all customers and subscribers is exactly the same. Some providers may offer the ability to run on one or two back level version. The only access available is through the browser or APIs. It is, therefore, crucial that you select a solution that best fits your enterprise need with minimum changes. According to Hestermann (2014), *"Instead of customizing the solution until all users feel satisfied, every user should be willing to accept the best practices built into the solution."* However, you cannot completely ignore the need to configure business processes, terminologies, user interface layout, reports, validation rules, etc. These configuration changes must be easily upgradable without loss of data or having to reconfigure them.

Additional Considerations

Apart from the above evaluation criterion, the desire to avoid vendor lock-in and spread the risk across multiple service providers introduces additional considerations e.g.

- **Learning Curve:** The developers working with IaaS or PaaS services from more than one provider will encounter provider specific interface and processes to order, provision, configure and access these resources. This, in turn, will increase the developers' learning curve.
- **Service Management:** The IT operations team will have to deal with cloud provider specific monitoring systems and dashboards in addition to the ones used for on-premises.
  - The IT operations cost will go up with higher staffing needs to monitor across on-premises and various cloud providers.
  - The added complexity might negatively impact the ability of the operations team to act in a timely manner. This, in turn, will impact the availability and quality of services.
  - The threshold and alerting policies and remediation actions across these environments have the risk of being inconsistent. This will introduce variations in the Service Management processes further impacting availability and quality.
  - The developers would also want to reduce the time spent on manual activities through automation.
- **Governance:** The providers will have limited ability to enforce an enterprise's policies. As a result, developers can wind up ordering resources that may not be in compliance with the policies (e.g. order a plan which offers significantly discounted charges but comes with an expensive long-term commitment than a plan with higher charges but no commitment).
- **Cost Control:** The executives responsible for managing the IT spending will need to rely on manual aggregation and analysis of charges from multiple sources.
  - The executives want the ability to monitor the aggregate IT spend and assess how migrating to cloud is helping in reducing the overall expenditure.
  - They also want a breakdown by provider so they can maximize the spending with the strategic providers as opposed to the tactical ones.

Cloud Service Broker

This is where Cloud Service Broker (CSB) comes into the picture to help mitigate all the issues and challenges discussed above. Before diving into the details, let us look at the definition of CSB. Gartner (n.d.) defines CSB as

An IT role and business model in which a company or other entity adds value to one or more (public or private) cloud services on behalf of one or more consumers of that service via three primary roles including aggregation, integration and customization brokerage. A CSB enabler provides technology to implement CSB, and a CSB provider offers combined technology, people and methodologies to implement and manage CSB-related projects.

Markets and Markets (2015) defines CSB as one that

...serves as an intermediary between the CSPs [Cloud Service Provider] and cloud service consumers. CSB helps organizations by aggregating multiple cloud services ... CSB helps customer by consulting and recommending the best fit cloud services according to their business need by presenting them a short list of recommended CSPs to choose their service(s). Cloud brokers may be granted rights to negotiate with different service providers on behalf of their customers.

CSBs offer various capabilities that can help streamline an enterprise's journey to cloud. Let us understand these in detail to see how they can help. While every CSB will not offer all the capabilities listed below, you will need to factor capabilities that are important for you in your CSB evaluation and selection.

- **Search and Discover:** In order for a CSB to be an intermediary and recommend the best fit, it needs a rich ecosystem of cloud services that cover a wide variety of domains and industry verticals from many providers. Unfortunately this is one area where CSB has not matured yet. Unlike airline, hotel, and car reservations, there are no brokerage marketplaces that can provide a rich selection of cloud services. There are two ways to overcome this. One option is to setup your own private brokerage. There are many providers in this space e.g. BMC, HP, IBM's Gravitant, Parallels, Redhat, RightScale, and Scalr. Some sell the software and offer services to set it up while others offer this as-a-service which comes with software and fully managed service to on-board services from multiple providers into CSB, build reusable patterns, integrate them, setup governance, aggregate billing, aggregate service management as so on. For large enterprises, the central IT can play the role of an internal broker by creating an ecosystem of cloud services from various service providers. However, this will require significant investment of time and money.
  - Second option is to research on ones own to find services. A wide variety of SaaS applications are available in the market like Salesforce, Workday, SAP, NetSuite, Marketo, Cornerstone, Constant Contact, DocuSign, IBM Verse, IBM Blueworks Live, and IBM Watson Analytics. These cater to various domains like Customer Relationship Management (CRM), ERP, Human Resources Management (HRM), and Financial Accounting. These can be easily found on the web. Another source for finding services is through research and consulting firms e.g. Montclare. It produces SaaS 250 and SaaS 1,000 reports which identify the 250 and 1,000 most influential SaaS companies in the world respectively (http://www. montclare.com). There are several service provider owned marketplaces that showcase their services and ones from their partners e.g. Azure (http://azure.microsoft.com), IBM Cloud Marketplace (https://www.ibm.com/marketplace/cloud/us/en-us), Amazon Web Services

Figure 9. Cloud service broker capabilities

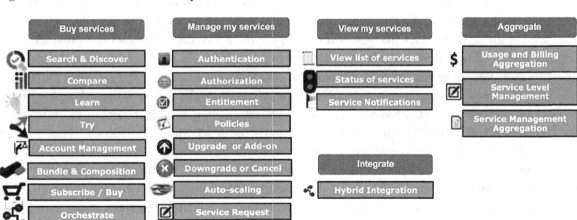

(AWS) Marketplace (http://aws.amazon.com/), and Google Compute (http://cloud.google.com).

- **Account Management:** One of the key paradigm shifts "born in the cloud" services bring is self-service. The entire sales and engagement cycle is shifting from high contact sales to consumers directly signing up for services. This introduces two issues. One, managing multiple accounts and keeping track of who has access to which accounts is a completely manual process. A central system to manage registrations with the providers will streamline this process. Second, without a central management system you run the risk of multiple accounts for the same service when it is not desired. For one of my clients, every sales team went on their own and signed up for the same SaaS service and they ended up with over 50 small and independent contracts. A centralized system would have given visibility to existing relationships and allowed other teams to extend the relationship to onboard additional teams. You not only have leverage for better pricing structure with a larger contract but you also have only one relationship team to deal with from the service provider. RightScale (n.d. a), for example, provides a hierarchical account structure that "lets you control on a granular level which users have access to which cloud accounts."

- **Bundle and Composition:** Bundling is a way to cluster two or more services primarily for cost efficiency. Bundles are a way to communicate to the enterprise users the savings from the bundle so they can make an informed decision before buying. Compositions, on the other hand, are also a form of bundling but are primarily to describe a deployment pattern of services. For example, in the beginning of the dot-com era many enterprises were deploying Linux, Apache Web Server, MySQL Database, and PHP for their web applications. This became a standard pattern and is widely known as the LAMP stack. You can create a composition to provision this entire stack with one click instead provisioning each of the components separately. Further, a CSB may support such a pattern that crosses multiple cloud service providers e.g. a database server from SoftLayer and application servers from AWS. A more modern equivalent is a MEAN stack (MongoDB, Express, AngularJS, and Node.js). With Gravitant's brokerage software, for example, you can "*combine the infrastructure requirements, application stack, and configuration details into a single container*" (Gravitant, n.d. b). Such pattern-based compositions have two key advantages. First, it can considerably speed up the provisioning of the entire stack compared to provisioning of one component at a time. Second, it enables consistent reuse of tried, tested, and approved architectures instead of everyone inventing his or her own. Such reuse will reduce governance overhead and ensure the systems are compliant with the enterprise's architecture, security requirements, and policies.

- **Subscribe and Buy:** A CSB can simplify the entire subscription and buy process through a single pane of glass. Without a CSB, you will have to use the interfaces of each service provider to order the services. A CSB may also provide the ability to define workflows to manage the approval processes tied to the subscription of bundles or compositions. For example, AddDirect allows you to "*subscribe to the applications you need and easily manage their subscriptions though a single, secure self-service portal. You can customize each subscription as needed, upgrading, purchasing additional seats, tracking usage, and more*" (AppDirect, n.d.). Similarly, with Gravitant you can "*manage multiple provider offerings through a robust IT-as-a-Service catalog, which can be complemented with your own pre-designed, complete, and compliant solutions*" (Gravitant, n.d. a).

- **Orchestration:** Orchestration extends the benefits of defining and subscribing to bundles and compositions to control and coordinate the fulfillment of the subscription request across all the services providers. In the above example, the orchestration engine will coordinate the order in which the subscriptions need to be sent between the provider of database service and the provider of the web server service. It will also take care of invoking any automation script to automatically configure the web servers and point them to the database server. Such automation can significantly increase the speed to market for the entire lifecycle – development, testing, staging and production. The days of developers waiting for machines to start even simple experiments are numbered. Enterprises will be able to quickly instantiate services, do their experiments, and finally destroy these services when they are done with their experiments.

- **Authentication:** Similar to how the authentication went out of control with traditional IT with each system having its own set of ID and password, moving to cloud introduces the same risk. You will end up with various different forms of authentication from different providers. CSB can provide capabilities to integration with your enterprise single sign on to the authentication mechanism of various cloud services. CSB can also provide capabilities like centrally storing encrypted credentials, repository to store SSH keys, etc. For end users who are dealing with multiple devices these days – laptop, tablets, and smartphones – this can help reduce their frustration and lower the helpdesk's cost of dealing with IDs and password resets.

- **Authorization:** Authorization primarily deals with what modules and functions the user has access to e.g. are you allowed to create purchase orders, are you allowed to approve requests, and are you allowed to update list price. Employees within an enterprise often move and change roles. Keeping track of their privileges across various cloud services will be a challenge. Similar to authentication, a centralized control to manage authorization will be critical.

- **Entitlement:** While authorization deals with functions and features you have access to, entitlement deals with the resource dimensions within the functions and features e.g. it is not sufficient to control whether you are allowed to approve a request, are you allowed to approve a request greater than $10,000. Most traditional IT systems have very limited entitlement checks implemented or the checks are done manually through gates in the process. These traditional methods of entitlement verification will not work in the fast paced cloud environment. Further, defining entitlement rules within each cloud service can lead to high maintenance overhead. A CSB can enable cost control through centralize entitlement rules for infrastructure, middleware, and storage type services. Further, it can simplify the procurement process by enforcing entitlement rules e.g. you cannot order additional VMs if you exceed your quota of $5,000 per month.

- **Policies:** A policy engine takes the access, authorization, and entitlement capabilities to the next level. It parses data and analytics and compares against the policies to automate governance, compliance, and security. For example, a user might be authorized to provision VMs and entitled to provision them in all regions and may not have any dollar limit. However, the enterprise may have a policy not to deploy VMs for production in United States because the datacenter may not meet the European Union's privacy requirements. A CSB's policy engine will take this policy into consideration and either not offer the choice of selecting a region in United States for production VMs or it may detect a violation and trigger follow-on actions to bring the environment back to compliance.

- **Upgrade or Add-On:** There are many instances where a service may offer add-on capabilities depending upon some base service you have subscribed to. For example, an infrastructure service may offer monitoring and security services. If you did not subscribed to these services initially, you will need the ability to subscribe to them in future through the CSB instead of going back to each provider to sign-up or even to learn that these add-ons exists. Similarly, you may have opted for a lower tier of service. If your organization's needs change, you should be able to upgrade to a higher tier of service through the CSB.

- **Downgrade or Cancel:** Similar to the upgrade or add-on, you should be able to downgrade your service and even cancel through the CSB.
- **Auto-Scaling:** Elastic computing is one of the biggest benefits of virtualization. It offers the ability to grow and shrink on-demand automatically. Unfortunately not every cloud service offers the ability to scale up and down automatically. Further, even if the service offers some elasticity, it may be workload driven; it might only look at up/down status or fixed parameters like day of the week or time of the day. A CSB can help with a central management of auto-scaling configuration and policies. Further, a CSB may have its own set of proxy scaling capability to augment the capabilities of the underlying cloud service providers.
- **Service Request:** Traditionally, Service Request is a ticket process that LOBs and IT teams have used to submit requests for IT resources. The self-service paradigm in cloud will significantly reduce the need to manually create tickets and will automate fulfillment of the requests. Only complex requests like advise, architecture support, best practice guidance, and API support will require manual ticket processing. A single pane of glass to submit the requests, track status, and view responses will provide clear visibility and reduce confusion.
- **View List of Services, Status of Services, and Service Notifications:** Central IT has struggled with tracking the usage, state, relationships, ownership etc. of IT resources or Configuration Items (CIs) within the enterprise. The challenge is going to get even bigger with hundreds of virtualized resources being created and destroyed on a daily basis or even hourly. The traditional Configuration Management Database (CMDB), which relies on a single physical database to track all CIs, is not going to be suitable for this new paradigm. The future CMDB will be logical and real time federation of information for a wide variety of resources. Unlike traditional data center where after a server is built, only some paper trail or monitoring dashboard knows the existence of the server, the new cloud services offer an up-to-date dashboard of all instances. For example, infrastructure service providers have a dashboard or portal showing all VMs and its status. A CSB can provide a federated dashboard showing all services you have subscribed, all instances of infrastructure and applications, their statuses, and any notifications associated with the services or the instances.
- **Usage and Billing Aggregation:** According to a CEB CIO Leadership Council (2014d) survey, IT cost is under scrutiny for most companies but they are ill equipped to manage it efficiently. Most CSBs offer capabilities to aggregate usage and cost information across service providers. Further, the ability to slice and dice the usage by provider, by type of services, by LOBs etc. can provider great insight into areas that have high spending. This insight can help narrow the focus on high cost areas and look for alternatives.
- **Service Level Management Aggregation:** The ease of consumption of the cloud services and diverse range of niche providers will dramatically increase the number of service providers you will need to deal with. Having visibility to how these services are performing against the promised service level agreements is not going to be easy. A CSB can help track and aggregate service level data from multiple service providers. It can also become a single pane of glass for accountability and control. The ability to reconcile the service level data against the invoice can help uncover any missing credits or discounts. Finally, the ability to compare the performance of multiple providers against the service level will give you the ability to demand better service quality or better price.

- **Service Management Aggregation:** This is potentially the most important aspect of a CSB. In an in-house data center where all IT resources are within your control and you have the ability to standardize on service management tools like monitoring, event correlation, dashboard, remediation, and ticketing. With cloud, you do not own the resources and also have very limited architectural control over them. This is both good and bad. On one hand, in a SaaS example, you do not have to worry about infrastructure and software while you lose visibility of failures. You no longer have a monitoring system that generates a ticket that your IT operations team is watching. The IT operations team will have to watch multiple status pages to keep track of status. A CSB can aggregate this information to improve the visibility and control. Monitoring service status is just one example of Service Management aggregation. The same would apply to network performance, application response time, backup status, batch job status etc.

- **Hybrid Integration:** Apart from aggregating various forms of data discussed earlier, integration with existing service management, compliance, release management, and disaster recovery systems is crucial specially when dealing with IaaS and PaaS. In these cases, the cloud service provider does not monitor above the virtualization layer. You will still be responsible for monitoring your VMs, middleware instances, and applications running on those. In order to integrate monitoring into your correlation engine or ticketing tool you will have to build your own integration using the APIs provide by the cloud service provider. A CSB can help simplify this with abstract API and hide the multi-cloud complexity. RightScale, for example, provides the ability to *"tie together operational data by hooking into and integrating cloud data for systems monitoring, application monitoring, logging, and SIEM [Security Information and Event Management] tools"* (RightScale, n.d. a)

Build Prototype

Now that we have covered Cloud Service Broker in detail, let us continue to our next step: to build the prototype. There are going to be many choices to solve the pain points identified during the exploration phase. The cloud computing services in the market are typically categorized into IaaS, PaaS, and SaaS.

In an IaaS or PaaS, the service provider is only responsible for the Service Level of the infrastructure or the platform layer respectively. You, as the consumer, will be responsible for the Service Level of the software or applications you build or install on top of the IaaS or PaaS. In other words, you will be responsible for monitoring, patching, upgrading, backing up, troubleshooting, and remediating the application layer. Figure 10 illustrates how the responsibilities for various Service Management functions will shift. Similar transformation will happen in other process domains like compliance, release management, disaster recovery etc. One of the most obvious challenges of taking this approach is how to manage the IT resources across on-premises and various cloud service providers. An enterprise can end up with a development system for a component on AWS, a training system for another might be more suitable to host in SoftLayer, and a mission critical application running on-premises.

A SaaS application, therefore, is an attractive first choice to implement all your ideas. A SaaS first approach will allow you to focus on your core business expertise instead of worrying about complex IT issues. With SaaS, the service provider completely manages the Service Level e.g. monitoring to ensure the service is up and running, redundancy for high availability, scaling up and down to meet the performance levels, patching underlying Operating System (OS) and middleware, backing up the configuration and data to ensure recoverability and so on. As a consumer, you consume the service as a

Figure 10. Cloud computing model and service management

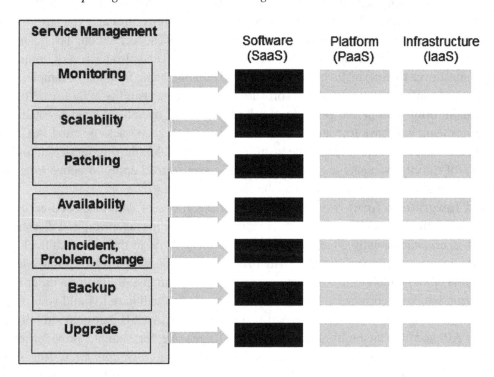

black box and pay for your usage of the service. However, do not underestimate the challenges of deploying a SaaS based solution. A CEB CIO Leadership Council (2014b) survey of 68 member institutions found that security, migration challenges, integration challenges, and regulatory were amongst the top barriers for SaaS adoption.

SaaS can greatly simplify implementation, reduce effort, and reduce the time to market, and reduce the time to implementation. However, you can realize these benefits only when the SaaS application is standalone or needs to be integrated with other SaaS applications. Applications within an enterprise are integrated with many applications. In my experience, each application on an average has 3-4 integrations. When you migrate one of those applications to SaaS, integrating them back to the remaining applications on-premises is complex. This is because you need to take into account connectivity, performance, data mapping, data cleansing, customization or extension to existing applications, and so on.

Let us consider few different scenarios to demonstrate how your prototype phase might look different based on the type of problem you are trying to solve.

- **Scenario 1:** The primary pain point of the current business application is capacity and availability. Your prototyping options could look like the following:
  - Evaluate IaaS services and simulate load to see if the infrastructure can scale up and down. Measure how quickly the service responds to changes in demand and improvement in expected user experience.

- ○ If your current business application is based on middleware technologies for which relevant PaaS services are available, this could be a better alternative. As this will reduce your overhead to monitor and patch the middleware layer.
- ○ Finally, if your business application is based on COTS and the software vendor now offers the same software as SaaS, before diving into function feature comparison first evaluate whether the SaaS version can handle your current workload. Often teams make the mistake to dive into function and feature comparison and forget about the reason for the assessment. The vendor might be in early stages of building its SaaS offering and may not be targeting enterprise your size. Hence, it is important that you first focus the evaluation on the capacity and availability. Once you are comfortable that it can meet your needs, then identify the customizations you have made to the COTS for your environment. As explained earlier, focus on embracing the best practices in the SaaS instead of discarding the SaaS option purely because your current requirements cannot be met with the SaaS.

- **Scenario 2:** The primary pain point of the current business application is speed and agility with which new requirements are implemented. Your prototyping options could look like the following:
  - ○ The reason for lack of speed and agility could be that the development team is still using waterfall software development life cycle (SDLC) method and relies on heavy planning and documentation. In such a case, embracing agile development method will bring speed and agility. This is not to suggest that you should not be looking at automation tools, but process, people and culture changes are as important as technology in solving problems.
  - ○ Evaluate devOps tools for the whole lifecycle:
    - **Development:** Version control tool for developers to manage code and other artifacts.
    - **Build:** Tools to automate the build process.
    - **Deploy:** Tools to deploy code into test and staging environments.
    - **Testing:** Automated testing tools to do integration testing and user acceptance testing.
    - **Release:** Tools to release the changes into the production environment.
  - ○ As described in Scenario 1, you may also want to investigate a SaaS alternative.
- **Scenario 3:** The primary pain point of the current business application could be the need for a modern platform or completely new business application for a new venture. Your prototyping options would involve multiple development platforms to find the one that best meet your needs. And it goes without saying that you need to investigate a SaaS alternative.

EVALUATE

It is highly recommended that you build the prototype iteratively instead of using a waterfall approach. Depending upon the size of your cupcake you may need several iterations to build it. Active participation of the users, throughout the process, is very important in assessing the prototype. Use the feedback from the users to prioritize other functions and features or adjust existing functions and features. In an unlikely situation where the solution does not make sense to the users or address their pain points then the solution is not worth pursuing further. You may have to go back to the Exploration stage and brainstorm other ideas or revisit the solutions that were voted out during the storyboard step.

In many cases, involvement of the cloud service providers will be critical simply because your team will not have the knowledge and skills necessary to work with the new services you are evaluating. Enterprises often make the mistake of handing over the prototype scenario to the service provider and have them build it all by themselves. Taking this approach will shut out your team from important learning about ease of setup, configurability, composability, learning curve, etc. Many times due to time pressure and the motivation to sell the providers development teams may take several shortcuts through hardcoding. Active involvement of your team with the providers' team will ensure right design choices are being made in building the prototype. If your solution involves multiple providers, make sure there is a clear understanding on ownership of who is responsible for implementing which portion.

Using the three scenarios described in the prototype phase, here are some potential outcomes of the evaluation:

- **Outcome 1:** Migrate current on-premises systems to one or more IaaS.
- **Outcome 2:** Migrate current on-premises applications to one or more PaaS.
- **Outcome 3:** Migrate current application to a SaaS.
- **Outcome 4:** Develop new applications using one or more PaaS.
- **Outcome 5:** Introduce a new SaaS application.

The subsequent sections will use these outcome scenarios to describe how to formulate, adopt and refine the transition to cloud.

FORMULATE

Once you have settled on your solution option, you need to formulate a plan for your transition. Let us look at various planning elements for the outcome scenario described in the previous section.

Outcome Scenario 1: Migrate Current On-Premises Systems to One or More IaaS

- Enterprises have many applications running on many variants of Unix operating systems like AIX, HP-UX, and Solaris etc. Not all applications in your current enterprise will seamlessly migrate to the Linux operating systems on cloud. Select the ones that are compatible and easy to migrate.
- Select highly underutilized systems like development, training and test for migration to the cloud first.
- Migrate standalone functions that are less critical compared to ones that are mission critical.
- Migrate internal applications and functions before the ones serving your external customers, partners, and vendors. This will reduce the risk of impacting your brand image or disrupting your supply chain if things were to go wrong.
- Migrate components like webservers and application servers before the database servers. The reason being: the compute functions for such components can be load balanced across several instances of virtual system. This will provide enterprises with the ability to scale up and down on-demand dynamically resulting in huge savings. The database servers in the legacy environment are mostly relational databases, which generally do not scale beyond one server. Many databases in the enterprise have grown large due to lack of archiving strategy. Therefore, leaving them on-premises initially is the best option. Once you have archived the historical data and brought it

down to a manageable shape, then consider moving it to cloud. However, care must be taken to test for any performance impact due to network latency and application's ability to tolerate this widely distributed deployment model.

Apart from application migration considerations, you will also have to plan for architectural considerations. In current datacenters it is not uncommon to find servers at varying version and patch levels of the operating systems. These servers also do not have any standard configuration. There are multiple ways to solve this with cloud. Most cloud providers let you take snapshots of your OS. You can create a new VM, install necessary middleware, and change the OS settings. A snapshot will save all this information in the form of an image. You can build an image library using this process. Scalr simplifies this process by letting you create these images on multiple clouds from the Scalr user interface (Orozco, 2014b). As per RightScale, the image approach does not work because images are too monolithic, opaque, too big, and too static (Eicken, 2010). RightScale's CSB has a feature called ServerTemplate which offers modular building blocks to manage server configuration. Scalr, too, has a similar feature called Roles where rule-based automation is applies to base image to build VMs.

If the compute needs of your workload has a lot of variability, auto scaling can significantly reduce cost. With auto scaling, the number of VMs will increase and decrease as the workload grows and shrinks. Not all providers natively support auto scaling. A CSB can enable auto scaling uniformly across providers even if they do not natively support this capability. Scalr lets you define scaling rules based on CPU load, free RAM, URL response, date and time, and network bandwidth (Orozco, 2014a). RightScale has a more sophisticated algorithm where servers vote whether to scale up or down (RightScale, n.d. c). RightScale monitors the votes and counts them to determine the action.

Outcome Scenario 2: Migrate Current On-Premises Applications to One or More PaaS

- For enterprise applications running on Unix variants, migrating to PaaS might offer a better choice. You no longer have to worry about OS compatibility issues.
- Unlike IaaS, with PaaS you cannot move just the development environment and leave the rest on-premises. All environments for a given application must maintain the same OS and middleware stack. This is because if some issue arises in production, you should be able to recreate this in your development or test environments. Further, you should be able to fix defects in the development environment, test them in the test environment, and release them into the production environment.
- If the middleware on PaaS is same as the middleware on-premises, then the migration would be the most easiest. You are primarily changing the hosting location. Majority of the work would be around connectivity and testing.
- If the middleware on PaaS is a newer version of the middleware on-premises, then it would be better to upgrade the on-premises version first. If you migrate and upgrade both at the same time, it will be difficult for you to isolate and troubleshoot any issue you might encounter.
- If the middleware on PaaS is a completely new middleware, then migration may involve rewriting some portions, extracting and importing data, and testing. This is going to be the most complex of the two options above.

Outcome Scenario 3: Migrate Current Application to a SaaS

- Migrating from an on-premises application to SaaS can eliminate many technical complexities of dealing with the OS and middleware incompatibility issues.
- If your on-premises application is now available as SaaS, the chances are that the vendor will provide some utility to make the migration easier.
- If you are migrating to an application from another vendor – you will have two major areas of work:
  - **Configuring the New System:** As described earlier, most enterprises make the mistake of configuring the new system to satisfy all users. The configuration of the system might go out of hand and increase the on-going maintenance cost.
  - **Transforming Data from Current System to the Target System:** In many cases, trying to migrate transactional data is cost prohibitive due to differences in data structure, validation rules, and processing logic. You will still need to transform the master data. Master data are supporting data necessary to create transactions e.g. employees, customers, suppliers, products, parts, and locations details. While at surface it sounds easy to migrate this data – often, poor data governance leads to poor quality, duplication, and incomplete data. You may have to do data cleansing to address these issues before you can load them in the new system. Further, the structure and type mismatch may introduce additional work. For example, if you current product code is alphanumeric but the new system only allows numeric, you will have to find a new numbering scheme.

Outcome Scenario 4: Develop New Applications using One or More PaaS

You may conclude that you will need to invest in building a new application using one or more PaaS. This approach will enable enterprises to experiment with modern technology platforms and deliver a more contemporary experience to its users. You will be able to build an application that can be accessible from multiple devices like desktop, laptop, tablet, and smartphone without coding a separate interface for each device.

Do not think of PaaS as simply middleware softare on IaaS. PaaS address issues like scalability and reliability and utilize new generation of software designed with cloud in mind. Unlike a relational database, simply by adding more database servers to the cluster can scale out a NoSQL database. The applications see the distributed database as a single database. A PaaS can abstract the underlying architecture to deliver your non-functional requirements and you only need to manage at the application layer.

Outcome Scenario 5: Introduce a New SaaS Application

There will be many situations where you are automating your current manual process with a SaaS offering. For example, you enterprise may have significantly grown and you need to automate the collaboration process of your finance department. When introducing automation for a completely new area, unlike a COTS, the key advantage of SaaS is that you are not locked-in any long-term commitments. It is recommended that you do a small pilot with a small number of users and a subset of your process before extending it to the entire team.

IMPLEMENT

In this phase you implement the ideas you have formulated. This is the most difficult phase. Depending upon the size of your transformation, it can be overwhelming. Agile methodology can help make this process less stressful. Agile is not just about software development, as many mistakenly believe. Let us look at one scenario where you have 100 highly underutilized development, training and test systems that you need to migrate to the cloud. Most enterprises would build one detailed project plan to migrate all 100 systems, identify all tasks the teams have to perform, the timeline, and the risks. Further, most of the teams e.g. system administrators, middleware administrators, application administrators work in silos for large enterprises. So hand-offs and coordination introduce risks and delays. Let us see how you would accomplish this with Agile. A detailed explanation of Agile is outside the scope of this book. There are many resources available online.

- First, you divide the 100 systems into different applications and environments. Now you could be looking at 40 different application environments you need to migrate instead of 100 systems. This is your product backlog – things you need to get done.
- Next, identify the skills needed to migrate the first environment. Create a single cross functional team with those skills to eliminate the hand-offs and coordination. The team members need to collaborate with each other directly. A co-located team is ideal. If they are not co-located, then can collaborate using audio, web, or video conferencing tools as appropriate. An ideal team size is less than 10.
- For the first environment, have the team collectively identify tasks to perform the migration. Often, teams make the mistake of trying to be perfect and try to foresee all types of problems they will encounter and build all kinds of contingencies in the plan. With agile, if you have 60% of your tasks identified, it is a good enough start. You can add tasks as you learn and discover. Further these tasks need to be at the right level of granularity. Do not define tasks that range from 1 hour to 5 days. Gathering status for fine-grained tasks is time consuming because you have too many things to check off. Similarly, keeping track of coarse-grained tasks is risky because team members often lose focus or get dragged into other things because there is "enough" time. It is best to stay at a granularity of tasks that can be accomplished in 4 or 8 hours by each team member. This way you find out sooner if there is a problem and gathering status is just a checkmark everyday against the tasks that were due.
- For a typical small development environment 2 weeks are likely to be sufficient to migrate the environment unless you have some complex software installation and configuration procedures to deal with. Start with 2 weeks as your time-box or Sprint to migrate each environment. As you get more experienced, you might start doing 2 or more environments in the same 2-week period.
- Now that your team has the tasks identified, they can start executing them. The team members are expected to collaborate together throughout the day as needed.
- One of the most important elements of Agile is a daily checkpoint or Daily Scrum. The entire team must meet everyday (in a physical or a virtual room) at the same time for 20 minutes. During these 20 minutes, each team member would go around and answer three questions – 1) What did I do yesterday 2) What will I do today and 3) What are my impediments. The purpose of this meeting is a quick checkpoint for the entire team to have visibility of status and for the entire team to be aware of any roadblocks. The meeting is not to solve any of the problems or go into long discus-

sion. It is likely that another team member may have an answer or know who can help. Keeping the meeting time-boxed to 20 minutes is critical for the team to get into the habit of only answering those 3 questions. Spending too much time on a topic will not give others the opportunity to share. Extending the meeting longer will waste time of others who may not care about the details. Any broader team discussion needs to be in a working session and kept outside of the Daily Scrum.

- Make sure the team is getting help in removing the impediments in order to keep the momentum of the daily tasks.
- At the end of the 2-week period or Sprint, the team should plan for a playback or a demo. This is to demonstrate the end results to the stakeholders to confirm that they accomplished the goals.
- Finally, the team should also internally meet to retrospect what went well and what went wrong. The team, as a whole, should also discuss and agree on how to overcome things that went wrong.

This approach will allow you to handle the whole migration in small chunks, lower the risk, and be more repeatable as you gain experience. If you are dealing with vastly different kinds of applications that need different skills, you may need to revisit the team composition and replace team members with more appropriate ones or form migration teams to deal with these differences e.g. one to deal with finance applications and another to deal with sales and marketing.

REFINE

This needs to be an ongoing activity in your environment. Implement regular lesson sharing mechanism e.g. wiki or discussion forum where teams share what's working and what's not working. During initial phases, have the teams meet once a week session to discuss their hurdles and think through options to resolve them. As things settle down, these sessions can be held once a month. This may require you to revisit the decisions made in exploration, prototyping, evaluation, and formulation phases. The advantage of using the approach described here is the ease with which you can make corrections to implementation plan without investing a lot of time recreating project plans and documents.

For example, during implementation you may experience that the IaaS service provider you selected is not able to meet your expectations. Using the approach described here you will uncover sooner rather than later. Instead of investing in weeks and months of planning, you would have only spent hours and days. The cost of rework will be much less too. Hopefully, you will discover the issues during your first 2-3 iterations of implementation.

CONCLUSION

In conclusion, your transition to the cloud needs to be well planned – technology like Cloud Service Broker is only one part of the picture. Inclusion of Line of Business users, understanding their pain point, iterating through solution options to make sure they address the pain points, prototyping the solutions, carefully evaluating the outcomes of these prototypes, formulating a plan to adopt the solution, using iterations to implement the solution, and finally a good feedback mechanism for ongoing improvement are all equally important. Implementing such a structure requires change in mindset and culture, which are not easy. There will be some failures and hiccups initially. However, do not let that deter you from the approach. Use the failures as learning opportunities. Do not aim for perfection – aim for execution.

REFERENCES

Anderson, E., & Mazzucca, J. (2015, February 18). *Survey Analysis: Cloud Adoption Across Vertical Industries Exhibits More Similarities Than Differences*. Gartner, Report number G00271486.

AppDirect. (n.d.). *Application Manager*. Retrieved from http://info.appdirect.com/products/appdirect-monetization-suite/marketplace-management-service/application-manager

CEB CIO Leadership Council. (2014a, August 21). *How to Promote IT's Climate of Openness*. CEB. Retrieved from https://www.executiveboard.com/member/applications/events/replays/14/how-to-promote-it-s-climate-of-openness.html?referrerTitle=Replays%20-%20CEB%20Applications%20Leadership%20 Council accessed on Sep, 19 2015

CEB CIO Leadership Council. (2014b, November 5). *The State of Enterprise SaaS Adoption*. CEB. Retrieved from https://www.executiveboard.com/member/applications/research/report/14/the-state-of-enterprise-saas-adoption.html?referrerTitle=Report%20-%20CEB%20Applications%20Leadership%20 Council

CEB CIO Leadership Council. (2014c, November 10). *Making Shadow IT Work for You*. CEB. Retrieved from https://www.executiveboard.com/member/applications/events/replays/14/making-shadow-it-work-for-you.html.html

CEB CIO Leadership Council. (2014d, December 23). *IT Cost Management Playbook*. CEB. Retrieved from https://www.executiveboard.com/member/finance-leadership/decision_supportcenter/it-cost-management-playbook.html

Decker, V. E. J. & Iervolino, C. (2015, August 18). *Critical CFO Technology Needs: 2015 Gartner FEI Study*. Gartner. Gartner Report number G00280250.

Fiscutean, A. (2015, August 12). *50 years and still going strong: Will we ever be ready to kill off CO-BOL?* ZDnet.com. Retrieved from http://www.zdnet.com/article/50-years-and-still-going-strong-will-we-ever-be-ready-to-kill-off-cobol/

Gartner. (n.d.). *IT Glossary*. Retrieved from http://www.gartner.com/it-glossary/cloud-services-brokerage-csb

Geier, B. (2015, March 11). *Apple's App Store outage is costing millions*. Retrieved from http://fortune.com/2015/03/11/app-store-apple-outage/

Gravitant. (n.d.a). *cloudMatrix 'IT Approved' Marketplace*. Retrieved from http://resources.gravitant.com/videos/cloudmatrix-approved-marketplace/

Gravitant. (n.d.b). *cloudMatrix Solution Blueprints*. Retrieved from http://resources.gravitant.com/videos/cloudmatrix-solution-blueprints/

Hestermann, C. (2014, July 8). *Define Your Customization Strategy for SaaS/ Cloud Business Applications*. Gartner. Report Number G00261452.

IBM. (n.d.a). *What is Cloud Computing?* Retrieved from http://www.ibm.com/cloud-computing/us/en/what-is-cloud-computing.html

IBM. (n.d.b). *IBM Designcamp*. Unpublished internal document. *IBM*.

Kelly, S. M. (2015, May 21). *Apple restores iCloud after outage impacts 200 million people.* Retrieved from http://mashable.com/2015/05/21/apple-icloud-down-some-users/

Markets and Markets. (2015, Jun 22). *Cloud Service Brokerage Market - Global Analysis & Forecast to 2020*. Author.

Ng, F., Anderson, E., & Anderson, D. S. (2015, Jan 13). *Cloud Service Providers Must Understand Deployment, Adoption and Buyer Complexity to Leverage Cloud Revenue Opportunities*. Gartner. Report number G00271022.

Normal, D. (n.d.). *Rethinking Design Thinking*. Retrieved from http://www.jnd.org/dn.mss/rethinking_design_th.html

Orozco, T. (2014a, June 12). *Scaling Metrics*. Scalr. Retrieved from https://scalr-wiki.atlassian.net/wiki/display/docs/Scaling+Metrics

Orozco, T. (2014b, November 6). *Roles and Images*. Scalr. Retrieved from https://scalr-wiki.atlassian.net/wiki/display/docs/Roles+and+Images

RightScale. (n.d.a). *API & Integrations*. Retrieved from http://www.rightscale.com/products-and-services/multi-cloud-platform/on-demand-architecture/cloud-api-and-integration

RightScale. (n.d.b). *Technical Overview*. RightScale. Retrieved from http://assets.rightscale.com/uploads/pdfs/RightScale-Technical-overview.pdf

RightScale. (n.d.c). Retrieved from http://support.rightscale.com/03-Tutorials/02-AWS/02-Website_Edition/How_do_I_set_up_Autoscaling%3F/index.html

Scuitto, J. (2015, July 10). *OPM government data breach impacted 21.5 million*. Retrieved from http://www.cnn.com/2015/07/09/politics/office-of-personnel-management-data-breach-20-million/

Terhune, C. (2015, February 5). *Anthem hack exposes data on 80 million; experts warn of identity theft*. Retrieved from http://www.latimes.com/business/la-fi-anthem-hacked-20150204-story.html

von Eicken, T. (2010, March 22). *RightScale Server Templates Explained*. RightScale. Retrieved from http://www.rightscale.com/blog/cloud-management-best-practices/rightscale-servertemplates-explained

KEY TERMS AND DEFINITIONS

Cloud Service Broker (CSB): It is an intermediary between the Cloud Service Providers and cloud service consumer to provide value-added services like aggregation, integration, consulting, negotiation etc.

Design Thinking: It is taking a human-centered approach to solve problems by exploring solution options to achieve extraordinary user experience.

Hybrid Cloud: Cloud systems that combine the use of private cloud infrastructure in combination with public cloud services.

IBM Design Thinking: It is IBM's approach to apply design thinking at the speed and scale the modern enterprise demands.

Lean: It is a continuous improvement process of removing "waste" within a manufacturing system. It was mostly derived from Toyota Production System. This method is now being applied in many businesses and across many processes.

Minimum Viable Product (MVP): Defining the minimum bare-bone product that would give value to the users.

Shadow IT: Describes a phenomena where Lines of Businesses (LOBs) bypass the central IT to lead technology projects and decisions.

Chapter 16
Risk and Governance Considerations in Cloud Era

Mohammad Ali Shalan
Jordan Engineers Association, Jordan

ABSTRACT

Cloud Computing (CC) has recently emerged as a compelling paradigm for managing and delivering computing services over the internet. It is rapidly changing the landscape of technology and ultimately turning the long-held promise of utility computing into a reality. Nevertheless, jumping into the cloud is never a trivial task. A special approach is required to discover and mitigate risks, also to apply controls related to the cloud jump. The main objective of this chapter is to specify some of the phenomena associated with the CC paradigm and associated business transformation. It looks at the motivations, contracting, obstacles and the agile project rollout methodologies. It then provides an in-depth analysis for the allied risks and governance directions. CC governance is being more crucial as the CC paradigm is still evolving. In this context, this chapter build few bricks toward a full Cloud Computing Risk and Governance Framework (CCRGF).

INTRODUCTION

Cloud Computing (CC) is increasingly asserted as the technology with the potential to change the way internet and information systems are being utilized into Client Enterprises (CEs). Cloud has emerged as a growing trend of scalable, flexible and powerful computing. Consequently, it is capable of introducing a paradigm shift in how technology is delivering value to the business. With significant global investments, Cloud Computing (CC) is showing the power to completely revolutionize the business mindset and promotes new business characteristics. On-demand services, shared computing resources, rapid provisioning and minimal intervention activities are just few trends to mention.

Cloud benefits are not coming hassle free, several risks, security concerns, contracting and compliance issues are surrounding the cloud models. The abridged availability of critical business processes, compromised confidentiality and reduced integrity are side effects of the CC utilizations. This is not surprising, since the concept of secure surrounding perimeter has been vanished by users and services

DOI: 10.4018/978-1-5225-0759-8.ch016

being more mobile. Internal or external service providers are introduced as a Middle Circle Contractors (MCCs) in the middle of the CC services. Additional substantially considerable effects exist due to moving company's key applications and certain corporate information to the cloud. More challenge raised because the adoption of cloud computing applications might begin outside the Technology Organization (TO), causing plenty of loose activities and associations.

This chapter aims to portray a picture for risk and compliance issues related to CC and to emphasize governance as a mechanism to orchestrate such a heterogeneous environment. Governance can set the rules and responsibilities, lead the way to uphold the cloud phenomena and manage the associated risks in a reliable and trustworthy way. This chapter will devote to invert the question facing the Chief Information Officer (CIO) when approaching the board to ask for a Governance, Risk and Compliance (GRC) implementation. Usually the CIO will be asked "how much it will cost, and what are the benefits?". Conversely, the right question in the cloud era should be "how much it will cost if we don't have a GRC practice, and what are the consequences?".

The chapter insight is putting risk and governance in the heart, while providing highly valuable experience to those looking for guidance to move their business infrastructure, processes and applications into the cloud. As a first step we aim to define cloud concepts and separate the potentially significant business benefits and threats, from the hype and hyperbole that are surrounding. This will increase navigation clarity through the fear, uncertainty and doubt. The native questions about the CE readiness for CC adoption are answered in a structured and systematic approach. One lesson learned from governance is that realizing value from new services requires a mature organization that can recognize associated benefits, set controls and own the relevant tools to measure. Because the cloud services are not yet mature, technology controls that exist today may be stretched or distressed if applied to the cloud and may be unable to cope with the demands placed on it. This chapter argued that new methodologies and mechanisms to control various cloud aspects need to be redesigned considering the associated risks and trends.

This chapter provides evidence-based insights into the CC benefits and challenges. Associated trends of elasticity, business transformation and value proposition are also conferred. The length and design of this chapter precludes extensive treatment of each area, consequently it appeals for both academics and practitioners. It highlights some key concepts and best practices to help smoothing the CC transition, the afterwards operation and the continuous enhancements. The main objective of this chapter is to highlight the risk and governance transformations in the cloud era and to provide real-world projections and effects. Notably, this chapter aims to help CEs rollout the CC projects, manage associated contracts smoothly and effectively follow the constructive trends including the agile methodologies.

BACKGROUND

Cloud Computing (CC) represents the network of business platforms (Baya, Mathaisel & Parker, 2010) as a new way to conceptualize and manage the integration between business and technology. There is no universal way to measure technology alignment with business (HBR, 2011; De Haes & Grembergen, 2009). Four major focusses can be identified in literature, those are technology transformation, governance, risk management and cloud computing, all are evolving with plenty of research dedicated to each topic individually or bi-combined with another (Aven, 2008; Ackermann, 2012; Goranson, 1999). Everyone comprehends these topics, but limited Client Enterprises (CEs) are doing all of it. The research correlating the four topics jointly are maturing. Risk and governance are gaining more space to reshape the cloud era.

With the business domains are reshaped significantly by CC and Technology Transformations (TTs), People should deliberate technology risks rather that IT risks (Menken & Blokdijk, 2008). The technology is involved in all business aspects within the CE and in not limited to its information. Usually we used to say that technology must support business strategy, nowadays, there are times when technology is leading us into the next realm of the previously unthinkable (Vice, 2015). Technology leadership is obvious today with many CEs establishing technology as the core of their operations (Turban, Leidner, McLean & Wetherbe, 2008).

Researchers agree that CEs are facing a continuously changing business environment including complex set of rules and regulations. This ignite multi-level cooperation to establish a governance model for CEs. Also there is an agreement that CC is here to stay and grow (Shawish & Salama, 2014). The movement towards cloud adoption is in line with the global trend of moving from product procurement to service procurement (Shelton, 2013). CC offers distributed utility driven, on-demand self-services which are location independent utilizing the elastic, pay-for-use, zero capex, zero ownership computing (Metheny, 2013). With such emphasis on CC future, board members are being directly accountable for technology behaviors in their CEs. They require strong CC governance in analogy to their responsibility for enterprise objectives and key assets (Hardy, 2006). With such speedy progressing and emerging, it becomes crucial to understand all aspects about the cloud associated technologies (Jayaswal, Kallakurchi, Houde & Shah, 2014).

Cloud chaos is everywhere; everyone is asking: What is a cloud service? Why do I need to move to the cloud? What is a service lifecycle? Who are service owners? The same story happened to data base administration in the early days. Cloud governance have to address all questions and provide the necessary clarity. The governance concept has developed over the past years, in a direct response to the financial crises and organizational failures coupled with significant disruption threats to information flow from hackers. Today cloud computing practitioners are trying to take a more structured approach to the art of governing to turn it, as much as possible, into a science. A mature governance paradigm that combine CC services lifecycle can be settled up throughout the CC maturity journey. (Brown & Laird & Gee & Mitra, 2008). Value proposition, service elasticity and scalability issues are discussed intensely but having a lot of noise around. This chapter is tailoring these concepts to fit the cloud era.

Risk Management (RM) is the process which enables the enterprise to set the risk tolerance, identify potential risks and prioritize them based on the enterprise's business objectives and internal controls (AAIRM, 2002). A broader and more inclusive risk process means that opportunities and risks will be sought proactively (Hillson, 2008). Various risk definitions exist in text books but some traditional risk definitions are inefficient and conceptually astringent. Plenty of books and articles have defined risks and enterprise risk management with few of them discussed the CC risks (Brotby, 2006; Davis, Schiller, & Wheeler, 2006; Schlarman, 2009).

Plenty of articles are trying to answer the practitioners' question that is why do we need this esoteric thing called governance in order to implement CC projects. They assume their project does not have time to factor-in the governance issues, and more importantly, it will not result in getting projects completed faster (Stantchev & Stantcheva, 2013). We among others are trying to clarify how governance derive the key benefits and provide measures on goal achievement (COSO, 2012). As governance applied, cloud benefits such as cost reduction, process flexibility, or improved fusion between business and technology, become clear to all stakeholders.

Information is no longer the sole domain of the technology functions. In the past years, many other business units have owned specialized technologies. The advent of cloud encouraged more of them to acquire software even without the need for technology organization (TO) support or capital (Marks, 2015). Role upgrade of modern business operations has accompanied the shift in technology concepts and techniques. Additionally, CC significantly enhanced the response to wide spread technologies. Business transformation and third party management exist prior to the cloud era; however, we are trying to align it to work efficiently in the cloud era.

In summary, it can be argued that recent progress in CC and technology environments has promoted a research on enterprise risk management, governance and enterprise transformation (Abram, 2009; Segal, 2011). The main differentiator of this chapter is to jointly address the related aspects and to orchestrate a wide spectrum of elements. This will help practitioners and researches to understand correlations and plan necessary enhancements across their CEs and Extensible Enterprises (EEs). CSPs, MCCs and their supporting third party vendors can benefit from this chapter as well. Better understanding will result in a well-developed risk and governance CC practice that is scalable with the business, repeatable across the CE, measurable, sustainable, defensible, continually improving, and cost-effective on an ongoing basis.

RISK TRANSFORMATION

As defined in COSO's 2004 "Risk is the possibility that an event will occur and adversely affect the achievement of objectives" (COSO, 2012), more generally the effect can be in a positive or negative manner.

Risk Management (RM) is the act of aligning the exposure to risk and the capability to handle information and technology with the stakeholders' risk tolerance. It acts as the primary means of decision support for technology resources. It is designed to protect the confidentiality, integrity, and availability of technology assets.

Risk practices are passing deep transformations as well. This section is meant to keep practitioners abreast of evolving risk transformations and informed on effective approaches, it includes an in-depth discussion about the challenges and tactics that can be helpful while jumping into the cloud.

Enterprise Risk Management

Due to the progressive nature of challenges, an RM program is necessary to provide CEs with the required flexibility to move ahead. Yet, implementation requires a tremendous amount of effort. "Risk Management is the process which enables the enterprise to set the risk tolerance, identify potential risks and prioritize them based on the enterprise's business objectives in association with internal controls" (Crouhy, Galai & Mark, 2006). Enterprise Risk Management (ERM) includes the methods and processes used by CEs to manage risks and seize opportunities to achieve their objectives.

Risks have a changing nature, also the CEs' risk tolerance and appetite changes over the time, in response of various changes. It is a must to conduct risk assessments periodically to identify areas that are high priority for the CE and to engage relevant stakeholders up to the board level. As a part of the business strategy conversation, stakeholders should be aware of major risks affecting the business. It is necessary to get business stakeholders including department managers, team leaders and senior executives to think about risks. Risk changes might consider major elements that are designed to establish common understanding and action triggers for management to limit risk deviation, these elements include:

- Likelihood rating that indicates the probability of a risk occurrence,
- Impact to evaluate the consequences of risk events if they are realized,
- Risk tolerance specifying the maximum risk that a CE is willing to take regarding each relevant risk,
- Risk appetite to determine the amount and type of risk a CE is willing to accept in pursuit of its business objectives in a comfortable manner with an acceptable degree of uncertainty to handle, and
- Risk capacity is a less popular term that considers enabling the CE to monitor the actual risk exposure against a risk threshold.

Risk parameters change over time in a dynamic and fluid behavior. Risk planning identify the CE's risk acceptance level at a point in time but it may change actively. RM requires buy-in from the top-down to provide continuous support for new initiatives and processes. Management usually selects a risk response strategy for every specific risks when identified and analyzed, this response may include:

- **Avoidance:** Thus exiting the activities arising the risk,
- **Mitigation:** By taking action to reduce the likelihood or impact,
- **Transfer:** Through sharing or insuring portion of the risk, or
- **Acceptance:** When a cost/benefit decision tends to favor no action to be taken.

Upholding Technology Risks

Managers and executives may be willing to take more risks but auditors are generally more conservative. Defining a baseline will encourage executives to discuss the areas they are willing to take more risks on. The baseline of acceptable risk level is somewhere between the two parties. Derived by the old philosophy that IT is a servant of business needs, some executives argue that "IT risks" should not exist in the board room. Fundamentally, the term "IT risks" causes people to astray as technology exists everywhere in every CE and it is leading the business innovation. The technology rapid advancement and heavy business involvement are promoting the abandonment of the "IT risk" term in favor of "Technology Risks" term. Moreover, prohibiting standalone IT risk elements from the board agenda could be counter-productive in several critical scenarios" (Marks, 2015).

ISACA (Information Systems Audit and Control Association) stands half-of-the-way into COBIT5 where it defined IT risk as "the business risks associated with the use, ownership, operation, involvement, influence and adoption of IT within an enterprise. IT risk consists of IT-related events that could potentially impact the business" (ISACA, 2013). "Business Technology Risk" seems to be more accurate, where information is no longer the sole domain of technology in CEs with plenty of business units own and operate specialized technologies without the need for IT capital or support. The term "technology risks" is promoted as a short term to summarize the situation. "This distinction occurs because what matters is the effect of a potential risk on the achievement of organizational objectives – not the effect on the IT functional objectives" (Marks, 2015).

Technology risks are off course matters to the Technology Organization (TO), nonetheless, what is more significant is how much should it matter to the board and executives? Some technology risks may seem significant to technical staff, but their importance pale when considered within the context of business objectives. Board cannot afford to consider risks only based on the IT silo technical assessment, however, a sort of specialization is required to classify the technology risks and mitigate them across the board (Vice, 2015). Similar situation occurs in CC services which involve large number of Middle Circle Contractors (MCCs). "The inclusion of risk management into external vendors' operation will lead to an improvement in achieving its Business-Level Objectives" (Fit´O & Guitart, 2014) but better judgement is still required.

Considering the disruptive nature of technology risks and the rapid changes they promote, they can be divided into three major categories based on their ability to withstand and affect the CE performance. These are:

- **Strategic Risks:** Focused on handling long or short term risks that have a specific strategic leverage and a thorough risk impact. They typically follow the archetypal 'risk-return' profile and their analysis can help executives to better align business objectives.
- **Tactical Risks:** Primarily concerned with CE performance focusing to measure the CE behavior against defined risk controls and to impose certain inline enhancements, though the business objectives are still paramount. Typically, they can be preventable risks with no strategic mileage
- **Operational Risks:** Where risk assessments, continuous monitoring and risk behaviors are measured. They also consider the compliance controls in place to find the gaps and add new tools. Some operational risks are pure external on which the CE has no significant handle.

This classification will help the entire CE stakeholders to manage risks more efficiently and effectively.

Risk in The Cloud Era

"With Cloud Computing poised to move from its nascent phase to a more robust growth phase, a systemic understanding of the risk space enveloping the cloud is becoming important" (Warrier, & Shandrashekhar, 2006). Risk definition continues to be "the occurrence of an event, which is associated with the adoption and use of cloud computing, and can have consequences or impacts" (Dutta, Peng & Choudhary, 2013). The types of risks are the same with systems in the cloud as they are with non-cloud technology solutions with some characteristics may be different. One major change occurs because technology is moving from being an enabler to business strategy to be a driver that leads into the next business realm of the previously unthinkable. This is not new as technology innovations have derived a lot of changes in business practices in the past and they are increasingly driving business decisions nowadays. This section is primarily focused to outline risk concepts and vectors that are generated by CC and technology effects.

While the CC delivery models have made substantive advances in the past few years, companion risk and governance activities have not matured at a similar rate. To deem a complete status, a mature study of CC risks must ensure that all risk factors are understood, mapped, segmented, weighted and monetized. The categorization of risks along functional lines is highly industry dependent, with no two industries have a common generic set of functional risks. The mapping of business risks is always required for the identification and segmentation of all challenges that impede the normal business flow. These challenges need first to be delineated in the functional space and then identified to accommodate the cloud factor.

When a technology is in the convergence mode, technology adoption can compound basic business risks. Usually, there could be problems associated with the newly emerging business models. CC affects critical focal points of risk assessment including the CE risk profile which encompasses the entire population of managed risks. This profile should be extended to include a subset of the service providers risk universe. When CC related solutions are adopted, the CE risk profile will change in most cases based on how and for what purpose the CC is utilized. This includes an increase or decrease of the likelihood and impact for inherited and residual risks based on multiple factors including the CSP associated behaviors. If a CSP cannot demonstrate comprehensive and effective risk management processes in association with its services, CEs should carefully consider contracting with that vendor. The CE capabilities to compensate for the potential risk management gaps should also be measured. Risk assessment approaches should be aligned between the CSP and the CE in impact analysis, measurement criteria and definitions. Both should jointly develop risk scenarios that is intrinsic to the CSP service design and aligned to the CE experience and expectations. "After the risk management plans are implemented, there is a need to follow-on actions as part of a comprehensive assessment and continuous monitoring program" (Alnuem, Alrumaih & Al-Alshaikh, 2015).

Risk assessment is crucial for management to evaluate the risk events associated with its CC strategy. It is important to determine the potential impact of risks associated to each CC option (Broder, 2006). RM can't follow one trend. Rules may formalize how the influencing factors can have an impact on the risks (Lamersdorf, et al, 2010). Some risks can be managed through a rule-based model; others will require alternative approaches. The ability to make risk assessment more accurate depends on whether the CE has a comprehensive, accurate and current inventory of risks. CEs who are looking to adopt CC should also ask whether their own management has defined risk tolerances with respect to cloud services and are willing to accept any residual risks. Board members need to be aware and prepared to evaluate these trends and consider their impact on current – and future – business plans. Unfortunately, "practice has shown that information and technology risks are often not well understood by the enterprise key stakeholders, including board members and executive management" (Shalan, 2010).

There are many variables, values and risks in any cloud opportunity or program that will affect the business decisions. For example, the dynamic scalability of cloud, which is defined as the possibility of quick upsizing and downsizing, can create roadblocks and efficiency risks. CE need to weigh those variables to decide on the appropriate solutions. For critical functionalities, there should be special considerations when utilizing cloud services. The RM approach for such functionalities should include identification and valuation of assets, deep analysis for threats, vulnerabilities and potential impacts. Additionally, risk incident scenarios, events' likelihood analysis and risk acceptance levels should be deliberated. The outcomes of risk treatment plans should be incorporated into service agreements and developed in consistency with functionality importance.

A combination of internal and external factors adds up to impede the efficiency of cloud operations, including the compliance strategies and risk based auditing. Business people and technology teams need to learn effective risk communication to share their risk objectives in a correlated and collective manner. The right balance should be selected and identified. Different categorization of risks may be utilized to help executives in understanding the qualitative distinctions between risk types facing the CE. Some categories already defined before the cloud era but they are now becoming more recognized and deep (Kaplan, & Mikes, 2012).

CLOUD GOVERNANCE PARADIGM

To be effective, a CE must establish clear responsibility chains to empower people while enhancing the measurement gauges and control mechanisms. Policies will be also required to guide the CE toward its goals and to ensure better compliance and communication to keep all stakeholders informed. Governance is a strategic lesson learned the hard way over the past decade, and it's a lesson that need to be revisited in the cloud era to handle all challenges and hurdles.

Governance Definitions and Pillars

Governance, as the term connotes, is the set of foundations, processes, policies, laws, and customs affecting the way a CE is directed, administered or controlled. It also addresses the relationship among the many stakeholders involved in achieving the CE goals. Governance enforces a solution to be operationally and legally feasible and ethically acceptable while respecting the rule of law. Governance is achieved by higher degrees of communication, comprehension and buy-in of all the stakeholders. Principles of good governance include transparency, effectiveness and efficiency, accountability, strategic focus, sustainability, equity and fairness. Among these principles there exist four major pillars;

- Accountability obligation to report, explain and be answerable for the consequences of decisions that are performed on behalf of the stakeholders.
- Transparency to enforce stakeholders understanding of the decision-making process and follow the rule of law consistently to achieve justice.
- Responsive to serve the entire stakeholders needs in a responsible manner while balancing competing interests in a timely and appropriate way. This includes responding changes positively and accurately.
- Fairness in utilizing the available human capital, time and resources to achieve the best possible effective and efficient results. Justice is required to implement processes and judge results honestly.

Good governance inspires the acceptance of the shareholders' rights as the true owners of the CE, and the role of senior management as trustees. Audit is always required to achieve continuous monitoring, better controls and constant enhancements. There exist plenty of governance models which follow similar basic principles and leading to "establishing chains of responsibility, authority, and communication to empower people carry out their roles and responsibilities while establishing measurements, policies and control mechanisms" (Brown, Moore, & Tegan, 2006). Auditing behaviors, board structures, management processes, corporate responsibility, information disclosure, ownership and structures are just few points to consider. In its participatory form, governance is the job of every stakeholder. The most vulnerable the stakeholder is; the more opportunities he should have to participate in the processes that can be affected by his decision.

Under the umbrella of corporate governance, technology governance should be considered as a main role for the board of directors. It should be considered prominently equal to the boards' responsibility in approving the CE's strategy, setting its policies, attracting high-level executives and ensuring the CEs' credibility to its shareholders and official bodies. Technology governance is almost voluntary with vast implementations analysis, performance and operational issues. To satisfy key business needs, it can provide flexible policies and practices to embrace both incumbent and new resources equally in a comprehensive way. The technology governance policies must be executed with formality, rigor and transparency to become a part of the of the CE defined fabric that is documented, communicated and repeatedly enhanced. With this approach, CEs can develop and maintain governance structure that address the current behaviors and policies needs while having enough flexibility to address evolving conditions.

Governance in The Cloud Era

Cloud governance is aimed as a constitution that is required to articulate a common agreement about cloud definitions, follow the best practices for decision making and to deliver well-defined solutions that satisfy structured stakeholders requirements. As CC invites more correlation between business and technology, governance aims to enhance both executives and non-executive spectacles. It helps the directors of business and technology organizations within the CE to fulfil their unlimited responsibilities utilizing the limited amount of time they can devote to their CEs. At the same time, it acts to stretch the visions, controls and business-technology alignments. CC governance need to start with the decision makers who are planning the cloud architecture, they need to incorporate effective, business-driven management tools and practices into the cloud services and applications from the ground up for maximum business value. Governance will help to minimize disruption of business and technology operations. Cohesion between stakeholders is required to provide a wide-spectrum governance that can handle systemic risks of the CC era.

CC governance activities is a sub-journey of the CE governance roadmap with long-term view to deliver short term solutions with a coherent vision. During the governance journey, plenty of questions might arise such as "What is cloud governance? How does it help CEs reaching their common agreement? How can it make a difference?". CC governance is a critical success factor to achieve standardization, reduce costs, improve business process flexibility and ultimately turning business agility from a platitude to reality. Typical CC governance paradigm includes requirements of technology infrastructure, employee behavior, and business processes. These components are often recorded, implemented and measured in organizational silos. For an effective governance in the cloud era, executives need to break down the walls between various silos and devise common approaches to manage policies, measure performance and ensure compliance. This will support the CE in reaching its goals more effectively.

There is a major difference between governance and management, this difference becomes more discrete in the cloud era. Management, in corporate context, is charged with directing and controlling people toward accomplishing a goal or goals. In the cloud era, that goal is to implement the processes required for the successful enactment and ongoing maintenance of CC architecture which includes providing the required resources and the associated services. These resources include people, processes, and technologies which are subject of management. Unlike management, governance is not charged with implementing the cloud architecture or managing the associated resources. It is charged to provide an oversight to certify that the cloud architecture is accomplished in a satisfactory approach. The optimal architecture must satisfy certain principles and policies as required to sustain the cloud environment in a successful and continual manner. Following its successful implementation, the governance model specifies the processes, polices, controls and mechanisms required to monitor and enhance the cloud architecture throughout its lifecycle. The governance model also concludes the organizational structure that defines associated roles and responsibilities while it is in practice.

Migration to the cloud is not an abdication of responsibility. Governance mechanisms are required to efficiently deal with risks, resolve trade-offs between diverse needs and interests and to deal with potential effects generated from new technologies. The evolution of governance mechanisms occurs much more slowly than the processes driving technological and operational change. The continuously generated risks in the cloud era prompts serious concerns from authorities, executives and other stakeholders. Progressive adoption and directed application of governance is a must to recognize the developing risks before they crystalize. The outsourcing of technology aspects is a key area that the CC governance should consider otherwise this will put the whole CE at risk of falling over technical and compliance barriers (Siepmann, 2014). Typically, concerns and challenges are reduced when a CE becomes more experienced in the governance practices. The cloud governance lifecycle describes the end-to-end requirements, from architecture planning and deployment to bursting, switching cloud providers, and off boarding from a cloud platform.

THE ELASTIC CLOUD COMPUTING NEXUS

Today, variety of consumer-driven forces challenge the CE information, technology and application development. CC among other innovations are converging to change CEs dramatically including their central technology shops. These forces are forming a highly disruptive nexus, that is a connected group of phenomena comprising several features to enable the change. Due to its nature and capabilities, CC is leading the change. Utilizing CC services, CEs can tap into powerful technologies without deep pocket investments, full-time data scientists or massive racks of servers. This will enable CEs to serve customers or partners with keen perception and timely actions. CC introduces new paramount ways for reaching or providing services and increasing flexibility. These ways have reduced time for system integration, increased the assets reuse and reduced time to market for solutions. CEs are responding in several ways, but overwhelmingly, the strategies for CC adoption across the world have multiple facets. This section is considering few aspects related to the CE elasticity as affected by the cloud.

Dissolved Security Perimeter

CC give workers new levels of flexibility and derived new levels of productivity, but they present unique security needs that do not fit the traditional endpoint paradigm. As a result of CC nexus, CEs are facing the phenomena of "dissolved security perimeter" introducing serious challenges of how to manage, monitor and secure their networks, systems, applications and data.

Security is the single biggest factor that kept some CEs, and some applications, away from the cloud. Many CEs cannot afford the moderate security infrastructure, which make them extremely vulnerable to malware attacks and data loss incidents. CC enables security delivery as a service, which is a different facet of cloud security. CC provides the scrambling TOs with efficient and secure ways to manage the CC utilization. Nonetheless, cloud security and privacy are sorely lacking, making it so important to understand what is at stake, when to trust data transfer to the cloud and what to do in order to secure virtual infrastructures and applications. This necessitate reviewing the current status of data security and storage in the cloud considering confidentiality, integrity, and availability.

Sometimes, cloud access security broker is introduced as a software or a service that resides between the CE end-user or on-premises infrastructure and the CSP infrastructure acting as a gatekeeper. This will produce a separation layer allowing the CE to extend their security policies reach beyond their own infrastructure. This broker ensures that network traffic between on-premises devices and the CSP complies with the CE security policies. This gatekeeper acting as an MCC should have the ability to give insights into cloud application usage across cloud platforms and any identity unsanctioned use.

Service Delivery Models

Cloud encompasses a variety of service delivery models to support on-demand computing. They can be provided in different forms that are spanning all service layers. Infrastructure-as-a-service, IaaS, is generally the CE first step into the cloud. IaaS enables the on-demand utilization of raw computing resources, processing power, network bandwidth and storage. Platform-as-a-service, PaaS, acts at the platform level as a cloud-based offering to provide CEs with an environment that supports rapid evolution. PaaS is required for the development of key business applications that need continuous changes to foster ongoing business innovation while keeping the cost under control.

Software-as-a-service, SaaS, is available at the application level via standard browsers. SaaS supports device independence and anywhere access. Database as a Service, DBaaS, is a cloud-based approach to store and manage the structured data with similar functionality to relational database management systems such as SQL Server. Middle Ware as a service, MWaaS, provides an end-to-end application development and deployment environment. It delivers a complete runtime environment that comprise all necessary services to deploy and run an enterprise-class applications. MWaaS may utilize the application hosting services, persistence store, application integration and application programmable interfaces (APIs) to enable programmed access to additional computing services and resources.

At the business level, cloud-based solutions provide the Business Process-as-a-Service, BPaaS, to offer an internet-enabled, externally-provisioned service for managing the entire business process including people processes such as contact centers. Additionally, CC ignite a wave of Identity and Access Management-as-a-Service, IAMaaS, where a middle circle contractor (MCC) can authenticate the user identity and privilege. The IAMaaS providers are an assortment of smaller vendors who deliver core IAM functions to the cloud or from the cloud. They implement a connector piece or provide a gateway for the CE employees or partners to enable the IAMaaS service through various means including the bio-identification.

Topology Deployment Models

For cloud services to cover the whole requirements of the CE spectrum, cloud imposes four main topology deployment models that cover a wide choice of cost and features. Private clouds are dedicated to a single CE for private usage of virtualized applications, infrastructures and communication services provided to the CE internal users and partners. They either can be built within the CE own data center or located off-premise and managed by an external third party. On the other hand, public clouds are owned and provided by external service providers who offer their services to multiple CEs over a network at an agreed upon cost that is based on actual consumption.

In between there exist the hybrid clouds that blend the benefits of public and private clouds enabling a CE to retain confidential information in a private cloud, while providing access to a wider choice of applications available in a public cloud. A special topology is the community clouds which employs collaborative resources that are shared between various CEs with common interests, perhaps being in the same industry. Community clouds can be hosted internally within a selected CE or externally at a third party premises with the costs to be shared across the participating CEs.

Scalability and Elasticity

With the increase in the amounts of data that CEs are processing, they can have troubles keeping up with the computing demands. Business analytics in particular have dynamic processing requirements. The number of users who need access to certain data can vary significantly at different points of the business cycle or there can be spikes in the amount of computing resources at certain times. This business scalability is one of the key differentiators for CEs that are transforming themselves.

CC affects heavily the cost distribution by introducing new pricing models for acquiring capabilities and resources. Businesses can pay for what they need instead of paying upfront for services. This is key for CEs who cannot afford to make a large initial investment in infrastructure that is often required to implement analytic and strategic solutions. When utility based payment options are used, flexible payment terms offer great cost savings and scalability. CC is elastic enough, thus CEs can evaluate cloud models that best suit their long term needs.

The pricing models for CC make it possible to deliver insights to a broader set of users or alternatively scale-up by providing more computing resources when needed. These resources will be scaled-down when they are not being utilized. This dynamic-scaling makes it easier to do short-term projects or proof of concepts to justify larger programs. In addition, small and medium CEs who have some difficulty making the upfront investments will be able to use CC resources to get started.

RISK AND GOVERNANCE PROJECTIONS

Risk is everywhere. It is inherited in the CC nature, that is still evolving with plenty of emerging technologies are being established and phased out (Soyata, 2015). Taking a broad approach to enhance the management of CC risks require moving toward more proactive approaches. To provide more visibility to detect anomalies across CC layers and seams, it will be required to continuously measure the activities against a baseline of expected behaviors.

The large magnitude of CC variables and parameters increase the risk that users encounter advanced obstacles. Some of these hurdles are technical in the origin while others are related to business process and usability. User experience complications are harder to detect, diagnose and resolve (Marcus, 2014). Auto-discovery capabilities may be required to identify risk parameters and classify them based on key risk factors to enforce different controls as necessary. This is especially important in regulated industries and enterprises.

Governance is acting as the beholder eye. It results in reducing the cost and complexity of business transformation and operation. Governance is particularly useful when provisioning new services in CEs with shadow operations or liberal policies that allow business units to procure and manage their own technology resources. Governance can resolve a host of legal questions around liability. For example, "if a self-driving car is involved in an accident, who is at fault? The device manufacturer? The coder of the algorithm? Or the human "operator"? (Daecher, & Galizia, 2015).

CC is not yet mature. CC specifications are being debated and espoused by several CEs, CSPs and regulatory bodies to increase efficiency and flexibility. However, one of the more obvious CC implications is the explosion of technology adoption especially in fields that are historically lacking connectivity and embedded intelligence. This leads to extensible enterprises and encourages the creation of large echo systems. To control extensible echo systems, CEs need to develop an effective strategy that establishes a virtual perimeter. Combined policies and procedures are required to manage various business scenarios and control devices that may access the business data. IAM (Identity and Access Management) structures are required to manage user roles and facilitate enterprise sign-on activities.

Effective audit and compliance are necessary to detect activities outside of anticipated norms and trigger the necessary range of responses. Technically plenty of measures or controls are required to generate data and analyze CC service usage. Considering the huge contracting and outsourcing that may be involved, running CC projects require special approaches for initiation and deployment. Over time, CC standards will develop, but in the near term complications are expected. Elegant approaches may eventually emerge to manage the interaction points across CC layers, CEs, MCCs and CSPs.

This section is viewing key areas in CC architecture, maturity, deployment and value proposition. Plenty of risks exist do exist lengthways on the CC roadmap. Governance can enhance navigation clarity and minimize the associated risks to make difference.

Maturity and Value Proposition

The National Institute of Standards and Technology (NIST) defines cloud computing as "a model for enabling ubiquitous, convenient, on-demand network access to a shared pool of configurable computing resources (e.g. networks, servers, storage, applications, and services) that can be rapidly provisioned and released with minimal management effort or service provider interaction" (Mell & Grace, 2011). The NIST definition is aimed towards a mature setup of CC, which is not the actual situation. Today, CC means various things to different practitioners: the developers often equate cloud and web services as one and the same, whereas designers view cloud as a set of implementation patterns that should be applied during development. Technology architects view cloud as another in the long line of architectural styles. Business executives and technology leaders consider cloud as a core underpinning to their information and technology strategy. Overall, CC is a critical enabler for business process management and transformation initiatives from different directions.

"Currently, the terminology of cloud service measurements is not well defined" (NIST, 2015). It is important to highlight the need for a shared vision and definition to achieve the promised CC benefits. Moreover, CEs should understand how to measure the cloud benefits and controls. This section provides CC insight considering its value proposition and maturity status in an attempt to identify a host of issues that is required by cloud entrepreneurs. This is important to respond many complexities and challenges associated with this new cloud era.

Maturity Status

To realize the benefits, there should be common agreement within the CE to define and establish the key goals and expectations from technology adoption. In new emerging mixed environments, maturity is playing a very important role to overcome shortcomings and stabilize the measurement parameters. Maturity will help to identify and mitigate risks that pertain to the cloud environment. Effective maturity valuation instruments are keys to support CEs in establishing technology roadmaps to improve their readiness for CC adoption. Additionally, there exists a relation between increasing maturity levels and the improvement of business practices.

Scanning the CC delivery models are showing clearly that some CSPs have achieved widespread take-up across many industries by providing SaaS and PaaS models. These CSPs have established themselves as disruptive ways to quickly deliver new functionalities in a reliable mechanism. Yet, MWaaS is still lagging due to the sensitivity of being in the middle of a runtime environment. Deploying and running enterprise-class application utilizing the MWaaS requires considering valid challenges while it is maturing. Still, MWaaS is facilitating cheaper and faster applications deployment by providing the capability that developers need not deal with the complexities of the underlying hardware and software components. For similar reasons, DBaaS is still one step behind although it provides a flexible, scalable, on-demand platform that is oriented toward self-service and easy management.

Monitoring capabilities are crucial to track the usage and performance of the CC services with a notification system to alert about potential issues and suggest enhancements. Middle Circle Contractors (MCCs) as key players in providing CC services necessitate effective mature management as well. Certain degree of data analytics is vital to manage CC components and to maintain the relations with all MCCs (Shalan, 2015). In addition, a solid enterprise architecture will be compulsory to provide the correct blueprint, define a set of standardized services and to support business agility. Project and portfolio management approaches should be mature as well to bring all CC demands under a holistic demand management as a single overall process. Managing components and stakeholders is critical to provide visibility to the business, communicate uniform value measurements and make clear trade-offs between the technology resource at the business-unit and enterprise levels.

With cloud service is yet immature, CEs should have a robust technology governance framework to enable the transition and operation into CC. The governance structures need to operate at the highest levels with a steering committee operating at the enterprise level. The CEO and board of directors should be involved where necessary to align with business strategy and enterprise architecture. All decision rights should be explicitly communicated and enforced to compensate for any immature area or weaknesses

Value Proposition

Cloud computing offers a value proposition that is different from traditional enterprise technology environments. By providing a way to exploit virtualization and aggregate computing resources, cloud computing can offer economies of scale that would otherwise be unavailable. One example, is the on-demand self-service-provisioning where a CE can provision computing capabilities including server time and network storage as per real time requirements. Such services are employed through a broad network access where these capabilities are available and accessed through standard mechanisms in an automatic fashion without a human interaction with the CSP. This promotes the usage of heterogeneous thin or thick client platforms including mobile phones and other digital devices (Campagna, Lyer and Krishnan, 2013).

CC also enables the resource pooling value, where a CSP computing resources may serve multiple CEs using a multi-tenant model with different physical and virtual resources. These resources including storage, processing, memory, network bandwidth and virtual machines can be assigned and reassigned according to consumer demand. This rapid elastic provisioning leads to quick scale-out and scale-in causing the resources to appear as unlimited and can be purchased in any quantity at any time (Shinder, 2013). Leveraging service metering capabilities and effective measurements is a necessity in CC to control and optimize resource usage automatically. Measurements will require a level of abstraction that is suitable to the service type being storage, processing, bandwidth or active user accounts. CSPs and CEs should monitor, control, and report on services with transparency, empowering the ability to precisely match expenses to IT demand.

Getting optimal value from cloud requires efforts both on a strategic level, through alignment and governance, and on operational level, by measuring and managing performance. It is this combination of activities, on all levels, that create the conditions for adequate value delivery with enabled monitoring of inherited risks.

Off-the-Shelf Services

During the early days of car manufacturing, the car owners and designers were required to design jointly or re-think to acquire every car element including screws, belts, leather, motor, mirror, etc. Following several iterations, they harmonize acquired parts and the car body is complete. Electrical components to be added and multiple polishing layers are performed before handing the car to a special driver to start its first journey. During this course multiple design, cost, delivery and integration aspects are considered. Following multiple standardization waves, today the car manufacturing industry is mature and the end user can acquire a car off-the-shelf from a wide selection of merchandises, brands and items.

The same car analogy exists for technology service structures. Technology providers are required to design platform structures, add networking, security and service layers prior to adding the business flavor for a service to be ready for use. "Cloud Computing represents a shift away from computing as a product that is purchased, to computing as a service that is delivered to consumers over the internet from large scale data centers or 'clouds'" (Tiwari, Sharma, & Mahrishi, 2014). CC is reshaping the computing behaviors and moving them toward off-the-shelf services. This movement is made possible by an architecture that is capable to support business flexibility and game-changing business models. Multiple scenarios, opportunities and threats still to be verified.

With business alignment in the core, off the shelf services along with dynamic CC architecture can support the lean enterprise environment. That is comprising moderate flexibility to business users and technology staff in association with robust standardization directions to control, stabilize and conform. The expected benefits of applying off-the-shelf services vary from improved operational efficiency to faster integration of core systems. This is achieved by deploying one or more shared functions across the CE, optimizing deployment cycles and reducing cost for business users. This scenario facilitates flexible dealings with business and creates new value from existing systems. However, to get the best value from off-the-shelf products, an optimal cloud architecture should be used to reduce risk exposure, improve visibility of business operations and provide a flexible business design.

Self-service provisioning and out-of-the-box concepts are boxed in the off-the-shelf service where users can monitor and administer services with minimal or no administrator intervention. Self-administration better manage the underlying resources to handle requests, decrease failure rates and avoid potential bottle-necks. Masked complexity simplifies the computing infrastructure so that more people can be data oriented to interact with the systems. Thanks to the CC advancements, analytics are delivered today in less sophisticated formats with its results can be utilized easily to optimize operational decisions.

Reliable management tools are crucial for creating, monitoring and managing off-the-shelf services. These tools are expected to enable automated resources baselining and discovery, integrated workflows and the repository for storing and retrieving documents, processes and provisioning profiles. Resource consumption metering and reporting is mandatory to track and charge users based on their chargeback plans. In-depth historical and on-demand reports can enable capacity planning including consolidation ratio, destination server utilization, server mapping and so on.

Audit and Compliance

Cloud enforced major changes in the audit arena. Recently, the external audit is stretched to a point where the degree of reliance that is placed upon it is out of proportion to the amount of work that actually goes into it. Internal audit is struggling, largely because many internal auditors are not the beneficiaries of the regard that they are owed. The cloud era promoted the continuous audit which is utilized with dynamic nature to monitor particular configurable items, provide an additional level of controls and to act as a metal control. Continuous audit activities are different from those taking place during the traditional one. Audit principles need to be re-conceptualized to place the auditor in the middle of the transaction flow. The implementation of continuous auditing consists of six procedural steps, which includes establishing priority areas, identifying monitoring and audit rules, determining the frequency of process, configuring continuous audit parameters, following up and the last is communicating results.

Similarly, the compliance behaviors are expected to bypass major changes to accommodate the cloud variables and challenges. The responsibility for regulatory compliance does not end at the boundary of the cloud. It should be propagated inside the CSP systems to avoid regulatory fines, increased risk and reputational damage. If built correctly cloud platforms should have the ability to implement system changes and refinements faster with more efficiency. This leads to cost-effective scenarios that can accelerate compliance and reduce disruption.

The service, and not just the CSP, should be the subject of risk audit. The usage of particular CC service and deployment models should be consistent with the CE risk management objectives, as well as with its business objectives. The landscape of the legal compliance environment changes with CSP and MCC support (JISC Legal Information, 2014). CE should act effectively to remove the unknown danger of control and governance loss to the external providers.

Business Transformation

Traditionally, to keep their leading edge, large enterprises maintain a unique architecture. They inevitably own a large number of computing systems that have been developed over a long period of time. These systems depend on different technologies, have different 'owners' within the CE and devise complex dependencies. This leads to multiple interactions between the systems themselves, the processed data, the middleware used and the platforms on which they run. Alongside, multiple business processes have evolved to make use of the available systems portfolio based on the specific features of each system (Pierantonelli, Perna & Gregori, 2015).

Nowadays, technology spending among Small and Medium Businesses (SMBs) is expected to grow strongly. The CC paradigm and associated technologies enables SMBs to ramp up or scale down with business in a manner that leapfrogs technology generations. This allows the SMBs to access cost-effective, highly-competitive resources so it can be compared against larger enterprises. Startup business may start fresh without facing many challenges as they have no legacy systems or existing business procedures.

CC is bridging the gaps to resolve the significant technology challenge facing CEs of all sizes. Off-the-shelf products and services are simplifying technical integration aspects. Integration between CC applications, infrastructures and legacy systems are expanding the functionality scope. Data management gateways like application programmable interfaces (APIs) among other tools are allowing programmers to join the movement and extend the value of existing technology investments. Additionally, CC is re-shaping the relation between the TO and business staff towards more involvement and integration. This section is trying to dive into business transformation to fitting the CC inside and navigate its risks and controls. This will help CEs to simplify integrating or building their systems in the cloud (Avasant, 2016).

Extensible Enterprise

Just as the Internet is a network of networks, cloud computing will become a network of business platforms (Baya & Mathaisel & Parker, 2010). The extensible-enterprise represents the successor of the slow, one-off ecosystem partnering and customer acquisition processes that was utilized in the pre-cloud era. It employs multiple cloud characteristics to enable a massive scalable partnering system with extended ecosystem capabilities. Multitenancy, scalability, elasticity, on-demand provisioning and adaptive business process mapping are just few added features. Extensible enterprise is responding the CE dependency on a growing number of partners, mobile users and connected devices to drive success. Ecosystem can utilize off-the-shelf products and common CC building blocks to attain the integration.

The first step to become an extensible enterprise is to assess if an existing or new process can represent capabilities to leverage other business partners. Process transformation plays a role to remove the strong interdependencies among the various activities in the process enabling the independent usage of their capabilities from inside or outside the CE. Those capabilities are exposed externally and made available to a broader ecosystem. This transformation will result in versatile processes that are provisioned in the cloud in a manner that supports the broadest range of use cases. Overall this will lead to exemplify strategic advantages, create effective collaboration and drive potential growth.

CEs do not need to act like a CSP to enable the extensible enterprise but they can establish a cloud-style platform that is created using own data centers, aggregated external cloud services or a combination of both. This will add more flexibility and enhance business value. Deep integration empowers looking much beyond the data exchange level to the integration of workflows or even to the integration and adoption of the overall user experience and capabilities. Application Programming Interfaces (APIs) play a critical role in functionality processing in a secure and reliable manner. It turns every CE to become data-powered business platforms and content publishers in their own right. This provides the CE with the ability to generate a "platform effect" by scaling and syndicating services for accelerated strategic business alignment.

In the overall, modularity in software services applied at multiple levels, from raw computing power up to the business processes of online services. It acts to break up internal capabilities or processes into modular service components that have standardized and open interfaces for integration with other business platforms. This permits the mix and match capabilities quickly and securely. "In truly scalable environment, architects dramatically re-design the software to be highly modular, such that when you hit any service, there are between tenths or hundreds of individual sub-services running inside the cloud, which dynamically on the fly come together to render that service" (Baya, Mathaisel & Parker, 2010).

Provisioning will be required while moving processes, that is originally internal or local, to a CC platform thus it can be shared and integrated with other cloud-resident processes. Being resident in the cloud enables the potential use in multiple contexts. However, this creates a risk that instantaneous process scaling can go viral, causing spikes in demand of business functions and processes. The CE is forced to model business activities more broadly to ensure their software in the extensible enterprise is robust to accommodate unexpected demands and exceptions. Waiting for manual activities or staff intervention to handle exceptions does not scale in the extensible enterprise.

Technology Organization Alignment

Technology trends and market forces mandate changes and innovations to keep the CE at the competitive edge. Conversely, many CEs still considering technology as an inhibitor to change. The tension between central technology provisioning and end users has been endless since the 1960s. Constant end-user complaints states that central services are unwilling or unable to respond quickly to changing business requirements. CC promotes different kind of conversation on two levels; the first is how the technology can partner with business proactively to decrease costs and improve efficiency levels and the second level is how technology can build assets for the CE that have longevity (Olson & Peters, 2011).

Technology provision is profoundly affected by political considerations with senior management usually set technology policies but they leave it to individual parties to enact in their own way. Managers naturally tend to adopt strategies that benefit their part of the CE without having a wide spectrum of other business units. The cloud era will require role changes and each member of the managerial suite to stretch in some way and to have sufficient knowledge of technology aspects. They will need to grapple with what CC opportunities can do for business growth and abandon the thinking of CC as strictly better solution to information technology. CE key members should also recognize the ramifications of the cloud risks. Business roles are changing to orchestrate awareness and plan appropriate responses to business changes. For example, the CIO role will continue to master the technology but will also need to acquire deeper understanding of the business opportunities. He need to coordinate more with business, rather than to manage the technology infrastructure. This promotes redefining the CIO as a Chief Integration Officer (Kark, & Vanderslice, 2015). CIO should serve as the critical link between business strategy and the technology agenda to identify, vet, and apply emerging technologies to the business roadmap. CIOs who do so intentionally have the best chance of success as technology leaders and as members of the business strategy team. Any discontinuity with business may result in catastrophic disasters beyond business continuity or safeguarding valuable company data.

The CC advent has enabled every CE to acquire technology, sometimes without the technology organization involvement, evaluation or support. This make the TO unaware about all the technology deployed across their CEs. The adoption of CC outside the TO without recognizing the enterprise governance structure may lead to plenty of issues including the creation of the next generation legacy system silos that are not integrated nor interoperable. This will regenerate the concept of "Shadow IT" which is a term often used to describe IT systems and solutions built and used inside the CE without formal approvals. Many people consider the "Shadow IT" as an important source of innovation arguing that shadow systems may turn out to be prototypes for future approved technology solutions. However, "shadow IT" solutions are not often in line with the CE requirements for control, documentation, security or reliability. It may cause fatal mistakes or huge data loss.

Fitting the Cloud Computing

CC is not simply about technological improvement of data centers, it is a fundamental change in how technology is provisioned and used. CEs need to consider the benefits, risks and the effects of CC on their business practices in order to make right decisions related to the CC adoption. Large CEs are inherently complex. In traditional situation, there are no individual or group within the CE who knows about all of the systems that are in use. Dependencies between systems are often discovered by accident when something simply stops working after a change. CC is aiming to change this silo mentality to produce a decoupled but unified solution that can be adapted under a CC governance framework. It is important to understand that "architecture is a key". Before choosing any type of CC solution, CEs need to think about how an architecture needs to morph toward functionally efficiency. CC should not be looked at as a new architecture, but another option for storing and running services. When utilizing multiple systems or topologies, cloud should be established as the core of all of them.

While shifting to the CC culture, various forces converge and thrive to provide a scalable, agile and fault tolerant applications that can use disparate services from inside and outside the CE. When choosing a CC solution to migrate certain application it should be verified to satisfy the requirements of key stakeholders and to deliver real value to the CE. To utilize services from off-the-shelf CC service solutions, CEs need to understand what qualities, characteristics and dependencies are associated with each service. Dependencies between services are major inhibitors that might impact the performance, therefore a flexible, decoupled services architecture is required. CEs should determine how a certain CC service can be best orchestrated into the existing environment considering the current architectural state. Following the implementation, CEs need to understand its detailed functional level and to figure out problem areas. Some cloud architectures are built on a publish-subscribe asynchronous pattern to combine data from multiple sources to infer events or patterns with complicated circumstances and to respond quickly to meaningful patterns and new business scenarios (Tarkoma, 2012).

One related risk is to find a proper middleware solution that can provide a proper messaging infrastructure to ensure durability, quality of service guarantees and to mediate services that provide routing, transformation and data integration for the event notifications. The middleware should also provide multiple types of events processing including simple and complex event processing. Another important aspect is to define common data, which is an overly complex task, especially where silos exist. It will be mandatory to look at information as a common asset, with proper understanding to figure out how all that detailed information is stored in back-end silos. Localization of the off-the-shelf CC services is yet another feature that is required to maintain the ease of use. CC services are expected to have various flavors in different geographies to cope with user expectation and demand. Measurement schemes and regional settings need to be adopted for different locations. Sometimes, different jurisdictions mean that the same system has to be used and supported in different ways when used in different countries.

A new generation of customer experience management analytics solutions designed during the cloud era creating the "Hyper digitization" phenomena. These new capabilities enable CEs to efficiently capture the complete user interactions, including social media communications. CEs are gathering data in many different formats and finding creative ways to use this data for deeper insights into customer behavior or market conditions. Once analyzed correctly big data provided by cloud and non-cloud solutions can be a primary collaboration set to deliver key insights. It can be used to truly understand the potential lifetime value of customers. The results of this analysis delivers unprecedented visibility into computing usage patterns and behaviors. This will enable CEs to pinpoint and resolve obstacles, make the right investment decisions and raise customer conversion and acquisition rates.

However, most CEs are still struggling to get the insight they need from new and existing sources of information. They are not always able to infuse analytics and insights they generate into their business processes or to deliver the insights to the right people who would benefit from them. To make better decisions, CEs are struggling with how to leverage this volatile and potentially noisy source of information.

Pervasive analytics that is powered by CC resources with more business-oriented interfaces may be required for developing insights using advanced analytics.

During the business transformation process, costs are important but so are customer relationships, public image, flexibility, business continuity and compliance. CEs need to understand how CC affects all of these. Other aspects should be well documented in the business transformation governance including the organizational change, the economic implications, the security, legal and privacy issues that are raised by CC.

Running Cloud Projects

The implementation of CC projects is unique in terms of the quantity of required correlations and inter-relations. Plenty of Middle Circle Contractors (MCCs) or "men-in-the-middle" exist in the CC deployments, they include the primary CSP, temporary contractors and service integrators. Managing such a number of MCCs is a key in achieving fruitful implementation. The success in cloud deployments boils down to one critical element whether the focus is external, from the public cloud, or within a private cloud, that element is trust (Hoda, Noble & Marshall, 2009).

CC deployments have direct effects on business transformations and strategy. CEs are facing significant roadblocks to deploy their CC initiatives. These includes technology and non-technology barriers related to people, processes, politics and other organizational issues. This flags the need to develop project management methodologies and processes to handle CC migrations and rollout. Agile methodologies are increasingly used to manage CC projects in a continuously progressive mechanism.

Stakeholders management is a key issue during the cloud adoption. The projects' overall decision-making committee structure is significant to address substances at the project, program and portfolio levels. Coordination with other business units or committees is crucial for the project success. Due to the incremental nature of CC projects, major CC implementation failures do not happen often. When such a failure occurs, it sometimes need to be part of the board agenda if the business strategy can be affected.

This section is shedding some lights on CC projects implementations, aspirations and correlation. It is also touching on the contracting and outsourcing of MCCs alongside with associated controls.

Initiation and Deployment

CC projects are usually initiated as an optimization projects which is usually applied to strategic systems. They often have significant user experience derives and innovation requirements. Usually, they are driven by the line of business rather than the technology organization. The difference between success and failure comes down to the ability to engage the user, in a sustained mechanism that requires delivering a customized experience to adapt to their needs in real-time. People have a vital input to determine how the CC structure should be populated. The rollout of CC projects must take into consideration the organizational accountabilities of involved stakeholders and how they translate into the project capital. A steering committee representing all necessary stakeholders and levels must be adequate to direct the CC portfolio, program or project. The overly large committees or destructed attitudes are the death of effective decision making. Once the structure and representation are addressed, the success of the CC deployment depends upon the quality of the information provided to the decision makers. The information flow should be tailored according to the needs of each committee, focused on optimizing the business requirements and in accordance to the engineering of sought outcomes.

The goal is to deploy a successful CC service that can adequately support the detailed requirements of business solutions. Plenty of critical requirements must be taken into consideration including deployment models, service structures and integration with existing systems. Other features including security, privacy, service level agreements, interoperability, legal and regulatory requirements should also be considered. Aggregated fulfillment of these requirements leads to a transition project to define the roll-out strategies and to manage related activities. Risk handling strategy is important to assess and detail the new CC services, how it will be managed? how it will interface to the legacy systems? and how it will be monitored and reported. Project governance must be associated to put the CC operated systems under the control of business stakeholders and the TO in an effective manner to achieve the CE goals.

Normalization of the existing portfolio is necessary to remove redundant applications or processes and to decide which application to migrate first into the CC environment. Actually this is an overly complex process that requires decision makers to transfer the most successful application along with their cloud architectures. Adaptation of an open strategy to align with business objectives and measure success is significant to achieve business transformation. It will enhance the CEs capacity to develop and track key metrics to measure the implementation and success of business objectives. Achieving the expected business value of released CC modifications require customer feedback, quality metrics, and progressive business requirements.

Adopting CC is a major first step to increase the CE ability to provision environments quicker and more frequently, but it is not enough. Alongside agile rollout methodologies should be followed to keep a competitive advantage, continue innovation and transform the new technology trends. Agile can take business ideas rapidly and transform them into a high performing activity to deliver new business functions at high quality (Beck, et. al., 2001). Agile project delivery methods enable better communication, collaboration and integration between technology organization and business professionals considering their interdependence especially in the cloud era (Abbas, Gravell & Wills, 2008). Agile also embraces the continuous delivery concept, in which fixes and enhancements arrive quickly, seamlessly and continuously with no disruption in service or loss of data. To effectively adopt agile delivery, CEs must address several challenges related to the lack of standards and poor configuration management. To avoid risky and error prone deployment, rapid provisioning will be required to handle traditional dependence on manual processes and tribal knowledge.

Cloud integration strategy differs from the typical enterprise approaches such as the Enterprise Service Bus (ESB) which was responsible for supporting connectivity, transport, protocol conversion, data transformation and routing. Flexible and secure integration model is required for the back-office systems to keep pace with this rapid change in the cloud platforms without custom coding. The cloud integration solutions should use preconfigured templates based on common integration scenarios to accelerate integration between legacy and cloud. Integration management tools and capabilities play a major role to facilitate any movements and adaptations.

Contracting and Outsourcing

There can be no effective business value to a service without the trust that a CC service will perform as promised in a secure and reliable way. Selecting and contracting a suitable supplier is a key success factor (Poppendieck & Poppendieck, 2013). This includes assessing appropriate business areas to be outsourced to the cloud its impact based on value, sustainability and quality. Writing up a CC service contract is a critical task that should manage unique risks including possibilities of data loss, lack of adequate internal controls, applied security and CSP or technology lock-in. In response to technology enhancement, cloud service contract should manage the expectations related to enhancement options as compared to other competitors.

Infrastructure is considered sometimes as part of the contracting, as CC performance results are dependent on the raw computation power. It is delivered by the underlying infrastructure and the navigation techniques through applications and databases. The underlying infrastructure and associated middleware layers are important for a highly available, reliable and secure service. Interoperability of CC services is another concern for CEs. A cloud-based service might offer significant economic benefits to the CEs, but concerns over lack of standards can result in vendor lock-in. What if a CE needs to switch the CSP or pull the service back in house? Asset inventories should account for supporting CC services and assets under the CSP control. Asset classification and valuation schemes should be consistent between CE and CSP.

More governments are adopting "sovereignty" laws that are intended to keep data in-country and dictate how it is handled. This may be the response to government spying, high-profile hacks and the realization that data is the next "natural resource". These laws typically specify what data can or cannot be stored outside the country, how it must be stored? who can access it? and What audit trails must be maintained? Complying with these laws can often be accomplished with an in-country presence, consequently CSPs may require to have data centers in every major financial market around the world. The more data centers and countries covered, the larger potential user base that can be optimally served. This will reduce the barrier to entry and encourage utilizing powerful CSPs with large geographic footprints to get more value. Additionally, the in-country presence shortens the last mile to enable providing better speed and to allow getting to the user more quickly. Storing and processing data at the "edge" minimizes latency and round-trip times from the client device and gives a distinct edge on the competition.

Whenever an MCC exist in the service loop, risk management and governance teams should be concerned. Plenty of questions should be answered, who has the responsibility to provide a sustainable risk management and governance? How the CC infrastructure will affect business risks? Who will assure adequate controls for compliance, privacy and long-term service continuity? Who will guarantee that the level of trust extended to a CSP or MCC is warranted? In an ideal world, the tactics used to engage a CSP would be commensurate with the level of risk to which the CE is exposed (CSA, 2015). If necessary, the tactics to judge if the CSP is worthy of trust and the quality procedures may be dictated by a risk and governance framework.

MCCs contracted by the CSP should be examined including their incident management, business continuity and disaster recovery policies, processes and procedures including the co-location and backup facilities. The CSP internal assessments of conformance to its own policies and procedures should be reviewed. CSP metrics should also be reviewed in relation to its internal controls, performance and effectiveness. If some CSP details cannot be reached, the CE management can make certain assumptions in order to complete the risk assessment.

Control and Confidence

Due to the lack of the CE physical control over the CSP infrastructure in many CC deployments, contract requirements, service level agreements (SLAs) and the CSP documentations may play a larger role in risk management than with traditional, enterprise owned infrastructure. CEs and CSPs should develop robust service control schema, regardless of the service or deployment model. This schema should be collaboration between both entities to achieve agreed-upon goals that supports the business mission and technology program. The service model may adjust the defined roles and responsibilities in collaborative schema based on the respective scope of control for the CE and the CSP. The controls may define accountability and expectations based on risk assessment.

Confidence is a key factor in the CE decision to participate in or engage with projects or programs to deliver the expected outcomes. In the CC deployments the confidence issue is further complicated by the interdependencies between CEs, CSPs and MCCs. The CE should view the CSP as supply chain loops, which means examining and assessing the CSP supply chain to the extent possible including its relationships and dependencies. When categories of stakeholders do not have sufficient confidence that a CSP is being controlled and directed toward their desired outcomes in a consistent manner, they are less likely to engage with CC projects. If this becomes an endemic system feature, the loss of confidence and participation in projects may affect many other stakeholders. This will increase the likelihood of external action to curtail the whole relationship between CEs, CSPs and MCCs.

There are times when, in spite of all care and consideration, deployments get so far off-the track, thus there is no alternative to pulling the plug. In CC deployments utilizing agile methodologies, this may occur at early stages with or without any functionality going live. Sometimes the failure is due to purely external challenges such as a CSP or an MCC is going out of business. This was rare case prior to the cloud, but it is more frequent in the cloud era. On the contrary, the traditional case when the original functional and technical specifications are inadequate is decreasing. Agile methodologies reduce wrong specifications scenarios or those cannot be adjusted to accommodate new business realities (Abrahamsson, Salo, Ronkainen, & Warsta, 2002). In the cloud era, top management and even the board need to have more awareness about the CC deployments status and consequences. They should be prepared to make decisions to protect business robustness, pursuing compensation or re-staging certain projects.

Every CE should carefully consider the monitoring mechanisms that are appropriate and necessary for its own circumstances. Due to the on-demand provisioning and multi-tenant aspects of CC, traditional forms of assessment may not be suitable or it may need some modifications. For example, some CSPs restrict vulnerability assessments and penetration testing, while others limit availability of service logs and activity monitoring. If those are required per internal policies, CE may need to seek alternative assessment options. The enterprise risk management framework may list specific contractual exceptions or alternative criteria that is better aligned with CC.

FUTURE RESEARCH DIRECTIONS

Technology is now everywhere and cloud computing (CC) is stretching the services so they can be used without significant capital expenditure. The relation between the Technology Organization (TO) and Business Units (Bus) is rephrased leading to a wide change in mentality and collaboration. BUs can acquire CC services without the TO involvement. These movements promote the term "Technology Organization (TO)" rather than "Information Technology (IT)". The CIO role should be renamed as Chief Integration Officer. Supported by the growth of CC services, both terms need to be reshaped as they are expected to spread out. A lot of business alignments and systems integrations are yet to come. Research should follow the trend and define new dimensions for "TO" and the new "CIO".

Cloud Computing (CC) and the associated technologies open a wide terrain and opportunities in theories and in real life. CC surges the dependency on external providers either for a limited scope or to have a long partnership. Handling the Cloud Service Providers (CSPs) and the Middle Circle Contractors (MCCs) is a big challenge that requires plenty of discussions about contracting and outsourcing.

The tactics to judge whether they are worthy of trust, the scope of controls required is two study topics. Similarly, is the deployment schemes of cloud projects, which requires a lot of agility, elasticity, optimization and acceleration techniques. Sometimes, CC research is considered as a part of the SMAC (Social, Mobile, Analytic and Cloud) arena as there exist a lot of dependencies and correlations.

Increasing the CC maturity levels is a must to achieve business stability and cultivate the benefits. This introduces fundamental changes in programming structure. Mini-services and extensible enterprise structures enhance business scalability, reduce costs and simplify management. They open a wide spectrum to orchestrate various components to minimize risk association and increase harmony. Likewise, is the establishment of self-standing services that can be utilized from everywhere. This leads to business transformation which involves a lot of standardization, harmonization and quality management. Maturity, standardization and business transformation invite advanced research to for better enhancement and utilization in the CC era.

Fostering business transformation is a challenge that requires the participation of a very wide range of stakeholders. Risk accompanies change, it is an inherited component of life. The willingness to take and accept risk is crucial for development and progress. Risk management is a key to track risk consequences and keep them under control. Governance is setting the rules to enable stakeholders benefiting from change without major deviation from the CE strategic directions. The right way may be dictated by a simple to use and easily to understood risk and governance framework. The development of an effective and acceptable risk and governance framework for CC is extremely necessary. Based on some understanding and practice, this chapter sheds few lights on CC risk and governance areas along with the associated business phenomena. The main recommendation out of this chapter is to establish a full Cloud Computing Risk and Governance Framework (CCRGF). This is a huge research project that should benefit from existing efforts and require the contribution of every stakeholder in order to be successful.

CONCLUSION

Cloud computing (CC) is reshaping the future, plenty of benefits are justifying its acceptance both from the technical and the management perspective. On the other hand, CC is not yet mature therefore it is important to re-invest the savings obtained from CC into more controls, ongoing detailed assessments and optimization. This will ensure that stakeholders requirements are continuously met, the benefits are measured and the accepted challenges are rewarded. CC services are undoubtedly forming the dynamic heart of the next enterprise transformation.

Practice has shown that associated CC technologies and risks are often not well understood by the key stakeholders in the client enterprise (CE), including board members and executive management. CC is characterized by direct correlation with business transformations. Without a clear understanding, senior executives have no point of reference for prioritizing and managing enterprise risks and objectives. Misunderstanding can be a major drawback, since these are the major stakeholders who should identify, monitor, control and govern major types of risk within the enterprise and manage its strategies. Executives should view cloud governance as a major sub-journey of the overall governance roadmap with long-term view to deliver short term solutions in a coherent vision. Governance benefits will be more recognized over the course of implementation and operation. However, the governance paradigm should apply equally to future components to govern new technology components as well as defined ones. It will help deriving the policies, standards, responsibilities, procedures, mechanisms, and metrics.

The CC phenomena have introduced several features and trigged major business transformations. Extensible enterprise, elastic CC nexus and the Middle Circle Contractors (MCCs) or the "men-in-the-middle" phenomena are just few disruptions. These have created new dimensions into the enterprise governance structure, processes, and controls. Transformation should be demonstrably risk-based and clearly support the enterprise governance objectives. As part of the CE due diligence, governance processes and capabilities of providers, partners and contractors should be assessed for sufficiency, maturity, and consistency. The rollout of cloud computing and associated business transformation projects is unique. It should utilize the best enterprise architecture and follow agile methodologies to move with sure steps to satisfy the integration and isolation rules. This will fit all business areas with conflicting behaviors while utilizing the "off-the-shelf" products and services to regenerate the CE processes and functionalities.

CC Governance has to achieve a seemingly impossible theme. That is to open and protect the CE processes and information effectively and balance risks with opportunities. In this challenging environment, a solid strategy will be required to facilitate quality risk management decisions and to support fact-based communication. This will lay the foundation for full risk assessment and disseminate a standardized methodology while promoting risk-related concepts. This chapter attempts to present some efforts in this direction and to ignite fruitful aspirations that will eventually lead to an increased number of research studies in the field of CC governance and risk. This can pave the way for a business transformation that can merging technology and business seamlessly as expected in the CC era. To achieve this, a full Cloud Computing Risk and Governance Framework (CCRGF) is required. This chapter is just few bricks to establish such a framework.

REFERENCES

AAIRM. (2002). *A risk management standard*. London UK: The Institute of Risk Management, the National Forum for Risk Management in the Public Sector and the Association of Insurance and Risk Managers.

Abbas, N., Gravell, A. M., & Wills, G. B. (2008). Historical roots of agile methods: where did agile thinking come from. In *Proceedings of 9th International Conference on Agile Processes in Software Engineering and Extreme Programming* (vol. 9, pp. 94-103). Heidelberg, Germany: Springer doi:10.1007/978-3-540-68255-4_10

Abrahamsson, P., Salo, O., Ronkainen, J. & Warsta, J. (2002). *Agile Software Development Methods*. Vuorimiehentie, Finland: VTT Technical Research Center of Finland.

Abram, T. (2009). The hidden values of it risk management. *Information Systems Audit and Control Association Journal, 2009*(2), 40-45.

Ackermann, T. (2012). *IT Security Risk Management: Perceived IT Security Risks in the Context of Cloud Computing*. Berlin, Germany: Springer-Gabler.

Alnuem, M., Alrumaih, H., & Al-Alshaikh, H. (2015). *Enterprise risk management from boardroom to shop floor*. Paper presented in The Sixth International Conference on Cloud Computing, GRIDs, and Virtualization, Nice, France.

Avasant. (2016). *Digital Enterprise Transformation: Rebooting Business Services for the New Global Economy.* El Segundo, CA: Create Space Independent Publishing Platform.

Aven, T. (2008). *Risk analysis: Assessing uncertainties beyond expected values and probabilities.* West Sussex, UK: John Wiely and Sons, Ltd. doi:10.1002/9780470694435

Baya, V., Mathaisel, B., & Parker, B. (2010). The cloud you don't know: An engine for new business growth. PWC Journal of Technology Forecast: Driving Growth with Cloud Computing, 1(4), 4-16.

Beck, K. (2001). *Manifesto for Agile Software Development.* Retrieved February 5, 2016, from http://agilemanifesto.org/

Broder, J. (2006). *Risk analysis and the security survey.* Burlington, MA: Butterworth-Heinemann Elsevier.

Brotby, W. (2006). *Information security governance: Guidance for boards of directors and executive management.* Rolling Meadows, IL: IT Governance Institute.

Brown, W. A., Moore, G., & Tegan, W. (2006). *SOA governance—IBM's approach.* Somers, NY: IBM Corporation.

Brown, W., Laird, R., Gee, C., & Mitra, T. (2008). *SOA Governance: Achieving and Sustaining Business and IT Agility.* Indianapolis, IN: IBM Press.

Campagna, R., Lyer, S., & Krishnan, A. (2013). *Mobile Device Security for Dummies.* Hoboken, NJ: John Wiley & Sons.

COSO. (2012). Enterprise Risk Management for Cloud Computing. Durham, NC: The Committee of Sponsoring Organizations of the Treadway Commission (COSO).

Crouhy, M., Galai, D., & Mark, R. (2006). *The essentials of risk management.* New York: McGraw-Hill Inc.

CSA (The Cloud Security Alliance). (2011). *Security guidance for critical areas of focus in cloud computing v3.0.* Retrieved September 09, 2015, from https://downloads.cloudsecurityalliance.org/initiatives/guidance/csaguide.v3.0.pdf

Daecher, A., & Galizia, T. (2015). *Ambient computing. Deloitte Journal of Tech Trends, 6(1),* 34–49.

Davis, C., Schiller, M., & Wheeler, K. (2006). *IT auditing: Using controls to protect information assets.* Emeryville, CA: McGraw-Hill Osborne Media.

De Haes, S., & Grembergen, W. (2009). *Enterprise governance of information technology: Achieving strategic alignment and value.* New York: Springer. doi:10.1007/978-0-387-84882-2

Dutta, A., Peng, G. C., & Choudhary, A. (2013). Risks in enterprise cloud computing: The perspective of IT experts. *Journal of Computer Information Systems, 53*(4), 39–48. doi:10.1080/08874417.2013.11645649

Fit'o, J., & Guitart, J. (2014). Introducing Risk Management into Cloud. *Journal of Future Generation Computer Systems, 32*(1), 41–53.

Goranson, H. (1999). *The agile virtual enterprise: Cases, metrics, tools.* New York: Quorum Books.

Hardy, G. (2006). New roles for board members on IT. *Governance Journal, 13*(151), 11–14.

HBR (Harvard Business Review). (2011). *Harvard Business Review on Aligning Technology with Strategy*. Boston: Harvard Business School Publishing.

Hillson, D. (2008). Why risk includes opportunity. *The Risk Register Journal of PMI's Risk Management Special Interest Group, 10*(4), 1–3.

Hoda, R., Noble, J., & Marshall, S. (2009). Negotiating Contracts for Agile Projects: A Practical Perspective. In *Proceedings of 10th International Conference on Agile Processes in Software Engineering and Extreme Programming*. Heidelberg, Germany: Springer. doi:10.1007/978-3-642-01853-4_25

ISACA. (2013). COBIT5 for Risk. Rolling Meadows, IL: Information Systems Audit and Control Association (ISACA).

Jayaswal, K., Kallakurchi, K., Houde, D., & Shah, D. (2014). *Cloud Computing Black Book*. New Delhi, India: Dreamtech Press.

JISC Legal Information. (2014). *User Guide: Cloud Computing Contracts, SLAs and Terms & Conditions of Use*. Retrieved February 5, 2016, from http://www.webarchive.org.uk/wayback/archive/20150703224546/ http://www.jisclegal.ac.uk/ManageContent/ViewDetail/ID/2141/User-Guide-Cloud-Computing-Contracts-SLAs-and-Terms-Conditions-of-Use-31082011.aspx

Kaplan, R., & Mikes, A. (2012). Managing Risks: A new framework. *Harvard Business Review, 90*(6), 48–63.

Kark, K., & Vanderslice, P. (2015). CIO as Chief Integration Officer. Deloitte Journal of Tech Trends, 6(1), 4-19.

Lamersdorf, A., Munch, J., Viso, A. F., Sanchez, C. R., Heinz, M., & Rombach, D. (2010). A Rule-Based Model for Customized Risk Identification in Distributed Software Development Projects.*Proceedings of the 5th IEEE International Conference on Global Software Engineering (ICGSE)*, (vol. 1, pp. 209–218). Los Alamitos, CA: IEEE Computer Society. doi:10.1109/ICGSE.2010.32

Marcus, A. (Ed.). (2014). *Design, User Experience, and Usability. User Experience Design for Diverse Interaction Platforms and Environments*. Heidelberg, Germany: Springer. doi:10.1007/978-3-319-07668-3

Marks, N. (2015). *The myth of IT risk*. Retrieved September 09, 2015, from https://normanmarks.wordpress.com/2015/08/28/the-myth-of-it-risk

Mell, P., & Grace, T. (2011). The NIST Definition of Cloud Computing, NIST Special Publication, 800-145, 2011. Gaithersburg, MD: National Institute of Standards and Technology (NIST).

Menken, I., & Blokdijk, G. (2008). *Virtualization: The complete cornerstone guide to virtualization best practices*. Brisbane, Australia: Emereo Pty Ltd.

Metheny, M. (2013). *Federal Cloud Computing: The Definitive Guide for Cloud Service Providers*. Waltham, MA: Elsevier.

NIST (National Institute of Standards and Technology). (2015). *Cloud computing service metrics description*. Retrieved September 09, 2015, from http://www.nist.gov/itl/cloud/upload/RATAX-CloudServiceMetricsDescription-DRAFT-20141111.pdf

Olson, D. & Peters, S. (2011). Managing Software Intellectual Assets in Cloud Computing, Part 1. *Journal of Licensing Executives Society International, H*(3), 160-165.

Pierantonelli, M., Perna, A., & Gregori, G. L. (2015). Interaction between Firms in New Product Development.*International Conference on Marketing and Business Development Journal, 1*(1), 144-152.

Poppendieck, M., & Poppendieck, T. (2013). *The Lean Mindset: Ask the Right Questions*. Westford, MA: Addison-Wesley.

Schlarman, S. (2009). IT risk exploration: The IT risk management taxonomy and evolution. *Information Systems Audit and Control Association Journal, 2009*(3), 27-30.

Segal, S. (2011). *Corporate Value of Enterprise Risk Management: The Next Step in Business Management*. Hoboken, NJ: John Wiley & Sons.

Shalan, M. A. (2010). Managing IT Risks in Virtual Enterprise Networks: A Proposed Governance Framework. In S. Panios (Ed.), *Managing Risk in Virtual Enterprise Networks: Implementing Supply Chain Principles* (pp. 115–136). Hershey, PA: IGI Global. doi:10.4018/978-1-61520-607-0.ch006

Shalan, M. A. (2016In press). Ethics and Risk Governance for the Middle Circle in Mobile Cloud Computing: Outsourcing, Contracting and Service Providers Involvement. In K. Munir (Ed.), *Security Management in Mobile Cloud Computing*. Hershey, PA: IGI Global.

Shawish, A., & Salama, M. (2014). Cloud Computing: Paradigms and Technologies. In F. Xhafa & N. Bessis (Eds.), *Inter-cooperative Collective Intelligence: Techniques and Applications* (pp. 39–67). Berlin, Germany: Springer-Verlag. doi:10.1007/978-3-642-35016-0_2

Shelton, T. (2013). *Business Models for the Social Mobile Cloud: Transform Your Business Using Social Media, Mobile Internet, and Cloud Computing*. Indianapolis, IN: John Wiley & Sons. doi:10.1002/9781118555910

Shinder, D. (2013). *Selecting a Cloud Provider*. Retrieved September 09, 2015, from http://www.cloudcomputingadmin.com/articles-tutorials/architecture-design/selecting-cloud-provider-part1.html

Siepmann, F. (2014). *Managing Risk and Security in Outsourcing IT Services: Onshore, Offshore and the cloud*. Boca Raton, FL: Taylor and Francis Group.

Soyata, T. (2015). *Enabling Real-Time Mobile Cloud Computing through Emerging Technologies*. Hershey, PA: IGI Global. doi:10.4018/978-1-4666-8662-5

Stantchev, V., & Stantcheva, L. (2013). Applying IT-Governance Frameworks for SOA and Cloud Governance. In M. D. Lytras, D. Ruan, R. D. Tennyson, P. Ordonez De Pablos, F. J. García Peñalvo, & L. Rusu (Eds.), *Information Systems, E-learning, and Knowledge Management Research* (pp. 398–407). Berlin, Germany: Springer-Verlag. doi:10.1007/978-3-642-35879-1_48

Tarkoma, S. (2012). *Publish / Subscribe Systems: Design and Principles*. Hoboken, NJ: John Wiley & Sons. doi:10.1002/9781118354261

Tiwari, A., Sharma, V., & Mahrishi, M. (2014). Service Adaptive Broking Mechanism Using MROSP Algorithm. In *Proceedings Advanced Computing, Networking and Informatics: Wireless Networks and Security* (vol. 2, pp. 383-392). Springer. doi:10.1007/978-3-319-07350-7_43

Turban, E., Leidner, D., McLean, E., & Wetherbe, J. (2008). *Information technology for management: Transforming organizations in the digital economy.* John Wiley and Sons Inc.

Vice, P. (2015). *Taking risk management from the silo across the enterprise.* Retrieved September 09, 2015, from http://www.aciworldwide.com/-/media/files/collateral/aci_taking_risk_mgmt_from_silo_across_enterprise_tl_us_0211_4572.pdf

Vice, P. (2015). *Should IT Risks Be Part of Corporate Governance?* Academic Press.

Warrier, S., & Shandrashekhar, P. (2006). A Comparison Study of Information Security Risk Management Frameworks in. Paper presented in the Asia Pacific Risk and Insurance conference, Tokyo, Japan.

ADDITIONAL READING

Aljawarneh, S. (Ed.). (2012). *Cloud Computing Advancements in Design, Implementation, and Technologies*. Hershey, PA, USA: IGI Global.

Antonopoulos, N., & Gillam, L. (Eds.). (2010). *Cloud Computing: Principles, Systems and Applications*. London, UK: Springer-Verlag. doi:10.1007/978-1-84996-241-4

Australian Government. (2013). Negotiating the cloud – legal issues in cloud computing agreements. Sydney, Australia.

Awad, M. A. (2005). *A Comparison between Agile and Traditional Software Development Methodologies*. (Unpublished master dissertation). The University of Western Australia, Perth, Australia.

Axelrod, C. W. (2004). *Outsourcing Information Security: Computer Security Series*. Norwood, MA: Artech House.

Ben Halpert, B. (2011). *Auditing Cloud Computing: A Security and Privacy Guide*. Hoboken, NJ, USA: John Wiley & Sons. doi:10.1002/9781118269091

Bento, A., & Aggarwal, A. (Eds.). (2013). *Cloud Computing Service and Deployment Models: Layers and Management*. Hershey, PA, USA: IGI Global. doi:10.4018/978-1-4666-2187-9

Biske, T. (2008). *SOA governance*. Birmingham, United Kingdom: Packt Publishing.

Booker, S., Gardner, J., Steelhammer, L., & Zumbakyte, L. (2004). What is your risk appetite? The risk-it model. *Information Systems Audit and Control Association (ISACA). Journal, 35*(2), 38–43.

Bostrom, A. (Ed.). French, S. (Ed.), & Gottlieb, S. (Ed.). (2008). Risk assessment, modeling and decision support: Strategic directions. Heidelberg, Germany: Springer-Verlag.

Braithwaite, J., Coglianese, C., & Levi-Faur, D. (2007). Can Regulation and Governance Make a Difference? *Regulation and Governance Journal. Wiley Publishing Asia Pty Ltd, 1*(1), 1–7.

Brown, D., & Wilson, S. (2005). *The Black Book of Outsourcing: How to Manage the Changes, Challenges, and opportunities*. Hoboken, NJ, USA: John Wiley & Sons.

Busby, J., & Zhang, H. (2008). How the subjectivity of risk analysis impacts project success? *Project Management Journal, 39*(3), 86–96. doi:10.1002/pmj.20070

Buyya, R., Broberg, J., & Goscinski, A. (Eds.). (2010). *Cloud Computing: Principles and Paradigms*. Hoboken, NJ, USA: John Wiley & Sons.

Chao, L. (Ed.). (2012). *Cloud Computing for Teaching and Learning: Strategies for Design and Implementation*. Hershey, PA, USA: IGI Global. doi:10.4018/978-1-4666-0957-0

Charette, R. (2005). Why software fails. *IEEE Spectrum, 42*(9), 42–49. doi:10.1109/MSPEC.2005.1502528

Cornelius, D. (2013, October). *SMAC and transforming innovation*. Paper presented at the meeting of the 2013 PMI Global Congress. New Orleans, Louisiana.

Dallas, G. (Ed.). (2004). Governance and risk. New York, USA: McGraw-Hill companies Inc.

Drucker, P. (1999). *Management challenges for the 21st century*. New York City, New York, USA: HarperCollins Publishers Inc.

Easwar, K. L. (2014). *Segmentation of Risk Factors associated with Cloud Computing*. Paper presented at 2nd International Conference on Cloud Security Management [ICCSM], Reading, UK.

Ferrier, M. (Ed.). (2015). *Leading in the SMAC age*. Bangalore, India: Wipro.

Franklin, T. (2008). Adventures in Agile Contracting: Evolving from Time and Materials to Fixed Price, Fixed Scope Contracts. In *Proceedings of IEEE Agile 2008 Conference* (vol. 1, pp. 269-273). Los Alamitos, CA: IEEE Computer Society. doi:10.1109/Agile.2008.88

Furht, B., & Escalante, A. (Eds.). (2010). *Handbook of Cloud Computing*. Berlin, Germany: Springer Science & Business Media. doi:10.1007/978-1-4419-6524-0

Grembergen, W. (Ed.). (2003). *Strategies for information technology governance*. Hershy, Pennsylvania, USA: Idea Group Publishing.

H°akansson, H., Ford, D., Gadde, L. & Snehota, I. (2003). *Managing Business Relationships*. Hoboken, NJ, USA:John Wiley & Sons.

Hogan, M., & Sokol, A. (Eds.). (2013). NIST Cloud Computing Standards Roadmap, NIST Special Publication, 500-291. Gaithersburg, MD, USA. National Institute of Standards and Technology (NIST).

Hoogervorst, J. (2009). *Enterprise governance and enterprise engineering*. Diemen, Netherlands: Springer. doi:10.1007/978-3-540-92671-9

Hubbard, D. (2009). *The Failure of Risk Management: Why It's Broken and How to Fix It*. Hoboken, NJ, USA: John Wiley & Sons.

IITP. (2013). Cloud computing code of practice version 2. Wellington, New Zealand: Institute of IT Professionals (IITP).

IRMA, Information Resources Management Association (Ed.). (2015). Cloud Technology: Concepts, Methodologies, Tools, and Applications (Vols. 1–4). Hershey, PA, USA: IGI Global.

Jamsa, K. (2012). *Cloud Computing*. Burlington, MA, USA: Jones & Bartlett Publishers.

Jordan, E., & Silcock, L. (2005). *Beating IT risks*. West Sussex, England: John Wiely and Sons, Ltd.

Khidzir, N, Z., Mohamed A. & Arshad, N. H. (2013). ICT Outsourcing Information Security Risk Factors: An Exploratory Analysis of Threat Risks Factor for Critical Project Characteristics. *Journal of Industrial and Intelligent Information Vol. 1, No. 4, December, 1*(4), 218-222.

Kunreuther, H. (2006). Risk and reaction: Dealing with interdependencies. *Harvard International Review: Global Catastrophe, 28*(3), 17–23.

Kunreuther, H. (2008). *The weakest link: Risk management strategies for dealing with interdependencies* (Working Paper # 2008-10-13). Philadelphia, Pennsylvania, USA: University of Pennsylvania, the Wharton School.

Kwak, Y. (2003). *Perception and practice of project risk management*. Paper presented in the Project Management Institute Global Congress North America, Baltimore, Maryland USA.

Laakkonen, K. (2014). *Contracts in Agile Software Development*. (Unpublished master dissertation). Aalto University, helsenki, Finland.

Larman, C., & Vodde, B. (2010). *Practices for Scaling Lean & Agile Development*. Boston, MA: Addison-Wesley & Pearson Education Inc.

Layton, M. C. (2012). *Agile Project Management for Dummies*. Hoboken, NJ, USA: John Wiley & Sons.

Lientz, B., & Larssen, L. (2006). *Risk management for IT projects*. Oxford, United Kingdom: Butterworth-Heinemann.

Liu, F., Tong, J., Mao, J., Bohn, R., Messina, J., Badger, L., & Leaf, D. (2011). NIST Cloud Computing Reference Architecture, NIST Special Publication, 500-292, Gaithersburg, MD, USA. National Institute of Standards and Technology (NIST).

Lööf, T. (2010). *Agile outsourcing: A Case Study*. (Unpublished bachelor dissertation). Gothenburg University, Göteborg, Sweden.

Lu, J., Yu, X., Chen, G., & Yu, W. (Eds.). (2016). *Complex Systems and Networks: Dynamics, Controls and Applications*. Heidelberg, Berlin: Springer. doi:10.1007/978-3-662-47824-0

Macintosh, R., Maclean, D., Stacey, R., & Griffin, D. (2006). *Complexity and Organization: Readings and Conversations*. New York, NY: Routledge.

Mastorakis, G., Mavromoustakis, C., & Pallis, E. (2015). *Resource Management of Mobile Cloud Computing Networks and Environments. Hershey, PA, USA: IGI Global. McDonald, K. (2010). Above the Clouds: Managing Risk in the World of Cloud Computing, Cambridge shire*. United Kingdom: IT Governance Ltd.

Moeller, R. (2008). *Enterprise risk management and the project manager*. Paper presented at Project Summit & Business Analyst World, Philadelphia, USA.

Moran, A. (2014). *Agile Risk Management*. New York, USA: Springer. doi:10.1007/978-3-319-05008-9

Moran, A. (2015). *Managing Agile: Strategy, Implementation, Organization and People*. Berlin, Germany: Springer. doi:10.1007/978-3-319-16262-1

Newman, M. (2004). Firewalls: Keeping the big, bad world out of your firm. *San Fernando Valley Business Journal, 9*(18), 21–22.

Niemann, K. (2008). *From Enterprise architecture to IT governance: Elements of effective IT management*. Wiesbaden, Germany: Springer-Verlag.

Ogheneovo, E. (2014). Software Dysfunction: Why Do Software Fail? Scrip *Journal of Computer and Communications, 2014*(2), 25-35.

Opelt, A., Gloger, B., Pfarl, W., & Mittermayr, R. (2013). *Agile Contracts: Creating and Managing Successful Projects with Scrum*. Hoboken, NJ, USA: John Wiley & Sons. doi:10.1002/9781118640067

Peltier, R. (2005). *Information security risk analysis*. Boca Raton, Florida, USA: Taylor and Francis. doi:10.1201/9781420031195

PMI. (2008). *A Guide to project management body of knowledge*. Newtown square, Pennsylvania, USA: Project Management Institute.

Raj, B. (2012). Cloud Enterprise Architecture, Poca Raton, FL, USA: CRC Press: Taylor & Francis Group. doi:10.1201/b13088

Ramirez, D. (2008). IT risk management standards: The bigger picture. *Information Systems Audit and Control Association (ISACA) Journal, 2008*(4), 35-39.

Renn, O. (2008). *Risk governance: Coping with uncertainty in a complex world*. London, United Kingdom: Earthscan Publications Ltd.

Rittinghouse, J., & Ransome, J. (2009). Cloud Computing: Implementation, Management, and Security, Poca Raton, FL, USA: CRC Press: Taylor & Francis Group. doi:10.1201/9781439806814

Rodrigues, J., Lin, K., & Lioret, J. (2013). *Mobile Networks and Cloud Computing Convergence for Progressive Services and Applications (Advances in Wireless Technologies and Telecommunication)*. Hershey, PA, USA: IGI Global.

Rothstein, H., Borraz, O., & Huber, M. (2013). Risk and the Limits of Governance. Exploring varied patterns of risk-based governance across Europe. *Regulation and Governance Journal. Wiley Publishing Asia Pty Ltd, 7*(2), 215–235.

Sargut, G., & McGrath, R. (2011). Learning to Live with Complexity. *Harvard Business Review*, *89*(9), 68–76. PMID:21939129

Sawyer, S., & Tapia, A. (2005). The sociotechnical nature of mobile computing work: Evidence from a study of policing in the United States. *International Journal of Technology and Human Interaction*, *1*(3), 1–14. doi:10.4018/jthi.2005070101

Schekkerman, J. (2006). *How to survive in the jungle of enterprise architecture frameworks*. Victoria, BC, Canada: Trafford Publishing.

Soili, N., Thomas, B., & Jaakko, K. (Eds.). (2015). *Flexibility in Contracting*. Rovaniemi, Finland: University of Lapland.

Sosinsky, B. (2011). *Cloud Computing Bible*. Indianapolis, IN, USA: John Wiley & Sons.

Thuraisingham, B. (2013). Developing and Securing the Cloud, Poca Raton, FL, USA: CRC Press: Taylor & Francis Group. doi:10.1201/b15433

Türke, R. (2008). *Governance: Systemic foundation and framework*. Heidelberg, Germany: Springer-Verlag. doi:10.1007/978-3-7908-2080-5

Udoh, E. (Ed.). (2011). *Cloud, Grid and High Performance Computing: Emerging Applications*. Hershey, PA, USA: IGI Global. doi:10.4018/978-1-60960-603-9

Vose, D. (2008). *Risk analysis: A quantitative guide*. West Sussex, England: John Wiley and Sons, Ltd.

Walewski, J., & Gibson, G. (2003). *International project risk assessment: methods, procedures, and critical factor (Research. Rep. No. 31)*. Austin, Texas: The University of Texas at Austin, Construction Industry Studies Centre.

Wells, J. (2013). *Complexity and Sustainability*. New York, NY: Routledge.

Westerman, G., & Hunter, R. (2007). *IT risk: Turning business threats into competitive advantage*. Boston, Massachusetts, USA: Harvard Business School Publishing.

Zhao, F. (Ed.). (2006). *Maximize business profits through e-partnerships*. Hershey, PA: IRM Press. doi:10.4018/978-1-59140-788-1

KEY TERMS AND DEFINITIONS

Agile Methodology: A development method that is people-focused, communication-oriented, leadership philosophy that encourages teamwork, self-organization and accountability to develop a dynamic service that can respond to change and continuously deliver business value.

Client Enterprise (CE): A business enterprise that use the professional, networking or computing services provided by Cloud Service Providers (CSPs). Services is provided according to a signed contract against some agreed financial charges.

Cloud Service Provider (CSP): An entity that provides cloud computing services based on their existing platforms and apply certain rules and charges for these services.

Governance: A set of processes, customs, policies, laws and institutions affecting the way an enterprise is directed, administered or controlled.

Middle Circle Contractor (MCC): An external or internal person, group or organization that is appointed to perform work or to provide goods/services at a certain price or within a certain time. The MCC appears as a middle person who may disappear after the specified task is complete usually.

Outsourcing: A common method whereby a third party performs a function on behalf of the Client Enterprise (CE), often when additional resources (either time, expertise, human resources, service, etc.) are needed. This may be usually an extended long relationship.

Risk Management: The act of handling the risk exposure through mitigation, acceptance, sharing and avoidance. It includes the ability to handle information and technology risks based on stakeholders' risk parameters.

Shadow IT: A term often used to describe technology systems and solutions built and used inside the CE without formal approvals or technology organization involvement.

SMAC: An acronym generated from the first letters of Social, Mobile, Analytics and Cloud words. These four technologies are currently driving business innovation, with multiple service categories and scenarios.

Technology Organization (TO): A team either inside the client enterprise (CE) or outside it, that is in charge of establishing, monitoring and maintaining technology systems and services. The "TO" need to support strategic planning to ensure that all technology initiatives aligned with business goals. Traditionally, "TO" was named as information technology (IT) department.

Chapter 17

A Survey and Taxonomy of Energy Efficient Resource Management Techniques in Platform as a Service Cloud

Sareh Fotuhi Piraghaj
The University of Melbourne, Australia

Rodrigo N. Calheiros
The University of Melbourne, Australia

Amir Vahid Dastjerdi
The University of Melbourne, Australia

Rajkumar Buyya
The University of Melbourne, Australia

ABSTRACT

The numerous advantages of cloud computing environments, including scalability, high availability, and cost effectiveness have encouraged service providers to adopt the available cloud models to offer solutions. This rise in cloud adoption, in return encourages platform providers to increase the underlying capacity of their data centers so that they can accommodate the increasing demand of new customers. Increasing the capacity and building large-scale data centers has caused a drastic growth in energy consumption of cloud environments. The energy consumption not only affects the Total Cost of Ownership but also increases the environmental footprint of data centers as CO2 emissions increases. Hence, energy and power efficiency of the data centers has become an important research area in distributed systems. In order to identify the challenges in this domain, this chapter surveys and classifies the energy efficient resource management techniques specifically focused on the PaaS cloud service models.

BACKGROUND

The numerous advantages of cloud computing environments, including cost effectiveness, on-demand scalability, and ease of management, encourage service providers to adopt them and offer solutions via cloud service models. In return, it encourages platform providers to increase the underlying capacity of their data centers to accommodate the increasing demand of new customers. One of the main drawbacks of the growth in capacity of cloud data centers is the need for more energy to power these large-scale

DOI: 10.4018/978-1-5225-0759-8.ch017

infrastructures. This drastic growth in energy consumption of cloud data centers is a major concern of cloud providers.

An average data center consumes as much energy as 25,000 households, as reported by Kaplan et al. (Kaplan, Forrest, & Kindler, 2008). This energy consumption results in increased Total Cost of Ownership (TCO) and consequently decreases the Return of Investment (ROI) of the cloud infrastructure. Apart from low ROI, energy consumption has a great impact on carbon dioxide (CO_2) emissions, which are estimated to be 2% of global emissions (Buyya, Beloglazov, & Abawajy, 2010).

The energy wastage in data centers are caused by various reasons such as inefficiency in data center cooling system (S. Greenberg, Mills, Tschudi, Rumsey, & Myatt, 2006), network equipment (Heller et al., 2010), and server utilization (A. Greenberg, Hamilton, Maltz, & Patel, 2008). However, servers are still the main power consumers in a data center (A. Greenberg et al., 2008). Both the amount of work and the efficiency with which the work is performed affects the power consumption of servers (Krioukov et al., 2010). Therefore, for improving the power efficiency of data centers, the energy consumption of servers should be made more proportional to their workload.

The power proportionality is defined as the proportion of the amount of power consumed comparing to the actual workload. The power proportionality can be achieved by either decreasing the servers idle power at hardware level (Barroso & Holzle, 2007) or efficient provisioning of servers through power aware resource management policies at software level. In this chapter, we solely focus on software level and the resource management techniques utilized for decreasing energy consumption in Cloud data centers considering four different service models (depicted in Figure 1):

- **Infrastructure as a Service (IaaS):** In this service a consumer has the ability to provision the required resources while running and deploying arbitrary software such as operating systems and applications. Using this model consumers do not need to worry about the underlying hardware.
- **Platform as a Service (PaaS):** This model has a higher level of abstraction in comparison to the IaaS model. By offering the application-hosting environment, the consumers do not need to have any control over the underlying infrastructure including storage, processing and network.
- **Software as a Service (SaaS):** Using this service model, a consumer is able to use the provider's applications which are hosted on the Cloud. Applications are accessible through web portals. This model has also made development and testing easy for providers via having access to the software.
- **Containers as a Service (CaaS):** This service is recently introduced and lies between IaaS and PaaS. While IaaS provides virtualized compute resources and PaaS provides application specific runtime services, CaaS is the missing layer that glues these two layers together.

Among the above-mentioned service models, this chapter mostly focuses on energy efficient resource management techniques for PaaS and CaaS.

PaaS POWER-AWARE RESOURCE MANAGEMENT

There is a large body of literature investigating energy management techniques for PaaS cloud service model that provides a platform for cloud customers to develop, run, and manage their applications without worrying about the underlying infrastructure and the required software. Both kinds of virtualization namely, OS level and System level virtualization, are considered and the newly introduced CaaS model

Figure 1. The container as a service cloud service model links the PaaS and IaaS layers

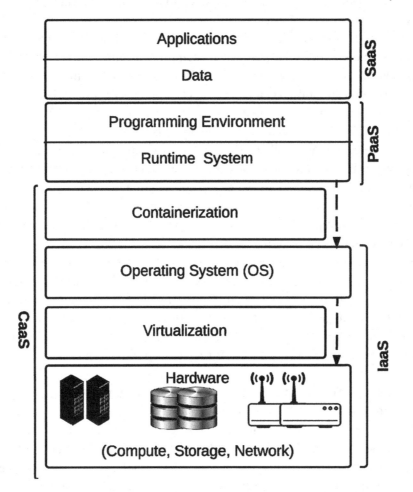

can be viewed as a form of OS level virtualization service. Since CaaS cloud model has been newly introduced, we grouped all the research with the focus on containerized (OS-level virtualized) cloud environments under the PaaS category.

The work in this area, as demonstrated Figure 2, is grouped in two major categories namely "Bare Metal, non-virtualized", and "Virtualized". The *Bare Metal* group contains the techniques in which the applications/tasks are mapped to the servers without considering virtualization technology, whereas the work investigating energy efficient techniques in a virtualized environment are all included in *Virtualized* group.

Bare Metal Environments

Servers are one of the most power-hungry elements in data centers, with CPU and memory as their main power consumers. The average power consumption of CPU and memory is reported to be 33% (Meisner, Gold, & Wenisch, 2009) and 23% (David, Fallin, Gorbatov, Hanebutte, & Mutlu, 2011) of the server's total power consumption respectively. Therefore, any improvement on processor and memory-level power

Figure 2. Power-aware PaaS resource management research breakdown

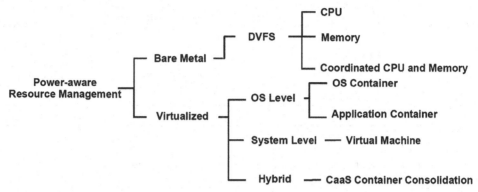

consumption would definitely reduce the total power consumption of the server, which also improves the energy efficiency of data center.

Dynamic Voltage and Frequency Scaling (DVFS) is an effective system level technique utilized both for memory and CPU in *Bare Metal* environments and it is demonstrated to improve the power consumption of these two elements considerably (Charles, Jassi, Ananth, Sadat, & Fedorova, 2009; David et al., 2011; Deng, Meisner, Ramos, Wenisch, & Bianchini, 2011; von Laszewski, Wang, Younge, & He, 2009). DVFS enables dynamic power management through varying the supply voltage or the operating frequencies of the processor and/or memory. Research in this area are summarized in Tables 2- 3.

Dynamic Voltage and Frequency Scaling of CPU

The technologies present in the market are AMD Turbo Core (AMD, 2016), Intel Turbo Boost (Charles et al., 2009), and Intel Enhanced Speed Stepping Technology (Intel, 2016), which dynamically adjust the CPU frequency and voltage according to the workload. Kim et al. (K. H. Kim, Buyya, & Kim, 2007), harnessed the DVFS capability of CPU in the proposed scheduling algorithm. DVS scheduling scheme considers the deadline of the Bag-of-Tasks applications as a constraint and the CPU frequency is adjusted so that the sub-tasks are finished by the deadline. An application made of a group of independent and identical tasks is an example of Bag-of-Task applications. DVS scheduling algorithms are provided for both time-shared and space-shared resource sharing policies. Proposed algorithm is validated through simulation and is shown to be more energy efficient when compared to the static voltage schemes.

Pietri et al. (Pietri & Sakellariou, 2014) also proposed an energy efficient scheduling algorithm utilizing the DVFS capability of CPU. The frequency of the CPU is adjusted with the objective of reducing the total energy consumption for the execution of tasks while meeting a user-specified deadline. Decreasing the overall energy consumption is considered as the objective of the algorithms, since DVFS is not always energy efficient, as scaling the CPU frequency may increase the execution time. Hence, it escalates the processors idle time. Based on the aforementioned objective, it is demonstrated that the lowest possible frequency is not always the most energy-efficient option. Therefore, the proposed approach only scales the frequency if the overall energy consumption can be minimized.

Table 1. Hardware virtualization taxonomy

Virtualization	Component	Communication with Hardware	Available Technologies
Operating System (OS)	OS Container (Lightweight VM)	System Standard Calls	LXC, OpenVZ, Linux VServer, FreeBSD Jails, Solaris zones
	Application Container		Docker, Rocket
System	Virtual Machine (VM)	Hypervisor	KVM, VMWare

Table 2. Energy efficient research considering bare metal environment

Authors	Workload	SLA	Energy Saving	Energy Model
David et al. (David et al., 2011)	SPEC CPU2006 benchmark workload	Application slow down	DVFS on Memory component for CPU intensive work- loads	Real-system measurements along with an analytically power reduction model for memory.
Deng et al.(Deng et al., 2011)	Memory Intensive, CPU Intensive, and balanced Workloads	User defined performance degradation limit.	DVFS on memory component	A power model is proposed to include the effect of the memory
Deng et al.(Deng et al., 2012)	Memory and CPU intensive and a combination of these workloads, The workload characteristics are known beforehand	Application performance degradation limit	DVFS on both CPU and memory component	System total energy model is proposed containing both CPU and memory frequency
Kim et al. (K. H. Kim et al., 2007)	Bag-of-Tasks	Task Execution time	DVFS on CPU component	$E = E_{dynamic} + E_{static} = k1V2\ L + k2(k1V2\ L) = \alpha V2\ L$
Leverich et al. (Leverich & Kozyrakis, 2010)	Hadoop's MapReduce workload	Throughput	Powering down idle nodes which are not accessed regularly, a set of nodes are considered as a backup to ensure the data availability.	Linear Power Model. (CPU only)
Lang et al. (Lang & Patel, 2010)	Workload Characteristics such as the expected resource consumption and performance goals of jobs are studied and considered as abstract meta-models	Response Time	Power down/up MR nodes to save energy in periods of low utilization.	An energy model is presented which incorporates the power drawn by both online and offline nodes during the workload execution.
Kaushik et al.(Kaushik et al., 2010)	One-month of Yahoo Hadoop's HDFS logs in a multi-tenant cluster are grouped according to creation date and access rate. Two main categories are considered namely hot and cold zones.	Response Time	Energy-efficient data-placement through dividing servers into two major groups namely Hot and Cold zones. Energy can be saved through harnessing the idleness in the Cold zone.	Power models are used for the power levels, transitions times of power states and the subsystems access time including the disk, the processor and the DRAM.

Table 3. Energy efficient research considering bare metal environment

Authors	Workload	SLA	Energy Saving	Energy Model
Chen et al. (Y. Chen et al., 2012)	MapReduce with interactive analysis (MIA) style workloads is classified using k-means clustering algorithm.	Response time	BEEMR (Berkeley Energy Efficient MapReduce) as an energy efficient MapReduce workload manager which is inspired by studying the Facebook Hadoop workload	Linear Power Model (CPU only).
Feller et al.(Feller et al., 2015)	Hadoop benchmarks including three micro-benchmarks namely TeraGen, TeraSort, and Wikipedia data processing are studied and the approach is applicable for both Bare metal and System level.	Application's completion time.	Achieved through considering the resource boundness of the tasks along with the differences between the map and reduce tasks.	Energy metered environment is utilized (Grid5000).
Lee et al.(Lee et al., 2015)	Bare Metal and System level Workflow applications Workload. Workload Characteristics is assumed to be a prior knowledge	Makespan	Improved the resource utilization.	NA
Pietri et al.(Pietri & Sakellariou, 2014)	Scientific Workflow applications	Makespan	DVFS on CPU component	Energy consumption pf is estimated considering each processors operating frequency f through a cubic model derived in [] Pf = Pbase + Pdif * (f − fbase/fbase)3 and the total power consumption is estimated adding Pf to the power consumed when the processor is idle.
Durillo et al.(Durillo et al., 2014)	Workflow applications	Makespan	Efficient Resource Allocation	Energy consumption of task A running on multi core systems is estimated through: $c.E_{core}+E_{share}$. Here, c is the number of active cores and E_{core} is the energy consumed in active cores while executing task A. E_{shared} is the energy consumption of all the shared subsystems which are active during the task execution.

Dynamic Voltage and Frequency Scaling of Memory

In addition to CPU, memory of servers also consumes a considerable amount of energy that is not proportional to the load (David et al., 2011). For memory-intensive workloads, system's memory speed is well tuned and optimized according to the peak computing power. However, there is still a place for improvement for other kinds of workloads that are less sensitive to the memory speed. For these kinds of workload, running at lower memory speed would result in less performance degradation and reduce the power consumption via running memory at a lower frequency.

David et al. (David et al., 2011) presented an approach utilizing the memory DVFS capability to tune the system's memory frequency based on the workload and consequently minimize the energy consumption. Additionally, a detailed power model is presented which quantifies dependency portions of memory power to the frequency and further proves the possibility of considerable power deduction through memory DVFS. Also, a control algorithm is proposed to tune frequency/voltage of memory considering its bandwidth utilization with the objective of minimizing performance degradation. The approach is evaluated through implementation on real hardware while SPEC CPU2006 is used to generate the workload. This work can further be extended for different types of workloads considering DVFS application for both CPU and memory components.

Deng et al. (Deng et al., 2011) introduces active lower-power modes (*MemScale*) for main memory to make it more energy proportional. In this respect, DVFS and dynamic frequency scaling (DFS) are applied on the memory controller and its channels and DRAM devices, respectively. *MemScale* is implemented as an operating system policy and, like David et al. (David et al., 2011) it identifies the DVFS/DFS mode for the memory subsystem according to the bandwidth utilization of memory. The objective of the research is also similar to the work by David et al. (David et al., 2011), which improves the energy consumption of the memory subsystem. This is important because it can reach up to 40% of the system's energy utilization (Hoelzle & Barroso, 2009). *MemScale* is evaluated through simulation considering a large set of workloads with less than 10% performance degradation while in (David et al., 2011) only one workload is studied.

Coordinated CPU and Memory DVFS

Deng et al. (Deng, Meisner, Bhattacharjee, Wenisch, & Bianchini, 2012) introduced *CoScale*, which jointly applies DVFS on memory and CPU subsystems with the objective of minimizing the systems total power consumption. *CoScale* is the first work in this area that coordinates DVFS on CPU and memory considering performance constraints. The frequency of each core and the memory bus is selected in a way that energy saving of the whole system is maximized. Therefore, the selected frequencies are not always the lowest ones.

As observed by Dhimsan et al. (Dhiman, Pusukuri, & Rosing, 2008), lowering the frequency sometimes results in more energy consumption. So *CoScale* always balances the system and component power utilization. It efficiently searches the space of available frequency settings of CPU and memory and sets the components voltage according to the selected frequencies. In this respect, the algorithm should consider $m * n * c$ possibilities in which m and c are the number of available frequency setting for memory and CPU respectively and n is the number of CPU cores. In order to accelerate the search process, a gradient-descent heuristic is proposed that iteratively estimates the frequencies of the components through the presented online models. Memory-intensive (MEM), compute-intensive (ILP), compute-memory balanced (MID), and a combination of workloads are applied as the input of the system. The results of *CoScale* is further compared with four different algorithms, namely *MemScale* (Deng et al., 2011), CPU DVFS, a fully uncoordinated, and a semi-coordinated algorithm. In the fully uncoordinated algorithm, both memory and CPU frequency are decided by their managers independently. In semi-coordinated policy, the CPU manager is aware of the degradation caused by the memory manager decision in the previous cycle through accessing overall performance slack. *CoScale* satisfies the performance target while being robust-across the search space parameter.

Virtualized Environments

Virtualization technology is one of the key features in cloud data centers that can improve the efficiency of hardware utilization through resource sharing, migration, and consolidation of workloads. The technology was introduced in the 1960's (Goldberg, 1974; Graziano, 2011) and exists in many levels. Of interested in this chapter, is virtualization at operating system level and at system level (Table 1).

In system-level virtualization, there exists the emulated hardware referred as "virtual machines" (VMs) that have their own operating system (OS) running on top of the host's hypervisor with independent kernels. However, on the operating system level, there exists the so called container that shares the same kernel with the host and is defined as lightweight virtual environment that provides a layer of isolation between workloads without the overhead of the hypervisor-based virtualization.

Considering these two virtualization types, techniques investigating power-aware resource management are divided into three main categories namely "Lightweight Container", "Virtual Machine", and "Hybrid". These groups are formed according to the environment in which applications execute. Therefore, the *Lightweight container* category contains techniques that assume that tasks/applications execute inside containers. In the *Virtual Machine* group, applications execute inside virtual machines. Finally in the *Hybrid* category, applications execute inside the containers while containers are mapped on virtual machines instead of servers.

Next, we discuss these three groups with more details and explore techniques that are applied to minimize the data center energy consumption considering the characteristics of each virtualized environment. The research in this area is summarized in Table 4.

Operating System (OS) Level Virtualization (Containers)

The Platform as a Service (PaaS) model has accelerated application development and eliminated the need for administration of the underlying infrastructure. In this service model, application isolation is achieved through the utilization of containers that can run both on PMs and VMs.

Containers are the building blocks of OS-level virtualization that offer isolated virtual environments without the need for intermediate monitoring media such as hypervisors, as shown in Figure 3.The container technology of the Linux Kernel are developed separately by four different resources including OpenVZ (OpenVZ, 2016) from Parallels, Google's *cgroups* (control groups), IBM's Dpar, and namespaces (Rosen, 2013). Among those, *cgroups* and *namespaces* presented solutions for resource management and per process isolation respectively and except for the Dpar, the other three are currently used (Bottomley, 2013).

Containerization technology has been implemented on large scale by cloud companies such as Google and Facebook. Containers are beneficial for cloud providers since they can be more densely packed when compared to VMs. The other benefit of containers is that they all share the host kernel. Therefore, the communication between containers and the hardware is performed through standard systems calls, which is much faster than hypervisor-based communication.

Operating System level virtualization or the containerization itself is categorized in two different types including OS containers and application containers and the energy management techniques which are applied to these environments are depicted in Figure 4.

OS containers can be taught of VMs that share the kernel of the host's operating system while providing isolated user space. Various OS containers with identical or different distributions can run together

Table 4. Energy efficient research considering os-level virtualization

Authors	Workload	SLA	Energy Saving	Energy Model
Dong et al. (Dong et al., 2014)	Google Cluster Data (OS Container)	NA	DVFS, Container Placement	Proposed a power model named as VPC
Pandit et al. (Pandit et al., 2014)	Synthetic workload (OS Container)	NA	Container placement, Simulated Annealing is applied.	NA
Hindman et al. (Hindman et al., 2011)	Synthetic workload (OS Container)	Response Time	Resource sharing between various programming models	NA
Spicuglia et al. (Spicuglia et al., 2015)	Primary Big Data application workloads (Shark [], YARN [J), and the background applications computing π. (Application Container)	Throughput	Power Capping (Considers a power constraint for running applications.)	Linear Power Model (CPU only)
Anselmi et.al (Anselmi et al., 2008)	Three Tier Application workload (Application Container)	Response Time	Efficient allocation of resources	NA
Rolia et al. (Rolia et al., 2003)	Enterprise application workload (Application Container)	NA	Efficient Allocation of Resources, Servers with fast migration ability is used	NA
Mohan et al. (Mohan Raj & Shriram, 2011)	Request arrival for web servers that follows Poisson distribution (Application Container)	Allowable pending requests for each application in the dispatcher queue	NA	Power Consumption of servers based on the number of VMS

Figure 3. Containerized virtual environment

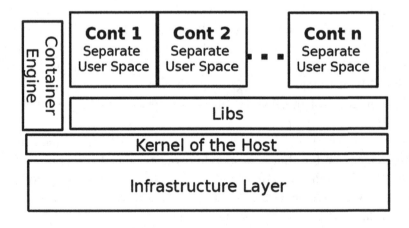

Figure 4. Energy management techniques which are applied to the OS level virtualization environments

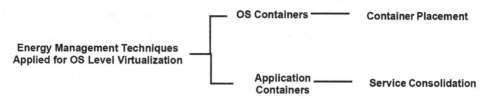

on top of the host operating system as long as they are compatible with the host kernel. The shared kernel improves the utilization of resources by the containers and decreases the overhead of container's startup and shutdown. OS containers are built up on the *cgroups* and namespaces, whereas application containers are built upon the existing container technologies. Application containers are specifically designed for running one process per container. Therefore, one container is assigned for each component of the application. Application containers, as demonstrated in Figure 5, are specifically beneficial for microservice architecture in which the objective is having a distributed and multi component system that is easier to manage if anything goes wrong.

Operating System (OS) Containers

OS containers based on *cgroups* and *namespaces* provide user space isolation while sharing the kernel of the host operating system. The development in OS containers is like VMs and one can install and run applications in these containers as he runs it on a VM. Like VMs, containers are created from templates that identify the contents (Nagy, 2015). Google cluster is an example of such systems that runs all its services in containers. As stated on Google open source blog (Brewer, 2016), Google launches more than 2 billion containers per week considering all of its data centers. The container technologies that support OS containers are LXC (Container, 2016), OpenVZ, Linux VServer (VServer, 2016), FreeBSD Jails and Oracle's Solaris zones (Price & Tucker, 2004).

Figure 5. The differences between the Application container and the OS container for a three tier application. Application containers are implemented to run a single service and by default has layered Filesystems
Source: Nagy, 2015

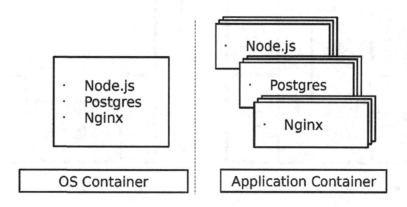

Energy efficient resource management techniques applied for OS container systems mostly focus on the algorithms for initial placement of the OS containers. In this respect, Dong et al. (Dong, Zhuang, & Rojas-Cessa, 2014) proposed a greedy OS container placement scheme, the most efficient server first or MESF, that allocates containers to the most energy efficient machines first. For each container, the most energy efficient machine is the server that shows the least rise in its energy consumption while hosting the container. Simulation results using an actual set of Google cluster data as task input and machine set show that the proposed MESF scheme can significantly improve the energy consumption as compared to the Least Allocated Server First (LASF) and random scheduling schemes. In addition, a new perspective on evaluating the energy consumption of a cloud data center is provided considering resource requirement of tasks along with task deadlines and servers' energy profiles.

Pandit et al. (Pandit, Chattopadhyay, Chattopadhyay, & Chaki, 2014) also explored the problem of efficient resource allocation focusing on the initial placement of containers. The problem is modeled utilizing a variation of multi-dimensional bin packing. CPU, memory, network and storage of PMs are all considered as each dimension of the problem. In a general n-dimensional bin-packing problem, there exist n sub-bins of different sizes that must be filled with objects. The resource allocation problem is different from the general form, since if any sub-bin of a bin reaches its capacity (e.g. CPU), then the bin is considered full while in the original problem this is not the case. Figure 6 demonstrates this difference. In order to design an efficient resource allocation algorithm, Pandit et al. (Pandit et al., 2014) applied Simulated annealing (SA). SA is a technique used to find optimal or sub-optimal solution for NP Hard problems such as the bin packing problem and it is often applied for discrete search space. The proposed resource allocation algorithm is demonstrated to be more efficient in terms of resource utilization when compared to the commonly used First Come First Serve (FCFS) allocation policy.

OS containers are also utilized in Mesos (Hindman et al., 2011) to provide the required isolation for workload. Mesos platform enables sharing commodity clusters between cluster computing frameworks

Figure 6. The difference between the original bin packing problem and its variation for the resource allocation
Source: Pandit et al., 2014

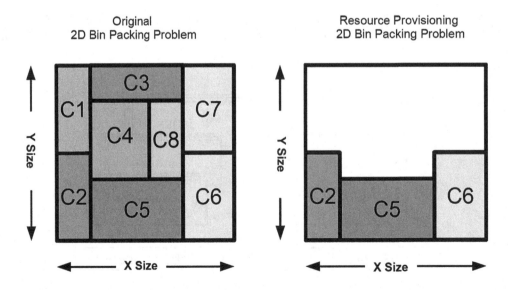

with different programming models. The main objective of Mesos is efficient utilization of resources through sharing and also avoiding data replication for each framework. Hindman et al. (Hindman et al., 2011) proposed a two-level scheduling for the Mesos platform called *resource offers*. For the first level of the scheduling, Mesos identifies the amount of required resources for each framework. The second level scheduling is performed by the scheduler of each framework, therefore the scheduler has the ability to accept or reject the resources while deciding about the placement of the tasks. Mesos used Linux Containers and Solaris technologies for the workload isolation. The framework is tested through applying both CPU and IO-intensive workloads derived from the statistics of Facebook cloud backend traces. The studied workloads are derived from the applications that are developed utilizing both Hadoop and MPI programming model. Results show that Mesos is highly scalable and fault tolerant and can improve the resource utilization with less than 4% overhead.

Application Containers

Contrary to OS containers that run multiple processes and services, application containers are dedicated to a single process and are built upon OS containers. The single process in each container is the process that runs the residing application (Nagy, 2015). Application containers can be considered a new revolution in the cloud era since containers are lightweight, easier to configure and manage, and can decrease the start-up time considerably. Docker(Merkel, 2014) and Rocket (Rocket, 2016) are examples of application containers. These containers are the building block of modern PaaS. Regular provisioning and de-provisioning of these containers, this happens during the auto-scaling, along with their unpredictable workloads results in cloud resource wastage and consequently more energy consumption. Therefore, like OS containers, designing optimal placement algorithms is the major challenge for container-based cloud providers.

Containers are fast to deploy because of their low overhead. Therefore, to simplify the development of applications, Spicuglia et al. (Spicuglia, Chen, Birke, & Binder, 2015) proposed OptiCA in which applications execute inside containers. The aim of the proposed approach is to achieve the desired performance for any given power and capacity constraints of each processor core. Although the focus in OptiCA is mainly on effective resource sharing across containers under resource constraints, it still reduces power consumption through considering energy as one of the constraints.

Anselmi et.al (Anselmi, Amaldi, & Cremonesi, 2008) investigated the Service Consolidation Problem (SCP) for multi-tier applications with the objective of minimizing the number of required servers while satisfying the Quality of Service defined by applications' response time. For modeling the data center, queueing networks theory is utilized since it is capable of capturing the performance behavior of service systems. A number of linear and non-linear optimization server consolidation problems are defined and solved through a number of heuristics. Heuristics are chosen as they solve the optimization problems in a shorter amount of time with a considerable accuracy when compared to the standard Integer Linear Programming (ILP) techniques. This work solves SCP and finds the best data-center configuration with the least cost while satisfying the required end-to-end response time of applications.

In the same direction, Rolia et al. (Rolia, Andrzejak, & Arlitt, 2003) investigated the SCP problem with the objective of minimizing the number of required servers through application consolidation. Enterprise applications are studied and their resource utilization is characterized. Like Anselmi et al. (Anselmi et al., 2008), linear integer programming is considered as one of the solutions and ILP is further compared with the genetic algorithms. The techniques are validated through a case study considering the workload of 41 servers. Results show that the linear integer programming model outperforms the genetic algorithm in terms of the required computation with a satisfactory accuracy in estimating the resource utilization. However, the proposed technique is not evaluated for large-scale data centers containing thousands of servers.

Mohan Raj et al. (Mohan Raj & Shriram, 2011) also focused on minimizing the energy consumption of the data center through consolidation of applications on physical machines (PM). An end-to-end Service-Level Agreement (SLA)-aware energy efficient strategy is presented in (Mohan Raj & Shriram, 2011) and the main objective is having an strategic workload scheduling for maximizing energy efficiency of the data center. Tasks are consolidated on virtual machines so that the number of active servers is reduced. Contrary to the previous discussed works (Anselmi et al., 2008; Rolia et al., 2003) synthetic workloads following the Poisson distribution are applied for the simulations to model the web server workloads. Containers are placed on the PMs that utilize the least energy rise. SLA is maintained through a control theoretic method and the requests of applications are accepted considering the SLA along with the data center capacity. The presented model is a queue-based routing approach and Holt-Winters forecasting formula is utilized for improving the SLA through decreasing the cost incurred by the times system waits for a PM to startup or to shut down. The proposed algorithm is also applicable in virtualized environments, where applications execute on virtual machines instead of directly on PMs.

System-Level Virtualization (Virtual Machines)

The virtual machine's idea originated from simulated environments offered for software development when testing on real hardware was unfeasible (Goldberg, 1974). In this respect, a specific environment was simulated considering the required processor, memory, and I/O devices. Later, this idea was improved to develop efficient simulators to provide copies of a server on itself. The improvement is done so that the program running on each copy can be executed directly on the hardware without requiring any software interpretation. These copies (simulated environments) are referred to as virtual machine systems, and the simulated software is referred as the virtual machine monitor (manager) (VMM) or the hypervisor (Goldberg, 1974). This kind of virtualization is referred as system-level virtualization.

In system-level virtualization, the VM communications happens through the hypervisor with more overhead than the OS standard calls for containers. However, communicating through VMM offers a stronger layer of isolation and is more secure than containers (Nagy, 2015). In addition, system-level virtualization enables VMs with any type of OS to be installed on a host (Figure 7). Moreover, this technology enables consolidating virtual machines (VM) on physical machines (PMs) to reach higher and efficient utilization levels of PMs. The virtualization technology also improves the deployment time, and the operating costs.

As depicted in Figure 8, energy management technique applied for system-level virtualization are categorized into five groups namely virtual machine consolidation, overbooking, VM placement, VM sizing, and DVFS. The research in this area is summarized in Table 5 - 7. In the rest of this section, we discuss these techniques with more details.

Figure 7. System level virtualization energy efficient management techniques

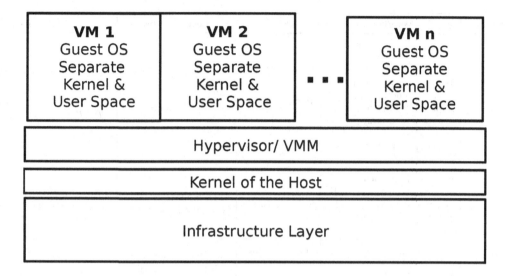

Figure 8. System-level virtualization energy efficient management techniques

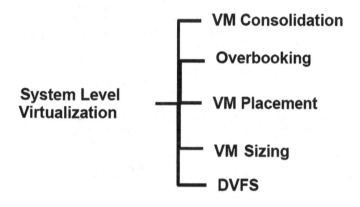

VM CONSOLIDATION

The hypervisor technology enables consolidation of virtual machines on physical servers. There is a vast body of literature investigating VM consolidation algorithms that can improve the energy consumption of data centers. The consolidation problem can be divided into three main sub-problems which are depicted in Figure 9. The techniques are grouped according to the sub problem it investigates.

Techniques Investigating Migration Triggers (When to Migrate?)

Virtual machine consolidation is shown to be an effective way to minimize the energy consumption of cloud data centers. However, identifying the right time to trigger migration is crucial especially when the host is overloaded. This ensures a certain level of Quality of Service (QoS).

Gmach et al. (Gmach, Rolia, Cherkasova, & Kemper, 2009) proposed an energy-efficient reactive migration controller that identifies situations in which the hosts are determined overloaded or underloaded.

Table 5. Energy efficient research considering system-level virtualization

Authors	Workload	SLA	Energy Saving	Energy Model
Urgaonkar et al. (Urgaonkar et al., 2010)	Synthetic Workloads that follow a uniform random distribution is studied. The proposed approach is independent of workload prediction and its statistics as it uses the queueing information to learn and adapt to unpredictable changes in the workload pattern	Throughput	DVFS (on CPU component)	The power-frequency relationship is presented as a quadratic model $P(f) = P_{min} + \alpha(f - f_{min})^2$.
Gmach et al.(Gmach et al., 2009)	Enterprise application workloads analysis is utilized for estimating the under-load and over-load situations for hosts	Response Time	VM Consolidation (When to migrate)	Linear Power Model (CPU only)
Beloglazov et al. (A. Beloglazov & R. Buyya, 2010)	PlanetLab Worklaod	The time during which host experience is identified overloaded	VM Consolidation (What triggers migration with fixed Under-load and Over-load thresholds)	Linear Power Model (CPU only)
Beloglazov et al. (Anton Beloglazov & Rajkumar Buyya, 2010)	PlanetLab Workload	The time during which host experience is identified overloaded	VM Consolidation (What triggers migration with automatic under-load and overload detection algorithms along with two VM selection approaches)	Linear Power Model (CPU only)
Beloglazov et al. (Anton Beloglazov & Buyya, 2012)	PlanetLab Workload, The approach is independent of workload including stationary and non-stationary workloads	A QoS goal as an input of consolidation algorithm	VM Consolidation (What triggers migration with optimally adjusting the overload threshold and selecting the right VM to migrate)	Linear Power Model (CPU only)
Meng et.al (Meng et al., 2010)	VM workloads of a commercial data center	Response time (Considering a performance constraint for each VM)	VM Consolidation (Where to migrate considering the Statistical Multiplexing approach)	NA

Table 6. Energy efficient research considering system-level virtualization

Authors	Workload	SLA	Energy Saving	Energy Model
Moreno et al. (Moreno, Yang, et al., 2013)	Google Workload is Classified based on task resource Usage patterns	QoS is insured through placing VMs based on their interference with the co-located VMs	VM Consolidation Where to migrate VMs? Interference Aware VM Placement	Linear Power Model (CPU only)
Caglar et al. (Caglar et al., 2013)	Google Workload	Response Time	VM Consolidation Where to migrate VMs? Interference Aware VM Placement	NA

continued on next page

Table 6. Continued

Authors	Workload	SLA	Energy Saving	Energy Model
Chen (M. Chen et al., 2011) et al.	The workload data of 5,415 servers from ten different companies is characterized via fitting distributions	A probabilistic function that contains the probability of a host being overloaded	VM Consolidation Where to migrate VMs? Statistical Multiplexing VM Placement	NA
Verma et al. (Verma et al., 2009)	Enterprise application workload from the production data center of a multi-national Fortune Global 500 company. A detail analysis of the workload is presented including the correlation between the workloads.	Number of time instances that an application demand is more than the server's capacity	VM Consolidation Where to migrate VMs? Statistical Multiplexing VM Placement	The power models are derived from actual measurements on the servers (Power vs CPU utilization).
Calheiros et al.(Calheiros & Buyya, 2014)	Bag of tasks applications considering CPU Intensive tasks	User defined deadlines	DVFS (CPU only)	The power consumption of each host is calculated considering the contribution of each CPU core.
Laszewski et al. (von Laszewski et al., 2009)	Worldwide LHC Computing Grid (WLCG) workload	Throughput	DVFS (CPU only)	Energy is estimated considering CPU frequency
Kim et.al (Jungsoo Kim et al., 2013)	Analyzed the characteristics of scale-out applications obtained from a data center.	Virtual machines are provisioned according to their peak load.	DVFS Efficient resource allocation placing VMs based on correlation analysis	Energy Model in [].
Tomas et al. (Tomas et al., 2014)	Real-life interactive workloads and non-interactive batch applications	Response Time	Overbooking resources	NA

Table 7. Energy efficient research considering system-level virtualization

Authors	Workload	SLA	Energy Saving	Energy Model
Klein et al. (Klein et al., 2014)	RUBiS and RUBBoS	Response time and throughput	Overbooking resources	NA
Forestiero et al. (Forestiero et al., 2014)	Logs of Eco4Cloud company www.eco4cloud.com	Avoiding any sites from being overloaded	Consolidating workloads on a multi-site platform (Geo-distributed cloud environment) Where to migrate?	NA
Khosravi et al.(Khosravi et al., 2013)	Lublin-Feitelson workload model is employed to generate the Web application and Bag-of-Tasks workload.	NA	Efficient placement of VMs	Modeled considering the frequency of CPU.
Assuncao et al. (Assuncao et al., 2012)	747 VM request workloads are classified.	Makes sure that most of the workloads can fit into selected templates	Efficient allocation of resources Decreasing the number of required templates	NA

Figure 9. The consolidation sub problems which need to be answered for a general consolidation problem

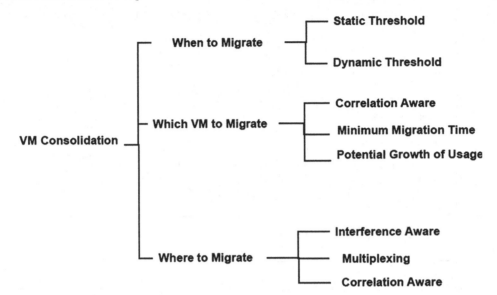

The overload and underload detection is defined when the server's CPU and memory utilization goes beyond or under a given fix threshold respectively. The same approach is applied in (A. Beloglazov, 2010) and the effect of these two thresholds on the overall data center energy consumption and SLA violations is studied. 30% and 70% is shown to be the efficient underload and overload threshold considering the total energy consumption and average SLA violations. Contrary to Gmach et al. (Gmach et al., 2009), the proposed approach (A. Beloglazov, 2010) is not dependent on the type of workload.

Beloglazov et al. (Anton Beloglazov & Rajkumar Buyya, 2010) improved the aforementioned approach (A. Beloglazov, 2010) so that the under-load and over-load thresholds are automatically adjusted. The previous approach for triggering the migration is modified since fixed values for thresholds are not suitable for cloud environments in which the workload's behavior is unknown and dynamic. The automation is performed through statistical analysis of the historical data from virtual machines workload. CPU utilization of the host is assumed to follow the t-distribution so that the sample mean and the standard deviation of the distribution can be used for determining the overload thresholds of each host. However, only one underload threshold is defined for the whole system. The adoptive approach shows a considerable improvement in terms of the QoS when compared to the fixed thresholds while it still saves energy.

Cloud providers should be able to ensure the Quality of Service (QoS) that they have promised to costumers. In the consolidation process, this QoS might be degraded because of the hosts being overloaded. In this respect, Beloglazov et al. (Anton Beloglazov & Buyya, 2012) proposed a technique for host overload detection that ensures QoS while saving energy. The proposed approach can find the optimal solution for the overload detection problem considering any known stationary workload. The main objective is maximizing the intermigration time considering a given QoS goal based on a Markov chain model. In order to handle the nonstationary workloads which are unknown, a heuristic-based approach is presented that utilizes the Multisize Sliding Window technique for workload estimation. The algorithm is validated through simulations considering PlanetLab VMs traces as the input workload. The technique is proven to provide up to 88% of the performance of the optimal offline algorithm.

Techniques for Choosing VMs to Migrate (What to Migrate?)

When migration is triggered, the second step is selecting the appropriate virtual machine to migrate. For under-load hosts, it is clear that all the VMs should be migrated so that the host can be shut down or put in a lower power state. For overloaded hosts only a couple of VMs are needed to be migrated so that the host is no longer overloaded.

Beloglazov et al. (Anton Beloglazov & Buyya, 2012), investigated the problem of VM selection policies in the consolidation process. Three different VM selection algorithms are studied namely random selection (RS), maximum correlation (MC), and the Minimum Migration Time (MMT) policies. The RS policy chooses VMs randomly until the host is not overloaded anymore. The MC policy chooses the VM with the maximum correlated workload with the other co-located VMs. The MMT policy selects the VM with the least migration time.

The performance of these policies are validated through simulation and the VM types are derived from Amazon EC2 instance Types (AWS, 2016). PlanetLab's workload (PlanetLab, 2016) is used as the CPU utilization of the VMs. Since the applied workload is for single core VMs, the VM types are all assumed to be single-core and the other resources are normalized accordingly.

The performance of the algorithms is compared considering the total energy consumption by the physical servers of the data center and the SLA violations. Considering the results, the MMT selection policy outperforms the MC and RS policies in terms of the total joint power consumption and the SLA violations. Minimization of the VM migration time is proven to be more important than the correlation between the VMs allocated to a host.

Beloglazov et al. (Anton Beloglazov & Rajkumar Buyya, 2010) also compared two other VM selection policies including Minimization of Migrations (MM) and Highest Potential Growth (HPG) with the RS. The MM algorithm selects the least number of VMs to migrate with the objective of decreasing the migration overhead. HPG chooses VMs with the lowest CPU usage compared to their requested amount, aiming at reducing the SLA violations through avoiding the total potential increase. It is shown that MM, which reduces the number of migrations, outperforms the other two algorithms in terms of the SLA violations and data center energy consumption.

TECHNIQUES INVESTIGATING MIGRATION DESTINATION (WHERE TO MIGRATE?)

When the migration is triggered and the virtual machines are selected for migration, it is the time to find a new destination for the selected VMs. Here, we describe techniques considered for finding new placement/destination for migrating virtual machines.

Interference-Aware VM Placement Algorithms

Virtualization improves resource utilization efficiency and consequently the energy consumption of cloud data centers by enabling multi-tenant environments in which diverse workload types can exist together. VM consolidation and resource overbooking improve energy savings in cloud environments. However, overbooking might affect the performance of virtual machines that are co-located on each server VM (Nathuji, Kansal, & Ghaffarkhah, 2010). The high-competitions for resource incurred between co-hosted

VMs and the resource sharing nature of virtualized environment might cause performance degradation and more energy consumption. The degradation effect of co-located VMs on the performance of each other's applications on the same VM is known as *performance interference* phenomenon.

Moreno et al. (Moreno, Yang, Xu, & Wo, 2013) investigated the impact of this phenomena on the energy efficiency in cloud data centers. The problem is formulated for the virtual machine placement and is modeled utilizing the Google cloud backend traces to leverage cloud workload heterogeneity. Google tasks are grouped according to their CPU, memory and length. Three types referred as small, medium and large are extracted through applying K-means clustering algorithm on the 18th day of the trace that has the highest submission rate. The VM placement decision is made considering the current performance interference level of each server. The interference aware VM placement algorithm is compared, via simulation, with the Google FCFS algorithm and shown to reduce the interference by almost 27.5% while saving around 15% of energy consumption.

As mentioned previously, the performance interference might degrade the QoS for real time cloud applications and consequently result in SLA violations and the placement/packing of VMs play an important role on the performance interference, since it is dependent on the workload of the co-located VMs. In this respect, Caglar et al. (Caglar, Shekhar, & Gokhale, 2013) presented an online VM placement technique included in the hALT (harmony of Living Together) middleware. hALT takes into account workload characteristics of the VMs along with the performance interference for finding placement for each VM. Machine Learning techniques are used for the online placement and the system is trained utilizing the results from an offline workload characterization. The presented framework contains three main parts, namely Virtual machine classifier, neural networks, and the decision making placement. A brief analysis of the Google cloud backend traces is presented. The analysis of the 3 days of the traces is utilized for training the classifier.

Each task in the Google traces is considered as a VM. CPU utilization, memory, and the CPI of tasks are used for the classification purpose. CPI attribute shows the `Cycle Per Instruction' metric and is used as a performance metric since it can well present the response time for compute-intensive applications (Zhang et al., 2013). Therefore, tasks that utilize more than 25% of the CPU and are compute intensive are considered for evaluation of the framework. Decrease CPI results in better performance, a result that had been demonstrated by the previous study.

Back propagation-based artificial neural networks (ANN) (Hecht-Nielsen, 1992) is used as the classifier that predicts the performance interference level. This is used to determine the best placement of the VM. The ANN is trained using the VM utilization patterns of each class of VMs, which is defined by the k-means clustering algorithm. The number of VM classes is estimated based on the maximum Silhouette value (Kaufman & Rousseeuw, 2009; Rousseeuw, 1987) and is determined to be 6 for the studied data set. The effect of the performance interference on the energy consumption is not investigated. The other drawback of the work is when the VM migration is triggered the ANN should run for every server in the data center, which may cause delays and overhead for large data centers. This can be avoided through new techniques in the search process.

Multiplexing Placement Algorithms

The other technique that is widely applied to find the new placement for selected VMs is Statistical Multiplexing. Multiplexing means sharing a resource between users with the objective of increasing the bandwidth utilization. This method has been applied to a variety of concepts including MPEG transport stream for digital TV (Haskell, Puri, & Netravali, 1997), UDP and TCP (Forouzan, 2002) protocols.

Meng et.al (Meng et al., 2010) applied the Statistical Multiplexing concept to VM placement in the server resources are multiplexed to host more VMs. In the proposed approach, called joint-VM provisioning, multiple VMs are consolidated together according to their workload patterns. Statistical multiplexing enables the VM to borrow resources from its co-allocated VMs while it is experiencing its workload spikes. In order to satisfy QoS requirements, a performance constraint is defined for each VM. This constraint ensures the required capacity for a VM to satisfy a specific level of performance for its hosted application. Three different policies are proposed for defining the performance constraint, selecting the co-located VMs, and estimating the aggregated resource demand of multiplexed VMs with complementary workloads. The VM workloads of a commercial data center are applied for evaluation purposes and the results show that the joint-VM provisioning is considerably efficient in terms of the energy consumption.

Chen et al. (M. Chen et al., 2011) investigated the problem of VM placement with the focus on consolidating more VMs on servers. The VM placement is formulated as a stochastic bin packing problem and VMs are packed according to their effective size (ES), which is defined considering Statistical Multiplexing principles. This principle takes into account the factors that might affect the servers aggregated resource demand on which the VM is placed. The effective size is originated from the idea of effective bandwidth; however it is extended to consider the correlation of VM workloads. In this respect, the ES of a VM is affected by its own demand and its co-located VMs considering the correlation coefficient. The proposed VM placement algorithm with the order of $O(1)$ is applied to find the best destination for VMs. Poisson and normal distributions are considered for the VM workloads. The system is also validated through simulation applying a real cloud workload trace. The effective sizing technique adds around 10% to 23% more energy saving than a generic consolidation algorithm. The optimization is performed considering only one dimension, which is CPU demand of VMs.

Correlation Aware VM Placement

Verma et al. (Verma, Dasgupta, Nayak, De, & Kothari, 2009) are among the first researchers to take into account correlation between workloads of co-allocated VMs in the proposed consolidation approach. The idea is initiated from a detail study of an enterprise server workload, the distribution of the utilization and spikes of the workload while considering workloads statistic metrics including the percentiles and average. According to the analysis, average is not a suitable candidate for sizing the applications since the tail of the distribution of the utilization does not decay quickly for most of the studied servers. Therefore, if the sizing is performed based on the average, it might result in QoS degradation. However, the 90-percentile and the cross correlation is shown to be fairly stable and consequently are the best metrics for application sizing purpose. Two correlation-aware placement algorithms, Correlation Based Placement (CBP) and Peak Clustering based Placement (PCP), are proposed considering the insights from the workload characterization. The placement algorithms are implemented as a part of a consolidation planning tool and further evaluated utilizing traces from a live production data center. PCP achieves more energy savings than PCB and also improves the QoS through an extra metric to ensure that co-allocated workloads' peak do not lead to violations.

Similarly, Meng et al. (Meng et al., 2010) also utilized correlation of VMs in their proposed joint-VM provisioning approach. In this approach, multiple VMs are consolidated in a way that the underutilized resources of one VM can be used by the co-located VM at its peak.

Quality of Service (QoS) is important in a cloud environment especially for scale-out applications (Ferdman et al., 2012) such as MapReduce (Dean & Ghemawat, 2008) and web searches. Therefore, Kim et.al (Jungsoo Kim, Ruggiero, Atienza, & Lederberger, 2013) investigated the VM consolidation problem concentrating on the aforementioned applications. Scale-out applications are different from HPC workloads in terms of the workload variance resulted from their user-interactive nature. This high variance is caused by external factors such as number of users and makes these workloads less predictable. The other difference is that scale-out applications are latency sensitive and should maintain users expectations and consequently satisfy the SLA.

In order to save power consumption, DVFS is considered in conjunction with the VM consolidation. The voltage and the frequency are defined considering the correlation between the VMs' workloads which ensures that the expected QoS is achieved. The approach is verified through real implementation of distributed web search applications. The approach is also validated for large scale cloud workloads and compared with a correlation aware placement approach (Verma et al., 2009). The comparison shows that this approach outperforms the aforementioned technique by 13.7% and 15.6% in terms of the energy saving and QoS improvements.

Overbooking

Overbooking is an admission control method to improve resource utilization in cloud data centers. In general, cloud users overestimate the VM size they need to avoid risk of resource shortage. This provides the opportunity for providers to include an overbooking strategy (Tomas, Klein, Tordsson, & Hernandez-Rodriguez, 2014) in their admission control system to accept a new user based on anticipated resource utilization and not on the requested amount. Overbooking strategies mostly rely on load prediction techniques and manage the tradeoff between maximizing resource utilization and minimizing performance degradation and SLA violation.

Based on the resources considered for overbooking, research works can be classified into two main categories. The first category (He, Ye, Fu, & Elnikety, 2012; Jinhan Kim, Elnikety, He, Hwang, & Ren, 2013) only considers CPU and the second category (Tomas et al., 2014; Tomás & Tordsson, 2014) considers I/O and memory along with CPU. Commonly, after the overbooking phase, the majority of approaches (Hu et al., 2013; Svärd, Hudzia, Tordsson, & Elmroth, 2011) mitigate the risk of overbooking by dealing with overload of VMs on a limited number of servers. However, when the data center is overloaded, such techniques are no longer effective.

One way to deal with such challenges (which is of interest for PaaS provider) is to collect the statistics regarding application performance metrics and then, based on the priority of application and users, degrade user experience and reduce utilization of resources. There are a number of application-aware approaches proposed in the literature (He et al., 2012; Jinhan Kim et al., 2013). However, they are application-specific and only consider CPU. To this end, Klein et al. proposed brownout (Klein, Maggio, & Hernández-Rodriguez, 2014), a programming paradigm that suits cloud environments and considers CPU, IO and memory. In a PaaS environment, brownout is integrated to an application in three phases. In the first phase, the application owner (with the incentive of receiving discount on service cost) reveals which part of the hosted application can be considered non-compulsory. This part of application can be discarded to decrease the resource requirements. In the second phase, brownout decides how often the non-compulsory computation can be discarded. Finally, in the last stage, when there is not enough capacity, brownout lessens the number of requests served with the non-compulsory part.

VM Placement

Among resource management policies, the initial placement of VMs plays an important role in the overall data center performance and energy consumption. A strategic placement of VMs can further improve the system overhead through decreasing the required number of migrations. Kabir et al. (Kabir, Shoja, & Ganti, 2014) investigated the issue assuming a hierarchical structure as a favoured deployment model for cloud service provider that consists of cloud, cluster, and hosts. This model helps in appropriately managing the geographical distributed infrastructure to achieve scalability. This hierarchical structure needs a VM placement approach that smartly provides cloud cluster, and node selection mechanisms to minimize resource fragmentation and improve energy efficiency.

In general, the placement strategies can be categorized into two classes, namely centralized and hierarchical. Khosravi et al. (Khosravi, Garg, & Buyya, 2013) proposed a centralized VM placement algorithm for distributed cloud data centers with the objective of minimizing both power consumption and carbon footprint. An information system that has the updated status regarding cloud, cluster, and host utilization is considered that enables centralized decision making and resource optimization. They considered distributed data centers with diverse carbon footprint rates and PUE values and provided a comprehensive comparison on energy efficiency of different combinations of bin-packing heuristics. They concluded that the proposed approach called energy and carbon-efficient (ECE) VM placement saves up to 45% carbon footprint and 20% of power consumption in data centers.

Similarly, Forestiero et al. (Forestiero, Mastroianni, Meo, Papuzzo, & Sheikhalishahi, 2014) proposed EcoMultiCloud, a hierarchical approach for workload management that offers an energy efficient VM placement in a multi-site data center. Their proposed architecture consists of two main layers. The upper layer is responsible for the assignment of workload (virtual machine requests) among remote sites and lower layer places virtual machines to hosts in each site. The proposed hierarchical approach achieves same energy efficiency as ECE (centralized solution), and offers more flexibility. This is because, as a hierarchical approach, it allows single data centers to select their internal VM placement algorithms.

VM Sizing

Virtualization technology provides the opportunity for applications to share the underlying hardware with secure isolation (Meng et al., 2010). Virtual machines configuration, in terms of the amount of resources (CPU, memory and I/O), are pre-defined by the cloud provider in most of the cloud service models. VM configuration is important for the resource allocation process where a host with enough resources need to be chosen to host the VM. Such VM placement process may ultimately affect the energy consumption of the data center.

Therefore, the efficiency of VM placement can be achieved by three different approaches. In the first approach, VMs are assigned to hosts according to their fix sizes and consolidated to less number of servers without change of configuration. This approach is discussed with details in the VM consolidation section (A. Beloglazov, 2010; Gmach et al., 2009)beloglazov_adaptive_2010 (Anton Beloglazov & Buyya, 2012) MorenoInference:2013 (Moreno, Yang, et al., 2013) . The second approach is tailoring virtual machine configuration to the workload, which can be achieved through characterization of the applications workload. These two approaches are considered as *Static VM Sizing* (Figure 10). Finally, the third approach is adjusting the VM's configuration to match its workload in runtime (Meng et al., 2010) and is known as *Dynamic VM Sizing* (As shown in Figure 10).

Static VM Sizing

Assuncao et al. (Assuncao et al., 2012) proposed *CloudAffinity*, a framework to match physical servers to VM instances called as *CloudMates*. This framework enables organizations to move their workloads to the cloud while choosing optimal number of available VM templates considering their budget constraint. *CloudAffinity* considers CPU, memory, and disk requirement of each server and chooses the optimal number of VM templates minimizing the user's cost based on the predefined Quality of Service (QoS). The QoS is defined as the percentage of the requests which are satisfied by each VM template. The effectiveness of the VM template matching is investigated through three metrics including cost, Euclidean distance, and Matching factor. The cost metric shows the amount of money that the user should pay to maintain a cloud instance and this cost differs from one instance to the other. The Euclidean distance metric is the distance between the cloud provider's template and the user's requirement in terms of the resources including CPU, memory and disk. The Matching factor metric shows the percentage of the difference between customer's requirement and what the template offers for each VM.

Piraghaj et al.(S.F. Piraghaj et al., 2015) also investigated the effect of virtual machine configurations on the total energy consumption of the data center. However, Piraghaj et al.(S.F. Piraghaj et al., 2015) tailored the VM configurations to the workload, instead of choosing from the available configurations which is the case of CloudAffinity (Assuncao et al., 2012).

In order to have efficient configurations, VM sizes are tailored to the workload. In this respect, an analysis of the system workload is inevitable. The work is carried out in three major steps, firstly the usage patterns of tasks are studied and the similarities in these patterns initiated the idea of grouping the tasks according to their utilization in terms of CPU and memory. In the second step, the clustering output is used for identifying the VM configuration for each group of tasks separately and in the third step, each group of tasks is mapped to a corresponding VM size. The presented approach is validated through simulation and Google backend data is utilized as the input workload. The efficiency of the identified VM sizes through the proposed technique is further compared with some of the Amazon EC2 instances. It is also provided that workload characterization and the utilized feature-set play an important role on the efficiency of the identified VM sizes. In this respect, two different feature sets are selected for clustering the tasks. The first set contains the scheduling class[1], submission rate and the length of the task along with the average resource utilization including memory and CPU, and disk. While the second

Figure 10. VM sizing techniques categorized in two major groups including static and dynamic sizing

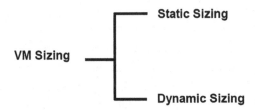

feature set only contains the average CPU and memory utilization of tasks during the studied period (1 day of the trace). The second clustering feature set is shown to identify more efficient VM sizes in terms of the required number of servers and the number of instantiated VMs.

Dynamic VM Sizing

In dynamic VM sizing, the approach estimates the amount of the resources that should be allocated to a VM with the objective of matching the VMs resources to its workload. The VM sizing should be carried out in a way that to avoid SLA violations resulted from under-provisioning of resources. Meng et al. (Meng et al., 2010), present a provisioning approach in which the less correlated VMs are packed together and an estimate of their aggregate capacity requirements is predicted. This approach applies statistical multiplexing considering dynamic VM resource utilization and it makes sure that the utilization peaks of one VM do not necessarily coincide with the co-allocated VMs. Hence, the amount of resources allocated to each VM varies according to its workload.

Chen et al. (M. Chen et al., 2011) also investigated the problem of VM sizing in the provisioning process, so that more VMs can be hosted on servers. The estimated VM sizes are referred as effective size (*ES*) ("OpenVZ Virtuozzo Containers Wiki,"), which is determined through Statistical Multiplexing principles. These principles take into account the factors that might affect aggregated resource demand of the server on which the VM is placed. The effective size of a VM is affected by both its own demand and its co-allocated VMs considering the correlation coefficient. This effective sizing technique is demonstrated to save more energy than a generic consolidation algorithm.

Dynamic Voltage and Frequency Scaling (DVFS)

In addition to the *Bare Metal* environment, Dynamic Voltage Scaling has also been applied to virtualized environments. Laszewski et al. (von Laszewski et al., 2009) focused on the design and implementation of energy-efficient VM scheduling in a DVFS-enabled compute clusters. Jobs are assigned to preconfigured VMs and the VMs are shutdown when the jobs finish. The solution is proposed for high performance cluster computing, however since they consider virtualization technology, it can be implemented in a cloud environment as well. The scheduling algorithm operates considering two main approaches. It either optimizes the processor power dissipating by running the CPU at lower frequencies with the minimum effect on the overall performances of the VMs or schedules the VMs on CPUs with low voltages and tries not to scale up the CPU voltage.

Urgaonkar et al. (Urgaonkar, Kozat, Igarashi, & Neely, 2010) investigated the problem of optimal resource allocation and power efficiency in cloud data centers through online control decisions.

These decisions are made utilizing available queueing information in the system and the Lyapunov optimization theory. Heterogeneous applications with volatile workloads are used to show that the presented approach can handle unpredictable changes in the workload since it is not dependent on any prediction or estimate of the workload. In the studied system, applications execute inside virtual machines and each application can have multiple instances running across different VMs. Dynamic Voltage and Frequency scaling of CPU is applied for improving the energy consumption of the data center. The frequency of CPU is decided according to the workload by the *Resource Controller*, which is installed on each server.

Authors conclude that DVFS does not always result in more energy savings and operators should also consider utilizing the low power modes available in modern processors which might provide better energy savings with the least performance degradation.

Hybrid

The hybrid virtualization model shown in Figure 11 is a combination of system and OS-level virtualization approaches. The containerization technology used in this model is mainly application containers such as Docker (Merkel, 2014), which was explained previously. This new model is currently provided by Google Container Engine and Amazon ECS as a new cloud computing service called Container as a Service. Running containers inside virtual machines provides an extra layer of isolation while ensuring the required security for users. Research in this area are summarized in Table 8.

As discussed, VM consolidation can be utilized for reducing energy consumption in data centers. However, VM consolidation is limited by the VMs memory (Tchana et al., 2015) and unlimited number of VMs can not be mapped on a physical machine (PM). Therefore, in order to save more energy, VM's resources should also be utilized efficiently. This problem is tackled in the hybrid model through consolidation of containers on VMs, which further improves the utilization of VMs resources. This approach is introduced by Tchana et al. (Tchana et al., 2015) and is called *Software/Service Consolidation* problem (*SCP*). In the *SCP* problem, several software/services are dynamically collocated on one VM. The objective is reducing the number of VMs and consequently decreasing the population of PMs along with the data center power consumption. In order to provide the required isolation, applications execute inside Docker containers. The problem is modeled utilizing Constraint Satisfaction Programming (CSP) and the *Software Consolidation* is carried out along with the VM consolidation. In order to accelerate the software consolidation process, the search domain is reduced considering a couple of boundaries

Figure 11. Hybrid virtual environment

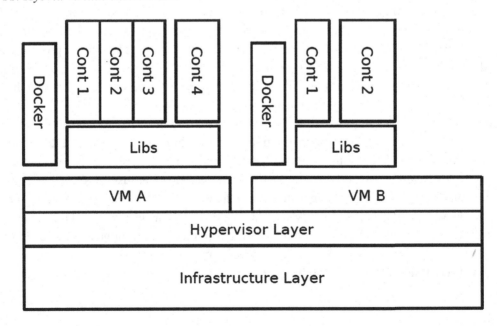

Table 8. Energy efficient research considering hybrid virtual environment

Authors	Workload	SLA	Energy Saving	Energy Model
Dhyani et al. (Dhyani et al., 2010)	Synthetic Workload	NA	Efficient allocation of resources	NA
Bichler et al. (Bichler et al., 2006)	Traces from 30 dedicated servers hosting different types of application services	NA	Efficient resource allocation, Decreasing the number of required servers for hosting applications	NA
Tchana et al. (Tchana et al., 2015)	An enterprise Internet application benchmark (SPECjms2007 benchmark http://www.spec.org/jms2007/)	Service degradation threshold defined at start time for each application	Software Consolidation	NA
Yaqub et al. (Yaqub et al., 2014)	High variability datasets from Google are characterized for OpenShift cloud which can span multi-domain IaaS.	SLA violation (SLAV) is modeled as upper bound estimate considering performance degradation due to both migration (PDM) and contention on machine's resources (PDC)	Software Consolidation, Container migration	Linear Power Model (CPU only)
Almeida et al. (Almeida et al., 2006)	Transactional web services workload is classified into independent Web service (WS) classes.	Response time	Efficient resource allocation	NA

such as containers collocation constraints. One of the limitations of this approach is the OS of the VM hosting the container, since unlike virtual machines, containers share the OS with their host.

Yaqub et al. (Yaqub et al., 2014) also investigated SCP in PaaS Clouds. This problem is framed leveraging the Google definition of Machine Reassignment model for the ROADEF/EURO challenge Roadef (2016) and was extended for RedHat's public PaaS (OpenShift (OpenShift, 2016)). Four Meta-heuristics are applied to find solutions for (re)allocations of containers. The solutions are then compared and ranked considering SLA violations, energy consumption, resource contention, migrations, machine used, and utilization metrics for four different cloud configurations. Contrary to (Tchana et al., 2015), no boundaries are considered to reduce the search domain for the Meta-heuristics to speed up the consolidation process.

Almeida et al. (Almeida, Almeida, Ardagna, Francalanci, & Trubian, 2006) investigated the SCP problem in a Service-Oriented Architecture. The problem was divided into two related sub-problems, short-term resource allocation and long-term capacity planning. The short-term resource allocation problem has a short-term impact on the revenue and its solution determines the optimal resource allocation to different services while increasing the revenue obtained through SLA contracts. However, the answer to long-term problem determines the optimal size of the service center that maximizes the long-term revenue from SLA contracts along with decreasing the Total Cost of Ownership (TCO). These problems are modelled in the proposed framework and a deep analysis of effects of short-term resource allocation is provided. A model is presented for identification of the optimal resource allocation in order to maximize the revenues of the service provider while meeting the required QoS. Resource utilization and the associated costs are also taken into account. The proposed optimal model is fast in terms of the computation speed, which makes it a good candidate for online resource management. Transactional Web services are considered as the hosted applications in the data center. The services are categorized into sub-classes because of the volatility of the web server workloads. Each VM is responsible for one class of web servers (WS). In order to insure the quality of service for each class of the WS, admission control is employed on top of each VM which decides to accept or reject the requests.

Dhyani et al. (Dhyani, Gualandi, & Cremonesi, 2010), introduced a constraint programming approach for the SCP problem. The research objective is decreasing data center cost through hosting multiple services running in VMs on each host. The SCP is modeled as an Integer Linear Programming (ILP) problem and compared with the presented solution through constraint programming. The constraint programming approach can find the solution in less than 60 seconds. However, ILP could find a better solution if it could meet the 60 seconds deadline. Therefore, constraint programming is found as a better solution comparing to ILP for SCP problem considering the algorithm speed.

Bichler et al. (Bichler, Setzer, & Speitkamp, 2006) also investigated the problem of capacity planning. An IT service provider hosting services of multiple customers is investigated in a virtualized environment. Three capacity planning models are proposed for three allocation problems. These problems are solved through multi-dimensional bin-packing approximate algorithms and the workloads of 30 services are applied as the input of the system.

Piraghaj et al. (S. F. Piraghaj, Dastjerdi, Calheiros, & Buyya, 2015), investigated energy-efficient resource management algorithms for container as a Service (CaaS) cloud model. A framework is presented to tackle the energy efficiency issue in the context of CaaS through container consolidation. The CaaS environment is modeled and four sets of simulation experiments are carried out and their impact on system performance and data center energy consumption is evaluated. Four placement algorithms are utilized for identifying the destination host.

A container selection algorithm is responsible for selecting the containers to migrate from an overloaded host. Three selection algorithms including random, correlation aware, which selects the most correlated container with the host load, and the most utilized container in terms of CPU are compared. The algorithm which selects the most correlated container is identified the most efficient one in terms of the energy consumption.

WORKLOAD CHARACTERIZATION AND MODELING

There is a growing body of research on resource management techniques with the focus on minimizing the energy usage in cloud data centers (Kansal, Zhao, Liu, Kothari, & Bhattacharya, 2010; Nathuji & Schwan, 2007). These techniques should be applicable for dynamic cloud workloads. However, because of the competitiveness and security issues, cloud providers do not disclose their workloads, and as a result there are not many publicly available cloud back-end traces. Therefore, most of the research lacks the study of the dynamicity in users demand and workload variation. The availability of cloud backend traces makes researchers able to model real cloud data center workloads. The obtained model can be applied for proving the applicability of the proposed heuristics in real world scenarios.

In 2009, Yahoo released traces from a production MapReduce M45 cluster to a selection of universities (Yahoo, 2010). In the same year, Google made the first version of its traces publicly available and this publicity resulted in a variety of research investigating the problems of capacity planning and scheduling via workload characterisation and statistical analysis of the planet's largest cloud backend traces (Reiss, Wilkes, & Hellerstein, 2011).

Workload Definition

The performance of a system is affected not only by its hardware and software components but also by the load it has to process (Calzarossa & Serazzi, 1993). As stated by Feitelson (Feitelson, 2015), understanding the workload is more important than designing new scheduling algorithms. If the tested systems do not have its input workload chosen correctly, the result of the proposed policies or algorithms might not work as expected when applied to real world scenarios.

The computer workload is defined as the amount of work allocated to the system that should be completed in a given time. A typical system workload consists of tasks and group of users who are submitting the requests to the data center. For example, in Google workload tasks are the building block of a job. In other words, a typical job consists of one or more tasks (Reiss et al., 2011). These jobs are submitted by the users, which are in this case the Google's engineers or its services.

Workload Modeling Techniques

In order to characterize the workload, the drive or input workload of the studied system should also be investigated. For measuring the performance of a computer system, input workload[2], should be the same as the real one. As stated by Ferrari (Ferrari, 1972), there are three types of techniques for obtaining the input workload:

- **Natural Technique:** Natural technique utilizes real workloads obtained from the log file of the system without any manipulation. Urgaonkar et al. (Urgaonkar et al., 2010), utilized real traces from heterogeneous applications to investigate the problem of optimal resource allocation and power efficiency in cloud data centers. Anselmi et.al (Anselmi et al., 2008) also applied real workloads from 41 servers to validate their proposed approach for Service Consolidation Problem (SCP). PlanetLab VMs traces are applied as the input workload to validate the consolidation technique in several works (Anton Beloglazov & Buyya, 2012; Buyya et al., 2010; S. F. Piraghaj et al., 2015).
- **Artificial Technique:** Artificial technique involves the design and application of a workload that is independent of the real one. Mohan Raj and Shriran (Mohan Raj & Shriram, 2011) apply synthetic workloads following the Poisson distribution to model web server workloads.
- **Hybrid Technique:** Hybrid technique involves sampling a real workload and constructing the test workload from the parts of the real workload. Hindman et al. (Hindman et al., 2011) evaluate Mesos the application of both CPU and IO-intensive workloads that are derived from the statistics of Facebook cloud backend traces and running applications utilizing Hadoop and MPI.

Workload Modelling

As stated by Calzarossa and Swerazzi (Calzarossa & Serazzi, 1993), the workload modeling process can be constructed through three main steps. The first step is the formulation in which the basic components such as submission rates for users and their descriptions are selected. In addition to this, for evaluating the proposed model, a criteria is considered. During the second step, the required parameters for modeling are collected while the workload executes in the system. Finally in the last step, a statistical analysis is performed on the collected data.

In selecting the workload modeling technique, the considered parameters for defining the requests play an important role (Agrawala, Mohr, & Bryant, 1976). In a distributed system, a user request is mainly defined via three main parameters including:

1. **t:** The time **t** is when the request is submitted to the system.
2. **l:** The location **l** is where the request is submitted from.
3. **r:** The request vector **r** contains the amount of resources needed in terms of CPU, memory and disk.

When time and spatial distribution of the user requests are ignored, e.g., only one day of the trace is studied, requests population are likely to have similarities and can be presented in the form of relatively homogeneous classes (Agrawala et al., 1976). Such kind of workload modeling is explored by Mishra et al. (Mishra, Hellerstein, Cirne, & Das, 2010) and Chen et al. (Y. Chen, Ganapathi, Griffith, & Katz, 2010) on the first version of the Google cluster traces. Mishra et al. (Mishra et al., 2010) applied the clustering algorithm K-means for forming the groups of tasks with more similarities in resource consumption and duration, while Chen et al. (Y. Chen et al., 2010) classified jobs instead of tasks. In addition to these approaches, Di et al. (Di, Kondo, & Cappello, 2013) characterized applications running in the Google cluster. Like (Y. Chen et al., 2010; Mishra et al., 2010), K-means is chosen for the clustering purpose. In our previous (Sareh Fotuhi Piraghaj, Calheiros, Chan, Dastjerdi, & Buyya, 2016), we proposed an end-to-end architecture aiming at efficient resource allocation and energy consumption in cloud data centers. In the presented architecture, the knowledge obtained from the analysis of the cloud backend workload is utilized to define customized virtual machine configuration along with maximum task capacity of each VM. Like the other aforementioned works (Moreno, Garraghan, Townend, & Xu, 2013; Solis Moreno, Garraghan, Townend, & Xu, 2014), the availability of virtualization technology is considered and the tasks are executed on top of virtual machines instead of physical servers. Unlike other approaches, the aim is decreasing energy by defining the virtual machines configurations along with their maximum task capacity.

If the time and location of the requests are considered, the workload can be modeled via a stochastic process such as Markovian model or time series models such as the technique applied by Khan et al. (Khan, Yan, Tao, & Anerousis, 2012). Khan et al. (Khan et al., 2012) presented an approach based on Hidden Markov Modeling (HMM) to characterize the temporal correlations in the clusters of VMs that are discovered and to predict the patterns of workload along with the probable spikes.

Workload-Based Energy Saving Techniques

Study of the characteristics of the workload and its fluctuations is crucial for selecting energy management techniques. For example in Intel Enhanced Speed Stepping Technology (Intel, 2016), the CPU frequency and voltage are dynamically adjusted according to the servers workload. From the analysis of the workload, one can decide if a power management methodology is applicable for the system. As stated by Dhiman et al. (Dhiman et al., 2008), DVFS does not always result in more energy savings and operators should also consider utilizing low power modes available in modern processors that might provide better energy savings with the least performance degradation considering the workload. The workload type is also important for DVFS on memory component because, as stated previously, in non-memory intensive workloads running at lower memory speed would result in less performance degradation than memory-intensive workloads. Therefore, reducing power consumption can be obtained through running memory at a lower frequency with the least effect on the application performance (David et al., 2011). The energy efficient resource management techniques in PaaS environments are grouped into two major categories namely workload aware and workload agnostic as depicted in Figure 12.

Beloglazov et al. (Anton Beloglazov & Buyya, 2012) applied Markov chain model for known stationary workloads while utilizing a heuristic-based approach for unknown and non-stationary workloads. Apart from this work, the analysis of workloads of co-existing/co-allocated VMs motivated new algorithms and management techniques for saving energy in cloud data centers. These techniques contain the interference-aware (Caglar et al., 2013; Moreno, Yang, et al., 2013; Nathuji et al., 2010) and correlation-aware and multiplexing (M. Chen et al., 2011; Ferdman et al., 2012; Meng et al., 2010; Verma et al., 2009) VM placement algorithms, virtual machine static (Assuncao et al., 2012) and dynamic sizing techniques (Meng et al., 2010), which were discussed previously. The workload study also motivated the idea of overbooking resources to utilize the unused resources allocated to the VMs (Hu et al., 2013; Svärd et al., 2011; Tomas et al., 2014; Tomás & Tordsson, 2014).

APPLICATION-BASED ENERGY SAVING TECHNIQUES

The type of application (Figure 13) plays an important role in selecting the energy management technique. For scale out applications, turning on/off cores, which is called dynamic power gating, is not practical since these applications are latency sensitive and their resource demand is volatile, therefore the transition delay between power modes would degrade the QoS. In this respect, Kim et al. (Jungsoo Kim et al., 2013) considered the number of cores according to the workloads peak and achieved power efficiency through DVFS.

Web Applications

Web applications deployed in cloud data centers have highly fluctuating workloads. Wang et al. (D. Wang et al., 2013) measured the impact of utilizing DVFS for multi-tier applications. They concluded that response time and throughput are considerably affected as results of bottlenecks between the database and application servers. The main challenge is identifying the DVFS adjustment period, which is not

Figure 12. The energy efficient resource management techniques in PaaS environment are grouped based on the approach awareness of the cloud workload and its characteristics

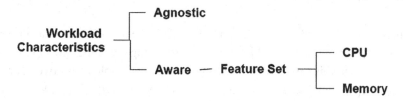

Figure 13. Application types supported in energy management systems

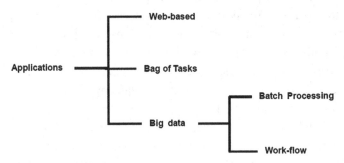

synchronized with workload burst cycles. Therefore, they proposed a workload-aware DVFS adjustment method that lessens the performance impact of DVFS when a cloud data center is highly utilized. VM consolidation methods also have been used along with DVFS for power optimization of multi-tier web applications.

Wang et al (L. Wang, Tao, von Laszewski, & Chen, 2010) proposed a performance-aware power optimization that combines either DVFS or VM consolidation. To achieve the maximum energy efficiency, they integrate feedback control with optimization strategies. The proposed approach operates in two levels: 1) at the application level, it uses a multi-input-multi-output controller to reach the performance stated in SLA by dynamically provisioning VMs, reallocating shared resources across VMs and DVFS, 2) at the data center level, it consolidates VMs onto the most energy-efficient host.

Bag of Tasks

Bag-of-Tasks (BoT) applications are defined as parallel applications whose tasks are independent (Cirne et al., 2003). Kim et al. (K. H. Kim et al., 2007) investigated the problem of power-aware BoT scheduling on DVS-enabled cluster systems. Applying DVFS capability of processors, the presented space-shared and time-shared scheduling algorithms both saved a considerable energy while meeting the user-defined deadline.

Calheiros et al. (Calheiros & Buyya, 2014) proposed an algorithm for scheduling urgent, CPU intensive Bag of Tasks (BoT) utilizing processors DVFS with the objective of keeping the processor at the minimum frequency possible while meeting the user-defined deadline. An urgent application is defined as a High Performance Computing application that needs to be completed before the soft deadline defined by the user. Disaster management and healthcare applications are examples of this kind of applications. DVFS is applied at the middleware/Operating System level rather than at CPU level and maximum frequency levels are supplied by the algorithm during task execution. The approach does not require prior knowledge of the host workload for making decisions.

Big Data Applications

As indicated by International Data Corporation (IDC) in 2011, the overall information created and copied in the world has grown by nine times within five years reaching 1.8 zettabytes (1.8 trillion gigabytes) (Gantz & Reinsel, 2011) and this trend would continue to at least double every two year. The exceptional growth in the amount of produced data introduced the phenomenon named *Big Data*. There exist various definitions for Big Data. However, Apache Hadoop definition is the one which is close to the concept of this study. Apache Hadoop defines Big Data as "datasets that could not be captured, managed and processes by general computers within an acceptable scope". Big data analysis and processing along with the data storage and transmission require huge data centers that would eventually consume large amount of energy. In this respect, energy efficient power management techniques are really crucial for Big Data processing environments. In this section, we discuss batch processing and workflows as two examples of Big Data applications along with the techniques applied to make them more energy efficient (See Figure 13).

Batch Processing

Large-scale data analysis and batch processing are enabled utilizing data center resources through parallel and distributed processing frameworks such as MapReduce (Dean & Ghemawat, 2008) and Hadoop (Hadoop, 2016). The large scale data analysis performed by these frameworks requires many servers and this triggers the possibility of a considerable energy savings that can be obtained via resource management heuristics that minimize the required hardware.

As stated by Leverich et al. (Leverich & Kozyrakis, 2010), MapReduce is widely used by various cloud providers such as Yahoo and Amazon. Google executes on average one hundred thousand MapReduce jobs every day on its clusters("Google Open Source Blog: An update on container support on Google Cloud Platform,").The vast usage of this programming model, along with its unique characteristics, requires further study to explore any possibilities and techniques that can improve energy consumption in such environments.

The energy saving in a cluster can either be made by limiting the number of active servers to the workload requirement and shutting down the idle servers or matching the compute and storage of each server to its workloads. Due to the special characteristics of the MapReduce frameworks, these options are not useful in these environments. Powering down idle servers is not applicable, as in MapReduce frameworks data is distributed and stored on the nodes to ensure reliability and availability of data. Therefore, shutting down a node would affect the performance of the system and the data availability even if the node is idle. Moreover, in a MapReduce environment, the mismatch between hardware and workload characteristics might also result in energy wastage (e.g. CPU idleness for I/O workloads). Also, recovery mechanisms applied for hardware/software failures increases energy wastage in MapReduce frameworks.

Leverich et al. (Leverich & Kozyrakis, 2010) investigated the problem of energy consumption in Hadoop as a MapReduce style framework. Two improvements are applied to the Hadoop framework. Firstly, an energy controller is added that can communicate with the Hadoop framework. The second improvement is in the Hadoop data-layout and task distribution to enable more nodes to be switched off. The data-layout is modified so that at least one replica of a data block would be placed on a set of nodes referred as *Covering Set* (CS). These *Covering Sets* ensure the availability of the data block when the other nodes that store the other replicas are all shutdown to save power. The number of replicas in a Hadoop framework is specified by users and is equal to three by default.

Lang et al. (Lang & Patel, 2010) proposed a solution called All-In Strategy (AIS) that utilizes the whole cluster for executing the workload and then power down all the nodes. Results show that the effectiveness of the algorithms directly depend on both complexity of the workloads and the time it takes for the nodes to change power states.

Kaushik et al. (Kaushik, Bhandarkar, & Nahrstedt, 2010), presented GreenHDFS, an energy efficient and a highly scalable variant of the Hadoop Distribution File System (HDFS). GreenHDFS is based on the idea of energy-efficient data-placement through dividing servers into two major groups namely Hot and Cold zones. Data that are not accessed regularly are placed in the Cold zone so that a considerable amount of energy can be saved harnessing the idleness in this zone.

Long predictable, streaming I/O and parallelization and non-interactive performance are named as the characteristics of MapReduce workloads computations in Leverich et al. (Leverich & Kozyrakis, 2010). However, there exists MapReduce with interactive analysis (MIA) style workloads that have been widely used by organizations (Y. Chen, Alspaugh, Borthakur, & Katz, 2012). Since MapReduce makes storing and processing of large scale data a lot easier, data analysts are widely adopting MapReduce to process their data.

Typical energy saving solution obtained through maximization of server utilization is not applicable for MIA workloads because of two main reasons. Firstly, MIA workloads are dominated by human-initiated jobs that force the cluster to be configured to the peak load so that it can satisfy SLAs. Secondly, workload spikes are unpredictable and the environment is volatile because machines are added or removed from the cluster regularly. In this respect, Chen et al. (Y. Chen et al., 2012) proposed BEEMR (Berkeley Energy Efficient MapReduce) as an energy efficient MapReduce workload manager inspired by an analysis of the Facebook Hadoop workload.

Hadoop is the open source implementation of the MapReduce programming model. Apart from energy consumption, which is studied in a number of works (Y. Chen et al., 2012; Kaushik et al., 2010; Lang & Patel, 2010; Leverich & Kozyrakis, 2010) Hadoop performance for both collocated and separated compute services and data models (Figure 14) is investigated by Feller et al. (Feller et al., 2015). The separation of compute services and data is applied for virtualized environments. It is shown that the collocation of VMs on servers has a negative effect on the I/O throughput, which makes physical clusters more efficient in terms of the performance when compared to the virtualized clusters. The performance

Figure 14. Two MapReduce development models studied in Feller, Ramakrishnan, and Morin
Source: Feller, Ramakrishnan & Morin, 2015

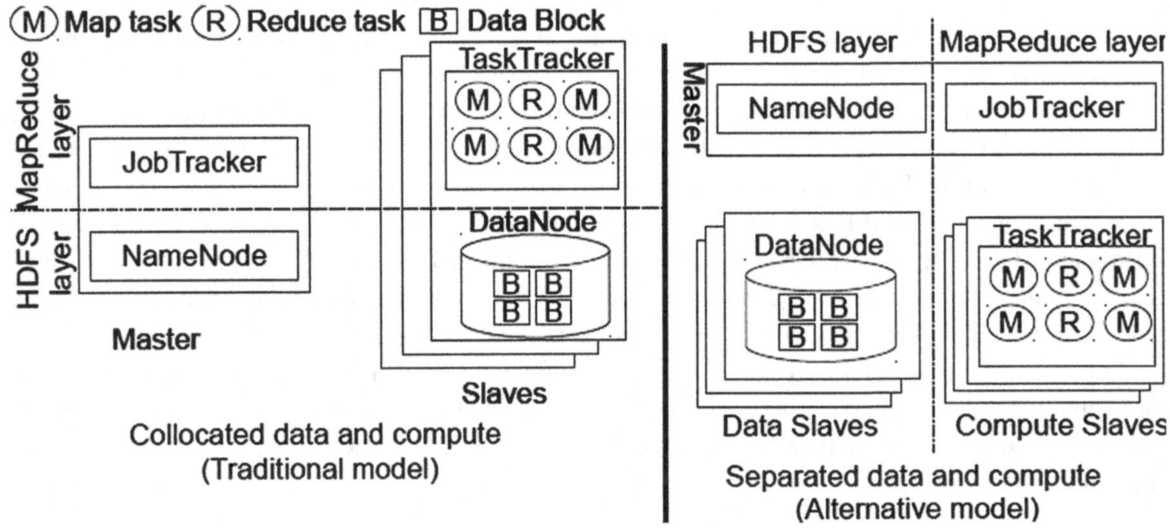

degradation is proven to be application-dependent and related to the data-to-compute ratio. There is also a trade-off between the application's completion time and the energy consumed in the cluster.

Workflow Applications

Workflows or precedence-constrained parallel applications are a popular paradigm for modeling large applications that is widely used by scientists and engineers. Therefore, there has been an increasing effort to improve the performance of these applications through utilizing distributed resources of Clouds. With the increase in the interest toward this type of applications, the energy efficiency of the proposed approaches also comes into the picture, as performance efficiency brought by excessive use of resources might result in extra energy consumption.

The inefficiency of provisioned resources for scientific workflows execution results in excessive energy consumption. Lee et al. (Lee, Han, Zomaya, & Yousif, 2015) addressed this issue through a resource-efficient workflow scheduling algorithm named MER. The proposed algorithm optimizes the resource usage of a workflow schedule generated by other scheduling algorithms. MER consolidates tasks that were previously scheduled and maximizes the resource utilization. Based on the trade-off between makespan (execution time) increase and resource utilization reduction, MER identifies the near optimal trade-off point between these two factors. Finding this point, the algorithm improves resource utilization and consequently reduces the provisioned resources and saves energy. The proposed algorithm can be applied to any environment in which scientific workflows of many precedence-constrained tasks are executed. However, MER is specifically designed for the IaaS cloud model.

As discussed earlier, Dynamic Voltage and Frequency Scaling (DVFS) is an effective approach to minimize the energy consumption of applications. As scientific workflows contain tasks with data dependencies between them, DVFS might not always result in desirable energy saving. Depending on system and workflow characteristics, decreasing the CPU frequency may increase the overall execution time and the idle time of the processors, which consequently deteriorates the planned energy saving. In addition, when the SLA violation penalty is higher than the power savings, adjusting the CPU to operate at the lowest frequency is not always energy efficient. In this situation, executing the tasks quickly with a higher frequency might result in less energy consumption (Freeh et al., 2007). In this respect, Pietri et al. (Pietri & Sakellariou, 2014) proposed an algorithm that identifies the best time to reduce the frequency in a way that the overall energy consumption is decreased. In the presented approach, the lowest possible frequency did not always result in the least energy consumption for completing the workflow execution. The algorithm considers various task runtime and processor frequency capabilities and it assumes an initial task placement on the available machines. Next, it determines the appropriate CPU frequency considering the time that the task can be stretched without violating the deadline (slack time). The proposed algorithm gradually scales down the frequency of the processor assigned for each task iteratively by the time the overall energy savings are increased. In each iteration, the CPU frequency is scaled down to the next available frequency mode. The algorithm performance is validated through simulation and the results demonstrated that the system can provide a good balance between energy consumption and makespan.

Durillo et al. (Durillo, Nae, & Prodan, 2014) proposed MOHEFT as an extension of the Heterogeneous Earliest Finish Time (HEFT) algorithm (Topcuoglu, Hariri, & Wu, 2002), which is widely applied for workflow scheduling. The proposed algorithm is able to compute a set of suboptimal solutions in a single run without any prior knowledge of the execution time of tasks. MOHEFT policy complements the HEFT scheduling algorithm through predicting task execution time based on the historical data obtained from real workflow task executions.

SLA AND ENERGY MANAGEMENT TECHNIQUES

The expectations of providers and costumers of a cloud service including the penalties considered for violations are all documented in the Service Level Agreement SLA) (Greenwood, Vitaglione, Keller, & Calisti, 2006; Hani, Paputungan, & Hassan, 2015; Yogamangalam & Sriram, 2013). Considering SLA, energy management techniques are categorized into two groups, namely SLA-Aware and SLA-Agnostic approaches (as shown in Figure 15).

SLA contains service level objectives (SLOs) including the service availability and performance in terms of the response time and throughput (W. Kim, 2013). Satisfying SLA in a cloud computing environment is one of the key factors that builds trust between consumers and providers. There has always been a trade-off between saving energy and meeting SLA in resource management policies, therefore it is really crucial to make sure that energy saving does not increase SLA violations dramatically.

The metrics utilized to measure SLA can be different based on the application type, for example SLA for workflow applications is defined in terms of the user-defined deadlines (Durillo et al., 2014; Lee et al., 2015; Pietri & Sakellariou, 2014) while in web and scale-out applications it is defined as the response time (Anselmi et al., 2008; Hindman et al., 2011; Lang & Patel, 2010). Anselmi et.al (Anselmi et al., 2008) consider the application response time as their SLA metric in their proposed solution for the Service Consolidation Problem (SCP) considering multi-tier applications.

In the studied scenario, the objective was minimizing the number of required servers while satisfying the Quality of Service. Similarly, Mohan et al. (Mohan Raj & Shriram, 2011) considered response time of the application as the SLA metric in their proposed energy efficient workload scheduling algorithm. The application request is accepted considering the data center capacity along with the SLA. The SLA is maintained through a control theoretic method. Holt-Winters forecasting formula is applied for improving the SLA through minimizing the incurred cost by the time in which the system waits for startup and shutdown delays of a PM/VM. Caglar et al. (Caglar et al., 2013) also considered response time as their SLA metric in the presented online VM placement technique. In a different approach, Beloglazov et al. (A. Beloglazov, 2010) utilized a combined metric considering both SLA violation and energy consump-

Figure 15. The energy efficient resource management techniques for PaaS environments are categorized in two groups, namely SLA Aware and SLA Agnostic considering SLA

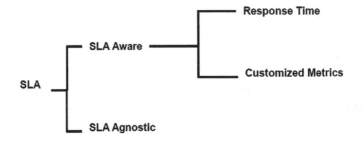

tion for their optimization problem. In the presented approach, SLA is violated during the time that a host is overloaded. This approach is application independent.

SUMMARY

According to the Refrigerating and Air Conditioning Engineers (ASHRAE) (Belady & Beaty, 2005), the Infrastructure and Energy Cost (I&E) has increased by 75% of the cost in 2014 while IT costs are only 25%("In the data center, power and cooling costs more than the it equipment it supports « Electronics Cooling Magazine – Focused on Thermal Management, TIMs, Fans, Heat Sinks, CFD Software, LEDs/ Lighting,"). This is a significant rise for I&E costs which was contributing up to 20% to the whole cost when IT costs where only 80% in the early 90's. This drastic rise of data center power consumption has made energy management techniques a non-separable part of the resource management in a cloud computing environment. In this respect, there is a large body of literature that consider energy management techniques for various cloud service models. In this chapter, we mainly focused on the PaaS service model in which the data center owner can obtain prior knowledge of the applications and their usage patterns. Further, we discuss the energy management techniques in both bare-metal and virtualized environments. In summary, research in this area concludes that selecting the right energy management technique is dependent on three main factors:

- **The Environment Where the Applications Run:** In this chapter, we covered various alternatives for execution environments including Bare Metal, containerized, and hypervisor-based virtualization.
- **The Workload and Application Type:** Applications are mainly different in terms of their workload patterns, latency sensitiveness, and etc. Understanding the workload characteristics can further improve the efficiency of the algorithms.
- **The Quality of Service:** The QoS for applications is defined through the Service Level Agreements (SLA) and the SLA metric can be different considering the applications nature. Considering SLA is important since energy management techniques might result in SLA violations and consequently degrade the performance of the system or increase the total costs for the applications execution.

Considering these factors, for future studies on this area, the following directions can further be developed:

- **Containerized Environment:** Further studies can be done on the consolidation of containers considering both the application and OS containers. The container migration capability can be studied deeply and might substitute VM migrations because of their smaller overhead and shorter startup delays.
- **Network-Aware VM/Container Consolidation:** The network element can be considered as one of the factors in the consolidation to decrease the communication overhead between VMs/ containers.

- **CaaS Environment:** The newly introduced cloud service model introduces new research directions that are required to explore with more details. The research directions in this area include joint VM-container consolidation algorithms along with new SLA metrics.

REFERENCES

Agrawala, A. K., Mohr, J., & Bryant, R. (1976). An approach to the workload characterization problem. *Computer*, *9*(6), 18–32. doi:10.1109/C-M.1976.218610

Almeida, J., Almeida, V., Ardagna, D., Francalanci, C., & Trubian, M. (2006). Resource Management in the Autonomic Service-Oriented Architecture*Proceedings of the 2006 IEEE International Conference on Autonomic Computing (ICAC 2006)* (pp. 84-92). doi:10.1109/ICAC.2006.1662385

AMD. (2016). *AMD Turbo Core Technology*. Retrieved 31 March, 2016, from http://www.amd.com/en-us/innovations/software-technologies/turbo-core

Anselmi, J., Amaldi, E., & Cremonesi, P. (2008). Service Consolidation with End-to-End Response Time Constraints*Proceedings of 34th Euromicro Conference on Software Engineering and Advanced Applications (SEAA 2008.)* (pp. 345-352). doi:10.1109/SEAA.2008.31

Assuncao, M. D., Netto, M. A. S., Peterson, B., Renganarayana, L., Rofrano, J., Ward, C., & Young, C. (2012). CloudAffinity: A framework for matching servers to cloudmates*Proceedings of the 2012 IEEE Network Operations and Management Symposium (NOMS 2012)* (pp. 213-220). doi:10.1109/NOMS.2012.6211901

AWS. (2016). *EC2 Instance Types – Amazon Web Services (AWS)*. Retrieved 31 March, 2016, from https://aws.amazon.com/ec2/instance-types/

Barroso, L. A., & Holzle, U. (2007). The Case for Energy-Proportional Computing. *Computer*, *40*(12), 33–37. doi:10.1109/MC.2007.443

Belady, C. L., & Beaty, D. (2005). Roadmap for Datacom Cooling. *ASHRAE Journal*, *47*(12), 52.

Beloglazov, A. (2010). *Energy Efficient Allocation of Virtual Machines in Cloud Data Centers*. Paper presented at the 10th IEEE/ACM International Conference on Cluster, Cloud and Grid Computing (CCGrid 2010). doi:10.1109/CCGRID.2010.45

Beloglazov, A., & Buyya, R. (2010). *Adaptive Threshold-based Approach for Energy-efficient Consolidation of Virtual Machines in Cloud Data Centers*. Paper presented at the 8th International Workshop on Middleware for Grids, Clouds and e-Science, Bangalore, India. doi:10.1145/1890799.1890803

Beloglazov, A., & Buyya, R. (2010). Energy efficient allocation of virtual machines in cloud data centers*Proceedings of the 10th IEEE/ACM International Conference on Cluster, Cloud and Grid Computing (CCGrid 2010)* (pp. 577 - 578). doi:10.1109/CCGRID.2010.45

Beloglazov, A., & Buyya, R. (2012). Optimal Online Deterministic Algorithms and Adaptive Heuristics for Energy and Performance Efficient Dynamic Consolidation of Virtual Machines in Cloud Data Centers. *Concurrent Computing: Practice and Experience, 24*(13), 1397–1420. doi:10.1002/cpe.1867

Bichler, M., Setzer, T., & Speitkamp, B. (2006). Capacity planning for virtualized servers*Proceedings of the 16th Annual Workshop on Information Technologies and Systems (WITS 2006).*

Bottomley, J. (2013, May). *Containers and The Cloud A Match Made in Heaven.* Academic Press.

Brewer, E. (2016). *Google Open Source Blog: An update on container support on Google Cloud Platform.* Retrieved from http://google-opensource.blogspot.com.au/2014/06/an-update-on-container-support-on.html

Buyya, R., Beloglazov, A., & Abawajy, J. (2010). Energy-efficient management of data center resources for cloud computing: a vision, architectural elements, and open challenges*Proceedings of 16th International Conference on Parallel and Distributed Processing Techniques and Applications (PDPTA 2010)* (pp. 6-17).

Caglar, F., Shekhar, S., & Gokhale, A. (2013). *A Performance Interference-aware Virtual Machine Placement Strategy for Supporting Soft Realtime Applications in the Cloud.* Institute for Software Integrated Systems, Vanderbilt University, Nashville, TN, USA, Tech. Rep. ISIS-13-105.

Calheiros, R. N., & Buyya, R. (2014). Energy-Efficient Scheduling of Urgent Bag-of-Tasks Applications in Clouds through DVFS*Proceedings of the 6th IEEE International Conference on Cloud Computing Technology and Science (CloudCom 2014)* (pp. 342-349). doi:10.1109/CloudCom.2014.20

Calzarossa, M., & Serazzi, G. (1993). Workload characterization: A survey. *Proceedings of the IEEE, 81*(8), 1136–1150. doi:10.1109/5.236191

Charles, J., Jassi, P., Ananth, N. S., Sadat, A., & Fedorova, A. (2009). Evaluation of the Intel\textregistered Core™ i7 Turbo Boost feature*Proceedings of the 2009 IEEE International Symposium on Workload Characterization (IISWC 2009)* (pp. 188-197). doi:10.1109/IISWC.2009.5306782

Chen, M., Zhang, H., Su, Y.-Y., Wang, X., Jiang, G., & Yoshihira, K. (2011). Effective VM sizing in virtualized data centers*Proceedings of the 2011 IFIP/IEEE International Symposium on Integrated Network Management (IM 2011)* (pp. 594-601). doi:10.1109/INM.2011.5990564

Chen, Y., Alspaugh, S., Borthakur, D., & Katz, R. (2012). Energy Efficiency for Large-scale MapReduce Workloads with Significant Interactive Analysis*Proceedings of the 7th ACM European Conference on Computer Systems* (pp. 43-56). doi:10.1145/2168836.2168842

Chen, Y., Ganapathi, A. S., Griffith, R., & Katz, R. H. (2010). *Analysis and lessons from a publicly available Google cluster trace.* EECS Department, University of California, Berkeley, Tech. Rep. UCB/EECS-2010-95, University of California, Berkeley.

Cirne, W., Brasileiro, F., Sauvé, J., Andrade, N., Paranhos, D., Santos-neto, E., & Gr, F. C. et al. (2003). Grid computing for of Bag-of-Tasks applications*Proceedings of the 3rd IFIP Conference on E-Commerce, E-Business and EGovernment.*

Container, L. (2016). *Linux Containers.* Retrieved 31 March, 2016, from https://linuxcontainers.org/

David, H., Fallin, C., Gorbatov, E., Hanebutte, U. R., & Mutlu, O. (2011). Memory Power Management via Dynamic Voltage/Frequency Scaling*Proceedings of the 8th ACM International Conference on Autonomic Computing* (pp. 31-40). doi:10.1145/1998582.1998590

Dean, J., & Ghemawat, S. (2008). MapReduce: Simplified Data Processing on Large Clusters. *Magazine Communications of the ACM, 51*(1), 107–113. doi:10.1145/1327452.1327492

Deng, Q., Meisner, D., Bhattacharjee, A., Wenisch, T. F., & Bianchini, R. (2012). CoScale: Coordinating CPU and Memory System DVFS in Server Systems*Proceedings of the 45th Annual IEEE/ACM International Symposium on Microarchitecture (MICRO 2012)* (pp. 143-154). doi:10.1109/MICRO.2012.22

Deng, Q., Meisner, D., Ramos, L., Wenisch, T. F., & Bianchini, R. (2011). MemScale: Active Low-power Modes for Main Memory*Proceedings of the 16th International Conference on Architectural Support for Programming Languages and Operating Systems (ASPLOS 2011)* (pp. 225-238). doi:10.1145/1950365.1950392

Dhiman, G., Pusukuri, K. K., & Rosing, T. (2008). Analysis of Dynamic Voltage Scaling for System Level Energy Management*Proceedings of the 2008 Conference on Power Aware Computing and Systems (HotPower 2008)* (pp. 9-9).

Dhyani, K., Gualandi, S., & Cremonesi, P. (2010). A Constraint Programming Approach for the Service Consolidation Problem. Integration of AI and OR Techniques in Constraint Programming for Combinatorial Optimization Problems, (pp. 97-101).

Di, S., Kondo, D., & Cappello, F. (2013). Characterizing Cloud Applications on a Google Data Center-*Proceedings of the 42nd International Conference on Parallel Processing (ICPP 2013)* (pp. 468-473). doi:10.1109/ICPP.2013.56

Dong, Z., Zhuang, W., & Rojas-Cessa, R. (2014). Energy-aware scheduling schemes for cloud data centers on Google trace data*Proceedings of the 2014 IEEE Online Conference on Green Communications (OnlineGreencomm 2014)* (pp. 1-6). doi:10.1109/OnlineGreenCom.2014.7114422

Durillo, J. J., Nae, V., & Prodan, R. (2014). Multi-objective energy-efficient workflow scheduling using list-based heuristics. *Future Generation Computer Systems, 36*, 221–236. doi:10.1016/j.future.2013.07.005

Feitelson, D. G. (2015). *Workload modeling for computer systems performance evaluation.* Cambridge University Press. doi:10.1017/CBO9781139939690

Feller, E., Ramakrishnan, L., & Morin, C. (2015). Performance and energy efficiency of big data applications in cloud environments: A hadoop case study. *Journal of Parallel and Distributed Computing, 79*, 80–89. doi:10.1016/j.jpdc.2015.01.001

Ferdman, M., Adileh, A., Kocberber, O., Volos, S., Alisafaee, M., Jevdjic, D., & Falsafi, B. et al. (2012). Clearing the Clouds: A Study of Emerging Scale-out Workloads on Modern Hardware. *ACM SIGPLAN Notices, 47*(4), 37–48.

Ferrari, D. (1972). Workload characterization and selection in computer performance measurement. *Computer, 5*(4), 18–24. doi:10.1109/C-M.1972.216939

Forestiero, A., Mastroianni, C., Meo, M., Papuzzo, G., & Sheikhalishahi, M. (2014). Hierarchical Approach for Green Workload Management in Distributed Data Centers*Proceedings of the 20th International European Conference on Parallel and Distributed Computing (Euro-Par 2014) Workshops* (pp. 323-334). doi:10.1007/978-3-319-14325-5_28

Forouzan, B. A. (2002). *TCP/IP protocol suite*. McGraw-Hill, Inc.

Freeh, V. W., Lowenthal, D. K., Pan, F., Kappiah, N., Springer, R., Rountree, B. L., & Femal, M. E. (2007). Analyzing the Energy-Time Trade-Off in High-Performance Computing Applications. *IEEE Transactions on Parallel and Distributed Systems, 18*(6), 835–848. doi:10.1109/TPDS.2007.1026

Gantz, J., & Reinsel, D. (2011, June). *Extracting Value from Chaos*. Retrieved 10 May, 2016, from https://www.emc.com/collateral/analyst-reports/idc-extracting-value-from-chaos-ar.pdf

Gmach, D., Rolia, J., Cherkasova, L., & Kemper, A. (2009). Resource Pool Management: Reactive Versus Proactive or Let's Be Friends. *Computer Networks, 53*(17), 2905–2922. doi:10.1016/j.comnet.2009.08.011

Goldberg, R. P. (1974). Survey of Virtual Machine Research. *Computer, 7*(9), 34–45. doi:10.1109/MC.1974.6323581

Graziano, C. D. (2011). *A performance analysis of Xen and KVM hypervisors for hosting the Xen Worlds Project*. Academic Press.

Greenberg, A., Hamilton, J., Maltz, D. A., & Patel, P. (2008). The cost of a cloud: Research problems in data center networks. *Computer Communication Review, 39*(1), 68–73. doi:10.1145/1496091.1496103

Greenberg, S., Mills, E., Tschudi, B., Rumsey, P., & Myatt, B. (2006). Best practices for data centers: Lessons learned from benchmarking 22 data centers*Proceedings of the ACEEE Summer Study on Energy Efficiency in Buildings* (pp. 76-87).

Greenwood, D., Vitaglione, G., Keller, L., & Calisti, M. (2006). Service Level Agreement Management with Adaptive Coordination*Proceedings of the 2006 International conference on Networking and Services* (pp. 45-45). doi:10.1109/ICNS.2006.99

Hadoop. (2016). *Welcome to Apache™ Hadoop®!* Retrieved 10 May, 2016, from http://hadoop.apache.org/

Hani, A. F. M., Paputungan, I. V., & Hassan, M. F. (2015). Renegotiation in Service Level Agreement Management for a Cloud-Based System. *ACM Computer Survey, 47*(3), 51:51-51:21.

Haskell, B. G., Puri, A., & Netravali, A. N. (1997). *Digital Video: An Introduction to MPEG-2*. Springer Science & Business Media.

He, Y., Ye, Z., Fu, Q., & Elnikety, S. (2012). *Budget-based control for interactive services with adaptive execution*. Paper presented at the 9th International Conference on Autonomic Computing. doi:10.1145/2371536.2371557

Hecht-Nielsen, R. (1992). *Theory of the Backpropagation Neural Network* (Vol. 2). Neural Networks for Perception.

Heller, B., Seetharaman, S., Mahadevan, P., Yiakoumis, Y., Sharma, P., Banerjee, S., & McKeown, N. (2010). ElasticTree: Saving Energy in Data Center Networks*Proceedings of the 7th USENIX Conference on Networked Systems Design and Implementation* (pp. 249-264).

Hindman, B., Konwinski, A., Zaharia, M., Ghodsi, A., Joseph, A. D., Katz, R., & Stoica, I. et al. (2011). Mesos: A Platform for Fine-grained Resource Sharing in the Data Center*Proceedings of the 8th USENIX Conference on Networked Systems Design and Implementation* (pp. 295-308).

Hoelzle, U., & Barroso, L. A. (2009). *The Datacenter As a Computer: An Introduction to the Design of Warehouse-Scale Machines*. Morgan and Claypool Publishers.

Hu, W., Hicks, A., Zhang, L., Dow, E. M., Soni, V., Jiang, H., & Matthews, J. N. et al. (2013). A quantitative study of virtual machine live migration*Proceedings of the 2013 ACM Cloud and Autonomic Computing Conference* (pp. 11). doi:10.1145/2494621.2494622

Intel. (2016). *Enhanced Intel SpeedStep Technology (EIST)*. Retrieved 31 March, 2016, from http://www.intel.com/cd/channel/reseller/asmo-na/eng/203838.htmoverview

Kabir, M. H., Shoja, G. C., & Ganti, S. (2014). VM Placement Algorithms for Hierarchical Cloud Infrastructure*Proceedings of the 6th IEEE International Conference on Cloud Computing Technology and Science (CloudCom 2014)* (pp. 656-659). doi:10.1109/CloudCom.2014.53

Kansal, A., Zhao, F., Liu, J., Kothari, N., & Bhattacharya, A. A. (2010). Virtual Machine Power Metering and Provisioning*Proceedings of the 1st ACM Symposium on Cloud Computing (SoCC 2010)* (pp. 39-50). doi:10.1145/1807128.1807136

Kaplan, J. M., Forrest, W., & Kindler, N. (2008). *Revolutionizing data center energy efficiency*. Academic Press.

Kaufman, L., & Rousseeuw, P. J. (2009). *Finding groups in data: an introduction to cluster analysis* (Vol. 344). John Wiley & Sons.

Kaushik, R. T., Bhandarkar, M., & Nahrstedt, K. (2010). Evaluation and Analysis of GreenHDFS: A Self-Adaptive, Energy-Conserving Variant of the Hadoop Distributed File System*Proceedings of the 2010 IEEE Second International Conference on Cloud Computing Technology and Science* (pp. 274-287). doi:10.1109/CloudCom.2010.109

Khan, A., Yan, X., Tao, S., & Anerousis, N. (2012). Workload characterization and prediction in the cloud: A multiple time series approach*Proceedings of the 2012 IEEE Network Operations and Management Symposium (NOMS 2012)* (pp. 1287-1294). doi:10.1109/NOMS.2012.6212065

Khosravi, A., Garg, S. K., & Buyya, R. (2013). Energy and carbon-efficient placement of virtual machines in distributed cloud data centers*Proceedings of the 19th International European Conference on Parallel and Distributed Computing (Euro-Par 2013)* (pp. 317-328). doi:10.1007/978-3-642-40047-6_33

Kim, J., Elnikety, S., He, Y., Hwang, S.-w., & Ren, S. (2013). *QACO: exploiting partial execution in web servers*. Paper presented at the 2013 ACM Cloud and Autonomic Computing Conference (CAC 2013). doi:10.1145/2494621.2494636

Kim, J., Ruggiero, M., Atienza, D., & Lederberger, M. (2013). Correlation-aware Virtual Machine Allocation for Energy-efficient Datacenters*Proceedings of the Conference on Design, Automation and Test in Europe* (pp. 1345-1350). doi:10.7873/DATE.2013.277

Kim, K. H., Buyya, R., & Kim, J. (2007). Power Aware Scheduling of Bag-of-Tasks Applications with Deadline Constraints on DVS-enabled Clusters*Proceedings of the 2007 IEEE Seventh International Symposium on Cluster Computing and the Grid (CCGrid 2007)* (pp. 541-548). doi:10.1109/CCGRID.2007.85

Kim, W. (2013). Cloud computing architecture. *International Journal of Web and Grid Services*, *9*(3), 287–303. doi:10.1504/IJWGS.2013.055724

Klein, C., & Maggio, M.-A. (2014). Brownout: building more robust cloud applications*Proceedings of the 36th International Conference on Software Engineering* (pp. 700-711).

Krioukov, A., Mohan, P., Alspaugh, S., Keys, L., Culler, D., & Katz, R. H. (2010). NapSAC: Design and Implementation of a Power-proportional Web Cluster*Proceedings of the First ACM SIGCOMM Workshop on Green Networking (Green Networking 2010)* (pp. 15-22). New York: ACM. doi:10.1145/1851290.1851294

Lang, W., & Patel, J. M. (2010). Energy Management for MapReduce Clusters. *Proceedings of the Very Large Data Bases Endowment Journal, 3*, 129-139. doi:10.14778/1920841.1920862

Lee, Y. C., Han, H., Zomaya, A. Y., & Yousif, M. (2015). Resource-efficient Workflow Scheduling in Clouds. *Knowledge-Based Systems*, *80*, 153–162. doi:10.1016/j.knosys.2015.02.012

Leverich, J., & Kozyrakis, C. (2010). On the Energy (in)Efficiency of Hadoop Clusters. *SIGOPS Operating Systems Review*, *44*(1), 61–65. doi:10.1145/1740390.1740405

Meisner, D., Gold, B. T., & Wenisch, T. F. (2009). PowerNap: Eliminating Server Idle Power. *SIGARCH Computer Architecture News*, *37*(1), 205–216. doi:10.1145/2528521.1508269

Meng, X., Isci, C., Kephart, J., Zhang, L., Bouillet, E., & Pendarakis, D. (2010). Efficient Resource Provisioning in Compute Clouds via VM Multiplexing*Proceedings of the 7th International Conference on Autonomic Computing* (pp. 11-20). doi:10.1145/1809049.1809052

Merkel, D. (2014). Docker: Lightweight Linux Containers for Consistent Development and Deployment. *Linux Journal, 2014*(239).

Mishra, A. K., Hellerstein, J. L., Cirne, W., & Das, C. R. (2010). Towards characterizing cloud backend workloads: Insights from Google compute clusters. *Performance Evaluation Review*, *37*(4), 34–41. doi:10.1145/1773394.1773400

Mohan Raj, V. K., & Shriram, R. (2011). Power aware provisioning in cloud computing environment*Proceedings of the 2011 International Conference on Computer, Communication and Electrical Technology (ICCCET)* (pp. 6-11). doi:10.1109/ICCCET.2011.5762447

Moreno, I. S., Garraghan, P., Townend, P., & Xu, J. (2013). An approach for characterizing workloads in Google cloud to derive realistic resource utilization models*Proceedings of the 7th IEEE International Symposium on Service Oriented System Engineering (SOSE 2013)* (pp. 49-60). doi:10.1109/SOSE.2013.24

Moreno, I. S., Yang, R., Xu, J., & Wo, T. (2013). Improved energy-efficiency in cloud datacenters with interference-aware virtual machine placement. *Autonomous Decentralized Systems (ISADS), 2013 IEEE Eleventh International Symposium on* (pp. 1-8). IEEE.

Nagy, G. (2015, May). *Operating System Containers vs. Application Containers*. Academic Press.

Nathuji, R., Kansal, A., & Ghaffarkhah, A. (2010). Q-clouds: managing performance interference effects for qos-aware clouds*Proceedings of the 5th European conference on Computer systems* (pp. 237-250). doi:10.1145/1755913.1755938

Nathuji, R., & Schwan, K. (2007). VirtualPower: Coordinated Power Management in Virtualized Enterprise Systems*Proceedings of 21st ACM SIGOPS Symposium on Operating Systems Principles (SOSP 2007)* (pp. 265-278). doi:10.1145/1294261.1294287

Open, V. Z. (2016). *OpenVZ Virtuozzo Containers Wiki*. Retrieved 31 March, 2016, from https://openvz.org/Main_Page

OpenShift. (2016). *OpenShift QuickStart · GitHub*. Retrieved from https://github.com/openshift-quickstart

Pandit, D., Chattopadhyay, S., Chattopadhyay, M., & Chaki, N. (2014). Resource allocation in cloud using simulated annealing.*Proceedings of the 2014 Conference on Applications and Innovations in Mobile Computing (AIMoC 2014)* (pp. 21-27). doi:10.1109/AIMOC.2014.6785514

Pietri, I., & Sakellariou, R. (2014). Energy-Aware Workflow Scheduling Using Frequency Scaling. *Proceedings of the 43rd International Conference on Parallel Processing Workshops (ICCPW 2014)* (pp. 104-113). doi:10.1109/ICPPW.2014.26

Piraghaj, S. F., Calheiros, R. N., Chan, J., Dastjerdi, A. V., & Buyya, R. (2016). Virtual Machine Customization and Task Mapping Architecture for Efficient Allocation of Cloud Data Center Resources. *The Computer Journal*, *59*(2), 208–224. doi:10.1093/comjnl/bxv106

Piraghaj, S. F., Dastjerdi, A. V., Calheiros, R. N., & Buyya, R. (2015). A Framework and Algorithm for Energy Efficient Container Consolidation in Cloud Data Centers.*2015 IEEE International Conference on Data Science and Data Intensive Systems* (pp. 368-375). doi:10.1109/DSDIS.2015.67

Piraghaj, S. F., Dastjerdi, A. V., Calheiros, R. N., Buyya, R., Piraghaj, S. F., Dastjerdi, A. V., . . . Buyya, R. (2015). Efficient Virtual Machine Sizing for Hosting Containers as a Service (SERVICES 2015). *Proceedings of the 2015 IEEE World Congress on Services* (pp. 31-38).

PlanetLab. (2016). *An open platform for developing, deploying, and accessing planetary-scale services*. Retrieved 31 March, 2016, from https://www.planet-lab.org/

Price, D., & Tucker, A. (2004). Solaris Zones: Operating System Support for Consolidating Commercial Workloads.*Proceedings of the 18th USENIX Conference on System Administration (LISA 2004)* (pp. 241-254).

Reiss, C., Wilkes, J., & Hellerstein, J. L. (2011). *Google cluster-usage traces: format+ schema*. Academic Press.

Roadef. (2016). *Challenge ROADEF/EURO 2012: Machine Reassignment*. Retrieved 10 May, 2016, from http://challenge.roadef.org/2012/en/index.php

Rocket. (2016). *Welcome to Rocket Diagram's documentation! — Rocket Diagram 0.1.0 documentation*. Retrieved 10 May, 2016, from https://rocketdiagram.readthedocs.io/en/latest/

Rolia, J., Andrzejak, A., & Arlitt, M. (2003). *Automating Enterprise Application Placement in Resource Utilities*. Self-Managing Distributed Systems. doi:10.1007/978-3-540-39671-0_11

Rosen, R. (2013, May). Resource management: Linux kernel Namespaces and cgroups. *Haifux*.

Rousseeuw, P. J. (1987). Silhouettes: A graphical aid to the interpretation and validation of cluster analysis. *Journal of Computational and Applied Mathematics*, *20*, 53–65. doi:10.1016/0377-0427(87)90125-7

Solis Moreno, I., Garraghan, P., Townend, P., & Xu, J. (2014). Analysis, Modeling and Simulation of Workload Patterns in a Large-Scale Utility Cloud. *IEEE Transactions on Cloud Computing*, *2*(2), 208–221. doi:10.1109/TCC.2014.2314661

Spicuglia, S., Chen, L. Y., Birke, R., & Binder, W. (2015). Optimizing capacity allocation for big data applications in cloud datacenters.*Proceedings of the 2015 IFIP/IEEE International Symposium on Integrated Network Management (IM 2015)* (pp. 511-517). doi:10.1109/INM.2015.7140330

Svärd, P., Hudzia, B., Tordsson, J., & Elmroth, E. (2011). Evaluation of delta compression techniques for efficient live migration of large virtual machines. *ACM Sigplan Notices*, *46*(7), 111–120. doi:10.1145/2007477.1952698

Tchana, A., Palma, N., Safieddine, I., Hagimont, D., Diot, B., & Vuillerme, N. (2015). Software Consolidation as an Efficient Energy and Cost Saving Solution for a SaaS/PaaS Cloud Model.*Proceedings of the 2015 European Conference on Parallel Processing (Euro-Par 2015)* (pp. 305-316). doi:10.1007/978-3-662-48096-0_24

Tomas, L., Klein, C., Tordsson, J., & Hernandez-Rodriguez, F. (2014). The Straw that Broke the Camel's Back: Safe Cloud Overbooking with Application Brownout.*Proceedings of the 2014 International Conference on Cloud and Autonomic Computing (ICCAC 2014)* (pp. 151-160). doi:10.1109/ICCAC.2014.10

Tomás, L., & Tordsson, J. (2014). An autonomic approach to risk-aware data center overbooking. *IEEE Transactions on Cloud Computing*, *2*(3), 292–305. doi:10.1109/TCC.2014.2326166

Topcuoglu, H., Hariri, S., & Wu, M.-Y. (2002). Performance-effective and low-complexity task scheduling for heterogeneous computing. *IEEE Transactions on Parallel and Distributed Systems*, *13*(3), 260–274. doi:10.1109/71.993206

Urgaonkar, R., Kozat, U. C., Igarashi, K., & Neely, M. J. (2010). Dynamic resource allocation and power management in virtualized data centers.*Proceedings of the 2010 IEEE Network Operations and Management Symposium (NOMS 2010)* (pp. 479-486). doi:10.1109/NOMS.2010.5488484

Verma, A., Dasgupta, G., Nayak, T. K., De, P., & Kothari, R. (2009). Server Workload Analysis for Power Minimization Using Consolidation.*Proceedings of the 2009 Conference on USENIX Annual Technical Conference* (pp. 28-28).

von Laszewski, G., Wang, L., Younge, A. J., & He, X. (2009). Power-aware scheduling of virtual machines in DVFS-enabled clusters.*Proceedings of the 2009 IEEE International Conference on Cluster Computing and Workshops (CLUSTER 2009)*. (pp. 1-10). doi:10.1109/CLUSTR.2009.5289182

VServer. (2016). *Overview - Linux-VServer.* Retrieved from http://linux-vserver.org/Overview

Wang, D., Ren, C., Govindan, S., Sivasubramaniam, A., Urgaonkar, B., Kansal, A., & Vaid, K. (2013). ACE: abstracting, characterizing and exploiting peaks and valleys in datacenter power consumption. *Proceedings of the ACM SIGMETRICS/International Conference on Measurement and Modeling of Computer Systems* (pp. 333-334). doi:10.1145/2465529.2465536

Wang, L., Tao, J., von Laszewski, G., & Chen, D. (2010). *Power Aware Scheduling for Parallel Tasks via Task Clustering.* Paper presented at the IEEE 16th International Conference on Parallel and Distributed Systems (ICPADS 2010). doi:10.1109/ICPADS.2010.128

Yahoo. (2010, November). *Yahoo! Expands Its M45 Cloud Computing Initiative.* Retrieved November, 2010, from https://yodel.yahoo.com/blogs/product-news/yahoo-expands-m45-cloud-computing-initiative-5065.html

Yaqub, E., Yahyapour, R., Wieder, P., Jehangiri, A. I., Lu, K., & Kotsokalis, C. (2014). Metaheuristics-Based Planning and Optimization for SLA-Aware Resource Management in PaaS Clouds.*Proceedings of the 7th IEEE/ACM International Conference on Utility and Cloud Computing (UCC 2014)* (pp. 288-297). doi:10.1109/UCC.2014.38

Yogamangalam, R., & Sriram, V. S. (2013). A Review on Security Issues in Cloud Computing. *Journal of Artificial Intelligence, 6*(1), 1–7. doi:10.3923/jai.2013.1.7

Zhang, X., Tune, E., Hagmann, R., Jnagal, R., Gokhale, V., & Wilkes, J. (2013). CPI2: CPU Performance Isolation for Shared Compute Clusters.*Proceedings of the 8th ACM European Conference on Computer Systems (EuroSys '13)* (pp. 379-391). doi:10.1145/2465351.2465388

ENDNOTES

[1]   The scheduling class shows how sensitive a task is to latency. In Google traces the scheduling class is an integer number between 0 and 3 and the higher the scheduling class is, the most latency sensitive the task

[2]   The input or drive workload is the workload under which the performance of the system is tested.

Chapter 18
Cost of Using Cloud Computing:
HaaS vs. IaaS

Ifeanyi P. Egwutuoha
The University of Sydney, Australia

Shiping Chen
CSIRO Data61, Australia

ABSTRACT

With the recent advancement in computing technologies, business and research applications are not only executed in the traditional systems such as enterprise systems and supercomputers (HPC systems) but also in the cloud. The traditional HPC systems are expensive and sometimes require huge start-up investment, technical and administrative support and job queuing. With the benefits of cloud computing, cloud services such as Infrastructure as a Service (IaaS) and Hardware as a Service (HaaS), enables business, scientists and researchers to run their business and HPC applications in the cloud without upfront investment associated with the traditional infrastructures. Therefore, in this paper we analyze the computational performance and dollar cost of running HPC applications in the cloud when IaaS or HaaS is leased. We find that HaaS significantly reduces the cost of running HPC application in the cloud by 20% compare to IaaS without significant impact to application's performance. We also found that there is a substantial improvement in computational performance in HaaS compare to IaaS.

INTRODUCTION

With the recent advancement in computing technologies, business and research applications are not only executed in the traditional systems such as enterprise systems and supercomputers but also in the cloud. Cloud computing is a revolutionary computing paradigm for storing data and running applications, including business and computation-intensive applications. It promises numerous benefits, which includes, no upfront investments. Cloud computing also reduces development time, staff (e.g., administrators), and hardware, resulting in better service and significant cost saving.

DOI: 10.4018/978-1-5225-0759-8.ch018

In research domain, cloud computing is also considered as a next generation of computing. It has been predicated that it will take a significant advancement in the next decade particularly for enterprise and HPC systems. This is possible due to the cloud computing architecture that provides four layers of services: Software as a Service (SaaS), Platform as a Service (PaaS), Infrastructure as a Service (IaaS); and Hardware as a Service (HaaS) and price model. Furthermore, the Amazon Elastic Compute Cloud (Amazon EC2) cluster recently appeared in TOP500 list, which shows that there is a great future for HPC systems in the cloud (Top500, n.d), (Armbrust, et al., 2010), (Evangelinos, C., & Hill, C., 2008), (Amazon, n.d.), (Baremetalcloud, n.d.) and (Softlayer, n.d.).

Today, cloud computing also offers new opportunities in business for small and medium-sized businesses to enterprise business. For example, financial institutions currently use cloud computing in real time modelling to make informed investment decisions. For small and medium-sized businesses to enterprise business, one of the most difficult challenges that faces both businesses are capital expenditures and running cost of computing technologies (e.g. hardware, IT staffers and business applications).

With cloud computing pay-as-you-go pricing model, businesses, scientists and researchers can lease cloud services such as Infrastructure as a Service (IaaS) and Hardware as a Service (HaaS) for business and computation-intensive applications. These services are relinquished when not in use. For business and researchers, this avoids capital expenditure and the job queuing, which is a common phenomenon in business and traditional HPC system respectively.

This book chapter aims to investigate, discuss, compare and contrast the dollar cost-benefits of clouds computing services for business and HPC in the cloud particularly when IaaS and HaaS is leased. This book chapter is targeted to academic readers and researchers. Furthermore, this book Chapter is an extension of our research works (Egwutuoha, I. P., Chen, S., Levy, D., & Calvo R, 2013) and (Egwutuoha, I. P., Schragl, D., & Calvo, R., 2013).

We address the following research questions:

1. What cloud service platform is more cost effective to researchers using HPC system in the cloud?
2. Compare and contrast dollar cost of running computation-intensive application in HPC Systems in the cloud when IaaS and HaaS are leased.

OVERVIEW OF CLOUD COMPUTING ARCHITECTURES FOR BUSINESSES AND RESEARCH COMMUNITIES

The published literature (Armbrust, et al., 2010), (Wang, Tao, Kunze, Castellanos, Kramer, & Karl, 2008), (Foster, Zhao, & Lu, 2008), (Mell, P. and Grance, T, 2011) and other sources (SYS-CON Medi Inc, n.d.) contain different definitions of cloud computing. We adopt the definition of Foster et al. Foster, Zhao, & Lu, (2008), which captures the four-layer architecture of cloud computing:

Cloud computing is a large-scale distributed computing paradigm that is driven by economies of scale, in which a pool of abstracted, virtualized, dynamically-scalable, managed computing power, storage, platforms, and services are delivered on demand to external customers over the Internet.

With the advent of cloud computing infrastructures, cloud services providers such as Salesforce.com (Salesforce, n.d), Amazon (Amazon, n.d.), Rackspace, Baremetalcloud (Baremetalcloud, n.d.), SoftLayer (Softlayer, n.d.), Google, and IBM offer different cloud services to cloud users. Some of these services offered are Software as a Service (SaaS), Platform as a Service (PaaS), Infrastructure as a Service (IaaS), Hardware as a Service (HaaS), Network as a Service (NaaS) and Storage as a Service (STaaS). Based on the capability provided by the cloud service provider, cloud computing services fall into four major competing categories (Rimal, Choi, & Lumb, 2009) and (Egwutuoha, Chen, Levy, Selic, & Calvo, 2012), *Software as a Service, Platform as a Service, Infrastructure as a Service and Hardware as a Service.* Figure 1 shows the architecture of the cloud computing services.

Software as a Service (SaaS)

Software as a Service (SaaS) is the highest abstraction level in the cloud. It offers cloud users ready-to-use online applications that are already deployed in the cloud. This layer is hidden from the users and managed by the SaaS providers. The users do not know where or how these applications are deployed, but simply use them. SaaS cloud applications can be accessed via the internet with any internet-ready device such as a laptops, smart phones, or iPads. This enables relatively dumb clients to perform complex tasks, by shifting the real work, transparently to the user, into the cloud. A good example of SaaS is the commonly used Gmail (email services) provided by Google.

Platform as a Service (PaaS)

Platform as a Service (PaaS) provides cloud users with a fully configured and managed computing platform, ready to run custom software developed by the users. Each PaaS platform is targeted to software developed in a specific programming language or software framework (e.g., Java EE) and ready to execute corresponding builds. PaaS cloud users deploy and run their software, without setting up servers and software stacks, without thinking about scalability or clustering, and often even without knowing how many computers or CPUs their application will run on.

Figure 1. Cloud layered architecture
Source: Evangelinos & Hill, 2008

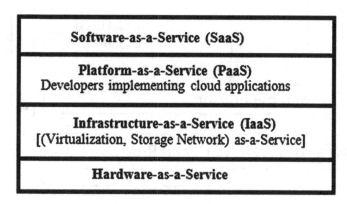

Infrastructure as a Service (IaaS)

Infrastructure as a Service (IaaS) is similar to HaaS, but virtual machines are rented out instead of real hardware. IaaS cloud users have to install, configure, and maintain the virtual machines they rent and are free to choose the operating system and software stack they install in their VMs. Often IaaS users make use of a pre-installed and preconfigured VM image supplied by their provider as base installation. Users do not have root access to the hardware. A good example of cloud provider that offers IaaS for HPC applications is Amazon (Amazon, n.d.). The Amazon Elastic Compute Cloud (Amazon EC2) offers cluster compute instances for HPC applications.

Hardware as a Service (HaaS)

Hardware as a Service (HaaS), in this case, the cloud provider basically rents out 'bare-metal' hardware (e.g., server/host and storage). Notable examples of cloud providers that offer HaaS are Baremetalcloud (Baremetalcloud, n.d.) and SoftLayer (Softlayer, n.d.). Cloud users connect to HaaS via the Internet, install and configure (e.g., VMs) the server they leased. Cloud users choose HaaS, because it gives them full control of the server, operating system, and software/hardware stack, as well as the number of VMs they execute on it. Research communities do lease HaaS for computation-intensive and/or data-intensive applications and configure HPC systems according to their needs (Evangelinos, C., & Hill, C., 2008) and (Egwutuoha, Chen, Levy, Selic, & Calvo, 2012). Consequently, computation-intensive applications that were traditionally run on HPC systems can now be executed in the cloud. Figure 2 shows the HaaS architecture and access level of the provider and user.

Figure 2. An example of HaaS architecture with level of involvement of key players

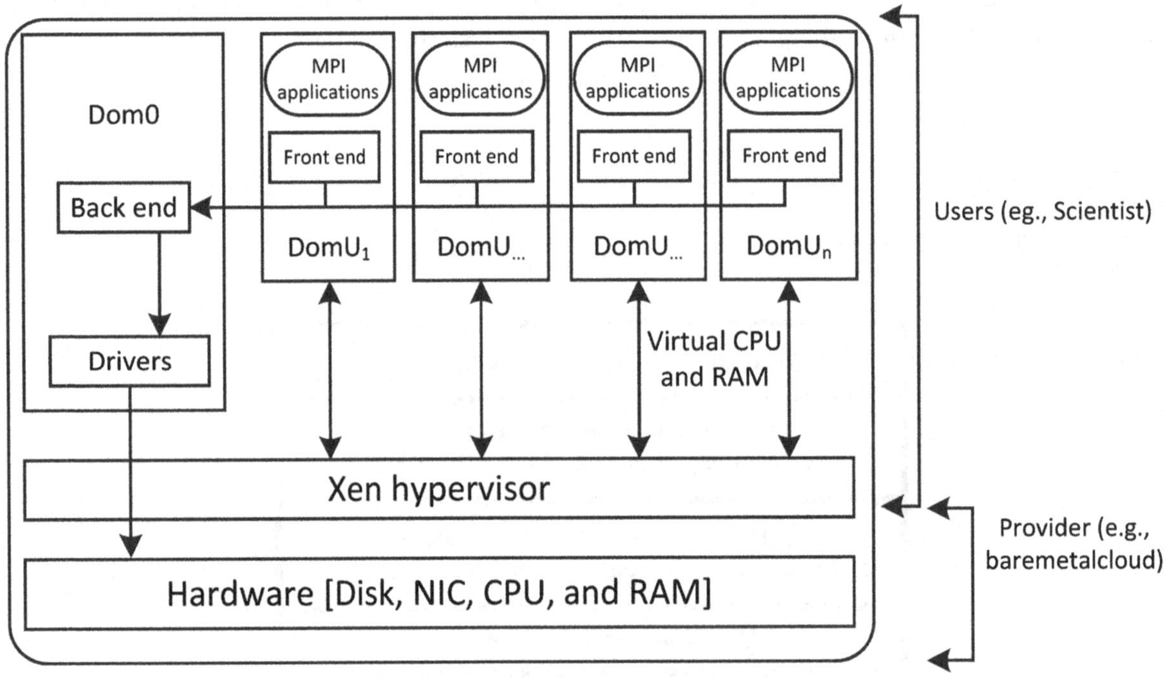

Each of these categories is implemented and offered by a number of cloud computing providers (some provider offer services in multiple categories). Providers also deliver different types of services to the cloud user, which can be used as building blocks and stacked as needed. By selecting a cloud provider from the category most suitable for organisation needs, companies can reduce their development time and achieve the same with less staff (e.g., administrators) and hardware, resulting in significant cost savings. Table 1 shows the summary of cloud services, configuration and the prices offered by the service providers (As at the time of writing this paper).

COST BENEFITS OF CLOUD COMPUTING FOR BUSINESSES AND RESEARCH COMMUNITIES

No Initial Investment Capital

An important benefit of cloud computing for Businesses and Research communities is the prevailing pay-as-you-go model, which eliminates the need for huge initial investments to build Information Technology infrastructure, because cloud users only have to pay for what they actually use. For example, an organization may choose to lease a server at a cost of $0.25 per hour for Hardware as a Service (HaaS) from cloud provider e.g. baremetalcloud (Baremetalcloud, n.d.) instead of investing about $35,000 to acquire server hardware. This gives businesses competitive advantages. The saved capital expenditure in IT can be invested in the core business area or used for other investments instead. If the capital would have to be borrowed, the interest the capital investment would have accrued is totally eliminated.

Table 1. Virtual and HaaS Instances from Cloud-A and Cloud-B as at 2013

Instance Type	Memory (GB)	CPU	Disk (GB)	Cost of Instances for Linux US$	Cost of Instance for Window
Ref-A Virtual Instance	30	2x2.0 GHz (sixteen-core)	500	$1.60 per hour	$1.80 per hour
Ref-B Virtual Instance	244	2 x Intel Xeon E5-2670 (eight-core)	240	$3.50 per hour	$3.83 per hour
Ref-C Virtual Instance	22	2 x Intel Xeon X5570 (quad-core)	1690	$2.10 per hour	$2.60 per hour
Ref-D Virtual Instance	23	2 x Intel Xeon X5570 (quad-core)	1690	$1.30 per hour	$1.60 per hour
Ref-E Virtual Instance	96	2 x 2.13 GHz E5606 (eight-core)	1000	$0.99 per hour	$1.19 per hour
Ref-F Virtual Instance	48	2 x 2.66 GHz X5650 (twelve-core)	300	$0.73 per hour	$0.93 per hour
Ref-G Virtual Instance	64	2 x 2.0 GHz E5-2650 OctoCore (sixteen-core)	500	$1.54 per hour	$1.59 per hour
Ref-H Virtual Instance	32	2 x 2.0 GHz (eight-core)	250	$1.25 per hour	$1.30 per hour

(Egwutuoha, I. P., Chen, S., Levy, D., & Calvo R, 2013)

Furthermore, leasing a cloud computer services eliminates the need to maintain an expensive data centre. As a result, pay-as-you-go model enables particularly start-ups and small businesses to offer their services with minimal upfront investments and costs, allowing them to scale their IT infrastructure and services as they find more customers (Reese, 2009) and to inexpensively test product or service ideas with low risk. While any company can enjoy this benefit, typically it is particularly important for start-ups and small businesses, as they tend to have limited funding and no existing data centres. This is probably why start-ups and small companies are the early adopters of cloud computing (Leavitt, 2009).

Scalability and the Need to Provision Demand

With cloud computing, the need to plan ahead for provisioning IT infrastructure is greatly reduced. It is difficult to forecast or predict IT service demand, because IT demand some times depends on unforeseeable events, coincidental and triggered events. For example, an article in a newspaper or on a news website may multiply prospective customers of a website within days. With cloud computing such surges in demand can be managed easily and without paying for idle just -in-case capacities. For example, Animoto (Jeff, n.d.) was able to manage the demand surge that occurred when its service was made available via Facebook. With Cloud Computing Animoto easily scaled its servers from 50 servers to 3500 servers within three days.

Fault-Tolerance and Disasters

Many providers have data centres distributed around the world, encapsulated from each other and far enough apart to warrant service, even if one or more locations are struck by disaster. By levering multiple data centres of a provider, a company can create inexpensive disaster proof systems, without upfront investments or even operating a single data centre, and with reduced response times for users, as servers can be placed, where the users are (e.g., Europe, USA, and Asia).

High Availability

Cloud providers offer highly available services, such as Amazon Web Services data storage S3, capable of sustaining the loss of up to two availability zones (an Amazon availability zone spans multiple data centres in a geographic region, isolated of each other). In research domain, High availability is one most desired feature in cloud computing because some computational intensive applications may take upto 12 weeks before completion of executions.

Performance and Elasticity of the Cloud

Clouds are pools of endless computing resources with unlimited performance that, provide endless amounts of resources at any time and automatically scale the performance of the system up and down as needed.

Mobility

Cloud computing services can be easily accessed through the Internet with any Internet enabled device like a PC, smart phone, or iPad, allowing users, employees, and administrators to access their systems from anywhere and at any time. To business owner, this means that staff can work any time and anywhere thereby maximizing business profits. However, there are certain risks and costs associated.

The cost benefits discussed in this section can mostly be realised when businesses and researchers choose cost effective cloud services. Our experimental result in this book chapter will help users to identify cost effective cloud service for their applications.

TYPES OF CLOUD COMPUTING

Without a good understanding of different types of cloud computing, it may be hard to realise the cost benefits described in Section 3. There are four types of cloud computing: public cloud, private cloud, community cloud, and hybrid cloud. Each of these cloud types offers different advantages to the businesses and research communities. A business can use one or more types of cloud computing to realize its organizational goals. Figure. 3 visualizes the four cloud computing types and their relationships.

Private Cloud

A private cloud is hosted in the data centre of a company and provides its services only to users inside that company or its partners. A private cloud provides more security than public clouds and cost saving in case it utilizes otherwise unused capacities in an already existing data centre (Aberdeen, n.d.). Making such unused capacities available through cloud interfaces allows to utilize the same tools as when working with public clouds and to benefit of the capabilities inherent in cloud management software, like a self -service interface, automated management of computing resources, and the ability to sell existing over capacities to partner companies. The Aberdeen Group (Aberdeen, n.d.) published a report, which concludes that organizations operating private clouds typically have about 12% cost advantage over organizations using public clouds.

Community Cloud

In community cloud computing, cloud services are provided to a specific group of organizations that share common goals or missions (such as security requirements, policy, or compliance considerations) (Marinos & Briscoe, 2009). The cost of running the cloud services is shared among the participants.

Figure 3. Types of Cloud Computing showing public cloud, private cloud, community cloud and hybrid cloud

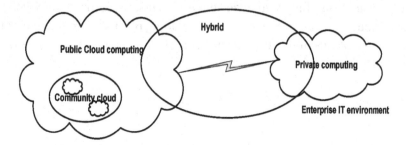

Community clouds can leverage service compliance to provide highly secure cloud environments among trusted communities (Yao, Chen, Wang, Levy, & Zic, 2011). Community clouds offer higher security and cost savings than public clouds, if managed properly, but less security than a private cloud.

Hybrid Cloud

This is a combination of private, public, or community clouds. Hybrid clouds allow organizations to find an optimal balance between cost of IT operations and inherent security risks by running highly confidential applications on private clouds and utilizing public clouds for peak loads or other computations. For example, a healthcare organization may use a private cloud managed by its internal IT unit to meet security requirements for healthcare data and public cloud services to fulfill organizational goals with lower security requirements. Hybrid clouds are still at an early stage in development and interoperability among clouds is a major challenge that has to be overcome to eventually allow users to manage their hybrid cloud environments without added complexity with the very tools they use to manage their private clouds (Searchcloudcomputing, n.d.).

RELATED TECHNOLOGIES

For completeness of this book chapter, this section outlines technologies that are often confused with cloud computing, namely:

Grid Computing

Computing grids are ancestors of clouds, and where built by connecting hundreds of servers in one or more data centres to provide aggregated computing power for long-running and computationally intense tasks (like scientific computations, such as weather or DNA folding simulations), which run multiple hours or days at a time. Similarly to private or community clouds, these computing grids were made for exclusive use by closed communities, like an organization or a few partner organisations (e.g., partner universities). Grids were specifically made for computing such long-running computationally intense tasks for closed communities and never developed the advanced means of manipulating and handling tasks. Clouds have to support all kinds of tasks, as they offer their services to a broader community, requiring more fine-grained means of task management, including the abilities to dynamically migrate tasks between servers depending on their loads, to distribute each resource (CPU cycles, memory, disk space, etc.) precisely among the given tasks, and to bill users based on their consumption of these resources. This higher level of refinement of clouds has mostly been enabled by the advancement of virtualization (clouds usually use fully virtualized environments, while grids were typically installed on physical machines). Clouds may use grid resources as building blocks to provide their cloud services to users. More in-depth discussions of the differences between cloud computing and grid computing have been published by Vouk et al (2008).

Utility Computing

Utility computing is another ancestor of cloud computing and has been inspired by how public utilities, such as electricity, water, and gas, are billed based on usage. Utility computing was developed after grid computing and provided computing resources to users through metered billing models. In grids, computing resources were often wasted, as users did not have incentives to control their resource usage. They did not pay for grid usage and their organizations did not pay based on the consumption, but contributed an agreed rate for being part of the grid partnership. Utility computing was introduced to make users aware of their consumption and more responsible. The major difference between utility and cloud computing lies in the underlying architecture and design, and how services are delivered to users. Clouds are fully virtualized and offer more advanced features to control tasks and computing resources than utility computing grids.

Virtualization

Virtualization allows installing multiple operating systems and software stacks (virtual machines (VMs)) on one physical computer, and executing them simultaneously but fully segregated from each other. It is the enabling technology for cloud computing, as it allowed operators of large data centres to consolidate existing unused resources and make use of these otherwise wasted resources. Cloud computing basically provisions a pool of virtualized computer resources on a pay-as-you-go model to its users. There are several competing virtualization technologies, most notably Xen (Xen, n.d) and Linux KVM (KVM, n.d.).

EXPERIMENTAL SETUP TO EVALUATE COMPUTATIONAL PERFORMANCE AND DOLLAR COST OF RUNNING COMPUTATION-INTENSIVE APPLICATION ON Iaas AND HaaS

We setup experimental environments to evaluate the computational performance and dollar cost of running computation-intensive application on IaaS and HaaS on HPC system. HPC systems in cloud covers most of the business and research applications. Our experimental setup includes two services we have leased from two cloud service providers; for the purpose of avoiding head-to-head comparison of the two cloud providers, we call them Cloud-A and Cloud-B. Cloud-A offers IaaS in different kind of cluster instances for HPC applications: for example, cluster compute instances. Cloud-B offers HaaS which can be configured to run HPC applications.

Cluster Compute Instances from Cloud-A (IaaS)

Cloud-A is one of the major cloud service providers of IaaS. When IaaS leased, only virtual machines (VMs) instances are provisioned to the users. Cloud-A 10provides IaaS in different instances for business and HPC applications. Table 1 shows a sample of cluster compute instances with price details of on-demand instances from cloud providers. The clusters compute instances are available with commonly used Operating System (OS) (Windows and Linux) in 32-bit and 64-bit platforms. For our experiments, we choose the Ref-C virtual instance in the Table 1 because it is widely used for HPC applications. The instances use Xen full virtualization. The I/O network communication between the cluster instance is 10 Gigabit Ethernet.

In order to compare the computational performance and dollar cost of running HPC applications when IaaS and HaaS services are leased. We leased a cluster compute instance with a total of 16 processors. The details of the leased cluster compute instance are shown in Table 2. We installed OpenMPI 1.6 on the node. OpenMPI is an open source implementation of the Message Passage Interface (MPI).

HPC SYSTEM ON HaaS IN THE CLOUD

As explained in Section 2, HaaS allows users to have full control of the system and control environment for measuring system performance and other available experiments. This enables users to determine the number of VMs to be deployed for HPC applications. We have leased an HaaS instance (Ref-G) with 64GB RAM from Cloud-B. Table 1 shows some of the cloud services that the HaaS providers offer that are similar to cluster compute instances that Cloud-A offers. The table also gives a summary of HaaS and price of the service leased. The communication network between each HaaS is a 1 Gigabit Ethernet.

The summary of the VM we provisioned on the HaaS is shown in Table 2. We installed Xen hypervisor (Xen, n.d) on the host. Xen hypervisor is an open source, industry standard virtualization technology. Linux Operating System (Ubuntu 12.4 64-bit) runs on top of the Xen hypervisor. We imported our pre-configured para-virtualised guest OS (Ubuntu 12.4 64-bit) on the HaaS instance. The preconfigured para-virtualised guest reduces the time to setup the HPC system on the HaaS instance. A paravirtualized OS uses a modified kernel, and reduces the size of the image. The VM is configured to have 16

Table 2. Computational environment for IaaS and HaaS

Cloud-A, VM of IaaS	Cloud-B, VM of HaaS
RAM: 24 GB	RAM: 60 GB
Architecture: x86_64	Architecture: x86_64
CPU op-mode(s): 32-bit, 64-bit	CPU op-mode(s): 64-bit
CPU(s): 16	CPU(s): 16
On-line CPU(s) 0-15	Thread(s) per core: 16, CPU socket: 1
Thread(s) per core: 2	Thread(s) per core: 16
Core(s) per socket: 4	Core(s) per socket: 1
NUMA node(s): 1	NUMA node(s): 1
Vendor ID: GenuineIntel	Vendor ID: GenuineIntel
CPU family: 6	CPU family: 6
Model: 26	Model: 26
Stepping: 5	Stepping: 5
CPU MHz: 2933.440	CPU MHz: 2266.78
Hypervisor vendor: Xen	Hypervisor vendor: Xen
Virtualization type: full	Virtualization type: para

(Egwutuoha, Chen, Levy, Selic, & Calvo, 2012)

processors with 60GB memory and 200GB hard drive. We installed OpenMPI on the node. This setup is almost equivalent to the cluster compute instances we leased from Cloud-A. The setup also allow us to have a good comparison environment for IaaS and HaaS in terms of computational performance and dollar cost. Table 2 shows both the IaaS and HaaS environments we used.

MPI APPLICATIONS AND BENCHMARK

We used a commonly used HPC benchmark and real HPC application to analyze and evaluate the MPI applications running on IaaS and HaaS services. The benchmark was the High Performance Linpack (HPL) benchmark (Petitet, Whaley, Dongarra, & Cleary, 2008) and the application was ClustalW MPI (Li, 2003). We describe them below. HPL (Petitet, Whaley, Dongarra, & Cleary, 2008) is a benchmark that is commonly used to evaluate the computational performance of HPC systems for example, Top500 (Top500, n.d). It measures the floating execution rate of linear equations based on the problem size. We executed the HPL benchmark with five different problem sizes of 2,000, 4,000, 6,000, 8,000 and 10,000 on the both cloud services on VMs from IaaS and on HaaS. The execution of each the problem sizes was carried twice and the average execution time calculated. The five different problem sizes enable us to obtain different wall clock execution times of HPL. We recorded the wall clock execution time for each problem size. We used the wall clock execution time to analyse the dollar cost and computational performance of the both platforms. Figure 4 show the results obtained on computational-performance.

Figure 4. Computational performance of high performance Linpack on 1 node with 16 processors

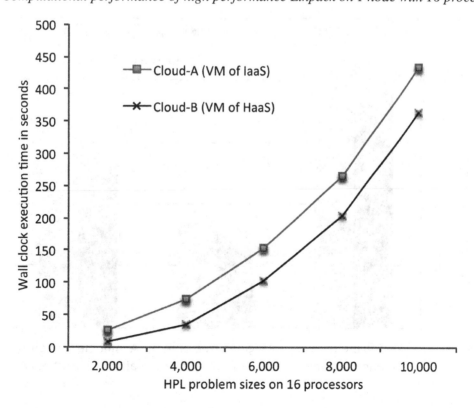

ClustalW MPI (Li, 2003) is a parallel implementation of ClustalW (Thompson, Higgins, & Gibson., 1994), which is based on MPI. ClustalW is a tool that is widely used in bioinformatics for multiple alignments of nucleic acid and protein sequences. It uses three alignments steps: pairwise alignment, guide-tree generation and progressive alignment. We ran a sample of 'A full multiple sequence alignment' 'A guide tree only sequence alignment' and 'A multiple sequence alignment out of an existing' on nodes from IaaS and from HaaS. We recorded the execution time of the three alignment steps to compare time to finish executions with both IaaS and HaaS. The results are shown in Figure 5.

RESULTS AND DISCUSSION

One of the major attractions to the Cloud-A cluster compute instance is that it is relatively easy to set up the clusters compared to setting up a cluster in HaaS. However, some level of technical knowledge is required to setup cluster on Cloud-A that will run HPC applications due to varying needs of HPC applications. In order to reduce the time to set up an HPC system on HaaS instances in the cloud, we uploaded our pre-configured para-virtualized image to the cloud. There are also similar VM images that can be downloaded from different sites. We estimated that this technique reduces the set up time by up to 80%. We did not compare the time to setup HPC system in Cloud-A (IaaS) cloud and in Cloud-B (HaaS) because setup time varies with individuals' technical experiences.

Figure 5. Performance of ClustalW-MPI application on 16 processors

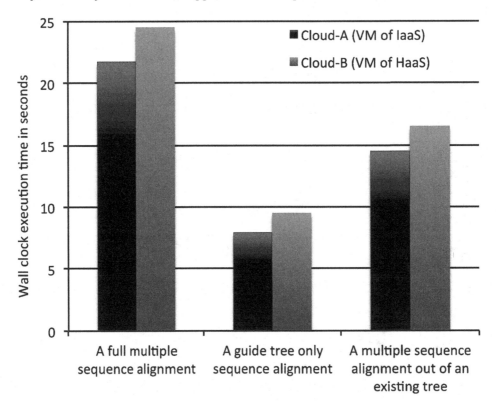

From the computational performance result of the HPL benchmark shown in Figure 4, we can see that the wall clock execution time of HPL benchmark on a provisioned instance on HaaS is shorter when compared to IaaS provided by Cloud-A. We achieved this because the memory of the virtual instances deployed on HaaS is 60GB. We chose to allocate this amount of memory to our virtual instance because we can predict the memory needed. This option is not available for the IaaS instance (users cannot change the memory of the virtual instance chosen). We also have full control of the Hardware instance and virtual instances.

As shown in Figure 4, executing the HPL on 1 node with 16 processor eliminates the bandwidth inequality on both providers. The virtual instances HaaS out performs IaaS. This is because we have full control of the applications running of our HaaS instance and we allocated higher memory to VM on HaaS. On IaaS, other VM instances may have been hosted on the hardware which may have affected the performance of the application running on our lease IaaS instance. As shown in (Ekanayake & Fox, 2010), high resource allocations on infrastructure affect applications running on VMs.

The ClustalW-MPI results is shown in Figure 4. Cloud-A IaaS uses 10 Gigabit Ethernet network, whereas HaaS we leased uses a 1 gigabit Ethernet with 16 processors network. We could have benchmarks with the same bandwidths, however the two major providers of HaaS do not have 10 gigabit Ethernet network. The results in Figure 5 show that there is no significant impact on application running on IaaS and on virtual instances on HaaS.

COST ANALYSIS

At the time of writing, Cloud-A offers different price models to their cluster compute instance customers; The primary price model which is widely used is called 'on-demand instances'. The on-demand instances price model allows users to pay hourly without contract while other price models may require up front payments and/or contracts.

Cloud-B offers their customers a pay-as-you-go price model, which is similar to on-demand instance prices offered by Cloud-A. Therefore we use on-demand price instance to compare the cost of running computation-intensive applications on both cloud services. In addition to the on-demand/pay-as-you-go instances prices, there are charges, which are charged for some cloud services such as network bandwidth and IP addresses which we do not consider to avoid complexity. We used the results obtained from HPL benchmarking to analyse the cost. As previously used in a similarly cost analysis (Deelman, Singh, Livny, Berriman, & Good, 2008), we assume that 1 second is equal to hourly rate which the both cloud providers offer. This also allows us to do the analysis without paying for the hours the experiment would have cost. We used the prices of the leased services as shown in Tables 1 and 2. The cost analysis computation of IaaS and HaaS is shown in Figure 6.

Based on the computational performance and cost analysis it appears that it is more cost effective to lease HaaS and configure the HPC systems. Cloud service users of HaaS have full control of the hardware as well as the VMs they provisioned. Application performance and other metrics can be easily measured. From the result, it seems that the cost of running HPC applications can be reduced by 20% when HaaS is leased.

Although, the price of IaaS and HaaS offered by the cloud provider Cloud-A and Cloud-B have varied over the period of time. Table 3 shows the current prices offered for IaaS and HaaS. Based on the prices offered by cloud service providers in 2013 and samples current prices, our experimental results showed

Figure 6. The cost analysis VM of IaaS and VM of HaaS

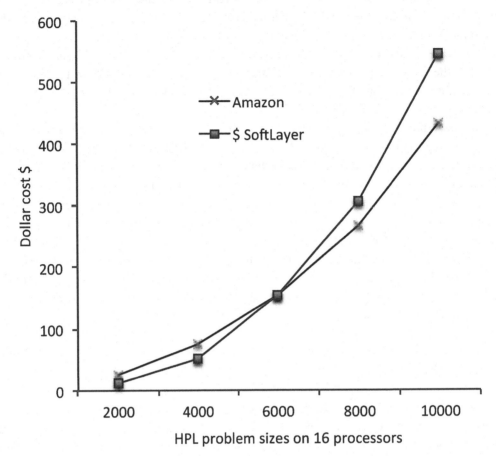

that it is cost effective to lease HaaS compare to IaaS, particularly for executing computation-intensive applications in the HPC systems in the cloud.

RELATED WORK

Cloud computing is a revolutionary computing paradigm for storing data, running applications, including computation-intensive applications. Cloud computing promises numerous benefits, which includes no up front investments for HPC applications, which is attractive, compared to traditional HPC systems. Many studies have evaluated the suitability of HPC systems in the cloud and showed that it is expected that more computation-intensive HPC applications will be run in the cloud HPC than traditional HPC systems (Carlyle, Harrell, & Smith., 2010). Furthermore, the Amazon Elastic Compute Cloud (Amazon EC2) cluster recently appeared in TOP500 list (Top500, n.d), which shows that there is a viable future for HPC systems in the cloud.

Many past researches evaluating of HPC applications on HPC systems in the Cloud with emphasis on Amazon EC2 have been carried out. These investigations focus on the performance of Amazon EC2

Table 3. Computational environment for IaaS and HaaS

Cloud Service Type: IaaS				
vCPU #	**vProcessor**	**vMemory (GB)**	**vStorage (GB)**	**$/Hour**
1	Intel Xeon E5-2670 v2	3.75	1 x 40 SSD	$0.07
2	Intel Xeon E5-2670 v2	7.5	1 x 32 SSD	$0.13
4	Intel Xeon E5-2670 v2	15	2 x 40 SSD	$0.27
8	Intel Xeon E5-2670 v2	30	2 x 80 SSD	$0.53
4	Intel Xeon E5-2680 v2	7.5	2 x 40 SSD	$0.21
8	Intel Xeon E5-2680 v2	15	2 x 80 SSD	$0.42
16	Intel Xeon E5-2680 v2	30	2 x 160 SSD	$0.84
32	Intel Xeon E5-2680 v2	60	2 x 320 SSD	$1.68
Cloud Service Type: HaaS				
Core #	**Xeon CPU**	**Ram**	**Harddrive**	**$/Hour**
8	2 x 2x2.0 GHz Gainestown E5504	44GB DDR3-1333	1 x 300.0GB 3.5" SCSI 10000RPM	$0.58
12	2 x 2x2.93 GHz X5670	64GB DDR3-1333	2 x 1000.0GB 2.5" SATA 5400RPM	$0.86
4	1 x 1x2.33GHz Quad Core L5410	8GB DDR2-667	2 x 147.0GB 2.5" SAS 15000RPM	$0.32
8	2 x 2x2.0 GHz Gainestown E5504	64GB DDR3-1333	1 x 300.0GB 3.5" SCSI 10000RPM	$0.68
4	1 x 1x2.13 GHz Harpertown E5506	24GB DDR3-1333	1 x 73.0GB 2.5" SAS 10000RPM	$0.37
8	2 x 2x2.0 GHz Gainestown E5504	44GB DDR3-1066	2 x 128.0GB 2.5" SSD 0RPM	$0.62

and Traditional HPC systems (Carlyle, Harrell, & Smith., 2010), (Deelman, Singh, Livny, Berriman, & Good, 2008), (Ekanayake & Fox, 2010), (Jinhui, Y., Chen, S., Nepal, S., Levy, D. and Zic, J.,, 2010).

Carlyle et al. (Carlyle, Harrell, & Smith., 2010) studied the cost effective HPC System. They show that it is cost effective for institutions like Purdue University to operate a community/traditional cluster than to lease HPC resources from Amazon EC2. This study clearly shows that Amazon on-demand cluster compute instances prices are not cost effective for HPC applications for some institutions. Their work focuses on Amazon EC2 service IaaS and traditional HPC systems.

Deelman et al (2008) The Cost of Doing Science on the Cloud: The Montage examples'; show that the cost of cloud services could be significantly reduced without significant impact on application performance, if the right storage and compute resources are provisioned. However, they did not consider different platforms like HaaS. We extended their work, demonstrating that HaaS can significantly reduce the cost of running computation-intensive application on HPC in the cloud.

Ekanayake & Fox, (2010) compare HPC applications with different needs and showed the performance of applications with latency. However, they did not compare the cost of executing computation-intensive application on different services such as IaaS and HaaS.

Jinhu et al, (2010) showed that optimal cost-performance ratio can be achieved with the appropriate cloud instance. However, they did not consider cost and computational performance when IaaS and HaaS are leased.

To the best of our knowledge, our work is different from other work in that we study the computational performance and dollar cost of running computation-intensive application in HPC in the cloud when IaaS and HaaS are leased. We experimentally show that the dollar cost of running computation-intensive application can be reduced as much as 20% with HaaS without significant impact to performance.

CONCLUSION AND FUTURE WORK

Due to the huge capital investment required to own a traditional HPC systems which typically involves job queuing, using an HPC system in the cloud is a good alternative. Cloud computing offers IaaS and HaaS for deployment of cluster instances, which can be used to run computation-intensive applications. IaaS provides almost ready to use clusters with minimal deployment installation tasks. With HaaS, virtual machines can be provisioned to run computation-intensive application. We have conducted experimental analysis to determine the performance and cost when cloud services IaaS and HaaS are leased to run computation-intensive application. We showed that the dollar cost of running computation-intensive application in the cloud can be reduced by as much as 20% when HaaS is leased. We showed that there is no significant impact in performance of the applications when executed on the leased HaaS.

ACKNOWLEDGMENT

The authors would like to thank Bran Selic for providing valuable comments and suggestions.

REFERENCES

Aberdeen. (n.d.). *Private Cloud*. Retrieved 2015, from http://v1.aberdeen.com/launch/report/perspective/8375-AI-private-cloud-virtualization.asp

Amazon. (n.d.). Retrieved 2015, from Amazon: https://aws.amazon.com/ec2

Armbrust, M., Fox, A., & Griffith, R. (2010). A view of cloud computing. *Communications of the ACM*, *53*(4), 50–58. doi:10.1145/1721654.1721672

Baremetalcloud. (n.d.). Retrieved 2015, from http://baremetalcloud.com/

Carlyle, A. G., Harrell, S. L., & Smith., A. P. (2010). Cost-effective HPC: The community or the cloud? *Cloud Computing Technology and Science (CloudCom)* (pp. 169-176). IEEE.

Deelman, E., Singh, G., Livny, M., Berriman, B., & Good, J. (2008). The cost of doing science on the cloud: The montage example.*SC '08: Proceedings of the 2008 ACM/IEEE conference on Supercomputing* (pp. 1–12). Piscataway, NJ: IEEE Press. doi:10.1109/SC.2008.5217932

Egwutuoha, I. P., Chen, S., Levy, D., & Calvo, R. (2013). Cost-effective Cloud Services for HPC in the Cloud: The IaaS or The HaaS? *Proceedings of the International Conference on Parallel and Distributed Processing Techniques and Applications (PDPTA).* (p. 217). The Steering Committee of The World Congress in Computer Science, Computer Engineering and Applied Computing (WorldComp).

Egwutuoha, I. P., Chen, S., Levy, D., Selic, B., & Calvo, R. (2012). A proactive fault tolerance approach to High Performance Computing (HPC) in the cloud. *Cloud and Green Computing (CGC),2012 Second International Conference* (pp. 268-273). IEEE. doi:10.1109/CGC.2012.22

Egwutuoha, I. P., Schragl, D., & Calvo, R. (2013). A brief review of cloud computing, challenges and potential solutions. *Parallel & Cloud Computing, 2*(1), 7–14.

Ekanayake, J., & Fox, G. (2010). *High performance parallel computing with clouds and cloud technologies.* Cloud Computing. doi:10.1201/EBK1439803158-c12

Evangelinos, C., & Hill, C. (2008). Cloud computing for parallel scientific HPC applications: Feasibility of running coupled atmosphere-ocean climate models on Amazon's EC2. ACM, 2(40), 2-34.

Foster, I., Zhao, I. R., & Lu, S. (2008). Cloud computing and grid computing 360-degree compared.*Grid Computing Environments Workshop, 2008. GCE08* (p. 110). IEEE. doi:10.1109/GCE.2008.4738445

Jeff, B. (n.d.). *Amazon.com CEO Jeff Bezos on Animoto.* Retrieved 2015, from https://animoto.com/blog/news/company/ amazon-com-ceo-jeff-bezos-on-animoto/

Jinhui, Y., Chen, S., Nepal, S., Levy, D., & Zic, J. (2010). TrustStore: Making Amazon S3 Trustworthy with Services Composition. *10th IEEE/ACM International Conference On Cluster, Cloud and Grid Computing} (CCGrid'2010)* (pp. 600-605). IEEE/ACM International Conference.

KVM. (n.d.). *Linux Kernel (Based Virtual Machine).* Retrieved March 2012, from http://www.linux-kvm.org/

Li, K.-B. (2003). *ClustalW-MPI: ClustalW analysis using distributed and parallel computing.* Academic Press.

Marinos, A., & Briscoe, G. (2009). Community cloud computing. *Cloud Computing,* 472-484.

Mell, P., & Grance, T. (2011). *The NIST Definition of Cloud Computingy.* National Institute of Standards and Technology.

Petitet, A., Whaley, R. C., Dongarra, J., & Cleary, A. (2008). *Benchmark.* Retrieved 2016, from HPL: http://www.netlib.org/benchmark/hpl/

Reese, G. (2009). *Cloud Application Architectures.* Reilly Media, Inc.

Rimal, B. P., Choi, E., & Lumb, I. (2009). A taxonomy and survey of cloud computing systems.*Fifth International Joint Conference on INC, IMS and IDC* (pp. 44-51). IEEE. doi:10.1109/NCM.2009.218

Salesforce. (n.d.). Retrieved 2016, from https://www.salesforce.com/

Searchcloudcomputing. (n.d.). *Hybrid cloud computing explained.* Retrieved 2012 йил Feb from http://searchcloudcomputing.techtarget.com/tutorial/Hybrid-cloud-computing-explained

Softlayer. (n.d.). Retrieved 2013, from http://www.softlayer.com/

SYS-CON Medi Inc. (n.d.). *Twenty-One Experts Define Cloud Computing*. Retrieved 2013, from http://cloudcomputing.syscon.com/node/612375/print

Thompson, J. D., Higgins, D. G., & Gibson, T. J. (1994). CLUSTAL W: Improving the sensitivity of progressive multiple sequence alignment through sequence weighting, position-specific gap penalties and weight matrix choice. *Nucleic Acids Research*, 22(22), 4673–4680. doi:10.1093/nar/22.22.4673 PMID:7984417

Top500. (2016). Retrieved 2016, from http://www.top500.org/

Vouk, M. A. (June2008). Cloud computing Issues, research and implementations. In *30th International Conference on Information Technology Interfaces (ITI 2008)*. doi:10.1109/ITI.2008.4588381

Wang, L., Tao, J., & Kunze, M. (2008). Scientific Cloud Computing: Early Definition and Experience. *10th IEEE International Conference on High Performance Computing and Communications*. IEEE. doi:10.1109/HPCC.2008.38

Xen. (n.d.). *Xen hypervisor*. Retrieved 2012 йил March from http://www.xen.org/products/xenhyp.html

Yao, J., Chen, S., Wang, Levy, D., & Zic, J. (2011). Modelling Collaborative Services for Business and QoS Compliance. *Proceedings of ICWS'2011* (pp. 299-306). Washington, DC: IEEE Computer Society. doi:10.1109/ICWS.2011.44

Compilation of References

AAIRM. (2002). *A risk management standard.* London UK: The Institute of Risk Management, the National Forum for Risk Management in the Public Sector and the Association of Insurance and Risk Managers.

Abbas, N., Gravell, A. M., & Wills, G. B. (2008). Historical roots of agile methods: where did agile thinking come from. In *Proceedings of 9th International Conference on Agile Processes in Software Engineering and Extreme Programming* (vol. 9, pp. 94-103). Heidelberg, Germany: Springer doi:10.1007/978-3-540-68255-4_10

Aberdeen. (n.d.). *Private Cloud.* Retrieved 2015, from http://v1.aberdeen.com/launch/report/perspective/8375-AI-private-cloud-virtualization.asp

Abrahamsson, P., Salo, O., Ronkainen, J. & Warsta, J. (2002). *Agile Software Development Methods.* Vuorimiehentie, Finland: VTT Technical Research Center of Finland.

Abram, T. (2009). The hidden values of it risk management. *Information Systems Audit and Control Association Journal, 2009*(2), 40-45.

Abrishami, Naghibzadeh, & Epema. (2013). Deadline-constrained workflow scheduling algorithms for Infrastructure as a Service Clouds. *Futur. Gener. Comput. Syst., 29*(1), 158–69. doi:10.1016/j.future.2012.05.004

Ackermann, T. (2012). *IT Security Risk Management: Perceived IT Security Risks in the Context of Cloud Computing.* Berlin, Germany: Springer-Gabler.

Advisory, C. E. R. T. CA-1998-01, Smurf IP Denial-of-Service Attacks. (1998). Available: http://www.cert.org/advisories/CA-1998-01.html

Agrawala, A. K., Mohr, J., & Bryant, R. (1976). An approach to the workload characterization problem. *Computer, 9*(6), 18–32. doi:10.1109/C-M.1976.218610

Aguilar, M. C., Bettaieb, S., Gaborit, P., & Herranz, J. (2011). *Improving Additive and Multiplicative Homomorphic Encryption Schemes based on Worst-Case Hardness Assumption.* Cryptology ePrint Archive Report 2011/607.

Alexander, C. (1979). *The Timeless Way of Building.* Oxford University Press.

Almeida, J., Almeida, V., Ardagna, D., Francalanci, C., & Trubian, M. (2006). Resource Management in the Autonomic Service-Oriented Architecture*Proceedings of the 2006 IEEE International Conference on Autonomic Computing (ICAC 2006)* (pp. 84-92). doi:10.1109/ICAC.2006.1662385

Alnuem, M., Alrumaih, H., & Al-Alshaikh, H. (2015). *Enterprise risk management from boardroom to shop floor.* Paper presented in The Sixth International Conference on Cloud Computing, GRIDs, and Virtualization, Nice, France.

Amazon Web Services. (2016). *Platform overview.* Retrieved from: https://aws.amazon.com/

Amazon. (n.d.). Retrieved 2015, from Amazon: https://aws.amazon.com/ec2

AMD. (2016). *AMD Turbo Core Technology*. Retrieved 31 March, 2016, from http://www.amd.com/en-us/innovations/software-technologies/turbo-core

An, Shekhar, Caglar, Gokhale, & Sastry. (2014). A cloud middleware for assuring performance and high availability of soft real-time applications. *J. Syst. Archit., 60*(9), 757–69. doi:10.1016/j.sysarc.2014.01.009

Anderson, E., & Mazzucca, J. (2015, February 18). *Survey Analysis: Cloud Adoption Across Vertical Industries Exhibits More Similarities Than Differences*. Gartner, Report number G00271486.

Andreolini, M., Casolari, S., Colajanni, M., & Messori, M. (2010). Dynamic Load Management of Virtual Machines in a Cloud Architectures. In *Lect. Notes Inst. Comput. Sci. Soc. Telecommun. Eng.* doi:10.1007/978-3-642-12636-9_14

Angeles, S. (2013, October 17). *8 Reasons to Fear Cloud Computing*. Retrieved March 07, 2016, from Business News Daily: http://www.businessnewsdaily.com/5215-dangers-cloud-computing.html

Anselmi, J., Amaldi, E., & Cremonesi, P. (2008). Service Consolidation with End-to-End Response Time Constraints*Proceedings of 34th Euromicro Conference on Software Engineering and Advanced Applications (SEAA 2008.)* (pp. 345-352). doi:10.1109/SEAA.2008.31

AppDirect. (n.d.). *Application Manager*. Retrieved from http://info.appdirect.com/products/appdirect-monetization-suite/marketplace-management-service/application-manager

Armbrust, Fox, Griffith, Joseph, Katz, Konwinski, Lee, Patterson … Zaharia. (2010). A view of cloud computing. ACM, 53(4), 50–58.

Armbrust, M., Fox, A., & Griffith, R. (2010). A view of cloud computing. *Communications of the ACM, 53*(4), 50–58. doi:10.1145/1721654.1721672

Assuncao, M. D., Netto, M. A. S., Peterson, B., Renganarayana, L., Rofrano, J., Ward, C., & Young, C. (2012). CloudAffinity: A framework for matching servers to cloudmates*Proceedings of the 2012 IEEE Network Operations and Management Symposium (NOMS 2012)* (pp. 213-220). doi:10.1109/NOMS.2012.6211901

Avasant. (2016). *Digital Enterprise Transformation: Rebooting Business Services for the New Global Economy*. El Segundo, CA: Create Space Independent Publishing Platform.

Aven, T. (2008). *Risk analysis: Assessing uncertainties beyond expected values and probabilities*. West Sussex, UK: John Wiely and Sons, Ltd. doi:10.1002/9780470694435

AWS. (2016). *EC2 Instance Types – Amazon Web Services (AWS)*. Retrieved 31 March, 2016, from https://aws.amazon.com/ec2/instance-types/

Bakshi, A., & Yogesh, B. (2010). Securing cloud from ddos attacks using intrusion detection system in virtual machine, in Communication Software and Networks, 2010. ICCSN'10. Second International Conference on. IEEE.

Banking and Finance. (2007). *Europe's Markets in Financial Instruments Directive (Mifid1 & 2). Investment Services and Regulatory Markets*. Retrieved from: http://ec.europa.eu/finance/securities/isd/index_en.htm.Europa.eu

Baremetalcloud. (n.d.). Retrieved 2015, from http://baremetalcloud.com/

Barroso, L. A., & Holzle, U. (2007). The Case for Energy-Proportional Computing. *Computer, 40*(12), 33–37. doi:10.1109/MC.2007.443

Basheer Nayef, A. D. (2005). *Mitigation and traceback countermeasures for DDoS attacks*. Iowa State University.

Baya, V., Mathaisel, B., & Parker, B. (2010). The cloud you don't know: An engine for new business growth. PWC Journal of Technology Forecast: Driving Growth with Cloud Computing, 1(4), 4-16.

Beck, K. (2001). *Manifesto for Agile Software Development*. Retrieved February 5, 2016, from http://agilemanifesto.org/

Begum, S., & Prashanth, C. (2013). Review of load balancing in cloud computing. *International Journal of Computer Science Issues, 10*(1), 343–352.

Behrendt, M. (2014). *CCRA 4.0 Overview Deck*. Retrieved March 2015, from, https://www.ibm.com/developerworks/community/files/form/anonymous/api/library/e1e5df30-d839-4965-97bb-b3f05fbe7dee/document/56af12bb-6259-4cc6-bf6d-2776682bd232/media/CCRA%204.0%20Overview_20140918_non_conf.pdf

Belady, C. L., & Beaty, D. (2005). Roadmap for Datacom Cooling. *ASHRAE Journal, 47*(12), 52.

Bellovin, S. (2000). The ICMP traceback message. Network Working Group, Internet Draft. Available at http://lasr.cs.ucla.edu/save/rfc/draft-bellovin-itrace-00.txt

Beloglazov, A. (2010). *Energy Efficient Allocation of Virtual Machines in Cloud Data Centers*. Paper presented at the 10th IEEE/ACM International Conference on Cluster, Cloud and Grid Computing (CCGrid 2010). doi:10.1109/CCGRID.2010.45

Beloglazov, A., & Buyya, R. (2010). Energy Efficient Resource Management in Virtualized Cloud Data Centers. *Clust. Cloud Grid Comput. (CCGrid), 2010 10th IEEE/ACM Int. Conf.* IEEE. doi:10.1109/CCGRID.2010.46

Beloglazov, A., & Buyya, R. (2010, November). Adaptive Threshold-Based Approach for Energy-Efficient Consolidation of Virtual Machines in Cloud Data Centers. In *Proc. 8th Int. Work. Middlew. Grids, Clouds E-Science*. doi:10.1145/1890799.1890803

Beloglazov, A., & Buyya, R. (2012). Optimal online deterministic algorithms and adaptive heuristics for energy and performance efficient dynamic consolidation of virtual machines in Cloud data centers. In Concurr. Comput. Pract. Exp., 24, 1397–1420. doi:10.1002/cpe.1867

Beloglazov, Abawajy, & Buyya. (2012). Energy-aware resource allocation heuristics for efficient management of data centers for Cloud computing. *Futur. Gener. Comput. Syst., 28*(5), 755–68. doi:10.1016/j.future.2011.04.017

Beloglazov, A., & Buyya, R. (2013). Managing overloaded hosts for dynamic consolidation of virtual machines in cloud data centers under quality of service constraints. *IEEE Transactions on Parallel and Distributed Systems, 24*(7), 1366–1379. doi:10.1109/TPDS.2012.240

Bergin, J. (2012). *Pedagogical Patterns: Advice For Educators*. CreateSpace Independent Publishing Platform.

Bhadauria, R. C. R., Chaki, N., & Sanyal, S. (2011). A survey on security issues in cloud computing. Retrieved from http://arxiv.org/abs/1109.5388

Bhuyan, K., Kashyap, H. J., Bhattacharyya, D. K., & Kalita, J. K. (2013). Detecting Distributed Denial of Service Attacks: Methods, Tools and Future Directions. *The Computer Journal, 57*(4), 537–556. doi:10.1093/comjnl/bxt031

Bichler, M., Setzer, T., & Speitkamp, B. (2006). Capacity planning for virtualized servers*Proceedings of the 16th Annual Workshop on Information Technologies and Systems (WITS 2006)*.

Biedermann, S., Mink, M., & Katzenbeisser, S. (2012). Fast dynamic extracted honeypots in cloud computing. In *Proceedings of the ACM Workshop on Cloud computing security workshop*. doi:10.1145/2381913.2381916

Bin, E., Biran, O., Boni, O., Hadad, E., Kolodner, E. K., Moatti, Y., & Lorenz, D. H. (2011). Guaranteeing high availability goals for virtual machine placement. In *Proc. - Int. Conf. Distrib. Comput. Syst.* IEEE. doi:10.1109/ICDCS.2011.72

Blanchard, B., Corti, G., Delaware, S., Kim, H. J., Plachy, A., Quezada, M., & Santos, G. (2014). *IBM PowerVC Introduction and Configuration*. Retrieved September 2014 from, http://www.redbooks.ibm.com/redpieces/pdfs/sg248199.pdf

Bobroff, N., Kochut, A., & Beaty, K. (2007). Placement of Virtual Machines for Managing SLA Violations. *2007 10th IFIP/IEEE Int. Symp. Integr. Netw. Manag.* IEEE. doi:10.1109/INM.2007.374776

Bottomley, J. (2013, May). *Containers and The Cloud A Match Made in Heaven*. Academic Press.

Brakerski, Z., & Vaikuntanathan, V. (2011). *Efficient Fully Homomorphic Encryption from (Standard) LWE*. Electronic Colloquium on Computational Complexity, Report No. 109 (2011).

Brakerski, Z., Gentry, G., & Vaikuntanathan, V. (2011). *Fully homomorphic encryption without bootstrapping*. Cryptology ePrint Archive, Report 2011/277.

Brandel, C., Grose, V., Hong, M., Imholz, J., Kaggali, P., & Mantegazza, M. (n.d.). *Cloud Computing Patterns of Expertise*. IBM Redbooks.

Breitgand, D. Marashini, & Tordsson. (2011). Policy-driven service placement optimization in federated clouds. Academic Press.

Breitgand, D., Dubitzky, & Epstein. (2012). Sla-aware resource over-commit in an iaas cloud. *Proc. 8th Int. Conf. Netw. Serv. Manag.* Retrieved from http://dl.acm.org/citation.cfm?id=2499406.2499415

Brewer, E. (2016). *Google Open Source Blog: An update on container support on Google Cloud Platform*. Retrieved from http://google-opensource.blogspot.com.au/2014/06/an-update-on-container-support-on.html

Broder, J. (2006). *Risk analysis and the security survey*. Burlington, MA: Butterworth-Heinemann Elsevier.

Brody, A. (2013). History of DDoS. Retrieved from: http://www.timetoast.com/timelines/history-of-ddos

Brotby, W. (2006). *Information security governance: Guidance for boards of directors and executive management*. Rolling Meadows, IL: IT Governance Institute.

Brown, W., Laird, R., Gee, C., & Mitra, T. (2008). *SOA Governance: Achieving and Sustaining Business and IT Agility*. Indianapolis, IN: IBM Press.

Brown, R. E. (2008). Impact of smart grid on distribution system design, in Power and Energy Society General Meeting-Conversion and Delivery of Electrical Energy.*2008 IEEE International conference*.

Brown, W. A., Moore, G., & Tegan, W. (2006). *SOA governance—IBM's approach*. Somers, NY: IBM Corporation.

Buckellew, P., Custis, K., Esposito, R., & Lesser, E. (2013). *The upwardly mobile enterprise: Setting the strategic agenda*. Retrieved from http://www-01.ibm.com/common/ssi/cgi-bin/ssialias?infotype=PM&subtype=XB&htmlfid=GBE03574USEN

Bundesinisterium der Justiz und fur Verbrauchenschutz. (2016). *What is Openstack*. Retrieved from: http://www.openstack.org/software/

Burch, H., & Cheswick, H. (2000). Tracing anonymous packets to their approximate source. Proceedings of USENIX LISA (New Orleans) Conference.

Buschmann, F., Meunier, R., Rohnert, H., Sommerlad, P., & Stal, M. (1996). *Pattern Oriented Software Architecture: A System of Patterns*. Wiley.

BusinessDictionary.com. (2016). *Service Provider definition*. Retrieved from; http://www.businessdictionary.com/definition/service-provider.html

Buyya, R., Beloglazov, A., & Abawajy, J. (2010). Energy-efficient management of data center resources for cloud computing: a vision, architectural elements, and open challenges*Proceedings of 16th International Conference on Parallel and Distributed Processing Techniques and Applications (PDPTA 2010)* (pp. 6-17).

Caglar, F., Shekhar, S., & Gokhale, A. (2013). *A Performance Interference-aware Virtual Machine Placement Strategy for Supporting Soft Realtime Applications in the Cloud.* Institute for Software Integrated Systems, Vanderbilt University, Nashville, TN, USA, Tech. Rep. ISIS-13-105.

Calcavecchia, N. M., Biran, O., Hadad, E., & Moatti, Y. (2012). VM Placement Strategies for Cloud Scenarios. In *2012 IEEE Fifth Int. Conf. Cloud Comput.* IEEE. doi:10.1109/CLOUD.2012.113

Calheiros, R. N., & Buyya, R. (2014). Energy-Efficient Scheduling of Urgent Bag-of-Tasks Applications in Clouds through DVFS*Proceedings of the 6th IEEE International Conference on Cloud Computing Technology and Science (CloudCom 2014)* (pp. 342-349). doi:10.1109/CloudCom.2014.20

Calzarossa, M., & Serazzi, G. (1993). Workload characterization: A survey. *Proceedings of the IEEE, 81*(8), 1136–1150. doi:10.1109/5.236191

Campagna, R., Lyer, S., & Krishnan, A. (2013). *Mobile Device Security for Dummies.* Hoboken, NJ: John Wiley & Sons.

Carl, G., Kesidis, G., Brooks, R. R., & Rai, S. (2006). Denial-of-service attack detection techniques. *IEEE Internet Computing, 10*(1), 82–89. doi:10.1109/MIC.2006.5

Carlyle, A. G., Harrell, S. L., & Smith., A. P. (2010). Cost-effective HPC: The community or the cloud? *Cloud Computing Technology and Science (CloudCom)* (pp. 169-176). IEEE.

Castañé, Núñez, Llopis, & Carretero. (2013). E-mc2: A formal framework for energy modelling in cloud computing. *Simul. Model. Pract. Theory, 39,* 56–75. doi:10.1016/j.simpat.2013.05.002

CEB CIO Leadership Council. (2014a, August 21). *How to Promote IT's Climate of Openness.* CEB. Retrieved from https://www.executiveboard.com/member/applications/events/replays/14/how-to-promote-it-s-climate-of-openness. html?referrerTitle=Replays%20-%20CEB%20Applications%20Leadership%20Council accessed on Sep, 19 2015

CEB CIO Leadership Council. (2014b, November 5). *The State of Enterprise SaaS Adoption.* CEB. Retrieved from https://www.executiveboard.com/member/applications/research/report/14/the-state-of-enterprise-saas-adoption. html?referrerTitle=Report%20-%20CEB%20Applications%20Leadership%20Council

CEB CIO Leadership Council. (2014c, November 10). *Making Shadow IT Work for You.* CEB. Retrieved from https://www.executiveboard.com/member/applications/events/replays/14/making-shadow-it-work-for-you.html.html

CEB CIO Leadership Council. (2014d, December 23). *IT Cost Management Playbook.* CEB. Retrieved from https://www.executiveboard.com/member/finance-leadership/decision_supportcenter/it-cost-management-playbook.html

Chaisiri, S., Lee, B.-S., & Niyato, D. (2012). Optimization of Resource Provisioning Cost in Cloud Computing. *IEEE Trans. Serv. Comput., 5*(2), 164–177. doi:10.1109/TSC.2011.7

Charles, J., Jassi, P., Ananth, N. S., Sadat, A., & Fedorova, A. (2009). Evaluation of the Intel\textregistered Core™ i7 Turbo Boost feature*Proceedings of the 2009 IEEE International Symposium on Workload Characterization (IISWC 2009)* (pp. 188-197). doi:10.1109/IISWC.2009.5306782

Chen, Joshi, Hiltunen, Schlichting, & Sanders. (2011). Using CPU gradients for performance-aware energy conservation in multitier systems. *Sustain. Comput. Informatics Syst., 1*(2), 113–33. doi:10.1016/j.suscom.2011.02.002

Chen, Y., Ganapathi, A. S., Griffith, R., & Katz, R. H. (2010). *Analysis and lessons from a publicly available Google cluster trace*. EECS Department, University of California, Berkeley, Tech. Rep. UCB/EECS-2010-95, University of California, Berkeley.

Chen, J., Wang, C., Zhou, B. B., Sun, L., & Lee, Y. C. (2011). Tradeoffs Between Profit and Customer Satisfaction for Service Provisioning in the Cloud. In *Proc. 20th Int. Symp. High Perform. Distrib. Comput. - HPDC '11*. New York: ACM Press. doi:10.1145/1996130.1996161

Chen, M., Zhang, H., Su, Y. Y., Wang, X., Jiang, G., & Yoshihira, K. (2011). Effective VM sizing in virtualized data centers. In *Proc. 12th IFIP/IEEE Int. Symp. Integr. Netw. Manag. IM 2011*. IEEE. doi:10.1109/INM.2011.5990564

Chen, Y., Alspaugh, S., Borthakur, D., & Katz, R. (2012). Energy Efficiency for Large-scale MapReduce Workloads with Significant Interactive Analysis*Proceedings of the 7th ACM European Conference on Computer Systems* (pp. 43-56). doi:10.1145/2168836.2168842

Chen, Y., Hwang, K., & Ku, W. S. (2006). Distributed change-point detection of DDoS attacks over multiple network domains.*Proceedings of the IEEE International Symposium on Collaborative Technologies and Systems*, (pp. 543–550). IEEE.

Choi, K., Chen, X., Li, S., Kim, M., Chae, K., & Na, J. (2012). Intrusion detection of nsm based dos attacks using data mining in smart grid. *Energies*, *5*(10), 4091–4109. doi:10.3390/en5104091

Chonka, A., Xiang, Y., Zhou, W., & Huang, X. (2012). Protecting Cloud Web Services from HX-DoS attacks using Decision Theory. IEEE International conference on communications in china: advanced internet and cloud (AIC). IEEE.

Chonka, A., Xiang, Y., Zhou, W., & Bonti, A. (2011). Cloud security defense to protect cloud computing against HTTP-DOS and XML-DOS attacks. *Journal of Network and Computer Applications*, *34*(4), 1097–1107. doi:10.1016/j.jnca.2010.06.004

Chunsheng, G. (2012). *Attack on fully homomorphic encryption over the integers*. Cryptology ePrint Archive Report 2012/157.

Cirne, W., Brasileiro, F., Sauvé, J., Andrade, N., Paranhos, D., Santos-neto, E., & Gr, F. C. et al. (2003). Grid computing for of Bag-of-Tasks applications*Proceedings of the 3rd IFIP Conference on E-Commerce, E-Business and EGovernment*.

Cler, C. (2013). *How to Use rPerfs for Workload Migration and Server Consolidation*. Retrieved September 22, 2015, from http://www.ibmsystemsmag.com/aix/tipstechniques/Migration/rperf_metric/

Cloud Computing and Hybrid Cloud. (n.d.). Retrieved May 09, 2016 from https://en.wikipedia.org/wiki/Cloud_computing#Hybrid_cloud

Cloud Security Alliance. (2010). Top Threats to Cloud Computing. Retrieved from http://www.cloudsecurityalliance.org/topthreats/csathreats.v1.0.pdf

Cloud Standard Customer Council. (2015). *Customer Cloud Architecture for Mobile*. Retrieved from http://www.cloud-council.org/CSCC-Webinar-Customer-Cloud-Architecture-for-Mobile-6-16-15.pdf

CloudFoundry. (2016). *What is CloudFoundry*. Retrieved from: https://www.cloudfoundry.org/

Columbus, L. (2015, September 27). *Forbes.com*. Retrieved March 07, 2016, from http://www.forbes.com/sites/louis-columbus/2015/09/27/roundup-of-cloud-computing-forecasts-and-market-estimates-q3-update-2015/#2b64aed56c7a

Container, L. (2016). *Linux Containers*. Retrieved 31 March, 2016, from https://linuxcontainers.org/

Coron, J. S., Mandal, A., Naccache, D., & Tibouchi, M. (2011). Fully homomorphic encryption over the integers with shorter public-keys. *Advances in Cryptology - Proc. CRYPTO 2011*, (LNCS), (vol. 6841). Springer. doi:10.1007/978-3-642-22792-9_28

Coron, J., S., Lepoint, T., & Tibouchi, M. (2012). *Batch fully homomorphic encryption over the integers.* Cryptology ePrint Archive Report 2013/036.

Corporate Governance of Information Technology. (n.d.). Retrieved May 09, 2016 from https://en.m.wikipedia.org/wiki/Corporate_governance_of_information_technology

COSO. (2012). Enterprise Risk Management for Cloud Computing. Durham, NC: The Committee of Sponsoring Organizations of the Treadway Commission (COSO).

Create, W.The Project? (n.d.). Retrieved on May 10, 2016 from https://www.hyperledger.org/

Crouhy, M., Galai, D., & Mark, R. (2006). *The essentials of risk management.* New York: McGraw-Hill Inc.

CSA (The Cloud Security Alliance). (2011). *Security guidance for critical areas of focus in cloud computing v3.0.* Retrieved September 09, 2015, from https://downloads.cloudsecurityalliance.org/initiatives/guidance/csaguide.v3.0.pdf

Daecher, A., & Galizia, T. (2015). *Ambient computing. Deloitte Journal of Tech Trends, 6(1)*, 34–49.

Dagley, R. (2011). *Data Centre Migration: Managing hidden business risks.* IBM. Retrieved from: https://www-935.ibm.com/services/uk/gts/pdf/GTW03030_GBEN_00.pdf

Darwish, M., Ouda, A., & Capretz, L. F. (2013) Cloud-based ddos attacks and defenses. In Information Society (i-Society), IEEE International Conference. Retrieved from http://staff.washington.edu/dittrich/talks/sec2000/timeline.html

David, H., Fallin, C., Gorbatov, E., Hanebutte, U. R., & Mutlu, O. (2011). Memory Power Management via Dynamic Voltage/Frequency Scaling*Proceedings of the 8th ACM International Conference on Autonomic Computing* (pp. 31-40). doi:10.1145/1998582.1998590

Davis, C., Schiller, M., & Wheeler, K. (2006). *IT auditing: Using controls to protect information assets.* Emeryville, CA: McGraw-Hill Osborne Media.

De Haes, S., & Grembergen, W. (2009). *Enterprise governance of information technology: Achieving strategic alignment and value.* New York: Springer. doi:10.1007/978-0-387-84882-2

Dean, J., & Ghemawat, S. (2008). MapReduce: Simplified Data Processing on Large Clusters. *Magazine Communications of the ACM, 51(1)*, 107–113. doi:10.1145/1327452.1327492

Decker, V. E. J. & Iervolino, C. (2015, August 18). *Critical CFO Technology Needs: 2015 Gartner FEI Study.* Gartner. Gartner Report number G00280250.

Deelman, E., Singh, G., Livny, M., Berriman, B., & Good, J. (2008). The cost of doing science on the cloud: The montage example.*SC '08: Proceedings of the 2008 ACM/IEEE conference on Supercomputing* (pp. 1–12). Piscataway, NJ: IEEE Press. doi:10.1109/SC.2008.5217932

Dempsey, K. (2014). *NIST Computer Security Division*csrc.nist.gov*Summary of NIST SP 800 - 53 Revision 4, Security and Privacy Controls for Federal Information Systems and Organizations.* NIST, NIST Computer Security Division csrc.nist.gov Summary of NIST SP 800 - 53 Revision 4, Security and Privacy Controls for Federal Information Systems and Organizations Kelley Dempsey. NIST.

Deng, Q., Meisner, D., Bhattacharjee, A., Wenisch, T. F., & Bianchini, R. (2012). CoScale: Coordinating CPU and Memory System DVFS in Server Systems*Proceedings of the 45th Annual IEEE/ACM International Symposium on Microarchitecture (MICRO 2012)* (pp. 143-154). doi:10.1109/MICRO.2012.22

Deng, Q., Meisner, D., Ramos, L., Wenisch, T. F., & Bianchini, R. (2011). MemScale: Active Low-power Modes for Main Memory*Proceedings of the 16th International Conference on Architectural Support for Programming Languages and Operating Systems (ASPLOS 2011)* (pp. 225-238). doi:10.1145/1950365.1950392

Dent, W., A. (2006). *Fundamental problems in provable security and cryptography*. Royal Society. Cryptology ePrint Archive Report 2006/278.

Dhiman, G., Pusukuri, K. K., & Rosing, T. (2008). Analysis of Dynamic Voltage Scaling for System Level Energy Management*Proceedings of the 2008 Conference on Power Aware Computing and Systems (HotPower 2008)* (pp. 9-9).

Dhyani, K., Gualandi, S., & Cremonesi, P. (2010). A Constraint Programming Approach for the Service Consolidation Problem. Integration of AI and OR Techniques in Constraint Programming for Combinatorial Optimization Problems, (pp. 97-101).

Diffie, W., & Hellman, M. E. (1976). New Directions in Cryptography. *IEEE Transactions on Information Theory*, *22*(6), 644–654. doi:10.1109/TIT.1976.1055638

Dijk, M. V., Gentry, C., Halevi, S., & Vaikuntanathan, V. (2010). Fully homomorphic encryption over the integers. *LNCS*, *6110*, 24–43.

Di, S., Kondo, D., & Cappello, F. (2013). Characterizing Cloud Applications on a Google Data Center*Proceedings of the 42nd International Conference on Parallel Processing (ICPP 2013)* (pp. 468-473). doi:10.1109/ICPP.2013.56

Do & Rotter. (2012). Comparison of scheduling schemes for on-demand IaaS requests. *J. Syst. Softw.*, *85*(6), 1400–1408. doi:10.1016/j.jss.2012.01.019

Doan, M. N., & Eui-Nam, H. (2011). A Collaborative Intrusion Detection System Framework for Cloud Computing. *Proceedings of the International Conference on IT Convergence and Security*, (pp. 91-109).

Dong, Z., Zhuang, W., & Rojas-Cessa, R. (2014). Energy-aware scheduling schemes for cloud data centers on Google trace data*Proceedings of the 2014 IEEE Online Conference on Green Communications (OnlineGreencomm 2014)* (pp. 1-6). doi:10.1109/OnlineGreenCom.2014.7114422

Dorothy, G. L., & Barton, S. W. (2015). *What's Lost When Experts Retire*. Retrieved September 23, 2015, from https://hbr.org/2014/12/whats-lost-when-experts-retire

DoS and DDoS Evolution. (n.d.). Retrieved from http://users.atw.hu/denialofservice/ch03lev1sec3.html

Doua, W., Chen, Q., & Chen, J. (2013). A confidence-based filtering method for DDoS attack defence in cloud environment. *Future Generation Computer Systems*, *29*(7), 1838–1850. doi:10.1016/j.future.2012.12.011

Douligeris, C., & Mitrokotsa, A. (2004). Ddos attacks and defense mechanisms: Classification and state-of-the-art. *Computer Networks*, *44*(5), 643–666. doi:10.1016/j.comnet.2003.10.003

Du, P., & Nakao, A. (2010). OverCourt: DDoS mitigation through credit-based traffic segregation and path migration. *Computer Communications*, *33*(18), 2164–2175. doi:10.1016/j.comcom.2010.09.009

Dupont, C., Schulze, T., Giuliani, G., Somov, A., & Hermenier, F. (2012). An energy aware framework for virtual machine placement in cloud federated data centres. In *Proc. 3rd Int. Conf. Futur. Energy Syst. Where Energy, Comput. Commun. Meet - E-Energy '12*. New York: ACM Press. doi:10.1145/2208828.2208832

Durillo, J. J., Nae, V., & Prodan, R. (2014). Multi-objective energy-efficient workflow scheduling using list-based heuristics. *Future Generation Computer Systems*, *36*, 221–236. doi:10.1016/j.future.2013.07.005

Dutta, A., Peng, G. C., & Choudhary, A. (2013). Risks in enterprise cloud computing: The perspective of IT experts. *Journal of Computer Information Systems*, *53*(4), 39–48. doi:10.1080/08874417.2013.11645649

Economist Intelligence Unit. (2015, May 14). *Economist Insights*. Retrieved March 07, 2016, from http://www.economistinsights.com/analysis/mapping-cloud-maturity-curve

Egwutuoha, I. P., Chen, S., Levy, D., & Calvo, R. (2013). Cost-effective Cloud Services for HPC in the Cloud: The IaaS or The HaaS? *Proceedings of the International Conference on Parallel and Distributed Processing Techniques and Applications (PDPTA)*. (p. 217). The Steering Committee of The World Congress in Computer Science, Computer Engineering and Applied Computing (WorldComp).

Egwutuoha, I. P., Chen, S., Levy, D., Selic, B., & Calvo, R. (2012). A proactive fault tolerance approach to High Performance Computing (HPC) in the cloud. *Cloud and Green Computing (CGC),2012 Second International Conference* (pp. 268-273). IEEE. doi:10.1109/CGC.2012.22

Egwutuoha, I. P., Schragl, D., & Calvo, R. (2013). A brief review of cloud computing, challenges and potential solutions. *Parallel & Cloud Computing*, *2*(1), 7–14.

Ekanayake, J., & Fox, G. (2010). *High performance parallel computing with clouds and cloud technologies*. Cloud Computing. doi:10.1201/EBK1439803158-c12

Erber, M. (2014, January 13). *Thoughts on Cloud*. Retrieved March 07, 2016, from http://www.thoughtsoncloud.com/2014/01/what-is-hybrid-cloud/

European Bank Authority. (2016). *Regulation and Policy*. Retrieved from: http://www.eba.europa.eu/regulation-and-policy

Evangelinos, C., & Hill, C. (2008). Cloud computing for parallel scientific HPC applications: Feasibility of running coupled atmosphere-ocean climate models on Amazon's EC2. ACM, *2*(40), 2-34.

Fabric Computing. (n.d.). Retrieved May 09, 2016 from https://en.wikipedia.org/wiki/Fabric_Computing

Fadlullah, Z. M., Fouda, M. M., Kato, N., Shen, X., & Nozaki, Y. (2011). An early warning system against malicious activities for smart grid communications. *IEEE Network*, *25*(5), 50–55. doi:10.1109/MNET.2011.6033036

Fang, Liang, Li, Chiaraviglio, & Xiong. (2013). VMPlanner: Optimizing virtual machine placement and traffic flow routing to reduce network power costs in cloud data centers. *Comput. Networks, 57*(1), 179–96. doi:10.1016/j.comnet.2012.09.008

Feitelson, D. G. (2015). *Workload modeling for computer systems performance evaluation*. Cambridge University Press. doi:10.1017/CBO9781139939690

Feller, E., Rilling, L., & Morin, C. (2011). Energy-Aware Ant Colony Based Workload Placement in Clouds. In *2011 IEEE/ACM 12th Int.Conf. Grid Comput.* IEEE. doi:10.1109/Grid.2011.13

Feller, E., Rohr, C., Margery, D., & Morin, C. (2012). Energy management in IaaS clouds: A holistic approach. In *Proc. - 2012 IEEE 5th Int.Conf. Cloud Comput. CLOUD 2012.* IEEE. doi:10.1109/CLOUD.2012.50

Feller, E., Ramakrishnan, L., & Morin, C. (2015). Performance and energy efficiency of big data applications in cloud environments: A hadoop case study. *Journal of Parallel and Distributed Computing*, *79*, 80–89. doi:10.1016/j.jpdc.2015.01.001

Feng, Y., Guo, R., Wang, D., & Zhang, B. (2009). *A comparative study of distributed denial of service attacks, intrusion tolerance and mitigation techniques, intrusion tolerance and mitigation techniques*. Academic Press.

Ferdman, M., Adileh, A., Kocberber, O., Volos, S., Alisafaee, M., Jevdjic, D., & Falsafi, B. et al. (2012). Clearing the Clouds: A Study of Emerging Scale-out Workloads on Modern Hardware. *ACM SIGPLAN Notices*, *47*(4), 37–48.

Ferguson, P., & Senie, D. (2001). Network ingress filtering: defeating Denial of Service attacks which employ IP source address spoofing. RFC 2827.

Ferrari, D. (1972). Workload characterization and selection in computer performance measurement. *Computer*, *5*(4), 18–24. doi:10.1109/C-M.1972.216939

Ferreto, Netto, Calheiros, & De Rose. (2011). Server consolidation with migration control for virtualized data centers. *Futur. Gener. Comput. Syst.*, *27*(8), 1027–34. doi:10.1016/j.future.2011.04.016

Fiscutean, A. (2015, August 12). *50 years and still going strong: Will we ever be ready to kill off COBOL?* ZDnet.com. Retrieved from http://www.zdnet.com/article/50-years-and-still-going-strong-will-we-ever-be-ready-to-kill-off-cobol/

Fit'o, J., & Guitart, J. (2014). Introducing Risk Management into Cloud. *Journal of Future Generation Computer Systems*, *32*(1), 41–53.

Foran, J. (2015). *Cloud computing licensing: Buyer beware*. Retrieved September 23, 2015, from http://searchcloud-computing.techtarget.com/feature/Cloud-computing-licensing-Buyer-beware

Forestiero, A., Mastroianni, C., Meo, M., Papuzzo, G., & Sheikhalishahi, M. (2014). Hierarchical Approach for Green Workload Management in Distributed Data Centers*Proceedings of the 20th International European Conference on Parallel and Distributed Computing (Euro-Par 2014) Workshops* (pp. 323-334). doi:10.1007/978-3-319-14325-5_28

Forouzan, B. A. (2002). *TCP/IP protocol suite*. McGraw-Hill, Inc.

Foster, I., Zhao, I. R., & Lu, S. (2008). Cloud computing and grid computing 360-degree compared.*Grid Computing Environments Workshop, 2008. GCE08* (p. 110). IEEE. doi:10.1109/GCE.2008.4738445

Freeh, V. W., Lowenthal, D. K., Pan, F., Kappiah, N., Springer, R., Rountree, B. L., & Femal, M. E. (2007). Analyzing the Energy-Time Trade-Off in High-Performance Computing Applications. *IEEE Transactions on Parallel and Distributed Systems*, *18*(6), 835–848. doi:10.1109/TPDS.2007.1026

Gagliordi, N. (2014, November 13). *ZDNET*. Retrieved March 07, 2016, from http://www.zdnet.com/article/forresters-2015-cloud-predictions-docker-rises-storage-pricing-war-claims-lives/

Gantz, J., & Reinsel, D. (2011, June). *Extracting Value from Chaos*. Retrieved 10 May, 2016, from https://www.emc.com/collateral/analyst-reports/idc-extracting-value-from-chaos-ar.pdf

Gao, Y., Guan, H., Qi, Z., Hou, Y., & Liu, L. (2013). A multi-objective ant colony system algorithm for virtual machine placement in cloud computing. J. Comput. *Syst. Sci.*, *79, 1230–42*. doi:10.1016/j.jcss.2013.02.004

Garg, S. K., Yeo, C. S., Anandasivam, A., & Buyya, R. (2009). *Energy-Efficient Scheduling of HPC Applications in Cloud Computing Environments*. Retrieved from http://arxiv.org/abs/0909.1146

Garg, Toosi, Gopalaiyengar, & Buyya. (2014). SLA-based virtual machine management for heterogeneous workloads in a cloud datacenter. *J. Netw. Comput. Appl.*, *45*, 108–20. doi:10.1016/j.jnca.2014.07.030

Gartner Inc. (2015, March 5). *Gartner Says By 2016, DevOps Will Evolve From a Niche to a Mainstream Strategy Employed by 25 Percent of Global 2000 Organizations*. Retrieved from www.gartner.com: http://www.gartner.com/newsroom/id/2999017

Gartner. (2014). *Gartner Identifies the Top 10 Technologies for Information Security in 2014*. Retrieved from http://www.gartner.com/newsroom/id/2778417

Gartner. (n.d.). *IT Glossary*. Retrieved from http://www.gartner.com/it-glossary/cloud-services-brokerage-csb

Geier, B. (2015, March 11). *Apple's App Store outage is costing millions*. Retrieved from http://fortune.com/2015/03/11/app-store-apple-outage/

Gentry, G. (2009). *A Fully Homomorphic Encryption Scheme* (PhD thesis). Stanford University. Retrieved from https://crypto.stanford.edu/craig/craig-thesis.pdf

Gentry, G., & Halevi, S. (2011). Implementing Gentry's fully homomorphic encryption scheme. EURO-CRYPT 2011, (LNCS). Springer. doi:10.1007/978-3-642-20465-4_9

Gentry, G. (2009). *Fully homomorphic encryption using ideal lattices*. ACM. doi:10.1145/1536414.1536440

Gentry, G. (2010). Computing arbitrary functions of encrypted data. *Communications of the ACM*, *53*(3), 97–105. doi:10.1145/1666420.1666444

Ghanti, S. R., & Naik, G. (2014). Protection of server from syn flood attack. *International Journal of Electronics and Communication Engineering & Technology*, *5*(11), 37–46.

Ghosh, R., & Naik, V. K. (2012). Biting Off Safely More Than You Can Chew: Predictive Analytics for Resource Over-Commit in IaaS Cloud. In *2012 IEEE Fifth Int. Conf. Cloud Comput.* IEEE. doi:10.1109/CLOUD.2012.131

Gibbens, R. J., & Kelly, F. P. (1999). Resource pricing and the evolution of congestion control. *Automatica*, *35*(12), 1969–1985. doi:10.1016/S0005-1098(99)00135-1

Gil, T. M., & Poletto, M. (2001). Multops: a data-structure for bandwidth attack detection. In *USENIX Security Symposium*.

Gmach, Rolia, Cherkasova, & Kemper. (2009). Resource pool management: Reactive versus proactive or let's be friends. *Comput. Networks, 53*(17), 2905–22. doi:10.1016/j.comnet.2009.08.011

Goel, S. (2015). Anonymity vs. security: The right balance for the smart grid. *Communications of the Association for Information Systems*, *36*(1).

Goldberg, R. P. (1974). Survey of Virtual Machine Research. *Computer*, *7*(9), 34–45. doi:10.1109/MC.1974.6323581

Gong, Z., & Gu, X. (2010). PAC: Pattern-driven application consolidation for efficient cloud computing. *Proc. - 18th Annu. IEEE/ACM Int. Symp. Model. Anal. Simul. Comput. Telecommun. Syst. MASCOTS 2010*. IEEE. doi:10.1109/MASCOTS.2010.12

Goranson, H. (1999). *The agile virtual enterprise: Cases, metrics, tools*. New York: Quorum Books.

Goudarzi, H., & Pedram, M. (2012). Energy-efficient virtual machine replication and placement in a cloud computing system. *Proc. - 2012 IEEE 5th Int. Conf. Cloud Comput. CLOUD 2012*. doi:10.1109/CLOUD.2012.107

Gravitant. (n.d.a). *cloudMatrix 'IT Approved' Marketplace*. Retrieved from http://resources.gravitant.com/videos/cloudmatrix-approved-marketplace/

Gravitant. (n.d.b). *cloudMatrix Solution Blueprints*. Retrieved from http://resources.gravitant.com/videos/cloudmatrix-solution-blueprints/

Graziano, C. D. (2011). *A performance analysis of Xen and KVM hypervisors for hosting the Xen Worlds Project*. Academic Press.

Greenberg, A., Hamilton, J., Maltz, D. A., & Patel, P. (2008). The cost of a cloud: Research problems in data center networks. *Computer Communication Review*, *39*(1), 68–73. doi:10.1145/1496091.1496103

Greenberg, S., Mills, E., Tschudi, B., Rumsey, P., & Myatt, B. (2006). Best practices for data centers: Lessons learned from benchmarking 22 data centers*Proceedings of the ACEEE Summer Study on Energy Efficiency in Buildings* (pp. 76-87).

Greenwood, D., Vitaglione, G., Keller, L., & Calisti, M. (2006). Service Level Agreement Management with Adaptive Coordination*Proceedings of the 2006 International conference on Networking and Services* (pp. 45-45). doi:10.1109/ICNS.2006.99

Grozev, N., & Buyya, R. (2014). Inter-Cloud architectures and application brokering: Taxonomy and survey. *Software, Practice & Experience*, *44*(3), 369–390. doi:10.1002/spe.2168

Guo, Y., Stolyar, A. L., & Walid, A. (2013). Shadow-Routing Based Dynamic Algorithms for Virtual Machine Placement in a Network Cloud. In *INFOCOM, 2013. 32nd IEEE Int. Conf. Comput. Commun.* doi:10.1109/INFCOM.2013.6566847

Gupta, C. P., & Sharma, I. (2013). *Fully Homomorphic Encryption Scheme with Symmetric Keys*. University College of Engineering, Rajasthan Technical University. Retrieved from http://arxiv.org/abs/1310.2452

Gupta, A., Kalé, L. V., Milojicic, D., Faraboschi, P., & Balle, S. M. (2013). HPC-aware VM placement in infrastructure clouds. In *Proc. IEEE Int. Conf. Cloud Eng. IC2E 2013*. IEEE. doi:10.1109/IC2E.2013.38

Hadoop. (2016). *Welcome to Apache™ Hadoop®!* Retrieved 10 May, 2016, from http://hadoop.apache.org/

Hahn, A., Ashok, A., Sridhar, S., & Govindarasu, M. (2013). Cyber-physical security testbeds: Architecture, application, and evaluation for smart grid. Smart Grid. *IEEE Transactions on*, *4*(2), 847–855.

Halder, K., Bellur, U., & Kulkarni, P. (2012). Risk Aware Provisioning and Resource Aggregation Based Consolidation of Virtual Machines. In *2012 IEEE Fifth Int. Conf. Cloud Comput.* IEEE. doi:10.1109/CLOUD.2012.86

Hamdaqa, M., & Tahvildari, L. (2014, November). The (5+ 1) architectural view model for cloud applications. In The IBM Centers for Advanced Studies Conference (pp. 46-60). IBM.

Hani, A. F. M., Paputungan, I. V., & Hassan, M. F. (2015). Renegotiation in Service Level Agreement Management for a Cloud-Based System. *ACM Computer Survey, 47*(3), 51:51-51:21.

Hardy, G. (2006). New roles for board members on IT. *Governance Journal*, *13*(151), 11–14.

Harreis, H., Lange, M., Machado, J., Rowshankish, K., & Schraa, D. (2015). *A marathon, not a sprint: Capturing value from BCBS 239 and beyond*. McKinsey & Company. Retrieved May 09, 2016 from http://www.mckinsey.com/~/media/mckinsey/business%20functions/risk/our%20insights/a%20marathon%20not%20a%20sprint%20capturing%20value%20from%20bcbs%20239%20and%20beyond/a_marathon_%20not_a_sprint_capturing_value_from_bcbs_239_and_beyond.ashx

Haskell, B. G., Puri, A., & Netravali, A. N. (1997). *Digital Video: An Introduction to MPEG-2*. Springer Science & Business Media.

HBR (Harvard Business Review). (2011). *Harvard Business Review on Aligning Technology with Strategy*. Boston: Harvard Business School Publishing.

He, Y., Ye, Z., Fu, Q., & Elnikety, S. (2012). *Budget-based control for interactive services with adaptive execution*. Paper presented at the 9th International Conference on Autonomic Computing. doi:10.1145/2371536.2371557

Hecht-Nielsen, R. (1992). *Theory of the Backpropagation Neural Network* (Vol. 2). Neural Networks for Perception.

Heiser, J. (2015, June 4). *Gartner Blogs*. Retrieved March 08, 2016, from http://blogs.gartner.com/jay-heiser/2015/06/04/saas-puppy/

Heller, B., Seetharaman, S., Mahadevan, P., Yiakoumis, Y., Sharma, P., Banerjee, S., & McKeown, N. (2010). ElasticTree: Saving Energy in Data Center Networks*Proceedings of the 7th USENIX Conference on Networked Systems Design and Implementation* (pp. 249-264).

Hermenier, F., Lorca, X., Menaud, J.-M., Muller, G., & Lawall, J. (2009). Entropy: a Consolidation Manager for Clusters.*Proc. 2009 ACM SIGPLAN/SIGOPS Int. Conf. Virtual Exec. Environ. - VEE '09*. doi:10.1145/1508293.1508300

Hestermann, C. (2014, July 8). *Define Your Customization Strategy for SaaS/ Cloud Business Applications*. Gartner. Report Number G00261452.

Hillson, D. (2008). Why risk includes opportunity. *The Risk Register Journal of PMI's Risk Management Special Interest Group, 10*(4), 1–3.

Hindman, B., Konwinski, A., Zaharia, M., Ghodsi, A., Joseph, A. D., Katz, R., & Stoica, I. et al. (2011). Mesos: A Platform for Fine-grained Resource Sharing in the Data Center*Proceedings of the 8th USENIX Conference on Networked Systems Design and Implementation* (pp. 295-308).

Hoda, R., Noble, J., & Marshall, S. (2009). Negotiating Contracts for Agile Projects: A Practical Perspective. In *Proceedings of 10th International Conference on Agile Processes in Software Engineering and Extreme Programming*. Heidelberg, Germany: Springer. doi:10.1007/978-3-642-01853-4_25

Hoelzle, U., & Barroso, L. A. (2009). *The Datacenter As a Computer: An Introduction to the Design of Warehouse-Scale Machines*. Morgan and Claypool Publishers.

Hosting. (2015). *Security Challenges Involved with Cloud Migration - HOSTING*. Retrieved September 23, 2015, from http://www.hosting.com/security-challenges-involved-with-cloud-migration/

Hu, J., Gu, J., Sun, G., & Zhao, T. (2010). A scheduling strategy on load balancing of virtual machine resources in cloud computing environment.*International Symposium on Parallel Architectures, Algorithms and Programming (PAAP)*.

Husson, T. (2015). *Five Myths about Mobile Apps*. Retrieved from http://blogs.forrester.com/thomas_husson/15-01-30-five_myths_about_mobile_apps

Hu, W., Hicks, A., Zhang, L., Dow, E. M., Soni, V., Jiang, H., & Matthews, J. N. et al. (2013). A quantitative study of virtual machine live migration*Proceedings of the 2013 ACM Cloud and Autonomic Computing Conference* (pp. 11). doi:10.1145/2494621.2494622

Iannucci, P., & Gupta, M. (2013). *IBM Smartcloud: Building a Cloud Enabled Data Centre*. Retrieved from: http://www.redbooks.ibm.com/redpapers/pdfs/redp4893.pdf

IBM Corporation. (2013). *IBM UrbanCode Deploy*. Retrieved from http://public.dhe.ibm.com/common/ssi/ecm/en/rad14132usen/RAD14132USEN.PDF

IBM. (2014). *IBM Mobile App Consumer Survey*, a commissioned study conducted by Forrester Consulting on behalf of IBM. Retrieved from http://www.ibm.com/mobilefirst/us/en/good-apps-bad-apps.html

IBM. (2014). *Simplifying cloud management and data center automation*. Retrieved from: https://www.viftech.com.pk/wp-content/uploads/2015/05/White-Paper-Simplifying-cloud-management-and-data-center-automation.pdf

IBM. (2015). *Implementing IBM Power Virtualisation Center in Your Data Center*. Retrieved September 2014 from, http://www.redbooks.ibm.com/technotes/tips1136.pdf

IBM. (2015, Jan 1). *IBM X-Force Threat Intelligence Quarterly, 1Q2015*. Retrieved Sep 30, 2015, from http://www-01. ibm.com/common/ssi/cgi-bin/ssialias?subtype=WH&infotype=SA&appname=SCTE_WG_WG_USEN&htmlfid=W GL03073USEN&attachment=WGL03073USEN.PDF#loaded

IBM. (2015a). *IBM Cloud AMM - migration service by IBM Cloud - Automated Modular Management | IBM*. Retrieved September 22, 2015, from https://marketplace.ibmcloud.com/apps/3933?restoreSearch=true#!overview

IBM. (2015b). *Managed Cloud: IBM Cloud Managed Services*. Retrieved September 22, 2015, from http://www.ibm. com/marketplace/cloud/managed-cloud/us/en-us

IBM. (2015c). *Softlayer: An IBM Company*. Retrieved September 22, 2015, from http://www.softlayer.com/info/ transparency?utm_source=google&utm_medium=cpc&utm_content=Brand_-_IBM_Softlayer&utm_campaign=PPC-AMS-Region-Brand&utm_term=ibmsoftlayer&matchtype=e

IBM. (n.d.a). *What is Cloud Computing?* Retrieved from http://www.ibm.com/cloud-computing/us/en/what-is-cloud-computing.html

IBM. (n.d.b). *IBM Designcamp*. Unpublished internal document. *IBM*.

IDC. (2014). *IDC Reveals Worldwide Mobile Enterprise Applications and Solutions Predictions for 2015*. Retrieved from http://www.idc.com/getdoc.jsp?containerId=prUS25350514

Intel. (2016). *Enhanced Intel SpeedStep Technology (EIST)*. Retrieved 31 March, 2016, from http://www.intel.com/cd/ channel/reseller/asmo-na/eng/203838.htmoverview

Internet of Things. (n.d.). Retrieved May 09, 2016 from https://en.wikipedia.org/wiki/Internet_of_Things

ISACA. (2013). COBIT5 for Risk. Rolling Meadows, IL: Information Systems Audit and Control Association (ISACA).

Isci, Hanson, Whalley, Steinder, & Kephart. (2010). Runtime Demand Estimation for effective dynamic resource management. In 2010 IEEE Netw. Oper. Manag. Symp. - NOMS 2010. doi:10.1109/NOMS.2010.5488495

IT Governance Institute. (2003). *Board Briefing on IT Governance* (2nd ed.). Rolling Meadows, IL: IT Governance Institute. Retrieved May 09, 2016 from http://www.isaca.org/restricted/Documents/26904_Board_Briefing_final.pdf

Jayaram, Peng, Zhang, Kim, Chen, & Lei. (2011). An empirical analysis of similarity in virtual machine images. In Proc. Middlew. 2011 Ind. Track Work. - Middlew. '11. New York: ACM Press. doi:10.1145/2090181.2090187

Jayasinghe, Pu, & Eilam. (2011). Improving performance and availability of services hosted on iaas clouds with structural constraint-aware virtual machine placement. *Serv. Comput.*, 72–79. doi:10.1109/SCC.2011.28

Jayaswal, K., Kallakurchi, K., Houde, D., & Shah, D. (2014). *Cloud Computing Black Book*. New Delhi, India: Dreamtech Press.

Jeff, B. (n.d.). *Amazon.com CEO Jeff Bezos on Animoto*. Retrieved 2015, from https://animoto.com/blog/news/company/ amazon-com-ceo-jeff-bezos-on-animoto/

Jeyarani, R., Nagaveni, & Vasanth Ram. (2012). Design and implementation of adaptive power-aware virtual machine provisioner (APA-VMP) using swarm intelligence. *Futur. Gener. Comput. Syst., 28*(5), 811–21. doi:10.1016/j. future.2011.06.002

Jiang, J. W., Lan, T., Ha, S., Chen, M., & Chiang, M. (2012). Joint VM placement and routing for data center traffic engineering. In Proc. - IEEE INFOCOM. IEEE. doi:10.1109/INFCOM.2012.6195719

Jian, L., Danjie, S., Sicong, C., & Xiaofeng, L. (2012). A Simple Fully Homomorphic Encryption Scheme Available in Cloud Computing.*Proceedings of IEEE CCIS2012*.

Jin, H., Xiang, G., & Zou, D. (2011). A VMM-based intrusion prevention system in cloud computing environment. *The Journal of Supercomputing*, 1–19.

Jinhui, Y., Chen, S., Nepal, S., Levy, D., & Zic, J. (2010). TrustStore: Making Amazon S3 Trustworthy with Services Composition. *10th IEEE/ACM International Conference On Cluster, Cloud and Grid Computing} (CCGrid'2010)* (pp. 600-605). IEEE/ACM International Conference.

JISC Legal Information. (2014). *User Guide: Cloud Computing Contracts, SLAs and Terms & Conditions of Use*. Retrieved February 5, 2016, from http://www.webarchive.org.uk/wayback/archive/20150703224546/http://www.jisclegal. ac.uk/ManageContent/ViewDetail/ID/2141/User-Guide-Cloud-Computing-Contracts-SLAs-and-Terms-Conditions-of-Use-31082011.aspx

Kabir, M. H., Shoja, G. C., & Ganti, S. (2014). VM Placement Algorithms for Hierarchical Cloud Infrastructure*Proceedings of the 6th IEEE International Conference on Cloud Computing Technology and Science (CloudCom 2014)* (pp. 656-659). doi:10.1109/CloudCom.2014.53

Kansal, A., Zhao, F., Liu, J., Kothari, N., & Bhattacharya, A. A. (2010). Virtual Machine Power Metering and Provisioning*Proceedings of the 1st ACM Symposium on Cloud Computing (SoCC 2010)* (pp. 39-50). doi:10.1145/1807128.1807136

Kaplan, J. M., Forrest, W., & Kindler, N. (2008). *Revolutionizing data center energy efficiency*. Academic Press.

Kaplan, R., & Mikes, A. (2012). Managing Risks: A new framework. *Harvard Business Review*, *90*(6), 48–63.

Karimazad, R., & Faraahi, A. (2011). An anomaly based method for DDoS attacks detection using rbf neural networks. In *Proceedings of the International Conference on Network and Electronics Engineering*.

Kark, K., & Vanderslice, P. (2015). CIO as Chief Integration Officer. Deloitte Journal of Tech Trends, 6(1), 4-19.

Katsaros, Subirats, Fitó, Guitart, Gilet, & Espling. (2013). A service framework for energy-aware monitoring and VM management in Clouds. *Futur. Gener. Comput. Syst., 29*(8), 2077–91. doi:10.1016/j.future.2012.12.006

Kaufman, L., & Rousseeuw, P. J. (2009). *Finding groups in data: an introduction to cluster analysis* (Vol. 344). John Wiley & Sons.

Kaushik, R. T., Bhandarkar, M., & Nahrstedt, K. (2010). Evaluation and Analysis of GreenHDFS: A Self-Adaptive, Energy-Conserving Variant of the Hadoop Distributed File System*Proceedings of the 2010 IEEE Second International Conference on Cloud Computing Technology and Science* (pp. 274-287). doi:10.1109/CloudCom.2010.109

Kelly, S. M. (2015, May 21). *Apple restores iCloud after outage impacts 200 million people*. Retrieved from http://mashable.com/2015/05/21/apple-icloud-down-some-users/

Kertesz, A. (2014). Characterizing Cloud Federation Approaches. In *Cloud Computing* (pp. 277–296). Springer International Publishing.

Khan, M., Hussain, S., & Imran, M. (2013). Performance Evaluation of Symmetric Cryptography Algorithms: A Survey. *ITEE Journal of Information Technology & Electrical Engineering, 2*(2).

Khan, A., Yan, X., Tao, S., & Anerousis, N. (2012). Workload characterization and prediction in the cloud: A multiple time series approach*Proceedings of the 2012 IEEE Network Operations and Management Symposium (NOMS 2012)* (pp. 1287-1294). doi:10.1109/NOMS.2012.6212065

Khiyaita, A., Zbakh, M., Bakkali, H., & Kettani, D. (2012). Load balancing cloud computing: state of art. In *Network Security and Systems (JNS2), National Days of*. IEEE. doi:10.1109/JNS2.2012.6249253

Khorshed, M., Ali, A. B. M. S., & Wasimi, S. A. (2012). A survey on gaps, threat remediation challenges and some thoughts for proactive attack detection in cloud computing. *Future Generation Computer Systems, 6*(28), 833–851. doi:10.1016/j.future.2012.01.006

Khosravi, A., Garg, S. K., & Buyya, R. (2013). Energy and carbon-efficient placement of virtual machines in distributed cloud data centers*Proceedings of the 19th International European Conference on Parallel and Distributed Computing (Euro-Par 2013)* (pp. 317-328). doi:10.1007/978-3-642-40047-6_33

Kim, Beloglazov, & Buyya. (2011). Power-aware provisioning of virtual machines for real-time Cloud services. *Concurr. Comput. Pract. Exp., 23*(13), 1491–1505. doi:10.1002/cpe.1712

Kim, J., Elnikety, S., He, Y., Hwang, S.-w., & Ren, S. (2013). *QACO: exploiting partial execution in web servers*. Paper presented at the 2013 ACM Cloud and Autonomic Computing Conference (CAC 2013). doi:10.1145/2494621.2494636

Kim, J., Lee, M., S., Yun, A., & Cheon, J., H. (2012). *CRT-based fully homomorphic encryption over the integers*. Cryptology ePrint Archive Report 2013/057.

Kim, J., Ruggiero, M., Atienza, D., & Lederberger, M. (2013). Correlation-aware Virtual Machine Allocation for Energy-efficient Datacenters*Proceedings of the Conference on Design, Automation and Test in Europe* (pp. 1345-1350). doi:10.7873/DATE.2013.277

Kim, K. H., Buyya, R., & Kim, J. (2007). Power Aware Scheduling of Bag-of-Tasks Applications with Deadline Constraints on DVS-enabled Clusters*Proceedings of the 2007 IEEE Seventh International Symposium on Cluster Computing and the Grid (CCGrid 2007)* (pp. 541-548). doi:10.1109/CCGRID.2007.85

Kim, S., & Narasimha Reddy, A. L. (2008). Statistical techniques for detecting traffic anomalies through packet header data. *IEEE/ACM Transactions on Networking, 16*(3), 562–575. doi:10.1109/TNET.2007.902685

Kim, W. (2013). Cloud computing architecture. *International Journal of Web and Grid Services, 9*(3), 287–303. doi:10.1504/IJWGS.2013.055724

Kim, W., Jeong, O.-R., Kim, C., & So, J. (2011). The dark side of the Internet: Attacks, costs and responses. *Information Systems, 36*(3), 675–705. doi:10.1016/j.is.2010.11.003

Kipnis, A., & Hibshoosh, E. (2012). *Efficient Methods for Practical Fully-Homomorphic Symmetric-key Encryption, Randomization, and Verification*. Cryptology ePrint Archive, Report 2012/637.

Klein, C., & Maggio, M.-A. (2014). Brownout: building more robust cloud applications*Proceedings of the 36th International Conference on Software Engineering* (pp. 700-711).

Kleineweber, C., Keller, A., Niehorster, O., & Brinkmann, A. (2011). Rule-Based Mapping of Virtual Machines in Clouds. In *Parallel, Distrib. Network-Based Process. (PDP), 2011 19th Euromicro Int. Conf.* IEEE. doi:10.1109/PDP.2011.69

Komviriyavut, T., Sangkatsanee, P., Wattanapongsakorn, N., & Charnsripinyo, C. (2009). Network intrusion detection and classification with decision tree and rule based approaches.*International Symposium on Communications and Information Technology (ISCIT)*, (pp. 1046-1050). doi:10.1109/ISCIT.2009.5341005

Kousiouris, Cucinotta, & Varvarigou. (2011). The effects of scheduling, workload type and consolidation scenarios on virtual machine performance and their prediction through optimized artificial neural networks. *J. Syst. Softw., 84*(8), 1270–91. doi:10.1016/j.jss.2011.04.013

Krioukov, A., Mohan, P., Alspaugh, S., Keys, L., Culler, D., & Katz, R. H. (2010). NapSAC: Design and Implementation of a Power-proportional Web Cluster*Proceedings of the First ACM SIGCOMM Workshop on Green Networking (Green Networking 2010)* (pp. 15-22). New York: ACM. doi:10.1145/1851290.1851294

KVM. (n.d.). *Linux Kernel (Based Virtual Machine)*. Retrieved March 2012, from http://www.linux-kvm.org/

Lamersdorf, A., Munch, J., Viso, A. F., Sanchez, C. R., Heinz, M., & Rombach, D. (2010). A Rule-Based Model for Customized Risk Identification in Distributed Software Development Projects.*Proceedings of the 5th IEEE International Conference on Global Software Engineering (ICGSE)*, (vol. 1, pp. 209–218). Los Alamitos, CA: IEEE Computer Society. doi:10.1109/ICGSE.2010.32

Landau, S. (n.d.). *Standing the Test of Time: The Data Encryption Standard*. Academic Press.

Lang, W., & Patel, J. M. (2010). Energy Management for MapReduce Clusters. *Proceedings of the Very Large Data Bases Endowment Journal, 3*, 129-139. doi:10.14778/1920841.1920862

Lee, Y. C., Han, H., Zomaya, A. Y., & Yousif, M. (2015). Resource-efficient Workflow Scheduling in Clouds. *Knowledge-Based Systems, 80*, 153–162. doi:10.1016/j.knosys.2015.02.012

Leigh, D. (2015, October 5). *Contributions and Peer Review*. IBM Senior Technical Staff Member, IBM Transformation and Operations Division.

Le, K., Bianchini, R., Zhang, J., Jaluria, Y., Meng, J., & Nguyen, T. D. (2011). Reducing electricity cost through virtual machine placement in high performance computing clouds.*2011 Int. Conf. High Perform. Comput. Networking, Storage Anal.* doi:10.1145/2063384.2063413

Leverich, J., & Kozyrakis, C. (2010). On the Energy (in)Efficiency of Hadoop Clusters. *SIGOPS Operating Systems Review, 44*(1), 61–65. doi:10.1145/1740390.1740405

Li, K.-B. (2003). *ClustalW-MPI: ClustalW analysis using distributed and parallel computing*. Academic Press.

Li, W., Tordsson, J., & Elmroth, E. (2011). Modeling for dynamic cloud scheduling via migration of virtual machines. In *Proc. - 2011 3rd IEEE Int. Conf. Cloud Comput. Technol. Sci. CloudCom 2011*. doi:10.1109/CloudCom.2011.31

Li, M., & Li, M. (2010). An Adaptive Approach for Defending against DDoS Attacks. *Mathematical Problems in Engineering*, 1–15.

Limwiwatkul, L., & Rungsawang, A. (2006). Distributed denial of service detection using TCP/IP header and traffic measurement analysis.*Proceedings of the IEEE International Symposium Communications and Information Technology*, (pp. 605–610).

List of Largest Companies by Revenue. (n.d.). In *Wikipedia*. Retrieved from https://en.wikipedia.org/wiki/List_of_largest_companies_by_revenue

Liu, F., Tong, J., Mao, J., Bonn, R., Messina, J., Badger, L., & Leaf, D. (2011). *NIST Cloud Computing Reference Architecture*. Retrieved August 2015 from http://www.nist.gov/customcf/get_pdf.cfm?pub_id=909505

Liu, L., Wang, H., Liu, X., Jin, X., He, W. B., Wang, Q. B., & Chen, Y. (2009). GreenCloud: A New Architecture for Green Data Center. In *Proc. 6th Int. Conf. Ind. Sess. Auton. Comput. Commun. Ind. Sess.* doi:10.1145/1555312.1555319

Lloyd, Pallickara, David, Lyon, Arabi, & Rojas. (2013). Performance implications of multi-tier application deployments on Infrastructure-as-a-Service clouds: Towards performance modeling. *Futur. Gener. Comput. Syst., 29*(5), 1254–64. doi:10.1016/j.future.2012.12.007

Lo, C. C., Huang, C. C., & Ku, J. (2010). A Cooperative Intrusion Detection System Framework for Cloud Computing Networks. In *39th International Conference on Parallel Processing Workshops*, (pp. 280-284). doi:10.1109/ICPPW.2010.46

Lonea, A. M., & Popescu, D. E. (2013). TianfieldDetecting DDoS Attacks in Cloud Computing Environment. Int J Comput Commun, (1), 70-78.

Lucas-Simarro, Moreno-Vozmediano, Montero, & Llorente. (2013). Scheduling strategies for optimal service deployment across multiple clouds. *Futur. Gener. Comput. Syst., 29*(6), 1431–41. doi:10.1016/j.future.2012.01.007

Lu, K., Roblitz, T., Yahyapour, R., Yaqub, E., & Kotsokalis, C. (2011). QoS-aware SLA-based Advanced Reservation of Infrastructure as a Service. In *2011 IEEE Third Int. Conf. Cloud Comput. Technol. Sci.* IEEE. doi:10.1109/CloudCom.2011.46

Lu, K., Wu, D., Fan, J., Todorovic, S., & Nucci, A. (2007). Robust and efficient detection of DDoS attacks for large-scale internet. *Computer Networks, 51*(18), 5036–5056. doi:10.1016/j.comnet.2007.08.008

Luke, M. (2015, October 5). *Contributions and Peer Review.* IBM Senior Technical Staff Member, Cloud Data Services DevOps Practice Lead in IBM Analytics.

Lunawat, S., & Patankar, A. (2014, February). Efficient architecture for secure outsourcing of data and computation in hybrid cloud. In *Optimization, Reliability, and Information Technology (ICROIT), 2014 International Conference on* (pp. 380-383). IEEE. doi:10.1109/ICROIT.2014.6798358

Luo, Z., & Qian, Z. (2013). Burstiness-aware server consolidation via queuing theory approach in a computing cloud. *Proc. - IEEE 27th Int.Parallel Distrib. Process. Symp. IPDPS 2013.* doi:10.1109/IPDPS.2013.62

Machida, F., Kawato, M., & Maeno, Y. (2010). Redundant virtual machine placement for fault-tolerant consolidated server clusters. In 2010 IEEE Netw. Oper. Manag. Symp. - NOMS 2010. IEEE. doi:10.1109/NOMS.2010.5488431

Mahajan, R., Bellovin, S. M., Floyd, S., Ioannidis, J., Paxson, V., & Shenker, S. (2002). Controlling high bandwidth aggregates in the network. *Computer Communication Review, 32*(3), 62–73. doi:10.1145/571697.571724

Maja, V., & Jinho, H. (2016, April). Cloud migration using automated planning. *NOMS 2016 - 2016 IEEE/IFIP Network Operations and Management Symposium* (pp. 96-103).

Malawski, M., Juve, G., Deelman, E., & Nabrzyski, J. (2012). Cost- and deadline-constrained provisioning for scientific workflow ensembles in IaaS clouds. In *2012 Int. Conf. High Perform. Comput. Networking, Storage Anal..* IEEE. doi:10.1109/SC.2012.38

Mann, V., Kumar, A., Dutta, P., & Kalyanaraman, S. (2011). VMFlow: Leveraging VM mobility to reduce network power costs in data centers.Lect. Notes Comput. Sci., 6640, 198–211. doi:10.1007/978-3-642-20757-0_16

Marcus, A. (Ed.). (2014). *Design, User Experience, and Usability. User Experience Design for Diverse Interaction Platforms and Environments.* Heidelberg, Germany: Springer. doi:10.1007/978-3-319-07668-3

Marinos, A., & Briscoe, G. (2009). Community cloud computing. *Cloud Computing*, 472-484.

Markets and Markets. (2014). *Bring Your Own Device (BYOD) & Enterprise Mobility Market Global Advancements, Market Forecast and Analysis (2014 – 2019).* Retrieved from http://www.marketsandmarkets.com/PressReleases/byod.asp

Markets and Markets. (2015, Jun 22). *Cloud Service Brokerage Market - Global Analysis & Forecast to 2020.* Author.

Marks, N. (2015). *The myth of IT risk.* Retrieved September 09, 2015, from https://normanmarks.wordpress.com/2015/08/28/the-myth-of-it-risk

Marshall, P., Keahey, K., & Freeman, T. (2011). Improving utilization of infrastructure clouds. In *Proc. - 11th IEEE/ACM Int. Symp. Clust. Cloud Grid Comput. CCGrid 2011*. IEEE. doi:10.1109/CCGrid.2011.56

Meiko, J., Jorg, S., & Nil, G. (2009). On technical issues in cloud computing.*IEEE International Conference on Cloud Computing*. IEEE.

Meisner, D., Gold, B. T., & Wenisch, T. F. (2009). PowerNap: Eliminating Server Idle Power. *SIGARCH Computer Architecture News*, *37*(1), 205–216. doi:10.1145/2528521.1508269

Mell, P., & Grace, T. (2011). The NIST Definition of Cloud Computing, NIST Special Publication, 800-145, 2011. Gaithersburg, MD: National Institute of Standards and Technology (NIST).

Mell, P., & Grance, T. (2011). The NIST Definition of cloud computing. National Institute of Standards and Technology Special Publication, 800-145. doi:10.6028/NIST.SP.800-145

Mell, P., & Grance, T. (2011). *The NIST definition of cloud computing*. Retrieved from: http://csrc.nist.gov/publications/nistpubs/800-145/SP800-145.pdf

Mell, P., & Grance, T. (2009). *Effectively and Securely Using the Cloud Computing Paradigm*. US National Institute of Standards and Technology.

Mell, P., & Grance, T. (2011). *The NIST Definition of Cloud Computingy*. National Institute of Standards and Technology.

Meng, X., Pappas, V., & Zhang, L. (2010). Improving the scalability of data center networks with traffic-aware virtual machine placement. In Proc. - IEEE INFOCOM. IEEE. doi:10.1109/INFCOM.2010.5461930

Meng, X., Isci, C., Kephart, J., Zhang, L., Bouillet, E., & Pendarakis, D. (2010). Efficient Resource Provisioning in Compute Clouds via VM Multiplexing*Proceedings of the 7th International Conference on Autonomic Computing* (pp. 11-20). doi:10.1145/1809049.1809052

Menken, I., & Blokdijk, G. (2008). *Virtualization: The complete cornerstone guide to virtualization best practices*. Brisbane, Australia: Emereo Pty Ltd.

Merkel, D. (2014). Docker: Lightweight Linux Containers for Consistent Development and Deployment. *Linux Journal*, *2014*(239).

Metheny, M. (2013). *Federal Cloud Computing: The Definitive Guide for Cloud Service Providers*. Waltham, MA: Elsevier.

Meulen, R. V. (2015, November 10). *Gartner Says 6.4 Billion Connected*. Retrieved May 05, 2016 from http://www.gartner.com/newsroom/id/3165317

Mihailescu, M., & Teo, Y. M. (2010). Dynamic resource pricing on federated clouds. In Cluster, Cloud and Grid Computing (CCGrid), IEEE/ACM International Conference, (pp. 513–517).

Mihailescu, M., Rodriguez, A., & Amza, C. (2011). Enhancing application robustness in Infrastructure-as-a-Service clouds. In *2011 IEEE/IFIP 41st Int. Conf. Dependable Syst. Networks Work*. IEEE. doi:10.1109/DSNW.2011.5958801

Minarolli, D., & Freisleben, B. (2011). Utility-based resource allocation for virtual machines in cloud computing. In *Proc. - IEEE Symp. Comput. Commun*. IEEE. doi:10.1109/ISCC.2011.5983872

Mindtools. (2015). *Stakeholder Management - Project Management Tools from MindTools.com*. Retrieved September 22, 2015, from https://www.mindtools.com/pages/article/newPPM_08.htm

Mirkovic, J., Prier, G., & Reiher, P. (2002). Attacking ddos at the source.*IEEE International Conference*, (pp. 312–321). IEEE.

Mirkovic, J., & Reiher, P. (2004). A taxonomy of ddos attack and ddos defense mechanisms. *Computer Communication Review, 34*(2), 39–53. doi:10.1145/997150.997156

Mishra, A. K., Hellerstein, J. L., Cirne, W., & Das, C. R. (2010). Towards characterizing cloud backend workloads: Insights from Google compute clusters. *Performance Evaluation Review, 37*(4), 34–41. doi:10.1145/1773394.1773400

Mitrokotsa, A., & Douligeris, C. (2007). Denial-of-service attacks. Network Security: Current Status and Future Directions, 117–134.

Modi, C., Patel, D., Borisaniya, B., Patel, H., Patel, A., Rajarajan, M., & Gujarat, N. S. (2013). A survey of intrusion detection techniques in Cloud. *Journal of Network and Computer Applications, 36*(1), 42–57. doi:10.1016/j.jnca.2012.05.003

Mohan Raj, V. K., & Shriram, R. (2011). Power aware provisioning in cloud computing environment*Proceedings of the 2011 International Conference on Computer, Communication and Electrical Technology (ICCCET)* (pp. 6-11). doi:10.1109/ICCCET.2011.5762447

Moore, G. (2011). *Systems of Engagement and the Future of Enterprise IT: A Sea Change in Enterprise IT*. Retrieved 2011, from http://www.aiim.org/

Moore, G. (2011). *Systems of Engagement and the Future of Enterprise IT: A Sea Change in Enterprise IT*. Retrieved from http://www.aiim.org

Moreno, I. S., Yang, R., Xu, J., & Wo, T. (2013). Improved energy-efficiency in cloud datacenters with interference-aware virtual machine placement. *Autonomous Decentralized Systems (ISADS), 2013 IEEE Eleventh International Symposium on* (pp. 1-8). IEEE.

Moreno, I. S., Garraghan, P., Townend, P., & Xu, J. (2013). An approach for characterizing workloads in Google cloud to derive realistic resource utilization models*Proceedings of the 7th IEEE International Symposium on Service Oriented System Engineering (SOSE 2013)* (pp. 49-60). doi:10.1109/SOSE.2013.24

Muda, Z., Yassin, W., Sulaiman, M.N., & Udzir, N.I. (2011). Intrusion detection based on K-Means clustering and Naïve Bayes classification. Emerging Convergences and Singularity of Forms, 1-6.

Nafi, K. W., Shekha, K. T., Hoque, S. A., & Hashem, M. M. A. (2012). A Newer User Authentication, File encryption and Distributed Server Based Cloud Computing security architecture. *International Journal of Advanced Computer Science and Applications, 3*.

Nagy, G. (2015, May). *Operating System Containers vs. Application Containers*. Academic Press.

Nathani, Chaudhary, & Somani. (2012). Policy based resource allocation in IaaS cloud. *Futur. Gener. Comput. Syst., 28*(1), 94–103. doi:10.1016/j.future.2011.05.016

Nathuji, R., Kansal, A., & Ghaffarkhah, A. (2010). Q-clouds: managing performance interference effects for qos-aware clouds*Proceedings of the 5th European conference on Computer systems* (pp. 237-250). doi:10.1145/1755913.1755938

Nathuji, R., & Schwan, K. (2007). VirtualPower: Coordinated Power Management in Virtualized Enterprise Systems*Proceedings of 21st ACM SIGOPS Symposium on Operating Systems Principles (SOSP 2007)* (pp. 265-278). doi:10.1145/1294261.1294287

National Institute of Science and Technology. (2015). *NIST 800-53 Controls*. Washington, DC: NIST.

National Institute of Standards and Technology. (2011). *Definition of Cloud Computing*. Retrieved from: http://nvlpubs.nist.gov/nistpubs/Legacy/SP/nistspecialpublication800-145.pdf

National Security Agency. (2015). *Defense in Depth, A practical strategy for achieving Information Assurance in today's highly networked environments*. Ft. Meade, MD: National Security Agency, Information Assurance Solutions Group – STE 6737. Retrieved May 09, 2016 from http://www.iad.gov/iad/library/reports/defense-in-depth.cfm

Net-centric. (n.d.). Retrieved May 09, 2016 from https://en.wikipedia.org/wiki/Net-centric

Net-Security. (2014, Feb 27). *Third-party programs responsible for 76% of vulnerabilities in popular software*. Retrieved Oct 1, 2015, from Help Net Security: www.net-security.org

Ng, F., Anderson, E., & Anderson, D. S. (2015, Jan 13). *Cloud Service Providers Must Understand Deployment, Adoption and Buyer Complexity to Leverage Cloud Revenue Opportunities*. Gartner. Report number G00271022.

Ni, J., Huang, Y., Luan, Z., Zhang, J., & Qian, D. (2011). Virtual machine mapping policy based on load balancing in private cloud environment. In *2011 Int. Conf. Cloud Serv. Comput*. IEEE. doi:10.1109/CSC.2011.6138536

NIST (National Institute of Standards and Technology). (2015). *Cloud computing service metrics description*. Retrieved September 09, 2015, from http://www.nist.gov/itl/cloud/upload/RATAX-CloudServiceMetricsDescription-DRAFT-20141111.pdf

Normal, D. (n.d.). *Rethinking Design Thinking*. Retrieved from http://www.jnd.org/dn.mss/rethinking_design_th.html

Oktay, U., & Sahingoz, O. K. (2013). Attack types and intrusion detection systems in cloud computing. 6th international information security & cryptology conference, (pp. 71-76).

Olson, D. & Peters, S. (2011). Managing Software Intellectual Assets in Cloud Computing, Part 1. *Journal of Licensing Executives Society International, H*(3), 160-165.

Online Retailers Expect to Increase Revenue. (2015). Retrieved from http://www.ebayenterprise.com/press-room/press-releases/online-retailers-expect-increase-revenue-17-percent-2015

Open, V. Z. (2016). *OpenVZ Virtuozzo Containers Wiki*. Retrieved 31 March, 2016, from https://openvz.org/Main_Page

OpenShift. (2016). *OpenShift QuickStart · GitHub*. Retrieved from https://github.com/openshift-quickstart

OpenStack Foundation. (2014a). *OpenStack Configuration Reference, icehouse*. Retrieved December 2014, from http://docs.openstack.org/icehouse/config-reference/config-reference-icehouse.pdf

OpenStack Foundation. (2014b). *OpenStack Operations Guide*. Retrieved from: http://docs.openstack.org/ops/

OpenStack Foundation. (2014c). *OpenStack Installation Guide for Ubuntu 12.04/14.04 (LTS), icehouse*. Retrieved September 2014 from, http://docs.openstack.org/icehouse/install-guide/install/apt/openstack-install-guide-apt-icehouse.pdf

Orozco, T. (2014a, June 12). *Scaling Metrics*. Scalr. Retrieved from https://scalr-wiki.atlassian.net/wiki/display/docs/Scaling+Metrics

Orozco, T. (2014b, November 6). *Roles and Images*. Scalr. Retrieved from https://scalr-wiki.atlassian.net/wiki/display/docs/Roles+and+Images

Palanisamy, B., Singh, A., Liu, L., & Jain, B. (2011). Purlieus. In *Proc. 2011 Int. Conf. High Perform. Comput. Networking, Storage Anal. - SC '11*. New York: ACM Press. doi:10.1145/2063384.2063462

Pandit, D., Chattopadhyay, S., Chattopadhyay, M., & Chaki, N. (2014). Resource allocation in cloud using simulated annealing.*Proceedings of the 2014 Conference on Applications and Innovations in Mobile Computing (AIMoC 2014)* (pp. 21-27). doi:10.1109/AIMOC.2014.6785514

Parag, K., Shelke, S. S., & Gawande, A. D. (2012). Intrusion Detection System for Cloud Computing. *International Journal of Scientific & Technology Research, 1*(4), 67–71.

Park, K., & Lee, H. (2001). On the effectiveness of route-based packet filtering for distributed dos attack prevention in power-law internets. *Computer Communication Review, 31*(4), 15–26. doi:10.1145/964723.383061

Parmar, R., McKenzie, I., Cohn, D., & Gann, D. (2014, January-February). The New Patterns of Innovation. *Harvard Business Review.*

Peng, T., Leckie, C., & Ramamohanarao, K. (2007). Survey of network-based defense mechanisms countering the dos and ddos problems. *ACM Computing Surveys, 39*(1), 1–42. doi:10.1145/1216370.1216373

Petitet, A., Whaley, R. C., Dongarra, J., & Cleary, A. (2008). *Benchmark.* Retrieved 2016, from HPL: http://www.netlib.org/benchmark/hpl/

Pettypiece, S. (2015). *Amazon Passes Wal-Mart as Biggest Retailer by Market Value.* Retrieved July 2015, from http://www.bloomberg.com/news/articles/2015-07-23/amazon-surpasses-wal-mart-as-biggest-retailer-by-market-value

Piao, J. T., & Yan, J. (2010). A Network-aware Virtual Machine Placement and Migration Approach in Cloud Computing. *2010 Ninth Int. Conf. Grid Cloud Comput.* IEEE. doi:10.1109/GCC.2010.29

Pierantonelli, M., Perna, A., & Gregori, G. L. (2015). Interaction between Firms in New Product Development. *International Conference on Marketing and Business Development Journal, 1*(1), 144-152.

Pietri, I., & Sakellariou, R. (2014). Energy-Aware Workflow Scheduling Using Frequency Scaling. *Proceedings of the 43rd International Conference on Parallel Processing Workshops (ICCPW 2014)* (pp. 104-113). doi:10.1109/ICPPW.2014.26

Piraghaj, S. F., Dastjerdi, A. V., Calheiros, R. N., Buyya, R., Piraghaj, S. F., Dastjerdi, A. V., . . . Buyya, R. (2015). Efficient Virtual Machine Sizing for Hosting Containers as a Service (SERVICES 2015). *Proceedings of the 2015 IEEE World Congress on Services* (pp. 31-38).

Piraghaj, S. F., Calheiros, R. N., Chan, J., Dastjerdi, A. V., & Buyya, R. (2016). Virtual Machine Customization and Task Mapping Architecture for Efficient Allocation of Cloud Data Center Resources. *The Computer Journal, 59*(2), 208–224. doi:10.1093/comjnl/bxv106

Piraghaj, S. F., Dastjerdi, A. V., Calheiros, R. N., & Buyya, R. (2015). A Framework and Algorithm for Energy Efficient Container Consolidation in Cloud Data Centers. *2015 IEEE International Conference on Data Science and Data Intensive Systems* (pp. 368-375). doi:10.1109/DSDIS.2015.67

PlanetLab. (2016). *An open platform for developing, deploying, and accessing planetary-scale services.* Retrieved 31 March, 2016, from https://www.planet-lab.org/

Ponemon Institute. (2015). *The State of Mobile Application Insecurity.* Retrieved from http://www.workplaceprivacyreport.com/wp-content/uploads/sites/162/2015/03/WGL03074USEN.pdf

Poppendieck, M., & Poppendieck, T. (2013). *The Lean Mindset: Ask the Right Questions.* Westford, MA: Addison-Wesley.

Pourya, S. (2014). C2DF: High Rate DDOS filtering method in Cloud Computing. *Computer Network and Information Security, 6*(9), 43–50. doi:10.5815/ijcnis.2014.09.06

Price, D., & Tucker, A. (2004). Solaris Zones: Operating System Support for Consolidating Commercial Workloads. *Proceedings of the 18th USENIX Conference on System Administration (LISA 2004)* (pp. 241-254).

Raden, N. (2005). Shadow IT: A Lesson for BI. *BI Review Magazine.*

Raj Kumar, P. A., & Selvakumar, S. (2011). Distributed denial of service attack detection using an ensemble of neural classifier. *Computer Communications*, *34*(11), 1328–1341. doi:10.1016/j.comcom.2011.01.012

Raj Kumar, P. A., & Selvakumar, S. (2012). M2KMIX: Identifying the Type of High Rate Flooding Attacks using a Mixture of Expert Systems. *Computer Network and Information Security*, *1*, 1–16.

Raj Kumar, P. A., & Selvakumar, S. (2013). Detection of distributed denial of service attacks using an ensemble of adaptive and hybrid neuro-fuzzy systems. *Computer Communications*, *36*(3), 303–319. doi:10.1016/j.comcom.2012.09.010

Randles, M., Lamb, D., & Taleb-Bendiab, A. (2010). A comparative study into distributed load balancing algorithms for cloud computing. In Advanced Information Networking and Applications Workshops (WAINA), IEEE International Conference on. doi:10.1109/WAINA.2010.85

Rao, T. V. N., Naveena, K., & David, R. (2015). A New Computing Environment Using Hybrid Cloud. *Journal of Information Sciences and Computing Technologies*, *3*(1), 180–185.

Reese, G. (2009). *Cloud Application Architectures*. Reilly Media, Inc.

Reiss, C., Wilkes, J., & Hellerstein, J. L. (2011). *Google cluster-usage traces: format+ schema*. Academic Press.

Reyhaneh, K., & Ahmad, F. (2011). An Anomaly-Based Method for DDoS Attacks Detection using RBF Neural Networks.*International Conference on Network and Electronics Engineering IPCST*.

RightScale. (n.d.a). *API & Integrations*. Retrieved from http://www.rightscale.com/products-and-services/multi-cloud-platform/on-demand-architecture/cloud-api-and-integration

RightScale. (n.d.b). *Technical Overview*. RightScale. Retrieved from http://assets.rightscale.com/uploads/pdfs/RightScale-Technical-overview.pdf

RightScale. (n.d.c). Retrieved from http://support.rightscale.com/03-Tutorials/02-AWS/02-Website_Edition/How_do_I_set_up_Autoscaling%3F/index.html

Rimal, B. P., Choi, E., & Lumb, I. (2009). A taxonomy and survey of cloud computing systems.*Fifth International Joint Conference on INC, IMS and IDC* (pp. 44-51). IEEE. doi:10.1109/NCM.2009.218

Roadef. (2016). *Challenge ROADEF/EURO 2012: Machine Reassignment*. Retrieved 10 May, 2016, from http://challenge.roadef.org/2012/en/index.php

Rocket. (2016). *Welcome to Rocket Diagram's documentation! — Rocket Diagram 0.1.0 documentation*. Retrieved 10 May, 2016, from https://rocketdiagram.readthedocs.io/en/latest/

Rolia, J., Andrzejak, A., & Arlitt, M. (2003). *Automating Enterprise Application Placement in Resource Utilities*. Self-Managing Distributed Systems. doi:10.1007/978-3-540-39671-0_11

Roschke, S., Cheng, F., & Meinel, C. (2009). Intrusion Detection in the Cloud. In *Eighth IEEE International Conference on Dependable, Autonomic and Secure Computing*, (pp. 729-734).

Rosen, R. (2013, May). Resource management: Linux kernel Namespaces and cgroups. *Haifux*.

Rousseeuw, P. J. (1987). Silhouettes: A graphical aid to the interpretation and validation of cluster analysis. *Journal of Computational and Applied Mathematics*, *20*, 53–65. doi:10.1016/0377-0427(87)90125-7

Salesforce. (n.d.). Retrieved 2016, from https://www.salesforce.com/

Savage, S., Wetherall, D., Karlin, A., & Anderson, T. (2001). Network support for IP traceback. IEEE/ACM Transaction on Networking, 9(3), 226-237.

Schlarman, S. (2009). IT risk exploration: The IT risk management taxonomy and evolution. *Information Systems Audit and Control Association Journal, 2009*(3), 27-30.

Scuitto, J. (2015, July 10). *OPM government data breach impacted 21.5 million.* Retrieved from http://www.cnn. com/2015/07/09/politics/office-of-personnel-management-data-breach-20-million/

Searchcloudcomputing. (n.d.). *Hybrid cloud computing explained.* Retrieved 2012 йил Feb from http://searchcloudcomputing.techtarget.com/tutorial/Hybrid-cloud-computing-explained

Segal, S. (2011). *Corporate Value of Enterprise Risk Management: The Next Step in Business Management.* Hoboken, NJ: John Wiley & Sons.

Senate and House of Representatives of the United States of America. (1990). *Germany's Federal Data Protection Act - known as Bundesdatenschutzgesetz or BDSG.* Retrieved from: http://www.gesetze-im-internet.de/bdsg_1990/index. html#BJNR029550990BJNE001503310

Serrano, N., Gallardo, G., & Hernantes, J. (2015). Infrastructure as a Service and Cloud Technologies. *IEEE Software, 32*(2), 30–36. doi:10.1109/MS.2015.43

Shalan, M. A. (2010). Managing IT Risks in Virtual Enterprise Networks: A Proposed Governance Framework. In S. Panios (Ed.), *Managing Risk in Virtual Enterprise Networks: Implementing Supply Chain Principles* (pp. 115–136). Hershey, PA: IGI Global. doi:10.4018/978-1-61520-607-0.ch006

Shalan, M. A. (2016In press). Ethics and Risk Governance for the Middle Circle in Mobile Cloud Computing: Outsourcing, Contracting and Service Providers Involvement. In K. Munir (Ed.), *Security Management in Mobile Cloud Computing.* Hershey, PA: IGI Global.

Sharma, S., Chugh, A., & Kumar, A. (2013). Enhancing Data Security in Cloud Storage. *International Journal of Advanced Research in Computer and Communication Engineering, 2*(5).

Shawish, A., & Salama, M. (2014). Cloud Computing: Paradigms and Technologies. In F. Xhafa & N. Bessis (Eds.), *Inter-cooperative Collective Intelligence: Techniques and Applications* (pp. 39–67). Berlin, Germany: Springer-Verlag. doi:10.1007/978-3-642-35016-0_2

Shelton, T. (2013). *Business Models for the Social Mobile Cloud: Transform Your Business Using Social Media, Mobile Internet, and Cloud Computing.* Indianapolis, IN: John Wiley & Sons. doi:10.1002/9781118555910

Shi, W., & Hong, B. (2011, December). Towards profitable virtual machine placement in the data center. In *Utility and Cloud Computing (UCC), 2011 Fourth IEEE International Conference on* (pp. 138-145). IEEE.

Shinder, D. (2013). *Selecting a Cloud Provider.* Retrieved September 09, 2015, from http://www.cloudcomputingadmin. com/articles-tutorials/architecture-design/selecting-cloud-provider-part1.html

Shrivastava, V., Zerfos, P., Kang-won, L., Jamjoom, H., Liu, Y.-H., & Banerjee, S. (2011). Application-aware virtual machine migration in data centers. In 2011 Proc. IEEE INFOCOM. IEEE. doi:10.1109/INFCOM.2011.5935247

Siepmann, F. (2014). *Managing Risk and Security in Outsourcing IT Services: Onshore, Offshore and the cloud.* Boca Raton, FL: Taylor and Francis Group.

Smart, N. P., & Vercauteren, F. (2010). Fully homomorphic encryption with relatively small key and ciphertext sizes. Public Key Cryptography – PKC 2010. doi:10.1007/978-3-642-13013-7_25

Smart, N., P., & Vercauteren, F. (2011). *Fully homomorphic SIMD operations.* IACR Cryptology ePrint Archive, Report 2011/133.

Snoeren, A. C., Partridge, C., Sanchez, L. A., Jones, C. E., Tchakountio, F., Kent, S. T., & Strayer, W. T. (2001). Hash-based ip traceback. *Computer Communication Review*, *31*(4), 3–14. doi:10.1145/964723.383060

Softlayer. (n.d.). Retrieved 2013, from http://www.softlayer.com/

Solis Moreno, I., Garraghan, P., Townend, P., & Xu, J. (2014). Analysis, Modeling and Simulation of Workload Patterns in a Large-Scale Utility Cloud. *IEEE Transactions on Cloud Computing*, *2*(2), 208–221. doi:10.1109/TCC.2014.2314661

Soyata, T. (2015). *Enabling Real-Time Mobile Cloud Computing through Emerging Technologies*. Hershey, PA: IGI Global. doi:10.4018/978-1-4666-8662-5

Specht, S. M., & Lee, R. B. (2004). Distributed Denial of Service: Taxonomies of Attacks, Tools, and Countermeasures. International Conference on parallel and Distributed computing Systems, International Workshop on Security in Parallel and Distributed Systems, (pp. 543–550).

Specht, S. M., & Lee, R. B. (2004). Distributed Denial of Service: Taxonomies of Attacks, Tools, and Countermeasures. *Proceedings of the International Workshop on Security in Parallel and Distributed Systems*, (pp. 543-550).

Spicuglia, S., Chen, L. Y., Birke, R., & Binder, W. (2015). Optimizing capacity allocation for big data applications in cloud datacenters.*Proceedings of the 2015 IFIP/IEEE International Symposium on Integrated Network Management (IM 2015)* (pp. 511-517). doi:10.1109/INM.2015.7140330

Spitzner, L. (2002). *Honeypots: tracking hackers* (Vol. 1). Addison-Wesley Reading.

Stantchev, V., & Stantcheva, L. (2013). Applying IT-Governance Frameworks for SOA and Cloud Governance. In M. D. Lytras, D. Ruan, R. D. Tennyson, P. Ordonez De Pablos, F. J. García Peñalvo, & L. Rusu (Eds.), *Information Systems, E-learning, and Knowledge Management Research* (pp. 398–407). Berlin, Germany: Springer-Verlag. doi:10.1007/978-3-642-35879-1_48

Subashini, S., & Kavitha, V. (2011). A survey on security issues in service delivery models of cloud computing. *Journal of Network and Computer Applications*, *34*(1), 1–11. doi:10.1016/j.jnca.2010.07.006

Sudevalayam & Kulkarni. (2013). Affinity-aware modeling of CPU usage with communicating virtual machines. *J. Syst. Softw.*, *86*(10), 2627–38. doi:10.1016/j.jss.2013.04.085

Svärd, P., Hudzia, B., Tordsson, J., & Elmroth, E. (2011). Evaluation of delta compression techniques for efficient live migration of large virtual machines. *ACM Sigplan Notices*, *46*(7), 111–120. doi:10.1145/2007477.1952698

Swaprava, N., Ekambaram, V. N., Anurag, K., & Vijay, K. P. (2012). Theory and Algorithms for Hop-Count-Based Localization with Random Geometric Graph Models of Dense Sensor Networks. *ACM Transactions on Sensor Networks*, *8*(4), 111–149.

SYS-CON Medi Inc. (n.d.). *Twenty-One Experts Define Cloud Computing*. Retrieved 2013, from http://cloudcomputing.syscon.com/node/612375/print

Taft. (2013). *IBM Secure Cloud Migration Tool Released*. Retrieved September 22, 2015, from http://www.eweek.com/cloud/ibm-secure-cloud-migration-tool-released.html

Tarannum, N., & Ahmed, N. (2014). *Efficient and Reliable Hybrid Cloud Architecture for Big Data*. arXiv preprint arXiv:1405.5200

Tarkoma, S. (2012). *Publish / Subscribe Systems: Design and Principles*. Hoboken, NJ: John Wiley & Sons. doi:10.1002/9781118354261

Tchana, Tran, Broto, DePalma, & Hagimont. (2013). Two levels autonomic resource management in virtualized IaaS. *Futur. Gener. Comput. Syst., 29*(6), 1319–32. doi:10.1016/j.future.2013.02.002

Tchana, A., Palma, N., Safieddine, I., Hagimont, D., Diot, B., & Vuillerme, N. (2015). Software Consolidation as an Efficient Energy and Cost Saving Solution for a SaaS/PaaS Cloud Model.*Proceedings of the 2015 European Conference on Parallel Processing (Euro-Par 2015)* (pp. 305-316). doi:10.1007/978-3-662-48096-0_24

Tebaa, M., El Hajji, S., & El Ghazi, A. (2012). Homomorphic Encryption Applied to the Cloud Computing Security. *Proceedings of the World Congress on Engineering.*

Temple, J. (2012). *A More Effective Comparison Starts With Relative Capacity.* Retrieved September 22, 2015, from http://ibmsystemsmag.com/mainframe/administrator/performance/relative_capacity/

Terhune, C. (2015, February 5). *Anthem hack exposes data on 80 million; experts warn of identity theft.* Retrieved from http://www.latimes.com/business/la-fi-anthem-hacked-20150204-story.html

The CAIDA UCSD. (2007). DDoS Attack 2007 Dataset. Retrieved from: http://www.caida.org/data/passive/ddos-20070804_dataset.xml

The Dodd-Frank Wall Street Reform and Consumer Protection Act (DFA). (2011). *Financial Stability Act.* Retrieved from: https://www.sec.gov/about/laws/wallstreetreform-cpa.pdf

The European Markets and Infrastructure Regulation (EMIR). (2012). *Derivatives/EMIR.* Retrieved from: http://ec.europa.eu/finance/financial-markets/derivatives/index_en.htm.Europa.eu

The Open Group. (2013). Cloud Performance Metrics: Performance Metrics for Evaluating Cloud Computing. Draft. Author.

The Open Web Application Security Project. (2013). *OWASP Top Ten Project.* Retrieved 09 28, 2015, from www.owasp.org: https://www.owasp.org/index.php/Category:OWASP_Top_Ten_Project

Thompson, J. D., Higgins, D. G., & Gibson, T. J. (1994). CLUSTAL W: Improving the sensitivity of progressive multiple sequence alignment through sequence weighting, position-specific gap penalties and weight matrix choice. *Nucleic Acids Research, 22*(22), 4673–4680. doi:10.1093/nar/22.22.4673 PMID:7984417

Thwe & Thandar. (2013). DDoS Detection System based on a Combined Data mining Approach.*4th International Conference on Science and Engineering.*

Thwe, O. T., & Thandar, P. (2013). A Statistical Approach to Classify and Identify DDoS Attacks using UCLA Dataset. *International Journal of Advanced Research in Computer Engineering & Technology, 2*(5), 1766–1770.

Tirthani, N., & Ganesan, R. (2014). *Data Security in Cloud Architecture Based on Diffie Hellman and Elliptical Curve Cryptography.* School of computing Sciences and Engineering, M. tech. – Computer Science, VIT, Chennai Campus.

Tiwari, A., Sharma, V., & Mahrishi, M. (2014). Service Adaptive Broking Mechanism Using MROSP Algorithm. In *Proceedings Advanced Computing, Networking and Informatics: Wireless Networks and Security* (vol. 2, pp. 383-392). Springer. doi:10.1007/978-3-319-07350-7_43

Tomas, L., Klein, C., Tordsson, J., & Hernandez-Rodriguez, F. (2014). The Straw that Broke the Camel's Back: Safe Cloud Overbooking with Application Brownout.*Proceedings of the 2014 International Conference on Cloud and Autonomic Computing (ICCAC 2014)* (pp. 151-160). doi:10.1109/ICCAC.2014.10

Tomás, L., & Tordsson, J. (2014). An autonomic approach to risk-aware data center overbooking. *IEEE Transactions on Cloud Computing, 2*(3), 292–305. doi:10.1109/TCC.2014.2326166

Tool, N. (n.d.). Retrieved from: http://ntwag.sourceforge.net/

Toosi, A. N., Calheiros, R. N., & Buyya, R. (2014). Interconnected cloud computing environments: Challenges, taxonomy, and survey. *ACM Computing Surveys*, *47*(1), 7. doi:10.1145/2593512

Top500. (2016). Retrieved 2016, from http://www.top500.org/

Topcuoglu, H., Hariri, S., & Wu, M.-Y. (2002). Performance-effective and low-complexity task scheduling for heterogeneous computing. *IEEE Transactions on Parallel and Distributed Systems*, *13*(3), 260–274. doi:10.1109/71.993206

Tordsson, Montero, Moreno-Vozmediano, & Llorente. (2012). Cloud brokering mechanisms for optimized placement of virtual machines across multiple providers. *Futur. Gener. Comput. Syst.*, *28*(2), 358–67. doi:10.1016/j.future.2011.07.003

Tsakalozos, K., Roussopoulos, M., & Delis, A. (2011). VM placement in non-homogeneous IaaS-clouds.Lect. Notes Comput. Sci., 7084, 172–87. doi:10.1007/978-3-642-25535-9_12

Turban, E., Leidner, D., McLean, E., & Wetherbe, J. (2008). *Information technology for management: Transforming organizations in the digital economy.* John Wiley and Sons Inc.

Udhayan, J., & Anitha, R. (2009). Demystifying and Rate Limiting ICMP hosted DoS/DDOS Flooding Attacks with Attack Productivity Analysis.*Advance Computing Conference. IACC 2009*, (pp. 558-564). doi:10.1109/IADCC.2009.4809072

Urgaonkar, R., Kozat, U. C., Igarashi, K., & Neely, M. J. (2010). Dynamic resource allocation and power management in virtualized data centers.*Proceedings of the 2010 IEEE Network Operations and Management Symposium (NOMS 2010)* (pp. 479-486). doi:10.1109/NOMS.2010.5488484

Van den Bossche, R., Vanmechelen, K., & Broeckhove, J. (2010). Cost-Optimal Scheduling in Hybrid IaaS Clouds for Deadline Constrained Workloads. In *2010 IEEE 3rd Int.Conf. Cloud Comput.* IEEE. doi:10.1109/CLOUD.2010.58

Van Den Bossche, Vanmechelen, & Broeckhove. (2013). Online cost-efficient scheduling of deadline-constrained workloads on hybrid clouds. *Futur. Gener. Comput. Syst.*, *29*(4), 973–85. doi:10.1016/j.future.2012.12.012

Van den Bossche, R., Vanmechelen, K., & Broeckhove, J. (2011). Cost-Efficient Scheduling Heuristics for Deadline Constrained Workloads on Hybrid Clouds. In *2011 IEEE Third Int. Conf. Cloud Comput. Technol. Sci.* IEEE. doi:10.1109/CloudCom.2011.50

Van, H. N., Tran, F. D., & Menaud, J.-M. (2009). SLA-Aware Virtual Resource Management for Cloud Infrastructures. In *2009 Ninth IEEE Int. Conf. Comput. Inf. Technol..* IEEE. doi:10.1109/CIT.2009.109

Varalakshmi, P., & Thamarai Selvi, S. (2013). Thwarting DDoS attacks in grid using information divergence. *Future Generation Computer Systems*, *29*(1), 429–441. doi:10.1016/j.future.2011.10.012

Varia, J., & Sajee, M. (2013). *Overview of AWS.* Retrieved September 28, 2015, from https://d36cz9buwru1tt.cloudfront.net/AWS_Overview.pdf

Vasanthi, S., & Chandrasekar, S. (2011). A study on network intrusion detection and prevention system current status and challenging issues. Advances in Recent Technologies in Communication and Computing, 181-183.

Venkatesh, M., & Sumalatha, M. (2012). *Improving Public Auditability, Data Possession in Data Storage Security for Cloud Computing.* ICRTIT.

Verma, A., Ahuja, P., & Neogi, A. (2008a). pMapper: Power and Migration Cost Aware Application Placement in Virtualized Systems. In Middlew. 2008 (LNCS), (vol. 5346, pp. 243–64). Berlin: Springer Berlin Heidelberg. doi:10.1007/978-3-540-89856-6_13

Verma, A., Ahuja, P., & Neogi, A. (2008b). Power-aware dynamic placement of HPC applications.*Proc. 22nd Annu. Int. Conf. Supercomput. ICS 08*. New York: ACM Press. doi:10.1145/1375527.1375555

Verma, A., Dasgupta, G., Nayak, T. K., De, P., & Kothari, R. (2009). Server Workload Analysis for Power Minimization Using Consolidation.*Proceedings of the 2009 Conference on USENIX Annual Technical Conference* (pp. 28-28).

Vice, P. (2015). *Should IT Risks Be Part of Corporate Governance?* Academic Press.

Vice, P. (2015). *Taking risk management from the silo across the enterprise*. Retrieved September 09, 2015, from http://www. aciworldwide.com/-/media/files/collateral/aci_taking_risk_mgmt_from_silo_across_enterprise_tl_us_0211_4572.pdf

Vissers, T., Somasundaram, T. S., Pieters, L., Govindarajan, K., & Hellinckx, P. (2014). DDOS defense system for web services in a cloud environment. *Future Generation Computer Systems*, *37*, 37–45. doi:10.1016/j.future.2014.03.003

VMware. (2015). *VMware Integrated OpenStack 1.0 Documentation*. Retrieved July 2015, from http://pubs.vmware. com/integrated-openstack-1/index.jsp

von Eicken, T. (2010, March 22). *RightScale Server Templates Explained*. RightScale. Retrieved from http://www. rightscale.com/blog/cloud-management-best-practices/rightscale-servertemplates-explained

von Laszewski, G., Wang, L., Younge, A. J., & He, X. (2009). Power-aware scheduling of virtual machines in DVFS-enabled clusters.*Proceedings of the 2009 IEEE International Conference on Cluster Computing and Workshops (CLUSTER 2009)*. (pp. 1-10). doi:10.1109/CLUSTR.2009.5289182

Vouk, M. A. (June2008). Cloud computing Issues, research and implementations. In *30th International Conference on Information Technology Interfaces (ITI 2008)*. doi:10.1109/ITI.2008.4588381

VServer. (2016). *Overview - Linux-VServer*. Retrieved from http://linux-vserver.org/Overview

Wang, L., Tao, J., von Laszewski, G., & Chen, D. (2010). *Power Aware Scheduling for Parallel Tasks via Task Clustering*. Paper presented at the IEEE 16th International Conference on Parallel and Distributed Systems (ICPADS 2010). doi:10.1109/ICPADS.2010.128

Wang, Niu, Li, & Liang. (2013). Dynamic Cloud Resource Reservation via Cloud Brokerage. In *2013 IEEE 33rd Int. Conf. Distrib. Comput. Syst.* IEEE. doi:10.1109/ICDCS.2013.20

Wang, D., Ren, C., Govindan, S., Sivasubramaniam, A., Urgaonkar, B., Kansal, A., & Vaid, K. (2013). ACE: abstracting, characterizing and exploiting peaks and valleys in datacenter power consumption.*Proceedings of the ACM SIGMETRICS/ International Conference on Measurement and Modeling of Computer Systems* (pp. 333-334). doi:10.1145/2465529.2465536

Wang, L., Tao, J., & Kunze, M. (2008). Scientific Cloud Computing: Early Definition and Experience.*10th IEEE International Conference on High Performance Computing and Communications*. IEEE. doi:10.1109/HPCC.2008.38

Warrier, S., & Shandrashekhar, P. (2006). A Comparison Study of Information Security Risk Management Frameworks in. Paper presented in the Asia Pacific Risk and Insurance conference, Tokyo, Japan.

Weiler. (2002). Honeypots for Distributed Denial of Service Attacks. International Workshops on Enabling Technologies: Infrastructure for Collaborative Enterprises (WETICE'02).

What is ITIL® Best Practice ? (n.d.). Retrieved on May 10, 2016 from https://www.axelos.com/best-practice-solutions/ itil/what-is-itil

Wikipedia. (2016). *Platform as a Service*. Retrieved from: http://en.wikipedia.org/wiki/Platform_as_a_service

Wikipedia. (2016, March 7). *Wikipedia*. Retrieved March 07, 2016, from https://en.wikipedia.org/wiki/Platform_as_a_service

Wood, Shenoy, Venkataramani, & Yousif. (2009). Sandpiper: Black-box and gray-box resource management for virtual machines. *Comput. Networks, 53*(17), 2923–38. doi:10.1016/j.comnet.2009.04.014

Xen. (n.d.). *Xen hypervisor*. Retrieved 2012 йил March from http://www.xen.org/products/xenhyp.html

Xia, Du, Cao, & Chen. (2012). An Algorithm of Detecting and Defending CC Attack in Real Time. Industrial Control and Electronics Engineering (ICICEE), (pp. 1804-1806).

Xiao, C. Y., Zeng, G. L., & Hoon, J. L. (2014). *An Efficient and Secured Data Storage Scheme in Cloud Computing Using ECC-based PKI*. ICACT.

Xiao, L., Bastani, O., & Yen, I. L. (2012). *An efficient homographic encryption protocol for multiuser systems, 2012*. Cryptology ePrint Archive Report 2012/193.

Xie, Zhang, Bai, Luo, & Xu. (2011). A Distributed Intrusion Detection System against flooding Denial of Services attacks. Advanced Communication Technology, 878-881.

Yahoo. (2010, November). *Yahoo! Expands Its M45 Cloud Computing Initiative*. Retrieved November, 2010, from https://yodel.yahoo.com/blogs/product-news/yahoo-expands-m45-cloud-computing-initiative-5065.html

Yang, Wang, Cheng, Kuo, & Chu. (2011). Green Power Management with Dynamic Resource Allocation for Cloud Virtual Machines. In *2011 IEEE Int. Conf. High Perform. Comput. Commun.* IEEE. doi:10.1109/HPCC.2011.103

Yao, J., Chen, S., Wang, Levy, D., & Zic, J. (2011). Modelling Collaborative Services for Business and QoS Compliance. *Proceedings of ICWS'2011* (pp. 299-306). Washington, DC: IEEE Computer Society. doi:10.1109/ICWS.2011.44

Yaqub, E., Yahyapour, R., Wieder, P., Jehangiri, A. I., Lu, K., & Kotsokalis, C. (2014). Metaheuristics-Based Planning and Optimization for SLA-Aware Resource Management in PaaS Clouds. *Proceedings of the 7th IEEE/ACM International Conference on Utility and Cloud Computing (UCC 2014)* (pp. 288-297). doi:10.1109/UCC.2014.38

Yellamma, P., Narasimham, C., & Sreenivas, V. (2013). Data Security in the Cloud Using RSA. *IEEE - 31661*. ICCCNT.

Yogamangalam, R., & Sriram, V. S. (2013). A Review on Security Issues in Cloud Computing. *Journal of Artificial Intelligence, 6*(1), 1–7. doi:10.3923/jai.2013.1.7

Younge, A. J., von Laszewski, G., Wang, L., Lopez-Alarcon, S., & Carithers, W. (2010). Efficient resource management for Cloud computing environments. In *Int. Conf. Green Comput.* IEEE. doi:10.1109/GREENCOMP.2010.5598294

Zhang, Q., Zhu, Q., & Boutaba, R. (2011). Dynamic Resource Allocation for Spot Markets in Cloud Computing Environments. In *2011 Fourth IEEE Int. Conf. Util. Cloud Comput.* IEEE. doi:10.1109/UCC.2011.33

Zhang, X., Tune, E., Hagmann, R., Jnagal, R., Gokhale, V., & Wilkes, J. (2013). CPI2: CPU Performance Isolation for Shared Compute Clusters. *Proceedings of the 8th ACM European Conference on Computer Systems (EuroSys '13)* (pp. 379-391). doi:10.1145/2465351.2465388

Zheng, Z., Wang, R., Zhong, H., & Zhang, X. (2011). An approach for cloud resource scheduling based on Parallel Genetic Algorithm. In *2011 3rd Int. Conf. Comput. Res. Dev.* IEEE. doi:10.1109/ICCRD.2011.5764170

Zhou, H., & Wornell, G. (2014). *Efficient Homomorphic Encryption on Integer Vectors and Its Applications*. Dept. Electrical Engineering and Computer Science, Massachusetts Institute of Technology. Retrieved from http://www.mit.edu/~hongchao/papers/Conference/ITA2014_HomomorphicEncryption.pdf

Index

A

Agile 16-17, 20, 22, 24, 26-28, 30-32, 34-36, 38, 47, 59, 99-100, 238, 262-263, 301, 327, 329-330, 338, 371, 376-377, 394-396, 398, 400, 408

Agile Edge 22, 24, 26-28, 30-32, 34-36, 38

Agile Methodology 371, 408

Algorithm 85, 131, 136-141, 143-147, 150, 189-190, 193-195, 197, 199-200, 204, 206-207, 211-214, 218-219, 224, 243, 245, 369, 387, 413, 416, 420, 422, 426-429, 431, 433, 436, 438, 440, 443-444

Analytics 1, 4-5, 7, 11, 13, 25-26, 30, 45, 47, 60, 69-71, 73-74, 84, 90, 92, 94, 96, 101, 174, 181, 265, 269, 282, 316, 338, 351, 387, 389-390, 394, 409

API 16, 28, 31, 38, 62, 76, 79, 123, 168, 172, 174, 179-181, 319

Application Container 23, 419

Application Migration 68, 258, 292, 369

Architectural Pattern 72, 94

Architecture 1-3, 8, 10-13, 15, 19, 21-23, 29-30, 36-37, 54, 57, 72, 88, 93, 97, 102, 140, 177, 179, 183, 193-194, 197, 224-226, 239, 241, 259, 270, 282, 287, 321, 329, 346, 350, 370, 384-385, 388-391, 394, 400, 419, 431, 435, 438, 456-458, 463

Assurance 99, 163, 174, 288, 302, 304

Asymmetric 189-190, 194, 205, 213, 215

Audit 26, 44, 80, 89, 101, 161-165, 171-172, 174-175, 181-182, 184-187, 260, 340, 345, 380, 383, 388, 391, 397

B

Banking 44, 47, 50-51, 53, 78, 82, 89, 98, 227

Blockchain 323-324

Broker 101, 116, 146, 304, 348, 360-361, 365, 372, 375, 385

Bus 9, 27, 396, 398, 416

Business Support 109, 112, 114, 116, 121-122, 129

Business Transformation 376-377, 379, 387, 391-392, 395-396, 399-400

C

CI 326-329, 331-332, 334-336, 339-340, 342-346

Client 2, 5-6, 9, 11, 15, 19, 28-29, 109, 116-117, 121-122, 124-125, 140, 147, 159-163, 165, 167-176, 180, 185-187, 192, 194, 196-197, 200, 244, 255, 285, 304, 313, 316, 331, 376-377, 389, 397, 399, 408-409

Client Enterprise (CE) 399, 408-409

Cloud 1, 5, 8-11, 13, 15-30, 32-64, 66-102, 105-131, 133-137, 139-140, 142-152, 159-163, 165, 167-187, 189-191, 193-194, 196-197, 199-202, 212-215, 222-227, 229, 232, 235-238, 241, 244, 254-256, 258-277, 279-280, 282-283, 285-289, 291-293, 300-313, 318, 320-323, 325-326, 330, 344, 348-352, 357, 360-361, 365-372, 375-379, 381-400, 408-412, 417, 420-421, 423, 426-441, 443-445, 455-470

Cloud Brokerage 21, 33, 101, 146

Cloud Computing 1, 9-10, 13, 15-16, 23, 26, 33, 38, 44-45, 47, 54-57, 71-74, 83, 106, 130, 159-160, 189-190, 193, 199, 222-227, 229, 234-236, 244, 258, 279, 293, 309, 325-326, 330, 344, 365-366, 376-378, 381, 385, 388-390, 392-393, 398-400, 408, 410, 434, 444-445, 455-457, 459-463, 468, 470

Cloud Data Centers 45, 64, 410-411, 417, 423, 427-428, 430-431, 433, 436, 438-439

Cloud Migration 177, 254, 258-259, 269, 271, 277, 279-280, 285-286

Cloud Provider 19-21, 35, 46, 54, 58, 62, 64, 80, 97, 100, 108, 130-131, 133, 137, 143-144, 148-149, 159-165, 167-175, 179-187, 190, 202, 225, 275, 286, 431-432, 458-459, 467

Cloud Security 25, 45, 159-160, 227, 234, 385

Cloud Service Broker (CSB) 360, 375

Cloud Service Provider (CSP) 41, 46, 49, 54, 116, 133, 143, 197, 232, 360, 408, 431, 457

Community 17, 39-40, 44-53, 89, 160, 309, 319, 325, 386, 462, 469

Compliance 6, 20, 26, 44, 69, 89, 91, 159-165, 167, 171, 177, 179, 182, 184-187, 255, 258, 260, 274-275, 301, 307-308, 315-316, 329-330, 335, 340, 342, 345, 365, 376-377, 382-385, 388, 391, 395, 397, 461-462

Connected 3, 94, 97, 117, 256, 264-265, 269, 303, 308, 310, 316, 321, 325, 385, 392

Container as a Service (CaaS) 436

Contracting 376, 382, 388, 395-398

Control(s) 9, 80, 93, 106, 124, 162-165, 167, 169-170, 172, 174-177, 179, 183, 185, 187, 341, 345, 376-379, 383-384, 387-388, 391-392, 395-400

Cross-Functional 330-331, 346-347

Cryptography 190-191, 194, 213, 215, 220

D

Dedicated 23, 41-42, 46, 52, 58, 75, 83-84, 93, 95, 108, 111, 115-117, 134, 161, 309, 316, 377, 386, 421

Defense in Depth 304, 324

Delivery 16-17, 23-24, 43, 72, 74-75, 78, 87-88, 91, 97, 120, 226, 256, 261-263, 268, 280, 304, 306, 318, 322, 325-328, 330, 334, 336, 342, 344, 346-348, 381, 385-386, 388, 390, 396

Deploy 23, 32, 54-55, 58, 64, 95, 97, 99, 101-102, 110, 126-127, 135, 145, 165, 183-185, 293, 305-306, 316, 334-335, 342-344, 386, 395, 421, 457

Deployment 23-24, 43, 56-57, 64, 68, 71, 75-77, 79-82, 84-85, 93, 95, 99-100, 102, 110, 123-127, 145-146, 148, 161, 172, 175, 177, 181-182, 184-185, 260, 282, 300, 302-313, 318-321, 323, 325, 328-329, 335, 338, 343, 385-386, 388-391, 395-397, 399, 422, 431, 470

Design Thinking 348, 350-351, 353-354, 375

Disaster Recovery 21, 36, 63-64, 71, 73, 77, 81, 89, 96, 99, 183, 255, 258, 271, 275-276, 292, 365, 397

Distributed Denial-of-Service (DDOS) 79, 222-224, 227-241, 244-246, 252

E

Elasticity 9, 56-57, 133, 222, 323, 377-378, 385, 387, 392, 399, 460

Energy Efficiency 138, 140, 413, 422, 428, 431, 436, 440, 443

Enterprise Mobility 1, 3-4

Extensible Enterprise 392, 399-400

F

Fabric 1, 99, 102, 113-114, 300, 304-305, 307, 310-311, 313, 319, 384

Filtering 224, 236-239, 246

Finance 69, 78, 81-82, 84, 89, 95, 98, 101, 355, 370, 372

Framework 10, 13, 15, 78, 89, 91, 129, 136, 140-141, 146, 149, 163, 169, 179, 183, 187, 200-201, 224, 300, 307, 319, 342, 344, 376, 389, 394, 397-400, 421, 428, 432, 435-436, 441, 457

Function 17, 28, 30-32, 34-36, 66, 83, 111, 115-116, 119-120, 137-140, 143-144, 149, 190, 194, 205, 212, 219, 223, 279, 307, 322-323, 325, 327, 331, 333, 347, 409

G

Governance 11, 43-44, 47, 49, 53, 78-79, 107, 159-161, 187, 261, 280, 300-308, 310-311, 313, 316-319, 321-323, 325, 350, 376-379, 381, 383-385, 387-391, 393-397, 399-400, 409

Government 44, 47, 69, 73, 84, 88-91, 95, 97-98, 107, 348, 397

Green Strategies 130

H

HaaS 455-459, 463-470

Healthcare 12, 69, 90-92, 440, 462

High Availability 16, 65, 77, 80-81, 89, 134, 142-143, 146, 150-151, 171, 183, 223, 232, 275, 288, 365, 410, 460

Homomorphic 189-191, 202-208, 211-214

HPC 87, 134, 137, 148, 430, 455-456, 458, 463-470

Hybrid 6, 9, 15-30, 33, 36-38, 43, 51, 68-69, 73, 75-76, 79, 82, 93, 95, 101-102, 105, 107, 109, 112, 119, 129, 135, 146, 148, 150, 159, 161-162, 175-176, 178-179, 181, 183, 185-186, 255, 264, 286, 288, 300-313, 317-323, 325, 349, 375, 386, 417, 434, 461-462

Hybrid Cloud 9, 15, 17-29, 33, 36-37, 43, 68-69, 76, 82, 93, 105, 107, 109, 112, 119, 129, 135, 146, 148, 150, 159, 161-162, 175-176, 178, 185, 286, 300-313, 318, 320-323, 325, 349, 375, 461-462

Hybrid Hosting 73

Hybrid IT 22, 25, 30, 38, 82, 102, 309

I

IBM 1-2, 4, 10, 42-43, 50-51, 54, 90, 111-112, 160, 177, 181-183, 254-256, 260, 264-266, 269, 274, 335, 348-349, 351, 353-354, 356-357, 375, 417, 457

IBM Design Thinking 348, 351, 375

Image Migration 264-265, 269, 273-275, 289-292

Industrialised 22, 24, 27-28, 30, 32, 34-36, 38

Industrialised Core 22, 24, 27-28, 30, 32, 34-36, 38

Inform 167-175, 186, 188

Information Divergence 224, 242, 246, 252

Infrastructure 2-5, 7, 16-17, 21, 23, 25, 42, 46, 49, 54, 56-58, 60-65, 67-69, 72, 78-80, 82, 88-89, 93, 95, 97, 99, 101-102, 106-115, 117-120, 122, 124, 126, 129-131, 134-135, 139, 144, 148, 150, 160-161, 163, 165, 169-172, 174-175, 177, 179-181, 185, 189, 223, 225, 235-236, 238-239, 255, 260, 265-266, 293, 300-301, 303-305, 308, 310, 312, 318, 323, 325-327, 333-334, 341, 344, 349-350, 354, 365, 375, 377, 384-385, 387, 390, 393-394, 397, 411, 417, 431, 445, 455-460, 467

Infrastructure as a Service (IaaS) 23, 28, 50, 54, 56-57, 68, 71-72, 93, 99, 107-108, 114-115, 130, 144, 146, 159-162, 165-167, 178, 189, 365, 368, 370, 372, 386, 412, 443, 455-458, 463-470

Integrity 24, 190, 197, 199, 212, 224, 304, 306, 310, 313, 320, 322-324, 376, 379, 385

Interconnected 91, 224, 308, 313, 319, 325

Internet of Things (IoT) 94, 300, 307, 309-310, 321, 325

Intrusion Detection System 224, 237

IT Architecture 22, 30, 72

ITIL 84, 255, 302, 304-305, 319-321, 325, 334

L

Lean 189, 375, 390

Lineage 304, 307, 313, 316, 320-324

M

Managed From 112, 129

Managed Services 89, 160, 254-255, 260, 277, 316, 325

Management 1, 5-7, 9, 12-13, 16, 21-22, 24-30, 32-33, 36, 54-55, 81-82, 84-85, 91-93, 100-101, 109-110, 112, 114-116, 118-125, 127, 129, 134, 136, 140, 146-148, 150-151, 160-161, 163, 165-175, 177, 179-186, 190, 200, 202, 222, 255, 258-261, 264-265, 267-269, 274, 302-304, 306-308, 310-312, 315-322, 325-330, 333-336, 338-339, 343-344, 346-347, 349, 351, 365-366, 377-384, 386-391, 393-400, 409-411, 413, 417, 419-420, 422-423, 431, 436, 438-441, 444-445, 461-462

Maturity 105, 163, 186, 323, 378, 388, 399-400

Middle Circle Contractor (MCC) 386, 409

Migration 38, 67-68, 71, 101, 128, 134, 136-137, 139, 141, 144, 147-151, 165, 177, 183, 254, 256-266, 268, 270-277, 279-283, 285-293, 295, 297, 348, 354, 366, 369, 372, 384, 417, 423, 426-428

Migration Project Plan 295

Minimum Viable Product (MVP) 375

Mobile Devices 3-4, 9-11, 13, 20, 26

Mobile Services 2-3

Monitoring 1, 25, 79-80, 84, 91, 109, 112, 115-116, 121, 129, 140, 161, 169, 173-174, 181, 184, 186, 197, 224, 230, 239, 260, 274, 305, 312, 322, 327, 330, 335, 339, 365, 382-383, 389-391, 398, 409, 417

N

Net-Centric 319, 325

Net-Centric 325

Network 5-6, 8-9, 16-17, 27-28, 41-42, 46, 54, 62, 64, 66, 68-69, 72-73, 75, 79, 81, 83-84, 87, 91, 95, 98, 100, 106, 108-114, 116-119, 121, 129, 131, 135, 137, 143-144, 146-148, 151, 160, 163, 165, 172, 175, 177, 181, 183, 222-224, 227, 232, 235-239, 241, 244, 252, 258, 261, 263, 265, 271-274, 282, 287-288, 302, 306, 308, 310, 319-320, 323, 325, 341, 369, 377, 385-386, 388-389, 392, 411, 420, 457, 464, 467

Network Aware 135, 146

Network Security 227

O

Operational Support 109, 114, 116, 121, 129

Operations 22-24, 28-29, 53, 61, 67, 69, 74, 78, 96, 99, 101, 112, 134, 185, 190-191, 200, 203-205, 207-209, 212-214, 220, 227-228, 236, 255, 277, 300, 302, 304, 308, 316, 318, 325, 327-328, 330-331, 339, 378-379, 382, 384, 387, 390, 462

Orchestration 21-22, 29-30, 33, 35-36, 99, 110, 112, 114-115, 117, 119, 121, 123, 125, 127, 129, 160, 259-260, 265, 327

Outsourcing 40, 149, 163, 316, 385, 388, 395-396, 398, 409

P

Patterns 9, 16, 56-57, 69, 71, 73, 75, 79, 81, 83, 87-88, 90-91, 93, 95, 97-98, 102, 136, 141, 144, 237, 274, 286-287, 293, 321, 329, 335, 338, 388, 394, 428-429, 432, 438, 445

Perform 6, 30, 35, 45, 65, 101, 110, 122, 124-125, 135-136, 139, 165, 167-172, 174-175, 185-186, 188, 190, 209, 213-214, 226, 239, 257, 265-266, 272, 285-286, 288-292, 335, 338, 371, 396, 409, 457

Placement Strategies 130, 134, 136-137, 140, 142, 146, 148, 151-152, 431

Platform as a Service (PaaS) 23, 27, 50, 54, 56-57, 72, 89, 108, 112, 114-115, 159-162, 165-166, 189, 261, 365, 369-370, 386, 388, 410-413, 417, 421, 430, 435, 439, 444-445, 456-457

Public 5, 9, 17, 23, 39-46, 49, 53, 56-58, 60, 62-64, 66-67, 69-71, 75-77, 82, 85, 87-88, 91, 93, 96-97, 100, 102, 106-107, 109, 112-113, 115, 117, 125, 127, 129, 135, 143, 149, 161, 190, 194, 196-197, 199-200, 205-206, 208, 210-212, 219, 236, 254, 256, 264-265, 309, 349-350, 360, 375, 386, 395, 435, 461-463

R

Reference Architecture 1-3, 10-13, 23

Regulation 69, 75, 79, 82, 84, 88-89, 95, 98

Regulatory Compliance 91, 345, 391

Responsibility (for a Control) 188

Retail 20, 34, 73-78, 92, 98, 101

Reuse 57, 260, 304, 385

Risk 4, 17, 26, 58, 67, 105-106, 124, 127, 145, 159-160, 162, 165, 177, 180-185, 187, 203, 257, 260, 263, 269, 272, 286-288, 333, 350, 359, 372, 376-382, 385, 387, 390-392, 394, 396-400, 409, 430, 460

Risk Management 26, 177, 184, 377-379, 381-382, 391, 397-400, 409

RPIE (Request, Perform, Inform, Evidence) 188

S

Security 1, 4-6, 8-10, 13, 22-27, 29-30, 42-47, 53, 55, 78-80, 84, 91, 94, 101, 110-112, 115-116, 120, 123-124, 127, 148, 159-165, 167, 171-172, 175-176, 179, 181-187, 189-191, 193-194, 196-197, 199-200, 202, 204, 206-207, 210-215, 222-223, 225, 227, 234, 236-237, 241, 246, 255, 258, 260, 264, 270-271, 274, 300, 302-304, 307-308, 312, 315-316, 319-320, 323-324, 326-332, 335, 339-343, 345, 348-350, 366, 376, 385-386, 390, 393, 395-396, 434, 436, 461-462

Service Management 29-30, 33, 36, 82, 84, 110, 115-116, 119, 121, 123, 125, 161, 168, 174, 180, 182, 184, 255, 326-330, 333-336, 338-339, 344, 346-347, 365-366

Service Provider 8, 16, 41, 46, 49, 54-55, 72, 83, 97, 107, 109, 114, 116, 133, 143, 197, 232, 360, 365, 368, 372, 388, 408, 431, 435-436, 457

Services 1-5, 7-13, 16-17, 20-23, 25-27, 29-30, 33-34, 36, 38, 40-45, 47, 50, 53-57, 63, 66, 69, 74, 78, 81, 83, 88-89, 94, 97-99, 101, 105, 107, 109-

119, 121-122, 124-130, 134-136, 143, 148, 151, 160-161, 163, 172, 174-177, 183, 187, 189, 223-224, 227, 229, 232, 235, 237-239, 254-255, 257, 259-260, 262-263, 265, 267-268, 274-277, 301, 303-306, 308-309, 312-313, 316, 318-323, 325, 331, 348-351, 360, 365, 367, 375-378, 381-382, 384-394, 396-400, 408-409, 419, 421, 434-437, 442, 455-457, 459-465, 467, 469-470

Shadow IT 301, 350, 375, 393, 409

Shared Responsibility Control 188

SMAC 399, 409

SOA 321, 323

Software as a SERVICE (SaaS) 23, 50, 54-57, 72, 89, 97, 108-109, 112, 114-115, 160-161, 165-166, 177, 182-184, 189, 265, 350, 352, 365-366, 370, 386, 388, 456-457

Symmetric 189-191, 200, 205, 211, 213-215

System Level Virtualization 411, 417, 423

System of Engagement 20, 38

System of Record 20, 31, 38

Systems-of-Insight 90, 92, 94

T

Technology 10, 13, 15-17, 23, 40, 45, 47, 54, 73-74, 78-79, 83-84, 86-88, 90-91, 94, 96, 100, 105-107, 128, 136, 140, 159, 162, 171, 177, 189, 219, 222-223, 234, 285, 289-290, 293, 300-308, 310, 312-313, 324-325, 330, 334, 348, 350, 354, 360, 370, 372, 375-385, 387-391, 393, 395-400, 409, 412-413, 417, 422-423, 431, 433-434, 438, 459, 463-464

Technology Organization (TO) 377, 379, 381, 398, 409

Telecommunications 86, 258

Transformation 10, 31, 98, 211-212, 254, 264, 266, 269-271, 275, 277, 280, 282, 287, 325, 348, 350-351, 354, 365, 371, 376-377, 379, 387-388, 391-392, 394-396, 399-400

Transition 29, 165, 254, 256, 258, 261, 264, 266, 271, 277, 305-306, 351, 368, 372, 377, 389, 396, 439

U

Use Case 1, 12, 19-21, 30-36, 52, 57-59, 61, 63, 65, 67, 69, 72-73, 91, 100, 114, 122-123, 134, 142, 176-177, 311

Use Cases 2, 15, 19, 21-22, 29, 32, 37, 51-52, 56-57, 65, 71, 73-74, 78-79, 82-83, 86-88, 90, 92-97, 102, 113, 117, 122-123, 134, 292, 308, 311, 321, 392

V

Virtual Machines 17, 41, 55, 62, 79, 83, 85, 87, 111, 121, 130-131, 133-144, 146-148, 150-152, 167, 174, 183, 226, 241, 244, 266, 389, 417, 422-423, 426-427, 431, 433-435, 438, 458, 463, 470

Virtualization 1, 6, 13, 41, 83-84, 107, 111-114, 116, 119-121, 127-129, 133, 136, 140, 163, 183, 226-227, 237-239, 252, 259, 389, 411-412, 417, 419, 422-423, 427, 431, 433-434, 438, 462-464

Virtualization Management 112, 121, 129

Visibility 115, 165, 174, 181, 186, 316, 331, 336, 338-339, 341, 345, 387, 389-390, 394

W

Wave Planning 101, 254, 256-257, 269-270, 274, 277, 280, 287-288, 296

Workflow 27, 32, 34-36, 114, 119, 122-125, 129, 180, 443-444

Workload 16, 19-21, 30, 35, 38, 42, 55, 65, 68, 73, 82, 85, 101-102, 107, 113, 117-118, 128, 134, 136-139, 144-146, 148-149, 151, 159-163, 165, 167, 169, 171-172, 175-176, 180-181, 184-185, 232, 235, 254, 258-260, 262-265, 279-280, 285, 288-289, 292, 369, 411, 413, 415-416, 420, 422, 426-433, 436-442, 444

Workload Characterization 428-429, 432, 436

X

XaaS 55, 109, 126

Printed in the United States
By Bookmasters